7/98

# Reference Library of

# BLACK
# AMERICA

*Reference Library of*

# BLACK
# AMERICA

VOLUME
## V

Edited by
## L. Mpho Mabunda

**Multiculture In Print**

*Reference Library of Black America is* based upon the seventh edition of *The African American Almanac*, published by Gale Research. It has been published in this 5-volume set to facilitate wider usage among students.

Linda Hubbard, *Managing Editor*
L. Mpho Mabunda, *Editor*
David G. Oblender, *Associate Editor*
Beth Baker, Craig Barth, Dawn Berry, Gene Brady, Carol Brennan, Melissa Walsh Doig, DeWitt S. Dykes, Jr., Kimberly Burton
Faulkner, Simon Glickman, Joyce Harrison, Bob Jacobson, Carmen Johnson, Michael Knes, Jeffrey Lehman, Sipho C. Mabunda,
William J. Moses, Anna Sheets, David Sprinkle, Stephen Stratton, Chris Tower, Aaron Turley, *Contributing Editors*

George Hobart, *Photo Researcher*

Marlene Hurst, *Permissions Manager*
Margaret McAvoy-Amato, *Permissions Assistant*

Victoria B. Cariappa, *Research Manager*
Barbara McNeil, Andrew Guy Malonis, Gary J. Oudersluys, *Research Specialists*
Norma Sawaya, Cheryl L. Warnock, *Research Associates*
Laura C. Bissey, *Research Assistant*

Mary Beth Trimper, *Production Director*
Evi Seoud, *Assistant Production Manager*
Shanna Heilveil, *Production Assistant*

Cynthia Baldwin, *Art Director*
Barbara J. Yarrow, *Graphic Services Supervisor*
Mark C. Howell, *Cover Designer*
Arthur Chartow, *Page Designer*
C.J. Jonik, *Desktop Publisher*
Randy Bassett, *Image Database Supervisor*
Robert Duncan, Mikal Ansari, *Imaging Specialists*
Pamela Hayes, *Photographic Coordinator*

Benita L. Spight, *Data Entry Supervisor*
Gwendolyn S. Tucker, *Data Entry Group Leader*
Beverly Jendrowski, *Senior Data Entry Associate*

The paper used in this publication meets the minimum requirements of American National Standard for
Information Sciences—Permanence Paper for Printed Library Materials, ANSI Z 39.48-1984.

ISBN 0-7876-1539-0 (Vol. 5)

Printed in the United States of America

# Advisory Board

# Contributors

**Stephen W. Angell**
Associate Professor of Religion, Florida A&M University

**Robin Armstrong**
Adjunct Lecturer, University of Michigan, Dearborn

**Claudette Bennett**
Bureau of the Census, United States Department of Commerce

**Allen G. Harris**
President, Air Force Association, General Daniel James Chapter

**Hayward Derrick Horton**
Assistant Professor of Sociology, Iowa State University

**George Johnson**
Professor of Law, Howard University School of Law

**Faustine C. Jones-Wilson**
Professor of Education, Howard University; Editor, *The Journal of Negro Education*

**Donald Franklin Joyce**
Director, Felix G. Woodward Library, Austin Peay State University

**Mark Kram**
Sportswriter, *Philadelphia Daily News*

**Robyn M. Lupa**
Assistant Branch Manager, Middle Village, Queens Borough Public Library

**Doris H. Mabunda**
Director of Youth Programs, YWCA-Grand Rapids, MI

**Ionis Bracy Martin**
Lecturer, Central Connecticut State University

**Marilyn Hortense Mackel**
Associate Professor, Western State University College of Law,
Judge Pro Tempore, Los Angeles County Superior Court, Juvenile Department

**Dan Morgenstern**
Director, Institute for Jazz Studies, Rutgers University

**Wilson J. Moses**
Professor of History, Pennsylvania State University

**Richard Prince**
National Association of Black Journalists

**Floyd Thomas, Jr.**
Curator of Fine Art and Military History, National Afro-American Museum and Cultural Center

**Michael D. Woodard**
Director, Los Angeles Institute for Multicultural Training;
Visiting Scholar, UCLA Center for Afro-American Studies

# Contents

## Volume 5

# Introduction

*The Reference Library of Black America* is based on the seventh edition of *The African American Almanac*, first published in 1967 as *The Negro Almanac* and since cited by *Library Journal* as an outstanding reference work.

## New Features in This Edition

All material was extensively reviewed by the editor and a board of prominent advisors, and, where appropriate, updated and/or expanded. In many instances, completely new topics were added to existing essays. Some chapters were totally rewritten to focus on issues facing contemporary African Americans. The most significant changes include the expansion of chapters three ("Significant Documents"), five ("Africa and the Black Diaspora"), 15 ("The Family"), and 19 ("Media"); and the revision of key essays within chapter ten ("Law"), chapter 11 ("Politics"), chapter 16 ("Education"), chapter 22 ("Blues and Jazz"), chapter 23 ("Popular Music"), chapter 24 ("Fine and Applied Arts"), chapter 25 ("Science and Medicine"); chapter 26 ("Sports"), and chapter 27 ("Military"). All 27 chapters were also made as current as possible, including chapter one ("Chronology") and chapter 2 ("African American Firsts").

Anyone familiar with earlier editions will be excited to find such new features such as a chronology current to April of 1996; coverage of newly anointed African American pioneers from 1994 and 1995; inclusion of "The Million Man March Mission Statement;" more and more useful information regarding the black diaspora; more extensive information regarding the origins of those enslaved in America; an essay on the history of federal judges in the United States; a brief history of African American involvement in the political system along with a list of addresses for current Congressional Black Caucus members; more profiles of trailblazing entrepreneurs both current and historical; coverage of more topics related to health and increased discussion of such issues related to family as marriage; a complete listing of African American chaired professors and endowed university chairs; summarization of the rash of black church fires; an accounting of black involvement on the information superhighway, including a list of more than 30 World Wide Web sites of interest to African Americans; new information on African American craft art, the Black Arts movement, and the role of historically black learning institutions in the preservation and presentation of African American art; more about black contributions to science and technology; more dynamic discussion of African American military participation in the Revolutionary War as well as the wars in Vietnam and the Persian Gulf; and better coverage of the blues, popular music, and sports.

## Content and Arrangement

Information in this edition appears in 27 subject chapters. Many chapters open with an essay focusing on historical developments or the contributions of African Americans to the subject area, followed by concise biographical profiles on selected individuals. Although the listees featured in this set represent only a small portion of the African American community, they embody excellence and diversity in their respective fields of endeavor. Where an individual has made a significant contribution in more than one area, his or her biographical profile appears in the subject area for which he or she is best known.

In order to facilitate further research, a bibliography is provided at the end of each volume of *The Reference Library of Black America*. The bibliography has been divided into two major divisions: "Africana" and "African Americana." Within these two divisions titles are arranged alphabetically by author under categories indicative of their subject matter.

Three appendixes provide timely information of special interest to students. The first lists African American winners of many popular and professional awards. The second identifies all the medalists at the centennial Olympic Games celebrated in Atlanta in 1996. The final one guides students in selecting a suitable college or university from among the many historically black institutions profiled in the same section.

More than five hundred maps and illustrations aid the reader in understanding the topics and people covered in the work. A name and keyword index provides access to the contents of the entire set.

# 23

# *Popular Music*

# ㉓

# *Popular Music*

◆ Gospel: The Root of Popular Music  ◆ The Rise of Rhythm and Blues
◆ Sweet Soul Music and Social Revolution  ◆ From Psychedelic Soul to Disco
◆ Rap: A Voice from the Subculture  ◆ Popular Music Gatekeepers

**by John Cohassey and Simon Glickman**

*Since the turn of the twentieth century, black music—whether gospel, rhythm and blues, soul, funk, or rap—has shaped American popular music. More recently, its impact can be heard in the emergence of world music coming out of Africa, South America, and the Caribbean Islands. From the church to the concert stage, thousands of gifted African American singers and musicians have bestowed upon America and the world a gift of unbounded spirit.*

## ◆ GOSPEL: THE ROOT OF POPULAR MUSIC

The foundation of twentieth-century black popular music is rooted in the sounds of several folk styles including black minstrel and vaudeville tunes, blues, and ragtime. However, the music of the African American church has played one of the most significant roles in the evolution of black popular music.

Inextricably bound to the spirituals sung by slaves, the gospel style came to dominate the black religious experience in America. By the turn of the century, gospel music had reached popularity as black religious songwriters began to publish their own compositions. One of the earliest and most influential of these writers was Charles Albert Tindley, a Maryland-born Methodist preacher, who was responsible for writing several gospel music classics. His song "I'll Overcome Someday" resurfaced more than a half decade later as "We Shall Overcome," the anthem of the 1960s civil rights movement. Tindley's 1905 composition "Stand By Me" became a major hit for singer Ben E. King during the 1960s.

Tindley's music subsequently influenced Thomas A. Dorsey, whose talents as a religious songwriter, accom-

panist, and choir director earned him the title "the father of gospel music." Before dedicating his life to the Baptist church, Dorsey spent his youth as an itinerant blues pianist, performing under the name Georgia Tom. Like other bluesmen/preachers such as Reverend Gary Davis, Blind Willie McTell, and Gatemouth Moore, Dorsey performed both secular and religious music. In 1928, for example, he not only co-wrote the blues hit "Tight Like That" with guitarist Hudson "Tampa Red" Whitaker, but also composed his first gospel song "If You See My Savior Tell Him You Saw Me."

Four years later, Dorsey abandoned his career as a blues and jazz pianist to devote himself to a form of religious music that historian Michael W. Harris describes as gospel-blues style melding black religious and popular music into a unique and passionate form of gospel. During the Great Depression, Dorsey's new style of gospel served as an uplifting spiritual release from the pervasive poverty experienced in the black community. The performance of two of Dorsey's songs at the 1930 National Baptist Convention created a wave of enthusiasm for gospel across the nation. In the following year, Dorsey organized the world's first gospel choir. In 1932, he began a 40-year career as choir director at Chicago's Pilgrim Baptist Church. During his stay at Pilgrim Baptist, he launched the golden age of gospel music (c. 1945–1960), training and accompanying singers from Sallie Martin to Mahalia Jackson.

### Gospel and the Recording Industry

The advent of the phonograph around the turn of the century helped to heighten the popularity of gospel music. The distribution of records helped break down the musical isolation imposed upon blacks since slav-

Thomas Dorsey with his group the Wandering Syncopators, 1923.

ery, allowing them to reach audiences outside their own communities. Recorded by the Victor label in 1902, the Jubilee and camp meeting shouts of the Dwinddie Colored Quartet appeared as one of the first black recordings. In the 1920s, black religious music became popular with the race record (a title designating the segregated sale of African American recordings). By 1924, Paramount Records sponsored its own Jubilee singers, and within three years Columbia Records began to send engineers into the field to record the richly complex harmonies of gospel quartets. Also popular were recorded sermons backed by occasional musical instruments, and evangelistic guitars, known commonly as "jack legs," which brought street singing gospel blues to a wider audience.

After a decline in recordings by evangelists during the 1930s and early 1940s, gospel music experienced an immense rise in popularity as hundreds of independent recording labels appeared after World War II. During the 1940s, numerous gospel quartets went on the road as full-time professionals, while thousands more sought work on weekends. Dressed in flowing robes and fashionably designed dress suits, quartets incorporated dance routines and expressive shouts into their performances.

Throughout the postwar period male gospel groups like the Five Blind Boys from Mississippi, the Mighty Clouds of Joy from Los Angeles, and the Sensational Nightingales from Memphis sang a capella (without instruments) on numerous recordings.

## ◆ THE RISE OF RHYTHM AND BLUES

As black veterans returned home from the Second World War, they found not only a new gospel sound, but an exciting blues style being played by small combos: jump blues. With its roots in boogie-woogie and the blues-swing arrangements of artists like Count Basie, Cab Calloway, Louis Jordan, and Lucky Millinder, this new blues style acquired an enormous following in black urban communities across the country. Unlike the swing-era big bands, jump blues groups featured fewer horns and a heavy rhythmic approach marked by a walking boogie bass line, honking saxophone solos, and a two-four drum pattern. Among the greatest exponents of postwar jump blues were guitarist T-Bone Walker, saxophonist Eddie "Cleanhead" Vinson, and blues shouter Big Joe Turner.

Louis Jordan had a profound impact on the emergence of rhythm and blues.

Soon many jump blues ensembles began to feature singers versed in a smooth gospel-influenced vocal style. In 1949, the popularity of this style led *Billboard Magazine* to change its black pop chart title to rhythm and blues, thus coining the name of this new music. Just as blues, religious spirituals, and hymns formed gospel, rhythm and blues drew upon gospel, electric urban blues, and swing jazz to create a vibrantly modern sound appealing to the younger generation of postwar blacks. Some of the early recordings exemplifying the gospel influence on rhythm and blues were Cecil Grant's 1945 hit "I Wonder," Roy Brown's 1947 classic "Good Rocking Tonight," and Wynonie Harris's 1949 disc "All She Wants To Do Is Rock."

It was not long before this kind of raw-edged rhythm and blues emerged from hundreds of independent recording labels that appeared across the country in the postwar era. With the increased availability of rhythm and blues recordings, a handful of black radio disc jockeys became locally famous as the first promoters and salesmen of this music. Bringing their colorful street language to the airwaves, pioneer black DJs such as Al Benson and Vernon Winslow not only helped to popularize rhythm and blues, but set the trend for modern pop radio.

## R&B and the Black Church

In the early 1950s, numerous gospel quartets and street corner singing groups set out to establish careers in the black popular music scene. Influenced by gospel music and the secular singing of groups like the Inkspots, vocal groups appeared that performed complex harmonies in *a capella* style. As they would for rap artists in decades to come, street corners in urban neighborhoods became training grounds for thousands of young aspiring African American artists. This music, known as doo-wop, first arrived on the scene with the formation of the Ravens in 1945. Not long afterward, there followed a great succession of doo-wop "bird groups" including the Orioles who, in 1953, scored a nationwide hit with "Crying in the Chapel"—a song which, for the first time in black popular music, walked an almost indistinguishable line between gospel and mainstream pop music. In the same year, Billy Ward formed the Dominoes, featuring lead singer Clyde McPhatter, the son of a Baptist minister.

In the wake of the success of these vocal groups, numerous gospel singers left the church to become pop music stars. In 1952, for example, the Royal Sons became the Five Royales, the Gospel Starlighters (with James Brown), and finally the Blue Flames. Five years later, a young gospel singer named Sam Cooke landed a number-one pop hit with "You Send Me," a song which achieved popularity among both black and white audiences.

The strong relationship between gospel and rhythm and blues was evident in the music of more hard-edged R&B groups like Hank Ballard and the Midnighters. Maintaining a driving blues-based sound, Ballard's music, while featuring gospel-based harmonies, retained secular themes, as evidenced in his 1954 hit "Work With Me Annie." However, the capstone of gospel R&B appeared in the talents of Georgia-born pianist and singer Ray Charles, who in 1954 hit the charts with "I Got a Woman," which was based upon the gospel song "My Jesus Is All the World to Me." Charles' 1958 recording "What I'd Say" is famed for its call-and-response pattern which directly resembled the music sung in Holiness churches.

## Rock and Roll

The rise of white rock and roll around 1955 served to open the floodgates for thousands of black R&B artists longing for a nationwide audience. A term applied to black R&B and its white equivalents during the mid-1950s, rock and roll represented a label given to a music form by the white media and marketplace in order to

Chuck Berry revolutionized rhythm and blues.

attract a mass multiracial audience. As black music writer Nelson George explained, naming this music rock and roll, "dulled down the racial identification and made young white consumers of Cold War America feel more comfortable." Taken from a term common among the Delta and electric blues cultures, rock and roll was actually rhythm and blues rechristened with a more "socially acceptable" title. Of course, the term "rock and roll" had sexual connotations as well; this, along with its roots in black culture, allowed white cultural conservatives of the time to demonize the form.

Thus, the majority of R&B performers never made the distinction between rhythm and blues and rock and roll. Ike Turner, a talent scout for the pioneering Sun Studios record label, was a formidable bandleader and guitarist; his 1951 cut "Rocket 88" has been considered by some to be the very first rock and roll record. The song's distorted guitar tone was achieved by accident—coming from a broken amplifier speaker—but would later influence the gritty sound of many subsequent rock and blues guitarists. Turner achieved mainstream success in collaboration with his wife, singer Tina Turner, who would later eclipse him in fame. One R&B artist who established a prosperous career in rock and roll was New Orleans-born pianist Antoine "Fats" Domino. Although he had produced a great amount of strong R&B material before his career in rock and roll, Domino did not hit the charts until 1955 with "Ain't That A Shame," followed by the classics "Blueberry Hill," "I'm Walkin'," and "Whole Lotta Loving." Another R&B pianist/singer to enter the rock and roll field was Little Richard Pennimen, a former Pentecostal gospel singer whose career in pop music began in 1956 with the hit "Tutti Frutti." Before entering a Seventh Day Adventist seminary in 1959, Little Richard produced a string of hits: "Long Tall Sally," "Rip It Up," "The Girl Can't Help It," and "Good Golly Miss Molly."

In 1955, as Fats Domino's New Orleans style R&B tunes climbed the charts, a young guitarist from St. Louis named Chuck Berry achieved nationwide fame when his country-influenced song "Maybelleine" reached number five on the charts. Backed by bluesman Muddy Water's rhythm section, "Maybelleine" offered a unique form of R&B, combining white hillbilly, or rockabilly, with jump blues; Berry revolutionized R&B by featuring the guitar as a lead, rather than a rhythm instrument. Modeled after his blues-guitar mentor T-Bone Walker, Berry's double string guitar bends and syncopated upstroke rhythm created a driving backdrop for his colorfully poetic tales of teenage life. A very eclectic and creative musician, Berry incorporated the sounds of urban blues, country, calypso, Latin, and even Hawaiian music into his unique brand of R&B. His classic "Johnny B. Goode," recorded in 1958, became a standard in almost every rock and roll band's repertoire, including 1960s rock guitar hero Jimi Hendrix.

Poly Styrene, a black woman, emerged in the 1970s as the leader of the punk group X-Ray Spec. Folk and soft rock maven Tracy Chapman became the Ritchie Havens of the late 1980s. In that decade and in the 1990s, black rock groups such as the Bus Boys, Living Colour, and Body Count had varying degrees of success. Blacks were also prominent in such musically hybrid groups as Bad Brains, Fishbone, and Skunk Anasie.

## Blacks and Country Music

Berry was not the only African American to take an interest in country music. Ray Charles' crossover into country music in the early 1960s caused controversy in many circles. In 1959, Charles recorded "I'm Moving On," a country tune by Hank Snow. Despite opposition, Charles went on to record a fine collection of songs in 1962 entitled *Modern Sounds in Country Music*. Filled with soulful ballads and backed by colorful string sections, the session produced two classic numbers "You Don't Know Me" and "I Can't Stop Loving You." Its popularity spawned a 1963 sequel *Modern Sounds in Country Music Volume 2*, producing several more hits including Hank Williams' "Your Cheating Heart" and "Take These Chains From My Heart."

Unlike other mainstream black country artists, Charles' renditions remained immersed in his unique gospel-blues sound. Before Charles' entrance into the country music field there had been many African American country artists like Dedford Bailey, a partially disabled harmonica player who became a regularly featured performer on the Grand Ole Opry from 1925 to 1941. However, it was not until 1965, when Charley Pride arrived on the country music scene with his RCA recordings "Snakes Crawl at Night" and "Atlantic Coastal Line," that a black artist emerged as a superstar in the country tradition. Pride's songs were so steeped in the country tradition that many radio listeners were astounded when they found out his racial identity. With the arrival of Pride, there appeared other black country artists like Linda Martel from South Carolina, O. B. McClinton from Mississippi, and Oklahoma-born Big Al Downing and Stoney Edwards. The most noted of these artists, Edwards recorded two nationwide hits in 1968 with Jesse Winchester's "You're On My Mind" and Leonard Cohen's "Bird on a Wire."

## ◆ SWEET SOUL MUSIC AND SOCIAL REVOLUTION

The tremendous social upheavals of the 1960s—including but not limited to the Civil Rights, Black Power, and women's movements and the coalescence

Ray Charles, one of the world's most popular musicians.

of a youth-based counterculture—were paralleled by numerous new musical forms. Perhaps no single genre of popular song encapsulated the highs and lows of this period more than soul music. Born in the black church, where testifying preachers and harmonizing choirs shepherded their congregations to weekly ecstasy, the form was escorted into the secular world by a handful of artists schooled simultaneously in gospel, jazz, country blues, R&B, and rock and roll.

Singer-keyboardist Ray Charles has been credited as one of the founders of the soul genre. His earliest hits— notably "What'd I Say" and "I Got a Woman"—brought the emotional testifying and call-and-response arrangements associated with gospel music into a non-religious context. He added the earthy pull of the blues and a jazz-influenced harmonic complexity to his distinctive musical blend. This hybrid of blue groove and spirit was the secular gospel known as soul music. Such innovations were controversial, but the sounds of soul sweetened and enriched rhythm and blues music from then on. Charles ruffled more feathers by mixing soul and country music. Blind "Brother Ray" became a cultural icon in the ensuing decades.

While R&B had functioned for some time as gospel's sinful, worldly counterpart—focusing largely on the concerns of the body while church music addressed the spirit—soul refused to deny either side of human experience. Even so, the young genre's exuberance and ambition made it ideal for reflecting the growing aspirations of America's black population. Inspired by the teachings and nonviolent organizing of Dr. Martin Luther King, Jr. and other civil rights leaders, African Americans also responded to songs that trumpeted change. "People Get Ready" and "We're a Winner" by Curtis Mayfield and the Impressions were early anthems; as soul grew and diversified many more would come.

Singer-bandleader James Brown, meanwhile, combined uplift and hard groove, gradually moving from heady soul/R&B into a new territory called funk with hits like "I Got You (I Feel Good)" and "Cold Sweat." Brown ran one of the tightest ships around, alternately inspiring and browbeating his musicians; turnover was high, but the ensemble was always a well-oiled machine. Though he would refine the funk style—driving rhythms emphasizing the "one" or first beat of each measure; repetitive vocal phrases and improvised, "churchy" shouts; and minimal, almost dissonant, instrumental figures—during the early 1960s, its content remained largely sexual for some time. Brown's political message did not fully materialize until the end of the decade. By then, his funky sermons championed black economic independence and freedom from addiction. Brown had a seismic effect on pop; not only funk artists but also scores of rock and rap musicians took his work as a point of departure.

Following Brown's lead, Sly and the Family Stone—led by Sylvester "Sly Stone" Stewart, a Northern California DJ and producer—lent a psychedelic rock tinge and communal good vibes to the bedrock funk groove. Featuring musicians black and white, male and female, the group offered one of the most inclusive visions in pop history. While "Dance to the Music" mapped out their utopia in musical terms, they trumpeted tolerance and equality in happy hits like "Everyday People," "Everybody Is a Star," and "You Can Make It If You Try." Stone's vision would darken substantially later on, however.

The syncopated rhythms of New Orleans were also fundamental to the development of modern funk. The Meters began as an instrumental foursome and eventually backed up acts as diverse as singer Lee Dorsey, vocal group The Pointer Sisters, and British popster Robert Palmer. During the 1960s they scored some instrumental hits—notably "Cissy Strut"—before add-

ing vocals in the 1970s. Though they eventually flew apart and were partly subsumed by soul survivors the Neville Brothers, the Meters were profoundly influential.

## Soul North and South: Stax/Volt, Atlantic, and Motown

Soul music's increasing hold on the public imagination during the 1960s had a great deal to do with two record companies, the Atlantic Records subsidiary Stax/Volt in the South and Motown in the North. Stax/Volt was a Memphis-based label that introduced the world to the rough-hewn "funky" sound of southern soul and R&B. The company's greatest successes came during the 1960s, thanks to a roster of powerful artists, gifted songwriters, and one of the greatest "house bands" in music history. The band in question, led by keyboardist Booker T. Jones, was a formidable mixed-race groove machine that not only backed the whole Stax roster and numerous acts on its parent label, Atlantic, but also achieved success as an instrumental recording act, Booker T. and the MG's. Their smoldering workouts "Green Onions" and "Hip Hug-Her" became signature themes of the era.

Stax's roster included vocal duo Sam and Dave, Rufus and Carla Thomas, Eddie Floyd, and Otis Redding. House songwriters Isaac Hayes and David Porter wrote hits like "Soul Man" and "Hold On, I'm Coming" for Sam and Dave; Hayes himself would later become a pop/soul superstar. Redding was both an extraordinary singer and a gifted tunesmith; he penned the luminous "Dock of the Bay" and the righteous "Respect." The latter song was transformed into an anthem of nascent feminism and black dignity thanks to the alchemy of Atlantic Records' Aretha Franklin, a gospel-bred singer turned pop maven; Franklin would become the "Queen of Soul" and one of the most enduring figures in popular music. While Franklin made "Respect" and other celebrated recordings—tracks like "Chain of Fools," the incandescent "(You Make Me Feel Like a) Natural Woman," and "I Never Loved a Man"—at the Fame studios in Muscle Shoals, Alabama, other Atlantic soul stars came to Memphis to make their hit records. The Stax crew collaborated with Wilson Pickett on hugely successful singles like "In the Midnight Hour" and "Land of 1000 Dances." Ultimately, however, Stax lost its commercial momentum; and by the 1970s was struggling to compete with a panoply of rivals.

As soul music gained a mass following in the black community, a black-owned and family-run Detroit record company emerged as one of the largest and most successful African American business enterprises in the United States. In 1959, Berry Gordy, a Detroit entrepreneur, songwriter, and modern jazz enthusiast, established the Motown Record Corporation.

James Brown, the "Godfather of Soul."

With its headquarters located in a modest two-story home, the company proudly displayed a sign on its exterior reading Hitsville USA. Taking advantage of the diversity of local talent, Gordy employed Detroit-based contract teams, writers, producers, and engineers. Motown's studio became a great laboratory for technological innovations, advancing the use of echo, multitracking, and over-dubbing. In the studio, Gordy employed the city's finest jazz and classical musicians to accompany the young singing talent signed to the company.

Unlike the soul music emerging in studios like Stax and Muscle Shoals, Motown's music was also marketed at the white middle class; Gordy called his music "The Sound of Young America," and sought to produce glamorous and well-groomed acts. "Blues and R&B always had a funky look to it back in those days," explained Motown producer Mickey Stevenson. "We felt that we should have a look that the mothers and fathers would want their children to follow."

Thus, Motown set out to produce a sound which it considered more refined and less "off-key" than the music played by mainstream soul and blues artists. In its early years of operation, Motown retained a R&B influ-

ence as evidenced in songs like the Marvelettes' "Please Mister Postman" (1961), Mary Wells' "You Beat Me to the Punch" (1962), and Marvin Gaye's "Pride and Joy" (1963).

One of the main forces responsible for the emergence of a unique "Motown sound" appeared in the production team of Brian and Eddie Holland, and Lamont Dozier, or H-D-H, as they came to be known. Utilizing the recording techniques of Phil Spector's "wall of sound," the H-D-H team brought fame to many of Motown's "girlgroups" such as Martha and the Vandellas, and the Supremes, featuring Diana Ross.

During 1966 and 1967, H-D-H began to use more complex string arrangements based upon minor chord structures. This gave rise to what has been referred to as their "classical period." As a result, many Motown songs reflected the darker side of lost love and the conditions of ghetto life. This mood was captured in such songs by the Four Tops as "Reach Out, I'll Be There," "Bernadette," and "Seven Rooms of Gloom."

After the Holland-Dozier-Holland team left Motown in 1968, the company, faced with numerous artistic and economic problems, fell into a state of decline. A year later, Gordy signed the Jackson Five, the last major act to join the label before its demise. The Jacksons landed 13 consecutive hit singles including "ABC" and "I'll Be There." In 1971, Gordy moved the Motown Record Corporation to Los Angeles, where the company directed its efforts toward film making. Through the late 1970s and early 1980s, Motown continued to sign such acts as the Commodores, Lionel Richie, and DeBarge. But in 1984, Gordy entered into a distribution agreement with MCA records and eventually sold Motown to an entertainment conglomerate.

## ◆ FROM PSYCHEDELIC SOUL TO DISCO

Disillusionment after the deaths of Dr. King and black power advocate Malcolm X, along with the lingering trauma of the Vietnam War and the worsening plight of America's inner cities, had a marked influence on soul's direction. Curtis Mayfield projected a vision of wary hope in his early 1970s work. His landmark soundtrack for the "Blaxploitation" film *Superfly* reflected the new soul paradigm: at once gritty and symphonic, encompassing soul's far-reaching ambition and funk's uncompromising, earthy realism. Isaac Hayes's theme from *Shaft*, another urban action film, earned an Academy Award. Much of the funk and soul of this period drew not only on the percolating rhythms developed by Brown but also on the trailblazing guitar work of Jimi Hendrix.

Hailed by many as the greatest electric guitarist of all time, Hendrix had toiled as a sideman for numerous R&B acts but emerged as a rocker of the first order during the mid-1960s. By the time of his death in 1970, he had revolutionized lead guitar playing forever; his use of the wah-wah pedal, an effect that lent a powerful percussive dimension to the instrument, became a staple of funk. His melding of psychedelic rock, hard blues, and soul tropes, meanwhile, influenced the "psychedelic soul" that emerged in his wake.

Commercial soul addressed the tenor of the times. Trailblazers Sly and the Family Stone focused less on the rainbow-colored sentiments of the preceding era and more on urban turmoil with their landmark album *There's a Riot Going On*, as did Marvin Gaye with hits like "Trouble Man" and "What's Goin' On." The O'Jays enjoyed chart success with such anxious singles as "Backstabbers" and "For the Love of Money," and the Temptations wrapped their prodigious vocal chops around inner-city woes on "Papa Was a Rolling Stone," among other smashes.

The 1970s did not lack for more traditionally romantic performers, however. Apart from Marvin Gaye, the period's most seductive male vocalists were arguably Al Green and Barry White. Green's rich falsetto and inti-

Jimi Hendrix redefined the sound of the electric guitar.

mate phrasing on hits like "Let's Stay Together" and "Love and Happiness" quickly established him as a visionary in the genre; though he left pop music to sing gospel music and preach, he remained a beloved figure in the soul world and returned to the fold for a 1995 album. White's bedroom soundtracks, meanwhile, kept lovers in thrall with an intoxicating blend of his baritone vocals and symphonic arrangements.

During the mid-1970s, club dance-floors were increasingly dominated by the pulsating sounds of disco. With its thumping beat and lush arrangements, the music was viewed by many as a saccharine and escapist form that betrayed the mission of funk and soul. While a number of powerful performers emerged from the disco scene, few could approach the star power of diva Donna Summer, who enjoyed a wave of hits before a religious conversion moved her into gospel. Though disco's "crossover" success meant that a number of artists who scored in that format were white, several all-black acts, notably Chic, Kool and the Gang, and LaBelle, flourished during this period.

These commercial laments were outstripped in daring—though not in sales—by the work of Detroit's Funkadelic. Fronted by singer and hairstylist George

Clinton, who led a doo-wop group called The Parliaments in the 1950s, Funkadelic mixed acid rock's cosmic guitar excursions with funk's relentless grooves; a danger existed in their work that limited its commercial appeal, but profoundly influenced rock and rap.

Eventually, Clinton established another group, Parliament, which focused on horn-driven funk and elaborate, fantasy-oriented concept albums. Funkadelic and Parliament, though manifestly different at first, gradually moved into similar territory as "P. Funk"; the "P" meaning "pure." Soon P. Funk was the umbrella term for a family of bands that included Bootsy's Rubber Band, The Brides of Funkenstein, and Parlet. Clinton scored in the 1980s as a solo artist, most notably with the mega-hit "Atomic Dog." P. Funk was so influential that for a time Parliament found itself competing with acts that appropriated its sound and themes, including hitmakers like the Ohio Players, Rick James, George Duke, and Earth, Wind and Fire. Though funk declined during the 1980s, artists like Prince took it in a new, eclectic direction.

## ◆ RAP: A VOICE FROM THE SUBCULTURE

While funk sold millions of records and received extensive radio airplay in the mid-1970s, rap music emerged within a small circle of New York artists and entertainers. In neighborhoods in Upper Manhattan and the South Bronx, disc jockeys at private parties discovered how to use "little raps" between songs to keep dancers on their feet. From behind the microphone, DJs created a call and response pattern with the audience. Taking advantage of their master of ceremonies status, they often boasted of their intellectual or sexual prowess. "Soon a division of labor emerged," explained Jefferson Morley. "DJs concentrated on perfecting the techniques of manipulating the turntables, while master of ceremonies (MCs or rappers) concentrated on rapping in rhymes." Through the use of a special stylus, rappers moved records back and forth on the turntable in order to create a unique rhythmic sound, known within the rap culture as needle rocking and later as "scratching."

Long before the modern rap, or hip-hop, culture appeared, however, African American artists existed who performed in a rap-style idiom. In 1929, for instance, New York singer-comedian Pigmeat Markham gave performances representative of an early rap-style.

Rap music is also rooted in the talking jazz style of a group of ex-convicts called the Last Poets. During the 1960s, this ensemble of black intellectuals rapped in complex rhythms over music played by jazz accompa-

nists. Last Poet member Jalal Uridin, recording under the name Lightning Rod, released an album entitled *Hustler's Convention.* Backed by the funk band Kool and the Gang, Uridin's recording became very influential to the early New York rappers.

Among one of the first New York rap artists of the early 1970s was Jamaican-born Clive Campbell, aka Kool Herc. A street DJ, Herc developed the art of sampling, the method of playing a section of a recording over and over in order to create a unique dance mix. Others to join the New York scene were black nationalist DJ Africa Bambaataa from the southeast Bronx and Joseph Saddler, known as Grandmaster Flash, from the central Bronx. Flash formed the group Grandmaster Flash and The Three MCs (Cowboy, Kid Creole, and Melle Mel). Later he added Kurtis Blow and Duke Bootee who founded the Furious Five.

However, rap music did not reach a broad audience until 1980, when the Sugar Hill Gang's song "Rapper's Delight" received widespread radio airplay. Small record companies began to affect the development of pop for the first time in years. Def Jam spearheaded the rise of influential rappers LL Cool J, Run-DMC, and Public Enemy, while Tommy Boy Records contributed to the rise of electro-funk. As rap groups assembled during the decade, they began to use their art to describe the harsh realities of inner city life. Unlike early rap music which was generally upbeat and exuberant in tone, the rap style of the 1980s exhibited a strong sense of racial and political consciousness. Grandmaster Flash's "The Message" was the first blatantly political rap hit; its yearning and desperation recalled the angst-ridden soul records of the preceding decade and hinted as rap's potential. Toward the end of the decade, rap came to express an increasing sense of racial militancy. Inspired by the Nation of Islam and the teachings of martyred race leader Malcolm X, rap groups like Public Enemy turned their music into voice supporting black power. Public Enemy's second LP *It Takes A Nation of Millions to Hold Us Back* sold more than one million copies. Their song "Fight the Power" appeared in director Spike Lee's film *Do the Right Thing.* The group's third album *Fear of a Black Planet* was released in 1990. While it is a statement against "western cultural supremacy," explained group member Chuck D., it is also "about the coming together of all races" in a "racial rebirth." Rapper KRS-One of Boogie Down Productions provided eloquent, barbed political commentary as well.

Women have also played a role in the shaping of rap music. Rap artists such as Queen Latifah, MC Lyte, and the group Salt-N-Pepa represent a growing number of female rappers who speak for the advancement of black women in American society. Queen Latifah has emerged as critic of male dominance in the music industry and the sexist image of women presented by some male rap artists.

The late 1980s also saw the birth of the "Native Tongues" school of rap, the graduates of which employed an eclectic array of samples and more heavily relied on humor and baroque rhymes than did their hardcore and political brethren. The best-known groups of this school were De La Soul, A Tribe Called Quest, and The Pharcyde; Digital Underground, meanwhile, openly aspired to be "Sons of the P." and wove elaborate Parliament-esque concepts. Artists with a more bohemian bent began to rely heavily on jazz; some, like Digable Planets and US3, sold briskly. A few, like Arrested Development and Spearhead, stayed close to their soul and funk roots.

The biggest story in rap during the 1990s was the rise of "Gangsta" rap, which utilized old-school funk beats and dwelt on hustling and violence—usually without soul's veneer of guarded optimism. The group N.W.A. (Niggaz With Attitude) upset social conservatives with their megahit "F— Tha Police," and its alumni Dr. Dre, Ice Cube, and Eazy-E would all become major solo artists. Ice-T put a slightly more deliberative spin on his gangster tales, but it was Dre's protege Snoop Doggy Dogg and former Digital Underground member Tupac Shakur who would become the biggest crossover acts of all. Snoop's laid-back style in particular earned him pop status with cuts like "Gin and Juice," "Murder Was the Case," and "Doggy Dogg World." The crossover success of these recordings was so worrisome to aforementioned conservatives that gangsta rap lyrics became a staple in political speeches, and politicians and activist groups threatened to take action against record companies that released such material.

Some pop rappers, like MC Hammer (who eventually dropped the "MC") and DJ Jazzy Jeff and the Fresh Prince, enjoyed periodic success and then faded from the charts. Those who retained a bit more street-level credibility, on the other hand, such as Naughty By Nature, who had a mega-smash with "O.P.P." and Coolio, who ruled the charts and scored a Grammy Award for his "Gangster's Paradise," enjoyed a longer reign.

In the mid-1990s, creative rhyme styles and techniques were perpetuated by Das Efx, Fu-Schnickens, Mystikal, Bone Thugs-N-Harmony, and Busta Rhymez, among others. With its array of styles and points of view, rap has emerged as a primary cultural form for young African Americans. Like the music of its predecessors, rap is filled with artistic energy and descriptions of the human experience. No longer considered a fad, rap has become a subculture.

## Soul's New Directions

Perhaps in part to counter the increasing dominance of hardcore hip-hop in the marketplace, R&B and Soul moved in a softer direction during the 1980s; as bands were replaced by sequenced keyboards and drum machines, recordings in this genre were increasingly dominated by producers and vocalists. Even longtime soul legends like Aretha Franklin and Chaka Khan moved in a glossier direction. This period saw the rise of a handful of phenomenally successful singers, notably Whitney Houston, whose mother Cissy had sung with Franklin and many others. Following a monster debut, Houston collected a string of hits and awards; her apotheosis came with the gargantuan sales of the soundtrack to the film *The Bodyguard*, in which she also had a starring role. Houston's athletic vocal chops paved the way for a number of other new soul divas, including Toni Braxton, Mariah Carey, and Mary J. Blige. Producers L. A. Reid and Babyface were among the preeminent hitmakers of this era; like Babyface, R. Kelley was successful both as producer and recording artist.

While the soft-edged trend continued through the 1990s, some artists within the fold, like the smash groups TLC and En Vogue, flirted with old-school soul. Meanwhile, "alternative" soul emerged at the margins, thanks to artists like bassist/singer-songwriter Me'Shell Ndegeocello, Arrested Development refugee Dionne Farris, and Marvin Gaye-disciple D'Angelo.

According to the Recording Industry Association of America (RIAA)—the bestower of gold, platinum, and multi-platinum plaques—among the top black record sellers with units including CDs, cassettes, albums, and singles as tallied between 1985 and 1996 were Michael Jackson, Whitney Houston, Mariah Carey, Prince, Janet Jackson, Boyz II Men, Hammer, TLC, Luther Vandross, Lionel Richie, and Nigerian-born British singer Sade.

## ◆ POPULAR MUSIC GATEKEEPERS

**Nicholas Ashford (1943– )**
**Valerie Simpson (1948– )**
*Singers, Songwriters*

One of the most enduring songwriting teams to emerge from Motown has been Nicholas Ashford and Valerie Simpson. For over a quarter of a century, the team has written hit songs for artists from Ray Charles to Diana Ross.

Nicky Ashford was born in Fairfield, South Carolina, on May 14, 1943, and Valerie Simpson was born in the Bronx section of New York City on August 26, 1948. The two met in the early 1960s while singing in the same choir at Harlem's White Rock Baptist Church. With Ashford's gift for lyrics and Simpson's exceptional gospel piano and compositional skills, the two began to write for the staff of Scepter Records in 1964. Two years later, their song "Let's Go Get Stoned" became a hit for Ray Charles.

In 1962, Ashford and Simpson joined Motown's Jobete Music, where they wrote and produced hit songs for Marvin Gaye and Tammi Terrell, including "Ain't Nothing Like the Real Thing," "Good Loving Ain't Easy to Come By," and the "Onion Song." Next, they worked with Diana Ross who had just set out to establish a solo career producing such hits as "Remember Me," "Reach Out (and Touch Somebody's Hand)," and an updated version of "Ain't No Mountain High Enough."

Ashford and Simpson's success as songwriters led them to release their own solo recording *Exposed* in 1971. After signing with Warner Brothers in 1973, they recorded a number of hit LPs: *Is It Still Good To Ya* (1978), *Stay Free* (1979), *A Musical Affair* (1980), and their biggest seller *Solid* in 1985. More recently, the singing and songwriting duo have collaborated on projects with producer Quincy Jones and artists like Gladys Knight and Chaka Khan.

### Anita Baker (1958– )
*Singer*

One of the most sophisticated soul divas to emerge in the 1980s, Baker considers herself "a balladeer" dedicated to singing music rooted in the tradition of gospel music and jazz. Inspired by her idols Mahalia Jackson, Sarah Vaughan,, and Nancy Wilson, Baker brings audiences a sincere vocal style which defies commercial trends and electronic overproduction.

Born on January 26, 1958, in Toledo, Ohio, Baker was raised in a single-parent middle class family in Detroit. She first sang in storefront churches, where it was common for the congregation to improvise on various gospel themes. After graduating from Central High School, Baker sang in the Detroit soul/funkgroup Chapter 8. Although Chapter 8 recorded the album *I Just Want To Be Your Girl* for the Ariola label, the group's lack of commercial success caused it to disband, and for the next three years, Baker worked as a receptionist in a law firm.

In 1982, Baker, after signing a contract with Beverly Glen, moved to Los Angeles, where she recorded the critically acclaimed solo album *Songstress*. Following a legal battle with Glen, Baker signed with Elektra and recorded her debut hit album *Rapture* in 1986. As the album's executive producer, Baker sought "a minimalist approach" featuring simple recording techniques which captured the natural sounds of her voice. The LP's single "Sweet Love" brought Baker immediate crossover success. Baker's follow-up effort, the multi-platinum

Anita Baker

selling *Giving You the Best I Got* is considered one of the finest pop music albums of the 1990s. Her third effort *Compositions*, recorded in 1990, featured a number of back-up musicians including Detroit jazz guitarist Earl Klugh.

After a nearly four-year hiatus, Baker released the double-platinum *Rhythm of Love* in 1994. Winner of five Grammys, two NAACP Image awards, two American Music awards, two Soul Train awards, and a star on Hollywood's Walk of Fame, Baker has brought her audiences music of eloquence and integrity that sets her apart from most of her contemporaries.

### Chuck Berry (1926– )
*Singer, Songwriter, Guitarist*

The first guitar hero of rock and roll, Chuck Berry's 1950s jukebox hits remain some of the most imaginative poetic tales in the history of popular music. Influenced by bluesmen like Aron T-Bone Walker and the picking styles of rockabilly and country musicians, Berry's solo guitar work brought the guitar to the forefront of rhythm and blues. His driving ensemble sound paved the way for the emergence of bands from the Beach Boys to the Rolling Stones.

Born on October 18, 1926, in San Jose, California, Charles Edward Anderson Berry was raised in a middle class neighborhood on the outskirts of St. Louis. Berry first sang gospel music at home and at the Antioch Baptist Church. Although Berry was drawn to the sounds of bluesmen such as Tampa Red, Arthur Crudup, and

Muddy Waters, he did not become serious about music until he was given a guitar by local rhythm and blues musician Joe Sherman. Taken by the sounds of rhythm and blues, Berry formed a trio with Johnny Jones on piano and Ebby Harding on drums. Hired to play back-yard barbecues, clubs, and house parties, the trio expanded their repertoire to include Nat "King" Cole ballads and country songs by Hank Williams.

By 1955, the 28-year-old Berry had become a formidable rhythm and blues guitarist and singer. While in Chicago, Berry visited a club to hear his idol, Muddy Waters, perform. At the suggestion of Waters, Berry visited Chess Studios where he eventually signed with the label. Berry's first hit for Chess was "Maybellene," a country song formally entitled "Ida May." In 1956 Berry continued on a path toward superstardom with the hits "Roll Over Beethoven," "Oh Baby Doll," followed by "Rock and Roll Music," and the guitar anthem "Johnny B. Goode."

Released from the Indiana Federal Prison in 1964 after serving a sentence for violating the Mann Act, Berry resumed his musical career, recording "Nadine" and "No Particular Place to Go." Since the 1970s, Berry has continued to record and tour. Berry's 1972 release of

Chuck Berry

the novelty tune "My-Ding-a-Ling" became his best-selling single. In 1988, Taylor Hackford paid tribute to the guitar legend in his film *Hail! Hail! Rock 'n Roll.* Berry was also a featured performer at the opening of Cleveland's Rock and Roll Hall of Fame and Museum in 1995.

### Bobby Brown (1966– )
*Singer*

Savvy and street smart, singer Bobby Brown possesses a charismatic charm which has earned him numerous million-selling records. A founding member of the Boston-based group New Edition, Brown remained with the group from 1984 to 1987. His solo debut album *Kind of Strange* featured the single "Girlfriend." Brown's second release *Don't Be Cruel* produced the single "Don't Be Cruel" and the video hits "My Prerogative" and "Every Little Step."

In 1990, Brown embarked on a worldwide tour. After playing a small role in the box office smash film *Ghostbusters II.* In July of 1992 Brown married singer/actress Whitney Houston in a star-studded ceremony. Two years later, the two solo artists performed together for the first time on the televise 1994 Soul Train Music Awards program. Aside from maintaining a burgeoning music career, Brown is the owner of B. Brown Productions, as well as his own private recording studio. Brown's violent temper and brushes with the law have been the subject of much publicity in the 1990s, even eclipsing the release of his 1993 recording *Remixes in the Key of B.*

### James Brown (1933– )
*Singer, Bandleader*

James Brown's impact on American and African popular music has been of seismic proportion. His explosive onstage energy and intense gospel music and R&B-based sound earned him numerous titles such as "The Godfather of Soul," "Mr. Dynamite," and "The Hardest Working Man in Show Business." During the 1960s and early 1970s, Brown's back–up group emerged as one of the greatest soul bands in the history of modern music, one that served as a major force in the development of funk and fusion jazz.

Born in Barnell, South Carolina on May 3, 1933, Brown moved to Augusta, Georgia at the age of four. Although he was raised by various relatives in conditions of economic deprivation, Brown possessed an undaunted determination to succeed at an early age. When not picking cotton, washing cars, or shining shoes, he earned extra money by dancing on the streets and at amateur contests. In the evening, Brown watched shows by such bandleaders as Louis Jordan and Lucky Millinder.

James Brown

At 15, Brown quit school to take up a full-time music career. In churches, Brown sang with the Swanee Quartet and the Gospel Starlighters, which soon afterward became the R&B group the Flames. During the same period he also sang and played drums with R&B bands. While with the Flames, Brown toured extensively, performing a wide range of popular material including the Five Royales' "Baby Don't Do It," the Clover's "One Mint Julep," and Hank Ballard and the Midnighters hit "Annie Had a Baby."

In 1956, Brown's talents caught the attention of Syd Nathan, founder of King Records. In the same year, after signing with the Federal label, a subsidiary of King, Brown recorded "Please Please Please." After the Flames disbanded in 1957, Brown formed a new Flames ensemble, featuring former members of Little Richard's band. Back in the studio the following year, Brown recorded "Try Me," which became a Top 50 pop hit. On the road, Brown polished his stage act and singing ability, producing what became known as the "James Brown Sound." His 1965 hit "Papa's Got a Brand New Bag" earned him a Grammy for best rhythm and blues recording, a feat he repeated in 1986 with "Living in America," a song that appeared on the soundtrack of the film *Rocky IV*.

After the release of "Out of Sight," Brown's music exhibited a more polyrhythmic sound as evidenced in staccato horn bursts and contrapuntal bass lines. Each successive release explored increasingly new avenues of popular music. Brown's 1967 hit "Cold Sweat" and the 1968 release "I Got the Feeling" not only sent shock waves through the music industry, they served as textbooks of rhythm for thousands of aspiring musicians. In 1970 Brown disbanded the Flames and formed the JBs, featuring Bootsy Collins. The group produced a string of hits like "Super Bad" and "Sex Machine." 1993's *Universal James* was Brown's 79th album.

Despite the negative publicity generated by the oft "in trouble" performer, Brown's career remained effervescent in the late 1980s to 1990s. Inducted into the Rock and Roll Hall of Fame in 1986, the ever-popular, Brown received the Ray Charles Lifetime Achievement Award from the Rhythm & Blues Foundation as part of the organization's Pioneer Awards program in 1993. Later that year, he awarded for his lifetime achievements at the Black Radio Exclusive awards banquet in Washington, DC. Steamboat Springs, Colorado voted to name a bridge after the soulster and Brown's hometown of Augusta, followed suit by naming a street after him. Perhaps the sweetest tribute paid to Brown has been the promotion of James Brown Cookeez by a Georgia-based cookie company. Many of his recordings were reissued in the 1990s.

### Shirley Caesar (1938– )
*Singer*

The leading gospel music singer of her generation, Shirley Caesar was born in Durham, North Carolina, in 1938. One of 12 children born to gospel great "Big Jim" Caesar, Shirley sang in church choirs as a child. By age 14, Caesar went on the road as a professional gospel singer, touring the church circuit on weekends and during school vacations. Known as "Baby Shirley," Caesar joined the Caravans in 1958. Featured as an opening act in the show, Caesar worked the audience to a near fever pitch. When Inez Andrews left the Caravans in 1961, Caesar became the featured artist who provided crowds with powerful performances of such songs as "Comfort Me," "Running For Jesus," and "Sweeping Through the City."

After leaving the Caravans in 1966, Caesar formed her own group, the Shirley Caesar Singers. Her sheer energy and pugnacious spirit made her one of the reigning queens of modern gospel. Her first album *I'll Go* remains one of her most critically acclaimed. In 1969, she released a ten-minute sermonette with the St. Louis Choir that earned her a gold record. A six-time Grammy winner, Caesar conducts weekly sermons at the Mount

Calvary Holy Church in Raleigh, North Carolina, between performances and recording dates.

## Reverend James Cleveland (1932–1991)
*Singer, Pianist, Composer*

Known by such titles as "King James" and the "Crown Prince," the Reverend James Cleveland emerged as a giant of the postwar gospel music scene. Likened to the vocal style of Louis Armstrong, Cleveland's raw bluesy growls and shouts appeared on more recordings than any other gospel singer of his generation.

Born on December 5, 1932, in Chicago, Illinois, James Cleveland first sang gospel under the direction of Thomas Dorsey at the Pilgrim Baptist Church. Inspired by the keyboard talents of gospel singer Roberta Martin, Cleveland later began to study piano. In 1951 Cleveland joined the Gospelaires, a trio which cut several sides for the Apollo label. With the Caravans, Cleveland arranged and performed on two hits "The Solid Rock" and an up-tempo reworking of the song "Old Time Religion."

By the mid-1950s, Cleveland's original compositions had found their way into the repertoires of numerous gospel groups, and he was performing with such artists as the Thorn Gospel Singers, Roberta Martin Singers,

Reverend James Cleveland

Mahalia Jackson, the Gospel Allstars, and the Meditation Singers. In 1960 Cleveland formed the Cleveland Singers featuring organist and accompanist Billy Preston. The smash hit "Love of God," recorded with the Detroit-based Voices of Tabernacle, won Cleveland nationwide fame within the gospel community. Signing with the Savoy label, Cleveland, along with keyboardist Billy Preston, released a long list of classic albums including *Christ Is the Answer*, and *Peace Be Still*. As a founder of the Gospel Workshop of America in 1968, Cleveland organized annual conventions which brought together thousands of gospel singers and songwriters. A year later, he helped found the Southern California Community Choir.

In 1972, Charles was reunited with former piano understudy Aretha Franklin, who featured Cleveland as a guest artist on the album *Amazing Grace*. Recipient of the NAACP Image Award, Cleveland also acquired a honorary degree from Temple Baptist College. Although the commercial gospel trends of the 1980s had caused a downturn in Cleveland's career, he continued to perform the gutsy blues-based sound which brought him recognition from listeners throughout the world. Cleveland died February 9, 1991, in Los Angeles, California.

## George Clinton (1942– )
*Singer, Songwriter, Bandleader, Producer*

The father of "P. [i.e.'pure'] Funk," George Clinton spun the funk formula refined by James Brown into an institution. His groups Parliament and Funkadelic and a panoply of offshoots kept the rest of the R&B world straining to keep up during the 1970s; by the 1990s, the prodigious body of work recorded under the P. Funk moniker exercised a huge influence on rap, soul, and rock. Though he relied heavily on a group of talented musicians to bring his visions to life, Clinton was the visionary behind the legendary "Parliafunkadelicment Thang."

Born in North Carolina, Clinton moved with his family to New Jersey during his adolescence; there he helped form a doo-wop group called The Parliaments. After years of struggling and move to Detroit, the group managed to sell some songs to other artists, but never achieved success on its own. With the advent of psychedelic rock in the mid-1960s, The Parliaments began to change in form; they morphed into Funkadelic by 1968, adding hard rock guitar and spacy grooves. The early Funkadelic albums, notably *Maggot Brain*, became classics of untamed funk-rock.

Clinton deployed Parliament as a slightly more conventional funk vehicle in the early 1970s, emphasizing horns and more dance-oriented arrangements. By the middle of the decade, Parliament had become a major hitmaker with its fantasy-themed concept albums and its circus-like performances. Songs like "Flash Light," "Bop Gun (Endangered Species)," "Mothership Connection," and "Aqua Boogie" became funk staples.

Funkadelic began to take a more commercial turn, particularly after signing with Warner Bros. Records; its biggest hits came with the albums *One Nation Under a Groove* and *Uncle Jam Wants You*. Clinton helped his bassist Bootsy Collins become a funk legend in his own right, and oversaw albums by such P. Funk enterprises as The Brides of Funkenstein, Parlet, and the P. Funk All-Stars, among many others. He also released a slew of solo recordings; his biggest hit in this capacity was the boisterous "Atomic Dog." Though business declined for these acts during the 1980s, Clinton's influence were constant in black pop; by the 1990s, P. Funk recordings were among the most sampled in hip-hop. Clinton went so far as to set up an easy licensing system for rap artists who wanted to lift from his work. Thanks to the adoration of everyone from Dr. Dre to rockers like the Red Hot Chili Peppers, Clinton became a ubiquitous figure on the pop culture scene. He fronted the P. Funk All-Stars at the Lollapalooza rock festival, and appeared in numerous films and television commercials.

Nat "King" Cole

## Nat "King" Cole (1919–1965)
*Singer, Pianist*

Nat Cole was born on March 17, 1919, in Montgomery, Alabama (the family name was Coles, but Cole dropped the "s" when he formed the King Cole Trio years later). When he was five, the family moved to Chicago, and he was soon playing piano and organ in the church where his father served as minister. While attending Phillips High School, Cole formed his own band, and also played with small combos, including one headed by his brother Edward, a bassist.

In 1936, Cole joined the touring company of *Shuffle Along*. After the show folded, he found work in small clubs in Los Angeles. In 1937, the King Cole Trio was formed when the drummer in his quartet failed to appear for a scheduled performance. That same year, Cole made his singing debut when a customer insisted he sing "Sweet Lorraine" (a number he later recorded with great success).

Cole's first record was made in 1943, "Straighten Up and Fly Right," which sold more than 500,000 copies. Over the years, one hit followed another in rapid succession—"Paper Moon," "Route 66," "I Love You for Sentimental Reasons," "Chestnuts Roasting on an Open Fire," "Nature Boy," "Mona Lisa," "Too Young," "Pretend," "Somewhere Along the Way," "Smile," and many others. Cole died of cancer in 1965.

## Natalie Cole (1950– )
*Singer*

With five gold records and her star on Hollywood Boulevard, Natalie Cole has emerged since the 1980s as a major pop music star. Born on February 6, 1950, in Los Angeles, Natalie was the second daughter of jazz pianist and pop music legend Nat "King" Cole. During the early 1970s, Cole performed in nightclubs, while pursuing a degree in child psychology at the University of Massachusetts. In 1975, she recorded her first album *Inseparable* at Curtis Mayfield's Curtom Studios. Her other albums include *Thankful*(1978), *I'm ready* (1983), *Good to Be Back* (1989), *Take a Look* (1993), and *Holly and Ivy* (1994), which coincided with her PBS special *Natalie Cole's Untraditional Traditional Christmas*.

In 1991, Cole released a 22-song collection of her father's hits. The album, which contains a re-mixed version of the original title-track "Unforgettable," features a duet between Cole and her father and earned her "Record of the Year" and "Album of the Year" Grammys, complementing the Grammys she won in 1976 for best new artist and in 1976 and 1977 for best rhythm and blues female vocal performance. Cole also won two NAACP Image awards in the mid-1970s and an American Music Award in 1978.

## Sean "Puffy" Combs (1971– )
*Record Company Executive*

Sean Combs was born in New York, New York in 1971. His ear for rap and hip hop combined with his production skills are a proven combination. He began to be noticed at the age of 19 in New York's hip-hop scene. As an intern at Uptown Records, Combs's talents earned him a permanent position. He headed up Uptown's Artist & Repertoire department where his primary responsibilities signing and developing new talents.

Luck took a turn for the worst as Combs was involved in an unfortunate event. In 1991, anxious fans for a charity basketball game rushed the entrance killing nine people. The event, staged by Combs, put a black mark on his young career. Media attacks and mayoral investigations pushed Combs into a depression. Unable to work, Combs confined himself to his Mt. Vernon, New York home. Within a year, Combs was fired from Uptown.

Frustration and rejection inspired Combs to pursue his life's dreams. Comb's talent had earned him a reputation prompting Arista Records to sign him to a deal. Combs called this division of Arista Records Bad Boy Entertainment. Success soon followed as Bad Boy released hits by rappers Craig Mack and the Notorious B.I.G., both of whom Combs is credited for discovering.

The ability to find such talent is what sets Combs apart from most other hip-hop producers. The success of Bad Boys hip-hop artists has lead to the development of new artists. Various projects, including the 1996 release of singer Faith Evans's debut keep Combs busy. Success and the drive instilled in Combs should keep Bad Boy on the rise.

## Sam Cooke (1931-1964)
*Singer, Songwriter*

Sam Cooke's sophisticated vocal style and refined image made him one of the greatest pop music idols of the early 1960s. One of the first gospel music artists to crossover into popular music, Cooke produced songs of timeless quality, filled with human emotion and spiritual optimism.

Born in Clarksdale, Mississippi, on January 2, 1931, Sam Cooke grew up the son of a Baptist minister in Chicago, Illinois. At the age of nine, Cooke, along with two sisters and a brother, formed a gospel group called the Singing Children. While a teenager, he joined the gospel group the Highway QCs which performed on the same bill with nationally famous gospel acts.

By 1950, Cooke replaced tenor Rupert H. Harris as lead singer for the renowned gospel group the Soul Stirrers. Cooke's first recording with the Soul Stirrers, "Jesus Gave Me Water," was recorded for Art Rupe's Specialty label. Although the song revealed the inexperi-

Sam Cooke

ence of the 20–year–old Cooke, it exhibited a quality of immense passion and heightened feeling. Under the pseudonym Dale Cooke, Sam recorded the pop song "Loveable" in 1957. That same year, in a session for producer Bumps Blackwell on the Keen label, Cooke recorded "You Send Me" which climbed to number one on the rhythm and blues charts. On the Keen label, Cooke recorded eight more consecutive hits including "Everyone Likes to Cha Cha Cha," "Only Sixteen," and "Wonderful World," all of which were written or co-written by Cooke.

After his contract with the Keen label expired in 1960, Cooke signed with RCA, and was assigned to staff producers Hugo Peretti and Luigi Creatore. In August, Cooke's recording "Chain Gang" reached the number two spot on the pop charts. Under the lavish production of Hugo and Luigi, Cooke produced a string of hits such as "Cupid" in 1961, "Twistin' the Night Away," in 1962, and "Another Saturday Night" in 1963. Early in 1964, Cooke appeared on the "Tonight Show", debuting two songs from his upcoming LP which included the gospel-influenced composition "A Change Is Gonna Come." On December 11, Cooke checked into a three-dollar-a-night motel where he demanded entrance into the night manageress's room. After a brief physical struggle, the manageress fired three pistol shots which mortally wounded Cooke. Despite his tragic death, Cooke left behind a catalogue of classic recordings and over 100 original compositions including the hit "Shake" which was posthumously released in 1965.

## Andrae Crouch (1942- )
*Singer, Pianist*

An exponent of a modern pop-based gospel style, Andrae Crouch became one of the leading gospel singers of the 1960s and 1970s. Born on July 1, 1942, in Los Angeles, Andrae Crouch grew up singing in his father's church. Along with his brother and sister, Crouch formed the Crouch Trio, which performed at their father's services as well as on live Sunday-night radio broadcasts. In the mid-1960s Crouch was "discovered" by white Pentecostal evangelists and subsequently signed a contract with Light, a white religious record label. Over the last three decades, Crouch has written numerous songs, many of which have become standards in the repertoire of modern gospel groups. Among his most famous songs are "I Don't Know Why Jesus Loved Me," "Through it All," and "The Blood Will Never Lose Its Power." In recognition for this work, Crouch received an ASCAP Special Songwriter Award.

During the late 1960s Crouch, inspired by the modern charismatic revival movement, began adopting street smart language and informal wardrobe. After forming the Disciples in 1968, Crouch recorded extensively and toured throughout the United States and Europe. His California style of gospel music combines rock, country music, and soul with traditional gospel forms. The Disciples won Grammys in 1975, for *Take Me Back* and in 1979, for *Live in London*, which also received a Dove Award. *This Is Another Day* garnered a Dove Award in 1976, as did Crouch's 1984 solo recording *No Time to Lose.*

Since the 1970s, Crouch's back–up groups have incorporated both electronic and acoustic instruments, including synthesizers. The new approach earned Grammys in 1980 and 1981. As the decade ensued, Crouch recorded as a solo artist and was bestowed the Gospel Music Excellence Award for best male vocalist in 1982, for *More of the Best.*

On September 23, 1995, Crouch assumed the pastorship of the Christ Memorial Church of God in Christ in Pacoima, California, the same pulpit once manned by his father. Nearly one year earlier, Crouch—a two-time NAACP Image Award recipient and one-time Golden Halo awardee-released *Mercy!*, his first album since 1984; others were reissued. His return was well-received.

## Dr. Dre (1965?– )
*Rap singer, Producer*

From the time he was four years old, Dr. Dre, born Andre Ramelle Young, was playing DJ at his mother's parties. In 1981, he heard a song by Grandmaster Flash that inspired him to change his name in honor of basketball star Julius "Dr. J." Erving and become a DJ. Dr. Dre began spinning records at a Los Angeles nightclub, producing the dance tapes in the club's four-track studio. In addition to using the rap trademarks of sampling, scratching, and drum machines, he added keyboards and vocals.

In 1982, when Dre was 17 years old, he formed the World Class Wreckin' Cru with another DJ. Their first independently released single sold 50,000 copies. The following year, Dre graduated from Compton, California's Centennial High School and was offered a mechanical drafting position with an aircraft firm, he turned it down to devote himself to music. In 1985, Dr. Dre joined the newly formed group, N.W.A. (Niggaz with Attitude), along with Ice Cube, Eazy-E, Yella, M. C. Ren, and Arabian Prince. That year he also produced Eazy-E's first platinum album, *Eazy-Duz-It.*

N.W.A's successful yet controversial ouvre included the multi-platinum *Straight Outta Compton*, released in 1989 on Eazy-E and Dr. Dre's Ruthless Records. Dr. Dre produced the D.O.C., a rapper he had discovered in Texas. The result, *No One Can Do It Better*, went to Number One on Billboard's R&B album chart. Dre also produced a platinum album for Michel'le, another Number One recording.

In January of 1990, Ice Cube left N.W.A. over a financial dispute; N.W.A. recorded the last of their four recordings without him in 1991. Later that year, Dre left Ruthless to cofound Death Row Records with Suge Knight. Dre's first solo effort, *The Chronic* was released in 1993. The work, featuring such budding rap artists as Snoop Doggy Dogg, sold three million copies. He went on to produce Snoop's debut, *Doggystyle.*

In 1994, Dre received a Grammy Award for best rap solo performance. At the *Source* awards, he was named best producer, solo artist, and *The Chronic* was named best album. The following year he was named "One of the Top Ten Artists That Mattered Most, 1985-1995" by *Spin.* In 1996, Dre stunned the hip-hop community by announcing that he was leaving Death Row.

## Fats Domino (1928- )
*Singer*

Antoine Domino was born on February 26, 1928, in New Orleans. As a teenager, Domino received piano lessons from Harrison Verret. In between playing night clubs, Domino worked at a factory and mowed lawns around New Orleans. At age 20, he took a job as a pianist with bassist Billy Diamond's combo at the Hideaway Club.

In 1949, while playing with Diamond's group, Domino was discovered by producer and arranger David Bartholomew, a talent scout, musician, and producer for the Imperial label. During the following year, Domino hit the charts with the autobiographical tune "Fat Man." After the release of "Fat Man," he played on tour backed by Bartholomew's band.

Although Domino released a number of sides during the early 1950s, it was not until 1955 that he gained national prominence with the hit "Ain't That A Shame." In the next six years, Domino scored 35 top hits with songs like "Blueberry Hill" (1956), "Blue Monday" (1957), "Whole Lotta Lovin" (1958), and "I'm Walkin" (1959). Domino's recording success led to his appearance in several films in the 1950s including *The Girl Can't Help It*, *Shake Rattle and Roll*, *Disc Jockey Jamboree*, and *The Big Beat*.

After Domino's contract with Imperial expired in 1963, he signed with ABC where he made a number of commercial recordings. In 1965 Domino moved to Mercury and then to Reprise in 1968. In the early 1970s, Domino began to tour with greater regularity than he had during the peak of his career. Today Domino continues to tour and make occasional television appearances.

### Kenneth "Babyface" Edmonds (1958?– )
*Songwriter, Producer*

Edmonds was born in the late 1950s in Indianapolis, Indiana, and spent his high school years finagling interviews with pop star idols like the Jackson 5 and Stevie Wonder. After performing in a number of R&B bands, Edmonds began a collaboration with Antonio "L.A." Reid in 1981; they were then members of an act called the Deele, but soon gained acclaim writing and producing songs for other artists such as Shalamar and Bobby Brown.

In 1989, Edmonds and Reid formed their owned company, LaFace Records, backed by the Arista label. They continued their success in writing and producing pop, soul, and R&B hits for such artists as Paula Abdul and Whitney Houston, and Edmonds and Reid are also credited with giving considerable start to the careers of TLC and Toni Braxton. The duo has won numerous Grammy Awards, including one for producer of the year for the 1993 soundtrack to the Eddie Murphy film *Boomerang*, and have shared several songwriter of the year honors from Broadcast Music Inc. (BMI).

Edmonds is also a popular solo artist and performer in his own right, with three well-received releases to his name including the 1993 release *For the Cool in You*, a

platinum-seller whose hit "When Can I See You" brought him the 1993 Grammy for best male R&B vocalist. For several months between 1994 and 1995 Edmonds was on the road, performing as an opening act for Boyz II Men, yet another one of the enormously successful groups he has written for and produced. In late 1995 he gained further accolades for producing for the soundtrack to the acclaimed film *Waiting to Exhale*. Edmonds won an Essence Award in 1996.

### Roberta Flack (1939– )
*Singer, Pianist*

Born in Asheville, North Carolina, on February 10, 1939, Roberta Flack moved to Washington, DC with her parents at the age of nine. Three years later she studied classical piano with prominent African American concert musician Hazel Harrison. After winning several talent contests, Flack won a scholarship to Howard University, where she graduated with a bachelors degree in music education. During the early 1960s, Flack taught music in the Washington, DC public school system.

While playing a club date in 1968, Flack was discovered by Les McCann whose connections resulted in a contract with Atlantic Records. Flack's first album *First Take* appeared in 1970 and included the hit song "The First Time Ever I Saw Your Face." Throughout the 1970s, Flack landed several hits such as "Killing Me Softly With His Song" and "The Closer I Get to You," a duet with Donny Hathaway; both songs earned Grammys, and "Killing Me Softly" was remade in 1996, by the rappers The Fugees. In the early 1980s, Flack collaborated with Peabo Bryson to record the hit "Tonight I Celebrate My Love For You." More recently, Flack has been involved in educational projects, and in 1994, she recorded the album *Roberta*.

### Aretha Franklin (1942– )
*Singer, Pianist, Songwriter*

During the 1960s, the collaboration of Aretha Franklin and Atlantic Records producer Jerry Wexler brought forth some of the deepest and most sincere popular music ever recorded. As "Queen of Soul," Franklin has reigned supreme for the last three decades. Her voice brings spiritual inspiration to her gender, race, and the world.

Daughter of the famous Reverend Charles L. Franklin, Aretha was born on March 25, 1942, in Memphis, Tennessee. Raised on Detroit's east side, Franklin sang at her father's New Bethel Baptist Church. Although she began to study piano at age eight, Franklin refused to learn what she considered juvenile and simple tunes. Thus, she learned piano by ear, occasionally receiving instruction from individuals like the Reverend James Cleveland. Franklin's singing skills were modeled after gospel music singers and family friends, including Clara Ward and R&B artists like Ruth Brown and Sam Cooke.

At 14, Franklin quit school to go on the road with her father's Franklin Gospel Caravan, an endless tour in which the family traveled thousands of miles by car. After four years on the road, Aretha traveled to New York City to establish her own career as a pop artist. In 1960, she signed with Columbia Records talent scout John Hammond. Her six year stay at Columbia, however, produced only a few hits and little material that suited Franklin's unique talents.

In 1966, Franklin signed with Atlantic Records, and, in the following year, recorded a session for Wexler that resulted in the hit "I Never Loved a Man (The Way That I Loved You)." That same year, Franklin's career received another boost when her reworking of the Otis Redding's song "Respect" hit the charts. Franklin's first LP *I Never Loved a Man* was followed by a succession of artistically and commercially successful albums: *Aretha Arrives, Lady Soul, Aretha Now!,* and *This Girl's In Love With You.* Her prominence grew so great that Franklin appeared on the cover of *Time* magazine in 1968. That year she performed at Martin Luther King, Jr.'s funeral and at the Democratic National Convention.

Aretha Franklin

During the 1970s, Franklin continued to tour and record. In 1971, she released the live LP *Aretha Live at the Fillmore West* backed by the horn and rhythm section of Tower of Power. Her next release, *Amazing Grace,* featured Reverend James Cleveland and the Southern California Community Choir. In 1977, she performed at U.S. president Jimmy Carter's inauguration, later doing the same for U.S. president Bill Clinton in 1993.

In 1980, Franklin appeared in the film *The Blues Brothers.* No stranger to television, she appeared in the specials *Aretha, Aretha Franklin: The Queen of Soul,* and *Duets,* in 1986, 1988, and 1993, respectively. The 1980s also saw Franklin score her first big commercial success in more than a decade with the album *Who's Zooming Who?,* featuring the single "Freeway of Love." In 1988, she released a double-live LP *One Lord, One Faith*—an effort dedicated to her father who passed away the previous year.

Franklin has won 15 Grammy awards in her career, including the lifetime achievement award, which was bestowed upon her in 1995. Other of her honors include an American Music Award and an *Ebony* magazine American Black Achievement Award, both in 1984; declaration as a "natural resource" of the State of Michigan in 1985; induction into the Rock and Roll Hall of Fame in 1987; an Essence Award in 1993; and a Kennedy Center Honors Award in 1994. Only Janet Jackson has matched Franklin's record of 14 gold singles, the most by a female solo artist.

Franklin stayed active in the 1990s, a decade in which many of her classic recordings were reissued. She was a headliner at the 1994 New Orleans Jazz and Heritage Festival and lent a track to the 1995 *Waiting to Exhale* soundtrack. Franklin also embarked on a new venture, launching her own label, World Class Records in 1995.

### Marvin Gaye (1939–1984)
*Singer, Songwriter*

The son of a Pentecostal minister, Marvin Gay was born on April 29, 1939, in Washington, DC (the final "e" on his surname was not added until the early 1960s). Raised in a segregated slum-ridden section of Washington, D.C., Gaye experienced a strict religious upbringing. As Gaye later recalled: "Living with my father was like living with a king, a very peculiar, changeable, cruel, and all-powerful king." Thus Gaye looked to music for release. Around the age of three, he began singing in church. While attending Cardoza High School, Gaye studied drums, piano, and guitar. Uninspired by his formal studies, Gaye often cut classes to watch James Brown and Jackie Wilson perform at the Howard Theatre.

Marvin Gaye

Soon afterward, Gaye served a short time in the Air Force, until obtaining a honorable discharge in 1957. Returning to Washington, DC, Gaye joined the doo-wop group the Marquees. After recording for Columbia's subsidiary label, Okeh, the Marquees moved to the Chess/Checker label where they recorded with Bo Diddley. Although the Marquees performed their own compositions and toured regularly, they failed to gain popularity. It was not until they were introduced to Harvey Fuqua, who was in the process of reforming Moonglows, that the Marquees attracted notice in the pop music world. Impressed by their sound Fuqua hired the Marquees to form a group under the new name Harvey and the Moonglows. Still under contract at Chess, Fuqua brought the Moonglows to the company's studio in Chicago to record the 1959 hit the "Ten Commandments of Love."

In 1960, Fuqua and Gaye traveled to Detroit where Fuqua set up his own label and signed with Motown's subsidiary, Anna. After a stint as a back-up singer, studio musician, and drummer in Smokey Robinson's touring band, Gaye signed a contract with Motown as a solo artist. Released in 1962, Gaye's first album was a jazz-oriented effort entitled *The Soulful Moods of Marvin Gaye*. With his sights on a career modeled after the ballad singer Frank Sinatra, Gaye was not enthusiastic when Motown suggested he record a dance record of rhythm and blues material. Nevertheless, Gaye recorded the song "Stubborn Kind of Fellow" in 1962 which entered the top ten R and B charts. This was followed by a long succession of Motown hits, such as "Hitch Hike,"

"Pride and Joy," "Can I Get a Witness," and "Wonderful One."

Motown's next projects for Gaye included a number of vocal duets, the first of which appeared with singer Mary Wells on the 1964 album *Together*. In collaboration with singer Kim Weston, Gaye recorded the 1967 hit LP *It Takes Two*. His most successful partnership, however, was with Tammi Terrell. In their two year association, Gaye and Terrell recorded, under the writing and production team of Ashford and Simpson, such hits as "Ain't No Mountain High Enough" and "Your Precious Love" and "Ain't Nothing Like the Real Thing" in 1968.

Back in the studio as a solo act, Gaye recorded the hit "Heard It Through the Grapevine." With his growing success, Gaye achieved greater creative independence at Motown, which led him to co-produce the 1971 hit album *What's Going On,,* a session producing the best selling singles "What's Going On," "Mercy Mercy (the Ecology)," and "Inner City Blues (Make Me Wanna Holler)."

After his last LP for Motown, *In Our Lifetime*, Gaye signed with CBS Records in April 1981, and within the next year released the album *Midnight Lover*, featuring the Grammy award-winning hit "Sexual Healing." On Sunday, April 1, 1984 Gaye was shot dead by his father in Los Angeles, California. Despite his public image, Gaye had suffered from years of inner conflict and drug abuse. "This tragic ending can only be softened by the memory of a beautiful human being," described longtime friend Smokey Robinson. "He could be full of joy sometimes, but at others, full of woe, but in the end how compassionate, how wonderful, how exciting was Marvin Gaye and his music."

### Berry Gordy, Jr. (1929– )
*Songwriter, Producer*

From assembly line worker to impresario of the Motown Record Corporation, Berry Gordy, Jr. emerged as the owner of one of the largest black-owned businesses in American history. A professional boxer, songwriter, producer, and businessman, Gordy, has been a self-made man. Through his determination and passion for music, the living legend helped to create one of the most celebrated sounds of modern music.

The seventh of eight children, Berry Gordy was born on November 28, 1929, in Detroit. Berry Gordy, Sr., the owner of a grocery store, a plastering company, and a printing shop, taught his children the value of hard work and family unity. Despite his dislike for manual labor, Berry possessed a strong desire to become commercially successful. After quitting high school to become a professional boxer, Berry won several contests before leaving the profession in 1950. A year later, Gordy was drafted into the U.S. Army, where he earned a high school equivalency diploma.

Upon returning from a military tour of Korea in 1953, Berry opened the 3-D Record Mart, a jazz-oriented retail store. Forced into bankruptcy, Berry closed the store in 1955, and subsequently took a job as an assembly line worker at the Ford Motor Company. His nightly visits to Detroit's thriving jazz and rhythm and blues scene inspired Gordy to take up songwriting. In 1957, one of Gordy's former boxing colleagues, Jackie Wilson, recorded the hit "Reet Petiti," a song written by Berry, his sister Gwen, and Billy Davis. Over the next four years, the Berry-Gwen-Davis writing team provided Wilson with four more hits, "To Be Loved," "Lonely Teardrops," "That's Why (I Love You So)," and "I'll Be Satisfied."

By 1959, Billy Davis and Gwen Gordy founded the Anna label, which distributed material through Chess Records in Chicago. Barret Strong's recording of "Money (That's What I Want)," written by Gordy and Janie Bradford, became the label's biggest selling single. With background as a writer and producer with the Anna label, Gordy decided to start his own company. In 1959, he formed Jobete Music Publishing, Berry Gordy, Jr. Enterprises, Hitsville USA, and the Motown Record Corporation. Employing a staff of local studio musicians, writers, and producers, Berry's label scored its first hit in 1961 with Smokey Robinson's "Shop Around." By the mid-1960s, Gordy assembled a wealth of talent including the Supremes, the Four Tops, the Marvelettes, Marvin Gaye, and Stevie Wonder.

In 1971, Gordy relocated the Motown Recording Corporation to Los Angeles. Although most of the original acts and staff members did not join the company's migration to the West Coast, Gordy's company became one of the country's top black-owned businesses. Throughout the 1970s and 1980s, Motown continued to produce artists like the Jackson Five, the Commodores, Lionel Richie, Rick James, and DeBarge. Gordy also tried his hand at producing feature films. *Lady Sings the Blues* (1972), *Mahogany* (1975), and *The Last Dragon* (1985) were not critical successes, but attracted the participation of such celebrities as Diana Ross, Billy Dee Williams, Richard Pryor, and Vanity. Faced with financial problems, Gordy signed a distribution agreement with MCA in 1982, and sold the label in entirety to the giant six years later.

Gordy's induction into the Hall of Fame in 1988, brought recognition to a giant of the recording industry who helped transform the sound of popular music. He was honored with a lifetime achievement award at the 1993 Black Radio Exclusive awards banquet ceremony. One of *Forbes* 400 richest Americans in the mid-1980s, Gordy authored his autobiography, *To Be Loved: The Music, the Magic, the Memories of Motown* in 1994.

## Al Green (1946– )
*Singer, Songwriter, Preacher*

Possessing one of the supplest voices in popular music, Al Green launched a series of hits up the soul charts during the 1970s. But the Arkansas native turned his back on pop later in that decade, singing gospel and preaching in a Memphis church. His influence on the development of soul was such, however, that he was tempted back to the secular realm for a 1996 album.

Green spent his early years singing gospel in the south, but switched to pop and scored a hit, "Back Up Train," in 1967. It wasn't until he hooked up with producer Willie Mitchell, however, that he found his niche. Recording for Mitchell's Hi Records in Memphis with an ace band, Green managed a remarkable synthesis of intimate, romantic pop and gritty soul. The fruits of this happy union included "Tired of Being Alone," "Love and Happiness," "Let's Stay Together," and "I'm Still in Love With You." His smoldering "Take Me to the River" was covered by numerous other artists.

Though he was "born again" into Christianity in 1973, Green continued to record largely secular music—albeit with a religious tinge—for several years. After founding his own church, the Full Gospel Tabernacle, in Memphis, he returned to gospel music. His recordings won regular honors in gospel circles and even a Grammy Award, but his presence continued to be felt in the soul/R&B world. Apart from the occasional duet, however, he steered clear of pop until his return in 1995 with *Your Heart's In Good Hands*.

## Andre Harrell (1962?– )
*Record Company Executive, Producer, Musician*

Andre O'Neal Harrell was born in the Bronx, New York. While growing up with hard times in the housing projects there, young Harrell developed a desire to succeed. As a teenager, Harrell teamed up with Alonzo Brown to form the playful rap duo Dr. Jekyll (Harrell) and Mr. Hyde (Brown). Before long, they had three top 20 hits under their belts and were carving a niche for themselves in rap.

Despite the his early rap success, Harrell enrolled in classes at the Bronx's Lehman College. After three years of study in communications and business management, Harrell met Russell Simmons in 1983. Simmons lured Harrell to come work for him at Rush Management, a company that helped define the hip-hop of the day. Within two years, Harrell had worked his way up vice-president and general manager and was instrumental in building the career of such rap icons as LL Cool J, Run-DMC, and Whodini.

Success continued to follow Harrell wherever he went. He left Rush Management to begin his own record company, Uptown Records. In 1988, the achievements of Uptown Records prompted a $75,000 record deal from music mega-company MCA. Artists like Al B Sure!, Guy, and Heavy D all prospered under Harrell's direction. By 1992, Uptown and their artists had blazed a shiny trail of gold and platinum albums and had landed an unprecedented $50 million multimedia agreement with MCA. Soon projects like the television show *In Living Color* and a showcase of Uptown recording artists, including Mary J. Blige and Jodeci on MTV's *Unplugged* were in the works. In 1995, Harrell left the reigns of Uptown to became the new president of Motown Records.

## Issac Hayes (1942– )
### Singer, Pianist, Producer

Born on August 20, 1942, in Covington, Tennessee, Issac Hayes moved to Memphis at age seven, where he was introduced to the sounds of blues, country western, and the music of idol Sam Cooke. Through the connections of saxophonist Floyd Newman, Hayes began a career as a studio musician for Stax Records in 1964. After playing piano on a session for Otis Redding, Hayes formed a partnership with songwriter Dave Porter. Together they were responsible for supplying a number of hits to Carla Thomas, William Bell, and Eddie Floyd.

The first real break for the Hayes-Porter team came when they were recruited to produce the Miami-based soul duo Sam and Dave. In the span of four years, Hayes and Porter succeeded in making Sam and Dave Stax's hottest selling act, producing such hits as "Hold On I'm Coming," "Soul Man," and "I Thank You!" During this period Hayes and Porter continued to perform in a group that established them as an underground legend in the Memphis music scene.

In the late 1960s, Hayes's solo career emerged in an impromptu fashion, when a late night session with drummer Al Jackson and bassist Duck Dunn prompted Stax to release his next effort. Hot Buttered Soul went double platinum in 1969 Featuring a soul version of the country song, "By the Time I Get to Phoenix," Hayes's rendition set a trend for the disco/soul sound of the 1970s. Following the release of the albums *To Be Continued* and *Issac Hayes Movement*, Hayes recorded the soundtrack for the "blaxplotation" film *Shaft* and the album *Black Moses*. In 1971, "Theme from *Shaft*" won an Academy Award for best song in a motion picture and Grammy awards for best instrumental and best original score for a motion picture. *Black Moses* earned a Grammy, too, this one for best pop instrumental performance.

Hayes left the Stax label to join ABC in 1974. Hayes recorded a series of disco albums. In 1977, the commercial downturn in Hayes's career forced him to file bankruptcy. Though he composed Dionne Warwick's "Déjà Vu,"—nominated for a Grammy in 1978—his last gold record, "Don't Let Go," was released on the Polydor label in 1979. Hayes moved into the 1980s and 1990s appearing on television shows and in such films as the futuristic thriller *Escape From New York* (1981) and the comedy-spoof *Robin Hood: Men in Tights* (1993).

Winner of a 1994 Georgy Award, as bestowed by the Georgia Music Hall of Fame, Hayes has heavily influenced the music of the late 1980s and early 1990s; together with James Brown, Hayes has been one of the most-frequently sampled artists by purveyors of rap. Choosing not to jump ship, however, Hayes has stuck to his own brand of "hot buttered soul." In 1995, he issued his first new recordings in seven years—*Branded* and *Raw and Refined*—and contributed a track to the Hughes brothers' film *Dead Presidents*.

## Jimi Hendrix (1942–1970)
### Guitarist, Songwriter

When Jimi Hendrix arrived on the international rock music scene in 1967, he almost single-handedly redefined the sound of the electric guitar. Hendrix' extraordinary approach has shaped the course of music from jazz fusion to heavy metal.

On November 25, 1942, in Seattle, Washington, Johnny Allen Hendrix was born to an enlisted Army soldier and a teenage mother. Four years later, Johnny Allen was renamed James Marshall Hendrix. Because of his mother's fondness for night club life and his father's frequent absences, Hendrix was a lonely, yet creative, child. At school he won several contests for his science fiction-based poetry and visual art. At the age of eight, Hendrix, unable to afford a guitar, strummed out rhythms on a broom. Eventually, he graduated to a fabricated substitute made from a cigar box, followed by a ukelele, and finally an acoustic guitar that was purchased by his father.

By the late 1950s, Hendrix began to play in local bands in Seattle. While a teenager, he played along with recordings by blues artists like Elmore James and John Lee Hooker. After a 26-month stint (1961–1962) in the 101st Airborne Division, Hendrix played in the Nashville rhythm and blues scene with bassist Billy Cox. For the next three years, Hendrix performed under the name Jimi James, backing up acts such as Little Richard, Jackie Wilson, Ike and Tina Turner, and the Isley Brothers.

In 1964 Hendrix moved to New York City where he performed in various Greenwich Village clubs. While in New York he formed the group Jimi James and the Blue

Jimi Hendrix

Flames. After being discovered by producer and manager Chas Chandler, the former bassist with the Animals, Hendrix was urged to leave for England. Arriving in England in 1966, Hendrix, along with bassist Noel Redding and drummer Mitch Mitchell, formed the Jimi Hendrix Experience. In 1967, after touring Europe, the trio hit the charts with a cover version of the Leaves song "Hey Joe." In the same year, the group released the ground-breaking album *Are You Experienced?*.

In 1968 the Experience recorded *Axis Bold As Love* which led to extensive touring in the U.S. and Europe. On the Experience's next LP, *Electric Ladyland*, Hendrix sought to expand the group's trio-based sound. A double record effort, *Electric Ladyland* featured numerous guest artists such as keyboardists Steve Winwood and Al Kooper, saxophonist Freddie Smith, and conga player Larry Faucette. The record also contained "All Along the Watchtower," a song written by Hendrix's musical and poetic idol Bob Dylan.

After the Experience broke up in 1969, Hendrix played the Woodstock Music and Arts Festival with the Gypsy Sons and Rainbows, featuring bassist Billy Cox. Along with drummer Buddy Miles, Hendrix and Cox formed the Band of Gypsys, and in 1970 the group

released an album under the same title. Months later, Mitchell replaced Miles on drums. In August, the Mitchell-Cox line-up played behind Hendrix at his last major performance held at England's Isle of Wight Festival. On September 18, 1970, Hendrix died in a hotel room in England.

### Whitney Houston (1963– )
*Model, Singer, Actress*

A multiple Grammy Award-winner whose face has graced the covers of magazines from *Glamour* to *Cosmopolitan*, Whitney Houston emerged as one of the most vibrant popular music talents during the 1980s. A talented singer, model, and actress, Houston dominated the pop charts into the 1990s. Her biggest successes were associated with two motion pictures in which she had major roles.

Born on August 9, 1963, Houston grew up in East Orange, New Jersey. As a member of the New Hope Baptist Choir, she made her singing debut at age 11. Later, Houston appeared as a back-up singer on numerous recordings, featuring her mother Cissy Houston and cousin Dionne Warwick. Despite her success as a fashion model, Houston found the profession "degrading," and, subsequently, quit in order to seek a career in music. She backed up the likes of Chaka Khan, Lou Rawls, and the Neville Brothers.

By age 19, Houston had received several recording contract offers. In 1985, she released her debut album on the Arista label entitled *Whitney Houston*, which produced four hits: "Saving All My Love for You," which won the Grammy for best female pop performance; "You Give Good Love"; "How Will I Know," which earned an MTV Video Music Award for best female video; and "The Greatest Love of All." The album won seven American Music awards, a feat she would duplicate in 1994. Houston's second LP, *Whitney*, appeared in 1987, and like her first effort, the work spawned a number of hits, including "I Wanna Dance With Somebody," "Didn't We Almost Have It All," "So Emotional," "Where Do Broken Hearts Go?," and "Love Will Save the Day." The album received four American Music awards. Following the success of her second record, Houston released *One Moment In Time* (1988) and the slickly produced *I'm Your Baby Tonight* (1990).

In 1992, Houston married singer Bobby Brown and made her acting debut in the film *The Bodyguard*, costarring Kevin Costner. The first single from the soundtrack, a remake of Dolly Parton's "I Will Always Love You," spent 14 weeks straight on the top of the pop singles chart; according to statistics from *Billboard* magazine, Houston set a record for the most time spent at the top of the charts, edging out Boyz II Men's "End of the Road" (13 weeks) and Elvis Presley's "Don't Be

Cruel" (11 weeks). Her vocal performance on the soundtrack won her seven American Music Awards, including the 1994 Award of Merit; four Grammy awards, including record of the year, album of the year, and best female pop performance; two Soul Train Music awards, including the Sammy Davis, Jr. Entertainer of the Year Award and the female R&B single award for "I Will Always Love You"; four NAACP Image awards; and the National Association of Black Owned Broadcasters' lifetime achievement award. Later in the year, AT&T signed Houston as the spokesperson for the corporation's "True Voice" campaign; Houston sang in two of the company's commercials.

Houston's next offering was not long in coming. With Angela Bassett, Lela Rochon, and Loretta Devine, Houston costarred in the 1995 film adaption of Terry McMillan's *Waiting to Exhale*. A box-office winner, the movie's soundtrack was written by producer Babyface and featured, in addition to Houston, such performers as Aretha Franklin and Toni Braxton. Houston sang the very successful first single, "Exhale (Shoop Shoop)."

### Ice Cube (1969– )
*Singer, Actor*

Behind his oft misogynistic and racist gangster image, rapper Ice Cube is a serious artist. Dedicated to black pride, he is a staunch spokesperson for black nationalism. Ice Cube looks upon his music as a means of launching a "mental revolution" in order to awaken African American youth to the value of education and the creation of private black economic enterprises.

Born Oshea Jackson, Ice Cube grew up in the west side of South Central Los Angeles. While in the ninth grade Jackson wrote his first rhyme in typing class. Prompted by his parents to pursue an education after high school, he attended a one-year drafting course at the Phoenix Institute in 1988. In the following year, Ice Cube achieved great commercial success as a member of N.W.A. (Niggas With Attitude). One of the group's founding members, along with Dr. Dre and Eazy-E, Ice Cube wrote or cowrote most of the material for N.W.A.'s first two albums. *Boyz-n-the-Hood* was released in 1986. Ice Cube's authoritative baritone won him a legion of fans for his N.W.A. rap anthem "Gangsta Gangsta." He also scripted much of Eazy's first solo work, *Eazy-Duz-It*, followed by N.W.A.'s platinum *Straight Outta Compton*, which included the controversial single, "F— tha Police."

Though he still worked sporadically with Dr. Dre after leaving N.W.A., Ice Cube released his 1990 solo album *AmeriKKKa's Most Wanted*, produced with Public Enemy's Chuck D. and the Bomb Squad; the recording went gold within three months. He then formed Street Knowledge, a record production company and

produced female rapper Yo Yo's *Make Way for the Motherlode*. During the same year, Ice Cube also made his acting debut in director John Singleton 's film *Boyz N' the Hood*. The rapper-actor went on to star in a number of films, including 1992's *Tresspass*, with Ice-T; *Higher Learning*, Singleton's vehicle of 1994; the 1995 comedy *Friday*, which he cowrote and co-produced; and Charles Burnett's 1995 work, *The Glass Shield*.

Having recorded his own *Kill at Will* and *Death Certificate* in 1991, Ice Cube remained active in Yo Yo's career, serving as executive producer of her *Black Pearl* in 1992, and worked with other artists, directing videos including one for blues-rock artist Ian Moore in 1993. Ice Cube stayed on top of his own music game as well, releasing *The Predator* in 1992; the recording debuted at number one on two *Billboard* charts—pop and R&B—at the same time, the first to do so since 1976 and Stevie Wonder's *Songs in the Key of Life*. In 1992, Ice Cube figured in the lineup of Lollapalooza II, an annual traveling rock festival. 1993's *Lethal Injection* featured the smash single "It Was a Good Day." Ice Cube also issued *Bootlegs & B-Sides*, and, in 1995, he contributed to the *Streetfigher* motion picture soundtrack. In 1996, he was working on a concept album with fellow rappers Mack 10 and WC.

### Janet Jackson (1966– )
*Singer*

The youngest child of a family of talented children, Janet Jackson is a tremendously energetic performer, whose singing and dance styles have reached immense popularity around the world. She is one of the most successful of a family of highly successful performers, including her brother Michael, the so-called "King of Pop." In the 1990s, she has fully emerged from his shadow and has become a full-fledged sex symbol and role model.

Born on May 16, 1966, in Gary, Indiana, Janet Jackson began performing with her brothers at age six, doing impressions of famous stars like Mae West and Cher. She made her first professional singing debut at one of the Jackson Five's shows in the Grand Hotel in Las Vegas. Before she was ten years old, Jackson was spotted by television producer Norman Lear, resulting in her appearances on such television shows as *Good Times*, *Different Strokes*, and *Fame*.

In 1982, Jackson's debut album for the A&M label *Janet* contained only a few minor hits. Teamed with producers Jimmy Jam and Terry Lewis, Jackson released her more commercially successful LP *Dream Street*. Her 1986 release *Control* scored six hit singles, including "What Have You Done For Me Lately," "Nasty," "When I Think of You," "Control," "Let's Wait Awhile," and "Pleasure Principle." Under the direction of Jam and Lewis, Jackson released the dance-oriented album *Janet Jackson's Rhythm Nation 1814* in 1989, which went quadruple platinum. Among the record's numerous singles were "Miss You Much," "Come Back To Me," and "Black Cat."

After an extensive world tour in 1990, Jackson left the A&M label to sign a contract with Virgin Records in 1991. The four-album contract was worth an estimated $80 million with $50 million guaranteed up-front. Two years later, she starred alongside Tupac Shakur in John Singleton's *Poetic Justice*. Jackson played a soul-searching hairdresser prone to writing poetry; Maya Angelou, who was also featured in the film, provided the poems Jackson's character read. In 1994, Jackson released *janet*. Critically acclaimed, the album did well commercially, too. The single "Any Time, Any Place" earned Jackson her fourteenth gold single, the most by any female solo artist other than Aretha Franklin. The following year, Jackson collaborated with her brother Michael on a track entitled "Scream." The visually stunning video associated with the single was the most expensive ever made. Later in 1995, her *Design of a Decade: 1986–1996* made a splashy debut. She also contributed a song to the soundtrack for *Ready to Wear*.

Jackson has earned much recognition throughout her career. Between 1986 and 1992, she garnered four *Billboard* awards; seven American Music awards; two MTV Video Music awards; one Grammy Award; three Soul Train awards; a BMI Pop Award; and the 1992 Sammy Davis, Jr. Award or Entertainer of the Year. In 1990, she acquired a star on Hollywood "Walk of Fame," and, in 1992, the NAACP gave her its Chairman's Award. Three years later, she received an Essence Award.

## Mahalia Jackson (1912–1972)
*Gospel Singer*

Hailed as the world's greatest gospel singer, Mahalia Jackson's rich contralto voice became a national institution. Through live performances, recordings, and television appearances, Jackson elevated gospel music to a level of popularity unprecedented in the history of African American religious music.

The third of six children, Jackson was born on October 26, 1912, in New Orleans, Louisiana. Growing in New Orleans, Jackson absorbed the sounds of parade music and brass bands. She later discovered the blues, a music labeled the "devil's music" by regular churchgoers, and listened secretly to recordings of singers like Mamie Smith and Bessie Smith.

In 1927, at the age of 13, Jackson moved to Chicago where she joined the Greater Salem Baptist Church. Two years later, Jackson met the gospel musician and songwriter Thomas A. Dorsey who invited her to sing at

Mahalia Jackson

the Pilgrim Baptist Church. In 1937 Jackson recorded four sides for the Decca label including the song "God's Gonna Separate the Wheat From the Tares."

Jackson's big break did not come until 1947 when she released gospel music's first million-selling record "Move on Up a Little." In 1949 her song "Let the Holy Ghost Fall on Me" won the French Academy's Grand Prix du Disque. Soon afterward, she toured Europe and recorded the gospel hit "In the Upper Room." During the 1960s, Jackson became a musical ambassador. Not only did she perform at the White House and at London's Albert Hall, but she sang at Martin Luther King's 1963 March on Washington, as well as his funeral ceremony in 1968.

On January 27, 1972, Jackson died of a heart condition in Chicago. At her funeral at Great Salem Baptist, some 45,000 mourners gathered to pay their respects to a woman who brought gospel music into the hearts and homes of millions of listeners.

### Michael Jackson (1958– )
*Singer, Composer*

From child singing star with the Jackson Five to his success as a solo performer in the 1980s, Michael Jackson has amassed the largest following of any African American singer in the history of popular music. Jackson has an audience that transcends the boundaries of nations and bridges the gaps brought about by generational differences. Despite some missteps in the early 1990s, the "King of Pop" reigns supreme.

The fifth of nine children, Michael Jackson was born on August 29, 1958, in Gary, Indiana. As a child, Michael, along with his brothers Tito, Jermaine, Jackie, and Marlon, comprised the Jackson Five. Under the tutelage of their father, Joe, the five boys learned to sing and dance. On weekends the family singing group traveled hundreds of miles to perform at amateur contests and benefit concerts.

After two years on the road, the group landed an audition with Motown records. Upon signing with the label in 1969, the Jackson Five hit the charts with the

Michael Jackson

number one hit "I Want You Back," a song arranged and produced by Berry Gordy, Jr. On recordings and television shows, Michael's wholesome image and lead vocal style attracted fans from every racial and age group. During the group's six-year stay at Motown, the Jackson Five scored 13 consecutive top 20 singles such as "ABC," "The Love You Save," and "I'll Be There."

While lead vocalist for the Jackson Five, Michael had signed a separate contract with Motown in 1971, formalizing a solo career that produced the hits "Got to Be There" in 1971, "Ben" in 1972, and "Just a Little Bit of You" in 1975. When cast in the role of the scarecrow in the 1975 Motown film *The Wiz*, Jackson met producer Quincy Jones who later collaborated with him to record the 1979 hit LP *Off the Wall* on the Epic label. Two years later, Jackson, guided by the production skills of Jones, recorded the biggest selling album of all time, *Thriller*. The seven hit singles included "Beat It," "Billie Jean," "Wanna Be Startin' Something," and the title track, which featured a voice–over by horror-cult figure Vincent Price. The video for the song was almost a mini-movie staring Jackson as a dancing werewolf run amok, with special effects that rivaled any full-length feature film.

In 1985, Jackson cowrote the song "We Are the World" for the U.S.A. for Africa famine relief fund. After joining Jones to produce the *Bad* in 1987, Jackson led the most commercially successful tour in history. Four years later, Jackson released *Dangerous*, which includes the hit single "Black or White."

In 1993, Jackson announced that the progressive lightening of his skin has been the result of a skin disorder known as vitiligo and not from intentional bleaching. The public declaration was one of many Jackson would find himself making about various topics in the ensuing years. Scandal-ridden, Jackson hit a backslide in his career following allegations of child molestation—charges that were dropped—and the coming to light of a pain medication addiction brought about by poor health.

Coming on the heels of such devastating disclosures, 1995's *HIStory: Past, Present, and Future, Book I* featured hits from the past as well as new works. Compared to his previous recordings, sales were disappointing and the recording was not considered a commercial success. Fan loyalty to the gifted musician, however, drove some of the new songs into chart contention, including "The Earth Song," the controversial "They Don't Care About Us," and the lilting ballad "You Are Not Alone." The compilation also gave Jackson a chance to work with his sister Janet, when the two collaborated on the duet "Scream," the first single to be released. The ensuing video for "Scream" cost $7 million, making it one of the most expensive, albeit eye-catching, videos ever produced.

Jackson had made headlines in 1994, when he announced his betrothal to Lisa Marie Presley, daughter of the late rock legend Elvis Presley. The marriage of Jackson and Presley was considered highly unusual, and many critics dismissed it as a publicity stunt. On June 14, 1995, Jackson and Presley were interviewed by Diane Sawyer on ABC's *Prime Time Live*. During the interview, the two insisted they were deeply in love and planned to eventually have children. However, in January of 1996, Lisa Presley announced that she was divorcing Jackson.

Jackson's business ventures have had more staying power. An astute business man, he entered into a $600 million joint publishing deal with Sony in 1995. The deal combined Sony's music publishing division with Jackson's ATV Music Catalog, which once owned the rights to the entire Beatles ouvre.

More importantly, Jackson continues to garner acclaim, despite his setbacks. In 1993, he received three American Music awards, including the first-ever International Artist Award and was recognized at the World Music Awards ceremony in Nonte Carlo, Monaco. In addition, he received special Grammy honors that year. Two years later, he won three MTV Video awards. While many argue that his work has been uneven, his contribution to modern pop has been enormous. Indeed, Jackson redefined stardom for the video era. Popular culture will never be the same.

## Quincy Jones (1933– )
*Trumpeter, Arranger, Producer*

Winner of 20 Grammy Awards and the writer of more than 52 film scores, Quincy Jones is popular music's quintessential musician/producer. Aside from performing trumpet with the likes of jazzmen Lionel Hampton and Dizzy Gillespie, Jones has produced for artists from Frank Sinatra to Michael Jackson.

Quincy Jones was born on March 14, 1933, in Chicago, Illinois. At age ten, Jones moved to Bremerton, Washington. As a member of Bump Blackwell's Junior Orchestra, Jones performed at local Seattle social functions. In 1949, Jones played third trumpet in Lionel Hampton's band in the local Seattle club scene. After befriending jazz bassist Oscar Pettiford, Jones established himself as an able musician and arranger.

From 1950 to 1953, Jones became a regular member of Hampton's band, and, subsequently, toured the United States and Europe. During the mid-1950s, Jones began to record jazz records under his own name. In 1956, he toured the Middle East and South America with the U.S. State Department Band headed by Dizzy Gillespie.

Quincy Jones

In 1961, Jones was appointed musical director at Mercury Records. In search of new musical horizons, Jones began producing popular music, including Leslie Gore's 1963 hit "It's My Party." Jones's growing prestige at Mercury led to his promotion to vice president of the company, marking the first time an African American had been placed in an executive position at a major label. During this time, Jones also began to write and record film scores. In 1967, he produced the music score for the movie *In the Heat of the Night*. He also produced the music score for Alex Haley's television mini-series *Roots* and co-produced the film adaptation of Alice Walker's *The Color Purple* with Steven Spielberg.

After his production of the 1978 Motown-backed film *The Wiz*, Jones went on to produce the film's star, Michael Jackson, on such recordings as the 1979 release *Off the Wall* and the 1985 record-breaking hit *Thriller*. Jones's 1989 release *Back on the Block*, a Grammy winner, was praised by critics and was no doubt a sign of Jones's continuing role in the future development of African American popular music. Two years later, Jones sat down with his old buddy Miles Davis. The musical encounter was recorded and released in 1993 as *Miles & Quincy Live at Montreaux*, along with a video documentary of the same name. In 1995, Jones released his album *Q's Juke Joint*, featuring updated versions of tunes popularized in post-slavery roadhouses.

Jones is also influential in the media industry. He is chairman of Quest Broadcasting; in 1994, the group partnered with Chicago's Tribune Co. to buy television stations in Atlanta and New Orleans. His joint venture with Time Warner—*Vibe* magazine, which Jones founded—has been very successful. The publication covers urban music and culture and has a high readership among blacks and Latinos.

## Louis Jordan (1908–1975)
*Singer, Alto-Saxophonist, Bandleader*

Louis Jordan led one of the most popular and influential bands of the 1940s. The shuffle boogie rhythm of his jump blues ensemble, the Tympany Five, had a profound impact on the emergence of rhythm and blues. As guitarist Chuck Berry admitted, "I identify myself with Louis Jordan more than any other artist." For it was Jordan's swinging rhythms, theatrical stage presence, and songs about everyday life that made him a favorite among musicians and listeners throughout the 1940s.

Born in Brinkley, Arkansas, July 8, 1908, Jordan was the son of a bandleader and music teacher. He received his music education in the Brinkley public schools and the Baptist College in Little Rock. Jordan's early music career as a clarinetist included stints with the Rabbit Foot Minstrels and Ruby Williams's orchestra. Soon after moving to Philadelphia in 1932, Jordan joined Charlie Gains' group; sometime around 1936, he joined drummer Chick Webb's band.

After Webb's death in 1938, Jordan started his own group. Because Jordan performed for both white and black audiences, he, to use his own words, learned to "straddle the fence" by playing music ranging from blues to formal dance music. Signing with Decca records during the same year, Jordan began a recording career which, by the early 1940s, produced a string of million selling recordings such as "Is You Is or Is You Ain't (My Baby)," "Choo Choo Ch'Boogie," "Saturday Night Fish Fry," and "Caledonia." Aside from working with artists like Louis Armstrong, Bing Crosby, and Ella Fitzgerald, Jordan appeared in several films such as the 1949 release *Shout Sister Shout*.

Although failing to achieve the success he experienced during the 1940s, Jordan fronted a big band in the early 1950s. During the 1960s and 1970s, he continued to tour the United States, Europe, and Asia. His career came to an end in 1975 when he suffered a fatal heart attack in Los Angeles.

## Eddie Kendricks (1939–1992)
*Singer*

As a member of the Temptations in the 1960s, Eddie Kendricks' articulate soulful falsetto provided Motown with a number of pop music classics. Kendricks' gospel music background "enabled him to bring an unusual earnestness to the singing of love lyrics," wrote music historian David Morse. "He can be compared only with Ray Charles in his ability to take the most threadbare ballad and turn it into a dramatic and completely convincing statement."

Born on December 17, 1939, in Birmingham, Alabama, Kendricks grew up with close friend and Temptations' member Paul Williams. In 1956 Kendricks and Williams quit school and traveled northward to become singing stars in the tradition of their idols Clyde McPhatter and Little Willie John. In Detroit, Kendricks and Williams formed the doo-wop singing group the Primes which performed at talent contests and house parties. In 1961 the Primes recorded the songs "Mother of Mine" and the dance tune "Check Yourself" for Berry Gordy's short-lived Miracle label.

Upon the suggestion of Berry Gordy, the Primes changed their name to the Temptations and after adding David Ruffin as lead vocalist, they set out to become one of the most successful groups on the Motown label. Throughout the decade, Kendricks sang lead on several songs including the classics "My Girl" in 1965, "Get Ready" in 1966, and "Just My Imagination (Running Away With Me)" in 1972.

In June of 1971, Kendricks pursued a solo career and eventually recorded two disco-influenced hits "Keep on Truckin" in 1973, and "Boogie Down" in 1974. Kendricks' career soon fell into decline. Unable to find material to suit his unique artistic sensibility, Kendricks switched record labels several times before reuniting with the Temptations in 1982. After the reunion, Kendricks performed with the Temptations on the Live Aid broadcast and on the album *Live at the Apollo Theater with David Ruffin and Eddie Kendricks*. In 1987 Ruffin and Kendricks signed a contract with RCA and recorded the aptly titled LP *Ruffin and Kendricks*. Stricken by lung cancer, Kendricks died in October 1992.

## Gladys Knight (1944– )
*Singer*

Born May 28, 1944, in Atlanta, Georgia, Gladys Knight was raised in a family which valued education and the sounds of gospel music. At age four, Knight began singing gospel music at the Mount Moriah Baptist Church. When she was eight, Knight won first prize on the television program "Ted Mack's Amateur Hour" for a rendition of the song "Too Young." Between the years 1950 to 1953, Knight toured with the Morris Brown Choir of Atlanta, Georgia. Around this same time, Knight joined her sister Brenda, brother Merald, and cousins William and Eleanor Guest to form a local church singing group. In 1957 the group took the name the Pips upon the suggestion of cousin and manager James "Pips" Woods.

Louis Jordan and the Tymphany Five, 1946.

Two years later Langston George and Edward Patten replaced Brenda Knight and Eleanor Guest. Though Gladys periodically left the group, she rejoined in 1964. After recording for several record labels, the Pips finally signed with Motown's subsidiary, Soul. Despite the lack of commercial success, the group released a number of fine recordings under the supervision of Motown's talented production staff including Norman Whitfield and Ashford and Simpson. In 1967 the group released the single "I Heard It Through the Grapevine" which reached number two on the Billboard charts. Following a long string of hits on Motown, the Pips signed with the Buddah label in 1973, releasing the album *Imagination* which provided the group with two gold singles, "Midnight Train to Georgia" and "I've Got to Use My Imagination."

By the late 1970s the group, faced with legal battles and contract disputes, began to fall out of popular vogue. For three years the group was barred from recording or performing together. As a result of an out-of-court settlement in 1980, the Pips signed a new contract with CBS, where they remained until 1985. Joined by Dionne Warwick and Elton John, Knight recorded the Grammy award winning gold single "That's

What Friends Are For" in 1986. Released in 1988, the title cut of the Pip's *Love Overboard* album became their biggest selling single in decades. That same year, Knight recorded the theme for the James Bond film *License To Kill*. Released on the MCA label, Knight's 1991 album *Good Women* features guest stars Patti Labelle and Dionne Warwick.

## Suge Knight (1966– )
*Record Company Executive*

Born Marion Knight, Jr. in 1966, Knight grew up in the rough neighborhood of Compton, California. Despite being surrounded by violence, Knight picked up the nickname "Suge"—short for "Sugar"—because of his basic good-natured temperament. While in high school, Knight devoted his time to playing football with the hopes of gaining an athletic scholarship to college. Standing more than 6' tall and weighing nearly 300 pounds, Knight took his talents to the University of Nevada in Las Vegas. There he won several awards, including the Rookie of the Year on defense and a spot on the dean's list for academics. After college, Knight was drafted by the NFL's Los Angeles Rams but decide to pursue different avenues.

Gladys Knight and the Pips at the 1989 American Music Awards.

A string of run ins with the law almost put an end to any hopes Knight had. Between the years of 1987 and 1990, Knight was arrested for several crimes, including auto theft, battery, and attempted murder. His luck soon changed as he made a name for himself while working as a bodyguard for musicians. Eventually, Knight formed a publication company and made a significant amount of money from ownership rights to several of white rapper Vanilla Ice's songs.

Based on the success of his publishing company, Knight decided to venture into artist management. This led to Knight meeting Dr. Dre, formerly of N.W.A. At that time, Dre was managed by Ruthless Records, but Knight pulled some strings and signed Dre and two other Ruthless artists to new contracts. Controversy surrounded the transaction as Knight was accused of using force to finalize the deal. Together with Dr. Dre, Knight founded Death Row Records. Blistering success quickly followed as the label grossed more than $60 million in 1993. An already impressive artist roster, including Dr. Dre, Snoop Doggy Dogg, and Warren G. quickly improved with the signing of Mary J. Blige and Jodeci. With three multi-platinum albums under his belt, Knight

began to refer to Death Row Records as "the Motown of the 90s."

In luring top artists to Death Row, Knight often doubles their royalty rates, offers more creative control for the musician, and upgrades their contracts. In 1995, Knight even bailed jailed rapper Tupac Shakur out of prison in order to add more talent to the Death Row cluster. Despite the success Knight has enjoyed, many are skeptical of his tactics, but his peers simply view him as a master of the art of negotiation.

### KRS-One (1965?– )
*Rap singer*

A self-described teacher whose Boogie Down Productions (BDP) was an important influence on hardcore rap, KRS-One survived street life, prision, homelessness, the murder of a close friend, and negative criticism to emerge as one of rap's most powerful figures. Born as Lawrence Parker c. 1965 in Brooklyn, New York, KRS-One (initially representative of "Kris, Number One," later an acronym for Knowledge Reigns Supreme Over Nearly Everyone") also went by Krishna Parker or Kris Parker. Leaving home at 13, he lived on the streets, taking odd jobs when available and hanging out in public libraries. Self-educated, he served a short stin in jail for selling marijuana. Upon his release, the 19-year-old met Scott Sterling, a social worker and DJ who worked under the name Scott LaRock. Together the two formed BDP.

BDP recored one album, *Criminal Minded* before LaRock was killed while trying to break up a fight. Perservering, KRS-One kept their music alive, recording several critically aclaimed works with the various musicians who comprised the BDP crew. In 1990, he created H.E.A.L., or Human Education Against Lies, an afro-centric, pro-educational organization. KRS-One also founded Edutainer Records that year. In 1991, he recorded *Live Hardcore Worldwide*, one of the first live rap albums ever and produced such artists as Queen Latifah and the Neville Brothers.

## Little Richard (1932– )
### Singer, Pianist

Flamboyantly dressed, with his hair piled high in a pompadour, Little Richard is a musical phenomenon, an entertainer hailed by pop superstar Paul McCartney as "one of the greatest kings of rock and roll." Richard's image, mannerisms, and musical talent set the trend for the emergence of modern popular music performers from Jimi Hendrix to Prince.

One of 12 children, Richard Wayne Penniman was born on December 5, 1932, in Macon, Georgia. As a child in Macon, Richard heard the sounds of gospel music groups, street musicians, and spiritual-based songs emanating from homes throughout his neighborhood. Nicknamed the "War Hawk" for his unrestrained hollers and shouts, Richard's voice projected with such intensity that he was once asked to stop singing in church. Richard's first song before an audience was with the Tiny Tots, a gospel group featuring his brothers Marquette and Walter. Later Richard sang with his family in a group called the Penniman Singers; they appeared at churches, camp meetings, and talent contests.

In high school, Richard played alto saxophone in the marching band. After school he took a part-time job at the Macon City Auditorium, where he watched the bands of Cab Calloway, Hot Lips Page, Lucky Millinder, and Sister Rosetta Thorpe. At age 14, Richard left home to become a performer in Doctor Hudson's Medicine Show. While on the road, he joined B. Brown's Orchestra as a ballad singer performing such compositions as "Good Night Irene" and "Mona Lisa." Not long afterward, he became a member of the traveling minstrel show of Sugarfoot Sam from Alabama.

Richard's first break came in 1951, when the RCA label recorded him live on the radio, producing the local hit "Every Hour." Traveling to New Orleans with his band the Tempo Toppers, Richard's group eventually played the Houston rhythm and blues scene, where he attracted the attention of Don Robey, president of Peacock Records. After cutting some sides for the Peacock label, Richard sent a demo tape to Art Rupe's Los Angeles-based Specialty label. Under the direction of Specialty's producer Bumps Blackwell, Richard recorded the 1956 hit "Tutti Frutti" at J&M Studios in New Orleans. Richard's subsequent sessions for Specialty yielded a long list of classic hits such as "Long Tall Sally," "Lucille," "Jenny, Jenny," and "Keep a Knocking." In 1957, Richard appeared in the films *Don't Knock Rock* with Billy Haley and *The Girl Can't Help It* starring Jane Mansfield.

In the following year, Richard quit his rock and roll career to enter the Oakland Theological College in Huntsville, Alabama. Between 1957 to 1959 Richard released several gospel recordings and toured with artists like Mahalia Jackson. In 1962, Richard embarked on a tour of Europe with Sam Cooke. One year later Richard hired an then-unknown guitarist, Jimi Hendrix, who went under the pseudonym of Maurice James. In Europe Richard played on the same bills as the Beatles and Rolling Stones.

By the 1970s, Richard pursued a career as a full-fledged evangelist and performer. In 1979, he set out on a nationwide evangelist tour. In the following decade, he appeared in the film *Down and Out in Beverly Hills* and recorded "Rock Island Line" on the tribute LP to Leadbelly and Woody Guthrie entitled *Folkways: A Vision Shared.*

Richard's continuing activity in show business represents the inexhaustible energy of a singer who had a profound impact on the careers of artists like Otis Redding, Eddie Cochran, Richie Valens, Paul McCartney, and Mitch Ryder. Having earned special Grammy honors in 1993, Richard was honored with a lifetime achievement award by the Rhythm & Blues Foundation the following year. Later that year, he headlined the 1994 New Orleans Jazz and Heritage Festival. He was called upon by the House of Blues Foundation to assist in the organizations Blues School House program in 1995.

## Curtis Mayfield (1942– )
### Singer, Songwriter, Producer

Born on June 3, 1942, in Chicago, Illinois, Curtis Mayfield learned to sing harmony as a member of the Northern Jubilee Singers and the Traveling Souls Spiritualist Church. In 1957, Mayfield joined the Roosters, a five-man doo wop singing group led by his close friend Jerry Butler. Renamed the Impressions, the group released the 1958 hit "Your Precious Love," featuring Butler's resonant baritone and Mayfield's wispy tenor. But in the following year, Butler left the group to pursue a solo career. In search of material, Butler collaborated with

Little Richard

Mayfield to write the hit songs "He Will Break Your Heart" and "I'm a-Telling You."

In 1960, Mayfield recruited Fred Cash to take Butler's place in the newly reformed Impressions. In the next year the Impressions hit the charts with the sensual soul tune "Gypsy Women." In collaboration with Butler, Mayfield also established the Curtom Publishing Company. With the loss of original members Richard Brooks and Arthur Brooks, the three remaining members of the Impressions, Mayfield, Cash, and Sam Goodman continued to perform as a trio. Under the direction of jazz musician/arranger Johnny Pate, the Impressions recorded "Sad Sad Girl" and the rhythmic gospel-based song "It's All Right" released in 1963.

During this time, Mayfield also wrote a number of songs for his Chicago contemporaries, including "Monkey Time" for Major Lance, "Just Be True" for Gene Chandler, and "It's All Over Now" for Walter Jackson. Writing for the Impressions, however, Mayfield turned to more socially conscious themes reflecting the current of the civil rights era. Mayfield's finest "sermon songs" were "People Get Ready" (1965), "We're a Winner" (1968), and "Choice of Colors" (1969).

After leaving the Impressions in 1970, Mayfield released his debut album *Curtis*. On his 1971 LP *Curtis Live!*, Mayfield was accompanied by a tight four-piece back-up group, which included guitar, bass, drums, and percussion. Mayfield composed the score for the 1972 hit film *Superfly*. The soundtrack became Mayfield's biggest commercial success, providing him two hits with the junkie epitaph "Freddie's Dead" and the wah-wah guitar funk classic "Superfly." Despite his commercial success, Mayfield spent the remainder of the decade in collaboration with other artists, working on such projects as the soundtrack for the film *Claudine*, featuring Gladys Knight and the Pips, and the production of Aretha Franklin's 1978 album *Sparkle*.

Throughout the next decade, Mayfield continued to record such albums as *Love Is the Place* in 1981, and *Honesty* in 1982. Joined by Jerry Butler and newcomers Nate Evans and Vandy Hampton, the Impressions reunited in 1983, for a 30-city anniversary tour. In 1983, Mayfield released the LP *Come in Peace With a Message of Love*. But in August of 1990, while performing at an outdoor concert in Brooklyn, New York, Mayfield received an injury that left him paralyzed from the neck down. In the following year, Mayfield's contributions to popular music were recognized when the Impressions were inducted into the Rock and Roll Hall of Fame. In 1994, Mayfield was presented with the Grammy Legend Award. Earlier that year a number of his peers, including Aretha Franklin, got together to record *All Men Are Brothers: A Tribute to Curtis Mayfield.*

### Charley Pride (1939– )
*Singer*

The first African American superstar of country music, Charley Pride is a three-time Grammy Award winner whose supple baritone voice has won him international fame. He was the first black to perform at the Grand Ole Opry. A prolific artist, Pride has recorded more than 30 albums.

Born on March 18, 1939, in Slege, Mississippi, Charley Pride grew up listening to late night radio broadcasts of the Grand Ole Opry, country music's most famous showcase. Although he taught himself guitar at age 14, Pride soon turned his attention to a professional baseball career. At age 16, he left the cotton fields of Slege for a stint in the Negro American baseball league. During his baseball career, Pride sang on public address systems and in taverns. In 1963, country singer Red Sovine heard Pride and arranged for him to attend an audition in Nashville one year later. This led to a recording contract with the RCA label and produced the 1964 hit "Snakes Crawl at Night."

Throughout the 1960s, Pride toured incessantly, appearing at concert dates and state fairs, as well as on radio and television. In 1967, Pride debuted at the Grand Ole Opry and within the same year hit the charts with singles "Does My Ring Hurt Your Finger?" and "I Know One." With the release of 1969's *The Sensational Charley Pride* and the subsequent year's *Just Plain Charley,* Pride found himself entering the decade of his greatest recognition. By the time he received the Country Music Award for Entertainer of the Year in 1970, Pride had already achieved tremendous success as a major figure in the popular cultural scene of the United States. Other honors included *Billboard's* Trendsetter Award and the Music Operators of America's Entertainer of the Year Award.

In the 1980s, Pride not only continued to find success as a music star, he became a successful entrepreneur. Making his home on a 240-acre estate in North Dallas, Texas, Pride emerged as a majority stockholder in the First Texas Bank and part owner of Cecca Productions. Pride made more history in the 1993, when he became the first black to join the cast of the Grand Ole Opry since DeFord Bailey's presence nearly 52 years earlier. The following year, Pride published his autobiography entitled *Pride: The Charley Pride Story.*

Charley Pride

### Prince 1958-
*Singer, Songwriter, Producer*

Son of a jazz pianist, Prince Rogers Nelson was born on June 7, 1958, in Minneapolis, Minnesota. By age fourteen Prince taught himself to play piano, guitar and drums. His eclectic taste that led to Prince's creation of the Minneapolis sound. After forming the band Grand Central in high school in 1973, Prince renamed the group Champagne and eventually recruited the talents of Morris Day. In 1978 Prince signed with Warner Brothers and recorded his debut album *For You.* His follow-up album *Prince* featured the hit "I Wanna Be Your Lover." Rooted in the music of Sly and the Family Stone and Jimi Hendrix, Prince's third LP *Dirty Mind* was released in 1980.

Two years later, Prince achieved superstardom with his album *1999,* an effort that was followed by a spectacular tour comprised of Prince and the Revolution, the Time, and the bawdy girl trio Vanity 6. Prince's 1984 film soundtrack *Purple Rain,* which received rave reviews for Prince's portrayal of a struggling young musician, grossed sixty million dollars at the box office in the first two months of its release. Near the end of 1985 Prince established his own record label Paisley Park, the warehouse/studio located in the wooded terrain of Chanhassen, Minnesota. That same year, Prince released the album *Around the World in a Day* featuring the hit singles "Raspberry Beret," "Paisley Park," and "Pop Life."

Prince's next film project *Under the Cherry Moon*, filmed in France, was completed under his direction. The soundtrack *Parade Music from Under the Cherry Moon* produced a number of hit singles including "Kiss" and "Mountains." After re–forming the Revolution, Prince released *Sign of the Times* in 1987, which included a duet with Sheena Easton, "I Could Never Take the Place of Your Man." Following the LP *Lovesexy*, Prince recorded several songs which appeared on the soundtrack for the film *Batman*. This was followed by another film soundtrack *Graffiti Bridge* in 1990.

In September of 1992, Prince signed a six–album contract with Warner Brothers. Backed by his new first rate ensemble the New Power Generation, Prince embarked on a nationwide tour in April of 1993, which proved the most impressive since his commercial breakthrough in the early 1980s. Prince has not only become an owner of his own nightclub, the Grand Slam, he has contributed a set of original music to the Joffery Ballet's production of "Billboards," which opened in January of 1993 to rave reviews.

Prince

That year, the eccentric performer also changed his name to an unpronounceable symbol and announced the retirement of "Prince" from recording. In 1994, The Artist Formerly Known as Prince (TAFKAP) debuted interactive CD-ROM software and New Power Generation retail establishments. Two years later, the long-time bachelor married on Valentine's Day and commissioned a symphony from his band to commemorate the occasion.

## Public Enemy
### *Rap group*

As spokesmen of racial pride, and proponents of militant public activism, Public Enemy have redefined the sound and the lyrical message of rap music. The formation of Public Enemy centered around Adelphi University in Long Island, New York, where the group's founder Carlton Ridenhour a.k.a Chuck D., a graphic design major, joined fellow students Hank Shocklee and Bill Stephney at radio station WBAU. First appearing on Stephney's radio show, Ridenhour soon hosted his own three-hour program. Ridenhour's powerful rap voice attracted a number of loyal followers. Ridenhour soon recruited the talents of William Drayton a.k.a Flavor Flav, Norman Rodgers a.k.a Terminator X, and Richard Griffin a.k.a Professor Griff to form Public Enemy. Shocklee and his production-oriented peers in the group came to be known as the Bomb Squad and their talents were often sought by other artists.

In 1987, Public Enemy released the debut album *Yo! Bum Rush the Show*, which sold more than 400,000 copies. Two years later Professor Griff, the group's "minister of information," was fired by Chuck D. for making anti-Semitic comments. Under the leadership of Chuck D. the group went on to record the song "Fight the Power" for director Spike Lee's film *Do The Right Thing*. The group's second album *It Takes a Nation of Millions to Hold Us Back* became a million-seller.

Public Enemy's 1990 release *Fear of a Black Planet* featured themes regarding a world struggle for the advancement of the black race. The controversial "911 Is a Joke" led to widespread discourse over the song's allegations that emergency personnel respond slower, if at all, to calls originating from inner city or predominantly black areas. The follow-up, *Apocalypse '91: The Enemy Strikes Black*, was a startling statement of social and racial consciousness and featured a collaboration with the heavy metal band Anthrax on "Bring the Noise," a track that originally appeared on *It Takes a Nation*. Another single, "By the Time I Get to Arizona," sparked another nation-wide debate over the refusal of Arizona state officials to recognize Martin Luther King, Jr.'s birthday as a legal holiday.

*Greatest Misses*, a hits compilation released in 1992, seemed to single the end of an era for the Public Enemy camp. In a departure from their earlier work, 1994's *Muse Sick n Hour Mess Age* traded the sonic dissonances of the Bomb Squad for samples from classic soul recordings. Meanwhile, most of the members had established themselves as solo artists or developed other career directions in the early 1990s, but overall the group's popularity seemed to wane as "gansta" rap commandeered the airwaves.

### Queen Latifah (1970– )
*Singer, Actress*

Born Dana Owens, rap artist Queen Latifah was raised in East Orange, New Jersey, and began performing in high school as the human beat box for the rap group Ladies Fresh. In 1989, she launched her solo recording career with the album *All Hail the Queen*, an afrocentric, pro-woman work. Her other recordings include 1991's *Nature of a Sista'*, featuring the single "Latifah Had It Up 2 Here, and 1993's *Black Reign*, which spawned the feminist anthem "U.N.I.T.Y."

Latifah manages the careers of other rap artists through her New Jersey-based Flavor Unit Records and Management Company, of which she is the CEO. In addition, she is a regular on the Fox network's *Living Single*, along with costars Kim Fields, Erika Alexander, and Kim Coles. She has also made appearances on *The Fresh Prince of Bel-Air* and in such films as the Hudlin Brothers' *House Party II*, Spike Lee's *Jungle Fever*, and Ernest Dickerson's *Juice*.

### Otis Redding (1941–1967)
*Singer, Songwriter*

Born on September 9, 1941, in Dawson, Georgia, Otis Redding moved with his parents at age three to the Tindall Heights housing project in Macon. In grade school Redding played drums and sang in a church gospel group. A few years later he learned the vocals and piano style of his idol Little Richard. Quitting school in the tenth grade, Redding went on the road with Little Richard's former band, the Upsetters. But Redding's first professional break came when he joined Johnny Jenkins and the Pinetoppers. Redding's debut single was a Little Richard imitation tune "Shout Bamalama." Accompanying Jenkins to a Stax studio session in Memphis, Redding was afforded some remaining recording time. Backed by Jenkins on guitar, Steve Cropper on piano, Lewis Steinburg on bass, and Al Jackson on drums, Redding cut "Hey Hey Baby" and the hit "These Arms of Mine."

Signed to the Stax label, Redding released the 1963 album *Pain in My Heart*. Backed by members of Book-

Otis Redding

er T. and the MGs, Redding's follow-up LP *Otis Blue (Otis Redding Sings Soul)* featured the 1965 hit "Respect." In the next year, Redding broke attendance records at shows in Harlem and Watts. After releasing a cover version of the Rolling Stones' song "Satisfaction" in 1966, Redding embarked on a European tour which included his appearance on the British television show "*Ready Steady Go!*"

In August 1966, Redding established his own record company, Jotis, which was distributed through the Stax label. Following a few commercially unsuccessful ventures, Redding recorded singer Arthur Conley who provided the label with the million-selling single "Sweet Soul Music." Redding's recordings "Try a Little Tenderness," and the vocal duet "Tramp," featuring Carla Thomas, hit the charts in 1967. On June 16 Redding, backed by the MGs, performed a stunning high-paced set at the Monterey Pop Festival. On December 10, Redding's career came to an tragic end when the twin engine plane carrying him to a concert date in Wisconsin crashed in Lake Monona, just outside Madison. As if in tribute, Redding's song "Sitting on the Dock of the Bay," released a few weeks after his death, became his first gold record.

## Lionel Brockman Richie (1949– )
*Singer, Songwriter, Pianist*

Lionel Brockman Richie was born on June 20, 1949, on the campus of Tuskegee Institute in Alabama. Richie's grandmother Adelaide Foster, a classical pianist, became his music instructor who introduced him to the works of Bach and Beethoven. While a freshman at the Tuskegee Institute, Richie formed the Mighty Mystics who, along with members of the Jays, became the Commodores. Combining gospel, classical, and country-western music, the Commodores emerged as a formidable live act throughout the 1960s and 1970s. After signing with the Motown label, the group landed its first hit in 1974 with the song "Machine Gun." In 1981 Richie recorded the hit theme song for Franco Zefferelli's film *Endless Love.*

A year later, Richie released his first solo album *Lionel Richie* which featured the hits "Truly," "You Are," and "My Love." His follow-up release *Can't Slow Down* produced five more hits: "All Night Long (All Night)," "Running with the Night," "Hello," "Stuck on You," and "Penny Lover." In collaboration with Michael Jackson, Richie co-wrote "We Are the World" for USA for Africa, the famine relief project organized and produced by Quincy Jones. In 1985 Richie received an Oscar nomination for "Best Original Song" for his composition "Say You, Say Me." A year later, Richie's third album *Dancing on the Ceiling* provided him with the hits "Dancing on the Ceiling," "Love Will Conquer All," "Ballerina Girl," and "Se La."

## Smokey Robinson (1940– )
*Singer, Songwriter, Producer*

Proclaimed by Bob Dylan as one of America's greatest poets, Smokey Robinson is a pop music legend. He has risen to fame as a brilliant songwriter, producer, and singer. His instantly recognizable falsetto voice continues to bring Robinson gold records and a legion of loyal fans.

William Robinson, Jr. was born in Detroit, on February 19, 1940. After his mother died when he was ten years old, Robinson was raised by his sister. Nicknamed "Smokey" by his uncle, Robinson was a bright student who enjoyed reading books and poetry. A reluctant saxophone student, Robinson turned his creative energy to composing songs that he collected in a dime store writing tablet. While attending Detroit's Northern High School in 1954, Robinson formed the vocal group the Matadors, which performed at battle-of-the-band contests and at recreation centers.

Robinson's introduction to Berry Gordy in 1957, resulted in the Matadors' first record contract with George Goldner's End label. Upon joining the newly formed

Motown label in 1960, the group changed their name, upon the suggestion of Gordy, to the Miracles. Although the Miracles' debut album failed to attract notice, they provided Motown with its first smash hit "Shop Around" in 1961, a song written and coproduced by Robinson.

In close collaboration with Gordy, Robinson spent the following decade as one of Motown's most integral singers and producers. With the Miracles he recorded such hits as "You Really Got a Hold On Me" in 1963, "Tracks of My Tears" in 1965, "I Second That Emotion" in 1967, and "Tears of a Clown" in 1970. As a writer he provided the label with hits like "My Guy" for Mary Wells, "I'll Be Doggone" for Marvin Gaye, and "My Girl" for the Temptations.

In 1972, Robinson left the Miracles to launch a solo career. Despite the moderate success of his records during the disco craze of the 1970s, Robinson continued to perform and record. In 1979, Robinson experienced a comeback with the critically acclaimed hit "Cruisin." Three years later, Robinson appeared on the NBC-TV special *"Motown 25: Yesterday, Today, and Tomorrow." Between 1986 and 1991, Robinson released five more albums including Smoke Signals, One Heartbeat,* and *Love, Smokey.* He was inducted into both the Rock and Roll Hall of Fame and the Songwriters Hall of Fame in 1986, and, in 1987, he won a Grammy for his vocal performance on "Just to See Her." In 1995, Robinson was signed by Music by Design, a U.K. company that solicits artists to create original music for television and radio commercials.

## Diana Ross (1944– )
*Singer, Actress*

One of six children, Diane Ross was born in Detroit, on March 26, 1944. An extremely active child Ross swam, ran track, and sang in church. In 1959, she joined the Primetes, a group comprised of Mary Wilson, Florence Ballard, and Barbara Martin. After failing to attract notice on the Lupine label, the group auditioned for Berry Gordy, Jr. who signed them to Motown. Upon the suggestion of Berry, the group changed its name to the Supremes. Released in 1961, the group's song, "I Want a Guy," featuring Ross on lead vocals, failed to attract notice. Not long afterward, following Martin's departure, the trio continued to record with Ross on lead vocal.

The Supremes did not find commercial success on the Motown label until 1964, when they were placed under the guidance of the Holland-Dozier-Holland production team. In 1964, H-D-H turned out the Supreme's first smash hit "Where Did Our Love Go?" followed by numerous hits, such as "Baby Love" in 1964, "I Hear a Symphony" in 1965, "You Can't Hurry Love" in 1966, and "Reflections" in 1967. With preferential treat-

Diana Ross makes her last appearance with the Supremes: Cindy Birdsong (left) and Mary Wilson (center), 1970.

ment by Gordy, Ross became the dominant figure of the group. By the mid-1960s Ross's emerging talent prompted Gordy to bill the group as Diana Ross and the Supremes.

In 1970, Ross left the Supremes to launch her solo career. Her debut album *Diana Ross* featured the writing and production talents of Ashford & Simpson, an effort that included the hit "Reach Out and Touch (Somebody's Hand)." One year later she made her film debut in the Motown-sponsored movie *Lady Sings the Blues* in which she won an Oscar nomination for her biographical portrayal of jazz singer Billie Holiday. Her role in the 1975 Motown-backed film *Mahogany* brought her not only an Oscar nomination, but the number one selling single "Do You Know Where You're Going To." In 1978, Ross starred in the film version of *The Wiz*, the last full-scale motion picture to be backed by Motown.

After leaving Motown in 1981, Ross signed a $20-million contract with the RCA label. Her debut album *Why Do Fools Fall in Love?* went platinum. This was followed by four more LP's for RCA, including *Silk Electric* in 1982, *Swept Away* in 1984, *Eaten Alive* in 1985. Two years later, Ross left RCA to sign with the

London-based EMI label, which produced the albums *Red Hot Rhythm 'n Blues* in 1987, *Working Overtime* in 1987, and *Greatest Hits, Live* in 1990. Meanwhile, Ross had returned to Motown Records as a recording artist and partial owner in 1989, one year after being inducted into the Rock and Roll Hall of Fame.

In the 1990s, the Grammy and Tony award-winning Ross continued to enjoy popularity around the world; She achieved tremendous success as the owner of her own multi-million-dollar corporation Diana Ross Enterprises. Her autobiography, *Secrets of a Sparrow: Memoirs*, was published in 1993, and a compilation called *Diana Extended/The Remixes* hit the stores in 1994.

### Russell Simmons (1957?– )
*Record Company Executive, Producer, Music Promoter*

Hollis, Queens, in New York City is the birth place of Russell Simmons. Although he grew up in a middle class neighborhood, Simmons got involved with gangs in his teens. The 1970s brought change to Simmons's life, however, as he enrolled in classes at the Harlem branch of City College of New York. While studying sociology, Simmons began noticing the influence rap music had on young inner-city blacks. The boasting and story telling skills of various rappers drew crowds on street corners and in neighborhood parks. Simmons found himself in the middle of a movement that would shape the sound of the music, particularly the rap genre.

Simmons left college to promote local rap artists. Hard work and perseverance led to the formation of Def Jam Records in 1984. Simmons and his partner, Rick Ruben, signed a deal with CBS Records to distribute their material. Simmons was primarily interested in promoting rap images that displayed the life and style of tough urban streets. Acts like the Beastie Boys, L.L. Cool J, and Run-DMC pushed Def Jam Records to early success. Other groups like Public Enemy enjoyed Simmons's input as their careers developed.

The music Simmons involved himself with not only revolutionized hip-hop but helped bring fashion to forefront as well. High top Addidas tennis shoes, black leather jackets, and t-shirts displaying the Def Jam Recording logo flooded the streets. These influences laid a foundation for Simmons's own line of clothing called Phat Pharm. Simmons furthered his own professional growth by getting involved in film production. He contributed to *Krush Groove* and *Tougher Than Leather* in the late 1980s. Simmons has moved into directing several music videos.

### Donna Summer (1948– )
*Singer*

One of the biggest stars of the disco era, Donna Summer first gained notice with a pulsatingly erotic

Euro-hit, then moved on to mainstream popularity. She ruled the charts through the late 1970s, though the fading of disco left her with no choice but to streamline her style. Although her popularity declined in the ensuing years, she has become one of the few stars of the era to transcend the kitsch that surrounds it.

Born Donna Gaines in Boston, the singer got her first break when she was cast in a traveling production of a rock musical. While in Germany she met Helmut Sommer, whom she married; she later made the acquaintance of Italian producer Giorgio Moroder, who produced her first hit, the throbbingly sexual "Love to Love You Baby." Summers's moans and groans were her initial route to stardom. Through the late 1970s, however, she continually expanded her range. Her hits included a cover version of the pop standard "Macarthur Park," "On the Radio," "Bad Girls," "Hot Stuff," and "Last Dance."

Summer became a born-again Christian in the early 1980s, and gradually turned toward inspiration music. She earned Grammy awards for Best Inspirational Performance in 1984 and 1985, but she surfaced less and less frequently in the pop world. On dancefloors throughout the world, however, she is accorded the status of a deity.

### Tina Turner (1939– )
*Singer*

With a music career spanning more than 30 years, Tina Turner has come to be known as the "hardest-working woman in show business." From soul music star to rock goddess, Turner's vocal style and energetic stage act remain a show-stopping phenomenon.

Born Annie Mae Bullock on November 25, 1939, in Brownsville, Tennessee, Turner moved to Knoxville with her parents at age three. Turner first sang in church choirs and at local talent contests. After moving with her mother to St. Louis at age 16, Turner met pianist Ike Turner, leader of the R and B group the Kings of Rhythm. Hired by the band to sing at weekend engagements, Annie Bullock married Ike Turner in 1958 and took the stage name Tina Turner. When the band's scheduled session singer failed to appear at a recording session in 1960, Tina stepped in to record the R and B song "Fool in Love" which became a million-seller.

With a major hit behind them, the Turners formed the Ike and Tina Turner Revue, complete with the Iketes. Major international success came for the Turners in 1966, when producer Phil Spector combined his "wall of sound" approach with a R and B sound to record the hit "River Deep, Mountain High." Subjected to years of physical abuse by her husband, Turner divorced Ike in 1976 and set out on a solo career. That same year she co-

Tina Turner

starred in The Who's rock opera film *Tommy* as the Acid Queen.

In 1984 Turner's career skyrocketed with the commercial success of the album *Private Dancer* which featured the hit singles "What's Love Got to Do With It?" and "Better Be Good." Turner's sensuously vibrant image soon appeared on high budget videos, magazine covers, and in films such as the 1985 release *Mad Max 3: Beyond the Thunderdome* in which she played the tyrannical Aunty Entity. With the immense commercial success of her 1989 album *Foreign Affair*, Turner closed out the decade as one of the most popular singers on the international music scene. In 1995 she was even tapped to perform the title track of that year's James Bond flick, *Goldfinger*.

### Luther Vandross (1951– )
*Singer, Composer, Producer*

One of the premier pop artists of the 1980s, Luther Vandross is responsible for the emergence of a new school of modern soul singers. Born in New York City on April 20, 1951, Vandross was the son of a gospel singer and a big band vocalist. Vandross received his musical education by listening to recordings of Aretha

Franklin and the Supremes. In high school Vandross formed numerous singing groups. Throughout the 1970s, he was great as a background singer, performing with such artists as David Bowie, Carly Simon, and Ringo Starr. He also sang advertising jingles like ATT's theme "Reach Out and Touch."

Following the release of his first album *Never Too Much* in 1981, Vandross was called upon to sing duets with a number of pop artists, including Aretha Franklin and Dionne Warwick. As a successful writer and producer, Vandross has released eight million-selling albums including the 1990 release *Best of Love*, which went multi-platinum.

### Mary Wells (1943–1992)
*Singer*

Born in 1943 and raised in her hometown of Detroit, Michigan, Mary Wells started her music career as a featured soloist in her high school choir. After attracting the notice of Berry Gordy, Jr. at age 17, Wells signed a contract with Motown in 1959. With Smokey Robinson as her main producer and writer, Wells scored a number of hits such as "I Don't Want to Take a Chance," in 1961, "You Beat Me to the Punch" in 1962, and "My Guy" in 1964. In the same year, she recorded the album *Together* with Marvin Gaye, and toured England with the Beatles.

At the peak of her career, Wells left the Motown label to become an actress. After relocating in Los Angeles, she signed a contract with the Twentieth Century Fox records. Unfortunately, Wells could never find a producer who equaled Robinson's ability to record her material. Her debut single in 1965 "Use Your Head" achieved only modest commercial success. In the 1970s Wells left music to raise her children. For a brief period she was married to Cecil Womack, brother of the R&B great Bobby Womack.

During the 1980s, Wells returned to music performing on the oldies circuit. In 1985 she appeared in "Motown's 25th Anniversary" television special. Diagnosed as having cancer of the larynx in August 1990, Wells, without medical insurance to pay for treatment, lost her home. Not long afterward, the Rhythm and Blues Foundation raised over $50,000 for Wells' hospital costs. Funds were also sent by artists like Bruce Springsteen, Rod Stewart, and Diana Ross. Despite chemotherapy treatments, Wells died on July 30, 1992 and was buried at Forest Lawn Memorial Park in Los Angeles.

### Jackie Wilson (1934–1984)
*Singer*

Between 1958 and 1963, Jackie Wilson reigned as one of the most popular R and B singers in America. Dressed in sharkskin suits and sporting a process hairstyle, Wilson exhibited a dynamic stage performance and a singing range which equaled his contemporaries James Brown and Sam Cooke.

Jack Leroy Wilson was born on June 9, 1934, in Detroit, Michigan. Wilson's mother sang spirituals and gospel songs at Mother Bradley's Church. As a youngster, he listened to the recordings of the Mills Brothers, Ink Spots, and Louis Jordan. In high school he became a boxer, and at age 16 he won the American Amateur Golden Gloves Welterweight title. But upon the insistence of his mother, Wilson quit boxing and pursued a career in music. While a teenager, Wilson sang with the Falcons in local clubs, and at talent contests held at the Paradise Theater. He also worked in a spiritual group with later members of Hank Ballard's Midnighters.

In 1953 Wilson replaced Clyde McPhatter as lead singer of the Dominoes. Wilson's only hit with the Dominoes was the reworking of the religious standard "St. Theresa of the Roses." Upon the success of the recording, Wilson signed a contract as a solo artist with the Brunswick label. Wilson's 1957 debut album *Rete Petite* featured the hit title track song which was written by songwriters Berry Gordy, Jr. and Billy Taylor. The

Jackie Wilson

songwriting team of Gordy and Taylor also provided Wilson with the subsequent hits "To Be Loved" in 1957, "Lonely Teardrops" in 1958, and "That's Why I Love You So," and "I'll Be Satisfied" in 1959.

During the early 1960s, Wilson performed and recorded numerous adaptations of classical music compositions in a crooning ballad style. This material, however, failed to bring out the powerful talent of Wilson's R and B vocal style. Although Wilson's repertoire contained mostly supper club standards, he did manage to produce the powerful pop classics "Dogging Around" in 1960 and "Baby Workout" in 1963. Teamed with writer/producer Carl Davis, Wilson also recorded the hit "Whispers" and the R and B masterpiece "Higher and Higher" in 1967.

Following Wilson's last major hit "I Get the Sweetest Feeling" in 1968, he performed on the oldies circuit and on Dick Clark's "Good Ol' Rock 'n' Roll Revue." In 1975 Wilson suffered a serious heart attack on stage at the Latin Casino in Cherry Hill, New Jersey. Forced into retirement, Wilson spent his last eight years in a nursing home until his death on January 21, 1984.

**Mary Wilson (1944– )**
*Singer*

As a member of the Motown supergroup the Supremes, Mary Wilson's musical career represents an American success story. Born on March 6, 1944, in Greenville, Mississippi, Wilson moved to Detroit at age 11. Raised in the Brewster-Douglas housing project on the city's east side, Wilson learned to sing by imitating the falsetto voice of Frank Lyman. Along with Barbara Martin and Betty Travis, Wilson formed the Primetes. Upon the departure of Travis, another neighborhood girl named Diana Ross joined the group. Appearing at talent shows and sock-hops, the Primetes went on to win first prize at the 1960 Detroit/Windsor Freedom Festival talent contest. Although the Primetes cut two singles on the Lupine label featuring Wilson on lead vocal, they failed to achieve commercial success.

On January 15, 1961, 16–year–old Wilson and Primete members Diana Ross, Florence Ballard and Barbara Martin signed with the Motown label as the Supremes. Wilson's effort to win the lead vocal spot, however, soon gave way to the dominance of Diana Ross. Released in 1964, the group's first gold single "Where Did Our Love Go?" made Wilson and the Supremes overnight celebrities. Between 1964 and 1968 Wilson sang background vocals on a number of hits, including "Baby Love," "You Can't Hurry Love," and "Reflections." Before leaving the group in 1976, Wilson also sang such recordings as "Love Child," "I'm Living in Shame," and "Someday We'll Be Together."

In 1983 Wilson was briefly reunited with the Supremes on "Motown's 25th Anniversary" television special. Making her home in Los Angeles, Wilson occasionally appears on the oldies circuit and at small Supremes revival shows.

**Nancy Wilson (1937– )**
*Singer*

Nancy Wilson was born in Chillicothe, Ohio, in 1937. Her musical talents were first noticed when, as a child, she performed for her family at various gatherings. The performances continued as Wilson became a member of her church choir. Influence from artists such as Billy Eckstine and Nat King Cole helped Wilson determine that singing would be her career. As a teen, Wilson and her family moved to Columbus, Ohio. Wilson soon became the host of her own radio show, Skyline Melody, during which she performed phoned in requests.

In 1955, Wilson enrolled in classes at Ohio's Central State College to pursue teaching credentials. Her stint in school was short lived, however, as Wilson dropped out to pursue her singing career. She spent the next three years touring the country as a member of Rusty Byrant's Carolyn Club Band. The experience Wilson gained while touring gave her the courage to go solo. New York City became Wilson's new home as her career began skyrocketing.

Shortly after her arrival in the Big Apple, Wilson obtained permanent work at a local night club. Word of her masterful performances soon spread all over the city prompting a recording session with Capitol records. 1960 marked the release of her debut album *Like in Love* and the recording of her first major hit, entitled "Save Your Love for Me." *How Glad I Am* won a Grammy in 1964, beginning a 30-year streak of acclaim.

Wilson's blend of rhythm and blues, jazz, and pop styles captivated thousands of fans around the world. Television executives began to take advantage of Wilson's talents as she was given her own weekly variety show. The Emmy Award-winning *The Nancy Wilson Show* was merely the beginning of Wilson's television appearances. Guest spots on *The Tonight Show*, *The Merv Griffin Show*, and *The Today Show* soon followed.

During the late 1970s and early 1980s, technology began to influence the fashion in which studio recordings were made. Wilson continued to record and tour despite differences with various recording companies issues of sound. Nonetheless, she was named Global Entertainer of the Year in 1986 by the World Conference of Mayors and the NAACP bestowed her with its Image Award that year as well.

Just as much heralded in the 1990s, Wilson's 54th full-length recording was completed in 1994. With a star on the Hollywood Walk of Fame, an Essence Award, a Martin Luther King Center for Social Change Award, and a Trumpet Award to her name, Wilson's bevy of honors is symbol of her timelessness and a testimony to the loyalty of her fans.

## The Winans
*Gospel singing group*

Detroit's first family of gospel music, the Winans have won a number of Grammy awards for their infectious modern pop gospel sound. Known as funky gospel, the Winans's music features electric keyboards, guitar, and bass, as well as saxophone accompaniment. David Jr., Michael, and twins Marvin and Carvin, first sang at their great-grandfather's Zion Congregational Church of Christ on Detroit's east side; their father, a minister and singer, David Winan, Sr. first organized the quartet. While attending Mumford High School, the group attracted large crowds at school talent contests. Originally called the Testimonials, the quartet released two locally-produced albums *Love Covers* in 1977 and *Thy Will Be Done* in 1978.

Upon being discovered by gospel singer Andraé Crouch, the group released its first national debut album *Introducing the Winans* in 1981, which was nominated for a Grammy award. The follow-up 1983 LP *Long Time Coming* also received a Grammy nomination. 1985's *Tomorrow* won a Grammy as did *Let My People Go*, recorded on Quincy Jones's ' Qwest label. Known to join secular pop artists in collaborative singing projects, the Winans featured Michael McDonald on their 1987 release *Decisions*. They also sang back-up on Anita Baker's Grammy-winning hit single "Ain't No Need To Worry" and provided vocal tracks for Michael Jackson's song "Man in the Mirror" featured on his *Bad*. *The Winans Live at Carnegie Hall* won a Grammy Award in 1988.

In 1992, the Winans appeared at "Culturefest 92" in West Africa. One year later they were invited to sing at U.S. president Bill Clinton's inauguration festivities. That year sisters Angie and Debbie became the newest additions to the family group, which has won Dove, Stellar, and Soul Train awards.

## Stevie Wonder (1950– )
*Singer, Pianist, Composer*

Popular music's genius composer and singer Stevie Wonder has remained at the forefront of musical change. His colorful harmonic arrangements have drawn upon jazz, soul, pop, reggae, and rap-derived new jack rhythms. Wonder's gift to pop music is his ability to create serious music dealing with social and political issues while at the same time revealing the soulful and deeper mysterious nature of the human experience.

Steveland Morris Judkins was born on May 13, 1950, in Saginaw, Michigan. Raised in Detroit, Steveland Morris first sang in the church choir. But the music that attracted him most were the sounds of Johnny Ace and B. B. King that he heard on late night radio programs. By age eight Wonder learned to play piano, harmonica, and bongos. Through the connections of Miracles member Ronnie White, Wonder auditioned for Berry Gordy, Jr. who, immediately signing the 13-year-old prodigy, gave him the stage name of Little Stevie Wonder. After releasing his first singles "Thank You (For Loving Me All the Way)" and "Contract of Love," In 1963, "Fingertips, Pt. 2" became the first live performance of a song to reach the top of the pop charts. That year Wonder also became the first recording artist to hold number one slots on the *Billboard* Hot 100, R&B Singles, and album charts, simultaneously. In the following year, Wonder hit the charts with the song "Hey Harmonica Man."

With the success of his recording career, Wonder began touring more frequently. Motown assigned Wonder a tutor from the Michigan School for the Blind, allowing him to continue his education while on the road. In 1964, he performed in London with the Motown Revue, a package featuring Martha and the Vandellas, the Supremes, and the Temptations. Wonder's subsequent recording of the punchy R&B single "Uptight (Everything's Alright)" became a smash hit in 1966. Wonder's growing commercial success at Motown brought him greater artistic freedom in the studio. In collaboration with Clarence Paul, Wonder produced a long succession of hits including Bob Dylan's "Blowing in the Wind" in 1966, "I Was Made to Love Her" in 1967, and "For Once in My Life" in 1968. In 1969, U.S. president Richard Nixon gave Wonder a Distinguished Service Award from the President's Committee on Employment of Handicapped People. That year, *My Cherie Amour* generated a single of the same name.

After recording the 1970 album *Signed, Sealed & Delivered*, featuring the title-track, Wonder moved to New York City, where he founded Tarus Production Company and Black Bull Publishing Company, both of which were licensed under Motown. With complete control over his musical career, Wonder began to write lyrics addressing social and political issues. Through the technique of over-dubbing, he played most of the instruments on his recordings including the guitar, bass, horns, percussion, and brilliant chromatic harmonica solos. *Music From My Mind, Talking Book,* and *Inversions* all feature Wonder distinctive synthesizer accompaniment.

Released in 1979, Wonder's *Journey Through the Secret Life of Plants* was an exploratory musical soundtrack for a film documentary. In 1984, Wonder's soundtrack for the film *Woman in Red* won him an

Stevie Wonder

Academy Award for Best Song with "I Just Called To Say I Love You." One year later, Wonder participated in the recording of "We Are the World" for U.S.A for Africa, the famine relief project. He also teamed up with Paul McCartney for "Ebony and Ivory." Wonder's 1985 album *Square Circle* produced the hit singles "Part Time Lover" and "Overjoyed" and won a Grammy. After the 15-time Grammy Award winner was inducted into the Rock and Roll Hall of Fame in 1989, he composed material for the soundtrack to Spike Lee's film *Jungle Fever*. Eight years in the making, 1995's *Conversation Piece* hit fans the same year as did the double-live recording *Natural Wonder*. He also contributed to the tribute-recording *Inner City Blues: The Music of Marvin Gaye* and to Quincy Jones's *Q's Jook Joint*. He won an *Essence* Award that year.

# 24

# *The Visual and Applied Arts*

# 24

# *The Visual and Applied Arts*

◆ An Enduring African Legacy ◆ Black Artists in Europe ◆ Black Artists in Early America
◆ African American Artists Interpreting Euro-American Traditions
◆ African American Artists in the Harlem Renaissance ◆ African American Artists Since the Depression
◆ The Search for an African American Identity ◆ The HBCU Connection
◆ African American Exhibitions ◆ Architecture and the Applied Arts
◆ Visual and Applied Artists ◆ Museums and Galleries

**by Ionis Bracy Martin and Floyd Thomas, Jr.**

*"The constructive lessons of African art are among the soundest and most needed of art creeds today. They offset with equal force the banalities of sterile, imitative classicism and the superficialities of literal realism. They emphasize intellectually significant form, abstractly balanced design, formal simplicity, restrained and unsentimental emotional appeal. Moreover, Africa's art creed is beauty in use, vitally rooted in the crafts, and uncontaminated with the blight of the machine. Surely the liberating example of such art will be marked as an influence in the contemporary work of Negro artists as it has been in that of the leading modernists: Picasso, Modigliani, Matisse, Epstein, Lipchitz, Brancusi and others too numerous to mention." (Alain Locke, Professor of Philosophy, Howard University, 1931).*

This comment by one of America's foremost art critics over sixty-five years ago underscores the problems and the promise encountered by African Americans interested in expanding their artistic skills throughout their history in the United States.

The problems and obstacles encountered by black artists in America have been enumerated and discussed by scholars and critics alike. It has been argued that a multiplicity of factors have combined to impede or preclude the development of black artists and their art. According to this line of thought, black Americans were torn from their cultural roots in Africa, while enslaved they were prevented from practicing artistic traditions associated with "pagan" religious beliefs, and even as

citizens they were denied opportunities, training, and patronage others received for their artistic endeavors. Additionally, because of their comparative economic deprivation, African Americans were historically discouraged from pursuing careers in the visual arts. The cumulative effects of these obstacles, according to this theory, proved so devastating to African American creativity in the visual arts, that the promise seemingly implied in a great African artistic tradition could not be realized in America.

Unfortunately, these arguments have been repeated with such frequency and "authority" that they were accepted into the cannon of American art history. The omission of black artists from standard art history texts, classroom discussions and museum collections has been rationalized by the erroneous assumption that African Americans had simply not produced a significant body of work that merited serious consideration. In consequence, African American artists have long been denied their rightful place in the history of American art.

Despite the obstacles and difficulties unique to them, African Americans have produced a remarkable body of work clearly worthy of consideration. Black Americans have faced and overcome bewildering obstacles in every field of creative endeavor—in literature, music, dance, and the visual arts. While it is certainly true that the odds stacked against black visual artists overwhelmed many along the way, many persevered. Lynn Moody Igoe's massive annotated bibliography, *250 Years of Afro-American Art*, published in 1981, contains over

1,200 pages of information pertaining to the accomplishments of 3,900 black American visual artists. That so few black artists have been acknowledged by the "mainstream" art establishment is less a reflection on African American artistic ability than a failure of the art establishment to comprehend the reality that aesthetic values are not universal and that unique cultural experience manifests itself in unique artistic expressions.

## ◆ AN ENDURING AFRICAN LEGACY

A growing number of scholars are challenging the once widely embraced assumption that the period of enslavement totally obliterated the African heritage, leaving African Americans devoid of cultural roots and artistic creativity. Surviving African aesthetic influences have been discussed by Nkiru Nzegwu (crafts), John Michael Vlach (architecture), Floyd Willis Coleman and Bamidele Demerson (painting), Alan Lomax (music), Katrina Hazzard-Donald (dance), Reginia Perry (folk art), and Robert Farris Thompson (sculpture), to name a few.

The supposition that slavery reduced African Americans to "cultural zero" fails to consider not only residual African influences, but also the factor of re-discovery and renewal. This process was first espoused by Alain Locke, who urged black artists to re-Africanize by adopting and adapting their ancestral arts. Locke believed that the amalgam of African and American influences would surely result in a new and unique art, representative of a new philosophy and cultural identity. As Bamidele Demerson points out:

> There always have been some African Americans who, fearing their ethnic group had lost too much of its ancestral culture and consequently its identification with Africa, led a variety of revitalization movements. In a society that anathematized the African American, such movements were part of a repertoire of strategies that allowed members of the imprecated ethnic group to: pridefully assert a glorious past that spanned millennia; selectively reclaim and adapt some aspects of African beliefs and behavioral codes; and zealously rescue their dignity. The message imparted by these movements was, "Remember you are African!"

According to artist/educator Willis "Bing" Davis, "Because our forebears' culture, right down to their names, was suppressed when they came to America as slaves, we have had to dig to link our cultural roots with Africa." (Quoted in Susan MacDonald, "From US to Slave House," *West Africa* 17 June 1985; 1223.) Evidence of an interest in Africa as a source of inspiration can be found in the murals painted by Aaron Douglas during the 1930s and in the work of Bing Davis, whose travels to the land of his ancestors has inspired and given direction to his art, both in clay and on canvas. Though much of his work is viewed as abstract and non-representational, his *Spirit Dance* series captures the colors and movements he experienced while watching dancers in West Africa.

African aesthetic values, forms and techniques are well represented in African American craft art. Blended with influences derived from an African American experience, craft art forms a vital link between African and African American creative expression. While Mary Jackson has retained an ancient African basket making tradition that has endured through the ages in coastal Carolina, she pushes the boundaries to create beautiful sea grass baskets that are both functional and truly unique.

> "A medium of artistic expression, these coiled sweet grass forms were also memory vessels. The coiling, the twilled, twined, checkerboard, and fine-bias weaves draw from centuries-old geometric and skeuomorphic patterns of West Africa and give them an American feeling. In these utilitarian objects, African American modifications amounted to an artistic exploration of the tensile strength of weaves and of the plasticity and structural potential of the natural fibers." (Nkiru Nzegwu, "A Circle of Dibias: Making Vessels of Memory and Life," *Uncommon Beauty in Common Objects: The Legacy of African American Craft Art*, 1993:9).

Yvonne and Curtis Tucker and David MacDonald are among a number of late twentieth century ceramists who continue the legacy of work in clay passed down through "Dave the Potter" and a lineage of enslaved Africans and their descendants. While inspired by African cultural traditions, these artists shape their work to reflect a history that is both African and African American. This melding of African cultural tradition and African American craft can also be found in the work of enslaved blacksmiths who incorporated African symbolism in their ornamental ironwork. This tradition has continued in Charleston, South Carolina, through the skill and imagination of master craftsmen such as Philip Simmons, his mentor Peter Simmons, and generations of now unknown black blacksmiths who preceded them in practicing this ancient African art form.

Another ancient West African metalworking process, lost-wax bronze casting has been preserved in the work of John Beckley, who has invented a portable table-top furnace to produce his sculptures. Beckley's *Me Myself*, which represents the two halves of his identity joined together, is a graphic representation of the African and African American influences that guide his art and his life. Another contemporary artist who works in metals, Andrew F. Scott, has created a series of stools fabricated in steel and outdoor steel sculptures that mix the iconography of traditional African art forms with the formal structure of totems. These reflect the compelling strength of Africa's influence and aesthetic values on a contemporary African American sculptor implying a continuum with an age-old African craft skill. His *Nkonde Totem III* was the first artwork to be installed in the sculpture garden of the National Afro-American Museum and Cultural Center in Wilberforce, Ohio.

The African tradition of woodcraft can be found in the cabinetry and carpentry that was so integral to the development of the early American economy and the built environment, including public buildings and private homes, particularly in the South. Known for his finely crafted furniture and architectural pieces, Thomas Day (c. 1800-1860) achieved aesthetic beauty and financial success by blending Euro-American period styles with African American craftsmanship, at times incorporating design features that appear to be African in origin. Contemporary artist Manuel Gomez has honed his woodcraft skills in creating "Afro combs" that continue a Ghanaian Akan tradition. Carved from exotic woods, these utilitarian objects are endowed with aesthetic beauty that reflects both cultural pride and African American sensibilities. Another woodcarver, the late Elijah Pierce (1892-1982), is among the most widely acknowledged African American "folk" artists. Nkiru Nzegwu has called his narrative wood carvings "sermons in wood." Whether his subject is sacred or secular, Pierce takes on the role of a contemporary African American *griot*, a historian who documents history in the stories his woodcarvings tell.

Carolyn Mazloomi and Michael Cummings are *griots* who preserve history through another craft skill with traditional African precedents—quilting. Both Mazloomi and Cummings chronicle the history of the African diaspora in the Americas with equal emphasis in their art on craftsmanship and aesthetic considerations as on the subject portrayed. Cummings incorporates a collage style and shapes inspired by Abomey applique. Through this medium, Mazloomi "raises socio-political issues of cultural identity and marginalization, visually forcing her audience's attention to key events in American history." (Nkiru Nzegwu, *Uncommon Beauty in Common Objects: The Legacy of African American Craft Art*, 1993:74). Mazloomi, Cummings, Peggy Hartwell, Carole Harris, Sandra German, and Faith Ringgold are among a growing number of artists who are taking the quilt from the bed to the wall. Concerned that a traditional African American art form was dying out, Mazloomi formed the Women of Color Quilter's Network, which presently has 600 members.

The link to African aesthetic values and inspiration can take unusual forms in African American craft art, as evident in the stylized aluminum, wood and leather "Zebra Chair" that is Richard Bennett's tribute to "the motherland, the mother continent where all life began."

## ◆ BLACK ARTISTS IN EUROPE

Two artists who excelled in Europe in the seventeenth century have been documented. They are Juan de Pareja and Sebastian Gomez. Pareja was a slave, apprentice, and pupil of the great master Velasquez. Many of Pareja's works were of such a quality that they were mistakenly accepted as Velasquez's own and hung in the great museums and mansions of western Europe. Today, Pareja's paintings, properly credited to him, hang in the Dulwich Gallery in London, the Prado in Madrid, the Munich Gallery, and the Hermitage in Leningrad. Pareja's talent was recognized in his lifetime and in 1652 he was manumitted by King Philip IV.

Another well-known seventeenth-century black artist, Sebastian Gomez, a servant of Murillo, was discovered painting secretly at night in his master's studio after Murillo's pupils had departed. Murillo made Gomez his student, and eventually Gomez, known as The Mulatto of Murillo, became famous for paintings and murals in Seville.

Although Pareja and Gomez were black artists, their genius was nurtured in a European setting and tradition. Cut off from their African heritage, they naturally worked in the same style and format as their white contemporaries. Their paintings were devoted to the religious themes and aristocratic portraits desired by the art world of that historical era.

## ◆ BLACK ARTISTS IN EARLY AMERICA

The first known African-American artists were from the eighteenth century. African slaves had many skills: metal tooling and smithing, furniture making, masonry, weaving, woodcarving, pottery making, clay sculpting and metal casting. The most talented crafts people were among the first to gain their freedom before emancipation and, needless to say, were among the most successful during Reconstruction and the years to follow.

As we approach the twenty-first century, will artists of African descent continue following and developing their art from lessons learned and based upon "Africa's art creed . . . beauty in use, vitally rooted in the crafts, and uncontaminated with the blight of the machine"? Or will African-American artists, like the members of AFRI-COBRA (African Commune of Bad Relevant Artists), continue to establish their own aesthetics, while still others follow mainstream American tastes in their pursuit to be a part of the American fabric?

*Newspaper Boy,* Edward Mitchell Bannister, 1869.

# ◆ AFRICAN AMERICAN ARTISTS INTERPRETING EURO-AMERICAN TRADITIONS

The only eighteenth-century African American artist in Colonial America presently known to have left a historical record was Scipio Morehead. His artistic endeavors appear to have been aided by two prominent women who lived in Boston where he was a slave. One was the wife of his clergyman master, the Reverend John Morehead, who was a patron of the arts, and the other, poet Phillis Wheatley, who was herself a slave. Morehead's style has been reported to have been in keeping with the period—classically allegorical, resembling the work of Romney and Reynolds, British masters of the era. Although no major work is known to have survived, a small portrait of Phillis Wheatley is believed to be Morehead's work.

Certainly, there were other black artists and craftsmen in the eighteenth century about whom history has left little trace. Fortunately, as scholars have more of a desire to understand the nature and development of the American culture, a more multi-ethnic pattern is beginning to emerge with the basic foundation being Western European, African, and Native American. Records indicate that blacks skilled as painters, silversmiths, cabinet and coach makers, ornamentalists, and shipwrights, were among the most successful in buying their freedom. Eugene Warbourg, for example, a black sculptor from New Orleans, became well known for his ornamental gravestones and eventually went to study in Europe. Much colonial iron work and metal work on eighteenth century mansions, churches, and public buildings were created and executed by blacks and occasionally reached heights that can be classified as fine art.

Emerging African American artists in the eighteenth and nineteenth centuries found that to be successful they had to simulate European artistic styles. Many were trained by white artists and they traveled to Europe to study and receive validation. Their works received some degree of popular acceptance, but racism kept them out of the mainstream. Most continued to work in the United States in spite of their status. Some were able to overcome immense obstacles and win recognition for their art. Joshua Johnston (1765-1830) is believed to be the first black American to gain recognition as a portrait painter. Robert S. Duncanson (1821-1872), who captured the beauty and wonder of nature in romantic views of the land, won praise at home and abroad. He is recognized as among the greatest landscape artists in American history. Edward Mitchell Bannister (1828-1901) also excelled in romantic interpretations of nature. Edmonia Lewis (1843-1900?) was the first African American woman to receive recognition as

an artist in the United States and in Europe. The influence of Greco-Roman sculpture she studied in Rome can be seen in her later works that are strongly neoclassical. Meta Vaux Warrick (Fuller) (1877-1968) is best known for sculptures that express pathos in her interpretations of humanity.

Some African American artists attempted to escape the classical tradition into which they were confined and expressed themes closer to their heritage and existence. Some fine portraits of black freedmen were painted by talented but obscure black artists in the rural South during the period from 1870 through the early part of the twentieth century. Henry Ossawa Tanner's paintings in the 1880s of poor blacks, for example, stem from this unheralded school of African American art. But he gained his greatest recognition for paintings that reflected his father's strong religious influence. Tanner, who went to Paris to study art and decided to stay, won many prestigious honors, including membership in the National Academy of Design. In 1923, he was designated a chevalier of the French Legion of Honor.

Patrick Reason (1817-1850) was among the earliest African American artists whose work was directed toward social objectives. Though a free man, Reason was keenly aware of the injustice and inhumanity of slavery. He devoted his energies to the anti-slavery cause by employing his talents as a draftsman and printmaker. His "Kneeling Slave" and other engravings and lithographs were widely published in abolitionist literature.

The turn of the century brought few changes in the approach of most African American artists to their work. They continued to look toward Western Europe for their themes and development of expression, and there was little emphasis given to demonstrating an ethnic consciousness. Two important developments in art helped to push black artists towards cultural and social awareness and a visual aesthetic: the 1913 Armory Show of works by European cubist and modernist painters revealed an interest in, and influence from, African abstraction of form, and the mainstream American art world developed an interest in genre subjects. These movements toward social realism and abstract formalism in art opened the doors to new interpretations and values in artistic expression.

The period of transition, from 1900 to the 1920s showed a continued interest on the part of black artists, in expressing themselves in imitative styles. They felt that the interest in African American culture was sincere in Europe and many traveled there to study. New trends, showing expressions of personal dignity and ethnic awareness began. The artists of this period—Palmer Hayden, Archibald Motley, Malvin Gray John-

*Hagar in the Wilderness,* Edmonia Lewis.

son, William Edouard Scott, Meta Warrick Fuller, and Laura Wheeler Warring—were among the major contributors to this new awareness.

## ◆ AFRICAN AMERICAN ARTISTS IN THE HARLEM RENAISSANCE

This new respect for the African idiom and negritude that began to manifest itself after World War I can be attributed directly to cultural activities that developed in several important cities during the 1920s—Cleveland, Chicago, and New York being the major active centers.

From Karamu House, a center for cultural activities founded in 1915 in Cleveland, came such artists as Hughie Lee-Smith, Zell Ingrams, Charles Sallee, Elmer Brown, William E. Smith, and George Hulsinger. In 1924, the Spingarn Awards were established. Three years later, in 1927, the Harmon Foundation was established by philanthropist William E. Harmon to aid African-American artists. The foundation offered financial awards and exhibitions and encouraged the growth of art education programs in many black institutions throughout the country. The Harmon Foundation was to become one of the major organizations involved in the perpetuation and presentation of African-American art in the United States and continued to exist until the mid-1960s. A major exhibition on the Harmon Foundation and its pioneering support of African American artists was organized by Gary A. Reynolds with the assistance of Beryl J. Wright at The Newark Museum in 1989.

The 1930s brought the depression and the Works Project Administration. Black artists abandoned by the white philanthropists of the 1920s were rescued by the WPA. Aaron Douglas, Augusta Savage, Charles Alston, Hale Woodruff, and Charles White created murals and other works for public buildings under this program. In 1939, the Baltimore Museum Show, the first exhibition of African-American artists to be held in a southern region, presented the works of Richmond Barthe, Malvin Gray Johnson, Henry Bannarn, Florence Purviance, Hale Woodruff, Dox Thrash, Robert Blackburn, and Archibald Motley. The Harlem Art Center and the Chicago South Side Community Art Center also began with the WPA.

Representation of the African American through art became an important imperative in the first three decades of this century. At the urging of Alain Locke, W. E. B. Du Bois, and others, creative artists began collaborating in literature, music, theatre, and art to promote an important cultural heritage. Aaron Douglas was considered the leading painter of "The Negro Renaissance". Active in New York from 1923 to 1925, Douglas was the first to depict visual symbols, stylized African figures with overlays of geometric forms, that created movement and rhythm. The idea spread from Harlem's boundaries where many intellectuals and artists from the Caribbean and other parts of the United States had settled. This concept, while promoting ethnic awareness and pride, also counteracted the stereotypes and shallow interpretations prevalent in the popular culture.

## ◆ AFRICAN AMERICAN ARTISTS SINCE THE DEPRESSION

During this period, active artists continued to express the American social and political climate for

A mural by Hale Woodruff depicting the contribution of African Americans in the history of California.

African Americans. The Second World War seemed to bring a sense of urgency to the search for equality. When the armed services were integrated, a real sense of hope developed for equality in other areas of life. There was a great migration from the South to northern cities, documented by artists such as Romare Bearden, Beauford Delaney, Jacob Lawrence, and Hughie Lee-Smith. African Americans in search of self and a better life might be an appropriate interpretation of the 1940s and 1950s.

The influence of the previous decades shows in the continuation of muralist art. Samella Lewis in her book *Art: African American* (Handcraft Studios, Los Angeles, California) notes that African architectural traditions include exterior murals as an important aspect. Charles Alston, John Biggers, Jacob Lawrence, and Charles White became important muralists during this period. Inspired by Mexican mural artists (who advocated social change through their art), African American artists were especially drawn to the themes, bold forms, and bright colors of artists such as Diego Rivera, David Alfero Siqueiros, and Jose Clemente Orozco.

Conscious of the need to study the history, aesthetics, and formal qualities of art—like their successful white counterparts—African American artists contin-

ued to go abroad to Paris, Rome, and before the war, Germany. Most, however, stayed at home and attended classes at universities such as Columbia, Ohio State, and Pennsylvania State or some professional art schools such as the Art Institute of Chicago, the New York Art Students' League, and the Philadelphia Academy of Art. Black institutions such as Fisk, Hampton Institute, Howard, Morehouse, and Tuskegee emphasized art education as a means of survival, as well as the basis for continuing a future cultural aesthetic in the visual arts.

"Some historians and critics," Dr. Lewis notes, "have erroneously assumed that African American artists are unfamiliar with the formalized techniques of Western aesthetics." From the 1940s, more African Americans were being awarded degrees in art than ever before. Some turned to abstraction, non-objective art, and expressive forms as seen in many works by Norman Lewis who, for a time, was a part of the group known as the Action Painters. (Jackson Pollock, a European American artist, was an exponent of the Action Painters and listened to jazz as he worked). Romare Bearden studied Cubism, as did Aaron Douglas. Early on, they knew the African roots of this art form (long before American critics wrote about the significant influence of African

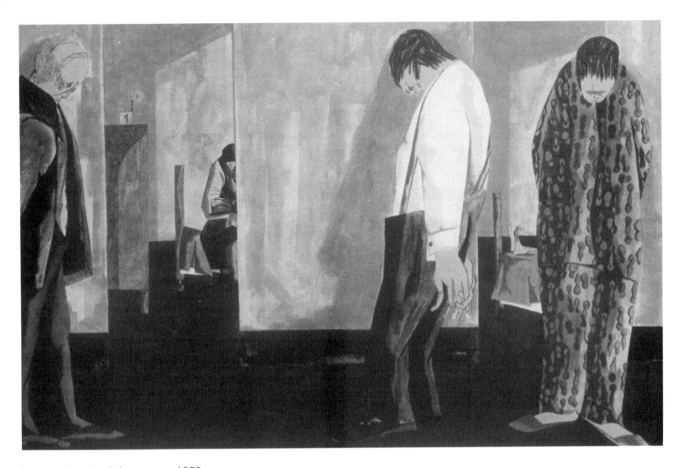

*Depression,* Jacob Lawrence, 1950.

art on the abstractionist painters of the twentieth century).

## ◆ THE SEARCH FOR AN AFRICAN AMERICAN IDENTITY

Following World War II, black soldiers came home to a land of greater opportunity by way of the G.I. Bill and employment possibilities previously denied to them. But victory abroad did not bring with it victory over racism and discrimination at home. This was a battle yet to be won. The civil rights movement employed legal challenges and civil disobedience to defeat segregation in the schools, at the lunch counter and on the bus. African American artists were there to document, to inspire, and to champion the "cause."

During the 1960s, many African American artists reassessed their role in and responsibility to the black community. Spiral Group was composed of New York artists who sought to reinforce the civil rights movement through their art. Reginald Gammon's *Freedom Now,* for example, incorporates an expressionistic technique to create a sense of unity and determination among marchers demanding their civil rights. Charles White challenged members of the newly formed National Conference of Artists (NCA) to create works that convey great ideas and great passions. Such groups profoundly affected many black artists, for they provided essential support, affirmation, and relief from creative isolation.

The transition from an emphasis on civil rights to the demand for "Black Power" and adherence to black aesthetic values is reflected in the development of AFRICOBRA (African Commune of Black Relevant Artists), and the rejection of art not directed toward the liberation of the black community. Jeff Donaldson, Wadsworth A. Jarrell, Nelson Stevens, Napoleon Jones Henderson, Murray N. DePillars and their fellow members of AFRICOBRA sought to create works "reflective of black visual ethos." (Robert L. Douglas, "Introduction," *Beyond 1984: Contemporary Perspectives on American Art,* Ohio University exhibition catalogue, 1985:n.p.). AFRICOBRA member Jeff Donaldson explained that AFRICOBRA members "strive for images inspired by African people/experience and images which African people can relate to directly without formal art training and/or experience." ("Ten in Search of a Na-

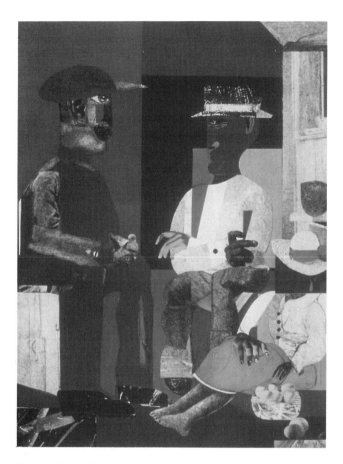

*Eastern Barn,* Romare Bearden, 1968.

tion," *Black World,* Oct. 1970:82). This philosophy was expressed earlier by members of OBAC (Organization of Black Artists in Chicago), who painted a huge mural depicting African American heroes on a building in the heart of Chicago's black community. Known as the *Wall of Respect,* the mural became a symbol of pride that was emulated by black artists who created murals in other major cities across the country.

Ron Karenga and others who espoused Black Cultural Nationalism, believed that "art must reflect and support the Black Revolution, and any art that does not discuss and contribute to the revolution is invalid." ("Ron Karenga and Black Cultural Nationalism," *Negro Digest,* Jan. 1968:18). Dana Chandler, an artist committed to the "Black Arts Movement," explained that he was not trying to be aesthetically pleasing; he was trying to be relevant. Widely acknowledged for his large murals painted on the exterior walls of buildings with the black neighborhoods of Boston, Chandler's concerns were "conceptual, didactic, and idealistic, not primarily aesthetic." He was not interested in pleasing the "art establishment." Rather, his objective was to inspire black unity, black dignity and respect "as the first steps in a long march toward social, economic and political

goals." (Carroll Greene, Jr. "Perspective: The Black Artist in America," *The Art Gallery,* Apr. 1970:26).

Proponents of the Black Arts Movement believed that the purpose of their art was to liberate man, in keeping with their ancient traditions and their contemporary needs. The Black Power movement stimulated artists to convey pride in African American heroes and accomplishments by correcting the historical record. Betye Saar, Murray DePillars, and other black artists of the period confronted negative stereotypes and re-shaped them from a militant African American perspective. In a series entitled "Exploding the Myth," Betye Saar transformed derogatory images such as Uncle Tom and Aunt Jemima by recasting them as militants in the black liberation movement. In this series, "Jemimas," "Toms," and "Little Black Sambos" are shown armed with guns instead of hoes and pancake turners. With the establishment of the Black Emergency Cultural Coalition, African American artists challenged the society and cultural institutions to acknowledge their work and its meaning.

Not all African American artists during this period subscribed to the Black Arts Movement or considered themselves Black Nationalists whose primary objective in art was political. Norman Lewis undoubtedly spoke for many artists who believed that "political and social aspects should not be the primary concern: aesthetic ideas should have preference." (Jeanne Siegal, "Why Spiral?" *Art News* Sep. 1966:48). Philosophical questions regarding the nature of African American art and aesthetics were at the forefront during this period—debated among artists, inside the African American community, within institutions of cultural conservation, and through the art press. While some artists emphasized that they were African American artists, others thought of themselves as artists who happened to be black. Such philosophical differences are reflected in the broad range of creativity expressed through the visual arts of the period.

During this period, emotions could not always be contained on canvas, channeled into familiar forms, or exhibited in traditional settings. Art literally took to the streets of the ghetto to meet with, appeal to, and celebrate the people, as was richly illustrated in Chicago and Detroit murals.

In 1972, in New York City, African American and Hispanic teenagers combined the spray paint can and street pride into a colorful art form, "wall graffiti." The content of the wall graffiti has often been no more than the name of a street gang or the nickname of the individual painter and the name and number of the street on which he lives, or to which he gives loyalty. On the other hand, the paintings can be seen as extravagant as a scene with cartoon characters and lavishly flamboyant lettering. Towards the end of the 1970s and well into the 1980s, this graffiti style became so popular its value increased. Several of the young street artists were welcomed into the mainstream art world, making a few famous for a short period and promoting one young artist, Jean-Michael Basquiat, into a superstar.

There were also mainstream artists who took on the graffiti style and made it their own, such as artist Keith Haring, and galleries such as the Paula Cooper Gallery opened their doors to this new and defiant art. Choreographer Twyla Tharp choreographed a ballet for the Joffrey Company, "Deuce Coupe," showing dancers moving against a background provided by boys painting with spray cans on ceiling-hung sheets of paper.

Moving into the 1990s, multimedia art forms (developed in the 1960s and 1970s; expanded by video and computers in the 1980s) came to the forefront. Artists who were experimenting with combining traditional modes of artistic expression (painting, printmaking, sculpture) with dance, drama and other performance arts to emphasize the importance and place of process in the visual arts were finding alternative spaces as well, in the environment, factories and school buildings. Stones, hair, elephant dung, twigs, bricks, discards, and other objects often replace traditional materials. Words, symbols, and numbers of images have a new emphasis, along with the purely gestural marks of some artists.

Multicultural considerations (how groups of people see themselves and others) are dominant themes in the 1990s. Through an enormous range of Native, African, Asian, European, and Hispanic American intercultural sharing, and African American identity is still evolving.

## ◆ THE HBCU CONNECTION

Traditionally, black educational institutions have played a major role in the preservation and presentation of African American art. Many historically black colleges and universities were collecting art by African Americans when most museums and private collectors were not interested in their work. Hampton University, which has one of the strongest collections of African American art in existence, began collecting in 1892. Through the years these institutions have amassed over 5,000 works, constituting the largest body of art by African Americans in our nation. These collections contain work that was previously ignored, but is recognized today as being of great aesthetic and historic significance. To celebrate this art, Edmond Barry Gaither, Director and Curator of the Museum of the National Center of Afro-American Artists in Boston, organized an exhibit entitled *Our Commonwealth, Our Collections: Works from Traditionally Black Colleges and Universities.*

Historically black colleges and universities have played another crucial role in the history of African American art by establishing art programs and hiring faculty who were master artists and exceptional role models and mentors for their students. John Biggers, Claude Clark, Aaron Douglas, David Driskell, James V. Herring, Lois Mailou Jones, Jack Jordan, James Amos Porter, and Hale Woodruff are among the faculty members who have fit this mold. Their guidance and inspiration have stimulated the development of generations of young African American artists.

## ◆ AFRICAN AMERICAN EXHIBITIONS

During the late 1960s and early 1970s, leading mainstream museums began to respond to the demands being made by African American artists to open their doors and hire African American scholars as curators and administrators. At the time of the intensive demonstrations, Kynastan McShine, a young West Indian who had already established his reputation as a strong curator at the Jewish Museum, moved on to become the assistant curator of painting and sculpture at the Museum of Modern Art. Howardena Pindell had just begun her career at the Museum of Modern Art as the assistant curator of drawings and prints, would later move on to become the associate curator, and would in 1980 resign from that position to pursue her career as an artist. However, this progress was not satisfactory to the artists who demonstrated and wrote letters demanding that jobs be made available to black art historians.

In 1968, Gylbert Coker became the first African American to be hired at the Guggenheim Museum in an administrative trainee position. She later went on to work at the Museum of Modern Art as cataloguer in the museum's registration department. In 1976, she received the Rockefeller Fellowship in Museum Education and spent one year at the Metropolitan Museum of Art. The following year, she became curator of The Studio Museum in Harlem where she set up their registration department and organized such important exhibitions as The Bob Thompson Exhibition and the Hale Woodruff Retrospective, before leaving to pursue a career as a freelance critic and curator. In 1980 and again in 1982, Coker co-directed *Art Across the Park*, an outdoor exhibition created by the artist David Hammons. The project was so popular that several groups in New York tried to copy the concept. It was the first large-scale exhibit that openly encouraged all artists to take part, and it was in this exhibition that the term *multiethnic* was coined.

From the Whitney Museum's Museum Studies Program came Faith Weaver and Horace Brockington. Faith Weaver went on to teach American Art History at the School of Visual Arts. Brockington gained recognition for his exhibition *Another Generation* for The Studio Museum in Harlem in 1978, which set the stage for *African American Abstraction*, presented two years later at P.S. 1, an alternative art center.

Regina Perry was invited by the Metropolitan Museum of Art in 1976 to produce an exhibition called *Selections of Nineteenth-Century Afro-American Art*. It was an exhibition which highlighted, for the first time, many early African American portrait painters and landscape artists, and it even made attempts to document some important slave artifacts and put them into an aesthetic rather than sociological perspective. David C. Driskell's traveling exhibition *Two Centuries of Black American Art*, organized by the Los Angeles County Museum in 1976, brought national attention to the beauty and diversity of African American art. The exhibit included examples of craft art as well as paintings and sculpture and the exhibit catalogue is an excellent resource for the study of African American art. In 1987, Driskell and Mary Schmidt-Campbell curated *Harlem Renaissance: Art of Black America*, for the Studio Museum in New York. Also in 1976, Lowery Sims put together an exhibition of selected works by twentieth-century African American artists from the Metropolitan Museum of Art collection for the Bedford-Stuyvesant Restoration Corporation. Three years later, in 1979, Sims mounted another exhibition of African American paintings from the twentieth-century collection. This time, the exhibition was inside the Metropolitan Museum.

*Against the Odds: African American Artists and the Harmon Foundation* was another major exhibition organized by a "mainstream" institution, the Newark Museum, in 1989. The exhibit celebrated the art and artists represented in the historic Harmon Foundation exhibitions, and provided many of the artists and their work with broader exposure than they received in the original Harmon Foundation exhibitions. The Newark Museum held its first black exhibition in 1944. That exhibition included the works of Richmond Barthe, Romare Bearden, and William Edmonson. In 1974, the museum presented *Black Artists: Two Generations*, curated by Paul Waters.

*Facing History: The Black Image in American Art 1710-1940* was a major exhibit curated by Guy C. McElroy, who also wrote a catalogue with an essay by Henry Louis Gates, Jr. This exhibit, organized by the Corcoran Gallery of Art in Washington, D.C., chronicled the way black people have been portrayed by American artists and perceived by American society. The Wadsworth Atheneum in Hartford, Connecticut, opened its first African American Gallery (believed to be the first in the country in a major "mainstream" museum, according to its curator) with an exhibit from the National Museum of American Art, *Free Within Ourselves: African American Art in the Collection of the National Museum of*

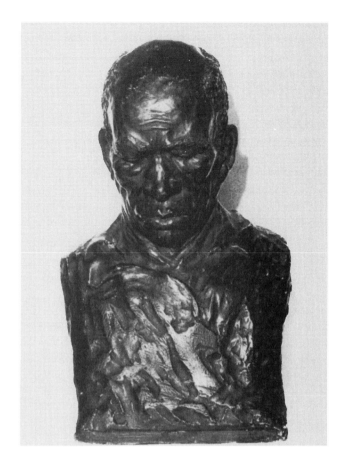

Bust by Richmond Barthe.

*American Art*, curated by Linda Roscoe Hartigan. The catalogue was written by Regenia Perry of the National Museum of Art, Smithsonian Institution.

In 1989, the Dallas Museum organized *Black Art: Ancestral Legacy* with an impressive exhibition staff that included Alia J. Wardlaw, chief curator; Regenia Perry and Edmund Barry Gaither, curators; David Boxer, David C. Driskell, William Ferris, and Robert Farris Thompson, advisers. The exhibit explored the impact of African culture on artists in the African diaspora, the Caribbean (Haiti, Jamaica, and the Bahamas), as well as the United States.

*Black Folk Art in America: 1930-1980)*, organized by The Corcoran Gallery of Art in 1982, was a pioneering exhibition on a then neglected topic in African American art. Curated by Jane Livingston and John Beardsley, the exhibit featured many artists whose works are recognized today as national treasures. The catalogue, which includes an essay by Regenia Perry, features the work of twenty black "folk" artists.

The National Afro-American Museum and Cultural Center in Wilberforce, Ohio, organized *Uncommon Beauty in Common Objects: The Legacy of African American Craft Art*, in 1993. This exhibition, catalogue, and companion issue of the *International Review of African American Art* focused national attention on another important but little known aspect of African American creative genius. Created by Willis "Bing" Davis, the exhibit included the work of over one hundred contemporary African American craft artists, and traveled to major venues across the country. An earlier show, *The Afro-American Tradition in the Decorative Arts*, curated by John Michael Vlach and organized by The Cleveland Museum of Art, explored the "tradition" of African American craft, and included early examples of musical instruments as well as carved walking sticks, face jugs, ceramic jars, wrought iron work, etc. The McKissick Museum, University of South Carolina, organized *Row Upon Row: Sea Grass Baskets of the South Carolina Lowcountry*, curated by Catherine Wilson Horne, in 1986.

In terms of photographic exhibits, *Black Photographers Bear Witness: 100 Years of Social Protest*, is particularly noteworthy. It was curated by Deborah Willis and Howard Dodson, and organized by Williams College Museum of Art in 1989. *Songs of My People: African Americans: A Self Portrait*, is another major photographic exhibit, organized by the Smithsonian Institution in 1992.

The Seattle Museum launched a major retrospective in 1986 of the work of Jacob Lawrence—often referred to as the "Dean of the Black Painters." In 1991, the Philadelphia Museum of Art organized a retrospective of the works of its native son, Henry Ossawa Tanner. The Columbus (Ohio) Museum of Art honored a native son in 1992 with *Elijah Pierce: Woodcarver*.

By the 1990s, mainstream museums across the country, from Brooklyn, New York and Hartford, Connecticut in the East, to Detroit, Michigan, Atlanta, Georgia, and Dallas, Texas, and on to San Francisco, California, and Seattle, Washington in the West, were sponsoring major exhibits of African Americans and artifacts designed to appeal to black audiences.

Major funders of these exhibits included the National Endowment for the Arts, private charitable trusts and foundations, state and local arts commissions, universities, and private corporations such as IBM, Ford Motor Co., and Philip Morris Corp.

It is hoped that the audiences that have been introduced to museums through these exhibitions will support them through volunteerism, memberships, and gifts, and that members of the black community will be placed in positions of governance. More and more volunteers are working as docents, serving on committees and boards. If museums can come through this rite of passage, to become more inclusive and not just for the wealthy in our population, African American art will continue to enter the mainstream.

# ◆ ARCHITECTURE AND THE APPLIED ARTS

## Architecture

Africans brought to America many skills in metalwork, woodcarving, masonry and toolmaking, to name a few. They built dwellings in Virginia and other parts of the Americas like rondavels found in Mali, Africa. These round brick slave quarters were topped with conical roofs and date from the eighteenth century. In the nineteenth century they built homes now called "shotgun houses," a part of the legacy from the Yoruba people of Western Africa. These came to Louisiana by way of Haiti. These mostly urban houses were narrow, frame dwellings 10' to 14' wide, with two or more rooms, varying in length from 22' to 65', and with ceilings from 6' to 12' in height. Slaves also built many mansions and public buildings. One built entirely by slaves was a courthouse in Vicksburg, Mississippi, which later became a museum.

Like other Africans, before and after emancipation, black craftsmen in the trades, interested in technology and art, sought to copy their European counterparts and were trained as slave labor or apprentices. They too, in time, began to do original works in wrought iron (later cast iron), wood and other metals.

The first African American to receive a degree from the Massachusetts Institute of Technology (in 1892) was Robert Taylor, who opened the first school of architecture in an African American school at Tuskegee Institute. In 1901, John A. Lankford built the Pythian Building, constructed entirely by African Americans. It was an office and social building designed by Lankford who was the first recorded African American architect with an office. The first African American to be accepted in the American Institute of Architects was Paul R. Williams (1926). The first African American woman to be elected was Norma Merrick Sklarek (1966).

Today, there are over eight hundred registered architects in the United States who are African American. The major schools of architecture in predominantly African American universities include: Florida A&M University, Tallahassee, Florida; Hampton University, Hampton, Virginia; Howard University, Washington, D.C.; Morgan State University, Baltimore, Maryland; Prairie View A&M University, Prairie View, Texas; Southern University, Baton Rouge, Louisiana; Tuskegee University, Tuskegee, Alabama; University of the District of Columbia, Washington, D.C.

In 1991, New York architect Jack Travis edited a book on thirty-three outstanding African American architects, which included a chronology of African Americans in architecture since 1868 by Vinson McKenzie of Auburn University, Auburn, Alabama. (*African American Architects in Current Practice*, Jack Travis, editor, Princeton Architectural Press.)

### The Applied Arts: Crafts, Illustration, Fashion Design, and Automobile Design

The artistic heritage of African Americans includes dressmaking and tailoring, quilting, weaving, silversmithing, engraving, and ceramic production, as well as jewelrymaking, stitchery, stained-glass, blown glass, mosaics, and enameling. Many slaves learned their crafts in Africa. As these skills were discovered, the slave masters put these skilled workers to use and trained their slaves in new skills as needed.

The twentieth century saw a revival of functional art. There was a great crafts revival, and many artists began to employ traditional crafts methods and materials in their art. The line between art and craft has practically disappeared. Faith Ringgold and Michael Cummings are two artists/quilters, for example.

In illustration, the graphic artists Jerry Pinkney and Larry Johnson are examples of successful African Americans, among others, who have used their skills for designing postage stamps, children's books, editorial cartoons, and illustrations for other publications.

African American artists in fashion design include Stephen Burrows, Gordon Henderson, and Willi Smith. Historically, some household slaves were excellent dressmakers and tailors who turned these skills into self-supporting businesses after becoming free men and women.

In automobile design, Emeline King and Edward T. Welburn are successful artists. Careers in industrial design, unlike in the previous century, are filled by trained artists who combine engineering studies with art.

### ◆ VISUAL AND APPLIED ARTISTS

#### Charles Alston (1907-1972)
*Painter, Sculptor, Muralist*

It was the murals of painter Charles Alston that established his reputation and insured his fame as a black American artist of importance.

Born in Charlotte, North Carolina in 1907, Alston studied at Columbia University in New York, receiving

Stephen Burrows

B.A. and M.A. degrees. He was later awarded several fellowships and grants to launch his painting career.

Alston's paintings and sculpture are in such collections as those of IBM and the Detroit Institute of Arts. His murals depicting the history of medicine adorn the facade of Harlem Hospital in New York. Alston was a member of the National Society of Mural Painters. Notable works include *Exploration and Colonization* (1949); *Blues with Guitar and Bass* (1957); *Blues Song* (1958); *School Girl* (1958); *Nobody Knows* (1966); *Sons and Daughters* (1966); and *Frederick Douglass* (1968).

#### Benny Andrews (1930- )
*Painter*

Born in Madison, Georgia on November 13, 1930, Andrews studied at Fort Valley State College in Georgia and later at the University of Chicago. He was awarded a B.F.A. from the Art Institute of Chicago in 1958. During his career he has taught at the New York School of Social Research; New York City University; and Queens College in New York. His works have appeared in exhibitions around the country, including the Boston Museum of Fine Arts, The Martha Jackson Gallery in

New York City; and other museums and galleries too numerous to list.

Most notably, Andrews directed the Visual Arts Program for the National Endowment for the Arts, 1982-1984. He has directed the National Arts Program since 1985, offering children and adults an opportunity to exhibit and compete for prizes in many cities across the country.

Other honors include an Honorary Doctorate from the Atlanta School of Art, 1984; John Hay Whitney Fellowship, 1965–1967; New York Council on The Arts Grantee, 1971; NEA Fellowship, 1974; Bellagie Fellow, Rockefeller Foundation, 1987; National Endowment for the Arts Painting Fellowship, 1986. Notable works include *The Family; The Boxer; The Invisible Man; Womanhood; Flora;* and *Did the Bear.*

In late 1994, an exhibit of Andrews's work entitled "Benny Andrews: The America Series" appeared on display at the Wendell St. Gallery in Cambridge, Massachusetts.

### Edward Mitchell Bannister (1828-1901)
*Painter*

Born in Nova Scotia in 1828, Bannister was the son of a West Indian father and African-American mother. Both parents died when he was very young. Bannister moved to Boston in the early 1850s, where he learned to make solar plates and worked as a photographer.

Influenced by the Barbizon style popular at the time, Bannister's paintings convey his own love of the quiet beauty of nature and his pleasure in picturesque scenes with cottages, cattle, dawns, sunsets and small bodies of water. In 1871, Bannister moved from Boston to Providence, Rhode Island, where he lived until his death in 1901. He was the only nineteenth-century African-American artist who did not travel to Europe to study art, believing that he was an American and that he wished to paint as an American. Bannister became one of the most outstanding artists in Providence in the 1870s and 1880s, and in 1880 was to become one of seven founders of the Providence Art Club, which later became known as the Rhode Island School of Design. Notable works include *After the Storm; Driving Home the Cows;* and *Narragansett Bay.*

### Richmond Barthe (1901-1989)
*Sculptor*

Born on January 28, 1901, in Bay St. Louis, Mississippi, Barthe was educated at the Art Institute of Chicago from 1924 to 1928. He studied under Charles Schroeder and Albin Polasek. Barthe's first love was painting, but it

Richmond Barthe

was through his experiments with sculpture that he began initially to gain critical attention in 1927. His first commissions were busts of Henry Ossawa Tanner and Toussaint L'Ouverture. The acclaim resulting from them led to a one-man show in Chicago and a Rosenwald Fellowship for study in New York City.

Barthe's work has been exhibited at several major American museums. The Metropolitan Museum of Art in New York City purchased *The Boxer* in 1943. In 1946, he received the first commission given to a black for a bust of Booker T. Washington for New York University's Hall of Fame. A year later he was one of the committee of fifteen artists chosen to help modernize sculpture in the Catholic churches of the United States.

Barthe held membership in the National Academy of Arts and Letters. He died March 6, 1989, at his home in Pasadena, California at the age of eighty-eight. Notable works include *Singing Slave; Maurice Ens; Lot's Wife;* and *Henry O. Tanner.*

### Jean-Michel Basquiat (1960-1988)
*Painter*

In a brief, tragic career, Jean-Michel Basquiat gained attention from wealthy collectors as a young artist discovered by Andy Warhol and promoted by other art consultants. He was raised in Brooklyn and attracted the New York art world with his trendy personal appearance (tangled dreadlocks) as a musician and artist at the age of eighteen. His works are autobiographical and deliberately "primitive" in style. In February 1985 he was a featured artist on the cover of the *New York Times Magazine*, shoeless in a suit, shirt and tie.

The Whitney Museum of American Art in New York City owns many of the six hundred works this artist produced, reportedly valued in the tens of millions of dollars, one might say symbolic of the excesses of the eighties. Jean-Michel Basquiat, was the example of a popular artist of the 1980s. The Whitney Museum mounted a retrospective exhibit of his work, October 23, 1992-February 14, 1993.

Basquiat began his career illegally painting images on buildings throughout the city. SAMO (slang for "same old s___") was his signature and trademark. He often used it in his paintings to preserve his reputation as a street artist. Basquiat was quoted as saying that his subject matter was, "Royalty, heroism and the streets."

He reportedly died of a drug overdose. Notable works include *Self Portrait as a Heel #3; Untitled (History of Black People); Hollywood Africans*; and *CPRKR* (in honor of Charlie Parker).

## Romare Bearden (1914-1988)
*Painter, Collagist*

Romare Bearden was born on September 2, 1914, in Charlotte, North Carolina. His family moved to Pittsburgh and later to Harlem. Bearden studied with George Grosz at the Art Students League and later, on the G.I. Bill, went to Paris where he met Matisse, Joan Miro, and Carl Holty. A product of the new generation of Afro-Americans who had migrated from the rural areas of the South to the urban cities of the North, Bearden's work reflected the era of industrialization. His would become the visual images that would reflect the city life, the music jazz the city people. Bearden's earlier works belonged to the school of Social Realism, but after his return from Europe his images became more abstract.

In the 1960s, Bearden changed his approach to his picture-making and began to make collages, soon becoming one of the best known collagists in the world. His images are haunting montages of his memories of past experiences, of stories told to him by other people. They are for Bearden "an attempt to redefine the image of man in terms of the black experience." Notable works include *Street Corner; He Is Arisen; The Burial; Sheba*; and *The Prevalence of Ritual*.

## John Biggers (1924- )
*Painter*

John Biggers has been a leading figure in Social Realism as a painter, sculptor, printmaker, and teacher, as well as an outstanding surrealistic muralist.

Born in Gastonia, North Carolina in 1924, Biggers has derived much of his subject matter from the contributions made by blacks to the development of the United States. While teaching at Texas Southern University, Biggers has become a significant influence on several young black painters.

Some of his most powerful pieces have been created as a result of his study trips to Africa: *The Time of Ede, Nigeria*, a series of works done in the 1960s are prime examples. Notable works include *Cradle; Mother and Child; The Contributions of Negro Women to American Life and Education*; and *Shotgun, Third Ward, #1*.

## Camille Billops (1933- )
*Sculptor, Photographer, Filmmaker*

A sculptor of note in the art and retailing world, Camille Billops was born in California in 1933, graduated from California State College in 1960, and then studied sculpture on the west coast under a grant from the Huntington Hartford Foundation. In 1960, she had her first exhibition at the African Art Exhibition in Los Angeles, followed in 1963 by an exhibit at the Valley Cities Jewish Community Center in Los Angeles. In 1966, she participated in a group exhibition in Moscow. Since then, her multifaceted artistic talents, which include poetry, book illustration, and jewelry making, have earned the praise of critics throughout the world, particularly in Sri Lanka and Egypt, where she also has lived and worked.

Billops has also taught extensively. In 1975, she was active on the faculties of the City University of New York and Rutgers at Newark, New Jersey. In addition, she has conducted special art courses in the New York City jail (the Tombs) and in 1972 lectured in India for the United States Information Service on black American artists. She participated in an exhibit at the New York Cultural Center in 1973.

Billops is a printmaker, filmmaker, and photographer who has also been active in the mail–art movement which has made art more accessible to the public. She has written articles for the *New York Times, Amsterdam News* and *Newsweek*.

Her grants for film include the New York State Council on the Arts, 1987, 1988; NYSCA and New York Foundation for the Arts, 1989, Rockefeller Foundation, 1991, and National Endowment for the Arts, 1994.

*Pepper Jelly Lady,* Romare Bearden, 1980.

In 1992, Billops won the prestigious Grand Jury Prize for Best Documentary at the Sundance Film Festival, *Finding Christa*, an edited combination of interviews, home movies, still images and dramatic acting. Notable works include *Tenure; Black American; Portrait of an American Indian* (all three are ceramic sculptures); *Year after Year* (painting). *Older Women and Love* (film); *Suzanne, Suzanne* (film); *A String of Pearls* (film); and *The K.K.K. Boutique Ain't Just Rednecks* (film).

Billops is also the author of *The Harlem Book of the Dead*, with James Van der Zee and Owen Dodson.

## Robert Blackburn (1921- )
*Printmaker*

Robert Blackburn was born in New York City in 1921. He studied at the Harlem Workshop, the Art Students League, and the Wallace Harrison School of Art. His exhibits include Art of the American Negro, 1940; Downtown Gallery, New York; Albany Museum; Contemporary Art of the American Negro, 1966; and numerous print shows in the United States and Europe. His work is represented in the Library of Congress, the Brooklyn and Baltimore museums, and the Atlanta University Collections. He is a member of the art faculty of Cooper Union.

Along with his other accomplishments, in 1949 he founded The Printmaking Workshop as an artist-run cooperative. In 1971, it was incorporated as a non-profit printmaking studio for work in lithography, etching, relief and photo-processes. The workshop, a magnet for third-world and minority artists that reflects Mr. Blackburn's warmth and encouraging personalty, remains a haven for artists "to turn out prints for the love of it" and to do anything from experimental hodgepodge to polished pieces. In 1988, Bob Blackburn and the Printmaking Workshop were given the Governor's Art Award for making "a significant contribution to the cultural life of New York State". Notable works include *Boy with Green Head* and *Negro Mother*.

## Selma Burke (1900-1995)
*Sculptor, Educator*

Selma Burke was an artist whose career spanned more than sixty years. She was born in Mooresville, North Carolina on December 31, 1900. She received a bachelor of arts degree from Winston-Salem University, and RN degree from St. Augustine College in 1924, an MFA from Columbia University in 1941, and a PhD from Livingston College in 1970. Burke received her training

as a sculptor at Columbia University in New York. She also studied with Maillol in Paris and in Vienna with Povoley.

Burke worked as an instructor in art & sculpture at Friends School/George's School/Forrest House in New York City from 1930 until 1949. From 1963 until 1976, she served as an instructor in art & sculpture at the Sidwell School, Haverford College, Livingston College, and Swarthmore College. The A.W. Mellon Foundation hired Burke as a consultant from 1967 until 1976. Burke founded New York City's Selma Burke School of Sculpture in 1940 and the Selma Burke Art Center in Pittsburgh in 1968, where she taught and supported many young artists.

In 1987, Burke received the Pearl S. Buck Foundation Women's Award. She also received honorary degrees from Livingston College, the University of North Carolina, and Moore College of Art.

Burke is best known for her relief sculpture rendering of Franklin Delano Roosevelt that was minted on the American dime. On August 29, 1995, she died of cancer.

The Pearl S. Buck Foundation Woman's Award was given to her in 1987 for her professional distinction and devotion to family and humanity. Notable works include *Falling Angel; Peace;* and *Jim*.

## Stephen Burrows (1943- )
*Fashion Designer*

On September 15, 1943, in Newark, New Jersey, Stephen Burrows was born. He studied at his grandmother's knee as a boy and started making clothes at quite a young age. He later studied at the Philadelphia Museum College of Art and the Fashion Institute of Technology in New York City.

With a partner, he opened a boutique in 1968. He worked for Henri Bendel from 1969 to 1973 and returned to Bendel's in 1977. From 1974 to 1977 he tried, with a partner, to run a Seventh Avenue firm.

Known for his unique color combinations, he used patches of cloth for decorative motifs in the 1960s. Topstitching of seams in contrasting threads, top stitched hems, known as "lettuce hems" because of their fluted effect, were widely copied. He preferred soft, clinging, easy-moving fabrics such as chiffon and matte jersey. He also liked asymmetry. His clothes were adopted readily by disco dancers, for whom he designed using natural fabrics with non-constricting, light and airy qualities. He won a Coty American Fashion Critics' Award in 1974 and a special Coty Award in 1977.

Robert Blackburn

## Elizabeth Catlett (1919- )
*Sculptor, Painter*

Elizabeth Catlett was born on April 15, 1919. The granddaughter of North Carolina slaves, Catlett was raised in the northwest district of Washington, DC. As a young woman she attempted to gain admission into a then all-white art school, Carnegie Institute of Technology in Pittsburgh, Pennsylvania. She was refused entry and instead went to Howard University and graduated as an honor student in 1937. In 1940, she went on to study at the University of Iowa, where she became the first of their students to receive an M.F.A.

Her exhibition history dates back to 1937 and includes group and solo presentations at all the major American art museums as well as institutions in Mexico City, Moscow, Paris, Prague, Tokyo, Beijing, Berlin and Havana. Catlett's public sculpture can be found in Mexico City; Jackson, Mississippi; New Orleans; Washington, DC and New York. Her work is represented in the permanent collection of over twenty museums throughout the world. The artist resides in Cuernavaca, Mexico.

Catlett accepted teaching positions at various black colleges in order to earn a living, but by 1946 she had moved to Mexico, where she eventually settled. Always a promoter of human struggle—visually concerned with the recording of economic, social, and political themes-Catlett became involved with the Civil Rights Movement so deeply that it contributed greatly to her philosophy of life and art. Between 1941 and 1969, Catlett won eight prizes and honors, four in Mexico and four in America. Notable works include *Black Unity* (1968); *Target Practice* (1970); *Mother and Child* (1972); and *Woman Resting* (1981).

In 1993, Catlett worked with James Weldon Johnson on the book *Lift Every Voice and Sing*. An exhibition of her works entitled "Elizabeth Catlett: Works on Paper, 1944-1992" was on display at the Studio Museum in Harlem, New York in 1994.

Catlett was presented with an honorary doctorate of human letters from Morgan State University in 1993. In 1995, the New School for Social Research presented her with an honorary doctorate of fine arts.

## Dana Chandler (1941- )
*Painter*

Dana Chandler is one of the most visible, outspoken, and provocative black painters on the American scene.

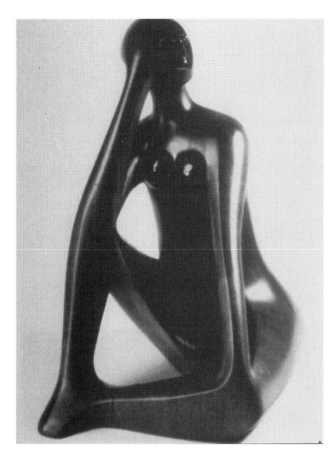

*Woman Resting,* Elizabeth Catlett.

Chandler's huge, colorful black power murals can be spotted throughout the ghetto area of Boston, a constant reminder of the resolve and determination displayed by the new breed of young black urban dwellers.

"All this stuff whites are buying," Chandler says, "tells the black man a lot about where the white community is at, namely, nowhere." Chandler's easel works are bold and simple. One, *The Golden Prison,* shows a black man with a yellow and red striped flag "because America has been yellow and cowardly in dealing with the black man." *Freddie Hampton's Door* shows a bullet-splintered door bearing a stamp of U.S. government approval.

Born in Lynn, Massachusetts, in 1941, Chandler received his B.S. from the Massachusetts College of Art in 1967. Chandler has worked as a critic of Afro American art for Simmons College in Boston, an assistant professor of art and art history at Bay State Banner, and an artist in residence at Northeastern University. Notable works include *Fred Hampton's Door; Martin Luther King, Jr. Assassinated; Death of Uncle Tom; Rebellion '68; Dynamite; Death of a Bigot;* and *The Golden Prison.*

Chandler is a member of the National Conference of Black Artists, Boston Black Artists Association, National Conference of Artists, Boston Union of Visual Artists, and the American Association of University Professors.

### Robert Colescott (1925- )
*Painter*

Robert Colescott was born in California in 1925. He received his B.A. in 1949 from the University of California and later his M.A. in 1952, from the same university. In 1953, Colescott studied in Paris with Fernand Leger. His exhibitions include: The Whitney Museum of American Art 1983 Biennial; the Hirshorn Museum and Sculpture Garden, in Washington, DC, 1984; and the Institute of Contemporary Art at the University of Pennsylvania in 1985.

His works are in the Metropolitan Museum of Art, the Portland Art Museum, the Delaware Museum of Art, the Baltimore Museum of Art and the University of Massachusetts' fine art collection.

One of the most controversial artists, criticized by both African American groups and traditionalists, Colescott's work questions the "heroic" and "pushes the standards of taste." He has substituted black figures in place of white figures in famous European paintings as he explores racism and sex in his works, along with other taboos and stereotypes. Notable works include *Homage to Delacroix: Liberty Leading the People; Eat Dem Taters; Shirley Temple Black and Bill Robinson White;* and *The Power of Desire; The Desire for Power.*

### Houston Conwill (1947- )
*Performance Artist, Environment Artist*

Born in Kentucky in 1947, Conwill spent three years studying for the priesthood. His strong Catholic upbringing and Catholic ritual play a part in his art that draws from both American and African myths and religions. In his explorations, he mostly uses non-traditional materials (he substitutes latex for canvas). The environments that he builds, paints, and fills with real chalices, candlesticks, carpets, or sand are works to which he adds his own personal iconography as well as some ancient symbols. Notable works include *The Cakewalk Manifesto; Passion of St. Matthew; East Shout; JuJu Funk.*

### Aaron Douglas (1899-1988)
*Muralist, Illustrator*

Born in Topeka, Kansas in 1899, Aaron Douglas achieved considerable eminence as a muralist, illustrator, and academician. As a young man, Douglas studied at the University of Nebraska, Columbia University Teachers College, and l'Academie Scandinave in Paris. He had one-person exhibits at the universities of Kansas and Nebraska and also exhibited in New York at the Gallery of Modern Art. In 1939, Douglas was named to the faculty of Fisk and later became head of its Department of Art.

Douglas died on February 2, 1988. In 1992, Fisk opened a new gallery in his memory. Douglas is considered the most important painter and illustrator of the "Negro Renaissance" now known as the Harlem Renaissance. Notable works include murals at Fisk and in the Countee Cullen branch of the New York City Public Library; illustrations in books by Countee Cullen, James Weldon Johnson, Alain Locke, and Langston Hughes; Alexander Dumas, Marion Anderson, and Mary McLeod Bethune are among the many African Americans he painted or rendered in charcoal.

## Emilio Cruz (1938- )
*Painter*

Emilio Cruz was born in New York City in 1938. His education includes work at the Art Students' League under Edwin Dickinson, George Grosz and Frank J. Reilly. Cruz has exhibited widely since 1959. Recent exhibits have included the Anita Shapolsky Gallery, 1986, 1991; The Studio Museum in Harlem, 1987; the Portland Museum of Art in 1987; and the Rhode Island School of Design, 1987; Gwenda Jay Gallery, Chicago, 1991; G.R. N'amdi Gallery, Birmingham, Michigan, 1991; and others.

An artist whose works are narrative and formalistic (emphasizing color and forms as the dominant elements), he combines these two theoretical approaches often with figurative subjects.

His awards include the Cintas Foundation Fellowship, 1965-66; John Hay Whitney Fellowship, 1964-65; Walter Gutman Foundation Award, 1962. Notable works include *Silver Umbrella; Figure Composition 6*; and *Striated Voodoo.*

## Roy DeCarava (1919- )
*Photographer*

Roy DeCarava is an urban man. His existence in New York City prepared him for his destined work as a photographer. He began as a commercial artist in 1938 by studying painting at Cooper Union. This was followed by classes at the Harlem Art Center from 1940 to 1942, where he concentrated on painting and printmaking. By the mid–1940s, he began to use photography as a convenient method of recording ideas for his paintings. In 1958, DeCarava gave up his commercial work and became a full-time freelance photographer. Edward Steichen, a very important photographer at this time, began to study his work and suggested that he apply for a Guggenheim Fellowship. Winning the award allowed DeCarava the financial freedom to take his pictures and tell his story. One of DeCarava's photographs from this

body of work appeared in Steichen's exhibition, "Family of Man", at the Museum of Modern Art. Later, Langston Hughes worked with DeCarava to create the book *Sweet Flypaper of Life.*

DeCarava has worked as a photographer for *Sports Illustrated* and taught photography at Hunter College, New York. His work can be found in many important collections throughout the country, among them: Andover Art Gallery, Andover–Phillips Academy, Massachusetts; Art Institute of Chicago, Chicago, Illinois; Atlanta University, Atlanta, Georgia; Belafonte Enterprises, Inc., New York; Center for Creative Photography, University of Arizona; the Corcoran Gallery of Art, Washington, DC; Harlem Art Collection, New York State Office Building, New York; Lee Witkin Gallery, New York; Menil Foundation, Inc., Houston, Texas; Metropolitan Museum of Fine Arts, Houston, Texas; The Museum of Fine Arts, Houston, Texas; Museum of Modern Art, New York; Olden Camera, New York; Joseph E. Seagram & Sons, Inc., New York; Sheldon Memorial Art Gallery, University of Nebraska, Nebraska.

DeCarava received a Distinguished Career in Photography Award in 1991 from the Friends of Photography. That same year, the American Society of Magazine Photographers presented him with a Special Citation for Photographic Journalism. DeCarava has also received honorary doctorates from The Maryland Institute, Rhode Island Institute of Fine Arts, and Wesleyan University.

## Beauford Delaney (1910-1979)
*Painter, Illustrator*

Born in Knoxville, Tennessee, in 1910, Beauford Delaney was described by his elder brother Samuel as a "remarkably dutiful child." His father, the Reverend Samuel Delaney, and his mother, Delia Johnson Delaney, understood and recognized Beauford Delaney's artistic talent, as well as that of his brother Joseph, and when the time came they encouraged them in the development of their skills. For Beauford Delaney, recognition came by way of an elderly white artist of Knoxville, Lloyd Branson. Branson gave him lessons and after a time urged him to go to a city where he might study and come into contact with the art world.

In 1924, Beauford Delaney went to Boston to study at the Massachusetts Normal School, later studying at the Copley Society, where he took evening courses while working full-time at the South Boston School of Art. From Boston, Delaney moved on to New York and was swept up like many artists.

It was in New York that Delaney took on the life of a bohemian, living in the village in coldwater flats. Much of his time was spent painting the portraits of the personalities of the day, such as Louis Armstrong, Ethel

Roy DeCarava

Waters, and Duke Ellington. In 1938, Beauford Delaney gained national attention when *Life Magazine*, in an article on "negroes," featured a photograph of him surrounded by a group of his paintings at the annual outdoor exhibition in Washington Square in New York. In 1945, Henry Miller wrote the essay "The Amazing and Invariable Beauford Delaney," which was later reprinted in *Remember to Remember*. The essay describes Delaney's bohemian lifestyle in New York during the 1940s and 1950s.

In the 1950s, Delaney left New York with the intention of studying in Rome. Taking the *Ile de France*, he sailed to Paris, next visiting Greece, Turkey, Northern Italy—but he never got to Rome. Returning to Paris for one more visit, Delaney began to paint, make new friends, and create a new social life filled with the famous and the soon-to-be-famous, like James Baldwin, who at that time had not yet become a famous novelist. Paris was to become Beauford Delaney's permanent home.

By 1961, Delaney was producing paintings at such an intense rate that the pressure began to wear upon his strength, and he suffered his first mental collapse. He was confined to a clinic in Vincennes, and his dealer and close friends began to organize his life, hoping to help relieve some of the pressure; but it was of little use. For the rest of his life, Delaney was to suffer repeated breakdowns and by 1971 was back in a sanitarium, where he was to remain until his death in 1979.

Beauford Delaney's numerous exhibitions took place in such venues as Artists Gallery, New York in 1948; Roko Gallery, New York, 1950-1953; Musée d'Art Moderne, Paris, 1963; American Negro Exposition, Chicago, 1940; and Newark Museum, 1971. His work can be found in the collections of the Whitney Museum of American Art, New York; the Newark Museum, New Jersey; and Morgan State College in Baltimore, Maryland. Notable works include *Greene Street; Yaddo; Head of a Poet;* and *Snow Scene.*

### David Clyde Driskell (1931- )
*Painter, Historian*

Born in Eatonton, Georgia, in 1931, Driskell studied at Howard University and Catholic University of America (M.A., 1962). He also studied at the Skowhegan School of Painting and Sculpture and the Netherlands Institute for History of Art. He has taught at Talladega College, Fisk University, Institute for African Studies of the University of Ife in Nigeria, and the University of Maryland at College Park.

Immediately after the death of Alonzo Aden, Driskell was asked to direct the gallery housing the important Barnett-Aden collection of African-American Art. He has curated and mounted important exhibitions of African American Art, including the impressive *200 Years of African American Art*, shown at major museums to audiences across the country.

A recipient of many awards including the John Hope Award and prizes from the Danforth Foundation, American Federation of Arts, and Harmon Foundation, Driskell has exhibited at the Corcoran Art Gallery, National Museum, and Rhodes National Gallery in Salisbury, Rhodesia. Notable works include *Movement; The Mountain; Still Life With Gateleg Table*; and *Shango Gone*.

### Robert Duncanson (1817-1872)
*Painter*

Robert Duncanson was the son of an African-American mother and a Scottish-Canadian father. Born in upstate New York in 1817, he was to spend much of his childhood in Canada. At some point in his youth, he and his mother moved to Mt. Healthy, Ohio, where in 1840 the Western Freedom's Aid Society, an anti-slavery group, raised funds to send him to Glasgow, Scotland, to study art. Returning to Cincinnati three years later, Duncanson turned to the local newspaper where he advertised as the proprietor of a daguerreotype studio. Even though he seemed to have been gaining a reputation as a painter, he continued to work at his daguerreotype until 1855, when he began to devote all of his time to his painting. Like many landscape artists of this time, Duncanson traveled around the United States drawing his compositions from the images of nature before him. In 1853, he made his second trip to Europe—this time to visit Italy, France and England.

Although Duncanson was active during and after the Civil War, with the exception of his painting of *Uncle Tom and Eva*, he made no attempts to present the turmoil that was taking place within America or the social pressures that he experienced. In September 1872, Duncanson, while at the height of his success, suffered a severe mental breakdown and ended his life on December 21 in the Michigan State Retreat in Detroit. Notable works include murals in the Taft Museum and *Bishop Payne*.

### William Edmonson (1882-1951)
*Sculptor*

William Edmonson was a stonecutter and self-taught sculptor. Born in Nashville, Tennessee, in 1882, he supported himself, working as a hospital orderly at

Baptist Hospital and other menial jobs. His work was discovered by Mrs. Meyer Dahl-Wolfe, who had an extensive private collection, and who brought him to the attention of the Museum of Modern Art. In an exhibition of self-taught artists, his work was received extremely well. In 1937 he was the first African American to have a one-person exhibit at the museum. Private collectors and museums have purchased his few sculptures, which are vigorously executed and original.

Inspired by biblical passages, Edmonson worked on tombstones and his sculpture, which he did in limestone, at the home he shared with his mother and sister until their deaths. He continued to live alone and work there until his own death in 1951. Notable works include *Choir Girls; Lion* and *Crucifixion*.

### Elton Clay Fax (1909-1993)
*Illustrator, Writer*

Elton Fax was among America's leading fine artists and illustrators. He was also a noted essayist. Both his drawings and his writings reflect a proud interest in the African legacy of the American black.

Born in Baltimore in 1909, he graduated from Syracuse University (B.F.A., 1931). He taught at Claflin University from 1935 to 1936, and was an instructor at the Harlem Community Art Center from 1938 to 1939. His work has been exhibited at the Baltimore Art Museum, 1939; American Negro Exposition, 1940; the Metropolitan Museum of Art; and Visual Arts Gallery, New York, 1970. Examples of his work hang in some of the nation's best university collections, including Texas Southern, the University of Minnesota, and Virginia State University.

Publications by Fax are *Africa Vignettes; Garvey; Seventeen Black Artists*; and *Black Artists of the New Generation. The Portfolio Black and Beautiful* features his art work, and he has written *Hashar*, about the life of the peoples of Soviet Central Asia and Kazakhstan. Notable works include *Steelworker; Ethiopia Old and New; Contemporary Black Leaders*; and *Through Black Eyes*.

### Tom Feelings (1933- )
*Illustrator*

Born in Brooklyn, New York, on May 19, 1933, Thomas Feelings grew up in the Bedford-Stuyvesant neighborhood of the city. Starting to draw cartoons at the age of four, his art work flourished under the guidance of teacher Thipadeux, a black artist, who encouraged Feelings to draw the people in his neighborhood. After high school, he attended the Cartoonists and Illustrators' School in New York City on a three-year scholarship. Feelings's art studies were interrupted by four years of

Elton Fax

service for the U.S. Air Force in England, but upon completion of his military service, he continued his art studies at the New York School of the Visual Arts.

While in art school, Feelings produced "Tommy Traveler in the World of Negro History," a comic strip published in *New York Age*, a Harlem newspaper. Completing art school in 1961, Feelings shopped around his sizable portfolio to earn freelance assignments, and he began to get work with magazines of primarily black readership. In 1964, Feelings traveled to Tema, a city in

Ghana, with other African Americans enlisted by the Kwame Nkrumah, then head of Ghanian government, to help direct the newly-independent country toward the future. Africa changed Feelings's art on a spiritual and stylistic level. But in 1966, he was forced to leave when the Nkrumah government fell.

Feelings returned to a United States embroiled in a civil rights movement hungry for work by and depicting African Americans, especially children's books, Feelings's new specialty. In this new climate, Feelings illustrated such books as *To Be A Slave* (1968); and *Moja Means One: A Swahili Counting Book*, which won a Caldecott Honor Award in 1972. From 1971 to 1974, Feelings administered the Guyanese Ministry of Education's children's book project while living in Guyana. There he wrote his autobiography, *Black Pilgrimage*, published in 1972. After returning to the United States, Feelings illustrated more books spread over the next ten years, including *Now Sheba Sings the Song* (1987), a collaboration with the poet/writer Maya Angelou.

While serving as an artist in residence at the University of South Carolina, Feelings has completed illustrations for two books. In 1993, he finished illustrations for *Soul Looks Back In Wonder*, a book compiling the poems of many black authors. Two years later, he completed *The Middle Passage*, which portrays the passage of slave ships from Africa to the western hemisphere. Both books received Coretta Scott King awards from the American Library Association.

Feelings has earned many awards for his illustrations, including two Outstanding Achievement awards from the New York School of Visual Arts, Visual Artists Fellowship and National Endowment for the Arts grants, and Distinguished Service to Children Through Art Award from the University of South Carolina (1991). Feelings has earned three Coretta Scott King Awards.

## Meta Vaux Warrick Fuller (1877-1968)
*Sculptor*

Meta Vaux Warrick Fuller was a part of the transitional period between the artists who chose to simulate Euro-American subjects and styles and the later periods to follow. Her subjects of *The Wretched*, exhibited at the Paris Salon, of African-American figures, shown in 1903 and 1904, did not suit popular tastes but they were sincere expressions of the talented artist.

Born in 1877, in Philadelphia and educated at the School of Industrial Art and the Pennsylvania Academy, Fuller's interest in sculpture led her to study with Charles Grafly and at the Academie Colarossi in Paris with Rodin. She was the first African-American woman to become a professional artist.

She married and settled in the Boston area where in 1910, most of her works were destroyed by fire. The Boston Art Club and the Harmon Foundation exhibited her works and today representative pieces of her sculpture can be found in the Cleveland Museum.

## Sam Gilliam (1933- )
*Painter*

Born in Mississippi in 1933, Sam Gilliam produces hanging canvases which are laced with pure color pigments rather than shades or tones. The artist bunches these pigments in weird configurations on drooping, drapelike canvases, giving the effect, in the words of *Time* Magazine, of "clothes drying on a line." His canvases are said to be "like nobody else's, black or white."

Gilliam received his M.A. from the University of Louisville, and was awarded National Endowment of Humanities and Arts grants. He has had one–man and group shows at the Washington Gallery of Modern Art; Jefferson Place Gallery; Adams–Morgan Gallery in Washington, DC; the Art Gallery of Washington University, St. Louis, Missouri; the Speed Museum, Louisville; the Philadelphia Museum of Art; the Museum of Modern Art; the Phillips Collection and Corcoran Gallery of Art, both in Washington, DC; the San Francisco Museum of Art; the Walker Art Center, Minneapolis, and the Whitney Museum of American Art. He is represented in the permanent collection of over forty-five American museums.

Gilliam has also been represented in several group exhibitions, including the First World Festival of Negro Arts in Dakar, Senegal (1966), "The Negro in American Art" at UCLA (1967), and the Whitney Museum's American Art Annual (1969).

In 1968, 1969 and 1970 his work was displayed in one-man shows at Washington, DC's Jefferson Place, and in 1971 he was featured in a one-man show at New York City's Museum of Modern Art.

In 1980, Sam Gilliam was commissioned, with thirteen other artists, to design an art piece for installation in the Atlanta, Georgia Airport Terminal, one of the largest terminals in the world and the first to install contemporary artwork on its walls for public viewing. Notable works include *Watercolor 4* (1969); *Herald* (1965); *Carousel Change* (1970); *Mazda* (1970); *Plantagenets Golden* (1984); and *Golden Element Inside Gold* (1994).

Gilliam's works have been on display at several exhibitions. In 1993, the Nancy Drysdale Gallery in Washington, D.C. hosted the exhibit "Sam Gilliam." The exhibition "Sam Gilliam: Bikers Move Like Swallows" was hosted by the Baumgartner Galleries in Washington, D.C. in 1994. Several works by Gilliam were included in the "Black Art" group exhibition at the Rockville Arts Place in Rockville, MD in 1995.

## Tyree Guyton (1955- )
*Multimedia Artist*

Born in Detroit, on August 24, 1955, Tyree Guyton has transformed the blighted urban pocket in which he has spent much of his life into an enormous ongoing art project that utilizes the detritus of the abandoned cityscape. Interested in the arts from a young age, after graduating from high school Guyton served in the U.S. Army and then worked at Ford Motor Company for several years. He also began a family and in his spare time took art classes.

In 1984, Guyton left his firefighting job to become a full-time artist and set to work transforming the small city block in which he and wife Karen Smith and their several children lived. His grandfather, a former housepainter, was both a source of early inspiration and an integral contributor to Guyton's artistic project. Using ordinary housepaint, a wealth of old toys, bicycles, and other found objects they salvaged from the junk piles that plague the city, Guyton transformed Heidelberg Street into a dynamic and unique art installation. A crack house, one of the many abandoned residences on the street, was painted in wild colors that discouraged the drug sales that even the narcotics squad raids had not been able to stop. A tree was nailed several yards high with vintage bicycles. Polka dots decorated the street, Guyton's own home, and nearly every other available surface. The combination of dots, stripes, lively patterning, and re-invention of found objects had been inspired by the style in which Guyton's mother had beautified their home on a tight budget when he was growing up.

Long heralded by the international artistic community, Guyton's art has periodically come under fire, however. Other residents of the east-side Detroit neighborhood dismiss the out-of-town visitors and laudatory praise heaped on the Heidelberg Project by the art critics and harken for the days of a neatly manicured lawn and more placid environs. In the fall of 1991, city bulldozers demolished several of the houses that Guyton had transformed, one of which had been slated for inclusion on a tour of local artistic sites. Ironically, that year he was named the Michiganian of the Year and the following year earned the Governor's Arts Award. Guyton sued the city—with the support of prominent members of Detroit's artistic community—but the dropped the suit when a more sympathetic mayoral administration came into power in 1994.

## Richard Hunt (1935- )
*Painter, Sculptor*

Richard Hunt was born in Chicago in 1935 and began his formal career after studying at the School of the Art Institute of Chicago, where he received a number of awards.

After graduating in 1957, Hunt was given the James Nelson Raymond Traveling Fellowship. He later taught at the School of the Art Institute of Chicago and at the University of Illinois. From 1962 to 1963, he pursued his craft while under a Guggenheim Fellowship.

Hunt's solo presentations have appeared at the Cleveland Museum of Art; Milwaukee Art Center; Museum of Modern Art; Art Institute of Chicago; Springfield Art Museum, Massachusetts; Indianapolis Museum of Art and a U.S.I.S.–sponsored show throughout Africa which was organized by the Los Angeles Museum of African American Art. Hunt sits on the board of governors at the School of the Art Institute of Chicago and the Skowhegan School of Painting and Sculpture; is a commissioner at the National Museum of American Art, Washington, DC; and serves on the advisory committee at the Getty Center for Education in the Arts, Malibu.

His works are in the Museum of Modern Art, New York; Cleveland Museum of Art, Ohio; Art Institute of Chicago; Milwaukee Art Center; Baltimore Museum of Art; Martin Gallery, Washington, DC; National Museum of American Art, Washington, DC; Hirshhorn Museum, Washington, DC; Museum of 20th Century Art, Vienna, Austria; the Albright Knox Gallery, Buffalo, New York; National Museum of Israel, Jerusalem; Terry Dintenfass Gallery, New York; Dorsky Gallery, New York; Whitney Museum of American Art, New York; and Howard University. He has had many other commissions. Notable works include *Man on a Vehicular Construct* (1956); *Linear Spatial Theme* (1962); *The Chase* (1965); and *Arching* (1986).

Some of Hunt's works appeared with those of Richmond Barthe at the "Richmond Barthe and Richard Hunt: Two Sculptors, Two Eras," exhibit at the Anacostia Museum in Washington, D.C. in 1993.

## Larry Johnson (1949- )
*Painter, Illustrator, Editorial Cartoonist*

Born in Boston, Massachusetts, in 1949, Larry Johnsonattended Boston Schools and the School of the Boston Museum of Fine Arts. He became a staff illustrator at *The Boston Globe* in 1968, where he covered many assignments, including courtroom sketches, sports events, entertainment, editorial sports cartoons and drawings, and other features. Johnson is now nationally syndicated through Universal Press Syndicate.

Barry Gaither, director of the National Center of African–American artists in Boston, says, "Johnson's works can be divided horizontally between commercial illustration and fine art, and vertically between drawings and paintings in acrylics and watercolor." In addition to working for the *Globe*, Johnson worked for the now defunct *National Sports Daily* and has designed book jackets for Little Brown. Commissioned by Pepsi-Cola, the *Old Farmer's Almanac*, the National Football League, *Fortune*, and others, he has left the *Globe* to freelance and run his own company, Johnson Editions, producer of fine arts prints and other multiples, such as greeting cards. Johnson was awarded the Associated Press Editorial Cartoon Award in 1985. Notable works include *Island Chisel; Rainbow*; and *Promises.*

In 1995, several of Johnson's photographs were included in the six-artist exhibition entitled "New Testament", which was hosted by the Marc Foxx Gallery in Santa Monica, California. The Margo Leavin Gallery in Los Angeles also hosted an exhibition of Johnson's art work in 1995.

### Lester L. Johnson (1937- )
*Painter, Educator*

Born in Detroit, Michigan, in 1937, Johnson attended the University of Michigan, where he received a B.F.A. in 1973, and an M.F.A. in 1974. He teaches at the Center for Creative Studies, College of Art and Design, in Detroit, Michigan.

His works are in many collections including: the Detroit Institute of Arts; Osaka University Arts, Japan; Johnson Publishers and The Masonite Corp., Chicago; Sonnenblick–Goldman Corp., New York; Taubman Co., Inc., Bloomfield Hills, Michigan; and St. Paul Co., St. Paul, Minnesota.

Commissions have included *Urban Wall Murals*, Detroit, 1974; New Detroit Receiving Hospital, 1980; and Martin Luther King Community Center. Johnson has exhibited at major institutions, including the Whitney Museum of American Art Biennial, 1973; National African–American Exhibit, Carnegie Institute, Pittsburgh, Pennsylvania; National Academy of Design, Henry Ward Ranger National Invitational, 1977.

Among his awards are the Andrew W. Mellon Foundation Grant, 1982 and 1984; and a Recognition Award, African–American Music Art Association.

In 1994, an exhibition of works by Lester Johnson was presented at the Edward Thorp Gallery in New York City.

### Sargent Johnson (1888-1967)
*Sculptor*

Sargent Johnson, who three times won the Harmon Foundation's medal as the nation's outstanding black artist, worked in stylized idioms, heavily influenced by the art forms of Africa in sculpture, mural bas-reliefs, metal sculpture, and ceramics.

Born in Boston in 1888, he studied at the Worcester Art School and moved west to the San Francisco Bay area in 1915, where his teachers were Beniamino Bufano and Ralph Stackpole. He exhibited at the San Francisco

Artists Annual, 1925-1931; Harmon Foundation, 1928-1931, 1933; Art Institute of Chicago, 1930; Baltimore Museum, 1939; American Negro Exposition, Chicago, 1940. He was the recipient of numerous awards and prizes.

From the beginning of his career he spoke of his sculpture as an attempt to show the "natural beauty and dignity of the pure American Negro" and wished to present "that beauty not so much to the white man as to the Negro himself. Unless I can interest my race, I am sunk." Notable works include *Sammy; Esther; Golden Gate Exposition Aquatic Park murals*; and *Forever Free.* He died in 1967.

### William Henry Johnson (1901-1970)
*Painter*

William H. Johnson was a pioneer black modernist whose ever-developing work went from abstract expressionist landscape and flower studies influenced by Vincent Van Gogh, to studies of black life in America, and finally to abstract figure studies in the manner of Rouault.

Born in Florence, South Carolina, on March 18, 1901, he studied at the National Academy of Design; Cape Cod School of Art, under Charles Hawthorne; in southern France, 1926-1929, and Denmark and Norway, 1930-1938. Exhibits include Harmon Foundation (Gold Medal in 1929); Aarlins, Denmark, 1935; Baltimore Museum, 1939; American Negro Exposition, Chicago, 1940. He produced one-person shows in Copenhagen in 1935, and at the Artists Gallery, New York, in 1938. Notable works include *Booker T. Washington; Young Man in Vest; Descent from the Cross*; and *On a John Brown Flight.* He died on April 13, 1970.

### Joshua Johnston (1765-1830)
*Painter*

Active between 1789 and 1825, Joshua Johnston is the first known black portrait painter from the Baltimore area. At least two dozen paintings have been attributed to this artist who was listed as a "free householder of colour, portrait painter". He was listed in the Baltimore directories in various studio locations.

It is believed Johnston may have been a former slave of Charles Wilson Peale, the artist who is also known for having started a drawing school in Maryland in 1795; or Johnston may have simply known the artist and his works. In either case, the artist was most likely self-taught. A portraitist in the true style of the period, his work now seems quaint and sensitive. Only one black subject has been attributed to him, *Portrait of a Cleric.*

*Going to Church,* William H. Johnson, c. 1940.

Notable works include *Portrait of Adelia Ellender, Portrait of Mrs. Barbara Baker Murphy* and *Portrait of Sea Captain John Murphy.*

## Ben Jones (1942- )
*Painter, Sculptor*

Ben Jones was born in Patterson, New Jersey, in 1942, and studied at the School of Visual Arts; New York University, where he received an M.A.; Pratt Institute; the University of Science and Technology, Ghana; and the New School of Social Research.

A professor of Fine Arts at Jersey City State College, Jones lives in New York. As a sculptor, his works (made during the height of the Black Art Movement in 1970) were cast in plaster from living models and painted in brightly colored patterns, as if inspired by traditional African symbols. Masks, arms and legs arranged in multiples or singly seem to have roots in African ceremony ritual and magic.

His pieces are in such collections as: the Newark Museum; Studio Museum in Harlem; Howard University; Johnson Publications, Chicago. His exhibits have included: The Museum of Modern Art; Studio Museum in Harlem; Black World Arts Festival, Lagos, Nigeria; Newark Museum; Fisk University, Nashville, Tennessee, and others.

Jones' awards have included grants from the National Endowment for the Arts; the New Jersey Arts Council; Delta Sigma Theta Sorority, and others. Notable works include *Five Black Face Images; High Priestess of Soul;* and *Untitled (6 Arms).*

## Karl Kani (1968?- )
*Fashion Designer*

Born Carl Williams, Kani and his friends were preoccupied with style even when very young. His fashion sense first became noticed on the streets of Flatbush, a neighborhood of Brooklyn, New York. While his peers were buying the latest clothes, Williams was busy purchasing material he would later bring to various tailors, instructing them to make garments exactly how he wanted for a relatively small price. As time passed, people who had seen Williams in one of his "originals" wanted their own made-to-order duds. Williams began taking orders and supplying the demand.

When the death of a close friend prompted him to search of a "positive endevour," Williams headed for

California. While working at Seasons Sportswear in South-Central Los Angeles, Williams developed the name Kani, based on the question "Can I?" as in "Can I do it?" In 1989, Kani met Carl Jones, cofounder of Threads 4 Life. Jones, who had already proven his ability to sell clothes with his Cross Colours line, agreed to help Kani get his designs out to the public. By 1992, the Kani line of clothing had added roughly $35 million dollars to the Threads 4 Life profit margin. Despite the success, Kani was not happy. Disagreements with Threads 4 Life led to Kani to venture off on his own.

Kani began "Karl Kani Infinity" in 1994. The thrill of the risk-taking and the fact that Kani wanted to work for himself fed his desire to succeed. While competition for hip-hop clothing had become fierce, Kani saw potential in the previously ignored market. With a staff of 15, Kani took on all competitors. Rap stars like Tupac Shakur began wearing his designs, and the Kani name was now in the public eye. In 1995, his designs were sold in more than 300 hundred stores nationwide.

## Emeline King
*Automobile Designer*

A native of Detroit, Michigan, Emeline King, the daughter of a Ford employee, acquired an ambition at an early age to design cars. King is a designer at the Ford Motor Company's Mustang studio.

King joined the company in 1983 after she graduated from Wayne State University where she majored in industrial design. She also studied in Detroit at the Center for Creative Studies. The Art Center College of Design in Pasadena, California awarded her a Bachelor of Science degree in transportation.

King was instrumental in the design of the 1994 Ford Mustang.

## Jacob Lawrence (1917- )
*Painter*

Born on September 7, 1917, in Atlantic City, New Jersey, Jacob Lawrence received his early training at the Harlem Art School and the American Artist School. He honed his craft under the watchful eye of notable artists such as Charles Alston, Henry Bannarn, Anton Refregier, Sol Wilson, Philip Reisman, and Eugene Moreley. His rise to prominence was ushered in by his painting of several series of biographical panels commemorating important episodes in African-American history. A narrative painter, Lawrence creates the "philosophy of Impressionism" within his work. Capturing the essential meaning behind the natural appearance of a historical moment of personality, Lawrence creates a formal series of several dozen small paintings which relate to the course of a particular historic event in American

history, such as *The Migration Series* ("...and the Migrants keep coming"), which traces the migration of the African-American from the South to the North, or the discussion on the course of a man's life (e.g., Toussant L'Ouverture and John Brown).

Jacob Lawrence is a visual American historian. His paintings record the African American in trade, theater, mental hospitals, neighborhoods, or running in the Olympic races. Lawrence's works are found in such collections as the Metropolitan Museum of Art, Museum of Modern Art, Whitney Museum of American Art, the National Museum of American Art, and the Wadsworth Atheneum in Hartford, Connecticut.

Lawrence lives in Seattle, Washington. Notable works include *The Life of Toussaint L'Ouverture* (forty one panels-1937); *The Life of Harriet Tubman* (forty panels-1939); and *The Negro Migration Northward in World War* (sixty panels-1942). He has also produced commissioned book and magazine illustrations, murals, posters, drawings, and prints. Among these are a 1976 print for the United States Bicentennial, illustrations for a 1983 special edition of John Hersey's book *Hiroshima*, and a 1984 poster for the National Urban League.

In 1970, Lawrence was awarded the NAACP's Spingarn Medal. He also received an invitation to paint the 1977 presidential inauguration of Jimmy Carter. President George Bush bestowed on Lawrence the National Medal of Arts in 1990. He is also the recipient of numerous honorary degrees.

Lawrence wrote and illustrated the book "The Great Migration: An American Story" in 1993.

## Hughie Lee-Smith (1915- )
*Painter*

Hughie Lee-Smith was born on September 20, 1915, in Eustis, Florida. He studied at the Cleveland Institute of Art and Wayne State University, where he received his B.S. in Art Education in 1953.

From childhood, Lee-Smith was encouraged to pursue his art and he has enjoyed a long and productive career. He worked for the Ohio Works Progress Administration and the Ford Factory at River Rouge during the 1930s and 1940s. He did a series of lithographic prints and painted murals at the Great Lakes Naval Station in Illinois. He taught art at Karamu House in Cleveland, the Grosse Pointe War Memorial in Michigan, Princeton Country Day School, Howard University, the Art Students League, and other institutions.

Lawrence's works can be seen in museums, schools, galleries, and collections across the United States, in-

*Tombstones,* Jacob Lawrence, 1942

Jacob Lawrence

cluding the American Negro Exposition, Chicago; Southside Community Art Center; Snowden Gallery; Detroit Artists Market; Cleveland Museum of Art; Whitney Museum of American Art; Museum of Modern Art; the June Kelly Gallery, New York City, and the Evans-Tibbs Collection, Washington, DC. His painted environments are often of decaying or ghetto environments in the state of revitalization peopled by a single or sometimes double-figured occupant. His subjects seem to suggest desolation or alienation, but waving banners or balloons in the scene counter the expression in their symbolism of hope and gaiety.

Lee-Smith's one-person shows and exhibitions are too numerous to list. He has received more than a dozen important prizes, including the Founders Prize of the Detroit Institute of Arts (1953), Emily Lowe Award (1957, 1985), Ralph Fabri Award, Audubon Artists, Inc. (1982), Binny and Smith Award (1983), and Len Everette Memorial Prize, Audubon Artists, Inc. (1986). He is a member of the Allied Artists of America, the Michigan Academy of the Arts, Sciences & Letters, and the Artists Equity Association. Notable works include *Portrait of a Sailor; Old Man and Youth; Waste Land; Little Diana;* and *Aftermath.*

In 1995, Bristol-Myers Squibb in Princeton, New Jersey featured the exhibit "Hughie Lee-Smith: An Overview, 1949-1995."

### Edmonia Lewis (1845-1890)
*Sculptor*

Edmonia Lewis was America's first black woman artist and also the first of her race and sex to be recognized as a sculptor. Born on July 4, 1845 in Albany, New York, she was the daughter of a Chippewa Indian woman and a free black man. From 1859 to 1863, under the patronage of a number of abolitionists, she was educated at Oberlin College, the first American college to admit women on a nonsegregated basis.

After completing her schooling, Lewis moved to Boston, where she studied with Edmund Brackett and did a bust of Colonel Robert Gould Shaw, the commander of the first black regiment organized in the state of Massachusetts during the Civil War. In 1865, she moved to Rome, where she soon became a prominent artist. Returning to the United States in 1874, she fulfilled many commissions, including a bust of Henry Wadsworth Longfellow that was executed for the Harvard College Library.

Edmonia Lewis

Her works are fine examples of the neo-classical sculpture that was fashionable during her lifetime. It is believed that she died in Rome in 1890. Notable works include *Hagar in the Wilderness*, *Forever Free*, and *Hiawatha*.

## Norman Lewis (1909-1979)
*Painter*

Norman Lewis was born in New York City in 1909. Lewis studied at Columbia University. He also studied under Augusta Savage, Raphael Soyer, Vaclav Vytacil, and Angela Streater. During the Great Depression he taught art through the Federal Art Project from 1936 to 1939 at the Harlem Art Center. He received a Carnegie International Award in Painting in 1956 and has had several one-person shows at the Willard Gallery in New York.

As one of the artists to develop the abstract movement in the United States, Lewis participated in many group shows in such institutions as the Whitney Museum of American Art, the Metropolitan Museum of Art, and the Art Institute of Chicago. Notable works include *Arrival and Departure* and *Heroic Evening*.

## Ionis Bracy Martin (1936- )
*Painter, Printmaker, Educator*

Born on August 27, 1936, in Chicago, Illinois, Ionis Bracy Martin attended the Junior School of the Art Institute of Chicago before going to Fisk University, where she studied with Aaron Douglas and earned her B.S. in 1957. Martin received an M.Ed. degree from the University of Hartford (1969) and an M.F.A. from Pratt Institute, Brooklyn, New York (1987). She is a Trustee of the Wadsworth Atheneum, 1977, co-founder of the Artists Collective (with Jackie McLean, Dollie McLean, Paul Brown, and Cheryl Smith), 1972, co-trustee and chairperson of the Ella Burr McManus Trust for the Alfred E. Burr Sculpture Mall, 1985, and a member of the advisory board of the CRT Craftery Gallery, Hartford, 1973.

Exhibiting widely in the Hartford area, Martin has also exhibited in New York; Springfield, Boston, and Northampton, Massachusetts; Fisk University, Nashville, Tennessee; and the University of Vermont, Burlington, Vermont. Among her many prizes and honors are a grant from the Connecticut Commission on the Arts (1969); a graduate fellowship in Printmaking, Pratt Institute (1981); a Summer-Six Fellowship from Skidmore College (1987); and a fellowship with the WEB DuBois Institute, Harvard University (1994).

A teacher at Weaver and Bloomfield High Schools since 1961, and lecturer in African-American art at Central Connecticut State University since 1985, Martin also lectures on and demonstrates serigraphy. Notable works include *Mother and Child; Allyn's Garden; Gran' Daddy's Garden*; and *Little Women of the Amistad: Series*.

## Geraldine McCullough (1928- )
*Sculptor*

Geraldine McCullough's steel and copper abstraction *Phoenix* won the George D. Widener Gold Medal at the 1964 exhibition of the Pennsylvania Academy of Fine Arts. In earning this award, she added her name to a roster of distinguished artists who have already won the same honor, including Jacques Lipchitz and Theodore Roszak. Of further note is the fact that this was her first showing in a major national exhibition.

A native of Arkansas, McCullough (b. 1928) has lived in Chicago since she was three and is a 1948 graduate of the Art Institute there. She also studied at the University of Chicago, DePaul University, Northwestern University, and the University of Illinois.

McCullough taught at Wendell Phillips High School (from 1950 to 1964) in Chicago and at Rosary College in River Forest, Illinois. Currently, she works and resides in Oak Park, Illinois. She has received many awards and commissions. Her works are represented in collections at Howard University; in Oak Park, Illinois; the Oakland, California museum, and many others. Notable works include *Bessie Smith; View from the Moon; Todd Hall Front; Atomic Rose; Phoenix;* and *Martin Luther King.*

### Evangeline J. Montgomery (1933- )
*Jeweler, Photographer, Sculptor*

Evangeline Montgomery was born in New York City on May 2, 1933. She received an associate's degree from Los Angeles City College in 1958 and her B.F.A. from the California College of Arts and Crafts in 1969; she also studied at the University of California, Berkeley and California State University.

Montgomery has worked as a freelance artist, an art consultant to museums, community organizations, and colleges for EJ Associates, and program director for Arts America. Known primarily for her metal boxes, incense burners, and jewelry, Montgomery has also been awarded prizes for her photography. Her works are in collections at the Oakland Museum and the University of Southern Illinois.

Active with many organizations, Montgomery has served on the San Francisco Art Commission, the advisory board of Parting Ways Ethnohistory Museum, and the board of directors of the Museum of the National Center of Afro-American Artists. She is currently a member of the Michigan Chapter of the National Conference of Artists, the College Art Association, the American Museums Association, and the Women's Art Caucus. Montgomery is also on the board of directors of the DC Arts Center.

Her awards have included a Smithsonian Fellowship and a museum grant from the National Endowment for the Arts. In 1989, Montgomery was presented with a Special Achievement Award from Arts America. Notable works include *Ancestor Box 1* and *Justice for Angela Davis.*

### Archibald Motley (1891-1980)
*Painter*

Archibald Motley touched on many topics and themes in his work but none was more gratifying to him than his candid depictions of black Americans.

Born in New Orleans in 1891, Motley's artistic talent was apparent by the time he attended high school. His father wanted him to become a doctor, but Archibald insisted on art and began formal education at the Art Institute of Chicago, earning his subsistence by working as a day laborer. During this time Motley came in contact with the drifters, scavengers, and hustlers of society, who are now immortalized in his street scenes. His genre scenes are highly stylized and colorful and are often associated with the *Ash-Can* school of art, which was popular in the 1920s.

In 1928, Motley had a one-person show at the new galleries in downtown New York and became the first artist, black or white, to make the front page of the *New York Times.* He was awarded a Guggenheim Fellowship in 1929 and studied in France. He was the recipient of a Harmon Foundation award for an earlier, more literal portrait. Notable works include: *The Jockey Club; The Plotters; Parisian Scene; Black Belt;* and *Old Snuff Dipper.* Motley died in 1980.

### John Wilfred Outterbridge (1933- )
*Sculptor*

John Wilfred Outterbridge was born in Greenville, North Carolina, on March 12, 1933. He studied at Agricultural and Technical University, Greensboro, North Carolina; the Chicago Art Academy; the American Academy of Art, Chicago; and the Art Center School of Design, Los Angeles.

From 1964 until 1968, Outterbridge worked as an artist/designer for Traid Corporation. He worked as artistic director and co-founder of the Communicative Arts Academy from 1969 until 1975. He has also taught at California State University and Pasadena Art Museum. Outterbridge was director of the Watts Towers Art Center, Los Angeles, from 1976 until 1992.

Outterbridge's sculptures are assemblages constructed from discarded materials. Some of his works are tributes to African ancestors and their descendants in Los Angeles and in other communities. Outterbridge is known for making and helping others create "Street Art," a combination of painting, relief sculpture, and construction that incorporates words and symbols expressing community goals and social ideas.

Outterbridge was featured in *Black Artists on Art,* Volume I (Selma Lewis/Ruth Waddy, Los Angeles Contemporary Crafts, 1971, 1976). Notable works include *Shoeshine Box; Mood Ghetto;* and *Ethnic Heritage Group.*

In 1990, Outterbridge was presented with the Malcolm X Freedom Award by the New Afrikan People's Organization and the Lifetime Achievement Award from the 1st Annual King Blvd. Memorial Project. The National Endowment for the Arts awarded Outterbridge with its Visual Arts Fellowship in 1994. That same year, he was presented with an honorary doctorate of fine arts by the Otis College of Arts and Design and the J. Paul Getty Visual Arts Fellowship.

### Gordon Parks (1912- )
*Photographer, Composer, Writer, Director*

Parks was born on November 30, 1912 in Fort Scott, Kansas. After the death of his mother, Parks went to St.

Archibald Motley with one of his paintings, 1932

Paul, Minnesota to live with relatives. While there he attended Central and Mechanical Arts high schools. Despite having fond childhood memories of his father on the family farm, Parks had a dysfunctional upbringing. Parks worked at a variety of jobs including janitor, busboy, and semi-pro basketball player. Always interested in the arts, Parks also tried sculpting, writing and touring with a band, but these artistic endeavors were largely without focus.

In 1933, Parks joined the Civilian Conservation Corps and in the late 1930s, while working as a railroad porter, he became interested in photography as a medium on which he could finally concentrate his considerable artistic talents. After purchasing a used camera, Parks worked as a freelance photographer and as a photojournalist. In 1942, he became a correspondent for the Farm Security Administration, and from 1943 to 1945 he was a correspondent for the Office of War Information. After the war he worked for Standard Oil Company of New Jersey, and in 1948 he became a staff photographer for *Life* magazine. He soon achieved national acclaim for his photographs and in the mid-1950s he began doing consulting work on Hollywood productions. In the 1960s Parks began doing television docu-

mentaries, and in 1966 he published his biography *A Choice of Weapons.*

Parks is also the author of *Flash Photography* (1947), *Camera Portraits: The Techniques and Principals of Documentary Portraiture* (1948), *The Learning Tree* (1963), *A Poet and His Camera* (1968), *Born Black* (1971), *Gordon Parks: Whispers of Intimate Things* (1971), *Moments without Proper Names* (1975), *Flavio* (1977), *To Smile in Autumn* (1979), *Shannon* (1981), *Voices in the Mirror* (1991), *Arias in Silence* (1994). In 1968 Parks produced, directed, and wrote the script and music for the movie production of *The Learning Tree.* Parks also directed and scored the movies *Shaft* (1971), *Shaft's Big Score* (1972), *The Super Cops* (1974), *Leadbelly* (1976), *Odyssey of Solomon Northrup* (1984) and *Moments Without Proper Names* (1986).

Parks is a recipient of the NAACP's Spingarn Award (1972), the Rhode Island School of Design's Presidents Fellow Award (1984), and Kansan of the Year (1986). In 1988 President Ronald Reagan presented him with the National Medal for the Arts. That same year, Parks won the World Press Photo Award. In 1989, he was awarded the Library of Congress National Film Registry Classics film honor for *The Learning Tree.* He was also present-

Gordon Parks

Marion Perkins

ed with the New York Mayor's Award and the Artist of Merit Josef Sudek Medal in 1989.

Parks is a member of the NAACP, Urban League, Newspaper Guild, Association of Composers and Directors, Writer's Guild, AFTRA, ASCAP, International Mark Twain Society, American Film Institute, Academy of Motion Pictures Arts and Sciences, and the American Society of Magazine Photographers.

On July 7, 1995, the Library of Congress announced that it had acquired the archives of Gordon Parks. The archives include roughly 15,000 manuscript pages of Parks's poems, novels and screenplays, as well as several thousand photographs and negatives.

## Marion Perkins (1908-1961)
### Sculptor

Born in Marche, Arkansas, in 1908, Perkins was largely a self-taught artist. His early works were composed while he tended a newspaper stand on Chicago's South Side. He later studied privately with Simon Gordon, and the two men became close friends.

Perkins's work has been exhibited at the Art Institute of Chicago, American Negro Exposition (1940), Xavier

University, and Rockland College, Illinois (1965). As artist in residence at Jackson State College in Mississippi, where much of his sculpture is housed, Perkins founded a scholarship fund for art students. Perkins died in 1961.

## Howardena Pindell (1943- )
### Painter

Born in Philadelphia on April 14, 1943, Howardena Pindell received her education at Boston University (B.F.A., 1965) and Yale University (M.F.A., 1967). She first gained national recognition for her artistic skills in 1969 with the exhibition "American Drawing Biennial XXIII" at the Norfolk Museum of Arts and Sciences in Virginia. By the mid–1970s, Pindell's work began appearing in such exhibitions as "Eleven Americans in Paris," Gerald Piltzer Gallery, Paris, 1975; "Recent Acquisitions; Drawings," Museum of Modern Art, New York, 1976; and "Pindell: Video Drawings," Sonja Henie Onstad Foundation, Oslo, Norway, 1976.

Around this same time, Pindell began to travel around the world as a guest speaker. Some of her lectures included "Current American and Black American Art: A Historical Survey" at Madras College of Arts and Crafts,

Madras, India, 1975; and "Black Artists, U.S.A.," Academy of Art, Oslo, Norway, 1976. She is currently a professor of art at State University of New York at Stony Brook.

Her work is part of the permanent collection in over thirty museums including the Brooklyn Museum, High Museum in Atlanta, Newark Museum, Fogg Museum in Cambridge, Massachusetts, Whitney Museum of American Art, Museum of Modern Art, and the Metropolitan Museum of Art. Pindell has received two National Endowment for the Arts Fellowships and a Guggengeim Fellowship.

Pindell has received numerous awards throughout her career. In 1990, she won the College Art Association Award for Best Exhibitor. She received the Studio Museum in Harlem Award and Joan Mitchell Fellowship in 1994. In 1996, the Women Caucus for Art presented Pindell with its Distinguished Contribution to the Profession Award.

## Jerry Pinkney (1939- )
*Illustrator*

Born in Philadelphia on December 22, 1939, Jerry Pinkney studied at the Philadelphia Museum College of Art. Pinkney has exhibited in illustrator shows throughout the country and is best known for his illustrations for children's books and text books.

From his studio in his home in Croton–on–Hudson, New York, Pinkney has been a major contributor to the United States Postal Service's stamps in the Black Heritage Series. Benjamin Banneker, Martin Luther King, Jr., Scott Joplin, Jackie Robinson, Sojourner Truth, Carter G. Woodson, Whitney Moore Young, Mary McLeod Bethune, and Harriet Tubman stamps were designed by this Citizens' Stamp Advisory Committee member.

A recipient of many honors, he has created illustrations in children's books that have been outstanding. For example, *The Talking Eggs*, written by Robert San Souci, was given a Caldecott Honor of Medal (Pinkney's second such honor) in 1989, received a Coretta Scott King Honor Book Award, was named an American Library Association Notable Book, and won the Irma Simonton Black Award from the Bank Street College of Education. In 1994, Pinkney won the Caldecott Medal for his illustrations in the book *John Henry*. That same year, he won two Parent's Choice Awards for the books *John Henry* and *The Sunday Outing*.

Pinkney has worked in Boston as a designer and illustrator. He is one of the founders of Kaleidoscope Studio in Boston, where he also worked for the National Center of Afro–American Art. For a while he was a Visiting Critic for the Rhode Island School of Design. He has taught at Pratt Institute, the University of Delaware

and in the Art Department at the State University of New York at Buffalo. Notable works include *The Tales of Uncle Remus*, published by Dial Brooks; *Call It Courage*, written by Armstrong Sperry and published by Aladdin Books; *Self Portrait*; and *Back Home*, written by his wife, Gloria Jean Pinkney.

## Horace Pippin (1888-1946)
*Painter*

Horace Pippin has been ranked in the company of Henri Rousseau due to his accomplishment as a self-taught artist. Born on February 22, 1888, in West Chester, Pennsylvania, Pippin began painting in 1920, and continued until his death on July 6, 1946. Among his most vivid portrayals on canvas are the battle scenes that he remembered from his own experience in World War I, during which he was wounded and partially paralyzed.

Pippin's earliest works are designs burned into wood with a hot poker. He did not make his first oil painting until 1930—after working on it for three years. This task was complicated by his wartime injury; he had to guide his right arm with his left hand in order to paint. He painted family reunions, Biblical stories, and historical events. Notable works include *John Brown Goes to a Hanging; Flowers with Red Chair; The Den; The Milk Man of Goshen;* and *Dog Fight Over the Trenches.*

## James A. Porter (1905-1971)
*Art Historian, Painter*

James A. Porter was a painter of considerable scholarship who also earned acclaim as a writer and educator. Born in Baltimore in 1905, he studied at Howard University (B.S., 1927); Art Students League, New York; Sorbonne; and New York University (M.A.). He was awarded numerous travel grants that enabled him to study African and European art firsthand.

Among his ten one-person shows are exhibits at Port-au-Prince, Haiti, 1946; Dupont Gallery, Washington, DC, 1949; and Howard University, 1965. His works are in the collections of Howard University; Lincoln University, Missouri; Harmon Foundation; IBM; and others. The first African-American art historian, he wrote the classic *Modern Negro Art* (1943) as well as numerous articles.

In 1953, he became chairman of the Department of Art and director of the Gallery of Art at Howard University, a position he held until his death. He was a delegate to the UNESCO Conference on Africa held in Boston in 1961, and to the International Congress of African Art and Culture in Salisbury, Southern Rhodesia, 1962. In 1965, at the twenty-fifth anniversary of the founding of the National Gallery of Art, he was named "one of

America's Most Outstanding Men of the Arts." His notable works include: *On a Cuban Bus*, *Portrait of F. A. as Harlequin*, *Dorothy Porter*, and *Nude.*.

## Martin Puryear (1941- )
*Sculptor*

Martin Puryear was born in Washington, DC, in 1941. He attended Catholic University of America and received an M.F.A. from Yale University in 1971; he has studied in Sweden and worked in Sierra Leone with the Peace Corps from 1964 to 1966.

Representing the United States in the 1989 Sao Paulo Bienal in Brazil he received first prize. His work has been described as post-minimalist, but it really defies categorizing. Puryear executes his own large pieces in wood and metal.

Puryear was the only black artist in the contemporary section of the exhibit, "Primitivism in Twentieth-Century Art: Affinity of the Tribal and Modern", at the Museum of Modern Art 1984; his other exhibits include Brooklyn Museum, 1988-1989, the Whitney Biennal, 1989, and New York Galleries, since 1987.

Puryear studied in Japan in 1987 on a Guggenheim Fellowship. Notable works include *For Beckwith; Maroon Desire; Sentinel;* recent works (since 1985) have been untitled.

## Faith Ringgold (1930- )
*Painter, Fiber Artist*

Committed to a revolutionary perspective both in politics and in aesthetics, Faith Ringgold is a symbolic expressionist whose stark paintings are acts of social reform directed toward educating the consciousness of her audience. Her most intense focus has been upon the problems of being black in America. Her works highlight the violent tensions which tear at American society, including the discrimination suffered by women. Ringgold is also known for her distinctive story quilts. These quilts feature paintings on canvas that are bordered with quilted textiles and handwritten strips of white fabric that contain fanciful stories.

Born in Harlem on October 8, 1934, she was raised by parents who made sure she would enjoy the benefits of a good education. She attended the City College of New York, receiving her B.S. in 1955 and her masters in Fine Arts in 1959. She is a professor of Art at the University of California at San Diego.

Ringgold's boldly political work has been well-received and widely shown. She has had several one-person shows, the first in 1968, and her paintings are included in the collections of the Chase Manhattan Bank, New York City; the Museum of Modern Art, the Bank Street College of Education, New York City; and the Solomon R. Guggenheim Museum.

In 1972, Ringgold became one of the founders of the Women Students and Artists for Black Liberation, an organization whose principal goal is to make sure that all exhibitions of black artists give equal space to paintings by men and women. In line with her interest in sexual parity, she has donated a large mural depicting the roles of woman in American Society to the Women's House of Detention in Manhattan.

Aesthetically, she believes that "black art must use its own color, black, to create its light, since that color is the most immediate black truth." Her most recent paintings have been an attempt to give pictorial realization to this vision.

Her first quilt, *Echoes of Harlem, Tar Beach* was completed in 1980. Other quilts produced by Ringgold include *The Sunflower Quilting Bee at Arles* and *Who's Afraid of Aunt Jemima*. In 1991, she illustrated and wrote a children's book, *Tar Beach* . This book was followed in 1992 by *Aunt Harriet's Underground Railroad in the Sky*. Notable artistic works include *The Flag Is Bleeding; Flag for the Moon; Die Nigger; Mommy & Daddy*; and *Soul Sister, Woman on a Bridge*.

Ringgold has received several awards for her work, including honorary doctorates from Moore College of Fine Art, Wooster College, Massachusetts College of Art, and City College of Art. In 1996, she received an award from the National Museum of Women in the Arts.

## Betye Saar (1926- )
*Painter, Sculptor*

Betye Saar was born in California on July 30, 1926. She went to college, got married, and raised her children—all while creating artwork, images built upon discarded pieces of old dreams, postcards, photographs, flowers, buttons, fans, and ticket stubs. Her motifs range from the fetish to the everyday object. In 1978, Saar was one of a select group of American female artists to be discussed in a documentary film entitled *Spirit Catcher: The Art of Betye Saar*. It appeared on WNET-13 in New York as part of "The Originals: Women in Art" series. Her exhibitions include an installation piece especially designed for The Studio Museum in Harlem in 1980, and several one-person exhibitions at the Monique Knowlton Gallery in New York in 1981.

Saar studied at Pasadena City College, University of California (B.F.A. in 1949), Long Beach State College, University of Southern California, San Fernando State College, Valley State College, California, and the American Film Institute. She was a teacher in–residence at Hayward State College, California. She has exhibited throughout the United States. In 1994, Saar's works were displayed with over 200 other artists at Brazil's Bienal, a biannual art exhibition featuring the works of artists from over 71 countries. Notable works include *The Vision of El Cremo; Africa; The View from the Sorcerer's Window*; and *House of Gris Gris*, a mixed-media installation (with daughter Alison Saar).

## Augusta Savage (1900-1962)
*Sculptor*

A leading sculptor who emerged during the Harlem Renaissance, Augusta Savage was one of the artists represented in the first all-black exhibition in America, sponsored by the Harmon Foundation at International House in New York City. In 1939, her symbolic group piece *Lift Every Voice and Sing* was shown at the New York World's Fair Community Arts Building.

Savage was born in Green Cove Springs, Florida, on February 29, 1900, studied at Tallahassee State Normal School, at Cooper Union in New York City, and in France as the recipient of Carnegie and Rosenwald fellowships. She was the first black to win acceptance in the National Association of Women Painters and Sculptors.

In the 1930s she taught in her own School of Arts and Crafts in Harlem and helped many of her students take advantage of Works Progress Administration projects for artists during the Depression. Notable works include: *Lift Every Voice and Sing; The Chase; Black Women; Lenore; Gamin; Marcus Garvey*; and *W.E.B. DuBois*.

## Charles Searles (1937- )
*Painter, Educator*

Born in Philadelphia, Pennsylvania, in 1937, Searles studied at Fleicher Art Memorial, Penn Academy of Fine Arts (1968-1972). His works have been exhibited at the Dallas, the Brooklyn, Philadelphia, Reading, High, Milwaukee, Whitney, and Harlem Studio Museums; Columbia University; and many other galleries and museums.

Searles has traveled to Europe and Africa. He has taught at the Philadelphia College of Art, the Philadelphia Museum Art Studio Classes, University of the Arts, Brooklyn Museum Art School, Jersey State College, and Bloomfield College in New Jersey.

He was commissioned to execute several murals, including the U.S. General Service Administration interior; *Celebration* (1976) for Wm. J. Green Federal Building; *Play Time* (1976) for Malory Public Playground; Newark, New Jersey Amtrak Station wall sculpture (1985); Dempsy Service Center wall sculpture (1989).

His works are in the collections of the Smithsonian Institute, Washington, DC; New York State Office Building; Philadelphia Museum of Art; Federal Railroad Administration; Ciba-Gigy, Inc.; Dallas Museum of Art;

*Gamin*, Augusta Savage, 1930.

Montclair Art Museum; Phillip Morris, Inc.; and Howard University.

The human figure, color and rhythmic patterns dominate his paintings. Notable works include *Cultural Mix; Rhythmic Forms; Play Time*; and *Celebration*.

## Lorna Simpson (1960- )
*Photographer, Conceptual Artist*

Simpson was born in Brooklyn, New York, on August 13, 1960, and attended the School of Visual Arts, where she earned her B.F.A. in 1982. She received her M.F.A. from the University of California, San Diego, in 1985. Her works are concerned with language and words, especially those with double and contradictory meanings, and stereotypes and cliches about gender and race.

Simpson is among the new young photographers who have broken into the mainstream of conceptual based art; her work has been shown at the Museum of Modern Art and the Wadsworth Atheneum. She is on the advisory board of the New Museum, New York City, and also on the board of Artists Space.

In 1990, Simpson became the first African American woman to have her work featured in the Venice Biennale, a prestigious international art exhibition. Her work has been shown in exhibitions thoroughout the United States, Europe, Latin America, and Japan. Several institutions have offered exhibitions of her work, among them the Ansel Adams Center in San Francisco, the Whitney Museum of American Art in New York City, and the Milwaukee Art Museum. Her works have also been exhibited in the Just Above Mid-Town Gallery, Mercer Union (Toronto), and the Wadsworth Atheneum Museum's Matrix Gallery. Notable works include *Outline; Guarded Conditions; Easy for Who to Say; Flipside; Bio; Untitled ("prefer/refuse/decide")*; and the interactive multimedia composition *Five Rooms.*

### Norma Merrick Sklarek (1928- )
*Architect*

Sklarek was born on April 15, 1928 in New York City, and received a B.A. in architecture from the Barnard College of Columbia University in 1950. In 1954, she became the first African American woman to be licensed as an architect in the United States. In 1966, Sklarek became the first African American woman to be named a fellow of the American Institute of Architects.

Sklarek's career began at Skidmore, Owens, Merrill, where she worked as an architect from 1955 until 1960. She also served on the faculty of New York City College from 1957 until 1960. In 1960, she took a position with Gruen and Associates in Los Angeles, California, where she worked for the next twenty years. She also served as a faculty member at UCLA from 1972 until 1978. Sklarek became vice president of Welton Becket Associates in 1980 and worked there until 1985. From 1985 until 1989, Sklarek was a partner in the firm Siegel, Sklarek, and Diamond, the largest female-owned architectural firm in the United States. In 1989, she began working as a principal for The Jerde Partnership, retiring in 1992. Sklarek remains active by conducting classes and seminars.

Among the notable structures designed by Sklarek are the American Embassy in Tokyo; Courthouse Center, Columbus, Indiana; City Hall, San Bernardino, California; and Terminal One, Los Angeles International Airport.

### Moneta Sleet, Jr. (1926- )
*Photographer*

Moneta Sleet was born on February 14, 1926, in Owensboro, Kentucky. He studied at Kentucky State College under Dr. John Williams, a family friend who was dean of the college and an accomplished photographer. In 1947, he received his bachelor's degree from Kentucky State College. He earned a master's degree from New York University in 1950.

Sleet taught photography at Maryland State College from 1948 until 1949. He moved to New York City in 1950 to work as a sportswriter for *Amsterdam News*. He also worked as a photographer for *Our World* from 1951 until 1955. Sleet moved to Chicago and took a job with the Johnson Publishing Company, where he has been staff photographer for *Ebony* and *Jet* magazines since 1955.

In 1969, Moneta Sleet became the first African American to win a Pulitzer Prize in Photography. Although employed by *Ebony*, he was eligible for the award because his photograph of Coretta Scott King at her husband's funeral was picked up by a wire service and published in daily newspapers throughout the country. He has also received awards from the Overseas Press Club of America, National Urban League, and the National Association of Black Journalists. In 1989, the University of Kentucky inducted Sleet into its Kentucky Journalism Hall of Fame.

His work has appeared in several group exhibitions at museums, including The Studio Museum in Harlem and Metropolitan Museum of Art. In 1970, solo exhibitions were held at the City Art Museum of St. Louis and at the Detroit Public Library. Other solo exhibitions of Sleet's work have been held at the New York Public Library, Newark Public Library, Chicago Public Library Cultural Center, Milwaukee Public Library, Martin Luther King Jr. Memorial Library, Albany Museum of Art, New York State Museum, and the Schomberg Center for Research in Black Culture.

Sleet is a member of the NAACP and the Black Academy of Arts and Letters.

### Willi Smith (1948-1987)
*Fashion Designer*

Born on February 29, 1948, in Philadelphia, Pennsylvania, Willi Smith studied at the Parsons School of Design on a scholarship and became popular during the 1960s. He was known for his designer wear in natural fibers, that were fun, cross seasonal, and affordable. His clothes were sportswear pieces that mixed readily with Willi-wear from previous years as well as other clothes. Smith innovated in mixing and matching plaids, stripes, and vivid colors. He designed for both men and women. Smith had his clothes manufactured in India, traveling there several times a year to supervise the making of his functional and practical collections.

Willi Smith

In 1983 Willi Smith received the Coty American Fashion Critics Award for Women's Fashion. He died in 1987.

## Nelson Stevens (1938- )
*Muralist, Painter, Graphic Artist*

Born in Brooklyn, New York, in 1938, Stevens studied at Ohio University (B.F.A. 1962) and Kent State University (M.F.A. 1969).

An active member of AFRICOBRA—a group exploring the aesthetics of African-American art which includes the use of the human figure, bright colors, African inspired patterns, text, letters and other symbols relating to the black experience—he is also a member of the National Conference of Artists.

Stevens is a professor of art at the University of Massachusetts in Amherst, Massachusetts. He has exhibited at the National Center of Afro-American Artists, Boston; The Studio Museum in Harlem; Howard University; Kent State University. Notable works include: *Madonna and Child*, for a 1993 calendar, *Art in the Service of the Lord*; *Malcolm—King of Jihad*; and *A Different Kind of Man*.

## Henry Ossawa Tanner (1859-1937)
*Painter*

Alain Locke called Henry Ossawa Tanner the leading talent of the "journeyman period" of black American art. Born in Pittsburgh on June 21, 1859, Tanner chose painting rather than the ministry as a career, overcoming the strong objections of his father, an African Methodist Episcopal bishop. After attending the Pennsylvania Academy of Fine Arts, he taught at Clark University in Atlanta, supplementing his salary by working as a photographer. Some of Tanner's most compelling work—such as *The Banjo Lesson* (1890)—was produced during this period, with Tanner himself emerging as the most promising black artist of his day.

In 1891, however, Tanner abandoned black subject matter and left the United States for Paris, where he concentrated on religious themes. In 1896, his *Daniel in the Lion's Den*, a mixture of realism and mystical symbolism, won honorable mention at the Paris Salon. The following year, the French government purchased his *Resurrection of Lazarus*. In 1900, Tanner received the Medal of Honor at the Paris Exposition and the Lippincott Prize.

Tanner died in 1937. Notable works include *Flight into Egypt, The Annunciation, Thankful Poor* and *The Sabot Makers.*

## Alma W. Thomas (1891-1978)
*Painter*

Born in Columbus, Georgia, in 1891, Alma Thomas moved to Washington, DC with her family when she was a teenager. She enrolled at Howard University and was the first graduate of its Art Department (1924). In 1934 she received her M.A. degree from Columbia University. She later studied at American University.

Retiring after a thirty-eight-year teaching career in public schools, Thomas concentrated solely on her painting. She is best known for her non-objective, mosaic-like works which emphasize color, pattern, and space. The optical relationships of her colors in flat shapes create three-dimensional forms, enlivening the painted surfaces with movement and pulsating rhythms. It is this later work that brought her many prizes and awards.

Her works are in the collections of the National Museum of American Art at the Smithsonian Institute, Howard University, Concord Gallery, Metropolitan Museum, La Jolla Museum, and private corporations. Notable works include *The Eclipse; Arboretum Presents White Dogwood; Elysian Fields; Red Sunset;* and *Old Pond Concerto.*

*Abraham's Oak,* Henry Ossawa Tanner, 1905.

## Bob Thompson (1937-1966)
*Painter*

The death of Bob Thompson marked the loss of an outstanding African-American painter from the art world, a man who had studied extensively in the United States and traveled widely in Europe and North Africa, living in Paris (1961-1962), Ibiza (1962-1963), and Rome (1965-1966).

Born in Louisville, Kentucky, in 1937, Thompson studied at the Boston Museum School in 1955 and later spent three years at the University of Louisville. In 1960, Thompson participated in a two-person show at Zabriskie Gallery and two years later received a John Hay Whitney Fellowship. For the next several years, Thompson had several one-person exhibitions in New York and Chicago. His work was also seen in Spain. He died in Rome at the age of twenty-nine.

Thompson's work is in several permanent collections around the country, including the Chrysler Museum in Provincetown, Massachusetts. In 1970, Thompson's work was featured in the African-American Artist exhibition at the Boston Museum of Fine Arts. Notable works include *Ascension to the Heavens; Untitled Diptych; The Dentist* (1963); and *Expulsion and Nativity* (1964).

## James VanDerZee (1886-1983)
*Photographer*

James VanDerZee was born on June 29, 1886, in Lenox, Massachusetts. His parents had moved there from New York in the early 1880s after serving as maid and butler to Ulysses S. Grant, who then resided on 34th Street in New York City. The second of six children, James grew up in a family filled with creative people. Everybody painted, drew, or played an instrument, so it was not considered out of the ordinary when, upon receiving a camera in 1900, VanDerZee became interested in photography.

By 1906 VanDerZee had moved to New York, married, and took odd jobs to support his growing family. In 1907, he moved to Phoetus, Virginia, where he worked in the dining room of the Hotel Chamberlin in Old Point Comfort, Virginia. During this time he also worked as a photographer on a part-time basis. In 1909, he returned to New York.

By 1915, VanDerZee had his first photography job as assistant in a small concession in the Gertz Department Store in Newark, New Jersey. With the money he saved from this job he was able to open his own studio in 1916, on 135th Street. World War I had begun and many young

James Van Der Zee

soldiers came to the studio to have their pictures taken. Over the course of a half-century, James VanDerZee would record the visual history of Harlem. His subjects included Marcus Garvey, Sweet Daddy Grace, Father Divine, Joe Louis, Madame Walker, and many other famous African Americans.

In 1969, the exhibition "Harlem On My Mind," produced by Thomas Hoving, then director of the Metropolitan Museum of Art, brought James VanDerZee international recognition. He died in 1983.

## Laura Wheeler Waring (1887-1948)
*Painter*

Born in 1887 in Hartford, Connecticut, this portrait painter and illustrator received her first training at the Pennsylvania Academy of Fine Arts, where she studied for six years. In 1914, she won the Cresson Memorial Scholarship, which enabled her to continue her studies at the Academie de la Grande Chaumiere in Paris.

Waring returned to the United States as an art instructor at Cheyney State Teachers College in Pennsylvania, eventually becoming head of the art department there. Her work, particularly portraiture, has been exhibited at several leading American art galleries. In 1927,

she received the Harmon Award for achievement in fine art. With Betsy Graves Reyneau, Waring completed a set of twenty-four re-paintings of a variety of their works titled *Portraits of Outstanding Americans of Negro Origin* for the Harmon Foundation in the 1940s.

Waring was also the director in charge of the black art exhibits at the Philadelphia Exposition in 1926 and was a member of the national advisory board of Art Movements, Inc. She died in 1948. Notable works include: *Alonzo Aden; W.E. Burghardt DuBois; James Weldon Johnson;* and *Mother and Daughter*

## Carrie Mae Weems (1953- )
*Photographer, Conceptual Artist*

Carrie Mae Weems was born in Portland, Oregon, in 1953, and went to California Institute of the Arts (B.F.A., 1981) and the University of California at San Diego (M.F.A., 1984). She received an M.A. in African-American Folklore from the University of Carlifornia at Berkeley.

A young artist who explores stereotypes, especially those of black women, Weems has exhibited widely in the last few years. Formerly a photo documentarian, Weems also teaches film-making and photography at Hampshire College in Amherst, Massachusetts. Her new works are "about race, gender, class and kinship."

She has exhibited at the Rhode Island School of Design, and Wadsworth Atheneum, Hartford, Connecticut. Notable works include *Mirror, Mirror; Black Woman With Chicken; High Yella Girl; Colored People; Family Pictures and Stories;* and *Ain't Jokin'.*

## Edward T. Welburn (1950- )
*Automobile Designer*

Chief designer of automobiles at the Oldsmobile Studio for General Motors, Edward T. Welburn had one of the outstanding car designs on the market with the 1992 Achieva model. Welburn was born on December 14, 1950 and graduated with a bachelor of fine arts degree from Howard University in 1972. He is also a graduate of the Skip/Barber School for Auto Race Drivers.

Welburn began his career with the GM Design Staff as a creative designer in 1972, advancing to the positions of senior creative designer and assistant chief designer. While a member of the GM Design Staff, he designed the Cutlass Supreme, Cutlass Ciera, and the Oldsmobile Calais. In 1989, he moved to the Oldsmobile Studio as chief designer.

In 1985, the Indianapolis 500 pace car was designed by a team on which Welburn served. He was named Alumni of the Year in 1989 by the Howard University Student Association. Welburn won the Industrial De-

1993 Oldsmobile *Achieva SC,* Edward Welburn.

signers Society of America Award for Design Excellence for his part in the design for *Oldsmobile Aerotech* in 1992.

Welburn is a member of The Cabinet and the Founders Society of the Detroit Institute of Arts.

### James Lesesne Wells (1902-1993)
*Artist*

Born on November 2, 1902, in Atlanta, James Lesesne Wells was a pioneer of modern American printmaking and the inspiration for a generation of black artists. After graduating from high school, Wells lived with relatives in New York City and worked for two years to earn money for college. Meanwhile, he studied drawing at the National Academy of Design for one term from 1918 to 1919. Wells spend one year at Lincoln University before transferring to Teachers College at Columbia University in 1923 and earning a B.S. in 1927. He received an MS from Columbia in 1938.

Immediately after earning his undergraduate degree, Wells created black print illustrations for magazines. He also made connections with art dealer and gallery-owner J. D. Neumann, who included Wells's work in a 1929 exhibition of "International Modernists." These projects captured the attention of Howard University's James V. Herring, who invited Wells to join the prestigious school's art faculty that year. Thus began a 39-year career at the university, during which Wells established a graphics arts department and taught several soon to be well-known artists, including Charles Alston and Jacob Lawrence. Wells taught clay modeling, ceramics, sculpture, metals, and block printing.

During the Great Depression, Wells devoted himself to printmaking; his prints from this period involved African American history and industrial themes. The art form began rising to the level of admiration later enjoyed by painting in the 1970s. Despite a lack of critical recognition, Wells's work won numerous art competitions throughout the 1930s, including the George E. Haynes Prize in 1933. At this time, he also served as the director of a summer art workshop that preceded the Harlem Community Art Center.

After World War II, Wells spent a sabbatical year working at Stanley Hayter's famous Atelier 17, then the most innovative center of etching and printmaking in the United States. Wells continued to teach and win awards for his artwork in the 1950s and 1960s. He moved the Washington, DC, and joined his brother-in-law Eugene Davidson, president of the local NAACP, in segregation protests. The harassment Wells suffered as a result of his outspokenness—a cross was burned in his yard in 1957—may have inspired the religious themes of much of his work from the era. He took first prize in a religious art exhibition sponsored by the Smithsonian in 1958.

After retiring from Howard in 1968, Wells continued to paint and make prints in the 1980s. In 1980, then-U.S. president Jimmy Carter bestowed Wells with a presidential citation for lifelong contributions to American art. Four years later, Washington, DC had a "James L. Wells Day." Designated a "Living Legend" by the National Black Arts Festival in 1991, Wells's work was featured in a retrospective exhibition by the Harmon Foundation, which had recognized him for his artwork as early as 1916, when he took a first prize in painting and second prize in woodworking. He died of congestive heart failure at the age of 90.

## Charles White (1918-1979)
*Painter*

White was an eminent exponent of social art. The subject matter of his paintings were the notable achievements of famous American blacks, as well as the suffering of the lowly and anonymous.

White was born in 1918 in Chicago and was influenced as a young boy by Alain Locke's critical review of the Harlem Renaissance, *The New Negro*. At the age of twenty-three, White won a Rosenwald Fellowship which enabled him to work in the South for two years, during which time he painted a celebrated mural depicting the black's contribution to American democracy. It is now the property of the Hampton Institute in Virginia.

The bulk of White's work is done in black-and-white, a symbolic motif which he felt gave him the widest possible purview. Notable works include *Let's Walk Together; Frederick Douglass Lives Again; Women;* and *Gospel Singer*.

## Paul Revere Williams (1894-1980)
*Architect*

Williams was born in Los Angeles, California, on February 18, 1894, and graduated from the University of California at Los Angeles. He later attended the Beaux Arts Institute of Design in Paris; he received honorary degrees from Howard, Lincoln, and Atlanta Universities as well as Hampton Institute.

Williams became a certified architect in 1915 and after working for Reginald Johnson and John Austin, distinguished designers and architects, he opened his own firm in 1923. Williams was known as America's

"architect to the stars" (*African Architects in Current Practice*, edited by Jack Travis, 1991). Williams designed some four hundred homes and a total of 3,000 buildings including homes for Cary Grant, Barbara Stanwyk, William Holden, Frank Sinatra, Betty Grable, Bill "Bojangles" Robinson, and Bert Lahr.

In 1926 he was the first black to become a member of the American Institute of Architects. He served on the National Monument Commission, an appointee of President Calvin Coolidge. Notable works include *Los Angeles County Airport; Palm Springs Tennis Club;* and *Saks Fifth Avenue at Beverly Hills*. He died on January 23, 1980.

## William T. Williams (1942- )
*Painter*

William T. Williams was born in Cross Creek, North Carolina, on July 17, 1942. He received his bachelor of fine arts degree from Pratt Institute in 1966 and his master of fine arts from Yale University in 1968.

In 1970, Williams taught painting classes at Pratt Institute and at the School of Fine Arts. Since 1971, he has been a professor of art at City University of New York, Brooklyn College. He also served as a visiting professor of art at Virginia Commonwealth University.

Critics have compared Williams' work more to Joseph Albers and the Bauhaus traditions from Europe than to his own statements about his work's relationships to the city, architecture, tension, things in flux, order from disorder, and to Africa and the United States.

Williams has been the recipient of several awards. In 1992, the Studio Museum in Harlem presented him with its Annual Award for Lifetime Achievement. He was also awarded the Mid-Atlantic Foundation Fellowship in 1994.

Exhibitions of Williams's work have been presented at, among others, The Studio Museum in Harlem, Wadsworth Atheneum, Art Institute of Chicago, and The Whitney Museum of American Art. Notable works include *Elbert Jackson L.A.M.F. Port II; Big Red for N.C.;* and *Buttermilk*.

## John Wilson (1922- )
*Painter, Printmaker*

Born in Boston on April 14, 1922, John Wilson studied at the Boston Museum of Fine Arts; Fernand Leger School, Paris; The Institute Politecnico, Mexico City; and the Escuela de las Artes del Libro, Mexico City. In 1947, Wilson received a bachelor's degree from Tufts University. He has been a teacher at Boston Museum, Pratt Institute, and Boston University.

William T. Williams

His numerous exhibits include the Albany Institute; the Library of Congress National (and International) Print Exhibit(s); Smith College; Carnegie Institute; and the American International College, Springfield, Massachusetts. His work is represented in the collections of the Museum of Modern Art; Schomburg Collection; Department of Fine Arts, French Government; Atlanta University; and Bezalel Museum, Jerusalem. Notable works include *Roxbury Landscape* (oil, 1944); *Trabajador* (print, 1951); and *Child with Father* (graphic, 1969).

Wilson created the Dr. Martin Luther King Jr. Monument in Buffalo, New York in 1983 and the Dr. Martin Luther King Jr. Commemorative Statue at the U.S. Capitol in Washington, D.C. In 1987, he completed the monument "Eternal Presence," which resides at the Museum of the National Center of Afro-American Artists, Boston, Massachusetts.

## Hale Woodruff (1900-1979)
### *Painter, Muralist*

Hale Woodruff's paintings were largely modernist landscapes and formal abstractions, but he has also painted rural Georgia scenes evocative of the "red clay" country. Born in Cairo, Illinois, in 1900, he graduated from the John Herron Art Institute in Indianapolis. Encouraged by a bronze award in the 1926 Harmon Foundation competition, Woodruff went to Paris to study at both the Academie Scandinave and the Academie Moderne, as well as with Henry Ossawa Tanner.

In 1931, he became art instructor at Atlanta University and five years later accepted a similar post at New York University. In 1939, he was commissioned by Talladega College to do *The Amistad Murals*, an episodic depiction of a slave revolt.

In 1948, Woodruff teamed with Charles Alston to work on the Golden State Mutual Life Insurance Company Murals in California, which presented the contribution of African Americans to the history of the development of California. Woodruff's last mural assignment came in 1950 when he developed the series of mural panels for Atlanta University entitled "The Art of the Negro."

Hale Woodruff died in 1979 after creating a body of work with styles that moved from the figurative, to the Impressionistic period of his Paris experience, to a brief exploration of the cubist visual concepts, to moving comfortably into the abstract style. With all of these stylistic developments, Hale Woodruff also became one of America's strongest mural painters. Notable works include: *Ancestral Remedies; The Little Boy*; and *The Amistad Murals.*

## Richard Yarde (1939- )
*Painter*

Richard Yarde was born in Boston, Massachusetts, on October 29, 1939. He studied at the School of the Museum of Fine Arts and at Boston University, where he received a B.F.A. in 1962 and an M.F.A. in 1964. He has taught at Boston University, Wellesley College, Amherst College, Massachusetts College of Art, Mount Holyoke College, and the University of Massachusetts.

Yarde has received numerous awards for his art, including Yaddo fellowships in 1964, 1966, and 1970, McDowell Colony awards in 1968 and 1970, and the Blanche E. Colman Award in 1970.

The Boston Museum of Fine Arts, Wadsworth Atheneum, Rose Art Museum, National Museum of African-American Artists, and Studio Museum in Harlem have all exhibited his works. He has held one-person shows at numerous galleries and universities. His works are in many collections, such as the Wadsworth Atheneum in Hartford, Connecticut. Notable works include *The Stoop, Passage Edgar and I, The Corner, Paul Robeson as Emperor Jones, Head and Hands I, Josephine's Baffle Triptych,* and *Richard's Cards.*

## ◆ MUSEUMS AND GALLERIES

The 1960s was an era which saw a great many radical changes in both the social and the cultural aspects of the United States. African Americans throughout the country were demanding political, social, and cultural recognition. No longer satisfied with the limited support of such philanthropic organizations as the Harmon Foundation, these artists looked for alternative forms of exposure. The result of their demands was an outpouring of galleries, community art centers, and community art galleries.

In New York City, the Acts of Art Gallery was established in 1969 by Nigel Jackson, a former artist turned administrator, and provided exhibition space for contemporary artists. A non-profit organization, the gallery was dedicated to promoting these artists and providing them with the opportunity to attract collectors interested in their work. The gallery exhibitions included the works of such artists as James Denmark, Dinga McCannon, Frank Wimberly, Ann Tanksley, Don Robertson, Lloyd Toomes, Lois Mailou Jones, Jo Butler, Robert Threadgill, and Faith Ringgold. Largely because of the politically volatility of the period, but also because of the gallery's aggressive action policy, in 1971 the Acts of Art Gallery

became the center for the controversial "Whitney Rebuttal Show."

The Studio Museum in Harlem began in 1969 under the direction of Edward Spriggs. Set up as a place for artists who needed working space, it eventually branched out into a cultural center where the artists could display their work, meet other artists and art supporters, and hold concerts, panel discussions, and other art related activities. The Studio Museum in Harlem had become by 1972, the cultural center of New York for the African-American community. Important retrospectives were presented including the works of Palmer Hayden, Hale Woodruff, Beauford Delaney, Bob Thompson, and James VanDerZee.

Also, the Lewis H. Michaux Book Fair took place for three years at the Studio Museum (1976-1979) under the direction of special program coordinator David Jackson. Lewis Michaux was a legend in the world of book selling, because he established a bookstore on 125th Street and Lenox Avenue which became a landmark for people from around the world who were interested in literature of or about African Americans, Africans, Caribbeans, and South Americans. The store opened in 1930 and continued to exist for the next forty-four years. It was called The National Memorial African Book Store.

While under the directorship of Edward Spriggs, the museum began the special holiday celebration Kwanzaa, a time during which the museum opened its doors to the entire neighborhood to share in dancing, singing, and eating with the artists. Dancer Chuck Davis would come to lead off the dancing, ending with the whole room filled with guests in the center of the floor dancing.

By 1980, the museum had grown out of its second floor loft space and moved into an old office building on 125th Street and 7th Avenue. The new space provided the museum with additional exhibition galleries, larger office areas, and space for its growing collection and the artist-in-residence program. In 1977, during this period of growth for the museum, a new director, Mary Campell Schmidt, took over the operations of the institution. In 1988, she was appointed commissioner of the Department of Cultural Affairs in New York. In January 1988, the Museum's deputy director Kinshasha Holman Conwill, wife of artist Houston Conwill, was named director. The Studio Museum has continued to expand its audience, exhibitions, and programs.

Just Above Midtown Gallery was the first organization to move into the gallery district in New York City. Established in 1976, it set up its operation base in a modest space on 57th Street in midtown Manhattan. Under the directorship of Linda Bryant, the organization

Two artists work with clay.

presented many of the leading contemporary artists of the 1970s including David Hammons, Senga Nengudi, Randy Williams, and Howardena Pindell. Placing the African American artists in direct competition with mainstream American artists was the objective of Bryant, her board, and her artists. No longer could art critics refuse to review these works because they could not get to Harlem, Queens, or Brooklyn. But the cost of running a gallery took its toll and in order to continue operations Bryant was forced to turn the gallery into a non-profit organization, adding educational programs for young artists, music concerts, performance programs, slide reviews and lectures.

By the end of 1979, Just Above Midtown moved from 57th Street to a larger space on Franklin Street in the Tribeca section of New York, changed its name to the Just Above Midtown/Downtown Alternative Art Center, and opened its doors to vanguard, new-wave artists.

The Schomburg Center for Research in Black Culture of the New York Public Library is one of the most widely used research facilities in the world and is devoted to the preservation of materials on black life. The Center's collections first won international acclaim in 1926 when the personal collection of the distinguished black scholar and bibliophile, Arthur A. Schomburg, was added to the Division of Negro Literature, History and Prints of the 135th Street Branch of the New York Public Library. Schomburg's collection included over 5,000 volumes, 3,000 manuscripts, 2,000 etchings and paintings, and several thousand pamphlets. He served as the curator in the Negro Division from 1932 until his death in 1938. Renamed in his honor in 1940, the collection grew steadily through the years. In 1972, it was designated as one of the Research Libraries of the New York Public Library and became The Schomburg Center for Research in Black Culture. Today, the Schomburg Center is the guardian of collections including over five million items, and provides services and programs for constituents from the United States and abroad.

The Cinque Gallery, another New York gallery, was the concept of three distinguished artists— Romare Bearden, Norman Lewis, and Ernest Crichlow. The gallery, which opened in 1969, was named after the famous African Joseph Cinque, who in 1839 led a successful revolt aboard the slave ship *Amistad*, won his freedom, and returned to Africa. It was the wish of Bearden, Crichlow, and Lewis to establish an exhibition space specifically for young African-American artists who needed to learn the process of being a professional artist. However, by the end of the 1970s it was decided that the gallery doors be opened to all new and emerging artists regardless of age.

The Weusi Ya Nambe Yasana Gallery, also in New York, was one of the few cooperative community galleries to come out of the late 1960s. Housed in a brownstone in Harlem, the gallery was established to present the art work of its members. Headed by Ademola Olagebefola, the other members included Otto Neals, Kay Brown, and Jean Taylor.

Genesis II was one of the alternative profit-making galleries that emerged out of the 1960s. Like many of its kind, the gallery functioned out of the dealer's apartment to cover the cost of overhead expenses. The dealer would invite his or her clients to come view the works in a living environment, so that they might better appreciate the art work. Also, at these gatherings, clients had the opportunity to meet other collectors as well as meet the artist and talk in detail about the work. The concept proved valuable for many African-American artists who needed to develop supporting collectors and to establish a real market for their work.

The New Muse Community Museum in Brooklyn began in the late 1960s, offering the African-American Brooklyn community the same kinds of art programs presented at the Studio Museum. In addition to the art programs, the New Muse also offered lessons in jazz with bassist Reggie Workman, who headed the program.

The Store Front Museum in Queens was established to satisfy the artistic needs of its community. Offering art classes in painting and drawing, its focus leaned more toward the performing arts—dancing and drama.

The Benin Gallery opened its doors in 1976. Director Edward Sherman operated the gallery as a non-profit, tax exempt corporation so that the public in Harlem would have a gallery to call its own. Located at 2366 Adam Clayton Powell, Jr., Boulevard in the St. Nicholas Historic District, the gallery focused on photography.

The Hatch-Billops Studio began in New York in 1968 as an organization designed to present multi-ethnic plays, performances and exhibitions. By 1973, the studio began collecting third world memorabilia. Based on the understanding that no one will protect your history or present your history the way you do, the collection became incorporated in 1975. Camille Billops and her husband Jim Hatch began taping the history of some black theater artists. Today the collection houses more than six hundred taped interviews and panel and media events about or by artists. There are well over 10,000 slides and 3,000 books, clippings, files, letters, memorabilia, programs, photographs, drawings, scrapbooks, and videotapes. This collection is one of the most complete reference centers focusing on African-American art—visual, literary, and theatrical. It is a collection available to artists, scholars, and students.

Meanwhile, galleries and museums for African-American artists were also developing in other parts of the country. In Los Angeles, Samella Lewis, a painter, art historian, and professor at Claremont College, founded the Contemporary Craft Center. Alonzo and Dale Davis established and directed the Brockman Galleries Productions, a nonprofit gallery showing contemporary African-American art and the work of other minority artists.

In Chicago, the Du Sable Museum was established in 1961 under the directorship of Margaret Burroughs to provide the South Side community with an art center. The museum grew out of an art center that was established under the Work-Progress Administration during the Depression. Some of the artists presented there include Charles White, Elizabeth Catlett, Gordon Parks, Rex Gorleigh, William McBride, Jr., and Eldzier Cortor.

In Boston, the museum of the National Center of Afro-American Artists, begun in 1969 under the curatorship of Edmond Barry Gaither, is a multi-media art center featuring dance, theater, visual arts, film, and educational programs.

In Washington, DC, the National Museum of African Art, formerly known as the Frederick Douglass Institute, was established in 1964 and until 1984 existed in a Victorian row house on Capitol Hill, nestled in the shadow of the United States Supreme Court. The house had belonged to Frederick Douglass, a former slave who became an advisor to President Lincoln. In 1984, the museum was moved to the Smithsonian Institute and the house was singularly devoted to early African-American art and memorabilia and continues to be known as the Frederick Douglass Institute. The museum was established to promote and familiarize Americans with the artistic heritage of Africa; today it includes a large and extensive collection devoted exclusively to African art and culture. One of the largest and most diverse of its kind in the United States, the collection consists of some 65,000 works including traditional carvings, musical instruments, and textiles with particular emphasis on works from Nigeria, Ghana, Liberia, the Ivory Coast, and Zaire. In the transition, the Smithsonian has also acquired the Eliot Elisofon Photographic Archives, which contains some 150,000 slides and motion pictures available to the public.

The Smith-Mason Gallery Museum located in Washington, DC is a four-story Victorian house established in 1968 to present its permanent collection, which features paintings, sculptures and graphics of African-American and Caribbean artists. The works remain on permanent display.

## Alabama

**George Washington Carver Museum**
1212 Old Montgomery Rd.
PO Drawer 10
Tuskegee Institute, AL 36087-0010
(205) 727-6390
Fax:(205) 727-4597

## California

**San Francisco African American Historical Society**
Fort Mason Center Bldg. C, No. 165
San Francisco, CA 94123
(415) 441-0640

**Brockman Gallery**
4334 Degnan Boulevard
Los Angeles, CA 90008
(213) 294-3766

**California Afro-American Museum**
600 State Drive; Exposition Park
Los Angeles, CA 90037
(213) 744-7432
Fax:(213)744-2050

**Ebony Museum of Art**
30 Jack Londo Boulevard, Ste. 209
Oakland, CA 94607
(415) 658-3158

**Museum of African-American Art**
4005 Crenshaw Boulevard, 3rd Floor
Los Angeles, CA 90008
(213) 294-7071

## Colorado

**Black American West Museum and Heritage Center**
3091 California St.
Denver, CO 80207
(303) 292-2566

## Connecticut

**Amistad Foundation and Gallery of African-American Art, Wadsworth Atheneum**
600 Main St.
Hartford, CT 06103
(203) 278-2670

**Artists, Collective, Inc.**
35 Clark St.
Hartford, CT 06120
(203) 527-3205

**Connecticut Afro-American Historical Society**
444 Orchard St.
New Haven, CT 06511

**CRT's Craftery Gallery**
1445 Main St.
Hartford, CT 06120
(203) 280-0170

## Delaware

**Afro-American Historical Society of Delaware**
512 E. 4th St.
Wilmington, DE 19801
(302) 984-1421

## District of Columbia

**Anacostia Museum**
1901 Fort Place SE
Washington, DC 20020
(202) 287-3306
Fax:(202) 287-3183

**Bethune Museum-Archives, National Historic Society**
1318 Vermont Ave. NW
Washington, DC 20005
(202) 332-1233
Fax:(202) 332-6319

**Black Film Institute, University of the District of Columbia**
Carnegie Building
8th St. and Mt. Vernon Pl. NW
Washington, DC 20001
(202) 727-2396

**Evans-Tibbs Collection**
1910 Vermont Ave., NW
Washington, DC 20001
(202) 234-8164

**Howard University Gallery of Art**
2455 6th St., NW
Washington, DC 20059
(202) 806-7070
Fax:(202) 806-6503

**Sign of the Times Cultural Workshop and Gallery, Inc.**
605 56th St., NE
Washington, DC 20019
(202) 399-3400

**Smithsonian Institute, National Museum of African Art**
950 Independence Ave., SW
Washington, DC 20560
(202) 357-4600
Fax:(202) 357-4879

## Florida

**Afro-Carib American Cultural Center**
4511 N.W. 25th Pl.
Lauderhill, FL 33313
(305) 739-1015

**Appleton Museum of Art/The Appleton Cultural Center**
4333 E. Silver Springs Boulevard
Ocala, FL 32670

**Black Archives Research Center and Museum, Florida A and M University**
c/o Florida A and M University
PO Box 809
Tallahassee, FL 32307
(904) 599-3020

**Black Heritage Museum**
PO Box 570327
Miami, FL 33257-0327
(305) 252-3535

**Gallery Antiqua**
5138 Biscayne Boulevard
Miami, FL 33137
(305) 759-5355

## Georgia

**Apex Museum**
135 Auburn Ave., NE
Atlanta, GA 30303
(404) 521-3739

**Hammonds House Galleries**
503 Peeples St., SW
Atlanta, GA 30310
(404) 752-8730

**Herndon Home**
587 University Pl. NW
Atlanta, GA 30314
(404) 581-9613

**King-Tisdell Cottage of Black History Museum**
502 E. Harris St.
Savannah, GA 31401
(912) 234-8000

**Martin Luther King Jr. Center, Cultural Affairs Program**
449 Auburn Ave., NE
Atlanta, GA 30312
(404) 524-1956

**McIntosh Gallery**
One Virginia Hill
587 Virginia Ave.
Atlanta, GA 30306
(404) 892-4023

**National Black Arts Festival**
70 Fairlie St., NW, Ste. 250
Atlanta, GA 30303
(404) 730-7315

**Uncle Remus Museum**
PO Box 184
Eatonton, GA 31024
(404) 485-6856

**US National Park Service, Martin Luther King Jr. National Historic Site and Preservation District**
522 Auburn Ave., NE
Atlanta, GA 30312
(404) 331-5190

## Illinois

**Afro-American Arts Alliance of Chicago**
7558 S. Chicago Ave.
Chicago, IL 60619
(312) 288-5100

**Afro-American Genealogical and Historical Society, Du Sable Museum of African American History**
740 E. 56th Place
Chicago, IL 60637
(312) 947-0600

**Isobel Neal Gallery Ltd.**
200 W. Superior
Chicago, IL 60610
(312) 944-1570

## Indiana

**Indiana University Art Museum**
Bloomington, IN 47405
(812) 855-5445
Fax:(812) 855-1023

## Kansas

**First National Black Historical Society of Kansas**
601 N. Water
Wichita, KS 67201
(316) 262-7651

## Maryland

**Baltimore's Black American Museum**
1765 Carswell St.
Baltimore, MD 21218
(301) 243-9600

**Great Blacks in Wax Museum**
1601-03 E. North Ave.
Baltimore, MD 21213
(410) 563-3404
Fax:(410) 675-5040

**Maryland Museum of African Art**
5430 Vantage Point Rd.
Columbia, MD 21044-0105
(410) 730-7105
Fax:(410) 715-3047

## Massachusetts

**Cousens-Rose Gallery**
Circuit Ave.
Oak Bluffs, Martha's Vineyard, MA 02568

**Liz Harris Gallery**
711 Atlantic Ave.
Boston, MA 02111
(617) 338-1315

**National Center of Afro-American Artists**
300 Walnut Ave.
Boston, MA 02119
(617) 442-8614

**Wendell Street Gallery**
17 Wendel St.
Cambridge, MA 02138
(617) 864-9294

## Michigan

**Detroit Black Arts Alliance**
13217 Livernois
Detroit, MI 48238-3162
(313) 931-3427

**Museum of African-American History**
301 Frederick Douglass St.
Detroit, MI 48202
(313) 833-9800
Fax:(313) 832-7933

**G.R. N'namdi Gallery**
161 Townsend
Birmingham, MI 48009
(313) 642-2700

**Your Heritage House**
110 E. Ferry
Detroit, MI 48202
(313) 871-1667

## Minnesota

**Pillsbury House/Cultural Arts**
3501 Chicago Ave. S.
Minneapolis, MN 55407
(612) 824-0708

## Mississippi

**Smith Robertson Museum and Cultural Center**
PO Box 3259
Jackson, MS 39207
(601) 960-2070

## Missouri

**Black Archives of Mid-America**
2033 Vine St.
Kansas City, MO 64108
(816) 483-1300
Fax:(816) 483-1341

**Vaughn Cultural Center**
1408 N. Kings Highway, Ste. 205
St. Louis, MO 63113
(314) 361-0111

## Nebraska

**Great Plains Black Museum**
2213 Lake St.
Omaha, NE 68110
(402) 345-2212

## New Jersey

**African Art Museum of the S.M.A. Fathers**
23 Bliss Ave.
Tenafly, NJ 07670
(201) 567-0450

**Merabash Museum**
PO Box 752
Willingboro, NJ 08046

**Newark Museum**
49 Washington St.
Newark, NJ 07101-0540
(201) 596-6550
Fax:(201) 642-0459

## New York

**African-American Cultural Center of Buffalo**
350 Masten Ave.
Buffalo, NY 14209
(716) 884-2013

**African-American Culture and Arts Network**
2090 Adam Clayton Powell, Jr. Boulevard
New York, NY 10027
(212) 749-4408

**African-American Institute Museum**
833 United Nations Plaza
New York, NY 10017
(212) 949-5666
Fax:(212) 682-6174

**African American Museum of Nassau County**
110 Franklin St.
Hempstead, NY 11550

**Aunt Len's Doll and Toy House Inc.**
6 Hamilton Terrace
New York, NY 10031
(212) 281-4143

**Bedford-Stuyvesant Restoration Center for Arts and Culture**
1368 Fulton, Ste. 4G
Brooklyn, NY 11216
(718) 636-6948

**Black Fashion Museum**
157 W. 126 St.
New York, NY 10027
(212) 666-1320

**Black Filmmaker Foundation**
Tribeca Film Center
375 Greenwich St., Ste. 600
New York, NY 10013
(212) 941-3944
Fax:(212) 941-3943

**Black Spectrum Theater Co.**
119 Roy Wilkens Park
Jamaica, NY 11434
(718) 723-1800

**Center for African Art**
52-54 E. 68th St.
New York, NY 10021
(212) 861-1200

**Cinque Gallery**
560 Broadway
New York, NY 10012
(212) 966-3464

**Community Folk Art Gallery**
2223 Genessee St.
Syracuse, NY 13210
(315) 424-8487

**Genesis II Museum of International Black Culture**
509 Cathedral Parkway
New York, NY 10025
(212) 666-7222

**Grinnell Gallery**
800 Riverside Dr.
New York, NY 10032
(212) 927-7941

**Harlem Cultural Council**
215 W. 125th St.
New York, NY 10027
(212) 316-6277

**Harlem Institute of Fashion**
157 W. 126th St.
New York, NY 10027
(212) 666-1320

**Harlem School of the Arts**
645 St. Nicholas Ave.
New York, NY 10030
(212) 926-4100

**Hatch-Billops Collection, Inc.**
491 Broadway
New York, NY 10012
(212) 966-3231

**International Agency for Minority Artists Affairs Inc.**
352 W. 71st St.
New York, NY 10023
(212) 873-5040

**June Kelly Gallery**
591 Broadway, 3rd Fl.
New York, NY 10012
(212) 226-1660

**Museum of African and African-American Art and Antiquities**
11 E. Utica St.
Buffalo, NY 14209
(716) 882-7676

**New Muse Community Museum of Brooklyn**
1530 Bedford Ave.
Brooklyn, NY 11216
(718) 774-2900

**Studio Museum in Harlem**
144 W. 125th St.
New York, NY 10027
(212) 864-4500
Fax:(212) 666-5753

**"Where We At" Black Women Artists**
1452 Bedford Ave.
Brooklyn, NY 11216
(718) 398-3871

## North Carolina

**African Heritage Center**
North Carolina A and T State University
Greensboro, NC 27411
(919) 334-7874

**African-American Atelier**
Greensboro Cultural Center
200 N. Davie St.
Greensboro, NC 27401
(919) 333-6885

**Afro-American Cultural Center**
401 N. Meyers St.
Spirit Square
Charlotte, NC 28202

**AM Studio**
1610 E. 14th St.
Winston Salem, NC 27105
(919) 725-4959

**Biggers Art Sales Traveling Gallery**
1404 N. Oakwood St.
Gastonia, NC 28052
(704) 867-4525

**Black Artists Guild**
400 N. Queen St.
P.O. Box 2162
Kinston, NC 28501
(919) 523-0003

**H C Taylor Gallery**
North Carolina A and T State University
Greensboro, NC 27411
(919) 334-7784

**Harambee Arts Festival**
Lenoir Recreation Department
PO Box 958
c/o Viewmont Community Center
Lenoir, NC 28645
(704) 754-3278

**Huff's Art Studio**
2846 Patterson Ave.
Winston-Salem, NC 27105
(919) 724-7581

**NCCU Art Museum**
PO Box 19555
Durham, NC 27707
(919) 560-6211
Fax:(919) 560-5012

**St. Augustine's College Art Gallery**
Department of Art
Saint Augustine's College
Raleigh, NC 27611
(919) 828-4451

**Selma Burke Gallery**
Winston-Salem State University
Winston-Salem, NC 27110

**Shaw University Art Gallery**
Shaw University Dept. of Art
Raleigh, NC 27602
(919) 755-4845

**Ubiquitous Gallery**
PO Box 34606
Charlotte, NC 28234-4606
(704) 376-6944

**Warehouse Arts**
862 W. 4th St.
Winston-Salem, NC 27101-2516
(919) 723-4800

**Winston-Salem State University Diggs**
601 Martin Luther King, Jr. Dr.
Winston-Salem, NC 27110
(919) 750-2458

**Young Men's Institute Cultural Center**
PO Box 7301
Asheville, NC 28802
(704) 252-4614

**Ohio**

**African American Museum**
1765 Crawford Rd.
Cleveland, OH 44106
(216) 791-1700

**Afro-American Cultural Center**
Cleveland State University
Black Studies Program
2121 Euclid Ave., UC 103
Cleveland, OH 44115
(216) 687-3655

**Art for Community Expressions**
772 N. High St.
Columbus, OH 43215
(614) 252-3036

**Black Historical Museum of Fashion Dolls, National Association of Fashion and Accessory Designers**
2180 E. 93rd St.
Cleveland, OH 44106
(216) 231-0375

**Cincinnati Art Museum**
Eden Park
Cincinnati, OH 45202-1596
(513) 721-5204
Fax:(513) 721-0129

**Karamu House**
2355 E. 89th St.
Cleveland, OH 44106
(216) 795-7070

**Malcolm Brown Gallery**
20100 Chagrin Boulevard
Shaker Heights, Ohio 44122
(216) 751-2955

**National Afro-American Museum and Cultural Center**
1350 Brush Row Rd.
PO Box 578
Wilberforce, OH 45384
(513) 376-4944
Fax: (513) 376-2007

**National Conference of Artists**
1624 Grand Ave.
Dayton, OH 45407
(513) 278-6793

**Resident Art and Humanities Consortium**
1515 Linn St.
Cincinnati, OH 45214
(513) 381-0645

**Watkins Academy Museum of Cultural Arts**
724 Mineola Ave.
Akron, OH 44320
(216) 864-0673

## Oklahoma

**Kirkpatrick Center Museum Complex**
2100 N.E. 52nd
Oklahoma City, OK 73111
(405) 427-5461

**NTU Art Association**
2100 N.E. 52nd St.
Oklahoma City, OK 73111
(405) 424-7760

**Theater North**
PO Box 6255
Tulsa, OK 74148
(918) 587-8937

## Pennsylvania

**Africamerica Festival**
2247 N. Broad
Philadelphia, PA 19132
(215) 232-2900

**African American Heritage, Inc.**
4601 Market St.
Philadelphia, PA 19139
(215) 748-7817

**African Cultural Art Forum**
237 S. 60th Street
Philadelphia, PA 19139
(215) 476-0680

**Afro-American Historical and Cultural Museum**
701 Arch St.
Philadelphia, PA 19106
(215) 574-0380

**Minority Arts Resource Council**
1421 W. Girard Ave.
Philadelphia, PA 19130
(215) 236-2688

## Rhode Island

**Rhode Island Black Heritage Society**
1 Hilton St.
Providence, RI 02905
(401) 751-3490

## South Carolina

**Avery Research Center for Afro-American History and Culture**
125 Bull St.
College of Charleston
Charleston, SC 29424
(803) 792-5742

**I.P. Stanback Museum and Planetarium**
South Carolina State College
300 College St., NE
Orangeburg, SC 29117
(803) 536-7174

**Mann-Simons Cottage: Museum of African-American Culture**
1403 Richland St.
Columbia, SC 29201
(803) 252-1770

**The Rice Museum**
Intersection of Front and Screven Sts.
PO Box 902
Georgetown, SC 29442
(803) 546-7423
Fax:(803) 533-3624

## South Dakota

**Black History Museum**
508 Cedar St.
Yankton, SD 57078

## Tennessee

**Black Cultural Exchange Center**
1927 Dandridge Ave.
Knoxville, TN 37915
(615) 524-8461

**Blues City Cultural Center**
415 S. Main
Memphis, TN 38114
(901) 525-3031

**Carl Van Vechten Gallery of Fine Arts**
Fisk University
Dr D B Todd Boulevard and Jackson St. N.
Nashville, TN 37203
(615) 329-8543

**Chattanooga African American Museum**
200 E. Martin Luther King, Jr. Boulevard
Chattanooga, TN 37203
(615) 267-1076
Fax:(615)267-1076

**Memphis Black Arts Alliance**
985 S. Bellevue Boulevard
Memphis, TN 38174
(901) 948-9522

**Tennessee State University Institute for African Affairs**
Tennessee State University
PO Box 828
Nashville, TN 37209
(615) 320-3035

### Texas

**African American Cultural Heritage Center**
Nolan Estes Educational Plaza
3434 S.R.L. Thornton Fairway
Dallas, TX 75224
(214) 375-7530

**African American Museum**
PO Box 150153
Dallas, TX 75315
(214) 565-9026
Fax:(214) 421-8204

**Black Art Gallery**
5408 Almeda Rd.
Houston, TX 77004
(713) 529-7900

**Black Arts Alliance**
1157 Navasota St.
Austin, TX 78702
(512) 477-9660

### Utah

**Utah Museum of Fine Arts**
101 ACC
University of Utah
Salt Lake City, UT 84122
(801) 581-7332
Fax:(801) 585-5198

### Virginia

**Alexandria Black History Resource Center**
20 N. Washington St.
Alexandria, VA 22314
(703) 838-4577

**Black Historical Museum and Cultural Center**
122 W. Leigh St.
Richmond, VA 23220
(804) 780-9093

**Harrison Museum of African American Culture**
523 Harrison Ave.
Roanoke, VA 24016
(703) 345-4818

**Task Force of Historical Preservation and Minority Communities**
500 N. 3rd St.
Richmond, VA 23219
(804) 788-1709

# 25

# *Science and Technology*

# 25

# Science and Technology

◆ Early African American Inventors ◆ Early African American Scientists
◆ African Americans in Medicine ◆ African Americans in Air and Space
◆ Modern Contributions to Science and Technology ◆ Discovery Gatekeepers

**by Lorna M. Mabunda**

*America's earliest African American scientists and inventors are largely unknown—their contributions to America buried in anonymity. While Benjamin Banneker's eighteenth-century successes in timepieces and urban planning are known and applauded, numerous achievements of seventeenth- and eighteenth-century blacks in architecture, agriculture, and masonry can not be identified. While historians increasingly recognize that blacks had a significant impact on the design and construction of plantations and public building in the South and that rice farming in the Carolinas might not have been possible without blacks, the individuals who spearheaded these accomplishments remain unknown.*

## ◆ EARLY AFRICAN AMERICAN INVENTORS

Perhaps in science more than in other areas, African Americans have been afforded few sanctioned opportunities to offer contributions. However, sheer will and exceeding intelligence helped a mass of individuals bring their ideas and dreams into the light, creating and perfecting them almost as if racial barriers did not exist. The industrial revolution swept blacks along just as dramatically as it did the white population. Though not all of them became household names, African Americans have made their mark in science and technology. For example, when Alexander Graham Bell invented the telephone, he chose Lewis Latimer, a black man, to draft the plans. Previously, Latimer had been a member of the Edison Pioneers, a group of inventors who worked for Thomas Edison from 1883 to the early 1900s.

One of the earliest stars of science was Benjamin Banneker, a free black who lived in the 1700s. Considered the first black scientist, Banneker's true forte lay in the areas of mathematics and astronomy, both of which he cultivated during his friendship with an influential white Quaker neighbor. In 1754, Banneker constructed what has been considered the first clock made in the United States. Later, Banneker and the Quaker's son were selected to survey the land that evolved into Washington, DC. Thus, not only was Bannker the first black to receive a presidential appointment, he was one of the first African American civil engineers. In the early 1790s, his almanac—a year-long calendar loaded with information such as the best planting times—was published with much success. New editions were issued for a succession of years.

In 1790, the U.S. government passed the U.S. Patent Act, legislation that extended patent rights to inventors, including free blacks. Slaves would not have this right until the passage of the 14th Amendment. In one of history's most absurd bureaucratic fiats, slaves could neither be granted patents nor could they assign patents to their masters. The underlying theory was that since slaves were not citizens they could not enter into contracts with their owners or the government. As a result, the efforts of slaves were dismissed, or when accepted, credited to their masters. One can only speculate on the extent to which slaves were active in invention. For example, Joe Anderson, a slave, was believed to have played a major role in the creation of a grain harvester his master Cyrus McCormick was credited with inventing, but available records are insufficient to determine the degree to which Anderson was involved. Similarly, Benjamin Montgomery, a slave belonging to Confederate President Jefferson Davis is thought to have concocted an improved boat propeller. Since the race of patent-seekers was rarely noted and other black inventions such as ice cream, created by Augustus Jackson of Philadelphia in 1832, were simply never patented, one cannot be sure how many inventions were made by free blacks either.

The first free blacks to have their inventions recorded were Thomas L. Jennings, whose dry-cleaning methodology received patent protection in 1821, and Henry Blair, who invented a seed planter in 1834. Free black Norbert Rillieux patented his sugar refining evaporator, thus revolutionizing the industry. The son of a French planter and a free black woman, Rillieux left his home in New Orleans to study engineering in Paris. After teaching mathematics there for a while, he created his vacuum pan evaporator. With his invention, a single person could do work that once required several people working at once. He returned to the United States and became wealthy as the device was implemented in sugar refineries in his home state and abroad in Cuba and Mexico.

In 1848, free black Lewis Temple invented the toggle-harpoon for killing whales, a major industry at the time. Temple's invention almost completely replaced the type of harpoon formerly used because it greatly diminished the mammal's ability to escape after being hooked. Prior to the Civil War, Henry Boyd created an improved bedframe, and James Foten, one of the few blacks that from era to gain extreme wealth from an invention, produced a device that helped guide ship sails. He used the money he earned in to build a sail factory.

The Reconstruction era unleashed a creativity that had been suppressed in blacks. Between 1870 and 1900, a time when nearly 80 percent of African American adults in the United States were illiterate, blacks were awarded several hundred patents. Many of the grantees were self-taught such as Elijah McCoy. Working as a locomotive fireman on a Michigan line, his job was to lubricate the hot steam engines during frequently scheduled train stops necessitated by the procedure. After years of work, in 1872, McCoy perfected and patented an automatic lubricator that regularly supplied oil, even as a train was in motion. The effect on the increasingly important railway system was profound as conductors were no longer forced to make oiling stops. McCoy adapted his invention for use on ships and in factories. When copycats tried to steal his thunder, the phrase "the real McCoy" came into vogue.

In 1884, Granville T. Woods invented a steam-boiler furnace in his Cincinnati electrical engineering shop. Three years later, Woods patented an "induction telegraphy" or synchronous multiplex railroad telegraph that allowed train personnel to communicate with workers on other trains while in motion. He was also responsible for what later became known as the trolley, when in 1888, he produced an overhead electrical power supply system for streetcars and trains. A prolific inventor, Woods, known as "The Black Edison," created more than 50 valuable inventions, including an airbrake, which he eventually sold to George Westinghouse, and an incubator.

Jan Matzeliger came to the United States from South America in 1877. Living in Lynn, Massachusetts, he obtained work in a shoe factory. There he witnessed the tedious process by which shoe soles were attached to shoe uppers by workers known as hand lasters. For six months he secretly labored at inventing a machine to automate the work. Unsatisfied with his original design, he spent several more years tweaking and perfecting his creation so that by the time he was granted a patent in 1883, the equipment was so successful that manufacturers the world over clamored for the gadgetry.

Progress has been a gift from women as well as men. For example, Sarah Goode is credited with creating a folding cabinet bed in 1996; Sarah Boone invented the ironing board in 1892; and photographer Claytonia Dorticus was granted several patents that were concerned with photographic equipment and developing solutions as well as a shoe dye. But Madame C. J. Walker, often regarded only as an entrepreneur, was one of the most successful female inventors. She developed an entire line of hair care products and cosmetics for blacks, claiming that her first idea had come to her in a dream.

During the next few years, Garret Morgan patented a succession of products, including a hair straightening solution that was still a best-seller in as late as the 1970s; a gas mask, or "breathing device" for firefighters, and an improved traffic signal. Morgan tried to pass himself off as Native American, but once his identity as a black man was discovered several of his purchase orders were canceled.

Nonetheless, the early inventors paved the way for future African Americans. All these men as well as the countless unknown ones were forced to endure the byproducts of racism. Whites were oftentimes hesitant to buy black inventions unless the smell of eventual monetary gains was too strong. McCoy, Woods, and several others died poor, although their creations sold like wildfire.

## ◆ EARLY AFRICAN AMERICAN SCIENTISTS

The contributions of African American scientists are better known than those of black inventors, partly

George Washington Carver

because of the recognition awarded to George Washington Carver, an agriculturalist, who, incidentally, refused to patent most of his inventions. Born into slavery in 1864, Carver was the first black to graduate from Iowa Agricultural State College, where he studied botany and agriculture. One year after earning a master's degree, Carver joined the Tuskegee Institute's agriculture department. In his role as department head, he engineered a number of experimental farming techniques that had practical applications for farmers in the area. His ideas, from crop rotation to replenish nutrient-starved soil to his advocacy of peanuts as a cash crop, Carver left an indelible mark in his field. An inventor at heart, he was behind the genesis of innumerable botanical products, by-products, and even recipes. Recognition of his efforts came in several forms, including induction into England's Royal Society of Arts and Manufacturing and Commerce in 1916. In 1923, he received an NAACP Spingarn Medal. Six years after his death, in 1949, Carver was the subject of a U.S. Postal Stamp.

Born approximately ten years before Carver earned his bachelor's degree, Ernest Everett Just was a pioneering marine biologist who had graduated *magna cum laude* from Dartmouth College in 1907. The first-

ever recipient of a Spingarn Medal in 1915, his first paper was published as "The Relation of First Cleavage Plane to the Entrance Point of the Sperm" in 1912. The work showed how the location of cell division in the marine worm *Nereis* is determined by the sperm's entry point on an egg. Teaching at Howard for several years, Just had a tenuous relationship with the school, paving the way for him to accept an offer to conduct research at the Kaiser Wilhelm Institute for Biology in Berlin, Germany. The first American to be invited to the internationally respected institution, he remained there from 1929 to 1933, at which point the Nazi regime was surging to power. Because he preferred working abroad to being shut out of the best laboratories in the United States on the basis of race, Just spent the rest of his career in France, Italy, Spain, and Portugal.

Blacks have had successes in the hard sciences, engineering, and mathematics as well. In 1876, Edward Bouchet became the first African American to earn a doctorate from a university in the United States, when he acquired a Ph.D in physics from Yale. In the twentieth century, Elmer Samuel Imes, husband of Harlem Renaissance writer Nella Larsen, received a doctorate in physics from the University of Michigan in 1918. In his dissertation, Imes took the works of white scientists Albert Einstein, Ernest Rutherford, and Niels Bohr, one step further, definitively establishing that quantum theory applied to the rotational states of molecules. His efforts would later play a role in space science, thus making Imes the first African American astro-industrial physicist.

Chemist Percy Julian carved a brilliant career for himself after obtaining a doctorate from Switzerland's University of Vienna in 1931. His specialty was creating synthetic versions of expensive drugs. Much of his work later in life was conducted at his Julian Research Institute in Franklin Park, Illinois. In the 1940s, another scientist, Benjamin Peery, switched his focus from aeronautical engineering to physics while still and undergraduate at the University of Minnesota. After garnering a Ph.D from the University of Michigan, Peery went on to a lengthy career teaching astronomy at Indiana University, the University of Illinois, and Howard University.

Between 1875 and 1943, only eight blacks were awarded doctorates in pure mathematics. One, David Blackwell, became the first black tenured professor at the University of California at Berkeley in 1955. An expert in statistics and probability, he has been a trailblazer despite a racially motivated setback he incurred soon after completing his doctoral work at the University of Illinois. Nominated for a Rosenwald fellowship from the Institute for Advanced Study at Princeton University, Blackwell was rejected because of his race. Undaunted, he went on to become the only African American mathe-

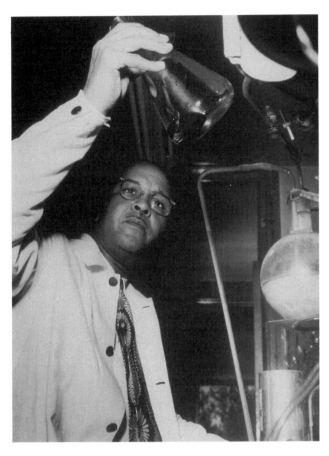

Dr. Percy Julian

matician to be elected into the National Academy of Sciences.

## ◆ AFRICAN AMERICANS IN MEDICINE

The medical profession has spawned a number of African Americans of high stature. As early as the 1860s, blacks had entered medical schools in the North and had gone on to practice as full-fledged physicians. In fact, during the Civil War, Dr. Alexander T. Augusta was named head of a Union army hospital and Rebecca Lee became the first female African American doctor by attending the New England Female Medical College in Boston. She was able to attend on a scholarship she received from Ohio Senator Benjamin Wade, an abolitionist. She used her schooling to provide health care to former slaves in the former confederate capital of Richmond, Virginia. Her 1883 *Book of Medical Discourses* taught women how to address their own health issues as well as those of their children.

Rebecca J. Cole was the second black woman to become a physician and the first African American graduate of the Woman's Medical College of Pennsylva-

nia. For the next 50 years she devoted her life to improving the lot of the poor. Her positions included performing a residency at the New York Infirmary for Women and Children and running Washington, DC's Government House for Children and Old Women and Philadelphia's Woman's Directory, a medical aid center.

In 1867, Susan McKinney Steward began studying at the New York Medical College for Women. Three years later she earned the distinction of being the third black female physician. Practicing in New York State, she specialized in homeopathic treatments and had black and white patients of both genders as clients. After opening a second office in New York City, she helped cofound the Brooklyn Woman's Homeopathic Hospital and Dispensary. She also served at the Brooklyn Home for Aged Colored People. A true humanitarian, Steward vigorously supported women's suffrage movement and conducted missionary work with her second husband, a chaplain for the Buffalo Soldier regiment. She ended her career by taking on the role of school doctor at Wilberforce University.

In 1868, Howard University opened its College of Medicine, the first black medical school in the country. The school nearly failed five years later when monetary problems arose and salaries for faculty were unavailable. Thanks to the efforts of Dr. Charles Parvis, who convinced the school to let him and his peers continue teaching on a nonpaid basis, the school survived the crisis. Parvis was later appointed chief surgeon of Washington, DC's Freedman's Hospital, a black institution, by U.S. president Chester Arthur. Parvis was thus the first African American to run a civilian hospital. He did so until 1894, when he began a private practice.

Meanwhile, Nashville's Meharry Medical College had emerged in 1876. Despite the decidedly low number of jobs for African American physicians who were routinely turned away from nearly every facility other than Freedman's Hospital, the school was a welcome addition to the slowly developing progress sought by black physicians, including Dr. Daniel Hale Williams, who replaced Parvis at Freedman's. Williams restored Freedman's to good health through internships, better nurses' training, and the addition of horse-drawn ambulances.

Williams had graduated from the Chicago Medical College in 1883 and entered into private practice almost immediately. Business was slow until 1890, when he met Emma Reynolds, an aspiring black nurse, whose skin color had kept her from gaining admission to any of the nursing schools in Chicago. Inspired by her unfortunate dilemma, Williams decided to operate his own hospital in hopes of initiating his own program for aspiring nurses. With 12 beds, Provident Hospital became the first black-operated facility in the United States, and Reynolds was the first to enroll in Williams's classes. Near the end of his career, Williams was appointed the first African American associate surgeon at Chicago's St. Luke Hospital and later was the only black charter member of the American College of Surgeons. During his career, Williams helped convince 40 hospitals to treat black patients.

Blacks in the South also received improved care in the late 1890s thanks to a dedicated black physician. In 1893, Alice Woodby McKane and her spouse, also a doctor, founded the first black-run health care center—a hospital, dispensary, and nursing school—in Savannah, Georgia. McKane had obtained her medical degree one-year earlier form the Woman's Medical College of Pennsylvania. Later the couple set up shop in Monrovia, Liberia, repeating their U.S. accomplishments.

Progress moved westward as another black woman used her training to benefit the region's black population though her patients transcended all racial barriers. From 1902 until nearly 50 years later, Denver's "Baby Doctor," Justina Ford, proudly served her community as the only black physician in Colorado. An obstetrician, she delivered more than 7,000 babies, making house calls whenever necessary.

Back East, Freedman's was the training ground for future head trauma authority Dr. Louis Wright, a Harvard Medical School graduate whose high academic standing meant nothing to Boston area hospitals that refused to hire blacks. When World War I erupted, Wright enlisted and found himself in charge of his unit's surgical ward. After the war, Wright, who had received a Purple Heart, became the first black physician to work in a New York City hospital when he was appointed to Harlem Hospital in 1919. Later he became directory of surgery, president of the medical board, and was admitted to the American College of Surgeons. Four years before his death in 1952, he founded the Cancer Research Foundation at Harlem Hospital. The son of two physicians, his father and his stepfather, the latter of whom was the first black graduate of Yale Medical School, Wright had two daughters who continued the family legacy by becoming doctors.

An almost legendary legacy was created by Dr. Charles R. Drew, a star high school athlete whose interest lay in medicine. A pathologist and expert on blood transfusions, Drew discovered that blood plasma was easier to store than whole blood. His experiments helped him become the first African American to receive a medical doctorate in 1940. During World War II, he helped Great Britain develop a national blood collection program and was later asked to do the same for the U.S. Armed

Forces. Unfortunately racism reared its ugly head again—black donors were first completely excluded from the program and later were only allowed to donate to other black servicemen. Frustrated, Drew withdrew from the program, briefly resuming his teaching career at Howard before joining the staff of Freedman's Hospital as medical director.

Howard continued developing new talents, however. Dr. Roland Scott, a physician at Howard University's College of Medicine, became a pioneer in the study and treatment of sickle cell anemia. His research was pivotal in drawing public attention to the disorder and prompting the U.S. government to devote money to more extensive study. Under the Sickle Cell Anemia Control Act passed in 1972, Congress forced the National Institutes of Health to set up treatment centers for patients. Scott was named director of the program that involved screening as well as treatment for those already afflicted.

## ◆ AFRICAN AMERICANS IN AIR AND SPACE

In 1920, Texan Bessie Coleman learned to fly at the École d'Aviation des Freres in France following a string of rejections from aviation schools in the United States. Having completed seven months of instruction and a rigorous qualifying exam, she earned her international aviator's license from the Federation Aeronautique Internationale the following year and went on to study further with aircraft designer Anthony H. G. Fokker. Known to an admiring public as "Queen Bess," Bessie Coleman was the first black woman ever to fly an airplane, the first African American to earn an international pilot's license, and the first black female stunt pilot. During her brief yet distinguished career as a performance flier, she appeared at air shows and exhibitions across the country, earning wide recognition for her aerial skill, dramatic flair, and tenacity. The tragic demise of the professional aviatrix occurred in 1926, when she was scheduled to parachute jump from a speeding plane at 2,500 feet. Ten minutes after take-off, however, the plane careened wildly out of control, flipping over and dropping Coleman, who plunged 500 feet to her death. Though he remained in the aircraft, the pilot, too, was instantly killed as the plane crashed to the ground. Later a service wrench mistakenly left behind in the engine was found to have been the cause of the accident.

Six years later, in 1932, pilot James Herman Banning and mechanic Thomas C. Allen flew from Los Angeles to New York City in 41 hours and 27 minutes. The transcontinental flight was followed by the first round-trip transcontinental flight the next year. That feat was accomplished by Albert Ernest Forsythe and Charles Alfred Anderson, who flew from Atlantic City to Los Angeles and back in 11 days, foreshadowing the advent of commericial flight.

Willa Brown-Chappell became the first black woman to hold a commercial pilot's license in the United States in 1934. Also the first African American woman to ascend to the rank of lieutenant, which she did as a member of the Civil Air Patrol Squadron; Brown-Chappell founded the National Airmen's Association of America, the first aviators group for blacks. With her husband, Cornelius R. Coffey, she established the first black-owned flying school—Coffey School of Aeronautics— and the first African American-owned school to receive certification from the Civil Aviation Authority. Brown-Chappell became the first African American member of the Federal Aviation Agency's Women's Advisory Council in 1972.

The second African American woman to earn a full commercial pilot's license was Janet Harmon Bragg, a Georgian nurse who took an interest in flying when she began dating Johnny Robinson, one of the first black aviation instructors. The first woman of any race to be admitted to Chicago's Curtiss Wright Aeronautical University, she was initially denied her commercial license despite having successfully fulfilled all preliminary requirements, including the airborne portion of the test. Her white instructor from the Federal Aviation Administration made it quite clear, however, that he would not grant a license to a black woman. Rather than give up, Bragg merely tested again with another instructor the same year and was granted her license in 1942. Along with a small group of black aviation devotees, she formed the Challengers Air Pilots Association (CAPA). Together, members of CAPA opened an airport in Robins, Illinois, the first owned and operated by African Americans.

Other black notables in the field of aviation include Perry H. Young, who, in 1957 became the first black pilot for a scheduled passenger commercial airline; New York Airways; Otis B. Young, Jr., who, in 1970, was the first African American pilot of a jumbo jet; and former naval pilot Jill Brown, who became the first black female to pilot for a major airline in 1987.

Military men were the first blacks to enter into the line of space exploration. In 1961, U.S. Air Force Captain Edward Dwight was invited by President John F. Kennedy to apply to test-pilot school. Two years later, Dwight was in the midst of spaceflight training when Kennedy was assassinated. Without the president's support, Dwight was pretty much ignored by National

Aeronautics and Space Administration (NASA). Air Force Major Robert H. Lawrence thus became the first African American astronaut a few years later. A doctor of nuclear chemistry, Lawrence was killed in a plane crash in December of 1967, just six months after his selection by NASA. Blacks would not make in-roads in space until the genesis of the space shuttle program. Grounded African American scientists were prevalent, however.

For example, Katherine Johnson joined the National Advisory Committee on Aeronautics, the precursor to NASA, in 1953. Initially all she was asked to do was basic number crunching, but in a kind of fluke, she spent a short period filling in at the Flight Research Division. There her valued interpretation of data helped in the making of prototype spacecraft, and she soon developed into a sage aerospace technologist. She developed trajectories for the Apollo moon-landing project and devised emergency navigational methods for astronauts. She retired in 1986.

Emergencies of another sort have been tackled by air force flight surgeon Vance Marchbanks, whose research showed that adrenaline levels could affect the exhaustion level of flight crews. His work brought him to the attention of NASA, and he became a medical observer for NASA's Project Mercury. Along with several other personnel scattered about the globe, Marchbanks, stationed in Nigeria, was responsible for monitoring pioneering white astronaut John Glenn's vital signs as he orbited the earth in 1962. Later, Marchbanks received the civilian post of chief of environmental health services for United Aircraft Corporation, where he had a hand in designing the space suit and life-support systems used in the Apollo moon shot.

Also specializing in design, aeronautical test engineer Robert E. Shurney spent nearly his entire career, from 1968 to 1990, at the Marshall Space Flight Center, specializing in design utility. His products included refuse disposal units that stored solids in the bottom and liquid in tubes to prevent any materials from floating openly and contaminating an entire cabin. The units were used in the Apollo program, Skylab, and on the first space shuttle missions. He also crafted strong, yet lightweight aluminum tires for the lunar rover. Much of his experimentation was conducted on KC-135 test planes in order to achieve the condition of "weightlessness."

Assertiveness enabled O. S. Williams to bring forth his own achievements. In 1942, Williams talked his way into employment at Republic Aviation as part of the technical staff. Better known as "Ozzie," he took the experience he earned there to NASA contractor Grumman Corporation. The small rocket engines he codeveloped saved the lives of the Apollo 13 astronauts when the ship's main rocket exploded during flight in 1970.

Three missions later, George Carruthers, a Naval Research Laboratory astrophysicist designed the far-ultraviolet camera/spectograph for use on Apollo 16. The semiautomatic device was able to photograph deep space—regions too far to be captured by regular cameras—once set up on the surface of the moon. Carruthers, who earned a Ph.D in aeronautical and astronautical engineering from the University of Illinois in 1964, was granted his first patent in 1969, for an electromagnetic radiation image converter. He was only 25 years old.

With a 1965 doctorate in atomic and molecular physics from Howard University, Carruther's contemporary, George E. Alcorn, has been one of the most prominent people working with semiconductors and spectrometers. By the early 1990s, he had eight patents to his name, including secret projects concerning missile systems.

In a less clandestine fashion, aerospace engineer Christine Darden has been a leading NASA researcher in supersonic and hypersonic aircraft. Her main goal has been the reduction of sonic boom, a phenomenon that creates an explosive burst of sound that can traumatize those on the ground. Darden works at manipulating an aircraft's wing or the shape of its nose, to try to control the feedback produced by air waves resulting from a plane's flight.

Dealing with people rather than machinery, directory of psychophysiology at NASA's Ames Research Center, Patricia Cowlings credentials are impressive; her post-doctoral work has touched upon such fields as aerospace medicine and bioastronautics. Since the late 1970s, she has assisted astronauts by teaching them autogenic feedback—how to impose mind over matter when zero gravity wreaks havoc with one's system. By studying physical and emotional problems that arise in such a setting, she can seek the cause and prescribe a therapy to alleviate stress. She was also the first woman of any race in the United States to receive astronaut training.

These individuals are joined by numerous others in the field of aviation and space flight, including chemical engineer Henry Allen, Jr., a liquid and solid rocket fuel specialist; missle expert and inventor extraordinaire Otis Boykin; environmental health office Julian Earls; aerospace technologist Isabella J. Coles; astrodynamicist Robert A. Gordon; and operations officer Isaac Gillam, IV, to name a few. Once the space shuttle program began in earnest, however, African Americans also took to the skies.

Traveling in the space shuttle *Challenger*, U.S. Air Force Colonel Guion "Guy" Bluford was the first black to fly in space, where he coordinated experiments and was in charge of deploying satellites. After his first mission in 1983, Bluford participated in three more. The second African American in space, Ronald McNair, was aboard the tragic *Challenger* flight of 1986, his second trip on the shuttle. The vehicle exploded 73 seconds after liftoff, killing all seven crew members. Charles Bolden's first mission was aboard the 1986 flight of the shuttle *Columbia*. He has also flown on the *Discovery*. The first African American to pilot a space shuttle was Frederick Gregory, who did so in 1985, on his very first journey to outer space. A veteran pilot of both helicopters and airplanes, Gregory became an astronaut in 1978. Gregory also made history on his fourth flight, when he commanded the first mission comprised of Russians and Americans. Mae Jemison went into space as a science specialist in 1992's joint U.S.-Japanese Spacelab-J project on the shuttle *Endeavor*. The following year, Bernard Harris took off in the shuttle *Columbia*. He served as a mission specialist in Spacelab-D2 alongside Germans and Americans.

## ◆ MODERN CONTRIBUTIONS TO SCIENCE AND TECHNOLOGY

The achievements of black inventors and scientists of the mid- to late twentieth century have been obscured by reasons more complex than blatant racial prejudice, among them the advent of government and corporate research and development teams. Such work, whether contracted or direct, often precludes individual recognition, regardless of a person's race. Nonetheless, in the corporate world as well as in academia, African American scientists and engineers play a substantial role in the development of solid state devices, high-powered and ultra fast lasers, hypersonic flight—two to three thousand miles per hour—and elementary particle science. Black engineers employed by NASA in managerial and research positions have made and continue to make considerable contributions.

African American manufacturing and servicing firms in various computer and engineering areas are sprouting and blossoming rapidly. For example, black entrepreneur Marc Hannah has made a niche for himself in the field of computer graphics as confounder of Silicon Graphics Incorporated. Principal scientist and vice president of the innovative company, Hannah has adapted his electrical engineering and computer science know-how to the medium of motion pictures since 1982. His computer-generated, 3-D special effects have been featured in such major films as *Terminator 2* (1991), *Aladdin* (1992), and *Jurassic Park* (1993).

Academia has more black science and technology faculty members, college presidents, and school of engineering deans than in the past. Many of these academics

Astronauts Guion Bluford, Ronald McNair, and Frederick Gregory, 1978.

are serving in the country's most prestigious institutions. As the United States faces the twenty-first century, a major challenge is being presented by European and Asian nations, with world leadership, maintenance of our position as a world super power, employment for our citizens, and our future standard of living at stake. A response has to come from America's young. In recent years, an increasing number of black students have demonstrated an interest in science. African American scientists and engineers already are an integral part of such institutions the National Aeronautics and Space Administration (NASA) and private research and development organizations such as Bell Laboratories. One area in which African Americans have been faltering, however, is medicine.

In the mid- to late 1990s, the number of black applicants to medical school was declining at an appalling rate. In a field thirsty for candidates, the search for African American physicians-to-be was nearing crisis-level status. The repercussions of this shortage includes difficulty for the poor and elderly in finding black attendants if they so desire. Primary care specialists—internists, pediatricians, obstetricians, gynecologists, etc.—were particularly in demand.

The health care profession began responding to this problem in 1991, when the Association of American Medical Colleges initiated Project 3000 by 2000—the primary aim being to graduate 3,000 minorities by the year 2000. As of 1996, the program was well on its way to success. In particular, Xavier University was the top school in the country for African American placement into medical school, gaining a reputation for placing an average of 70 percent of its premed seniors into medical schools each year. Meanwhile, black doctors already in practice were forming cooperatives amongst themselves in order to serve those African American patients who were discriminated against by Health Maintenance Organizations (HMOs) that considered them too poor or sick to be participants.

Similarly, the National Dental Association (NDA) launched the Networking Action Plan, an initiative aimed at addressing the dental needs of African Americans by emphasizing regular and routine dental care through the 6,000 dentists who are members. A second thrust involved recruiting partnerships with Howard University Dental School and Meharry Medical College in an effort to increase both students and faculty.

The situation is not nearly as dire in engineering, perhaps due in part to a mentoring program established in 1975, by the National Action Council for Minorities in Engineering (NACME). With industry backing, the council has focused on youngsters as early as at the fourth-grade level. More than 4,700 of their students have acquired engineering degrees and their graduates make up ten percent of all engineers from minority groups.

Still, the importance of role models with names and faces can not be overlooked. Some black scientists have entered into the public consciousness; for example, in 1973, Shirley Ann Jackson became the first black woman in the United States to earn a doctorate in theoretical particle physics as well as the first female African American to earn a Ph.D from the prestigious Massachusetts Institute of Technology (MIT). She has had a distinguished career, culminating with her appointment as chairwoman of the Nuclear Regulatory Commission by President Bill Clinton in 1995.

In 1996, Claude A. Verbal became the first African American president of the Society of Automotive Engineers (SAE) International. A General Motors (GM) Service Parts Operations plant manager, the business executive earned his engineering degree from North Carolina State University in 1964.

Another African American rose to the prominent rank of National Science Foundation (NSF) director, the highest science-related administrative post in the United States. Holder of a physics doctorate from St. Louis' Washington University, Walter Massey was able to create a number of programs to provide science-oriented training to young blacks. During his two-year stint at the NSF, from 1991 to 1993, Massey repeated the kind of success he had had when he began the Inner City Teachers Science program while teaching at Brown University.

In the field of medical research, Charles Whitten founded the National Association for Sickle Cell Disease in 1971. His work has been complemented more recently by Griffin Rodgers, chief of the Molecular Hematology Unit at the National Institutes of Health. In the 1990s, Rodgers was working on an experimental anticancer drug that could possibly provide benefits for sickle cell anemia patients.

Patients with prostate cancer have been encouraged by the work of Detroit-based urologist and oncologist Isaac Powell. In 1995, the Centers for Disease Control and Prevention named his screening program as the outstanding community health project of the year. Powell has been pursuing the idea of advanced diagnostic testing for black men. Through a partnership with the Karmanos Cancer Institute and area churches, nurses, and hospitals, Powell has been able to educate the public about the importance of undergoing prostate cancer screening. Benefitting from a prostate-specific antigen test, patients have had their cancer caught early enough to undergo successful surgery. In 1996, Powell's program was being exported to other cities in the United States.

The cancer research of Jill Bargonetti, a young African American biologist has garnered much attention. She discovered a correlation between a specific gene's ability to bind with the genetic matter known as DNA and its ability to suppress tumors. In 1996, she received a $300,000, 3-year grant from the American Cancer Society and a $200,000, 4-year award from the Department of Defense to pursue her study of breast cancer.

In the early 1990s, Alabama-based rural health-care provider Dr. Regina Benjamin uncovered a 1977 health-clinic law that distributed additional federal monies for qualified practices. Since then, other towns have sought the M.B.A.-holder's advice on how to establish facilities in their own areas.

Outside of medical research, one-time Olympic athlete and physicist Meredith Gourdine earned a Ph.D from the California Institute of Technology in 1960. The Olympic medalist then formed Gourdine Systems, a research and development firm geared towards producing electricity—from chemical and thermal energy or from flowing gas. Though blinded by diabetes in 1973,

Gourdine went on to launch Energy Innovations the next year. An inventor at heart, he has more than 70 patents in his name and was inducted into the Black Inventors Hall of Fame.

The energy of earthquakes motivates geophysicist Waverly Person. His interest in seismology paid off when he was named director of the U.S. Geological Survey's National Earthquake Information Center in 1977. The first African American earthquake scientist, Person is also the first black in more than 30 years to hold such a prominent position in the U.S. Department of the Interior.

Similarly, meteorolgist and climatologist Warren Washington has been concerned with the earth's exterior. Since 1987, the "greenhouse effect" expert has been director of the Climate and Global Dynamics Division of the National Center for Atmospheric Research. After seven years there, he was elected to a one-year term as the first African American president of the American Meteorological Society. Finishing up there, Washington cofounded the Black Environmental Science Trust, introducing black children to the joys of science.

Along with hundreds of other notable blacks, African American scientists have been working towards restoring scientific education at all levels. Their presence, whether inside or outside of the public eye, is felt. Younger blacks who learn of their endeavors are thus encouraged to free their creative science minds.

## ◆ DISCOVERY GATEKEEPERS

### Archie Alexander 1887-1958
*Civil Engineer*

Born in 1887, in Ottumwa, Iowa, Archie Alphonso Alexander graduated from the University of Iowa with a B.S. degree in civil engineering in 1912. During his collegiate years he was a star football player who earned the nickname "Alexander the Great" on the playing field. His first job was as a design engineer for the Marsh Engineering Company, which specialized in building bridges. Two years later, in 1914, Alexander formed his own company, A. A. Alexander, Inc. Most of the firm's contracts were for bridges and sewer systems. So successful was he that the NAACP awarded him its Spingarn Medal in 1928. The following year, he and formed Alexander and Repass with a former classmate. Alexander's new company was also responsible for building tunnels, railroad trestles, viaducts, and power plants. Some of Alexander's biggest accomplishments include the Tidal Basin Bridge and K Street Freeway in Washington, DC; a heating plant for his alma mater, the University of Iowa; a civilian airfield in Tuskegee, Alabama; and a sewage-disposal plant in Grand Rapids, Michigan.

A member of Kappa Alpha Psi, Alexander was awarded their "Laurel Wreath" for great accomplishment in 1925. Alexander received honorary civil engineering degrees from the University of Iowa in 1925 and Howard University in 1946. The following year, Alexander was named one of the University of Iowa's outstanding alumni and "one of the first hundred citizen of merit." Politically active, Alexander was appointed Governor of the Virgin Islands in 1954 by President Dwight Eisenhower though he was forced to resign one year later due to health problems. He died at his home in Des Moines, Iowa in 1958.

### Benjamin Banneker 1731-1806
*Mathematician/Statistician, Astronomer, Surveyor/ Explorer, Publisher*

Benjamin Banneker was born on November 9, 1731 in Ellicott, Maryland. His mother was a free woman and his father was a slave, who ultimately purchased his own freedom. At the age of 21, Banneker constructed a clock based upon a pocket watch he had seen, calculating the ratio of the gears and wheels and carving them from wood. The clock operated for more than 40 years.

Banneker's aptitude for mathematics and knowledge of astronomy enabled him to predict the solar eclipse of 1789. Within a few years, he began publishing an almanac which contained tide tables, data on future eclipses, and a listing of useful medicinal products and formulas. The almanac, which was the first scientific book published by an African American, appeared annually for more than a decade.

Banneker served as a surveyor on the six-person team that helped lay out the base lines and initial boundaries for Washington, DC. When the chairman of the committee, Major Pierre Charles L'Enfant, abruptly resigned and returned to France with his plans, Banneker was able to reproduce the plans in their entirety. He died on October 9, 1806.

### Andrew Jackson Beard 1850-1910
*Railroad Porter, Inventor*

While working in an Alabama railroad yard, Beard had seen men lose hands, even arms, in accidents occurring during the manual coupling of railroad cars. The system in use involved the dropping of a metal pin into place when two cars crashed together. Men were often caught between cars and crushed to death during this split-second operation. Beard's invention, the "Jenny Coupler" (patent 594,059), was an automatic device which secured two cars by merely bumping them together. In 1897 Beard received $50,000 for an invention which has since prevented the death or maiming of countless railroad men.

## Henry Blair 1804-1860
*Farmer, Inventor*

Maryland native Henry Blair was one the first black inventors to receive a U.S. patent. He was granted a patent for a corn-planting machine in 1834, and two years later, a second patent for a similar device used in planting cotton. In the registry of the Patent Office, Blair was designated "a colored man" the only instance of identification by race in these early records. Since slaves could not legally obtain patents, Blair was evidently a free man.

## Guion Stewart Bluford, Jr. 1942-
*Space/Atmospheric Scientist, Aerospace Engineer, Air Force Officer, Airplane Pilot*

Guy Bluford was born November 22, 1942, in Philadelphia. He graduated with a B.S. from Pennsylvania State University in 1964. He then enlisted in the U.S. Air Force and was assigned to pilot training at Williams Air Force Base in Arizona. Bluford served as a fighter pilot in Vietnam and flew 144 combat missions, 65 of them over North Vietnam. Attaining the rank of lieutenant colonel, Bluford received an M.S. from the Air Force Institute of Technology in 1974 and a Ph.D. in aeronautical engineering in 1978.

In 1979, Bluford was accepted in NASA's astronaut program as a mission specialist. On August 30, 1983, with the lift-off of the STS-8 Orbiter *Challenger* Bluford became the first African American in space. He flew two other space shuttle missions in 1985 and 1991 for a total of 314 hours in space. Bluford retired from NASA in 1993 to pursue a career in private industry.

Bluford has won numerous awards including the Distinguished National Science Award given by the National Society of Black Engineers (1979), NASA Group Achievement Award (1980, 1981), NASA Space Flight Medal (1983), and the NAACP Image Award in 1983. Some of his military honors include the National Defense Service Medal (1965), Vietnam Campaign Medal (1967), Air Force Commendation Medal (1972), Air Force Meritorious Service Award (1978), and the USAF Command Pilot Astronaut Wings (1983).

## Charles Frank Bolden, Jr. 1946-
*Airplane Pilot, Space/Atmospheric Scientist, Marine Officer, Operations and Systems Researcher/Analyst*

A graduate of the U.S. Naval Academy and the University of Southern California, Charles Bolden, Jr., has a bachelor of science degree in electrical science and a master of science degree in systems management. Bolden began his career as a second lieutenant in the U.S. Marine Corps, becoming a naval aviator by 1970. In 1973, he flew more than 100 sorties while assigned in

Major Charles Bolden

Thailand. Upon return to the United States, Bolden began a tour as a Marine Corps selection and recruiting officer. In 1979, he graduated from the U.S. Naval Test Pilot School, and was assigned to the Naval Test Aircraft Directorates.

Bolden was selected as an astronaut candidate by NASA in May of 1980, and in July of 1981 completed the training and evaluation program—making him eligible for assignment as a pilot on space shuttle flight crews. Bolden has served as pilot for the Hubble Space Telescope mission and was commander of the first American-Russian space shuttle mission. In 1994, he accepted a position at the Naval Academy. Bolden has been awarded the Defense Superior Service Medal, the Defense Meritorious Service Medal, the Air Medal, and the Strike/Flight Medal.

## Marjorie Lee Browne 1914-1979
*Mathematician/Statistician, Educator*

Browne was born September 9, 1914 in Memphis, Tennessee. She received a B.S. in mathematics from Howard University in 1935, an M.S. from the University of Michigan in 1939, and a Ph.D. in mathematics, again from the University of Michigan, in 1949. Browne taught at the University of Michigan in 1947 and 1948. She accepted the post of Professor of Mathematics at North Carolina Central University in 1949 and became department chairperson in 1951.

Browne's doctoral dissertation dealt with topological and matrix groups and she was published in the *American Mathematical Monthly*. She was a Fellow of the National Science Foundation in 1958-59 and again in 1965-66. Browne was a member of the American Mathematical Society, the Mathematical Association of America, and the Society for Industrial and Applied Mathematics. She died in 1979.

## George E. Carruthers 1940-
*Physicist*

Dr. George Carruthers is one of the two naval research laboratory people responsible for the *Apollo* 16 lunar surface ultraviolet camera/spectrograph, which was placed on the lunar surface in April 1972. It was Carruthers who designed the instrument while William Conway adapted the camera for the lunar mission. The spectrographs, obtained from 11 targets, include the first photographs of the ultraviolet equatorial bands of atomic oxygen that girdle the earth.

Carruthers, born on Chicago's south side in 1940, built his first telescope at the age of ten. He received his Ph.D. in physics from the University of Illinois in 1964, the same year that he started employment with the Navy. Carruthers is the recipient of the NASA Exceptional Scientific Achievement medal for his work on the ultraviolet camera/spectrograph.

## Ben Carson 1951-
*Neurosurgeon*

Born Benjamin Solomon Carson on September 18, 1951, in Detroit, Michigan, Dr. Carson has been recognized throughout the medical community for his prowess in performing complex neurosurgical procedures, particularly on children. Pediatric brain tumors have

been his main focus. Among his accomplishments are a number of faultless hemispherectomies, a process in which a portion of the brain of a critically ill seizure victim or other neurologically diseased patient is removed to restore normal functioning. Carson's most famous operation took place in 1987, earning him international acclaim. That year he successfully separated a pair of West German Siamese or conjoined twins, who had been attached at the backs of their heads. The landmark operation took 22 hours; Carson led a surgical team of 70 doctors, nurses, and technicians. Since then, he has saved thousands of childrens' lives worldwide.

Carson was raised in Detroit. A trouble-maker—he almost killed a peer during a knife fight when he was 14 years old—and a failing student, his mother imposed a reading program on him and limited his television viewing until his grades improved. In high school, he continued to excel and was accepted at Yale University in 1969, with a scholarship, when he had graduated. With a B.A. from that Ivy League institution, Carson entered the University of Michigan, where he obtained his M.D. in 1977. For one year he served as a surgical intern at the Johns Hopkins Hospital, later doing his residency there as well. From 1983 to 1984, Carson practiced at the Sir Charles Gairdner Hospital in Perth, Australia. In 1984, at 33 years of age, he became the youngest chief of pediatric neurosurgery in the United States. Then, in 1985, Johns Hopkins named him director of pediatric neurosurgery. In the mid-1990s, he was an associate professor neurosurgery, plastic surgery, and oncology at the Johns Hopkins School of Medicine in addition to his duties at the hospital. In 1996, Carson, who penned an autobiography called *Gifted Hands*, was in the midst of establishing a scholarship fund, USA Scholars Program, with the aid of his wife.

## George Washington Carver 1864-1943
*Educator, Agricultural/Food scientist, Farmer, Maid/Housekeeper*

George Washington Carver devoted his life to research projects connected primarily with southern agriculture. The products he derived from the peanut and the soybean revolutionized the economy of the South by liberating it from an excessive dependence on cotton.

Born a slave on January 5, 1864 in Diamond Grove, Missouri, Carver was only an infant when he and his mother were abducted from his owner's plantation by a band of slave raiders. His mother was sold and shipped away, but Carver was ransomed by his master in exchange for a race horse.

While working as a farm hand, Carver managed to obtain a high school education. He was admitted as the first black student of Simpson College, Indianola, Iowa.

George Washington Carver

He then attended Iowa Agricultural College (now Iowa State University) where, while working as the school janitor, he received a degree in agricultural science in 1894. Two years later he received a master's degree from the same school and became the first African American to serve on its faculty. Within a short time his fame spread, and Booker T. Washington offered him a post at Tuskegee.

Carver revolutionized the southern agricultural economy by showing that 300 products could be derived from the peanut. By 1938, peanuts had become a $200 million industry and a chief product of Alabama. Carver also demonstrated that 100 different products could be derived from the sweet potato.

Although he did hold three patents, Carver never patented most of the many discoveries he made while at Tuskegee, saying "God gave them to me, how can I sell them to someone else?" In 1938 he donated over $30,000 of his life's savings to the George Washington Carver Foundation and willed the rest of his estate to the organization so his work might be carried on after his death. He died on January 5, 1943.

### W. Montague Cobb 1903-1990
*Anthropologist, Organization Executive/Founder, Medical Researcher, Educator, Editor*

W. Montague Cobb was born on October 12, 1903, in Washington, DC. For 51 years he was a member of the Howard University Medical School faculty, and thousands of medical and dental students studied under his

direction. At Howard, he built a collection of more than 600 documented skeletons and a comparative anatomy museum in the gross anatomy laboratory. In addition to a B.A. from Amherst College, an M.D. from Howard University, and a doctorate from Case Western Reserve, he received many honorary degrees. Cobb died on November 20, 1990, in Washington, DC.

As editor of the *Journal of the National Medical Association* for 28 years, Cobb developed a wide range of scholarly interests manifested by the nearly 700 published works under his name in the fields of medical education, anatomy, physical anthropology, public health and medical history. He was the first African American elected to the presidency of the American Association of Physical Anthropologists and served as the chairman of the anthropology section of the American Association for the Advancement of Science. Among his many scientific awards is the highest award given by the American Association of Anatomists. For 31 years was a member of the board of directors of the NAACP and served as the president of the board for many years.

### Price M. Cobbs 1928-
*Psychiatrist, Author, Management Consultant*

Cobbs was born in Los Angeles, California, in 1928, and followed in his father's footsteps when he enrolled in medical school after earning a B.A. from the University of California at Berkeley. He graduated from Meharry Medical College in 1958 and within a few years had established his own San Francisco practice in psychiatry.

With his academic colleague at the University of California, William H. Grier, Cobbs authored the groundbreaking 1968 study *Black Rage*. In it, the authors argued that a pervasive social and economic racism had resulted in an endemic anger that stretched across all strata of African American society, from rich to poor; this anger was both apparent—and magnified by—the social unrest of the 1960s. Cobbs and Grier also co-authored a second book, *The Jesus Bag*, that discussed the role of organized religion in the African American community.

A seminar Cobbs held in 1967 with other mental health care professionals eventually led him to found his own diversity training company, Pacific Management Systems (PMS). Since its inception, the company has been instrumental in providing sensitivity training for Fortune 500 companies, community groups, law enforcement bodies, and social service agencies. A member of numerous African American professional and community organizations as well as an assistant clinical professor at the University of California at San Francisco, Cobbs continues to guide PMS well into its third decade, a firm that has pioneered the concept of ethnotherapy, which uses the principles of group therapy to help seminar participants rethink their attitudes toward members of other ethnic groups, the disabled, and those of alternative sexual orientations.

## Elbert Frank Cox 1895-1969
*Educator, Mathematician/Statistician*

Cox was born in Evansville, Indiana on December 5, 1895. He received his B.A. from Indiana University in 1917 and his Ph.D. from Cornell University in 1925. His dissertation dealt with polynomial solutions and made Cox the first African American to be awarded a doctorate in pure mathematics. Cox was an instructor at Shaw University (1921-1923), a professor in physics and mathematics at West Virginia State College (1925-1929) and an associate professor of mathematics at Howard University from 1929 to 1947. In 1947, he was made full professor; he retired in 1966.

During his career, Cox speicalized in interpolation theory and differential equations.. Cox was a Brooks Fellow (1924, 1925) and an Erastus Brooks Fellow. He belonged to the Mathematical Society and the Physical Society. Cox died in 1969.

## Ulysses Grant Dailey 1885-1961
*Editor, Health Administrator, Organization Executive/Founder, Diplomat*

From 1908 to 1912, Ulysses Grant Dailey served as surgical assistant to Dr. Daniel Hale Williams, founder of Provident Hospital and noted heart surgeon. Born in Donaldsonville, Louisiana, in 1885, Dailey graduated in 1906 from Northwestern University Medical School, where he was appointed a demonstrator in anatomy. He later studied in London, Paris, and Vienna and in 1926 set up his own hospital and sanitarium in Chicago. His name soon became associated with some of the outstanding achievements being made in anatomy and surgery.

An associate editor of the *Journal of the National Medical Association* for many years, Dailey traveled around the world in 1933 under the sponsorship of the International Collége of Surgeons, of which he was a founder fellow. In 1951, and again in 1953, the U.S. State Department sent him to Pakistan, India, Ceylon, and Africa. One year later he was named honorary consul to Haiti.

## Charles Richard Drew 1904-1950
*Educator, Medical Researcher, Health Administrator, Surgeon/Physician*

Using techniques already developed for separating and preserving blood, Charles Drew pioneered further into the field of blood preservation and organized proce-

dures from research to a clinical level, leading to the founding of blood banks just prior to World War II. Born on June 3, 1904 in Washington, DC, Drew graduated from Amherst College in Massachusetts, where he received the Messman Trophy for having brought the most honor to the school during his four years there. He was not only an outstanding scholar but the captain of the track team and a star halfback on the football team.

After receiving his medical degree from McGill University in 1933, Drew returned to Washington, DC, to teach pathology at Howard. In 1940, while taking his D.Sc. degree at Columbia University, he wrote a dissertation on "banked blood" and soon became such an expert in this field that the British government called upon him to set up the first blood bank in England.

During World War II, Drew was appointed director of the American Red Cross blood donor project. Later, he served as chief surgeon at Freedmen's Hospital in Washington, DC as well as professor of surgery at Howard University Medical School from 1941-1950. He was killed in an automobile crash on April 1, 1950.

## Joycelyn Elders 1933-
*Physician, Endocrinologist, Former U.S. Surgeon General*

Dr. Joycelyn Elders was born Joycelyn Minnie Jones, on August 13, 1933, in Schall, Arkansas. The first of eight children, she grew up working in cotton fields. An avid reader, Jones earned a scholarship to the all-black, Philander Smith College in Little Rock, after graduating from high school. Jones studied biology and chemistry in hopes of becoming a lab technician. She was inspired towards greater ambitions after meeting Edith Irby Jones (no relation), the first African American to study at the University of Arkansas School of Medicine. After obtaining her B.A., Jones served as a physical therapist in the U.S. Army in order to fund her post-graduate education. She was able to enroll in the University of Arkansas School of Medicine herself in 1956. However, as the only black woman and one of only three African American students, she and the other two blacks were forced to use a separate university dining facility—the one provided for the cleaning staff.

Having married Oliver B. Elders in 1960, the newly dubbed Joycelyn Elders fulfilled a pediatric internship at the University of Minnesota, then returned to Little Rock in 1961 for a residency at the University of Arkansas Medical Center. Her success in the position led her to be appointed chief pediatric resident, in charge of the all-white, all-male battery of residents and interns. During the next 20 years, Elders forged a successful clinical practice, specializing in pediatric endocrinology, the study of glands. She published more than 100 papers in that period and rose to professor of pediatrics, a position she maintained from 1976 until 1987, when she was named director of the Arkansas Department of Health.

Over the course of her career, Elders's focus shifted somewhat from diabetes in children to sexual behavior. At the Department of Health, Elders was able to pursue her public advocacy in regards to teenage pregnancy and sexually transmitted diseases. Under Elders, 18 school clinics were opened with the mission bringing sex education to the youth. In 1989, her lobbying efforts finally paid off, and the Arkansas State Legislature mandated a kindergarten to 12th grade course curriculum encompassing instruction in hygiene, substance-abuse prevention, elevation of self-esteem, and contraceptive responsibility for males as well as females.

In 1993, U.S. president Bill Clinton nominated Elders for the U.S. surgeon general post, making her the second African American and the fifth woman to hold the cabinet position. Though her confirmation was not unchallenged—many decried her liberal stance—she was formally voted into approval for the position by the Senate on September 7, 1993. Within six months, Elders's first annual Surgeon General's Report was issued under the title, "Preventing Tobacco Use Among Young People." The effort was historical in that it was the first to focus just on kids.

During her short-lived tenure, Elders would do just that, i.e. advocating for children as well as for the poor. She attacked Medicaid for failing to help poverty-stricken women prevent unwanted pregnancies and faulted pharmaceutical companies for overpricing contraceptives. Between 1993 and December of 1994, Elders spoke out in support of the medicinal use of marijuana, in favor of studying drug legalization, family planning and against toy guns for children. Many of her stances were deemed controversial by conservative factions, but the biggest flak occurred when Elders was reported to have recommended that masturbation be discussed in schools as part of human sexuality. She was forced to resignation by Clinton in December of 1994.

Elders returned to the University of Arkansas Medical School, though the state's General Assembly budget committee tried to block her return. There she resumed teaching. In 1995, she was hosting a daily talk show on AM stations KYSG in Little Rock and WERE in Cleveland.

## Helene D. Gayle 1955-
*Epidemiologist, AIDS Researcher*

Helene Gayle was born in 1955 in Buffalo, New York, the third of five children of an entrepreneur father and social worker mother; her brother would also go on to become a doctor. After graduating from Barnard College in 1976, she then won acceptance to the University of Pennsylvania's medical school.

Having heard a speech once on the cure of smallpox inspired Gayle to pursue public health medicine, and her direction would prove a significant one in the years to come as the plague of AIDS came to decimate communities across the globe. She received her medical school degree from University of Pennsylvania as well as an M.A. in public health from Johns Hopkins both in 1981. After a residency in pediatrics, she was selected to enter the epidemiology training program in 1984 at the Centers for Disease Control in Atlanta, Georgia, the nation's top research center for infectious diseases.

For much of the 1980s Gayle was intensely involved in the CDC's research into AIDS and HIV infection through her work first in the center's Epidemic Intelligence Service and later as a chief of international AIDS research, a capacity in which she oversaw the scientific investigations of over three hundred CDC researchers. The physician has been instrumental in raising public awareness about the disease, and is especially driven to point out how devastating AIDS has been to the black community. Sex education, better health care for the poor, and substance abuse prevention are some of the proposals Gayle has championed that she believes will help reduce deaths from AIDS.

In 1992 Gayle was hired as a medical epidemiologist and researcher for the AIDS division of the U.S. Agency for International Development, cementing the physician's reputation as one of the international community's top AIDS scientists.

## Evelyn Boyd Glanville 1924-
*Author, Educator, Lecturer*

Born in 1924, Glanville attended Smith College from 1941 to 1946 and earned an A.B. and an M.A. in mathematics. She received a Ph.D. from Yale University in 1949. She was the first African American woman to be awarded a Ph.D. in pure mathematics. Glanville's first teaching position was as an instructor at New York University (1949-1950). She moved to Fisk University where she was an assistant professor (1950-1952) and then to the University of Southern California as a lecturer (1961-1973). Since then she has been an associate professor at California State University. Glanville is the author of *Theory of Applications of Math for Teachers.*

## Frederick Drew Gregory 1941-
*Airplane Pilot, Air Force Officer*

Gregory was born January 7, 1941 in Washington, DC. He is the nephew of the late Dr. Charles Drew, noted African-American blood plasma specialist. Under the sponsorship of United States Representative Adam Clayton Powell, Gregory attended the U.S. Air Force Academy and graduated with a B.S. in 1964. In 1977, he received an M.S.A. from George Washington University.

Gregory was a helicopter and fighter pilot for the USAF from 1965 to 1970 and a research and test pilot for the USAF and National Aeronautics and Space Administration (NASA) in 1971. In 1978 he was accepted into NASA's astronaut program. In 1985 he went into space aboard the Spacelab 3 *Challenger* Space Shuttle as a pilot. Currently, Gregory is with NASA's astronaut program at the Johnson Space Center in Houston, Texas, and he is a colonel in the USAF.

Gregory belongs to the Society of Experimental Test Pilots, the Tuskegee Airmen, the American Helicopter Society, and the National Technical Association. He has won numerous medals and awards including the Meritorious Service Medal, the Air Force Commendation Medal, and two NASA Space Flight Medals. He has twice received the Distinguished Flying Cross and is also the recipient of George Washington University's Distinguished Alumni Award, NASA's Outstanding Leadership Award, and the National Society of Black Engineers' Distinguished National Scientist Award.

## Lloyd Augustus Hall 1894-1974
*Research Director, Chemist*

Grandson of the first pastor of Quinn Chapel A.M.E. Church, the first African American church in Chicago, Lloyd Augustus Hall was born in Elgin, Illinois, on June 20, 1894. A top student and athlete at East High School in Aurora, Illinois, he graduated in the top ten of his class and was offered scholarships to four different colleges in Illinois. In 1916, Hall graduated from Northwestern University with a bachelor of science in chemistry. He continued his studies at the University of Chicago and the University of Illinois.

Hall served his country during World War I; as a lieutenant, his job was to inspect explosives at a Wisconsin plant. After the war, Hall joined the Chicago Department of Health Laboratories, where he quickly rose to senior chemist. In 1921, he took employment at Boyer Chemical Laboratory before becoming president and chemical director of the Chemical Products Corporation the following year. In 1924, he was offered a position with Griffith Laboratories. Within one year he was chief chemist and director of research.

There Hall entered the most unique and fruitful phase of his career. He discovered curing salts for the preserving and processing of meats, thus revolutionizing the meat-packing industry; discovered how to sterilize

spices; and researched the effects of antioxidants on fats. Along the way, he registered more than 100 patents for processes used in the manufacturing and packing of food, especially meat and bakery products.

In 1954, Hall became chairman of the Chicago chapter of the American Institute of Chemists. The following year, he was elected a member of the national board of directors, becoming the first African American man to hold that position in the institute's 32-year history. Upon his retirement from Griffith in 1959, Hall continued to serve as a consultant to various state and federal organizations. In 1961, he spent six months in Indonesia, advising the Food and Agricultural Organization of the United Nations. From 1962 to 1964, he was a member of the American Food for Peace Council, an appointment made by President John F. Kennedy.

## Matthew Alexander Henson 1866-1955
*Seaman, Explorer/Surveyor, Author*

Mathew Henson was born August 8, 1866, in Charles County, Maryland near Washington, DC. He attended school in Washington for six years but at the age of thirteen signed on as a cabin boy on a ship headed for China. Henson worked his way up to seaman while he

Matthew Henson

sailed over many of the world's oceans. Tiring of life at sea, Henson took a job in a Washington, DC clothing store. While there he met Nicaragua-bound, U.S. Navy surveyor Robert Edward Peary. He was hired on the spot as Peary's valet. Henson was not pleased at being a personal servant but nonetheless felt his new position held future opportunities.

Peary eventually became obsessed with arctic exploration. After numerous trips to Greenland between 1893 and 1905, Peary became convinced that he could become the first man to stand at the North Pole. Henson accompanied Peary on these trips to Greenland and became an integral part of Peary's plans. In 1906, along with a number of Inuits, Peary and Henson set out from Greenland on their first attempt to reach the North Pole. They came within 160 miles of their goal but were forced to turn back because unseasonably warm weather had created open sheets of water that could not be traversed by dogsled.

Undaunted, Peary and Henson tried again in 1909. Although Peary was undoubtedly the driving force of these expeditions he was increasingly reliant on Henson. Henson's greatest asset was his knowledge of the Inuit language and his ability to readily adapt to their culture. He was also an excellent dog driver and possessed a physical stamina that Peary lacked due to leukemia. Henson felt that he was serving the black race by his example of loyalty, fortitude, and trustworthiness.

By the end of March of 1909, they were within 150 miles of their goal. Henson, because of his strength, would break trail and set up camp for the night, while Peary followed. On April 6th, Henson thought he had reached the Pole. When Peary arrived later he asserted that they were three miles short. After a brief rest they both set out together and stopped when they thought they were in the area of the North Pole. There have been conflicting theories ever since as to who was the first man to reach the top of the world.

In 1912, Henson wrote *A Negro at the North Pole* but the book aroused little interest. He took work first as a porter and then as a customs official in New York. By the 1930s, however, Henson began receiving recognition for his contributions to arctic exploration. In 1937 he was the first African American elected to the Explorers Club in New York. In 1945 he and other surviving members of the expedition received the Navy Medal. In the early 1950s Henson received public recognition for his deeds from President Eisenhower. Henson died in 1955 and was buried in New York. In 1988 his remains were exhumed and buried with full military honors at Arlington National Cemetery next to the grave of Robert Peary.

## William Augustus Hinton 1883-1959
*Lecturer, Medical Researcher, Educator*

Long one of the world's authorities on venereal disease, Dr. William A. Hinton is responsible for the development of the Hinton test, a reliable method for detecting syphilis. He also collaborated with Dr. J. A. V. Davies on what is now called the Davies-Hinton test for the detection of this same disease.

Born in Chicago on December 15, 1883, Hinton graduated from Harvard in 1905. In 1912, he finished his medical studies in three years at Harvard Medical School. For three years after graduation, he was a voluntary assistant in the pathological laboratory at Massachusetts General Hospital. This was followed by eight years of laboratory practice at the Boston Dispensary and at the Massachusetts Department of Public Health. In 1919, Hinton was appointed lecturer in preventive medicine and hygiene at Harvard Medical School where he served for 34 years. In 1949, he was the first person of color to be granted a professorship there.

In 1931, at the Boston Dispensary, Hinton started a training school for poor girls so that they could become medical technicians. From these classes of volunteers grew one of the country's leading institutions for the training of technicians. Though he lost a leg in an automobile accident, Hinton remained active in teaching and at the Boston Dispensary Laboratory, which he directed from 1916 to 1952. He died in Canton, Massachusetts on August 8, 1959.

## Shirley Ann Jackson 1946-
*Lecturer, Physicist*

Born in Washington, DC, in 1946, Shirley Ann Jackson graduated as valedictorian of her class from Roosevelt High School in 1964. In 1968, she received a bachelor of science degree from Massachusetts Institute of Technology. In 1973 she became the first African American woman in the United States to earn a Ph.D. in physics, which she also earned from Massachusetts Institute of Technology.

Jackson's first position—as a research associate at the Fermi National Accelerator Laboratory in Batavia, Illinois and where she studied large subatomic particles—reflected her interest in the study of particles found within atoms. Jackson has worked as a member of the technical staff on theoretical physics at AT&T Bell Laboratories, as a visiting scientist at the European Organization for Nuclear Research in Geneva, and as a visiting lecturer at the NATO International Advanced Study Institute in Belgium. In 1995, President Bill Clinton named Jackson as chairperson of the Nuclear Regulatory Commission.

Dr. Mae Jemison

## Mae C. Jemison 1956-
*Physician/Surgeon*

Mae Jemison was born October 17, 1956, in Decatur, Alabama but her family moved to Chicago when she was three. She attended Stanford University on a National Achievement Scholarship and received a B.S. in chemical engineering and a B.A. in Afro–American studies in 1977. She then enrolled in Cornell University's medical school and graduated in 1981. Her medical internship was at the Los Angeles County/University of Southern California Medical Center in 1982. She was a general practitioner with the INA/Ross Loos Medical Group in Los Angeles until 1983, followed by two years as a Peace Corp medical officer in Sierra Leone and Liberia. Returning to the United States in 1985, she began working for CIGNA Health Plans, a health maintenance organization in Los Angeles.

In 1987, Jemison was accepted in NASA's astronaut program. Her first assignment was representing the astronaut office at the Kennedy Space Center in Cape Canaveral, Florida. On September 12, 1992, when the space shuttle *Endeavor* lifted off, Jemison was aboard and became the first African American woman in space. She served aboard the *Endeavor* as a science specialist.

Jemison resigned from NASA in 1993 to pursue personal goals related to science education and health care in West Africa. In 1994 Jemison founded the International Science Camp in Chicago to help young people become enthusiastic about science.

In 1988, Jemison won the Science and Technology Award given by *Essence* magazine and in 1990 she was Gamma Sigma Gamma's Woman of the Year. In 1991 she earned a Ph.D. from Lincoln University.

## Frederick McKinley Jones 1892-1961
*Mechanic*

In 1935, Frederick McKinley Jones built the first automatic refrigeration system for long haul trucks. Later, the system was adapted to various other carriers including railway cars and ships. Previously, foods were packed in ice so slight delays led to spoilage. Jones' new method instigated a change in eating habits and patterns of the entire nation and allowed for the development of food production facilities in almost any geographic location.

Jones was born in Cincinnati in 1892. His mother died when he was a boy and he moved to Covington, Kentucky, where he was raised by a priest until he was sixteen. When he left the rectory, Jones worked as a pin boy, mechanic's assistant, and finally, as chief mechanic on a Minnesota farm. He served in World War I, and in the late 1920s, his mechanical fame spread when he developed a series of devices to adapt silent movie projectors into sound projectors.

Jones also developed an air conditioning unit for military field hospitals, a portable x-ray machine, and a refrigerator for military field kitchens. During his life, a total of 61 patents were issued in Jones's name. He died in 1961.

## Percy Lavon Julian 1898-1975
*Educator, Medical Researcher, Research Director*

Born on April 11, 1898 in Montgomery, Alabama, Julian attended DePauw University in Greencastle, Indiana. He graduated Phi Beta Kappa and was valedictorian of his class after having lived during his college days in the attic of a fraternity house where he worked as a waiter. For several years, Julian taught at Fisk and Howard universities, as well as at West Virginia State College, before attending Harvard and the University of Vienna.

In 1935, Julian synthesized the drug physostigmine, which is used today in the treatment of glaucoma. He later headed the soybean research department of the Glidden Company and then formed Julian Laboratories in order to specialize in the production of sterols, which

Dr. Percy Julian

he extracted from the oil of the soybean. The method perfected by Julian in 1950 eventually lowered the cost of sterols to less than 20 cents a gram, and ultimately enabled millions of people suffering from arthritis to obtain relief through the use of cortisone, a sterol derivative. Later, Julian developed methods for manufacturing sex hormones from soya bean sterols: progesterone was used to prevent miscarriages, while testosterone was used to treat older men for diminishing sex drive. Both hormones were important in the treatment of cancer.

In 1953, after serving as director of research for the Glidden Company, he founded his own company, the Julian Institute, in Franklin Park, Illinois and Mexico. Years later, the institute was sold to Smith, Klein and French. In 1947, Julian was awarded the Spingarn Medal, and in 1968 he was awarded the Chemical Pioneer Award by the American Institute of Chemists. He died on April 19, 1975.

### Ernest Everett Just 1883-1941
*Editor, Zoologist, Marine Biologist*

Born in Charleston, South Carolina, on August 14, 1883, Ernest Just received his B.A. in 1907 with high honors from Dartmouth and his Ph.D. in 1916 from the University of Chicago. His groundbreaking work on the embryology of marine invertebrates included research on fertilization—a process known as parthenogenesis—but his most important achievement was his discovery of the role protoplasm palys in the development of a cell.

A member of Phi Beta Kappa, Just received the Spingarn Medal in 1914 and served as associate editor of *Physiological Zoology, The Biological Bulletin,* and *The Journal of Morphology.* Between 1912 and 1937, he published more than 50 papers on fertilization, parthenogenesis, cell division, and mutation. In 1930 Just was one of 12 zoologists to address the International Congress of Zoologists and he was elected vice president of the American Society of Zoologists.

### Samuel L. Kountz 1931-1981
*Physician/Surgeon, Medical Researcher*

Born in 1931 in Lexa, Arkansas, Samuel Kountz graduated third in his class at the Agricultural, Mechanical and Normal College of Arkansas in 1952. He pursued graduate studies at the University of Arkansas, earning a degree in chemistry. Senator J. W. Fulbright, whom he met while a graduate student, advised Kountz to apply for a scholarship to medical school. Kountz won the scholarship on a competitive basis and was the first black to enroll at the University of Arkansas Medical School in Little Rock. Kountz was responsible for finding out that large doses of the drug methylprednisolone could help reverse the acute rejection of a transplanted kidney. The drug was used for a number of years in the standard management of kidney transplant patients.

In 1964, working with Dr. Roy Cohn, one of the pioneers in the field of transplantation, Kountz made medical history by transplanting a kidney from a mother to a daughter—the first transplant between humans who were not identical twins. At the University of California in 1967, Dr. Kountz worked with other researchers to develop the prototype of a machine which is now able to preserve kidneys up to fifty hours from the time they are taken from the body of a donor. The machine, called the Belzer Kidney Perfusion Machine, was named for Dr. Folkert O. Belzer, who was Dr. Kountz's partner. Dr. Kountz died in 1981 after a long illness contracted on a trip to South Africa in 1977.

### Theodore K. Lawless 1892-1971
*Physician, Philanthropist*

Theodore Kenneth Lawless was born on December 6, 1892, in Thibodeaux, Louisiana. He received his bachelor's from Talladega College in 1914 and continued to further his education through 1924 at Northwestern

University, where he received his medical doctorate degree and on year of a master's in dermatology, which he finished at Columbia University from there he attended Harvard University, the University of Paris, the University of Freiburg, and the University of Vienna, where he continued his extensive work in dermatology.

Lawless started his own practice in the Chicago's predominantly black south side upon his return in 1924, which he continued until his death in 1971. He soon became one of the premier dermatologists in the country and earned great praise for researching treatments and cures for a variety of skin diseases, including syphilis, leprosy, and sporotrichosis. During the early years of his career, he taught dermatology at Northwestern University Medical School, where his research was instrumental in devising electropyrexia, a treatment for those suffering cases of syphilis in its early stages. Before he left his role at Northwestern in 1941, he aided in building the university's first medical laboratories.

After leaving Northwestern, Lawless entered the business world beginning as president of 4213 South Michigan Corporation, which sold low-cost real estate, and later as president of the Service Federal Savings and Loan Association. And by the 1960s, he was well-known as one of the 35 richest black men in the United States. During his lifetime, Lawless served on dozens of boards of directors and belonged to countless organizations. He served on the Chicago Board of Health, as senior attending physician at Provident hospital, as associate examiner in dermatology for the National Board of Medical Examiners as chairman of the Division of Higher Education, and as consultant to the Geneva Community Hospital in Switzerland. He was also recognized with many awards for his exemplary breakthroughs in medicine, public service, and philanthropy, including the Harmon Award in Medicine in 1929, the Churchman of the Year in 1952, the Springarn Medal from the NAACP in 1954, and the Daniel H. Burnham Award from Roosevelt University in 1963. He died in 1971.

### Lewis Howard Latimer 1848-1928
*Draftsperson, Electrical Engineer*

Lewis Howard Latimer was employed by Alexander Graham Bell to make the patent drawings for the first telephone, and later went on to become chief draftsman for both the General Electric and Westinghouse companies. Born in Chelsea, Massachusetts, on September 4, 1848, Latimer enlisted in the Union Navy at the age of 15, and began studying drafting upon completion of his military service. In 1881, he invented a method of making carbon filaments for the Maxim electric incandescent lamp; he later patented this method. He also supervised the installation of electric light in New York, Philadelphia, Montreal, and London for the Maxim-

Weston Electric Company. In 1884, he joined the Edison Company.

### Robert H. Lawrence, Jr. 1935-1967
*Astronaut, Airplane Pilot*

Air Force Major Robert H. Lawrence, Jr. was the first African American astronaut to be appointed to the Manned Orbiting Laboratory. Lawrence was a native of Chicago, and while still in elementary school he became a model airplane hobbyist and a chess enthusiast. Lawrence became interested in biology during his time at Englewood High School in Chicago. As a student at Englewood, Lawrence excelled in chemistry and track, placing top in the 440 and 880. When he graduated, he placed in the top ten percent of the class.

Lawrence entered Bradley University, joining the Air Force Reserve Officer's Training Corps and attaining the rank of lieutenant colonel, the second highest ranking cadet at Bradley. Lawrence was commissioned a second lieutenant in the United States Air Force in 1956 and soon after received his bachelors degree in chemistry. Following a stint at an air base in Germany, Lawrence entered Ohio State University through the Air Force Institute of Technology as a doctoral candidate.

Major Robert H. Lawrence, Jr.

Lawrence's career came to an end in 1967 when his F-104D Starfighter jet crashed on a runway in a California desert.

## Arthur C. Logan 1909-1973
*Community Activist, Civil Rights/Human Rights Activist, Physician/Surgeon*

Arthur Logan was born in Tuskegee, Alabama in 1909. When he was ten his family moved to New York City, where he received his middle school and high school education. After attending Williams College in Williamstown, Massachusetts, he went to medical school at Columbia University College of Physicians and Surgeons, graduating in 1934. Wishing to work among his people, Logan interned at Harlem Hospital and was affiliated with the hospital for the rest of his life.

In addition to his many years of medical service to Harlem residents and others, Logan also headed New York City's Council Against Poverty in 1965 at the request of Robert F. Wagner, then mayor of the city. Logan was a board member of New York City's Health and Hospital Corporation, as well as a longtime activist in the civil-rights movement, and a strong supporter of a wide range of community causes. He was active with the National Urban League and the NAACP Legal Defense Fund, and was an intimate friend of Martin Luther King, Jr., Whitney Young, and Roy Wilkins. His home in New York was often a meeting place for major figures in the civil-rights movement in the 1960s.

## Miles Vandahurst Lynk 1871-1956
*Publisher, Physician/Surgeon, Educational Administrator*

Miles Vandahurst Lynk was born on June 3, 1871, near Brownsville, Tennessee. He was founder, editor, and publisher of the first black medical journal, the *Medical and Surgical Observer*, first published in December OF 1892. At the age of nineteen, Lynk received his M.D. degree from Meharry Medical College. Lynk was one of the organizers of the first black national medical association; the organization later became the National Medical Association. He also founded and was president of the School of Medicine at the University of West Tennessee.

## Jan Matzeliger 1852-1889
*Inventor, Shoemaker/Leather Worker*

Born in 1852 in Paramaribo, Dutch Guiana, Matzeliger found employment in the government machine works at the age of 10. Eight years later, he immigrated to the United States, settling in Philadelphia, where he worked in a shoe factory. He later moved to New England, settling permanently in Lynn, Massachusetts. The Indus-

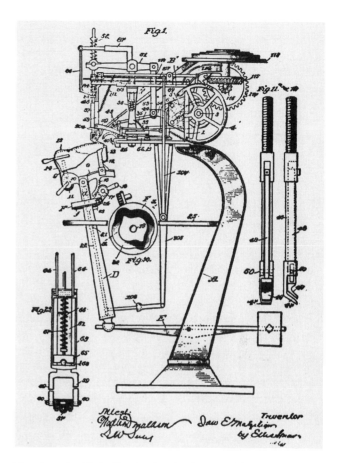

Drawings for Matzeliger's shoe lasting machine.

trial Revolution had by this time resulted in the invention of machines to cut, sew, and tack shoes, but none had been perfected to last a shoe. Seeing this, Matzeliger lost little time in designing and patenting just such a device, one which he refined over the years to a point where it could adjust a shoe, arrange the leather over the sole, drive in the nails, and deliver the finished product—all in one minute's time.

Matzeliger's patent was subsequently bought by Sydney W. Winslow, who established the United Shoe Machine Company. The continued success of this business brought about a 50 percent reduction in the price of shoes across the nation, doubled wages, and improved working conditions for millions of people dependent on the shoe industry for their livelihood. Between 1883 and 1891, Matzeliger received five patents on his inventions, all which contributed to the shoe making revolution. His last patent was issued in September 1891, two years posthumously.

Matzeliger died in 1889 at the age of 37, long before he had the chance to realize a share of the enormous profit derived from his invention. He never received any money. Instead, he was issued stock in the company which did not become valuable until after his death.

## Elijah McCoy
*Inventor, Machinist*

Born in Canada, McCoy moved to Ypsilanti, Michigan, after the Civil War, and over the next 40 years, acquired some 57 patents for devices designed to streamline his automatic lubrication process.

Elijah McCoy's inventions were primarily connected with the automatic lubrication of moving machinery. Perhaps his most valuable design was the "drip cup," a tiny container filled with oil whose flow to the essential moving parts of heavy-duty machinery was regulated by means of a "stopcock." The drip cup was a key device in perfecting the overall lubrication system used in large industry today.

## Ronald E. McNair 1950-1986
*Astronaut*

Ronald McNair was born on October 12, 1950, in Lake City, South Carolina. He was graduate of North Carolina A&T State University with a B.S. degree in physics. He also received a Doctor of Philosophy in Physics from Massachusetts Institute of Technology. He was presented an honorary Doctorate of Laws from North Carolina A&T in 1978.

McNair was working in optical physics when he was selected by NASA in 1978 to train as an astronaut. In August 1979, he completed a one-year training and evaluation period that made him eligible for assignment as mission specialist on space shuttle flight crews. He presented papers in the areas of lasers and molecular spectroscopy and gave many presentations in the United States and Europe. He was the second African American to orbit the earth on a NASA Mission.

Despite the rigorous training in the NASA program, he taught karate at a church, played the saxophone, and found time to talk to young people. McNair was aboard the flawed shuttle *Challenger* that exploded shortly after lift-off from Cape Kennedy and plunged into the waters off the Florida coast on January 28, 1986. The shuttle had a crew of seven persons, including two women, a mission specialist, and a teacher-in-space participant.

## Garrett Augustus Morgan 1877-1963
*Inventor*

Born in Paris, Kentucky, in 1877, Morgan moved to Cleveland at an early age. His first invention was an improvement on the sewing machine which he sold for

Dr. Ronald McNair

Garret Morgan

$150. In 1923, having established his reputation with the gas inhalator, he was able to command a price of $40,000 from the General Electric Company for his automatic traffic signal.

The value of Garrett Morgan's "gas inhalator" was first acknowledged during a successful rescue operation of several men trapped by a tunnel explosion in the Cleveland Waterworks, some 200 feet below the surface of Lake Erie. During the emergency, Morgan, his brother, and two other volunteers—all wearing inhalators—were the only men able to descend into the smoky, gas-filled tunnel, and save several workers from asphyxiation.

Orders for the Morgan inhalator soon began to pour into Cleveland from fire companies all over the nation, but as soon as Morgan's racial identity became known, many of them were canceled. In the South, it was necessary for Morgan to utilize the services of a white man to demonstrate his invention. During World War I the Morgan inhalator was transformed into a gas mask used by combat troops. Morgan died in 1963 in Cleveland, the city which had awarded him a gold medal for his devotion to public safety.

### Norbert Rillieux 1806-1894
*Inventor, Mechanical Engineer*

Norbert Rillieux's inventions were of great value to the sugar-refining industry. The method formerly used called for gangs of slaves to ladle boiling sugarcane juice from one kettle to another—a primitive process known as "the Jamaica Train." In 1845, Rillieux (1806-1894) invented a vacuum evaporating pan (a series of condensing coils in vacuum chambers) which reduced the industry's dependence on gang labor and helped manufacture a superior product at a greatly reduced cost. The first Rillieux evaporator was installed at Myrtle Grove Plantation, Louisiana, in 1845. In the following years, factories in Louisiana, Cuba, and Mexico converted to the Rillieux system.

A native of New Orleans, Rillieux was the son of Vincent Rillieux, a wealthy engineer, and Constance Vivant, a slave on his plantation. Young Rillieux's higher education was obtained in Paris, where his extraordinary aptitude for engineering led to his appointment at the age of twenty-four as an instructor of applied mechanics at L'Ecole Centrale. Rillieux returned to Paris permanently in 1854, securing a scholarship and working on the deciphering of hieroglyphics.

When his evaporator process was finally adopted in Europe, he returned to inventing with renewed interest—applying his process to the sugar beet. In so doing, he cut production and refining costs in half. Rillieux died in Paris on October 8, 1894, leaving behind a system which is in universal use throughout the sugar industry, as well as in the manufacture of soap, gelatin, glue, and many other products.

### Mabel K. Staupers 1890-1989
*Nursing Executive, Civil Rights/Human Rights Activist*

Staupers was born in Barbados in 1890, and moved with her family to Harlem as a teenager. She graduated from Washington, DC's Freedmen's Hospital School of Nursing in 1917, returned to Harlem, and, by 1920, had cofounded a tuberculosis clinic for African American sufferers there. She served as the director of nursing at the clinic—named after Booker T. Washington—before deciding she could better serve in the profession as an educator.

The racism Staupers witnessed in a white hospital she became involved with—during her stint as superintendent of nursing at Mudget Hospital in Philadelphia—convinced her to work toward eradicating prejudice in the profession. Returning to New York, she served as executive secretary of the Harlem Committee of the New York Tuberculosis and Health Association from 1922 to 1934 before taking on a post of the same name at the National Association of Colored Graduate Nurses (NACGN), an organization that worked to improve working conditions for and erase racism toward African American nurses. With the outbreak of World War II, Staupers began enjoining the military branches to accept African American nurses into its medical Corps units.

The U.S. Army Nurse Corps was the first to integrate, but only grudgingly, with a quota system in place. Staupers fought—with the help of First Lady Eleanor Roosevelt—to end the quotas and win these African American nurses wishing to serve their country more equal assignments. By the war's end, the quota system had been eliminated and the Navy Nurse Corps had also been integrated. She dissolved the NACGN in 1951—shortly after serving as its president—because, as she said at the time, its aims had been accomplished. That same year Staupers was awarded the NAACP's distinguished Spingarn Medal. She recounted her life in the 1961 autobiography *No Time for Prejudice: A Story of the Integration of Negroes in Nursing in the United States*. Staupers died in 1989 a few months short of what would have been her one hundredth birthday.

### Lewis Temple 1800-1854
*Inventor*

The toggle harpoon invented by Lewis Temple so improved the whaling methods of the nineteenth century that it more than doubled the catch for this leading New England industry. Little is known of Temple's early background, except that he was born in Richmond,

Virginia, in 1800 and had no formal education. As a young man he moved to New Bedford, Massachusetts, then a major whaling port. Finding work as a metal smith, Temple modified the design of the whaler's harpoon, and in the 1840s, manufactured a new version of the harpoon which allowed lines to be securely fastened to the whale. Using the "toggle harpoon," the whaling industry soon entered a period of unprecedented prosperity. Temple, who never patented his harpoon, died destitute.

## Vivien Thomas 1910-1985
*Surgical Research Technician*

Born in Nashville, Tennessee, in 1910, Thomas had dreamed of a career as a physician since childhood. As a teenager, he worked as a carpenter and as an orderly to earn money for college, and enrolled in Tennessee Agricultural and Industrial College in 1929. Sadly, the stock market crash later that year eradicated Thomas's savings, and he was forced to quit school.

The following year, he was hired for a research assistant post at Vanderbilt University Medical School; he would be trauma researcher and surgeon Alfred Blalock's assistant. For the next decade, Thomas worked long hours in the lab, conducting medical experiments for Blalock that eventually led to lifesaving advances in medicine during World War II, especially in the use of blood transfusions.

When Blalock was hired by the prestigious medical school at Johns Hopkins University in 1940, he would accept the post only if they hired Thomas as well. Thomas then served as director of the medical school's Hunterian Surgical Research Laboratory, where he continued to test out the scientific theories Blalock presented. One of their most significant achievements together was a surgical procedure that restructured an infant's heart if the child was in danger of death due to poor circulation of blood into the lungs. Thomas virtually instructed the surgeon on some parts of the procedure he had already performed many times on dogs, and was present for the university's first 100 trials of the surgery.

Thomas became a well-known, and well-regarded figure on the campus of Johns Hopkins, and ironically became known as an unofficial expert in veterinary medicine because of his long research experience with lab dogs. He remained at the institution even after his mentor passed away in 1964, and in 1971 was honored by graduates of its medical school for his achievements. He became a medical school faculty member in 1977, but perhaps received more personal satisfaction from the honorary degree the university had awarded him. Thomas passed away in 1985, the same year a recounting of his life was published with *Pioneering Research*

*in Surgical Shock and Cardiovascular Surgery: Vivien Thomas and His Work with Alfred Blalock.*

## Levi Watkins, Jr. 1945-
*Surgeon, Educator*

Watkins was born in Kansas in 1945 but grew up in Montgomery, Alabama, where through his involvement in local churches became acquainted with civil rights leaders Dr. Ralph David Abernathy and the Reverend Martin Luther King. Both were prominent members of the Montgomery community, as was Watkins's own father, a college professor. The teenager's participation in civil rights issues did not stop him from excelling academically, and he graduated as valedictorian of his high school class and went on to earn a 1966 honors degree from Tennessee State University.

Watkins's awareness of issues of racial inequality led him to apply to Vanderbilt University Medical School, and he first learned of his acceptance as its first African American student by reading the newspaper headline announcing the breakthrough. He graduated in 1970, and began his internship and surgical training at the prestigious medical school at Johns Hopkins University. Watkins also studied at Harvard University Medical School for a time, and there conducted research that led to the lifesaving practice of prescribing angiotensin blockers for patients susceptible to heart failure.

In 1978, Watkins became Johns Hopkins's first African American chief resident in cardiac surgery and became a faculty member that year as well. Two years later, he made medical history with the successful surgical implantation of an AID (Automatic Implantable Defibrillator) device, which has been credited with saving countless lives by its ability to keep the heart pumping blood at a normal rate. In 1991 he became a full professor of cardiac surgery at Johns Hopkins, another first for the institution. For several years, however, Watkins had been working to increase minority presence at this elite medical school, and he instituted a special minority recruiting drive when he was appointed to the medical school's admissions committee. Watkins was known for writing personal letters enjoining qualified minority applicants to apply to the school, and because of his work, minority enrollment increased 400 percent in four years. Such accomplishments lend an added import to the campus birthday celebration Watkins organizes annually on Martin Luther King, Jr. Day.

## Daniel Hale Williams 1856-1931
*Surgeon/Physician*

A pioneer in open heart surgery, Daniel Hale Williams was born in Holidaysburg, Pennsylvania, on January 18, 1856. His father died when he was 11, and his mother

Dr. Daniel Hale Williams

deserted him after apprenticing him to a cobbler. He later worked as a roustabout on a lake steamer and as a barber before finishing his education at the Chicago Medical College in 1883.

Williams opened his office on Chicago's South Side at a time when Chicago hospitals did not allow African American doctors to use their facilities. In 1891 Dr. Williams founded Provident Hospital which was open to patients of all races. At Provident Hospital on July 10, 1893, Williams performed the operation upon which his later fame rests. A patient was admitted to the emergency ward with a knife wound in an artery lying a fraction of an inch from the heart. With the aid of six staff surgeons, Williams made an incision in the patient's chest and operated successfully on the artery.

For the next four days, the patient, James Cornish, lay near death, his temperature far above normal and his pulse dangerously uneven. An encouraging rally then brought him out of immediate danger, terminating the crisis period. Three weeks later, minor surgery was performed by Williams to remove fluid from Cornish's pleural cavity. After recuperating for still another month, Cornish fully recovered and was able to leave the hospital, scarred but cured.

Williams was instrumental in the forming of the Medico-Chirurgical Society and the National Medical Association. In 1913, he was inducted into the American Board of Surgery at its first convention. Williams died on August 4, 1931, after a lifetime devoted to his two main interests—the NAACP and the construction of hospitals and training schools for black doctors and nurses.

# 26

# *Sports*

# Sports

◆ Current Issues ◆ Baseball ◆ Football ◆ Boxing ◆ Basketball ◆ Other Sports
◆ Women in Sports ◆ Athletic Gatekeepers

**by Mark Kram and Craig Barth**

*The image of the black athlete continues to develop a positive face on some fronts. Several athletes are actively and positively involved in the community. Football legend Jim Brown operates the Amer-I-Can program which teaches self-esteem to prison inmates with the hope that they will positively change their lives upon release. Many other current and former stars are presently taking advantage of their popularity by reaching out to a society in need of guidance and support. As an example, the NBA's Terrell Brandon of the Cleveland Cavaliers has generously donated funds to his hometown of Portland and is actively doing his part to help revitalize an inner-city area there. This trend of "giving back" and remembering one's roots is both encouraging and significant.*

## ◆ CURRENT ISSUES

Much rhetoric abounds about the representation of African Americans in the sports arena. In a broad sense, it is generally difficult to gauge the inroads or lack thereof that blacks are making. Northeastern University's Center for the Study of Sport in Society issues an annual Racial Report Card that assesses the competency of the NBA, National Football League (NFL) and Major League Baseball in relation to the racial composition of those sports. The center's 1995 report is noteworthy and revealing.

Overall, minority coaching positions manned by blacks in the above mentioned leagues declined despite the addition of several expansion teams. Administrative positions (i.e. business operations, community relations, marketing and public relations) have also taken a

hit, most notably in the NBA and NFL. It is worth noting that playing great Isiah Thomas was recently appointed executive vice president of the NBA's expansion Toronto Raptors.

There is good news. African American assistant coaches employed by the National Basketball Association and Major League Baseball have reached an all-time high, with 40 and 18 percent representation, respectively. The center concludes its study by awarding final grades in the categories of front office and head-coach hiring practices. The NBA received Bs in top management and administrative positions and a B+ in coaching. The NFL received a C-, B-, and C+ respectively. Major League Baseball was granted a C in top management and B+ for managers.

*The Sporting News* annually ranks the 100 most powerful people in sports. The 1995 list includes nine African Americans, which is consistent with the prior year but does represent a 33 percent increase over 1992. The most recent tabulation includes Dr. Leroy Walker, president, United States Olympic Committee; Gene Upshaw, executive director, National Football League Players Association; Harold Henderson, executive vice president, National Football League; Bill Strickland, sports agent; and Rudy Washington, Head basketball coach at Drake University and the executive director of the Black Coaches Association, along with other figures. It is also worth noting that blacks are becoming increasingly prominent in broadcasting and as sports agents.

Other sports such as hockey, golf and horse racing continue to include only a smattering of African American participants. The reasons therefore are likely multifarious. One obvious cause is that these are traditionally "wealthy" sports. Many youths in American cities do not have the means to purchase equipment necessary to participate.

Basketball and football players continue to leave school early for the opulence of the NBA and NFL. Recently instituted rookie salary caps appear to be partially deterring early exits from college. However, the opportunity to receive more money than most young men have ever dreamed of is tempting. Some are now by-passing college entirely. This is not an entirely new trend, especially in the NBA. Historically, some have done so with great success (Moses Malone and Shawn Kemp). Others were somewhat less successful (Darryl Dawkins and Bill Willoughby). Minnesota Timberwolves' rookie Kevin Garnett was a Chicago high school senior in 1995 who has expressed some regret about his decision to forego a college education. Kobe Bryant, a prep phenom from Ardmore, Pennsylvania, announced his intention to enter the 1996 NBA draft. Other high school athletes are pondering a similar course of action.

Black attendance at sporting events continues to decline. In an ironic twist, the stratospheric salaries being paid to players such as Garnett have caused teams to raise ticket prices. This has made it virtually impossible for many inner city youths to attend games, reducing minority attendance. Another concern is the increasingly transient nature of sports franchises. Within the past year, four professional football teams have relocated, with several others considering similar moves. Often, ownership has to implement means beyond even lofty ticket prices, such as Personal Seat Licenses (PSL's), to raise funds to help defray the costs associated with these relocations. The upshot is to price less advantaged individuals and families almost entirely out of the market.

Drug abuse and more outwardly dangerous and degenerate behavior such as spousal abuse continue to pervade. These problems are obviously not limited to the African American community but are nonetheless a concern therein. Substance abuse policies exist in all major professional leagues, in varying degrees of severity. Unfortunately, reports of spousal abuse are prevalent. Recent incidents have involved athletes such as football's Warren Moon and Dan Wilkinson, baseball's Darryl Strawberry and basketball's Robert Parish and even a celebrated case involving University of Nebraska tailback Lawrence Phillips. The latter involved an abuse incident with a female student and stirred a maelstrom of controversy as Nebraska allowed Phillips to remain with the team. The fact that Nebraska won college football's 1995 national championship only served to fan the flames of the argument regarding the price of success and the exploitation of college athletes to reach that goal.

# ◆ BASEBALL

Long considered our "National Pastime," baseball was an incomplete entity prior to 1947. In an egregious miscarriage of justice that unfortunately was endemic of the era, African Americans were not permitted to participate in organized, professional baseball until 1945, when Jackie Roosevelt Robinson was signed to a minor league contract by the Brooklyn Dodgers organization and chief executive Branch Rickey, Sr., to play for the minor league Montreal Royals. Baseball's book on segregation in its Major Leagues finally began to close when Robinson took the field as a Dodger, at Ebbets Field, on April 15, 1947. Despite tremendous pressure and amid much hostility, Robinson persevered and was awarded baseball's rookie of the year award that season.

Unbeknownst to many, Robinson technically was not the first black to participate in professional baseball. Oberlin College's Moses Fleetwood Walker actually played with Toledo team of the American Association, then considered a major league, from 1884 until 1888, during which time baseball was actually integrated. However, a movement to purge blacks from baseball was initiated. Its leader was Adrian (Cap) Anson of the Chicago White Stockings, one of the great players of that era. His crusade gained momentum, and by the turn of the century, African Americans were essentially no longer represented in the Major Leagues.

Shortly after Robinson's arrival on the scene, also in 1947, Larry Doby became the first African American to appear in the American League, with the Cleveland Indians. Along with Robinson and Doby, other former Negro League stars, at various stages of their careers, had the opportunity to participate in the formerly all white Major Leagues, including Robinson's teammate Roy Campanella and Indians' pitcher Leroy (Satchel) Paige, long considered one of the sport's great characters.

Unfortunately, baseball's desegregation arrived too late for many. An all-time, all-star team of Negro Leaguers who, as victims of their birth dates, never appeared in the Major Leagues, could be assembled, which, arguably, would be comparable to any other. Catcher Josh Gibson; infielders Walter "Buck" Leonard, Judy Johnson and Ray Dandridge; outfielders James "Cool Papa" Bell and Oscar Charleston; and pitcher Andrew (Rube) Foster would have shone brightly in any era. Some baseball historians regard Gibson as the greatest baseball player of all-time, regardless of the league or era. Bell was perhaps the fastest player in history. It was said the he was so fast that "he could turn the switch off and be in bed before the room got dark." In all, 12 Negro Leaguers have been admitted to baseball's Hall of Fame on the basis of their careers in the Negro Leagues.

Josh Gibson was reputed to be the greatest hitter ever in the Negro baseball leagues of the 1930s.

After 1947, black baseball players began to make up for lost time as quickly as major league ownership would allow. By the 1970s, blacks dotted the rosters of every Major League team. Many have attained levels comparable to the greats of the early twentieth century and are now mentioned in the same breath with Babe Ruth, Ty Cobb, Lou Gehrig and other pre-1947 luminaries.

Remarkable achievements abound. Hank Aaron became baseball's all-time home run leader, considered the sport's most storied record, and has driven in more runs than anyone in history. Rickey Henderson is the stolen base king by a wide margin, with Lou Brock second. Lee Smith is the all-time leader in saves. Additionally, black players have been the recipients of the Most Valuable Player award in the American or National League over 35 percent of the time during the last half century. Center fielder Willie Mays is considered by many to be the greatest of all time at his position. Frank Robinson was the only player ever to win an MVP award in both the National and American League and was the first black named manager of a major league franchise. In 1996, Seattle's Ken Griffey Jr. became the highest paid player of all time, at over $8

million per year. Finally, many major leaguers, whose careers began after the desegregation of the sport, have found their rightful places in the Hall of Fame.

Curt Flood helped change the face of the game of baseball, but not because of his playing ability. In 1969, Flood decided to challenge his trade from the St. Louis Cardinals to the Philadelphia Phillies on the grounds that baseball's reserve clause—binding players to their existing teams—was in violation of Federal antitrust laws. A lawsuit brought by Flood was eventually heard by the U.S. Supreme Court, which decided that baseball could retain its posture as the only professional sport exempted from federal antitrust legislation. While Flood lost the case, he managed to open the door for the elimination of the reserve clause and the advent of free agency.

During the 1995 season, 19 percent of all players were African American, a decline from the peak seasons of the 1970s. One factor responsible for this change is the streamlining of inner city baseball programs and urban Little Leagues due to lack of financial support. The economic situation has become such in some American cities that even scholastic athletic programs are threatened with cutbacks or dissolution.

Baseball has made gradual, albeit modest, progress in the employment of blacks in top management positions. Although since deposed, Bill White was named president of the National League in 1988. The Colorado Rockies, San Francisco Giants and Toronto Blue Jays will begin the 1996 season with black field managers. Additionally, ten African Americans occupy top management positions.

The baseball landscape abounds with prominent black players. Aside from Griffey, current stars include Cincinnati's Barry Larkin, San Francisco's Barry Bonds, Cleveland's Albert Belle, Minnesota's Kirby Puckett, San Diego's Tony Gwynn, Boston's Mo Vaughn, Detroit's Cecil Fielder, and the Chicago White Sox' Frank Thomas. Cleveland's Eddie Murray and the recently retired Dave Winfield are likely to enter the Baseball Hall of Fame when eligible.

## ◆ FOOTBALL

Unlike the other major American sports, professional football was integrated from its inception. Beginning in 1919, with Fritz Pollard of the Akron Indians of the American Professional Football League as its first representative, African Americans participated until 1933. At that point, the National Football League initiated its eviction of blacks from professional football.

With the signing of Kenny Washington by the Los Angeles Rams in 1946, blacks began their re-emergence into professional football. The Cleveland Browns' full-back Marion Motley, who debuted that same year, was the earliest black superstar. Four years after the end of Motley's career, Syracuse University's Jim Brown began his career with the Browns and continued its legacy of great running backs. Considered by many observers to be the greatest at his position in the history of the NFL, he led the league in rushing for eight of his nine years and held the career mark for nineteen years after his retirement. Some consider Brown the greatest of all time, regardless of position.

By the end of Brown's career in the mid-1960s, several other black luminaries had emerged. New York Giants' safety Emlen Tunnel set the record for career interceptions while Chicago Bears running back Gale Sayers broke in as one of the league's most exciting and graceful players. Several other fine athletes were also dotting the NFL landscape.

African American stars continued to proliferate in the 1960s and 1970s. Charley Taylor was the first black to twice lead the league in receptions. Willie Wood was the first to lead the NFL in interceptions. In 1973, the Buffalo Bills' O.J. Simpson became the first player to rush for more than 2,000 yards in a single season. The visibility of blacks in the NFL became truly focalized with the popularity of certain teams' defensive lines and their familiar and catchy nicknames. The Minnesota Vikings offered the "Purple People Eaters", including Carl Eller, Alan Page and Jim Marshall. David "Deacon" Jones and Rosey Grier were mainstays on the Los Angeles Rams' "Fearsome Foursome". The great Pittsburgh Steeler defenses of the 1970s were fronted by the "Steel Curtain" which included "Mean" Joe Greene, among others.

During the 1980s, the Giants' Lawrence Taylor revolutionized the position of outside linebacker and made the quarterback sack popular lexicon for all football fans. In 1988, the Washington Redskins' Doug Williams became the first black to quarterback his team to a Super Bowl victory. During 1984, Walter Payton of the Bears eclipsed Jim Brown's record for career rushing yards and concluded his brilliant career in 1987 with more than 16,700 yards. Two current running backs, the Detroit Lions' dazzling Barry Sanders and the Dallas Cowboys' relentless Emmitt Smith have Payton's record in their sights. The San Francisco 49ers' record setting wide receiver Jerry Rice had scored an unparalleled 156 touchdowns at the conclusion of the 1995 season. Pittsburgh Steelers' cornerback Rod Woodson is an unquestioned superstar.

African Americans currently represent approximately 70 percent of those playing in the NFL. Minority representation in the NFL coaching fraternity as well as top management and administrative positions has re-mained somewhat constant in recent years. In the mid-1990s, the Philadelphia Eagles, Minnesota Vikings, and Tampa Bay Buccaneers employed black head coaches.

No discussion would be complete without mentioning the significant role played by predominantly black colleges in the development of football. Grambling's head coach Eddie Robinson continues to extend his record for victories by a head coach at any collegiate level and has now coached over 400 winners during his legendary career. Black colleges have also produced many all-time greats, including the above mentioned Payton, who starred at Jackson State. Currently, NFL teams feature several fine players from these schools.

## ◆ BOXING

Black athletes have been boxing professionally since colonial times. George "Little Chocolate" Dixon became the first African American to win a world boxing title, in 1886, and Jack Johnson became the first to win the heavyweight title, in 1908. In between, Joe Walcott captured the world lightweight and welterweight titles. Blacks have virtually dominated the sport since the 1930s, especially the most popular heavyweight division. Joe Louis held the world heavyweight title for a record 11 years and eight months in the 1930s and 1940s. Middleweight champion Sugar Ray Robinson is considered by many to be "pound for pound," the greatest boxer of all time. Henry Armstrong held three world titles at once-featherweight, lightweight, and welterweight-during the Great Depression.

Louis, Robinson and Armstrong were stars in what is considered the first Golden Age of blacks in boxing. A new Golden Age was ushered in on March 8, 1971, when Muhammad Ali and Joe Frazier drew the sport's first multimillion-dollar gate. Ali, a national figure since winning an Olympic gold medal in 1960, was one of the first athletes to exploit his position to comment on American political and social events. Almost single-handedly, he transformed boxing from a second-rank endeavor to a top drawing entertainment entity.

Other divisions too have featured stellar black fighters. During the 1970s and 1980s fans were thrilled by middle- and welterweight matchups featuring Sugar Ray Leonard, Marvin Hagler, and Thomas Hearns. When Ali was no longer able to defend his heavyweight crown, new challengers such as Larry Holmes and Leon Spinks ascended to the championship ranks.

As purses for major boxing events inched into the neighborhood of $100 million per match in the mid-

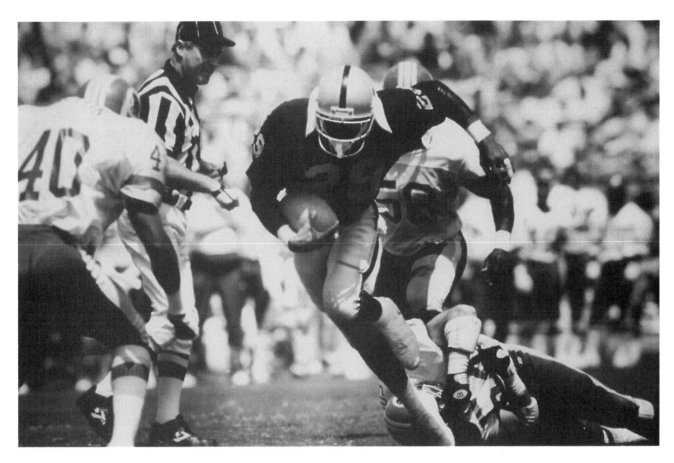

Eric Dickerson of the Los Angeles Raiders.

1980s, a new generation of fighters arose. "Iron" Mike Tyson, a tough youngster from Brooklyn, became the best known heavyweight champion since Ali and the wealthiest boxer of all time. His tumultuous reign ended with a knockout by James "Buster" Douglas, who in turn lost to Evander Holyfield. Holyfield was unseated in 1992 by Riddick Bowe, another product of the same Brooklyn projects in which Tyson had grown. Unlike the combative Tyson, Bowe earned a reputation for professionalism and social activism as he spoke against apartheid policies in South Africa and the need for more sports programs in the nation's ghettos. While other fighters, including Pernell Whitaker and Roy Jones Jr., have shone brightly in recent years, none have shone as brightly as Tyson, who regained the title in 1996, resoundingly defeating the Brit's Frank Bruno.

Top boxers can conceivably earn as much as $100 million for less than a dozen major ring events. The advent of pay-per-view television and cable network sponsorship has lead to soaring profits for the sport and its practitioners. Professional boxing features well-known black figures in all realms of the sport. Bowe, for instance, employs black trainers, including the well known Eddie Futch, and a black manager, Rock Newman.

Colorful entrepreneur Don King is both the most famous, wealthiest, and controverisal boxing promoter of the modern era. His powerful position in boxing's ranks, and his ability to ingratiate himself with champion after champion assure his continued success in the field.

The role of boxing's Golden Gloves Boxing Tournament cannot be overlooked in the development of the sport. Created in 1923 by *Chicago Tribune* sports editor Arch Ward, the Golden Gloves provided an organized forum for budding fighters to exhibit their skills. Integrated from the very beginning, the Golden Gloves served to bring the sport into the limelight as the boxers had a public platform to display their skills, in contrast to the dingy, shady clubs to which they were accustomed. For many, it became an avenue to great successes. To wit, future champions Joe Louis, Sugar Ray Robinson, Floyd Patterson, Muhammad Ali, and Sugar Ray Leonard all earned Golden Gloves titles.

Boxing is a brutal and dangerous sport, and it demands years of specialized training, rigorous conditioning, and singular dedication. The public appetite for major boxing events will continue to provide ample opportunities for talented athletes from all over the world.

Joe Frazier knocks down Jimmy Ellis, 1970.

## ◆ BASKETBALL

The integration of professional basketball saw its genesis in 1950, four years after the debut of the National Basketball Association. The initial African American representative in the league is arguable. Chuck Cooper, of Duquesne University, was the first to be drafted, by the Celtics, and owner Walter Brown. Nat "Sweetwater" Clifton was the first signed to a professional contract and is considered the most talented and colorful black player from that era. However, on October 31, 1950, when Earl Lloyd of the then Washington Capitols took the court, he became the first to actually participate in an NBA game.

Black presence in the game of basketball pre-dates those events. Until the NBA's formation, only loosely organized leagues existed, black or otherwise. The sport was more popular on the collegiate level. During 1916, educators, coaches, and faculty members from Hampton Institute, Shaw, Lincoln, Virginia Union, and Howard University formed the Central Interscholastic Ath-

Marvin Hagler

letic Association, the first black collegiate conference. Others soon followed, including the Southeastern Athletic Conference, Southwestern Athletic Conference and Southern Intercollegiate Athletic Conference.

Much of the legacy of black basketball history lies in its pioneers. Bob Douglas, who founded the Harlem Renaissance team during the 1920s, is considered the "Godfather of Black basketball." He was integral to the development of the game. His innovations included

Evander Holyfield

monthly player contracts; a custom designed team bus; and tours in the south, which was previously an untapped basketball bastion. John McLendon, legendary coach during the 1950s and 1960s is recognized as the strategic architect of the fast break and, furthermore, is the first African American to publish a book detailing his coaching philosophy. He is also the first to coach a national professional league team. Additionally, McLendon was a prominent advocate of the desegregation of intercollegiate athletics.

No discussion is complete without a mention of the world famous Harlem Globetrotters, basketball's "Ambassadors of Goodwill." From their inception in 1926, until the present, the Globetrotters have delighted basketball fans world-wide with their unique combination of skill and humor. Names such as "Meadowlark" Lemon, "Curly" Neal, "Goose" Tatum, and Marques Haynes are familiar to fans young and old.

A dazzling array of superstars has bridged the gap between the early years and today's NBA of Michael Jordan, Scottie Pippen, Shaquille O'Neal, Hakeem Olajuwon, David Robinson, Patrick Ewing, Karl Malone, Anfernee Hardaway, Charles Barkley, and others. Wilt Chamberlain once averaged more than 50 points per game in a single season and has more rebounds than any player in history. Bill Russell, considered the game's greatest defensive center, helped his Boston Celtics to an astounding 11 championships during the 1950s and 1960s. Kareem Abdul-Jabbar (formerly Lew Alcindor) holds the all-time record for points scored and games played in a career. Elgin Baylor and the remarkably versatile Oscar Robertson are considered among the best at their respective positions. Julius Erving revolutionized basketball with a rare combination of athleticism, style, and grace. All of these players have played roles in transforming the league into an exciting, fast paced affair that continues to gain in popularity globally.

African Americans now occupy more than 80 percent of the spots on NBA rosters, a figure that is increasing. Other areas indicate considerably less representation. Five teams began the 1996 season with black head coaches, although approximately 40 percent of NBA assistant coaches are African American. The Atlanta Hawks' Lenny Wilkens has won more games than any other coach in history, with more than 1,000 victories. Approximately 15 percent of top management and administrative positions are manned by blacks. It should be noted that in 1990, with the purchase of the Denver Nuggets, Bertram Lee and Peter C.B. Bynoe became the first African American owners of a professional sports franchise.

The NBA has received a spark from the recent comebacks of Magic Johnson, who retired in 1992, after testing positive for the HIV virus, and Michael Jordan,

Michael Jordan following one of the Chicago Bulls NBA championship victories.

Kareem Abdul-Jabbar

competitions. Their legacy began at the London Olympics of 1908, when John Baxtor Taylor became the first to capture a gold medal as part of the four by 400 meter relay team and was carried on via household names such as Jesse Owens, Bob Beamon, and Carl Lewis.

After lagging success during the decade of the 1920s, major strides were made in the following two decades. Prior to the 1930s, black colleges had been unable to offer quality track programs. Blacks therefore displayed their abilities at traditionally white colleges and in various clubs. During the 1930s and 1940s, African American track and field competitors ascended to the top of their sport, especially in the sprints and jumping events.

Jesse Owens was the beacon of the first half of the twentieth century. Owens is best known for his four gold medal performance at the "Hitler" Olympics in Berlin, Germany, in 1936, one of the most remarkable displays in Olympic history. However, it was on May 25, 1935, at Ann Arbor, Michigan, that Jesse Owens provided the greatest performance in track and field history at the Big Ten Championships as a member of Ohio State University. Owens began his day by equalling the world record in the 100-yard dash. He then proceeded to set the world records in the broad jump, 220-yard dash and 220-yard low hurdles, all in scarcely over one hour.

Others have left their imprints on the sport. At the Olympics of 1960, Ralph Boston broke Owen's long jump record, to win Olympic Gold. In so doing, he also became one of only two track stars to break a world record on six separate occasions. During the same games, Rafer Johnson set the standard for the decathlon. While Owens's day in 1935 is unmatched, Bob Beamon, at the 1968 Mexico City Games, provided the greatest singular achievement in track and field, and perhaps sports, history when he soared an astounding 29 feet, 2 1/2 inches to break his own world record in the

regarded by some as the greatest player in history. They have helped energize a sport that began to flourish in part with their original entry into the league. Their competitiveness and respect for the game is a welcome tonic for a league replete with precocious young stars and will only serve to enhance the sport.

## ◆ OTHER SPORTS

Black athletes have excelled in track and field, making an indelible mark at various Olympiads and other long jump by approximately two feet. Beamon's record would stand for a quarter of a century, until finally topped by Mike Powell. In 1984, in Los Angeles, Carl Lewis, "the world's fastest human," became the first athlete since Owens in 1936 to win four gold medals. Edwin Moses, one of the sport's most respected athletes, became the greatest 400-meter hurdler in history, dominating his competition well into the 1980s. Of late, 1992 Olympic Gold medalist Michael Johnson has been one of the sport's most impressive athletes. Johnson, a specialist in both the 200 and 400-meters also captured gold at the World Track and Field championships in 1991, when he broke his own record in the 200 meters. He was named male athlete of the year for 1990 by *Track and Field News.*

One of the most noteworthy events in Olympic history occurred not in competition but during an awards ceremony. In 1968, after finishing first and third respectively, in the 200-meter dash, Tommie Smith and John Carlos, while on the victory stand, raised their arms in unison in what has become known as the "Black power salute". Their purpose was to focus the world's attention on the plight of blacks in society and was a reflection of the climate of the times. The upshot was to forever alter the image of the African American athlete.

Other sports bear the enduring imprint of black athletes. The professional tennis community was basically devoid of blacks through World War II, a time when African Americans were not welcome by the U.S. Lawn Tennis Association (USLTA). In a sport primarily associated with the upper class, their only avenues were universities and colleges, clubs (if admitted) and various minor tournaments. Shortly after the war, the USLTA loosened its discrimination policy and, in 1948, Oscar Johnson became the first black player to win a USLTA-sanctioned event. Players began to sprinkle onto the scene. None bore the impact of Arthur Ashe, however.

With Althea Gibson having paved the way in the 1950s, Ashe became her male counterpart of the following two decades. The classy and congenial champion won the Australian Open in 1970, and the Wimbledon title in 1975, along with several less celebrated tournaments during his career. He represented his country as a member of the U.S. Davis Cup team ten times and was its captain from 1981 to 1984. As is the case with Gibson, no black male player has even approached Ashe's accomplishments. Ashe may have been an even greater champion off the court. Beyond even his significant contributions as a human rights activist, Ashe retained a dignity and grace, before and during his battle with AIDS, that won him the respect and admiration of people the world over, spanning all races and walks of life. The current hope to carry Ashe's torch on the court

is the University of Michigan's Mali Vai Washington, a young, promising talent.

African Americans' attempts to break into golf prior to World War II paralleled those of their tennis counterparts to a certain degree. However, the Professional Golfers Association (PGA) did not rescind its white-only policy until 1959, when Charlie Sifford became the first black to be issued a PGA card as an "approved player"—in fact, no black woman was approved as an LPGA member until Renee Powell's admission in 1967. Sifford was the best known of the initial participants on the tour. He was the first to win a predominantly white event with his victory at the 1957 Long Beach Open. Others soon followed. The notables were Lee Elder during the 1960s and 1970s and Calvin Peete during the 1970s and 1980s. Recently, teenager Tiger Woods, in amateur competition, has shown potential for future greatness.

African American luminaries exist in other sports. By winning the Brunswick Memorial World Open, George Branam became the first African Americn bowler to win a Professional Bowling Association (PBA) title. Hockey goaltender Grant Fuhr won five Stanley Cup championships as a member of the Edmonton Oilers. The Boston

Arthur Ashe holds the Wimbledon trophy, 1975.

Bruins Willie O'Rhee became the first to perform in the NHL, during the 1958 season. The great weightlifter John Davis was the first athlete of any race to win eight consecutive World and Olympic Championships, during a remarkable career spanning three decades. Superlative bodybuilder Lee Haney reached the top of his field by winning eight consecutive Mr. Olympia titles (1984-1991). Chris Dickerson won the same award in 1982. At one point, at the turn of the nineteenth century, cyclist Marshall Taylor, was among the three most celebrated black athletes in the world. During the same era, jockey Isaac Murphy, viewed as the greatest in the world at his craft, was part of a triumphant half century of African American jockeys. Oliver Lewis was a part of this tradition, winning the inaugural Kentucky Derby aboard Aristedes, in 1875. Special mention should go to one of the generation's greatest athletes, two-sport star Bo Jackson. Injuries derailed what would have been, in all likelihood, stellar careers in professional football and/or baseball. Before settling on football, Deion Sanders also played both football and baseball.

## ◆ WOMEN IN SPORTS

The world of sports has been greatly enriched by the accomplishments of many woman who have, in often anonymous fashion, attained greatness. Their contributions span the athletic spectrum, ranging from tennis, to figure skating, to basketball. Many such exploits occurred during the Olympic Games.

Alice Coachman became the first African American woman to capture an Olympic Gold with her performance in the high jump in 1948 and thus became the forerunner for future hopefuls. The valiant Wilma Rudolph, a model in perseverance, overcame debilitating childhood illnesses to win three golds at the 1960 Olympiad in Rome. Her teammate, 15-year-old Barbara Jones, became the youngest female to win a Gold Medal in track and field. In the 1968 games, Wyomia Tyus became the second African American to win more than one Gold Medal in one Olympiad as well as the first to set world records in two different events. Debi Thomas became the first African American woman to win an Olympic medal in figure skating, in 1988. Two years earlier, she accomplished her goal of becoming the first American black woman to win an International Senior singles title. Florence Griffith Joyner, the world's fastest woman, in a performance similar in significance to Rudolph's, won four medals during the 1988 Olympiad, including three golds. Not to be overlooked is Jackie Joyner-Kersee, owner of two Olympic gold medals, or the courageous Gail Devers, who has overcome the effects of Graves' disease to achieve a level of excellence that included a gold medal at the 1992 Olympic Games.

Florence Griffith Joyner

African American women have reached the top of their fields in other endeavors as well. Ironically, the first female black athlete to dominate her sport was tennis' Althea Gibson who did so in a traditionally "non-black" sport. A superb, all-around athlete, Gibson was named 1957's female athlete of the year during which she captured the prestigious Wimbledon singles' title and U.S. Lawn Tennis Association championship. She won both titles again in 1958, and was the undisputed number one women's player in the world for those years. This trailblazer had become the first black woman to capture a Grand Slam event in 1956 with her singles and doubles championships at the French Open. To date, no other black women has come close to matching Gibson's accomplishments. Zina Garrison-Jackson has enjoyed quite a bit of success in the sport, including a one-time Top 10 world ranking. She was also named Female Athlete of the Year in 1981. More recent talents have included Venus Williams and Lori McNeil.

The sport of basketball has abounded with unmatched female players since the 1970s. Indiana Pacers' star Reggie Miller may not even be the best player in his family; his sister, Cheryl's exploits have become legend-

Althea Gibson

ary in basketball circles. She was named All-American at the conclusion of each of her four years at the University of Southern California, was national player of the year three times, and was inducted in the Basketball Hall of Fame in 1995. The decade of the 1970s featured the great center Lusia Harris, the first woman to be inducted into the Basketball Hall of Fame. Others who have left their marks in basketball annals include University of Kansas star Lynette Woodard, perhaps best known as the first female member of the Harlem Globetrotters, having joined them in 1985. Pam and Paula McGee, teammates of Miller at Southern California, are world class performers. Most recently, Texas Tech's dazzling Sheryl Swoopes vaulted to the top of the game of women's college basketball as well as becoming the first woman to have a line of shoes bearing her name.

Notables in other sports include but are certainly not limited to the late volleyballer Flo Hyman; bodybuilder Lenda Murray, who had won the Ms. Olympia title six times as of 1995; and standout gymnast Dominique Dawes. Playing second base for the Indianapolis Clowns and Kansas City Monarchs from 1953 to 1954, Marcenia Lyle Alberga, a.k.a. Toni Stone, was the first woman in

the Negro Leagues. She boasted a .243 batting average as well as a career highpoint of hitting a single off a Satchel Paige fastball in 1953. More than 20 years later, another black milestone was reached when Wendy Hilliard became the first African American member of the U.S. National Rhythmic Gymnastics Team. And in 1994, Fredia "The Cheetah" Gibbs became the first African American to hold the Women's World Super Light Weight Kickboxing Championship title.

Unfortunately, very few women have the opportunity to display their talents on a professional level. Traditionally, women's athletics have long been hamstrung by the dearth of non-amateur forums in which black female athletes could participate. For many, the Olympic Games or intercollegiate athletics have been the final step of their careers, with the exception of basketball. Many find different ways of expressing their athleticism. Hilliard, for example, went on to coach the National Rhythmic Gymnastics Team; then in 1996, she became president of the nonprofit Women's Sports Foundation, an organization dedicated to improving the emotional, mental, and physical well-being of young girls and women by encouraging participation in sports and fitness-related activities.

As aforementioned, women basketball players have had better luck in entering sustained professional competition. One reason is that basketball has long been the top participant choice among U.S. high school girls. Many continue into their adulthood. For example, the 1996 U.S. Women's Olympic Basketball team included eight African Americans on the 11-member roster. Among them were U.S. Army Reserves First Lieutenant Ruthie Bolton, the first American woman to play professionally in Hungary and Sweden; Teresa Edwards, a two-time University of Georgia All-American and the first American basketball player of either gender to compete in four Olympics, winning gold in 1984 and 1988 and bronze in 1992; runway model Lisa Leslie; Katrina McClain, the world's highest-paid female basketball player, earning a $250,000 salary while playing on a Japanese team; Nikki McCray; Carla McGhee; Dawn Staley, two-time college player of the year and a professional player in Brazil, France, Italy, and Spain; and Sheryl Swoopes. Though these stars were formerly forced to play abroad, the American Basketball League (ABL) was slated to debut in October of 1996 with teams in eight to 12 U.S. cities. Players' salaries were expected to average $70,000 per year.

Women's athletics received a boost with the enactment of Title IX of the Education Amendment Act of 1972, which stipulated that any university receiving federal funds was obligated to varsity sports for women who wanted them. As Cheryl Miller once noted, "Without Title IX, I wouldn't be here." Women may never gain acclaim similar to their male sporting counterparts. However, our history has already been enriched by their accomplishments. As attitudes evolve, it is hoped that their place in America's sporting landscape will become even more visible.

# ◆ ATHLETIC GATEKEEPERS

### Hank Aaron (1934- )
*Baseball Player*

Born in Mobile, Alabama on February 5, 1934, Hank Aaron first played sandlot ball as a teenager. He later played for a team called the Black Bears, but soon thereafter signed a $200-per-month contract with the Indianapolis Clowns of the Negro American League.

In June of 1952, Aaron's contract was purchased by the Boston Braves. The following season, playing for their minor league team in Jacksonville, his .362 average led the South Atlantic League. This led, in 1954, to a promotion to the major league Braves, then based in Milwaukee, and the beginning of his brilliant career.

Aaron enjoyed perhaps his finest season in 1957, when he was named Most Valuable Player and led his team to a world championship. His stats that year included a .322 average, 44 homers, 132 RBIs, and 118 runs scored.

Aaron hit more home runs than anyone else in the history of major league baseball. He attained this plateau with his second home run of the 1974 season, a shot which marked his 715th career round-tripper and thus broke the previous record of 714 which had been held by Babe Ruth. Aaron finished that season with 20 homers and brought his career mark to a total of 733. He completed his career with a total of 755 home runs.

During his career, Aaron won a pair of batting titles and hit over .300 in 12 seasons. He won the home run and RBI crowns 4 times apiece, hit 40 or more homers 8 times, and hit at least 20 home runs for 20 consecutive years, a National League record. In addition, he was named to 20 consecutive all-star teams.

In January 1982, Aaron received 406 of 415 votes from the Baseball Writers Association, thereby being elected into the Baseball Hall of Fame. In the mid-1990s, he served as vice president/assistant to the president for the Braves.

### Kareem Abdul-Jabbar (1947- )
*Basketball Player*

Jabbar was born Ferdinand Lewis Alcindor, Jr. on April 16, 1947, in New York City. In high school, at 7'1/2'' tall, he was easily the most sought after basketball player, particularly after he established a New York City record of 2,067 points and 2,002 rebounds, leading

Hank Aaron, 1970.

Power Memorial High School to three straight championships. Power won 95 and lost only six games during Lew Alcindor's years with the team; 71 of these victories were consecutive.

Jabbar combined great height with catlike moves and a deft shooting touch to lead UCLA to three consecutive NCAA Championships. Twice, as a sophomore and a senior, he was chosen as the top collegiate player in the country. He finished his career at UCLA as the ninth all-time collegiate scorer, accumulating 2,325 points in 88 games for an average of 26.4 points per game. After leading UCLA to its third consecutive NCAA title, Jabbar signed a contract with the Milwaukee Bucks for $1.4 million.

In his rookie season, 1969-1970, he led the Bucks, a recently established expansion club, to a second place finish in the Eastern Division, only a few games behind the division winners—the New York Knickerbockers. Jabbar won personal acclaim for his outstanding play in the 1970 NBA All-Star game, combining with the Knicks' Willis Reed to lead the East to victory. After being voted Rookie of the Year, he went on to win the scoring championships in 1971 and 1972. He was one of the keys to the Bucks' world championship in 1971. In 1973, he finished second in scoring with a 30.2 point average, but he had become dissatisfied with life in Milwaukee. At the end of the 1974-1975 season he was traded to the L.A. Lakers. Jabbar enjoyed a very successful career with the Lakers, leading the team to NBA championships in 1980, 1982, 1985, 1987, and 1988.

A serious person both on and off the court, Abdul-Jabbar is a convert to the Hanafi Muslims. Greatly influenced by the life and struggles of Malcolm X, he believes that the Islamic religion (as distinct from the nationalistic Black Muslims) and determined effort have much to offer for a good life.

Abdul-Jabbar announced that his retirement after the 1988-89 season, one year after the Lakers had won back-to-back World Championships. He was inducted into the Baskeball Hall of Fame in 1995.

## Muhammad Ali (1942- )
*Boxer*

Born Cassius Clay, in Louisville, Kentucky, on January 17, 1942, Ali started boxing because he thought it was "the quickest way for black people to make it." After winning the 1960 Olympic gold medal as light-heavyweight, Cassius Clay turned pro. In 1963 he converted to Islam, although the faith strongly disapproves of boxing, and changed his name to Muhammad Ali.. A year later, Ali won the world heavyweight championship by knocking out Sonny Liston.

Nine successful title defenses followed before Ali's famous war with the Army began. Refusing to serve in the armed forces during the Vietnam War, Ali maintained that it was contrary to Muslim tenets. Stripped of his title and banned from boxing in the United States, Ali faced prison, but he refused to back down and was finally vindicated by the United States Supreme Court in 1970.

Coming back to the ring after a 3 1/2 year layoff, he worked his way up for another title shot. His biggest

Kareem Abdul-Jabbar

matches along the way were Superfights I and II against Joe Frazier in which Ali suffered his first loss, and, in a return match, evened the score.

Few fans gave Ali a chance against heavyweight champion George Foreman when they met in Zaire on October 30, 1974. A 4-1 underdog at ring time, Ali amazed the boxing world, knocking out his stronger, younger opponent. After regaining the crown, Ali knocked-out Chuck Wepner and Ron Lyle, and decisioned Joe Bugner.

In December of 1981, Muhammad Ali entered the ring and lost a bout against Canadian heavyweight Trevor Berbick. It was a rare defeat and an inauspicious end to a career for a fighter who had won the heavyweight title three times.

As he gets older, Ali's personal dedication to helping black people everywhere becomes increasingly more generous, and he now places special emphasis on setting a good example for black youth.

## Henry Armstrong (1912-1988)
*Boxer*

The only fighter ever to hold three titles at the same time is Henry Armstrong, who accomplished this feat on August 17, 1938, when he added the lightweight championship to the featherweight and welterweight titles which he had won earlier.

Armstrong was born on December 12, 1912 in St. Louis, Missouri. In 1929, while fighting under the name of Melody Jackson, he was knocked out in his professional debut in Pittsburgh. However, two weeks later he won his first fight. For the next eight years he traveled from coast to coast, fighting all comers until he was finally given a shot at the featherweight title on October 20, 1937, when he defeated Petey Sarron.

Less than a year later, on May 31, 1938, Armstrong picked up his second title with a decision over welterweight champion Barney Ross. Within three months he gained his own triple crown, winning a decision over lightweight champion Lou Ambers.

Armstrong was inducted into the Black Athletes Hall of Fame in 1975.

## Arthur Ashe (1943-1993)
*Tennis Player*

Born in Richmond, Virginia, Ashe learned the game of tennis at the Richmond Racket Club, which had been formed by local black enthusiasts. Dr. R.W. Johnson, who had also served as an advisor and benefactor to Althea Gibson, sponsored Ashe's tennis career, spending thousands of dollars and a great deal of time with him.

Muhammad Ali

Henry Armstrong

By 1958, Ashe reached the semifinals in the under-15 division of the National Junior Championships. In 1960 and 1961, he won the Junior Indoors Singles title. He was ranked 28th in the country even before he finished high school he was ranked 28th in the country.

In 1961, Ashe entered UCLA on a tennis scholarship. Ashe was on his way to winning the United States Amateur Tennis Championship and the U.S. Open Tennis Championship, in addition to becoming the first black man ever named to a Davis Cup Team.

In 1975, Ashe was recognized as one of the world's greatest tennis players, having defeated Jimmy Connors at Wimbledon as well as taking the World Championship Tennis (WCT) singles title over Bjorn Borg.

In 1979, at the age of 35, Ashe suffered a heart attack. Following quadruple bypass heart surgery, Ashe retired from active tennis. He began writing a nationally syndicated column and contributed monthly articles to *Tennis Magazine*. He wrote a tennis diary, *Portrait in Motion* and his autobiography, *Off the Court* and the book *Advantage Ashe*. In addition, he compiled the historical work, *A Hard Road to Glory: A History of the African-American Athlete*.

Arthur Ashe was named captain of the U.S. Davis Cup team in 1981. He was a former president and active member of the board of directors of the Association of Tennis Professionals, and a co-founder of the National Junior Tennis League. Late in his career, he also served as a television sports commentator.

In April 1992, Ashe announced that he had contracted AIDS as the result of a tainted blood transfusion received during heart-bypass surgery. He died on February 6, 1993.

### Ernie Banks (1931- )
*Baseball Player*

Nicknamed "Mr. Cub", Ernie Banks was a stellar shortstop and first baseman during his 19 year career, the entirety of which was spent with the Chicago Cubs. One of the most congenial and well-liked player the game has seen, Banks coined the now famous phrase "Let's play two"; an indication of his enthusiasm for the game.

Born in Dallas, Banks was slightly built at 6'1", 180 pounds but his powerful wrists help him produce a career total of 512 home runs. His 44 homers and five grand slams in 1955 were single season records for

Tennis great Arthur Ashe.

shortstops. His best season was 1958, during which he led the National League in at-bats (617), home runs (47), runs batted in (129), and slugging percentage (.614). He was named the league's Most Valuable Player after the 1958 and 1959 seasons.

Banks, who was moved to first base during the 1961 season at the age of 31 was durable, a fact illustrated by his 717 consecutive games played streak. He may have the somewhat dubious distinction of being the greatest player to never play in a World Series, as his Cubs rarely produced winning ballclubs during his tenure.

Banks, along with second baseman Gene Baker, formed the majors' first all black double play combination. He was the second African American to play for the Cubs, after Baker. Banks was elected to the Baseball Hall of Fame in 1977, and is also a member of the Texas Sports Hall of Fame.

After his playing career, Banks became a bank executive with Seaway National Bank. He remained very visible on the community scene, becoming a board member of the Chicago Transit Authority, the Chicago Metropolitan YMCA and of the Los Angeles Urban League, Banks also served in the U.S. Army.

## Elgin Baylor (1934- )
*Basketball Player*

Born on September 16, 1934, in Washington, DC, Elgin Baylor first became an all-American while attending Spingarn High School. While at Seattle University he was a college All-American. In 1959, Baylor made a sensational professional debut with the Minneapolis Lakers; he became the first rookie to be named Most Valuable Player in the All-Star Game. That same year, he was named to the All-League team, setting a scoring record of 64 points in a single game.

After five years as a superstar, Baylor injured his knee during a 1965 playoff game against the Bullets. Constant work brought him back to competitive form, but he never reached his former greatness. His career point total of 23,149 is fourth highest in NBA history, and his scoring average of 27.4 is second. His best year was 1961-62, when he averaged 38.2 points a game. When he retired in 1968, Baylor had made the All-Pro first team nine times and had played eight consecutive All-Star games.

Baylor was inducted into the Black Athletes Hall of Fame in 1975, and the Basketball Hall of Fame in 1976. He was head coach of the New Orleans Jazz in 1978-79. Since 1986, Baylor has been executive vice president-basketball operations for the Los Angeles Clippers.

## Lou Brock (1939- )
*Baseball Player*

Born in El Dorado, Arkansas, Lou Brock is one of the greatest base stealers of all-time. He stole 938 bases during a 19-year career which began in 1961, and was spent predominantly with the St. Louis Cardinals. Brock became the standard bearer for stolen bases on August 29, 1977, when the 893rd steal of his career eclipsed the mark that had been held by Ty Cobb for 49 years. In 1974, at the age of 35, Brock's 114 steals broke Mary Wills' single season mark, still a National League record in 1996. 1974 was one of the eight seasons in which he led the National League in steals. Brock registered at least 50 steals in 12 consecutive seasons and at retirement was the only player to hold both the Major League single season and career record in any major statistical category (stolen bases).

In 1967, Brock led the league in at-bats, runs scored and steals. The following season he set the pace in triples and steals, leading the Cardinals to pennants both seasons. With Brock, St. Louis also claimed a National League pennant in 1964, and World Championships in 1964 and 1967, over the New York Yankees and Boston Red Sox, respectively.

On June 6, 1964, in one of the most lopsided trades in baseball history, Brock was traded from the Chicago

Cubs to the Cardinals primarily for pitcher Ernie Broglio, who would win only 14 more games in the big leagues. Brock who went on to become a coach and business executive was presented with the Jackie Robinson Award by *Ebony* magazine as well as the Roberto Clemente award, in 1975. He was also the recipient of the B'nai B'rith Brotherhood award and was voted Man of the Year by the St. Louis Jaycees. Brock was inducted into the Baseball Hall of Fame in 1985.

## Jim Brown (1936- )
*Football Player*

James Nathaniel Brown was born February 17, 1936, on St. Simon Island, Georgia, but his family moved to Manhasset, Long Island, New York, when he was seven. While at Manhasset High School he became an outstanding competitor in baseball, football, track and field, basketball, and lacrosse; following graduation he had a choice of 42 college scholarships, as well as professional offers from both the New York Yankees and the Boston Braves. Brown chose Syracuse University, where he gained national recognition. An All-American performer in both football and lacrosse, he turned down the opportunity to compete in the decathlon at the 1956 Olympic games, since it would have conflicted with his football schedule. He also spurned a three-year $150,000 offer to become a professional fighter.

Brown's 1957 entry into professional football with the Cleveland Browns was emblematic of the manner in which he would dominate the game in the decade to come. He led the league in rushing; paced Cleveland to a division championship; and was unanimously named Rookie of the Year. Brown broke rushing and scoring records in both single season and lifetime totals, and he was All-League fullback virtually every season. His records include most yards gained, lifetime 12,312, and most touchdowns, lifetime 106. He was voted Football Back of the Decade for 1950-1960.

Brown announced his retirement in the summer of 1966, deciding to devote his time to a budding movie career, and to the improvement of black business. He has made several films, including *Rio Conchos*, *The Dirty Dozen*, and *100 Rifles*. In addition to his movie-making activities., he is president and founder of Amer-I-can.

## Roy Campanella (1921-1993)
*Baseball Player*

Born on November 19, 1921, in Philadelphia, Campanella began playing semi-professional baseball at the age of fifteen with the Bacharach Giants. In 1945, Campanella turned down the opportunity to become the first black in the major leagues, when he mistakenly understood Branch Rickey's offer to be a contract with a rumored black team in Brooklyn. A few days later, he learned from Jackie Robinson that the offer had involved the possibility of playing with the Brooklyn Dodgers of the National League.

In 1946, Campanella was signed by the Dodgers. However, before the year was out, Campanella was brought up to Brooklyn. Over the next eight years, the Dodger star played with five National League pennant winners, and one world championship team. He played on seven consecutive National League All-Star teams (1949-1955).

In January 1958, Campanella's career was ended by an automobile accident which left him paralyzed and confined to a wheelchair. In 1969, he was inducted into the Baseball Hall of Fame; he was inducted into the Black Athletes Hall of Fame in 1975.

## Wilt Chamberlain (1936- )
*Basketball Player*

Wilt Chamberlain was born in Philadelphia on August 21, 1936. By the time he entered high school, he was already 6'11". When he graduated from high school, he had his choice of 77 major colleges, and 125 smaller schools. He chose Kansas University, but left after his junior year with two years of All-American honors behind him.

Before joining the NBA in 1959, Chamberlain played with the Harlem Globetrotters. Although dominating the sport with the Philadelphia 76ers (1959-1967) and with the Los Angeles Lakers (1968-1972), Chamberlain was a member of only two championship teams, Philadelphia (1961) and Los Angeles (1972). For his gargantuan effort in defeating the Knicks in the latter series, including playing the final game with both hands painfully injured, he was voted MVP. At the start of the 1974 season, he left the Lakers to become player-coach of the San Diego Conquistadors (ABA) for a reported $500,000 contract.

Wilt Chamberlain holds most major records for a single game, including most points (100); field goals made (36); free throws (28); and rebounds (55). His season records include highest scoring average (50.4); highest field goal percentage (.727); and most rebounds (23,924). He was inducted into the Basketball Hall of Fame in 1978.

## Alice Coachman (1921- )
*Track and Field*

Alice Coachman, who attended both Tuskegee Institue and Albany State was the first African American to win an Olympic Gold medal and the only American woman to earn a gold medal at the 1948 Games, which she accomplished in the high jump. She was also an out-

Roy Campanella (right) with Sammy Hughes, 1942.

standing basketball player, earning All-American honors as a guard while at Tuskegee.

Hailing from Albany, Georgia, Coachman made a name for herself at a very early age, when, as a seventh grader, she high jumped 5'4 1/2", less than an inch from the world record. Very versatile, she won the Amateur Athletic Union (AAU) Outdoor 50-meter title four times; 100-meters three times; and the high jump ten times, dominating the latter event during her career. Indoors, Coachman won the 50-meter twice and the high jump on three occasions.

Coachman's ten victories without a loss, between 1939 and 1948, is an AAU record. She is a member of eight different Halls of Fame, including the National Track and Field Hall of Fame, the Black Athletes Hall of Fame, the Tuskegee Hall of Fame, and the Georgia State Hall of Fame.

### Willie Davis (1934- )
*Football Player*

Born in Lisbon, Louisiana, Willie Davis's career got off to an inauspicious start. After playing collegiately at Grambling, he was signed by the Cleveland Browns, where he was miscast as an offensive lineman during the first two years of his NFL career (1958-59). Moving to the Green Bay Packers in time for the 1960 season, Davis played for ten more seasons and enjoyed a magnificent decade on both a personal and team level.

Davis was an All-Pro during the 1962 and 1964 through 1967 seasons. He was an integral and inspirational cornerstone of a Packers dynasty, which included championships in 1961, 1962, 1965, 1966, and 1967 and did not miss a single game during his career with Green Bay. Following the conclusion of his illustrious career, Davis earned a master's degree in business administration from the University of Chicago—the impetus behind a very successful career in business and community relations.

Davis's off-field accomplishments rival those from the gridiron: He is president and owner of All-Pro Broadcasting, Inc. as well as serving on the Board of Directors of the Joseph Schlitz Brewing Company. Additionally, he is on the advisory board of the Black Peace Officers Association and president and director of the Los Angeles Urban League, among other endeavors. Davis speaks approximately once a week to a variety of civic and community groups.

Wilt Chamberlain

Lee Elder

Formerly a football analyst for NBC television, Davis has done public relations and promotional work for the Chrysler Corporation. He also toured Vietnam for the State Department in 1966, having previously served in the U.S. Army. He was named "Man of the Year" by the NAACP in 1978. Davis was elected to the Football Hall of Fame in 1981, and is also a member of the NAIA Hall of Fame.

### Lee Elder (1934- )
*Golfer*

Born Robert Lee Elder in Washington, DC, on July 14, 1934, Elder first picked up golf as a caddie at the age of fifteen. After his father's death during World War II, Elder and his mother moved to Los Angeles, where he met the famed black golfer Ted Rhodes. He was later drafted by the United States Army, where he sharpened his skills as captain of the golf team.

Following his discharge from the Army, he began to teach golf. In 1962, he debuted as a professional, winning the United Golf Association (a black organization) national title. Elder had played seventeen years with the United Golf Association, prior to his participation in the PGA, participating in close to fifty tournaments. He

debuted with the PGA in November 1967, finishing one stroke out of the money. In thirty PGA tournaments, Elder earned $38,000; he was the first black professional golfer to reach $1 million in earnings.

### George Foreman (1948- )
*Boxer*

Born in Marshall, Texas, George Foreman rose from a childhood of mischief and thievery to a championship career, eventually emerging as one of boxing's most endearing figures. During a turbulent childhood in Houston, Foreman was a truant, snatching purses and participating in petty larcenies. He claims to have been eventually saved by the Job Corps and football legend Jim Brown. His early success included a gold medal performance at the 1968 summer Olympic Games. Foreman was a physical presence in the ring, one of the fight game's most powerful punchers. His record featured 42 knockouts in his first 47 bouts.

Foreman captured the heavyweight title as a result of his victory over Joe Frazier, in Kingston, Jamaica, on January 22, 1973. Having twice defended his belt successfully, he prepared to face Muhammad Ali on October 30, 1974, in Kinshasa, Zaire, a fight that become known as the "Rumble in the Jungle." Despite being a three to one favorite, and considerably stronger than Ali, Foreman was out-strategized by the latter who used his "rope-a-dope" tactic to tire Foreman and victimize him in the eighth round. Ali spent much of the bout leaning against the ropes, protecting his head, and letting Foreman expend his energy. Ali took the crown.

Foreman eventually retired to become a minister and transformed his image into that of a congenial and very popular ex-champion. He initiated a comeback, which, after a series of tune-up bouts against overmatched opponents, resulted in a recapture of the heavyweight crown, when he defeated Michael Moorer on November 5, 1994.

### Julius "Dr. J." Erving (1950- )
*Basketball Player*

Julius Erving was born in Hempstead, Long Island, on February 22, 1950. As a player at Roosevelt High School, Erving made the All-County and All-Long Island teams. He was awarded an athletic scholarship to the University of Massachusetts, but after completing his junior year, he left college, hired the services of a management firm, and signed a $500,000, four-year contract with the Virginia Squires of the ABA. Voted Rookie of the Year in 1972, he renegotiated his contract and eventually signed with the New Jersey Nets for $2.8 million over four years.

In his first season with the Nets (1973), Erving led the league in scoring for the second consecutive year and led his team to the ABA championship. After being traded to the 76ers, Erving became a favorite with Philadelphia fans, leading his team to the NBA championship in 1983. Between his combined seasons with the two teams, he became the 13th player to score 20,000 points. Erving retired following the 1986-87 season. In the 1990s, the articulate Erving remained in the midst of a successful broadcasting career. He was inducted into the Basketball Hall of Fame in 1993.

### Althea Gibson (1927- )
*Tennis Player*

Althea Gibson was born on August 25, 1927, in Silver, South Carolina, but raised in Harlem, where she learned to play paddle tennis. After her paddle tennis days, she entered and won the Department of Parks Manhattan Girls' Tennis Championship. In 1942, she began to receive professional coaching at the interracial Cosmopolitan Tennis Club, and a year later, won the New York State Negro Girls Singles Title. In 1945 and 1946, she won the National Negro Girls Singles championship, and in 1948, began a decade of domination of the same title in the Women's Division.

A year later Gibson entered Florida A and M, where she played tennis and basketball for the next four years. In 1950, she was runner-up for the National Indoor Championship, and that same year became the first black to play at Forest Hills. The following year she became the first black to play at Wimbledon.

In 1957 Gibson won the Wimbledon singles crown, and teamed with Darlene Hard to win the doubles championship as well. In 1957 and 1958, Gibson won the U.S. Open Women's Singles title.

Gibson has served as a recreation manager, a member of the New Jersey State Athletic Control Board, the Governor's Council on Physical Fitness, and as a sports consultant. She is also the author of a book, *I Always Wanted to be Somebody*.

### Bob Gibson (1935- )
*Baseball Player*

Bob Gibson was born in Omaha, Nebraska into abject poverty. Fatherless, he was one of seven children, and lived in a four- room wooden shack. When able to sleep alone, he did so on an army cot. Denied a spot on Omaha Technical High School's baseball team because he was black, he was permitted to join the track and field and basketball teams; he became a star for each sport. During college at Creighton, he became the first black athlete there to play both basketball and baseball.

Gibson was proficient enough at basketball that he spent some time with the Harlem Globetrotters. While with them, he accepted an offer to join the St. Louis Cardinals minor league team at Omaha for a salary of $3,000 and a $1,000 bonus. Gibson debuted with the Cardinals in 1959, the start of a Hall of Fame career—he was inducted in 1981—that lasted 17 seasons and included five 20-victory seasons and 13 consecutive winning seasons. His highlights include a 1968 campaign in which he recorded a remarkable 13 shutouts, 22 victories, 268 strikeouts and an Earned Run Average of 1.12, still a National League record in 1996.

During his career, Gibson recorded 3,117 strikeouts, finishing with an ERA of 2.91. He was at his finest in the biggest games, winning seven and losing two games in three World Series appearances, with an ERA of 1.89. In Game 1 of the 1968 series he struck out 17 Detroit Tigers, though St. Louis eventually lost the series in seven games. Gibson did pitch the Cardinals to World Championships in 1964 and 1967.

Gibson, one of the most feared and intimidating pitchers of his era was considered sullen and difficult. Following his playing days, Gibson served as pitching coach with the New York Mets and Atlanta Braves. He currently is an announcer with the St. Louis Cardinals.

Althea Gibson, 1957.

### Josh Gibson (1911-1947)
*Baseball Player*

Josh Gibson has been considered by some to be the greatest baseball player who ever lived, regardless of race. He was a catcher whose entire 16-year career was spent in the Negro League, beginning in 1929. With the exception of a stint with the Pittsburgh Crawfords, between 1934 and 1936, and one season in Mexico, in 1941, Gibson played for with the Homestead Grays.

Gibson was born in Buena Vista, Georgia, in 1911, and subsequently moved to Pittsburgh, where he left school at the age of 14, eventually finding work with Gimbels Department store. Gimbels had a baseball team, which is where Gibson first attracted attention. His first game with Homestead took place on July 25, 1929, when, as a spectator, he was called out of the stands where he was watching a game versus the Kansas City Monarchs, to replace an injured starter.

A great catcher, Gibson was better known for his legendary power. Playing at Yankee Stadium, he once hit a homerun over the left field bullpen and out of the stadium. An even greater feat was a ball Gibson powered out of the same ballpark, to the top of the bleach- ers, an estimated 580 feet—the longest homerun ever seen to that date.

Gibson died in 1947, from a stroke thought to be brought on by his alcoholism. He was elected to the Hall of Fame in 1972.

### Lusia Harris (1955- )
*Basketball Player*

Born in 1955, in Minter City, Mississippi, Lusia Harris is the greatest center in women's basketball history. The seventh of nine children, the 6'3" Harris participated on the silver medal- winning Olympic basketball team in 1976, when women's basketball made its debut at the games and scored the first two points in Olympic history. In addition to the Olympics, where she scored the most points, she was also the high scorer in the 1975 World University Games and Pan American Games. In college, she led Delta State University to three Association for Intercollegiate Athletics for Women titles from 1975 to 1977. She was named Mississippi's first amateur athlete of the year in 1976. An acknowledged leader on campus, Harris was selected as Delta State's homecoming queen, the first black so honored.

Harris, the dominant female player of her era, broke hundreds of records and won countless American and international awards. As a graduate student, she became assistant basketball coach and admissions counselor at Delta State. She played briefly with the Houston Angels of the new Women's Professional League in 1980.

In the 1990s, Harris has been coaching basketball and teaching physical education in Mississippi. In 1992, along with Nera White, Harris became the first woman inducted into the Basketball Hall of Fame. Additionally, she spends time addressing groups as a motivational speaker.

### Larry Holmes (1949- )
*Boxer*

Larry Holmes was one of the most unheralded champions in boxing history. He lacked the flair of Muhammad Ali, the punching power of George Foreman, or the flamboyance of Sugar Ray Leonard. He was, however, one of the sport's most consistent and enduring champions.

Holmes was born in Cuthberth, Georgia, and turned professional at the age of 24. On June 9, 1978, he won the World Boxing Council heavyweight title from Ken Norton and defended it successfully seven times. On October 2, 1980, in Las Vegas, his conquest of Muhammad Ali by knockout unified the World title. The 38-year old Ali was no match for Holmes.

Holmes defended his title 12 times until losing to Michael Spinks on September 22, 1985, and again on

April 19, 1986, in 15-round decisions. In all, Holmes held the WBC/World heavyweight title for seven years, three months, and 13 days. A brief comeback attempt was stunted by a knockout at the hands of Mike Tyson on February 22, 1988. Holmes, who was voted one of the ten Most Outstanding Men in America by the Junior Chamber of Commerce, was currently in the throes of a second comeback attempt in the mid-1990s.

## Reggie Jackson (1946- )
*Baseball Player*

Because of his outstanding performance in the early fall, Reggie Jackson became known as "Mr. October." During his years with the Oakland Athletics and New York Yankees, Jackson captured or tied 13 World Series records to become baseball's greatest record holder for the fall classic. Reggie Jackson ranks among baseball's crop of players with proven superstar ability. His temperament, long reported to be as explosive and dynamic as his skill with the bat, gave him the drive to reach the top.

Born in Wynecote, Pennsylvania, on May 18, 1946, he followed his father's encouragement to become an all-around athlete while at Cheltenham High School, where he ran track, starred at halfback, and batted .550. An outstanding football and baseball collegian at Arizona State University, he left after sophomore year to join the Athletics (then located in Kansas City).

In 1968, his first full season with the Athletics, Jackson hit 29 homers and batted in 74 runs, but made 18 errors and struck out 171 times, the second worst seasonal total in baseball history. After playing a season of winter ball, under Frank Robinson 's direction, Jackson was back on track. His performance continued to improve, and, in 1973, he batted .293, led the league in home runs (32), RBIs (117), and slugging average (.531), and was selected Most Valuable Player (MVP).

While with Oakland, Jackson helped the Athletics to three straight World Series championships, from 1972 to 1974. Later, with the New York Yankees, Jackson participated in the 1977, 1978, and 1981 World Series, with New York winning the first two. In 1977, he was named series MVP, after hitting five home runs, including three, on three consecutive pitches, in the sixth and deciding game.

The first of the big money free agents, Jackson hit 144 homers, drove in 461 runs, and boosted his total career home runs to 425 while with the Yankees. Jackson retired as an active player in 1987, and has occasionally served as a commentator during baseball broadcasts. He has also continued to devote more time to his collection of antique cars.

## Earvin "Magic" Johnson, Jr. (1959- )
*Basketball Player*

Earvin Johnson, Jr. was born August 14, 1959 in Lansing, Michigan. He attended Everett High School, and, in 1974, made their varsity basketball team as a guard. While playing for Everett he picked up the nickname "Magic" because of his ball-handling abilities. While in high school, Johnson made the All-State Team and for three years was named the United Press International Prep-Player of the Year in Michigan.

In 1977, Johnson enrolled at Michigan State University and played college ball until 1979, when he was selected by the Los Angeles Lakers in the National Basketball Association draft. Johnson played with the Lakers until his forced retirement in 1991, when he tested positive for HIV, the virus that is closely associated with acquired immunodeficiency syndrome (AIDS).

Throughout his college and professional career, Johnson was an outstanding basketball player who brought much excitement, goodwill, and admiration to the game. He was the recipient of many awards and was chosen to play on many post-season all-star teams. He was All-Big Ten Team in 1977, and chosen as the NCAA Tournament-Most Valuable Player and consensus All-American (1979), NBA All-Rookie Team (1980), All-NBA Team (1982-89, 1991), NBA Finals Most Valuable Player (1987), and NBA All-Star Game Most Valuable Player (1990, 1992).

During his retirement, Johnson made appearances on the court, including playing on the U.S. Olympic Basketball Team in 1992, and the 1992 NBA All-Star game, where he won another Most Valuable Player award. He also coached the Lakers briefly at the end of the 1994 season, became team vice president, and had an ownership stake in the Lakers, which he was forced to surrender upon his return as a player in 1996.

## Jack Johnson (1878-1946)
*Boxer*

Jack Johnson, became the first black heavyweight champion, after winning the crown from Tommy Burns in Sydney, Australia on December 26, 1908.

Johnson was born in Galveston, Texas, on March 31, 1878, the son of a school janitor. He was so tiny as a boy that he was nicknamed "Li'l Arthur," a name that stuck with him throughout his career. As a young man, he "hoboed" around the country, making his way to Chicago, Boston, and New York, and learning the fighting trade by working out with veteran professionals whenever he could. When he finally got his chance at the title, he had already been fighting for nine years and had lost only three of approximately 100 bouts.

Reggie Jackson with the New York Yankees, 1977.

With his victory over Burns, Johnson became the center of a bitter racial controversy, as the American public clamored for the former white champion, Jim Jeffries, to come out of retirement and recapture the crown. When the two fought on July 4, 1910 in Reno, Nevada, Johnson knocked out Jeffries in the fourteenth round.

In 1913, Johnson left the United States because of legal entanglements. Two years later he defended his title against Jess Willard in Havana, Cuba and was knocked out in the twenty sixth round. His career record was 107 wins, 6 losses.

Johnson died on June 10, 1946, in an automobile crash in North Carolina. He was inducted into the Boxing Hall of Fame in 1954.

### Michael Jordan (1963- )
*Basketball Player*

Michael Jordan was born in Brooklyn, New York, on February 17, 1963, and attended the University of North

Earvin "Magic" Johnson

Carolina. As a rookie with the Chicago Bulls in 1985, Jordan was named to the All-Star team. A skilled ball-handler and a slam-dunk artist, he became the second NBA player in history to score more than 3,000 points in a single season in 1986.

Jordan was the NBA's individual scoring champ from 1987 through 1993. He was also named the NBA's Most Valuable Player at the end of the 1987-88 season. In 1991, Jordan led the Chicago Bulls to their first NBA Championship and was the league's Most Valuable Player. Under Jordan's leadership, the Bulls experienced repeat NBA championships in 1992 and 1993. In 1992 Jordan played for the 1992 United States Olympic basketball team, which captured the gold medal in Barcelona, Spain.

In October of 1993, Jordan announced his retirement from basketball to pursue another lifelong dream—to become a professional baseball player. His decision was made in part because of the stresses related with his basketball superstardom but also because of the pain of coping with his father's untimely death. (James Jordan, his father, was murdered in North Carolina shortly before the season ended.)

Michael Jordan began his professional baseball career with the Chicago White Sox's Class AA team, the Birmingham Barons, in 1994. Despite having only a .202 batting average for the year, Jordan was voted the most popular man in baseball in a national poll and remained at the top of Forbes magazine's list of the world's top paid athletes for the third consecutive year.

In 1995, Jordan expected to move up to Class AAA ball, but on March 18, 1995, Michael Jordan released a two-word announcement to the Chicago Bulls organization and the media—"I'm back"—simultaneously announcing his retirement from baseball and his return to the NBA late in the 1994-95 season. He was named the 1996 All-Star game MVP during the next season. Entering the 1995-96 campaign, Jordan, considered by many to be the greatest player in history, held the mark for the highest career scoring average at 32.2. On June 16, 1996, Jordan led the Bulls to their fourth NBA championship.

### Florence Griffith Joyner (1959- )
*Track and Field Athlete*

Born in Los Angeles on December 21, 1959, Florence Griffith started in track at an early age. She first attend-

Michael Jordan

Florence Griffith Joyner

ed California State University-Northridge, but later transferred with her coach Bob Kersee when he moved to UCLA. In 1987 she married 1984 Olympic gold medalist Al Joyner.

At the 1984 Olympic games she won a silver medal. She returned to the Olympic games in 1988, winning a gold medal in the 100 meter, 200 meter, 400 meter relay, and 1600 meter relay races. She set the world record for the 100 meter and 200 meter races that year.

### Jackie Joyner-Kersee (1962- )
*Track and Field Athlete*

Often touted as the world's greatest female athlete, Jackie Joyner-Kersee (b. 1962) won two gold medals at the 1988 Olympic games and a gold and a bronze medal at the 1992 games.

Born on March 3, 1962, in East St. Louis, Illinois, she studied previous outstanding woman athletes and soon teamed with her husband to pursue her dreams of success in the field of competition. Prior to winning the 1988 gold medal, she participated in the 1984 Olympics and came away with a silver medal for the heptathlon despite a torn hamstring muscle.

The only woman to gain more than 7,000 points in the heptathlon four times, she set a world record for the grueling two-day event with 7,215 points at the 1988 Olympic trials prior to the competition itself. Joyner-Kersee also earned another gold medal in the heptathlon and a bronze medal in the long jump at the 1992 Olympics in Barcelona, Spain.

### Dick "Night Train" Lane (1928- )
*Football Player*

Born in Austin, Texas on April 16, 1928, Dick "Night Train" Lane became one of the NFL's best-ever free agent finds. After attending Scottsbluff Junior College, Lane's 14-year career spanned three teams, the Los Angeles Rams (1952-53), Chicago Cardinals (1954-59), and Detroit Lions (1960-65), during which he earned All-Pro honors six times.

A cornerback, Lane twice led the NFL in interceptions, including a record 14 as a rookie. His 68 career interceptions place him third on the all-time NFL list. Lane, who was chosen as an all-time NFL All-Pro in 1969, and was voted All-Time Player of the Century in 1968, was inducted into the Pro Football Hall of Fame in 1974, and the Black Athletes Hall of Fame in 1977 .

Jackie Joyner-Kersee

Lane coached at Southern University and Central University in the early to mid-1970s. He was also an assistant NFL coach. Lane became the Detroit Police Athletic League Athletic Director in 1975. He is the founder of the Michigan Youth Development Foundation and is Past-President of the Detroit Varsity Club. He has been involved with the Boy's Club of Metro Detroit as well as the Booker T. Washington Businessmen's Association. During his playing days, Lane had directed youth programs in Chicago and Detroit.

### Carl Lewis (1961- )
*Track and Field Athlete*

Carl Lewis was born on July 1, 1961, in Birmingham, Alabama. In the 1984 Olympics in Los Angeles, Lewis became the first athlete, since Jesse Owens in 1936, to win four gold medals in Olympic competition.

An often controversial track and field performer, the New Jersey native went into the 1984 competition with the burden of tremendous expectations as the result of intense pre-Olympics publicity. He did not set any Olympic records, even as a gold medalist and found that his public image and statements were often the subject of public concern.

Lewis went to the 1988 Olympics in Seoul, South Korea, hoping to duplicate his four gold medal wins, and was the subject of widespread interest as he faced off against his arch-rival Canadian Ben Johnson.

Lewis won gold medals in the long jump and the 100-meter dash (but the latter prize came after Ben Johnson was disqualified following the race when he tested positive for steroid use) and a silver medal in the 200-meter dash. At the 1992 Olympics in Barcelona, Spain, Lewis won a gold medal for the long jump.

### Joe Louis (1914-1981)
*Boxer*

Joe Louis held the heavyweight championship, for more than 11 years, longer than anyone else and defended the title more often than any other heavyweight champion. His 25 title fights were more than the combined total of the eight champions who preceded him.

Born on May 13, 1914, in a sharecropper's shack in Lexington, Alabama, Louis moved to Detroit as a small boy. Taking up boxing as an amateur, he won 50 out of 59 bouts (43 by knockout), before turning professional in 1934. He quickly gained a reputation in the Midwest.

Carl Lewis

In 1935 Lewis came East to meet Primo Carnera, former boxing champion who was then staging a comeback. Louis knocked out Carnera in six rounds, earning his nickname, "The Brown Bomber." After knocking out ex-champion Max Baer, Louis suffered his lone prechampionship defeat at the hands of Max Schmeling, the German title holder who knocked him out in the twelfth round. Less than a month later, Louis knocked out another former champion, Jack Sharkey, in three rounds. After defeating a number of other challengers, he was given a title fight with Jim Braddock on June 22, 1937. He stopped Braddock in the eighth round, and began the long championship reign that was to see him defending his crown as often as six times in six months.

One of Louis' greatest fights was his 1941 come-from-behind thirteenth-round-knockout of Billy Conn. After winning a disputed decision over Joe Walcott in 1947, Louis knocked out the Jersey challenger six months later, and then went into retirement. Joe Louis died April 12, 1981 at the age of 67.

### Willie Mays (1931- )
*Baseball Player*

During his 21 seasons with the San Francisco Giants, Willie Mays hit more than 600 home runs. Besides being

Joe Louis, 1936.

a solid hitter, Mays also has been called the game's finest defensive outfielder and perhaps its best baserunner as well.

Born in Fairfield, Alabama on May 6, 1931, Mays made his professional debut on July 4, 1948, with the Birmingham Black Barons. He was signed by the New York Giants in 1950 and reached the major leagues in 1951, in time to become the National League's Rookie of the Year with 20 home runs, 68 RBIs, and the sensational fielding which contributed to his team's pennant victory.

After two years in the Army, Mays returned to lead the Giants to the World Championship in 1954, gaining recognition as the league's Most Valuable Player for his 41 homers, 110 RBIs and .345 batting average.

When the Giants moved to San Francisco, Mays continued his phenomenal home run hitting, and led his team to a 1962 pennant. A year later, *Sport* magazine named him "the greatest player of the decade." He won the MVP award again in 1965, after hitting 52 home runs and batting .317.

Traded to the New York Mets before the 1972 season, he continued to play outfield and first base. At the end of the 1973 season, his records included 2,992 games (3rd on the all-time list), 3,283 hits (7th), and 660 home runs (3rd). Willie Mays is one of only seven ballplayers to have hit four home runs in one game. After acting as a coach for the Mets, Mays left baseball to pursue a business career. He was elected to the Baseball Hall of Fame in 1979.

## Cheryl Miller (1964- )
*Basketball Player*

Cheryl Miller was born and raised in Riverside, California, and is thought by many as the greatest women's basketball player in history. She has occasionally been overshadowed by her brother, Reggie, a guard with the Indiana Pacers. Another brother, Darrell, played baseball professionally with the California Angels in the late 1980s.

The 6'3" Cheryl Miller began raising eyebrows at an early level, having once scored 105 points in a game while at Polytechnic High School. Miller was offered nearly 250 scholarships before deciding to enroll at the University of Southern California (USC). There she led the Trojans to two national titles, was All-American four times, and was named national player of the year three times.

Miller was a member of numerous national teams, including the U.S. Junior National Team in 1981, and the National Team the following year. She participated in the World Championships in 1983, the Pan American Games the same year, and, in 1984, was an integral component of the first American Olympic women's basketball team to claim a gold medal.

Since the end of her playing career, Miller has made numerous television appearances as a commentator. In 1993, she became the women's head basketball coach at her alma mater, USC, but announced her retirement in 1995, the same year she was voted into the Basketball Hall of Fame.

## Edwin Moses (1955- )
*Track and Field*

Born in Dayton, Ohio, in 1955, Edwin Moses became the greatest hurdler in track and field history. Having attended Morehouse College, he was the top ranked intermediate hurdler in the world as early as 1976. That same year he earned a gold medal at the Olympic Games, a feat to be duplicated eight years later. Moses also won a bronze medal at the 1988 Games. A world record holder in the 400-meter hurdles, his greatest accomplishment is undoubtedly his remarkable streak of 122 consecutive victories in competition. *Sports Illustrated* presented Moses with its Athlete of the Year award in 1984, one year after he won the Sullivan award, given annually to the best amateur athlete, regardless of sport.

Moses is currently an MBA-candidate and a partner in the Platinum Group. He is the chairperson of the U.S. Olympic Committee Substance Abuse Center and serves on the International Olympic Committee Athletes Commission.

## Jesse Owens (1913-1980)
*Track and Field Athlete*

The track and field records Jesse Owens set have all been eclipsed, but his reputation as one of the first great athletes with the combined talents of a sprinter, low hurdler, and broad jumper has hardly diminished with the passing of time.

Born James Cleveland Owens in Danville, Alabama, on September 12, 1913, Jesse and his family moved to Ohio when he was still young; the name "Jesse" derived from the way a teacher pronounced his initials, "J.C."

In 1932, while attending East Technical High School in Cleveland, Owens gained national fame with a 10.3 clocking in the 100-meter dash. Two years later, Owens entered Ohio State University, and for the next four years made track history, becoming universally known as "The Ebony Antelope." While competing in the Big Ten Championships at Ann Arbor, Michigan on May 25, 1935, Owens had what has been called "the greatest single day in the history of man's athletic achievements." In the space of about 70 minutes, he tied the world record for the 100-yard dash and surpassed the world record for five other events, including the broad jump, the 220-yard low hurdles, and the 220-yard dash.

In 1936, at the Berlin Olympics, Owens won four gold medals, at that time the most universally acclaimed feat in the history of the games. When Adolf Hitler refused to present him with the medals he had won in the various competitions, Owens' fame became even more widespread as a result of the publicity.

Willie Mays slides across home plate, 1956.

## Leroy Robert "Satchel" Paige (1906-1982)
*Baseball Player*

Long before Jackie Robinson broke the color barrier of "organized baseball," Satchel Paige was a name well-known to the general sports public. As an outstanding performer in "Negro baseball," Paige had become a legendary figure whose encounters with major league players added considerable laurels to his athletic reputation.

Paige was born in Mobile, Alabama on July 7, 1906. He began playing semi-professional ball while working as an iceman and porter. In the mid-1920s, he became a professional player with the Birmingham Black Barons, and later, while playing at Chattanooga, acquired the nick-name "Satchel" because of his "Satchel-sized feet."

For the next two decades, Paige compiled a phenomenal record. In 1933, he won 31 games and lost four. Paige also dominated winter ball in Latin America during the 1930s. In 1942, Paige led the Kansas City Monarchs to victory in the Negro World Series, and four years later he helped them to the pennant by allowing only two runs in 93 innings, a performance which included a string of 64 straight scoreless innings.

In 1948, when he was brought up to the major leagues, Paige was well past his prime, but he still was able to contribute six victories in Cleveland's pennant drive. Four years' later, while pitching for the St. Louis Browns, he was named to the American League All-Star squad.

Until the 1969 baseball season, Paige was primarily active on the barnstorming circuit with the Harlem Globetrotters and a host of other exhibition teams. In 1969 the Atlanta Braves, in an attempt to make Paige eligible for baseball's pension plan, signed him to a one-year contract as coach. Paige died in June 1982.

## Jim Parker (1934- )
*Football Player*

Born April 3, 1934 in Macon, Georgia, this guard from Ohio State University holds the distinction of being the first lineman ever inducted into the Pro Football Hall of Fame exclusively as an offensive player, an honor accorded him in 1973. He has also been elected to both the College and Georgia Halls of Fame.

While in college, Parker was the recipient of the Outland Trophy in 1956, awarded to the nation's outstanding lineman and was All-American in 1955 and 1966. A fine run-and-pass blocker, he provided protec-

Jesse Owens (left) with Ralph Metcalfe, 1936.

Jesse Owens (center) accepts the gold medal at the 1936 Olympic Games in Berlin, Germany.

tion for Hall of Fame teammate and quarterback Johnny Unitas during each of Parker's seasons in the NFL (1957-1967) and was named All-Pro eight consecutive years (1958-1965). The 6'3", 273 pound Parker was named to the first team Pro Football Hall of Fame Selection Committte" All-NFL 1960-1984 All-Star Team."

### Walter Payton (1954- )
*Football Player*

Walter Payton was born on July 25, 1954, in Columbia, Mississippi. When he retired as a running back for the Chicago Bears after the 1986 season, he was the National Football League's all-time leading rusher, breaking a record held for many years by Jim Brown.

A graduate of Jackson State University, Payton played his entire career in Chicago, receiving numerous awards and helping to lead the Bears to a victory in Super Bowl XX. Nicknamed "Sweetness," he broke O. J. Simpson 's single game rushing record after gaining 275 yards during a game with the Minnesota Vikings in 1977. Seven years later, during a game agains the New Orleans Saints, he surpassed Jim Brown's career rushing record and concluded his career with a total of 16,726.

Following his retirement, Payton continued his pursuit of a career in the auto racing industry and also fronted a group of businessmen in an attempt to bring a professional football team to the city of St. Louis.

### Calvin Peete (1943- )
*Golfer*

Born in Detroit, on July 18, 1943, Calvin Peete's ascendence to prominence is an unlikely story that finally landed him as the most accomplished African American golfer in history. During World War II, Peete moved with his family to Pahikee, Florida where he grew up. One of 19 children, he survived as a youth as a farm laborer and itinerant peddler, selling wares to farmers travelling up and down the east coast.

Constantly badgered by friends to take up golf, Peete's would respond "who wants to chase a little ball around under the hot sun." He finally relented, and at the age of 23, hit a golf ball for the first time, soon realizing that he possessed some aptitude for the sport. Unlike other black golfers of his era who were forced into caddying as a means of gaining entrance into the sport, Peete was able to move directly toward a professional career.

Walter Payton

Peete did, however, face the handicap of a left arm that he was unable to completely straighten; experts told him that he would never be successful.

After turning pro in 1971, Peete struggled. As late as 1978, he placed 108th in total money winnings on the PGA tour, but he soon made up for lost time. Peete's first tour victory came at the 1979 Greater Milwaukee Open, which he won again in 1982, along with the Anheuser-Busch Classic, BC Open, and the Pensacola Open. In 1981 and 1982, he finished first on the tour in the categories of driving accuracy and greens reached in regulation.

Despite his success, Peete was not considered fully accredited because the PGA does not recognize a golfer as such unless he has obtained a high school diploma. This was a requirement toward obtaining a spot on the prestigious Ryder Cup team. In 1982, with the assistance of his wife, a part-time teacher, Peete passed the Michigan General Equivalency examination 24 years after leaving high school. *Ebony* magazine rewarded him with a Black Achievement award, and, in 1983, Peete was presented with the Jackie Robinson award.

Peete captured two more PGA titles in 1983—the Georgia-Pacific Atlanta Classic and the Anheuser-Busch

Classic, for the third time. He was also asked to represent the U.S. as a member of the Ryder Cup team. That same year, he won the Ben Hogan award. The following year, Peete had the best scoring average on the PGA tour and was the most successful golfer of the decade to that point.

## Willis Reed (1943- )
*Basketball Player*

Born in Bernice, Louisiana, on June 25, 1943, Willis Reed spent his boyhood picking cotton around his hometown. He attended Grambling College, where he was discovered by Red Holzman, the chief scout for the New York Knicks. Reed led the Knicks in scoring and rebounding on his way to becoming Rookie of the Year in 1965.

In 1970, when the Knicks won their first NBA Championship, Reed received three separate MVP awards—one for the regular season, one for the All-Star game, and one for the playoffs.

At 6'9" and 240 pounds, Reed was not big for a center. However, he was named to the All Star team his first seven seasons. In 1973 he led the Knicks to their second NBA title and was again named Most Valuable Player. Unfortunately, knee problems ended his career. In 1981 Reed was elected to the National Memorial Basketball Hall of Fame.

## Jerry Rice (1962- )
*Football Player*

Born in Starkville, Mississippi, on October 13, 1962, San Francisco 49ers wide receiver Jerry Rice has been rewriting the NFL's record books at a dizzying pace. At a collegian at Mississippi Valley State, Rice set 18 Division II records. Drafted in the first round by the 49ers in 1985, the durable Rice, combined with quarterback Joe Montana to form the most elite pass-catching combination in pro football history.

Rice continues to add to his career record for touchdowns, regardless of position (156). His ten straight seasons with more than 1,000 receiving yards is also a league record. His best season was the strike-shortened 1987 campaign, during which he scored 22 touchdowns in only 12 regular season games. In that same year, Rice scored touchdowns in 13 straight games, including playoffs. In a 1990 contest with the Atlanta Falcons, Rice scored five touchdowns. He has been named to the Pro Bowl for ten straight seasons and was named the NFL's Player of the year by the *Sporting News* in 1987 and 1990. Rice was Most Valuable Player in the 49ers' Super Bowl XXIII victory over the Cincinnati Bengals.

Rice had helped lead the 49ers to Super Bowl victories after the 1988, 1989, and 1994 seasons and is known for his tireless work ethic. While on vacation, he has been known to travel with a parachute that he straps onto his back to add resistance while running on the beach. He traces the development of his superb hands to his childhood, during which his father would toss him bricks during construction work.

## Eddie G. Robinson (1919- )
*College Football Coach*

Life for Eddie G. Robinson began on February 13, 1919, in Jackson, Louisiana. Even at an early age, Robinson's knack for coaching was noticeable. Once while in grade school, several high school football players visited Robinson's class. All of the younger children swarmed the teens except Robinson. He was busy hanging around the coach.

As a gifted athlete in high school, Robinson earned a scholarship to Leland College in Louisiana. A star quarterback, Robinson got involved in his first coaching clinic there. After obtaining his bachelor's degree, Robinson took his first college coaching job in 1941. Though only 22 years old at the time, Grambling State gave Robinson the opportunity to run both offense and defense as he saw fit. The early success of Grambling State's football team earned Robinson much respect. Segregation, oppression, and a world war could not impede him. As the years passed, the wins for his football teams kept coming. By 1985, Robinson had surpassed Bear Bryant, the "winningest" coach in college football history in career victories.

## Frank Robinson (1935- )
*Baseball Player*

Born in Beaumont, Texas in 1936, Frank Robinson moved with his family to Oakland, California at the age of five. During his teens, he was a football and baseball star at McClyronds High School. After graduation in 1953, he signed with the Cincinnati Reds.

In 1956, Robinson made a smash debut in the major leagues, hitting 38 homers and winning Rookie of the Year honors. During the next eight years, he hit 259 homers and had 800 RBIs, an outstanding record, but one that was often underpublicized, because Robinson played in the shadow of such greats as Willie Mays and Hank Aaron.

In 1961, Robinson was named Most Valuable Player for leading Cincinnati to the National League pennant. Five years later, Robinson won the American League's Triple Crown and became the first player to win the MVP in both leagues. He retired as an active player after the 1976 season with a lifetime batting average of .294 in 2,808 games along with 2,943 hits, 1,829 runs, and 1,812 RBIs. His 586 home runs rank fourth all-time.

Frank Robinson was major league baseball's first black manager. Named to the head post of the Cleveland Indians in 1975, Robinson exhibited the same cool, confident demeanor that served him well during an 18-year career as a major league player.

Robinson left the Indians in 1977, and became the manager of the Rochester Red Wings, a minor league team, in 1978. In 1981, Robinson was hired by the San Francisco Giants, where he managed the team until 1984. He also managed the Baltimore Orioles during the late 1980s. He later became the assistant general manager of that team. Robinson was elected to the National Baseball Hall of Fame in 1982.

## Jackie Robinson (1919-1972)
*Baseball Player*

Born in Cairo, Georgia, on January 31, 1919, Robinson was raised in Pasadena, California. At UCLA he gained all-American honorable mention as a halfback, but he left college in his junior year to play professional football for the Los Angeles Bulldogs. After serving as an Army lieutenant during World War II, Robinson returned to civilian life with the hope of becoming a physical education coach. To achieve this, he felt he had to make a name for himself, and for this reason decided to spend a few seasons in the Negro baseball league.

In 1945, while he was playing with the Kansas City Monarchs, Branch Rickey of the Brooklyn Dodgers assigned him to the Montreal Royals, the team's top farm club, where he was to be groomed for a career in the majors. On April 10, 1947, the Dodgers announced that they had purchased Robinson's contract and the following day he began his major league career. During a 10-year career, he hit .311 in 1,382 games with 1,518 hits, 947 runs, 273 doubles, and 734 RBIs. He stole home 19 times, once in World Series play. He won the National League's Most Valuable Player award in 1949, and played on six National League pennant winners, as well as one world championship team. Robinson was inducted into the National Baseball Hall of Fame in 1962.

After his retirement from baseball, Robinson became a bank official, president of a land development firm, and a director of programs to combat drug addiction. He died on October 24, 1972 in Stamford, Connecticut.

## Oscar Robertson (1938- )
*Basketball Player*

Oscar Robertson was born in Charlotte, Tennessee in 1938, eventually moving to Indiana. As a teenager at Indianapolis' Crispus Attucks High School, he led his team to the prestigious Indiana state basketball title on two occasions and shortly thereafter became the first African American to play at the University of Cincinnati.

Brooklyn Dodger Jackie Robinson, 1949.

He helped Cincinnati reach the Final Four in 1959 and 1960, was named United Press International college player of the year for three consecutive seasons and set 14 major collegiate records. He is credited with attracting the recruits who led the school to two more Final Fours, including a championship in 1962. He also became the first to lead the NCAA in scoring for three consecutive seasons.

In 1960, and after participating on the U.S. gold medal winning Olympic basketball team as co-captain, Robertson signed a $100,000 contract with the Cincinnati Royals, earning Rookie of the Year honors during his initial season in the NBA. At 6'5", 210 pounds, he would become the NBA's first true "big guard". The multi-dimensional Robertson, known as the "Big O," was a textbook fundamental player and unyieldingly physical. During the 1962 season—only his second in the league—he led the NBA in assists, at 11.4 per game. His best season was the 1964 campaign in which he averaged 31.4 points per game, led once more in assists (868), shot free throws at a .853 clip and was named the league's Most Valuable Player.

Over the course of five separate seasons, Robertson, averaged more than 20 points and 10 assists per game,

something no other player in NBA history has accomplished. He was the Most Valuable Player of the 1961, 1964, and 1969 All-Star games. Robertson joined the Milwaukee Bucks in time to team with Kareem Abdul-Jabbar and lead the Milwaukee to their only NBA championship, in 1971.

Robertson became the President of the NBA Players Association. Under his leadership, the NBAPA established collective bargaining with the league's owners.

Florence Griffith Joyner and Wilma Rudolph, 1988.

Bill Russell

He was elected to the Basketball Hall of Fame in 1979, and was named to the NBA's 35th anniversary all-time team in 1980. Robertson was also elected to the Olympic Hall of Fame in 1984.

Robertson has remained extremely visible off the court, becoming a successful chemical company executive as President/CEO of ORCHEM, Inc. in 1981, and starting Oscar Robertson and Associates in 1983. He is a member of the NAACP Sports Board, a trustee of the Indiana High School and Basketball Halls of Fame, the National Director of the Pepsi-Cola Hot Shot Program and the President of the NBA Retired Players Association. Robertson was also the developer of affordable housing units in Cincinnati and Indianapolis. He served in the United States Army for eight years.

### "Sugar Ray" Robinson (1920-1989)
*Boxer*

Born Walker Smith, in Detroit on May 3, 1920, he took the name Robinson from the certificate of an amateur boxer whose identity enabled him to meet the age requirements for getting a match in Michigan; the "Sug-

ar" came from his having been dubbed "the sweetest fighter."

As a 10-year-old boy, Robinson had watched a Detroit neighbor, Joe Louis, train for an amateur boxing career. When Robinson moved to New York two years later, he began to spend most of his time at local gyms in preparation for his own amateur career. After winning all 89 of his amateur bouts and the 1939 Golden Gloves featherweight championship, he turned professional in 1940 at Madison Square Garden, fighting for the first time on a card headlined by the Fritzie Zivic-Henry Armstrong fight.

After several years of being "the uncrowned king of the welterweights," Robinson beat Tommy Bell in an elimination title bout in December 1946. He successfully defended the title for five years, and on February 14, 1951, took the middleweight crown from Jake LaMotta.

In July 1951, he lost the title to Randy Turpin, only to win it back two months later. Retiring for a time, Robinson subsequently fought a series of exciting battles with Carl "Bobo" Olsen, Carmen Basilio, and Gene Fullmer before retiring permanently, on December 10, 1965, with six victories in title bouts to his credit—more than any other fighter in history.

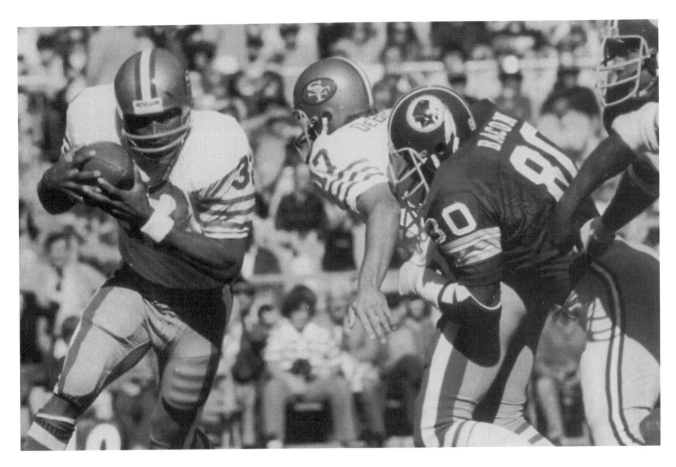

O.J. Simpson

Suffering from diabetes, hypertension and Alzheimer's disease, one month shy of his 69th birthday, Robinson died of apparent natural causes at the Brotman Medical Center in Culver City, California on April 12, 1989. Over his career, he won 174 of 201 professional bouts, including titles in three weight classes.

### Wilma Rudolph (1940-1994)
*Track and Field Athlete*

Wilma Rudolph was the only American woman runner ever to win three gold medals in the Olympic games. Her performance was all the more remarkable in light of the fact that she had double pneumonia and scarlet fever as a young child and could not walk without braces until age 11.

Rudolph was born on June 23, 1940, in St. Bethlehem, Tennessee, the 17th of 19 children, and soon moved with her family to Clarksville. At an early age, she survived polio and scarlet fever, only to be left with the use of one leg. Through daily leg massages administered in turn by different members of her family, she pro-

gressed to the point where she was able to walk only with the aid of a special shoe. Three years later, however, she discarded the shoe, and began joining her brother in backyard basketball games. At Burt High School in Clarksville, while a sophomore, Rudolph broke the state basketball record for girls. As a sprinter, she was undefeated in all her high school track meets.

In 1957, Rudolph enrolled at Tennessee State University and began setting her sights for the Olympic games in Rome. In the interim, she gained national recognition in collegiate meets, setting the world record for 200 meters in July of 1960. In the Olympics, she earned the title of the "World's Fastest Woman" by winning gold medals for the 100-meter dash, the 200-meter dash (Olympic record), and for anchoring the 400-meter relay (world record). She was named by the Associated Press as the U.S. Female Athlete of the Year for 1960, and also won United Press Athlete of the Year honors.

Rudolph served as a track coach, an athletic consultant, and assistant director of athletics for the Mayor's Youth Foundation in Chicago. She was also the founder of the Wilma Rudolph Foundation. Rudolph, a noted goodwill ambassador, was also a talk show hostess and

Bill White

active on the lecture circuit. On November 12, 1994, Wilma Rudolph died at her home in Brentwood, Tennessee of a malignant brain tumor.

### Bill Russell (1934- )
*Basketball Player*

Bill Russell, who led the Boston Celtics to 11 titles, including eight in a row, is regarded as the finest defensive basketball player in the game's history. The 6'10" star is also the first black to coach and play for a National Basketball Association team. His style of play is credited with revolutionizing basketball.

Russell was born on February 12, 1934, in Monroe, Louisiana. The family moved to Detroit when he was nine, but two years later the family continued on to Oakland, California. There, at McClyronds High School, Russell proved to be an awkward but determined basketball player who eventually received a scholarship to the nearby University of San Francisco.

In college, Russell came into his own, in his sophomore year becoming the most publicized athlete on the West Coast. Over the next two years, his fame spread across the nation as he led his team to 60 consecutive victories (a collegiate record) and two straight NCAA titles.

The Celtics had never won an NBA Championship before Russell's arrival in 1957. With the help of Russell's defensive capabilities, the Celtics became one of the most successful teams in the history of professional sports, winning the world championship eight years in a row. Russell himself was named Most Valuable Player on five separate occasions (1958, 1961-1963, 1965). In 1966, Russell became the Celtics player/coach.

After the 1968-1969 season, having led the Celtics to their eleventh NBA crown, Russell retired as both coach and player. He left the game as its all-time leader in minutes played (40,726), a record since surpassed by Kareem Abdul-Jabbar. In 1980, the Professional Basketball Writers Association of America selected Russell as the greatest player in NBA history.

After retirement, Russell was a color commentator on NBC-TV's NBA Game of the Week. In 1974, he accepted a lucrative contract to become head coach and

Willie Stargell

Michael Jordan

Charlie Joiner

general manager of the Seattle Supersonics. That year, he was inducted into the Basketball Hall of Fame. He remained at Seattle's helm through 1977 and returned to the coaching ranks ten years later for a one-year stint with the Sacramento Kings. He was named the team's director of player personnel in 1988.

## Gale Sayers (1943- )
*Football Player*

Gale Sayers was born into an impoverished Wichita, Kansas household on May 30, 1943. He proceeded to star not only in football but also in track while in high school and decided to enroll at Kansas University. He signed with the Chicago Bears before graduating but returned to finish and eventually earn a master's degree.

Sayers quickly made his mark, garnering All-Pro honors in his rookie season of 1965 and three of the next four. His graceful, shifty running style soon became admired by anyone who had the opportunity to watch him perform. His ability to make defenders "miss" was uncanny. Sayers led the league in rushing in 1969, and was also its highest paid player. In a 1965 game against the San Francisco 49ers, he tied an NFL record by scoring six touchdowns.

Sayers's career was ended prematurely after the 1971 season due to a knee injury which robbed him of much of his trademark mobility. His final totals included 56 touchdowns; 39 scored rushing, 9 receiving, six via kickoff returns (including a 103 yarder in 1967), and two on punt returns. He was named to the "All-NFL 1960-1984 All-Star Team" as a kick returner. Despite his brief career, he was recognized by virtue of his induction into the Pro Football Hall of Fame in 1977.

Following his playing career, Sayers was named assistant to the athletic director at Kansas and in 1981, became the athletic director at Southern Illinois University. Very active in the community, Sayers has been the commissioner of the Chicago Park District; the co-chairperson of the legal defense fund for sports, NAACP

Jesse Owens, 1936.

Coordinator; and an honorary chairman of the American Cancer Society in addition to his involvement in the Reach Out Program. In 1984, Sayers founded his own company, "Computer Supplies by Sayers."

### Charlie Sifford (1922- )
*Golfer*

The most famous African American golfer prior to 1970, Charlie Sifford, from Charlotte, North Carolina, was the first black to participate in a predominately white event, the 1957 Long Beach Open. Sifford's entry into golf began as a caddie at the age of nine. At 13, he won a caddie tournament shooting a 70. First prize consisted of $10 and a case of Pepsi-Cola. After moving to Philadelphia, Sifford worked as a teaching professional and chauffeur.

Sifford became the first African American to be awarded a PGA card as an approved player, in 1959, as the tour lifted its "Caucasian only" clause. He was also the first to win a major PGA event, the Los Angeles Open, in 1969. On the Seniors tour, Sifford triumphed at the PGA Seniors Open (1975), and the Suntree Seniors Open (1980). He also won the Negro National Title six times.

### O. J. Simpson (1947- )
*Football Player*

Orenthal J. Simpson may have been the finest running back in pro football. Nicknamed "The Juice," he made his mark by becoming the first back to gain more than 2,000 rushing yards in a season, amassing a total of 2,003 in 1973.

Born in San Francisco on July 9, 1947, Simpson starred at the University of Southern California, winning the Heisman Trophy in 1968. One year prior to that, he was a member of the USC relay team that set a world record of 38.6 seconds in the 440-yard run. One year after graduation, ABC Sports voted him College Player of the Decade. He signed with the Buffalo Bills in 1969, and three years later achieved his first rushing title, gaining more than 1,200 yards.

Simpson enjoyed his finest season in 1973. On opening day, he rushed for 250 yards against the New England Patriots, breaking the record of 247 yards held by Willie Ellison. His astonishing yardage total for the entire season surpassed the previous mark of 1,863 held by Jim Brown. In addition, he scored 12 touchdowns, averaged six yards per carry, and had more rushing yardage than 15 other NFL clubs. He was named Player of the Year and won the Jim Thorpe Trophy.

Simpson retired from football in 1978. He has appeared in several feature films and worked as a sports commentator for ABC-TV and NBC-TV. In 1995, a jury found Simpson not guilty of charges that he had brutally slain his ex-wife and a male friend who had been found dead outside of her California home in the summer of 1994, a decision that divided the nation as the so-called "Trial of the Century" was completed.

### Lawrence Taylor (1959- )
*Football Player*

Born in Williamsbug, Virginia, Lawrence Taylor is considered the best outside linebacker in professional football history and revolutionized the position. His style was so disruptive that opposing offenses occasionally would invariably design their game plans around stopping or at least slowing him down. His relentless forays to the quarterback popularized the term "quarterback sack," now an integral part of the football lexicon.

After an outstanding career at the University of North Carolina where he was named Atlantic Coast Conference Player of the Year in 1980, Taylor was taken by the New York Giants with the second pick of the 1981 draft, behind only running back George Rogers, chosen by the New Orleans Saints. Taylor amassed 132 1/2 career sacks, an NFL record that would eventually be broken by Reggie White, a defensive lineman. Taylor was an integral part of two Giants Super Bowl championships, following the 1986 and 1990 seasons. He was named to the NFL's All-Decade team for the 1980s.

### Debi Thomas (1967- )
*Figure Skater*

Born in Poughkipsee, New York, Debi Thomas is the premier African American figure skater. The graceful and creative Thomas was the winner at the 1985 National Sports Festival in Baton Rouge. The following year she captured the U.S. and World figure skating titles, becoming the first African American to capture an international singles meet. Having attended Stanford and majored in pre-med, she was an Olympic bronze medalist at the 1988 Games. In 1985, Thomas had been the winner at the National Sports Festival in Baton Rouge.

### Gene Upshaw (1945- )
*Football Player*

As a guard for Oakland/Los Angeles Raiders from 1967 to 1982, Gene Upshaw was an anchor on the Raiders offensive line. For 14 of those seasons, he teamed with future Raider coach Art Shell to form the greatest tandem guard/tackle in NFL history.

Born in Robstown, Texas, Upshaw attended Texas A&I University. He was named All-Pro or to the Pro-Bowl eight consecutive years, between 1967 and 1974, and received his induction to the Pro Football Hall of Fame in 1987.

Upshaw is currently the executive director of the National Football League Players Association, a post he has held since 1982. Under his leadership, the organization has expended considerable resources on education and rehabilitation for substance abuse. Upshaw is also the president of the Federation of Professional Athletes AFL-CIO as well as serving on the California Governor's Council on Wellness and Physical Fitness. He is the coordinator for voter registration and fundraising in Alameda, California county and served as the planning commissioner for that same county.

Upshaw was the recipient of the Byron (Whizzer) White Humanitarian award as voted by the NFL players in 1980. In 1982, he was presented with the A. Philip Randolph Award, by the A. Philip Randolph Institute. In a recent poll by the *Sporting News*, Upshaw was named the 45th most powerful figure in sports.

## Marshall W. "Major" Taylor (1878-1932)
*Cyclist*

Marshall W. "Major" Taylor became America's first black U.S. National Champion in 1899. Born in Indianapolis in 1878, the son of a coachman, he worked at a bicycle store part-time as a teen. After attending his first race, his boss suggested that Major enter a couple of races. To their surprise, he won a 10-mile race and proceeded to compete as an amateur.

By the time he was 16, he went to work in a factory owned by a former champion, and with his new boss's encouragement, competed in races in Canada, Europe, Australia and New Zealand.

During nearly 16 years of competition, he won numerous championships and set several world records. Years after he retired, he met President Theodore Roosevelt, who told him that he had followed his career with admiration. Taylor was inducted into the Bicycle Hall of Fame. He died in 1932.

## Bill White (1934- )
*National League of Professional Baseball Clubs President*

William DeKova White was born in Lakewood, Florida, on January 28, 1934. He began his major league career with the New York Giants in 1956 and spent thirteen years as a player with the San Francisco Giants, St. Louis Cardinals, and the Philadelphia Phillies. During his career, White was named to the National League All-Star team six times and won seven Gold Gloves. He retired form baseball in 1969, and in 1971 joined Phil Rizzuto as a television play-by-play announcer for the New York Yankees.

On April 1, 1989, Bill White became the first African American president of the National League.

## African American Olympic Medalists

| Place/Year | Athlete | Event | Place | Time or Distance |
|---|---|---|---|---|
| St. Louis, 1904 | George C. Poag | 200 m hurdles | 3rd | |
| | George C. Poag | 400 m hurdles | 3rd | |
| London, 1908 | J.B. Taylor | 1600 m relay | 1st | 3:29.4 |
| Paris, 1924 | Dehart Hubbard | Long jump | 1st | 24'5.125" |
| | Edward Gourdin | Long jump | 2nd | 23'10" |
| Los Angeles, 1932 | Eddie Tolan | 100 m dash | 1st | 10.3 |
| | Ralph Metcalfe | 100 m dash | 2nd | 10.3 |
| | Eddie Tolan | 200 m dash | 1st | 21.2 |
| | Ralph Metcalfe | 200 m dash | 3rd | 21.5 |
| | Edward Gordon | Long jump | 1st | 25' 0.75" |
| Berlin, 1936 | Jesse Owens | 100 m dash | 1st | 10.3 |
| | Ralph Metcalfe | 100 m dash | 2nd | 10.4 |
| | Jesse Owens | 200 m dash | 1st | 20.7 |
| | Matthew Robinson | 200 m dash | 2nd | 21.1 |
| | Archie Williams | 400 m run | 1st | 46.5 |
| | James DuValle | 400 m run | 2nd | 46.8 |
| | John Woodruff | 800 m run | 1st | 1:52.9 |
| | Fritz Pollard, Jr. | 110 m hurdles | 3rd | 14.4 |
| | Cornelius Johnson | High jump | 1st | 6'8" |
| | Jesse Owens | Long jump | 1st | 26' 5.75" |
| | Jesse Owens | 400 m relay | 1st | 39.8 |
| | Ralph Metcalfe | 400 m relay | 1st | 39.8 |
| London, 1948 | Harrison Dillard | 100 m dash | 1st | 10.3 |
| | Norwood Ewell | 100 m dash | 2nd | 10.4 |
| | Norwood Ewell | 200 m dash | 1st | 21.1 |
| | Mal Whitfield | 400 m run | 3rd | 46.9 |
| | Willie Steele | Long jump | 1st | 25' 8" |
| | Herbert Douglass | Long jump | 3rd | 25' 3" |
| | Lorenzo Wright | 400 m relay | 1st | 40.6 |
| | Harrison Dillard | 1600 m relay | 1st | 3.10.4 |
| | Norwood Ewell | 1600 m relay | 1st | 3.10.4 |
| | Mal Whitfield | 1600 m relay | 1st | 3.10.4 |
| | Audrey Patterson | 200 m dash | 3rd | 25.2 |
| | Alice Coachman | High jump | 1st | 5' 6.125" |
| Helsinki, 1952 | Andrew Stanfield | 200 m dash | 1st | 20.7 |
| | Ollie Matson | 400 m run | 3rd | 46.8 |
| | Mal Whitfield | 800 m run | 1st | 1:49.2 |
| | Harrison Dillard | 110 m hurdles | 1st | 13.7 |
| | Jerome Biffle | Long jump | 1st | 24' 10" |
| | Meredith Gourdine | Long jump | 2nd | 24' 8.125" |
| | Harrison Dillard | 400 m relay | 1st | 40.1 |
| | Andrew Stanfield | 400 m relay | 1st | 40.1 |
| | Ollie Matson | 400 m relay | 1st | 40.1 |
| | Bill Miller | Javelin | 2nd | 237 |
| | Milton Campbell | Decathlon | 2nd | 6,975 pts. |
| | Barbara Jones | 400 m relay | 1st | 45.9 |
| Melbourne, 1956 | Andrew Stanfield | 200 m dash | 2nd | 20.7 |
| | Charles Jenkins | 400 m run | 1st | 46.7 |
| | Lee Calhoun | 110 m hurdles | 1st | 13.5 |
| | Charles Dumas | High jump | 1st | 6" 11.25" |
| | Gregory Bell | Long jump | 1st | 25' 8.25" |
| | Willye White | Long jump | 2nd | 19" 11.75" |
| | Ira Murchison | 400 m relay | 1st | 39.5 |
| | Leamon King | 400 m relay | 1st | 39.5 |

| Place/Year | Athlete | Event | Place | Time or Distance |
|---|---|---|---|---|
| | Charles Jenkins | | | |
| | Lou Jones | 1600 m relay | 1st | 3:04.8 |
| | Milton Campbell | Decathlon | 1st | 7,937 pts. |
| | Rafer Johnson | Decathlon | 2nd | 7,587 pts. |
| | Mildred McDaniel | High jump | 1st | 5' 9.25" |
| | Margret Matthews | 400 m relay | 3rd | 44.9 |
| | Isabelle Daniels | 400 m relay | 3rd | 44.9 |
| | Mae Faggs | 400 m relay | 3rd | 44.9 |
| | Wilma Rudolph | 400 m relay | 3rd | 44.9 |
| Rome, 1960 | Les Carney | 200 m dash | 2nd | 20.6 |
| | Lee Calhoun | 110 m hurdles | 1st | 13.8 |
| | Willie May | 100 m hurdles | 2nd | 13.8 |
| | Hayes Jones | 110 m hurdles | 3rd | 14 |
| | Otis Davis | 400 m run | 1st | 44.9 |
| | John Thomas | High jump | 3rd | 7" 0.25" |
| | Ralph Boston | Long jump | 1st | 26' 7.75" |
| | Irvin Roberson | Long jump | 2nd | 26' 7.25" |
| | Otis Davis | 1600 m relay | 1st | 3:02.2 |
| | Rafer Johnson | Decathlon | 1st | 8,392 pts. |
| | Earlene Brown | Shot put | 3rd | 53' 10.25" |
| | Wilma Rudolph | 100 m dash | 1st | 11 |
| | Wilma Rudolph | 200 m dash | 1st | 24 |
| | Martha Judson | 400 m relay | 3rd | 44.5 |
| | Lucinda Williams | 400 m relay | 3rd | 44.5 |
| | Barbara Jones | 400 m relay | 3rd | 44.5 |
| | Wilma Rudolph | 400 m relay | 1st | 44.5 |
| Tokyo, 1964 | Robert Hayes | 200 m dash | 1st | 9.9 |
| | Henry Carr | 200 m dash | 1st | 20.3 |
| | Paul Drayton | 200 m dash | 2nd | 20.5 |
| | Hayes Jones | 110 m hurdles | 1st | 13.6 |
| | Robert Hayes | 400 m relay | 1st | 39.0 |
| | Paul Drayton | 400 m relay | 1st | 39.0 |
| | Richard Stebbins | 400 m relay | 1st | 39.0 |
| | John Thomas | High jump | 2nd | 7' 1.75" |
| | John Rambo | High jump | 3rd | 7' 1" |
| | Ralph Boston | Long jump | 2nd | 26' 4" |
| | Wyomia Tyus | 100 m dash | 1st | 11.4 |
| | Edith McGuire | 100 m dash | 2nd | 11.6 |
| | Marilyn White | 100 m dash | 3rd | 11.6 |
| | Edith McGuire | 200 m dash | 1st | 23 |
| | Marilyn White | 100 m dash | 3rd | 11.6 |
| | Edith McGuire | 200 m dash | 1st | 23 |
| | Wyomia Tyus | 400 m relay | 2nd | 43.9 |
| | Edith Mcguire | 400 m relay | 2nd | 43.9 |
| | Willye White | 400 m relay | 2nd | 43.9 |
| | Marilyn White | 400 m relay | 2nd | 43.9 |
| Mexico City, 1968 | Jim Hines | 100 m dash | 1st | 43.9 |
| | Charles Greene | 100 m dash | 3rd | 10.0 |
| | Tommie Smith | 200 m dash | 1st | 19.8 |
| | John Carlos | 200 m dash | 3rd | 20.0 |
| | Lee Evans | 400 m run | 1st | 43.8 |
| | Larry James | 400 m run | 2nd | 43.9 |
| | Ron Freeman | 400 m run | 3rd | 44.4 |
| | Willie Davenport | 110 m hurdles | 1st | 13.3 |
| | Ervin Hall | 110 m hurdles | 2nd | 13.4 |
| | Jim Hines | 400 m relay | 1st | 38.2 |
| | Charles Greene | 400 m relay | 1st | 38.2 |
| | Mel Pender | 400 m relay | 1st | 38.2 |

| Place/Year | Athlete | Event | Place | Time or Distance |
|---|---|---|---|---|
| | Ronnie Ray Smith | 400 m relay | 1st | 38.2 |
| | Wyomia Tyus | 400 m relay | 1st | 42.8 |
| | Barbara Ferrell | 400 m relay | 1st | 42.8 |
| | Margaret Bailes | 400 m relay | 1st | 42.8 |
| | Mildrette Netter | 400 m relay | 1st | 42.8 |
| | Lee Evans | 1600 m relay | 1st | 2:56.1 |
| | Vince Matthews | 1600 m relay | 1st | 2:56.1 |
| | Ron Freeman | 1600 m relay | 1st | 2:56.1 |
| | Larry James | 1600 m relay | 1st | 2:56.1 |
| | Edward Caruthers | High jump | 2nd | 7' 3.5" |
| | Bob Beamon | Long jump | 1st | 29' 2.5" |
| | Ralph Boston | Long jump | 3rd | 26' 9.25" |
| | Wyomia Tyus | 100 m dash | 1st | 11.0 |
| | Barbara Ferrell | 100 m dash | 2nd | 11.1 |
| | Madeline Manning | 800 m run | 1st | 2:00.9 |
| Munich, 1972 | Robert Taylor | 100 m dash | 2nd | 10.24 |
| | Larry Black | 200 m dash | 2nd | 20.19 |
| | Vince Matthews | 400 m run | 1st | 44.66 |
| | Wayne Collett | 400 m run | 2nd | 44.8 |
| | Rod Milburn | 100 m hurdles | 1st | 13.24 |
| | Eddie Hart | 400 m relay | 1st | 38.19 |
| | Robert Taylor | 400 m relay | 1st | 38.19 |
| | Larry Black | 400 m relay | 1st | 38.19 |
| | gerald Tinker | 400 m relay | 1st | 38.19 |
| | Randy Williams | Long Jump | 1st | 27' 0.25" |
| | Arnie Robinson | Long jump | 3rd | 26' 4" |
| | Jeff Bennet | Decathlon | 3rd | 7,974 pts. |
| | Wayne Collett | 400 m dash | 2nd | 44.80 |
| | Cheryl Toussain | 1600 m relay | 2nd | 3:25.2 |
| | Mable Fergerson | 1600 m relay | 2nd | 3:25.2 |
| | Madeline Manning | 1600 m relay | 2nd | 3:25.2 |
| Montreal, 1976 | Millard Hampton | 200 m dash | 2nd | 20.29 |
| | Dwayne Evans | 200 m dash | 3rd | 20.43 |
| | Fred Newhouse | 400 m run | 2nd | 44.40 |
| | Herman Frazier | 400 m run | 3rd | 44.95 |
| | Willie Davenport | 110 m hurdles | 3rd | 13.38 |
| | Edwin Moses | 400 m hurdles | 1st | 47.64 |
| | Millard Hampton | 400 m relay | 1st | 38.83 |
| | Steve Riddick | 400 m relay | 1st | 38.83 |
| | Harvey Glance | 400 m relay | 1st | 38.83 |
| | John Jones | 400 m relay | 1st | 38.83 |
| | Herman Frazier | 1600 m relay | 1st | 2:58.7 |
| | Benny Brown | 1600 m relay | 1st | 2:58.7 |
| | Maxie Parks | 1600 m relay | 1st | 2:58.7 |
| | Fred Newhouse | 1600 m relay | 1st | 2:58.7 |
| | Arnie Robinson | Long jump | 1st | 27' 4.75" |
| | Randy Williams | Long jump | 2nd | 26' 7.25" |
| | James Butts | Triple jump | 2nd | 56' 8.5" |
| | Rosalyn Bryant | 1600 m relay | 2nd | 3:22.8 |
| | Shelia Ingram | 1600 m relay | 2nd | 3:22.8 |
| | Pamela Jiles | 1600 m relay | 2nd | 3:22.8 |
| | Debra Sapenter | 1600 m relay | 2nd | 3:22.8 |
| Los Angeles, 1984 | Carl Lewis | 100 m dash | 1st | 9.9 |
| | Sam Graddy | 100 m dash | 2nd | 10.19 |
| | Carl Lewis | 200 m dash | 1st | 19.80 |
| | Kirk Baptiste | 200 m dash | 2nd | 19.96 |
| | Alonzo Babers | 400 m run | 1st | 44.27 |

| Place/Year | Athlete | Event | Place | Time or Distance |
|---|---|---|---|---|
| | Antonio McKay | 400 m run | 3rd | 44.71 |
| | Earl Jones | 800 m run | 3rd | 1:43.83 |
| | Roger Kingdom | 110 m hurdles | 1st | 13:20 |
| | Greg Foster | 110 m hurdles | 2nd | 13:23 |
| | Edwin Moses | 400 m hurdles | 1st | 47.75 |
| | Danny Harris | 400 m hurdles | 2nd | 48.13 |
| | Sam Graddy | 400 m relay | 1st | 37.83 |
| | Ron Brown | 400 m relay | 1st | 37.83 |
| | Calvin Smith | 400 m relay | 1st | 37.83 |
| | Carl Lewis | 400 m relay | 1st | 37.83 |
| | Sunder Nix | 1600 m relay | 1st | 2:57.91 |
| | Roy Armstead | 1600 m relay | 1st | 2:57.91 |
| | Alonzo Babers | 1600 m relay | 1st | 2:57.91 |
| | Antonio McKay | 1600 m relay | 1st | 2:57.91 |
| | Michael Carter | shot put | 1st | 21.09m |
| | Carl Lewis | Long jump | 1st | 8.54m |
| | Al Joyner | Triple jump | 1st | 17.26m |
| | Mike Conley | Triple jump | 2nd | 17.18m |
| | Evelyn Ashford | 100 m dash | 1st | 10.97 |
| | Alice Brown | 100 m dash | 2nd | 11.13 |
| | Valerie Brisco-Hooks | 200 m dash | 1st | 21.81 |
| | Florence Griffith | 200 m dash | 2nd | 22.04 |
| | Valerie Brisco-Hooks | 400 m run | 1st | 48.83 |
| | Chandra Cheeseborough | 400 m run | 2nd | 49.05 |
| | Kim Gallagher | 800 m run | 2nd | 1:58.63 |
| | Benita Fitzgerald-Brown | 100 m hurdles | 1st | 12.84 |
| | Kim Turner | 100 m hurdles | 2nd | 12.88 |
| | Judi Brown | 400 m hurdles | 2nd | 55.20 |
| | Valerie Brisco-Hooks | 1600 m relay | 1st | 3:18.29 |
| | Chandra Cheeseborough | 1600 m relay | 1st | 3:18.29 |
| | Lillie Leatherwood | 1600 m relay | 1st | 3:18.29 |
| | Sherri Howard | 1600 m relay | 1st | 3:18.29 |
| | Jackie Joyner | Heptathlon | 2nd | 6,386pts. |
| | Patrick Ewing | Men's basketball | 1st | |
| | Vern Fleming | Men's basketball | 1st | |
| | Michael Jordan | Men's basketball | 1st | |
| | Sam Perkins | Men's basketball | 1st | |
| | Alvin Robertson | Men's basketball | 1st | |
| | Wayman Tisdale | Men's basketball | 1st | |
| | Leon Wood | Men's basketball | 1st | |
| | Cathy Boswell | Women's basketball | 1st | |
| | Teresa Edwards | Women's basketball | 1st | |
| | Janice Lawrence | Women's basketball | 1st | |
| | Pamela McGee | Women's basketball | 1st | |
| | Cheryl Miller | Women's basketball | 1st | |
| | Lynette Woodard | Women's basketball | 1st | |
| Seoul, 1988 | Carl Lewis | 100 m dash | 1st | 9.92 |
| | Calvin Smith | 100 m dash | 2nd | |
| | Joe DeLoach | 200 m dash | 1st | 19.75 |
| | Carl Lewis | 200 m dash | 2nd | |
| | Steve Lewis | 400 m run | 1st | 43.87 |
| | Butch Reynolds | 400 m run | 2nd | |
| | Danny Everett | 400 m run | 3rd | |
| | Roger Kingdom | 110 m hurdles | 1st | 12.98 |
| | Tonie Campbell | 400 m hurdles | 3rd | |
| | Andre Phillips | 400 m hurdles | 1st | 47.19 |
| | Edwin Moses | 400 m hurdles | 3rd | |
| | Butch Reynolds | 1600 m relay | 1st | 2:56.16 |

| Place/Year | Athlete | Event | Place | Time or Distance |
|---|---|---|---|---|
| | Steve Lewis | 1600 m relay | 1st | 2:56.16 |
| | Antonia McKay | 1600 m relay | 1st | 2:56.16 |
| | Danny Everett | 1600 m relay | 1st | 2:56.16 |
| | Carl Lewis | Long jump | 1st | 28'7.25" |
| | Mike Powell | Long jump | 2nd | |
| | Larry Myricks | Long jump | 3rd | |
| | Flo Griffith Joyner | 100 m dash | 1st | 10.54 |
| | Evelyn Ashford | 100 m dash | 2nd | |
| | Flo Griffith Joyner | 200 m dash | 1st | 21.34 |
| | Shelia Echols | 400 m relay | 1st | 41.98 |
| | Flo Griffith Joyner | 400 m relay | 1st | 41.98 |
| | Evelyn Ashford | 400 m relay | 1st | 41.98 |
| | Alice Brown | 400 m relay | 1st | 41.98 |
| | Jackie Joyner-Kersee | Long jump | 1st | 24'3.5" |
| | Jackie Joyner-Kersee | Heptathlon | 1st | 7,291 pts. |
| | Denean Howard-Hill | 1600 m relay | 2nd | 3.15.51 |
| | Valerie Brisco | 1600 m relay | 2nd | 3.15.51 |
| | Diane Dixon | 1600 m relay | 2nd | 3.15.51 |
| | Flo Griffith-Joyner | 1600 m relay | 2nd | 3.15.51 |
| | Kim Mitchell | 800 m run | 3rd | |
| | Andrew Maynard | Boxing- heavyweight | 1st | |
| | Ray Mercer | Boxing- heavyweight | 1st | |
| | Kennedy McKinney | Boxing-bantamweight | 1st | |
| | Riddick Bowe | Boxing-super heavyweight | 2nd | |
| | Roy Jones | Boxing-middleweight | 2nd | |
| | Kenny Monday | Wrestling-freestyle | 1st | |
| | Nate Carr | Wrestling-freestyle | 3rd | |
| | Zina Garrison | Tennis-doubles | 1st | |
| | Zina Garrison | Tennis-singles | 3rd | |
| | Tom Goodwin | Baseball | 1st | |
| | Ty Griffin | Baseball | 1st | |
| | Cindy Brown | Women's basketball | 3rd | |
| | Vicky Bullett | Women's basketball | 3rd | |
| | Cynthia Cooper | Women's basketball | 3rd | |
| | Teresa Edwards | Women's basketball | 3rd | |
| | Jennifer Gillom | Women's basketball | 3rd | |
| | Bridgette Gordon | Women's basketball | 3rd | |
| | Katrina McClain | Women's basketball | 3rd | |
| | Teresa Weatherspoon | Women's basketball | 3rd | |
| | Willie Anderson | Men's basketball | 3rd | |
| | Stacey Augmon | Men's basketball | 3rd | |
| | Vernell Coles | Men's basketball | 3rd | |
| | Jeff Grayer | Men's basketball | 3rd | |
| | Hersey Hawkins | Men's basketball | 3rd | |
| | Danny Manning | Men's basketball | 3rd | |
| | J.R. Reid | Men's basketball | 3rd | |
| | Mitch Redmond | Men's basketball | 3rd | |
| | David Robinson | Men's basketball | 3rd | |
| | Charles D. Smith | Men's basketball | 3rd | |
| | Charles E. Smith | Men's basketball | 3rd | |
| Barcelona, 1992 | Dennis Mitchell | 100 m dash | 3rd | 10.04 |
| | Gail Devers | 100 m dash | 1st | 10.82 |
| | Mike Marsh | 200 m dash | 1st | 20.01 |
| | Michael Bates | 200 m dash | 3rd | 20.38 |
| | Gwen Torrence | 200 m dash | 1st | 21.81 |
| | Quincy Watts | 400 m run | 1st | 43.50 |
| | Steve Lewis | 400 m run | 2nd | 44.21 |
| | Johnny Gray | 800 m run | 3rd | 1:43.97 |

| Place/Year | Athlete | Event | Place | Time or Distance |
|---|---|---|---|---|
| | Mike Marsh | 400 m relay | 1st | 37.40 |
| | Leroy Burrell | 400 m relay | 1st | 37.40 |
| | Dennis Mitchell | 400 m relay | 1st | 37.40 |
| | Carl Lewis | 400 m relay | 1st | 37.40 |
| | Evelyn Ashford | 400 m relay | 1st | 42.11 |
| | Esther Jones | 400 m relay | 1st | 42.11 |
| | Carlette Guidry-White | 400 m relay | 1st | 42.11 |
| | Gwen Torrence | 400 m relay | 1st | 42.11 |
| | Tony Dees | 110 m hurdles | 2nd | 13.24 |
| | Kevin Young | 400 m hurdles | 1st | 46.78 |
| | Sandra Farmer | 400 m hurdles | 2nd | 53.69 |
| | Janeence Vickers | 400 m hurdles | 3rd | 54.31 |
| | Andrew Valmon | 800 m relay | 1st | 2:55.74 |
| | Quincy Watts | 800 m relay | 1st | 2:55.74 |
| | Michael Johnson | 800 m relay | 1st | 2:55.74 |
| | Steve Lewis | 800 m relay | 1st | 2:55.74 |
| | Natasha Kaiser | 800 m relay | 2nd | 3:20.92 |
| | Gwen Torrence | 800 m relay | 2nd | 3:20.92 |
| | Jearl Miles | 800 m relay | 2nd | 3:20.92 |
| | Rochelle Stevens | 800 m relay | 2nd | 3:20.92 |
| | Hollis Conway | High jump | 3rd | 7' 8" |
| | Carl Lewis | Long jump | 1st | 28' 5.5" |
| | Mike Powell | Long jump | 2nd | 28' 4.25" |
| | Joe Greene | Long jump | 3rd | 27' 4.5" |
| | Jackie Joyner-Dersee | Long jump | 3rd | 23' 2.5" |
| | Mike Conley | Triple jump | 1st | 59' 7.5" |
| | Charlie Simpkins | Triple jump | 2nd | 57'9" |
| | Jackie Joyner-Kersee | Heptathlon | 1st | 7,044 pts. |
| | Tim Austin | Boxing-flyweight | 3rd | |
| | Chris Byrd | Boxing-middleweight | 2nd | |
| | Kevin Jackson | Wrestling-middleweight | 1st | |
| | Charles Barkley | Men's basketball | 1st | |
| | Clyde Drexler | Men's basketball | 1st | |
| | Patrick Ewing | Men's basketball | 1st | |
| | Earvin Johnson | Men's basketball | 1st | |
| | Michael Jordan | Men's basketball | 1st | |
| | Karl Malone | Men's basketball | 1st | |
| | Scottie Pippen | Men's basketball | 1st | |
| | David Robinson | Men's basketball | 1st | |
| | Vicky Bullett | Women's basketball | 1st | |
| | Daedra Charles | Women's basketball | 1st | |
| | Cynthia Cooper | Women's basketball | 1st | |
| | Teresa Edward | Women's basketball | 1sts | |
| | Carolyn Jones | Women's basketball | 1st | |
| | Katrina McClai | Women's basketball | 1stn | |
| | Vickie Orr | Women's basketball | 1st | |
| | Teresa Weatherspoon | Women's basketball | 1st | |

Note: The United States did not attend 1980's Moscow games in protest of the Soviet Union's invasion of Afghanistan.

# 27
# *Military*

# 27

# *Military*

◆ The Colonial Period ◆ The Revolutionary War (1775-1783) ◆ The War of 1812 (1812-1815)
◆ The Civil War (1861-1865) ◆ The Indian Campaigns (1866-1890)
◆ The Spanish-American War (1898) ◆ World War I (1914-1918) ◆ The Interwar Years (1919-1940)
◆ World War II (1941-1945) ◆ The Korean War (1950-1953) ◆ The Vietnam War (1964-1973)
◆ Military Participation in the 1970s and 1980s ◆ The Persian Gulf War (1991)
◆ Outstanding Military Figures

**by Allen G. Harris and Floyd Thomas, Jr.**

*As with other aspects of American society, the role of African American people in the nation's armed forces has been evolutionary. It was shaped by the white majority of an infant republic that embraced and then rejected slavery. Next was an adolescent "separate but equal" era of racial segregation. Finally, the United States has matured—as an increasingly multicultural society—in its understanding of race and racism.*

Sadly, a nation's history is often shaped by its wars. Insofar as blacks and the American military are concerned, the historic linkage extends from before the Revolutionary War to the most recent military expeditions involving United States troops.

Based on European experiences, the early American colonists were wary of the military. Both the Declaration of Independence and the United States Constitution reflect the fear of a large and permanent military establishment. As a result, much of early American military history revolves around the locally recruited militia—now the National Guard of the states and territories.

## ◆ THE COLONIAL PERIOD

Fearful of Indian warfare and slave insurrection, colonial governments sought to reduce the risk of a confederation between Indians and slaves. Some colonial governments promised freedom and various other inducements to black slaves willing to help fight the Indian, and paid Indians to hunt down and return escaped slaves. As early as 1703, South Carolina authorities began to enlist slaves into its colonial militia. The

Massachusetts Bay government required that black men, free and slave alike, undergo militia training. Less concerned with an Indian attack than a slave uprising, Virginia forbid the arming of slaves. Though few in number, both enslaved and free blacks served in colonial militias and fought in the French and Indian War, 1754-1763.

As tensions mounted between England and the American colonies, confrontation led to bloodshed in the Boston Massacre, March 5, 1770. In protest against the manner of taxation and British authority, a crowd of angry Boston residents confronted a group of British soldiers charged with enforcing the laws of Great Britain. One of the soldiers fired on the crowd and an escaped slave leading the advance was struck. Crispus Attucks fell dead at the feet of the British soldiers, followed by four white citizens who with him became martyrs to the cause of American independence.

## ◆ THE REVOLUTIONARY WAR

In 1775, black men joined colonists in fighting the British during the battles of Lexington and Concord, the first battles of the Revolutionary War. A black man, Salem Poore, fought in the Battle of Bunker Hill. Credited with firing the shot that killed Major John Pitcairn, commander of the British force, Salem Poore received a commendation for gallantry. He would later serve with George Washington at Valley Forge.

Although a number of blacks were serving in New England units and proving themselves both capable and brave, Southern slave holders objected to their presence. In response to these critics, General Washington and his principal officers agreed to reject all slaves and bar free black veterans from reenlisting, a policy quickly ratified by the Continental Congress.

French and Spanish forces allied with the American colonists did not hesitate to enlist blacks into their ranks. The English also did not object to this valuable source of military manpower. When Lord Dunmore, the royal governor of Virginia, promised freedom to slaves who joined His Majesty's troops, he was able to organize an Ethiopian Regiment composed of approximately 300 men, "a mere fraction of those who gambled their lives on promises made by officers of King George III." (Nalty, p.18).

As it became increasingly difficult for the colonial militias and the Continental Army to meet recruiting needs, George Washington's initial belief that only whites should serve began to change. The success of the British in attracting black volunteers seeking to earn their freedom was a matter of concern. With troop strength dangerously low following the brutal winter at Valley Forge, Washington reversed his earlier policies and welcomed both free blacks and slaves into the Continental Army.

By 1778, the Continental Army was racially integrated. On average, each brigade contained 42 black soldiers. In the naval service, black sailors were engaged in nearly every phase of shipboard operations. In addition to cooking and cleaning, black seamen manned guns, joined boarding parties, and served as sharpshooters in Marine detachments. Ultimately, 5,000 blacks served in the war for American independence. Some won their freedom, others gained respect in their communities and a measure of economic security.

"The Revolutionary War thus lent credence to the belief, which later would become almost an article of faith among blacks, that military service in wartime represented a path toward freedom and greater postwar opportunity. Unfortunately, the conflict also set the pattern, followed for more than a century and a half, by which the American government used blacks in time of crisis and ignored them afterward. Only a handful of blacks succeeded in taking advantage of the mechanism the war provided for betterment. Despite the contributions of 5,000 blacks in the cause of liberty, their freedom was assured only in the handful of states that formally abolished slavery during the war or immediately afterward." (Nalty, p.18).

A memorial to the blacks who served the American cause during the Revolutionary War will be erected on the Mall in Washington, D.C. Ironically, that memorial honoring an eighteenth century contribution will be emplaced after similar recognition of the twentieth-century Tuskegee Airmen at the United States Air Force Academy, and the nineteenth-century "Buffalo Soldiers" at Fort Leavenworth, Kansas.

## ◆ THE WAR OF 1812 (1812-1815)

Following the Revolutionary War, the exclusion of blacks from military service was reinstituted. In 1792, Congress restricted military service to "free able-bodied white males." Six years later, the Secretary of War ordered the Commandment of the Marine Corps that "No Negro, mulatto or Indian is to be enlisted." However, when the need arose for recruits during the War of 1812, black sailors made up approximately twenty percent of Navy crews. Commodore Oliver Hazard Perry welcomed black sailors who served in his armada that defeated the British on Lake Erie.

While the Army and Marine Corps continued to exclude blacks, the Louisiana legislature authorized enlistments of free black land-owners. The combat bravery of these black troops was a key factor in the American victory at the Battle of New Orleans—though it was fought after the war had officially ended. Because blacks were not authorized to serve in the Army, their contributions went unrecognized by the United States Army.

## ◆ THE CIVIL WAR (1861-1865)

Only weeks after the Confederate assault on Fort Sumter in 1861 which initiated the Civil War, black men from Wilberforce College in Ohio answered Abraham Lincoln's call for volunteers to help subdue the Confederacy. Similar offers quickly came from Washington, D.C. and New York, where the governor was offered three black regiments to serve for the duration of the war, with their weapons, clothing, equipment, pay and provisions all to be provided by the black population of the state. These and other such requests to serve were spurned. Expecting a short war, Secretary of War Simon Cameron rebuffed the offers.

Although some Union leaders such as Major General John C. Fremont wanted to recruit blacks as soldiers, the Lincoln administration refused permission to proceed with the effort. Fearful that such action would antagonize slave-holding border states loyal to the Union, President Lincoln made it clear that this was a war to preserve the Union, not to free the slaves. Union General Benjamin Butler, who would later command black troops, offered Union soldiers to suppress a rumored slave uprising in Maryland. Meanwhile, the Confederacy enjoyed the fruits of slave labor in constructing fortifications and related combat service support roles.

As early as June 1861, some Southern states were recruiting free blacks for military service.

Though prohibited from enlisting blacks for military duty as troops, some Union generals began to use black fugitives from slave territory as teamsters, cooks, and laborers. Only after important military setbacks and considerable debate in the press and Congress did the legislature authorize the employment of black soldiers with the Militia Act of July 17, 1862. The War Department had not yet given permission to recruit black soldiers when General Jim Lane organized and trained the 1st Kansas Colored Volunteers and sent them into action against Confederate troops near Butler, Missouri in late October, 1862. The success of black troops in the first engagements in which they were permitted to fight for the Union, helped to reduce opposition to their recruitment.

## United States Colored Troops (USCT)

Following the Emancipation Proclamation of September 1862, systematic recruitment of blacks began throughout the country. Massachusetts was permitted to organize the 54th and 55th Massachusetts Infantry regiments. Raised by Colonel Robert Gould Shaw, the 54th led the Union attack on Fort Wagner, July 18, 1863. This strategically located Confederate position on Morris Island dominated the shipping channel leading into the Charleston harbor, South Carolina. Although access to Fort Wagner was restricted to a narrow road and subject to fire from three Confederate forts and batteries nearby, Union General Truman Seymour boasted that he could take it in one night. A reporter for the New York *Tribune* quoted the general as saying that he would have General George C. Strong's brigade take the lead and ". . . put those damned niggers from Massachusetts in the advance; we might as well get rid of them one time as another."

Under intense fire, the 54th made their charge with Shaw urging his men over an earthwork and into the fort. The black soldiers and their white officers were met with a barrage of artillery and rifle fire and grenades. As he crossed the fort's parapet, Shaw was shot dead. Half of the officers and men of his regiment were killed, wounded, or captured in the battle. Although eventually driven from the fort, the 54th Massachusetts Infantry came to symbolize the courage and determination of black troops.

Despite repeated demonstrations of their ability and courage, skepticism regarding the usefulness of black soldiers remained. General Benjamin Butler was determined to prove the black troops under his command were fit to bear arms. On the dawn of September 29,

1864, Butler ordered his troops of the XVII Corps to storm a fortified Confederate position at New Market Heights, Virginia. "With the caps removed from the nipples of their guns so that there could be no confused or confusing firing during the advance, the Negro soldiers moved across a stream, up the slope, through two lines of obstructions, and into the fortifications. The garrison fled before the bayonet assault and the works were in Union hands—at a cost of 1,000 casualties." (Dudley Taylor Cornish, *The Sable Arm*, p. 280.) Butler recorded in his memoirs that "the capacity of the Negro race for soldiers had then and there been fully settled forever." (Benjamin Franklin Butler, *Autobiography and Personal Reminiscences of Major-General Benj. F. Butler—BUTLER'S BOOK. A Review of His Legal, Political and Military Career.* (Boston, 1892, pp. 731-33.)

By July 1863, over thirty black regiments were being organized or were already on the field. These units and others previously organized except the 54th and 55th Massachusetts, were designated as United States Colored Troops (USCT). These soldiers were mustered directly into federal service and were fighting for the United States. Following the establishment of USCT regiments, blacks fought and died in every major Civil War action. For a period, they did so by being paid substantially less than white troops. While white privates received $13 per month plus $3.50 in clothing allowance, black troops of any rank were paid only $10 per month. In some units, black soldiers would not accept the lesser pay. Several men from a black Rhode Island artillery unit on duty in Texas were sentenced to hard labor for refusing their pay. When Sergeant William Walker persuaded the men of his South Carolina regiment company to refuse to perform any duty unless they received pay equal to that of white troops, he was brought up on charges of mutiny and executed by firing squad. After vigorous protests by prominent officers of black troops, newspaper editors, and legislators, the

Poster urging blacks to join the Union Army.

1864 Army Appropriation Act was enacted to provide identical pay scales for all soldiers.

The passions of the Civil War resulted in ignoring the then-emerging doctrines of land warfare on issues such as treatment of non-combatants and prisoners of war. The most serious documented breaches of land warfare law were committed by the Confederacy. The barbaric treatment of white Union prisoners of war at Andersonville Prison in Georgia, for example, retains military infamy. Black soldiers who fell into Confederate hands were either re-enslaved or summarily killed. One of the bloodiest such events was the Confederate butchery at Fort Pillow, Tennessee. Congressional Report No. 65, "Fort Pillow Massacre" (April 24, 1864), identified the Confederate leader responsible as General Nathan Bedford Forrest, who would later organize the Ku Klux Klan. According to the report:

> . . . the rebels commenced an indiscriminate slaughter, sparing neither age nor sex, white or black, soldier or civilian. The officers and men seemed to vie with each other in the devilish work; men, women, and even children, wherever found, were deliberately shot down, beaten, and hacked with sabres; some of the children not more than ten years old were forced to stand up and face their murderers while being shot; the sick and wounded were butchered without mercy, the rebels even entering the hospital building and dragging them out to be shot or killing them as they lay there unable to offer the least resistance.

Although somewhat exaggerated in the interest of propaganda, the report clearly established that black troops were murdered while attempting to surrender. The slaughter at Fort Pillow and the murder of captured and wounded black troops at the Battle of Poison Spring, Arkansas would not go unanswered. Black troops assaulted their Confederate enemy with ferocious intensity as they shouted their battle cry, "Remember Fort Pillow!" and "Remember Poison Spring!"

Many black men served in the Union cause, but very few were permitted to do so as officers. Despite strident public opposition and War Department policy unfavorable to the appointment of black officers, nearly one-hundred black men held commissions during the course of the Civil War. Over three-fourths of these commissions were awarded in General Butler's Louisiana regiments. Many blacks gained their appointment as officers in state militias. A few black surgeons and a large number of chaplains also received appointments. After Martin R. Delany, a black physician, had an audience with Abraham Lincoln, the President directed his Secretary of War to meet this "most remarkable black man." Shortly thereafter, on February 26, 1865, Martin R. Delany was commissioned a Major of Infantry, making him the highest ranking black field officer during the war. Before Delany had an opportunity to organize and command an "armee d'Afrique," the Civil War ended. Delany was detailed for duty with the freedmen. He retained the rank of major until 1868.

One black officer of the U.S. Colored Troops was commissioned because of his distinguished service with the Navy. Robert Smalls, a slave on board the *Planter*, took the helm of the 300-ton sidewheel Confederate steamer and with his followers delivered the ship to the Union Navy in May, 1862. Fitted with two guns and carrying four others as cargo, the ship was a welcome addition to the Union fleet. Having demonstrated his ability and leadership, the former slave served as pilot of the *Planter* for a time and later piloted the gunboat *Keokuk*. After the war, Robert Smalls was elected to the United States Congress as a representative from the state of South Carolina.

While not accepted into the Union forces, black women also played an important role during this critical era of American history. Many endured great hardship in their effort to keep their families together as their husbands, fathers, and sons marched off to war. While some black women served as volunteer nurses, others took a more aggressive role in support of the Union cause. Both Sojourner Truth and Harriet Tubman used their knowledge of Underground Railroad routes to guide Union forces operating in hostile territory. In one such instance, Miss Tubman led 300 Union cavalrymen on a raid in South Carolina that freed 800 slaves and destroyed cotton valuable to the Confederacy.

## The Medal of Honor

America's highest decoration for valor was established during the Civil War when Congress authorized issuance of a Medal of Honor on December 21, 1861. Issuance was initially limited to enlisted men of the Navy and the Marine Corps, but the award was expanded to include the Army on July 12, 1862. On March 3, 1863, commissioned officers also became eligible for the Medal of Honor. During the Civil War, 1,523 Medals of Honor were awarded, twenty-three to black servicemen. The first black recipient was Sergeant William H. Carney, 54th Massachusetts Infantry, for combat valor on July 18, 1863, at Fort Wagner, South Carolina. Fourteen of the medals went to black soldiers who fought in the battle of New Market Heights.

United States Colored Troops had constituted thirteen percent of the Union Army. By the end of the Civil War, over 37,000 black servicemen had died, constituting nearly thirty-five percent of all blacks who served in combat.

A rifle company of black Union soldiers.

# ◆ THE INDIAN CAMPAIGNS (1866-1890)

Post-Civil War America acquired a new appreciation of the importance of military power. In 1866, the 39th Congress passed legislation to "increase and fix the Military Establishment of the United States." The peacetime army would have five artillery regiments, ten cavalry regiments, and forty-five infantry regiments. This legislation also stipulated "That to the six regiments of cavalry now in service shall be added four regiments, two of which shall be composed of colored men..." Consequently, the nation gained its first all-black Regular Army regiments: The 9th and 10th Cavalry, and the 24th and 25th Infantry—the "Buffalo Soldiers." This nickname was bestowed on the soldiers by Plains Indians who saw a resemblance between their hair and that of the buffalo, an animal the Indians considered sacred. Although the term "Buffalo Soldiers" initially denoted these four post-Civil War regiments, it has been adopted with pride by veterans of all racially-segregated black Army ground units of the 1866-1950 era.

One Hollywood "oversight" involves their depiction of the United States Army of the post-Civil War westward expansion. Approximately twenty percent of Ar-

my soldiers on duty in the West were black. According to historian Gary Donaldson, "...even today, few Americans realize that when the cavalry came to the rescue of white settlers in the Old West that the rescuers, those gallant soldiers in blue, might well have been black." (1991, *The History of African-Americans in the Military*). The heroism of black soldiers is attested to the eighteen Medals of Honor they earned during what historians term both "The Indian Campaigns" and "The Plains War."

Black participation in the war against native American Indians was embedded in historical ironies, both in terms of fighting another race subjugated by Anglo-Americans, and in terms of anti-black sentiment within the United States military itself. One of many painful episodes for the original "Buffalo Soldiers" was the case of Second Lieutenant Henry Ossian Flipper. Born in Thomasville, Georgia on March 21, 1856, Flipper was the first black to graduate from the United States Military Academy at West Point, New York. He ranked fiftieth among the seventy-six members of the Class of 1887, and became the only black commissioned officer in the Regular Army. Assigned initially to Fort Sill, Oklahoma Territory, Lieutenant Flipper was eventually

The parents of Marine Private James Anderson, Jr. receive his Medal of Honor, awarded posthumously August 21, 1968.

sent to Fort Davis, Texas. He was assigned the duties routine to a newly-commissioned officer, such as surveying and supervising construction projects. Flipper also acquired some combat experience fighting Apache Indians led by Chief Victoria.

In August 1881, Lieutenant Flipper was arrested and charged with failing to mail $3,700.00 in checks to the Army Chief of Commissary. The young lieutenant was tried by court-martial for embezzlement and conduct unbecoming an officer. He was acquitted of the first charge (the checks were found in his quarters), but convicted of the second. Upon confirmation of his sentence by President Chester Arthur, Flipper was dismissed from the service on June 30, 1882. Returning to civilian life, Flipper used his West Point education as a surveyor and engineer in working for mining companies. He also published his memoirs as well as technical books dealing with both Mexican and Venezuelan laws. Additionally, Flipper served as a translator for the Senate Committee on Foreign Relations, and became a special assistant to the Secretary of the Interior.

Nearly a century after Flipper left West Point, a review of his record indicated that he had been framed by his fellow officers. His records were corrected and he was granted an honorable discharge from the Army. On the 100th anniversary of his graduation, his bust was unveiled and is now displayed in the Cadet Library at the Military Academy.

There were only two other nineteenth century black graduates of West Point: John H. Alexander (1864-1894) in the Class of 1887; and Charles A. Young (1864-1922) in the Class of 1889. It would be forty-seven years before another black cadet graduated from the United States Military Academy.

## ◆ THE SPANISH-AMERICAN WAR (1898)

America's "Ten Week War" with Spain marked the nation's emergence as a global colonial power. Although the United States had just completed its own "Indian Campaigns," the tension between the two nations arose from Spain's treatment of Cuba's indigenous population, who increasingly resisted autocratic Spanish rule on the island. In 1885, open rebellion by the Cuban people resulted in brutal suppression by the Spanish. The battleship USS Maine was sent to Cuba to protect United States interests there—and, clearly, as a reminder of America's intention to enforce the Monroe Doctrine.

On the evening of February 15, 1898, a gigantic explosion rocked the warship. It sank rapidly in Havana harbor, killing 266 American sailors—twenty-two of them African Americans. The cause of the Maine's sinking was undetermined, but inflamed American passions were represented by the slogan, "Remember the Maine, to hell with Spain."

On March 29th, the United States issued an ultimatum to Spain, demanding (1) release of Cubans from brutal detention camps, (2) declaration of an armistice, and (3) preparations for peace negotiations mediated by President McKinley. The Spanish government did not comply and, on April 19th, the United States Congress proclaimed Cuba free and independent. In its proclamation, Congress authorized the President to use United States troops to remove Spanish forces from Cuba.

In the annals of American military history, the Spanish-American War was of special significance for the black officer. It was the first time that black men served in every Army grade below general officer. This opportunity arose because of a geographically determined national security strategy. Separated from both Europe and Asia by oceans, the United States understood that those waters also provided a mobilization time cushion. Any perceived threat from either direction had to overcome United States naval power before touching the United States. Thus, the Navy became the "first line of defense." The small U.S. Army was really a cadre force.

9th Cavalry

Time would permit recruitment, training and deployment of volunteers—or draftees—who would fight on United States soil led by experienced Regulars. An additional mobilization asset was the various state militias composed of part-time citizen soldiers.

The war with Spain was an expeditionary campaign requiring maritime deployment to foreign soil. Instead of a mobilize-and-defend situation, the United States had to mobilize, transport to, and fight on foreign soil. It was the nation's first large-scale exposure to the complex logistics of overseas operations, experience that would evolve into occupation duty and related counterinsurgency warfare.

The Regular Army of only 28,000 men included the all-black 9th and 10th Cavalry regiments, and the 24th and 25th Infantry regiments. Shortly after arriving in Cuba, the 9th and 10th Cavalry and the 24th and 25th Infantry distinguished themselves in combat. On June 24, 1898, one squadron of the 10th Cavalry, two squadrons of Rough Riders, which were a regiment of U.S. cavalry volunteers recruited by Theodore Roosevelt, and a squadron from the Regular Army's 1st Cavalry, attacked and defeated twice their number of Spanish soldiers. When Rough Riders were pinned down by

Spanish fire while crossing open ground near Las Guasimas, 10th Cavalry troops and soldiers from the 1st Cavalry regiment arrived and silenced the enemy. John J. "Black Jack" Pershing, the 10th Cavalry's regimental quartermaster, credited his men with "relieving the Rough Riders from the volleys that were being poured into them from that portion of the Spanish line."

The 25th Infantry also took part in the action, storming the village of El Caney on the morning of July 1. Armed with a batter of Hotchkiss automatic guns, the 10th Cavalry figured prominently in taking Kettle Hill, and the 24th Infantry with the 71st New York Volunteers stormed San Juan Hill. Black soldiers manned trenches around Santiago de Cuba, which capitulated in mid-July, ending the war in Cuba, but not the danger to the troops stationed in occupation there.

Though hostilities between the United States and Spain were officially ended, American troops in Cuba faced an enemy more deadly than the Spanish forces. More than three of every four deaths among U.S. troops were attributed to disease, particularly typhoid and yellow fever. In the mistaken belief that people of African descent had a natural immunity to tropical disease, troops of the 24th Infantry were assigned work

10th Cavalry

details at a hospital treating victims of typhoid and yellow fever. Roughly half of the black troops assigned to the hospital contracted the illnesses. Many of the black female volunteer nurses who cared for the sick and dying became victims as well.

Black men also served in the United States Volunteer Infantry (USVI), a manpower augmentation of 175,000 troops from the federalized state militia/national guard reserves. The USVI was to include the nation's oldest all black national guard unit, which had its organizational roots in Chicago, Illinois. Formed in the wake of the 1871 Chicago fire, it was originally known as the Hannibal Guards. It became an Illinois militia unit on May 5, 1890 as the 9th Battalion, commanded by Major Benjamin G. Johnson, a black man. When the Spanish American War erupted, other all-black militia regiments were organized; the 3rd Alabama, the 23rd Kansas, the 3rd North Carolina, the 9th Ohio, and the 6th Virginia.

Until converted to artillery battalions in World War II, the 8th Illinois USVI was always commanded by a black officer; Colonel John R. Marshall was the highest ranking black officer of the Spanish American War, and commanded the 8th Illinois until 1914. John R. Marshall was born on March 15, 1859, in Alexandria, Virginia.

After attending public schools in Alexandria and Washington, D.C. he became an apprentice bricklayer. After moving to Chicago, he was appointed Deputy Clerk of Cook County. Marshall joined the Illinois National Guard, organized a battalion and served in it as lieutenant and as major. In June 1892, he was commissioned as a colonel and assumed command of the 8th Illinois USVI Regiment. He led the regiment to Cuba where it joined with the 23rd Kansas and 3rd North Carolina in occupation duty.

The Spanish-American War provided a small increase in the number of black Regular Army officers. Benjamin O. Davis served as a lieutenant in the 8th Illinois USVI. Upon his discharge, he enlisted on June 14, 1899 as a private in the 9th Cavalry. He was promoted to corporal, and then to sergeant major. Davis was commissioned a Regular Army second lieutenant of cavalry on February 2, 1901. Also commissioned as Regular Army officers that year were John R. Lynch and John E. Green. As the twentieth century began, the United States Army had four black commissioned officers (excluding chaplains): Captain Charles Young, and Lieutenants Davis, Green, and Lynch. In 1940, Davis would become the nation's first black general officer.

Although only ten weeks long, the Spanish-American War produced fifty-two Medals of Honor, six to black recipients—five from the 10th Cavalry, which fought as infantry in Cuba. A black sailor won the sixth medal for heroism aboard the USS Iowa in the waters off Santiago, Cuba.

# ◆ WORLD WAR I (1914-1918)

The nation's entry into World War I raised the question of how to utilize black troops. Of the more than 400,000 black soldiers who served during the war, only about ten percent were assigned to combat duty in two infantry divisions. The 92nd Infantry Division was composed mainly of draftees. Black men from the 8th Infantry of the Illinois National Guard and the 315th Infantry of the New York National Guard formed the 93rd Infantry Division (Provisional). The majority of black World War I soldiers were assigned to stevedore units at ports, or labor units as quartermaster troops.

The most difficult question for the War Department was the demand that blacks be trained as commissioned officers. Initially, the idea was dismissed as ludicrous. It was said to be "common knowledge" that black men inherently lacked leadership qualities.

Only the persistence of the NAACP, the Urban League, and black newspapers like *The Chicago Defender*, eventually changed War Department policy. An all-black Officer Training School was established at Fort Dodge, near Des Moines, Iowa. On October 14, 1917, the school graduated and commissioned 639 black officers. However, the War Department had an iron-clad rule: No black officer could command white officers or enlisted men.

In accordance with this rule, the War Department retired Lieutenant Colonel Charles Young, who some white officers feared would assume command of the 10th Cavalry. Pressured by these officers, the U.S. senators who represented them in Congress, and President Wilson, the War Department developed a strategy to eliminate Young from consideration. Although Young was the highest ranking black officer, a West Point graduate who had trained black troops for combat and led them in action, he was discharged from active duty ostensibly because of ill health. To prove his fitness for active duty, Young rode on horseback from his home in Wilberforce, Ohio to Washington, D.C. While Young received support from the black press and many powerful friends, the War Department relented only five days before the end of World War I. Therefore, he was not given the opportunity to command troops in Europe and contribute to the American victory in the World War. He

was also denied a chance to become the first black general officer in American history. White supremacy was to remain ensconced in the nation's armed services.

One solution to the issue of utilizing black officers and soldiers was characteristic of military racism at this date: several black regiments were "attached" to the allied French Army. Colonel William Hayward, commander of New York's 369th Infantry criticized General John J. Pershing for this decision. Colonel Hayward charged that Pershing "simply put the black orphan in a basket, set it on the doorstep of the French, pulled the bell, and went away" (1936, *From Harlem to the Rhine: The Story of New York's Colored Volunteers* Arthur W. Little).

Despite the imposed "orphan" status, it was the 369th Infantry Regiment (15th New York) that established the best World War I record of any United States Army infantry regiment. The 369th served for 191 consecutive days in the trenches and never lost a foot of ground to the Germans. The so-called "Harlem Hell Fighters" won their laurels attached to the French 4th Army—using French weapons—and wearing United States uniforms.

In 1919, Columbia University President Nicholas Murray Butler gave *Harper's Weekly* his assessment of the 369th Infantry Regiment: "No American soldier saw harder or more constant fighting and none gave better accounts of themselves. When fighting was to be done, this regiment was there." (*The Independent and Harper's Weekly*, XCII, February 26, 1919, p. 286).

Despite the "Jim Crow" atmosphere, black soldiers earned an impressive number of awards for combat bravery defeating German troops. Sergeant Henry Johnson of New York's 369th Infantry Regiment was the first American, black or white, to receive the French Croix de Guerre. France awarded its Croix de Guerre to thirty-four black officers and eighty-nine black enlisted men during the war. In the 92nd Division, fourteen black officers and thirty-four black enlisted men earned the United States Army Distinguished Flying Cross (DFC). Ten officers and thirty-four enlisted men of the 93rd Division were DFC recipients.

Although they were not permitted to serve in the armed forces, Black women also contributed to America's efforts in World War I. They made bandages, worked in hospitals and troop centers, promoted the purchase of Liberty Bonds to finance the war effort, and served in the Red Cross, YWCA and other relief organizations.

## Posthumous Medal of Honor Awarded

No Medal of Honor was awarded to a black serviceman during World War I. In 1988, the Department of the

A group of black World War I sailors.

Army researched the National Archives to determine whether racial barriers had prevented award of the nation's highest decoration for valor.

The archives search produced evidence that Corporal Freddie Stowers of Anderson County, South Carolina had been recommended for the award. For "unknown reasons," the recommendation had not been processed. Stowers was a squad leader in Company C, 371st Infantry Regiment, 93rd Division. On September 28, 1918, he led his squad through heavy machine gun fire and destroyed the gun position on Hill 188 in the Champagne Marne Sector, France. Mortally wounded, Stowers continued to lead his men through a second trench line.

On April 24, 1991, President George Bush belatedly presented Stowers's Medal of Honor to his surviving sisters in a White House ceremony.

## ◆ THE INTERWAR YEARS (1919-1940)

With the end of the war, the nation generally returned to applying the *Plessy v. Ferguson* doctrine—with a vengeance. Some senior white Army officers advocated

barring enlistment or re-enlistment of blacks altogether, an action that would have eventually abolished the four black Regular Army regiments by attrition.

A focal point of the Army's anti-black sentiment was the black commissioned officer. Despite countless well-documented cases of superb combat leadership, most black officers were eliminated from active duty following World War I.

An effective tool against retaining black officers was their alleged poor performance. That was buttressed by criticism of the black Officer Training School (OTS) class at Des Moines, Iowa. One of the severest critics was Major General Charles C. Ballou, commander of the World War I 93rd Infantry Division. Ballou emphasized that while white candidates were required to be college graduates, "only high school educations were required for... the colored... and in many cases these high school educations would have been a disgrace to any grammar school. For the parts of a machine requiring the finest steel, pot metal was provided" (Ballou letter, March 14, 1920).

However, there were combat-experienced white officers who held a decidedly different view of black

369th Infantry Regiment

officer training, such as Major Thomas A. Roberts. "As I understand the question," Roberts wrote in April 1920, "what the progressive Negro desires today is the removal of discrimination against him; that this can be accomplished in a military sense I believe to be largely possible, but not if men of the two races are segregated." Noting his appreciation of the "tremendous force of the prejudice against association between negroes and whites," Roberts declared "my experience has made me believe that the better element among the negroes desires the removal of the restriction rather than the

association itself" (Roberts letter to Asst. Comdt Gen. Staff College, April 5, 1920).

The anti-black campaign was also evident in the Army's civilian components, the National Guard and Officers Reserve. New York's 369th Infantry Regiment was maintained at full strength, although the 8th Illinois lost one battalion.

As for commissioned officers, the Reserve Officers' Training Corps (ROTC) detachments at Howard and Wilberforce Universities provided the bulk of new black second lieutenants. With no allocations for black officers to attend service schools, the lack of opportunity to maintain proficiency caused considerable attrition in the number of black reserve officers. To retain their commissions, other officers took advantage of correspondence and specially organized lecture/seminar courses.

# ◆ WORLD WAR II (1941-1945)

Less than two months after war began in Europe, the nation's preeminent black organizations, the NAACP and the National Urban League, had mobilized to defeat American racial segregation as well as Axis fascism. The black community clearly foresaw that the United States would eventually ally itself with Britain and France in war against Germany, Italy, and Japan.

Military mobilization began on August 27, 1940 with the federalizing of the National Guard, and activation of the Organized Reserve. When Japan attacked Pearl Harbor on December 7, 1941, there were 120,000 officers and 1,523,000 enlisted men on active duty in the Army and its Air Corps. On September 16, 1940, the nation began its first peacetime draft. By the end of World War II, the Selective Service System had inducted 10,110,104 men; 1,082,539 (10.7 percent) were black.

America's war effort required rapid expansion of both military and industrial power. Victory depended on the constant provision of ammunition, guns, planes, tanks, naval vessels, and merchant ships. The nation would have to unite to survive. A minority number of blacks, including Nation of Islam founder Elijah Muhammad, openly favored a Japanese victory; Muhammad's stance led to a four-year term in the United States Penitentiary at Milan, Michigan.

Essential to the desegregation activism of both the NAACP and the Urban League was the impact of black-owned weekly newspapers such as Robert S. Abbott's *Chicago Defender* and Robert Vann's *Pittsburgh Courier*. The rallying slogan was the "Double V"—victory against fascism abroad and racial discrimination in the United States. The goal was equal opportunity in both the armed services and within the civilian defense industries.

Soon, the NAACP and the Urban League were joined by the black activists of the March on Washington Movement led by A. Philip Randolph of the Brotherhood of Sleeping Car Porters and Maids. Randolph predicted that upwards of 100,000 blacks would march on Washington demanding equal employment opportunities in defense plant employment. On June 25, 1941, a week before the scheduled march, President Franklin D. Roosevelt forestalled the March by issuing Executive Order 8802. The President's order established a Committee on Fair Employment Practice "to provide for the full and equitable participation of all workers in defense industries, without discrimination." Of course, the Executive Order did not apply to the armed services.

The necessity of winning the war opened the economy to millions of black men and women who surged into defense plants, earning the same wages as their white co-workers. The war years thus brought economic upward mobility for many black civilians. Through the postwar benefits of the G.I. Bill of Rights, furthermore, the number of black college graduates and home owners would increase dramatically.

What has been largely ignored is that the United States Army took its first steps toward racial integration early in World War II. The obvious waste of duplicated facilities caused the Army to operate all of its twenty-four Officer Candidate Schools as racially-integrated institutions, where the primary quality sought was proven leadership capacity. The so-called "ninety-day wonders" who survived the standard three-month course were commissioned as second lieutenants in one the twenty-four Army branches ranging from the Army Air Forces Administrative School (Miami, Florida) to the Tank Destroyer School (Camp Hood, Texas). Of course, upon graduation, black officers were only assigned to black units.

## The Army Air Force (AAF)

The exception in racially-integrated Army officer procurement during World War II was the Army Air Force Aviation Cadet program that trained pilots, bombardiers, and navigators. Ironically, black non-flying officers graduated from the integrated AAF Officer Candidates School at Miami Beach.

A total of 926 black pilots earned their commissions and wings at the segregated Tuskegee Army Air Field (TAAF) near Chehaw, Alabama. The 673 single-engine TAAF pilot graduates would eventually form the four squadrons of the 332nd Fighter Group.

Led by Lieutenant Colonel Benjamin O. Davis, Jr., a 1936 West Point graduate, the 99th Fighter Squadron was assigned to the 33rd Fighter Group commanded by Colonel William M. Momeyer. The 99th's first operational mission was a June 2, 1943 strafing attack on the Italian island of Pantelleria. On this date, Captain Charles B. Hall scored the squadron's first air victory by shooting down a FW-190 and damaging a ME-109. The 99th then settled into normal operations—or so the men thought.

In September Colonel Davis was recalled to take command of the 332nd Fighter Group. That is when he and the black community discovered that the "Tuskegee Experiment" was about to be labeled a failure. To this

Brigadier General Benjamin Davis reviews troops, Camp Breckinridge, 1943.

effect, Colonel Meyer submitted an appraisal of the 99th Fighter Squadron that was extremely negative:

"Based on the performance of the 99th Fighter Squadron to date, it is my opinion that they are not of the fighting caliber of any squadron in this group. They have failed to display the aggressiveness and daring for combat that are necessary to a first class fighting organization. It may be expected that we will get less work and less operational time out of the 99th Fighter Squadron than any squadron in this group."

On October 16, 1943, squadron commander Davis appeared before the War Department's Committee on Special [Negro] Troop Policies to answer his group commander's allegations.

In his 1991 autobiography, written after his retirement as a retired Air Force lieutenant general, Davis describes the problem he faced at the Pentagon as a lieutenant colonel: "It would have been hopeless for me to stress the hostility and racism of whites as the motive behind the letter, although that was clearly the case. Instead, I had to adopt a quiet, reasoned approach, presenting the facts about the 99th in a way that would appeal to fairness and win out over ignorance and racism."

Davis presented such a convincing factual case that Army Chief of Staff General George C. Marshall ordered a G-3 [operations] study of the black squadron. The study's title, "Operations of the 99th Fighter Squadron Compared with Other P-40 Squadrons in the Mediterranean Theatre of Operations," precisely describes its contents. In his book, General Davis describes the G-3 study: "It rated the 99th according to readiness, squadron missions, friendly losses versus enemy losses, and sorties dispatched. The opening statement in the report was the clincher: 'An examination' of the record of the 99th Fighter Squadron reveals no significant general difference between this squadron and the balance of the P-40 squadrons in the Mediterranean Theatre of Operations.'"

On October 13, 1942, the Army had activated the 100th, 301st, and 302nd Fighter Squadrons. Combined with the 99th, the four squadrons would become the 332nd Fighter Group. Colonel Robert R. Selway, Jr., a white pilot, was its initial commanding officer. With the 99th vindicated by the G-3 study, Davis assumed command of the Fighter Group at Selfridge Army Air Field,

As for the 332nd Fighter Group, it became a famous flying escort for heavy bombers. It was the only AAF fighter group that never lost an escorted bomber to enemy planes. The wartime record of the 332nd Fighter Group was 103 enemy aircraft destroyed during 1,578 combat missions. In addition to more than 100 Distinguished Flying Crosses, the 332nd also earned three Distinguished Unit Citations.

The so-called "Tuskegee Experiment" thus proved that black men could fly "state-of-the-art" aircraft, and could also conduct highly successful combat operations meeting AAF standards. The fruit of the Tuskegee Airmen's efforts would be harvested in less than three years—the 1948 racial desegregation of the United States military.

## The Ground War

During World War II, the United States Army fielded two major black combat organizations: the 92nd Infantry Division in Europe, and the 93rd Infantry Division in the Pacific. Both of the Divisions suffered from avoidable impediments.

Just as in World War I, the 93rd Division was employed only in a fragmented manner. Major General Raymond G. Lehman's headquarters sailed from San Francisco, California on January 11, 1944; the artillery and infantry battalions and division headquarters assembled on Guadalcanal at the end of February. As Professor Ulysses Lee observed, "This was the last time until the end of the war that all elements of the division were gathered in the same location" (1966, *The Employment of Negro Troops*). The division would spend the rest of the war island-hopping, relieving units that had defeated Japanese troops. The 93rd Division World War II casualties were 12 killed in action; 121 wounded in action; and 5 who died of wounds.

Elements of the 93rd Division, primarily the 24th Infantry Regiment, performed well during the 1944 Bougainville campaign. Generally, the division's performance was considered adequate and acceptable. The usual after-action comments were made concerning the lack of initiative by junior officers, but overall the 93rd Division was described as well-disciplined and having good morale.

The 92nd Infantry Division, in contrast, gained a reputation as a chaotic outfit. During its preparation for deployment overseas, portions of the 92nd Division were sprinkled across the United States. While the division headquarters were at Fort Huachuca, Arizona, subordinate units were stationed at Fort McClellan, Alabama; Camp Robinson, Arkansas; Camp Breckinridge, Kentucky; and Camp Atterbury, Indiana. The division's

General Benjamin Davis, Sr. pins the Distinguished Flying Cross on son, Colonel Benjamin Davis, Jr.

Michigan. The 332nd departed for Italy on January 3, 1944 and absorbed the 99th as its fourth squadron.

During the period that the 99th was deployed and the 332nd was organizing, the TAAF program expanded to training two-engine B-25 pilots. While the fighter pilot fought alone, the B-25 "Mitchell" medium bomber required a five to six man crew that included two pilots and a bombardier-navigator. The 253 medium bomber pilots trained at TAAF, as well as 393 black navigators and bombardiers from Hondo and Midland Fields in Texas, formed the nation's second black flying organization when the Army Air Force activated the four squadron 477th Bombardment Group (Medium) in June 1943.

The 477th was plagued from the start by a shortage of enlisted aircrew members, ground technicians, and even airplanes. Fifteen months after activation, the 477th was still short twenty-six pilots, forty-three co-pilots, two bombardier-navigators, and all of its authorized 288 gunners. Moving from base to base for "operational training," the 477th logged 17,875 flying hours in one year without a major accident. Although finally earmarked for duty in the Pacific, the war ended before the 477th was deployed overseas.

World War II casualties figures were vastly different than those of the 93rd Division: 548 killed in action; 2,187 wounded in action; and 68 who died of wounds. From its training in the United States through combat in Europe, the division's main problem seemed to be its commander, Major General Edward M. Almond. Many veterans of the 92nd Division continue to blame General Almond for the division's reputation and casualties.

It appears that "Ned" Almond was a racist. In a 1984 interview, retired Lieutenant General William P. Ennis, Jr. gave a "warts and all" description of Almond. As a World War II brigadier general, Ennis had commanded the corps artillery that supported the 92nd Division. According to Ennis, Almond and many white Southern officers in the division were selected because "in theory, they knew more about handling Negroes than anybody else, though I can't imagine why because [Almond] just despised the ground they walked on" (1992, *The Journal of Military History*).

The contrast of attitude at the division's various posts was amazing. While Almond denigrated the competence of black officers, Officer Candidate School (OCS) commandants generally held opposite views. For example, Brigadier General H. T. Mayberry, who commanded the Tank Destroyer OCS, observed in a 1945 interview that "a considerable number of young, potentially outstanding Negro officers were graduated. It was surprising—to me, at least—how high the Negroes (those who graduated) stood in the classes."

Lieutenant Colonel Robert C. Ross, a field artillery battalion commander in the 92nd Division, reported to Almond on five black officers who completed the basic artillery course. Three were made course instructors, while two were selected "as outstanding students from the entire forty-eight officers, both white and colored, from the first Officers Basic School."

One black officer, Captain Hondon B. Hargrove, was a 1938 Wilberforce University ROTC graduate. After his wartime service in the division's 597th Field Artillery Battalion, he commented that Almond did not believe "any black, no matter what his file showed, or how much training he had, was able in an officer's position . . . . He firmly believed only white officers could get the best out of [Negro troops] . . . [and] just could not countenance black officers leading them."

General Almond established his headquarters at Viareggio, Italy on Oct. 5, 1944. Two days later, the division's 370th Infantry Regiment began its assault on Massa. Professor Lee described the 92nd Division's major weakness: "It was a problem in faith and lack of it—the wavering faith of commanders in the ability and determination of subordinates and enlisted men, and the continuation in the minds of enlisted men of training period convictions that they could not trust their leaders." Thus, the Massa attack degenerated into chaos. In what was to be a major charge against the division, the men began to "melt away" from the fighting. After Massa, there were increasing cases of mutinous behavior toward both black and white officers.

In February 1945, the 92nd became the focus of serious Pentagon scrutiny. The man who would examine the situation was Truman K. Gibson, Jr., a black insurance company lawyer from Chicago, and Civilian Aide to Secretary of War Henry L. Stimpson. In his assessment, Gibson refused to blame the victim, or to generalize about the capabilities of black soldiers based on the performance of General Almond's 92nd Division. In a March 14th news conference in Rome, Gibson maintained that "If the division proves anything, it does not prove that Negroes can't fight. There is no question in my mind about the courage of Negro officers or soldiers and any generalization on the basis of race is entirely unfounded."

On May 14, 1945, a week after Germany surrendered, Lieutenant Colonel Marcus H. Ray wrote a letter to Gibson. A Chicagoan, as was Gibson, Colonel Ray was a National Guard officer of the 8th Illinois when it was mobilized in 1940. He ended the war as commanding officer of the 600th Field Artillery Battalion of the 92nd Division. Colonel Ray closed his letter to Gibson by observing that "those who died in the proper performance of their assigned duties are our men of the decade and all honor should be paid them. They were Americans before all else. Racially, we have been the victims of an unfortunate chain of circumstances backgrounded by the unchanged American attitude as regards the proper 'place' of the Negro . . . . I do not believe the 92nd a complete failure as a combat unit, but when I think of what it might have been, I am heart-sick . . . ."

## The 761st Tank Battalion

The most highly acclaimed black ground combat unit of World War II was the 761st Tank Battalion. As an organization, it enjoyed the substantially better circumstances than the 92nd Division. Again, however, the "command climate" would be formative. Before the United States entered World War II, some white United States Army officers favored opening opportunities for black soldiers. They rejected the dogma of their colleagues who declared that modern weaponry was "too technical" for blacks. Fortunately, one such officer became the Commanding General of Army Ground Forces.

92nd Division, Ponsacco, Italy.

In this post, Lieutenant General Lesley James McNair spent most of his time visiting the nationwide array of ground forces training camps. When he visited the 761st at Camp Claiborne, Louisiana, he openly praised and encouraged the Army's first black tankers. When the 761st went ashore in France on October 10, 1944, the men believed that their outfit's existence was due mainly to McNair. (General McNair was killed by United States "friendly fire" on July 25, 1944 in France. The Joint Chiefs of Staff National Defense University is located at Fort Lesley J. McNair, named in his honor, in Washington, DC).

The 761st joined the 26th Division on October 31st and was welcomed by the division commander, Major General Willard S. Paul: "I am damned glad to have you with us. We have been expecting you for a long time, and I am sure you are going to give a good account of yourselves." Two days later, General George S. Patton visited and welcomed the 761st.

The 761st initial combat was on November 8, 1944 at Athaniville, France—the first of 183 continuous days of combat for the battalion. During their advance through six European countries, the 761st proved to be a stellar combat organization. The battalion is credited with killing 6,266 enemy soldiers, and capturing 15,818. Despite its outstanding combat record, the 761st did not receive a well-deserved Presidential Unit Citation until January 24, 1978.

The veterans of the 761st still pursue a World War II mission: posthumous Medal of Honor for Staff Sergeant Ruben Rivers, of Tecumseh, Oklahoma. Sergeant Rivers was severely wounded on November 16, 1944, when his tank ran over two mines near Guebling, France. With his lower thigh torn and his kneebone protruding, Sergeant Rivers refused evacuation. Instead, he remained with his tank and crew for three days of continuous combat. When his company was taken under fire by German heavy weapons, the company commander ordered his tanks to pull back below the crest of a hill. Sergeant Rivers' tank opened fire at the enemy and continued firing until it was hit in the turret by an armor piercing round that killed Sergeant Rivers.

The veterans of the 761st have been acknowledged— unfortunately, not without some controversy—by the Public Broadcasting System. On Nov. 11, 1992, PBS presented an hour-long documentary, "The Liberators," focusing on the exploits of the 761st Tank Battalion. Moreover, the broadcast asserted that the 761st helped liberate the most infamous of all Nazi concentration camps—Buchenwald and Dachau. Unquestionably, the 761st did liberate some concentration camps, but the assertion that the Battalion played a role in the liberation of those two specific camps has been challenged by some 761st veterans. The April 1945 after-action report of the 761st contains no entries concerning either of the two camps. Furthermore, the April 1945 location entries place the 761st miles from either camp. PBS therefore withdrew "The Liberators" from further exhibition pending additional research.

Smaller African American combat units made significant contributions in combat operations in both Europe and the Pacific. Fire from black artillerymen helped dislodge German troops as American forces fought to cross the Rhine River. For its defense of Bastogne, a strategic city in Belgium, the 969th Field Artillery Battalion received a Distinguished Unit Citation for meritorious service performed while attached to a white organization. Company C of the 614th Tank Destroyer Battalion became the first black ground unit to win this honor in World War II for driving off a German force that blocked the 411th Infantry in its advance on Climbach, Germany. Black antiaircraft outfits protected outposts in the Pacific and shot down German aircraft in Europe.

Because of a policy of racial segregation and discrimination, most of the one million African Americans in uniform during World War II were not assigned combat duty. Instead, they were assigned duty in the Service of Supply (SOS). In this capacity, they proved instrumental in the outcome of the war by operating bulldozers and cranes, setting up communications systems, and transporting essential supplies to the front. Over seventy percent of the truck companies in the Army's Motor Transport Service were black. Their role was critical in Europe because the railroads in France were destroyed by retreating German forces. Therefore, Allied forces had to be supplied by truck. The Red Ball Express was formed to meet this need in August, 1944, with an original route between St. Lo and Paris. "On an average day, 899 vehicles on the Red Ball Express traveled 1,504,616 ton-miles on the trip that took an average time of 54 hours." (Department of Defense *Black Americans in Defense of Our Nation*, n.d., p. 100).

The White Ball Route replaced the Red Ball Express in November, 1944. Four of the nine truck companies transporting supplies from Le Havre and Rouen to forward areas were black. Black truck companies also saw duty on the Antwerp-Brussels-Charleroi Route and the Green Diamond Route between Normandy and the Brest peninsula. The 3917th Gasoline Supply Company supplied the Third Army with up to 165,000 gallons of gas a day. Black truckers were also well represented among the twelve amphibian truck companies. Though assigned transport duty, black truckers were subject to hostile fire and were called upon to fight in emergencies. A number received military honors from both the United States and France for courage and meritorious service in combat.

## The Women's Auxiliary Army Corps

With the creation of the Women's Auxiliary Army Corps on May 14, 1942, black women could serve in the American military in greater numbers than ever before. Many of the 4,000 black volunteers were assigned duties unlike their white counterparts in the renamed Women's Army Corps. While white women typically typed in offices, most black women were assigned to clean-up details and laundry and mess duty. This was not always the case, however. Overseas, the 6888th Postal Battalion commanded by Major Charity Adams arrived in England in 1945. The unit was later sent to the European mainland where it improved the mail delivery system, a system invaluable to troop morale.

Black women also served in the Army Nurse Corps. Initially, these women were only permitted to care for black patients, but this policy proved impractical. The resentment generated when black women were assigned to care for German prisoners of war ultimately led to a change in policy, enabling black nurses to care for wounded Americans, regardless of race.

## The Sea Services

Following a decade of excluding blacks from enlistment, the United States Navy in 1932 decided upon a place for them—their own branch. The branch was known as the Stewards' Service, referred to in the black community as "sea-going bell hops." The 1940 Navy consisted of 170,000 men of whom 4,007 or 2.3 percent were blacks in the Stewards' Service. In addition to blacks, Navy stewards were also recruited from among Filipinos and other Asian-American populations.

The advent of World War II transformed this situation. President Franklin D. Roosevelt had served as assistant secretary of the Navy during World War I, and considered it "his branch" of the armed services. Therefore his January 9, 1942 memo to the Navy had tremendous impact. The President noted to then-Secretary of the Navy Frank Knox: "I think that with all the Navy activities, Bureau of Navy might invent something that colored enlistees could do in addition to the rating of messman."

The Navy did relent on April 7, 1942 by announcing it would accept 14,000 black enlistees in all ratings and branches. The initial training of black sailors was conducted at the Great Lakes Naval Training Station, north of Chicago, Illinois.

It was at Great Lakes that the Navy finally made a breakthrough in regard to black personnel. In January 1944, sixteen black petty officers began a special and intensive course of instruction that was conducted without public announcement. Three months later, the Navy announced the commissioning of twelve black ensigns and one warrant officer. They were then and are now the Navy's "Golden Thirteen" (1933, *The Golden Thirteen: Recollections of the First Black Naval Officers*. Annapolis, Maryland: Naval Institute Press).

Shortly after the "Golden Thirteen" were commissioned, the Navy opened the V-12 officer training programs to black men. Among the V-12 graduates who became Navy officers in World War II were Samuel L. Gravely, Jr. and Carl T. Rowan. Gravely became the Navy's first black admiral; Rowan is a syndicated columnist and broadcaster.

By the end of World War II, 165,000 blacks had served in the Navy; 17,000 in the Marine Corps; 5,000 in the Coast Guard; 12,000 in Construction Battalions (Sea Bees); and 24,000 in the Merchant Marine. These African American soldiers served with distinction. Notable among them is the mess steward Dorie Miller, who on December 7, 1941 manned a machine gun aboard the *USS Arizona* as Japanese aircraft attacked Pearl Harbor. Miller destroyed two of the attackers and, after some delay, was awarded the Navy Cross. He was also promoted to mess attendant first class. Miller died when the escort aircraft carrier *USS Liscome Bay* was sunk on November 24, 1943. Three other black mess attendants received the Navy Cross during World War II: Eli Benjamin (*USS Intrepid*); Leonard Harmon (*USS San Francisco*); and William Pinkney (*USS Enterprise*). Dorie Miller is memorialized by one of the three Navy warships named for black Americans: the frigates *USS Miller* and *USS Jesse L. Brown*, and the missile submarine *USS George Washington Carver*.

## Desegregation of the Military

As the Allied victory of World War II approached, the highest levels of the United States government recog-

nized that a new domestic racial era had emerged. The war to defeat Fascism had, indeed, involved the entire United States population.

One impetus for change of military policy toward blacks was an August 5, 1945 letter from Colonel Noel F. Parrish, commander of Tuskegee Army Air Field, to Brigadier General William E. Hall, Headquarters Army Air Forces. (1986. Bernard C. Nalty. *Strength For the Fight* New York: The Free Press, 213-214). Colonel Parrish recommended "that future policy, instead of retreating defensibly further and further, with more and more group concessions, openly progress by slow and reasonable but definite steps toward the employment and treatment of Negroes as individuals which law requires and military efficiency demands."

Although Secretary of War Henry L. Stimson often revealed racist tendencies, his assistant, John R. McCloy, was considerably more liberal. Stimson was succeeded by Robert P. Patterson who adopted McCloy's suggestion for a study of future use of blacks in the military. The study was made by a board of three Army generals: Lieutenant General Alvan C. Gillem, Jr., a former corps commander; Major General Lewis A. Pick, who built the Ledo Road in Burma; and Brigadier General Winslow C. Morse, of the Army Air Force. During a six week period, the so-called Gillem Board took testimony from more than fifty witnesses toward forming the Army's postwar racial policy. Two key individuals who worked with the Gillem Board were the two black Chicagoans who served sequentially as Civilian Aide to the Secretary of War: Truman K. Gibson, Jr. and the recently-discharged Lieutenant Colonel Marcus H. Ray. It is noteworthy that racial desegregation of the military was driven by the considerable political and economic influence of black Chicago.

The Gillem Board's findings leaned toward more "efficient" use of Negro manpower, but did not advocate actual desegregation.

That vagueness reactivated the pre-war coalition of the NAACP, the National Urban League, and the grassroots labor forces led by A. Philip Randolph.

The advent of the Cold War led to the National Security Act of 1947. One of the major elements of the new law was the establishment of the Department of Defense (DOD), with the subordinate Departments of Army, Navy and, Air Force. The other new entity created was the Central Intelligence Agency (CIA).

In the continuing movement toward desegregation of the armed forces, 1947 brought two important black personnel shifts within the Department Of Defense: Lieutenant Colonel Marcus H. Ray returned to active duty as senior advisor on racial matters in Europe and in the Pentagon, Dr. James C. Evans, a Howard University professor and Department of Army official, moved to the new post of Special Assistant to the Secretary of Defense. As the highest-ranking black civilian in the Department Of Defense, Dr. Evans served under ten secretaries of Defense until his retirement in 1970.

The demand for desegregation of the military became a key political issue in black America. As preparations for the 1948 presidential election intensified, President Truman faced a campaign against Republican Thomas E. Dewey, States Rights segregationist Strom Thurmond, and the Communist Party-supported Progressive Party of former Vice-President Henry A. Wallace. In such a fragmented situation, the black vote became crucial.

By May 1948, President Truman had decided to desegregate the armed forces by an Executive Order. Dr. Evans guided the politically sensitive staff coordination effort through the Pentagon. In other Executive branch and Capitol Hill offices, two political concessions were required. First, no deadlines would be imposed. Second, the order would not denounce racial segregation. With a final sign-off by the Attorney General, President Truman issued Executive Order No. 9981, which signalled a policy to end segregation in the military.

## ◆ THE KOREAN WAR (1950-1953)

On June 25, 1950, North Korean forces surged across the 38th parallel and invaded South Korea. The United States ground forces in Korea were savaged by the North Koreans and driven south. At the start of the Korean War, the Air Force was the only branch of the military that was desegregated.

The first United States victory of the Korean War was won by black soldiers of the 24th Infantry Regiment on July 20, 1950, at Yechon. Captain Charles M. Bussey, a World War II Tuskegee Airman, was the ground commander and earned a Silver Star at Yechon. Two black soldiers were awarded posthumous Medals of Honor during the Korean War: Private First Class William Thompson and Sergeant Cornelius H. Charlton, both of the 24th Infantry Regiment.

Thompson distinguished himself by bravery and determination above and beyond the call of duty in action against the enemy on August 6, 1950, near Haman,

Korea. While his platoon was reorganizing under cover of darkness, enemy forces overwhelmed the unit with a surprise attack. Johnson set up his machine gun in the path of the onslaught and swept the enemy with fire, momentarily pinning them down and thus permitting the remainder of his platoon to withdraw to a more secure position. Although hit repeatedly by grenade fragments and small-arms fire, he resisted his comrades' efforts to induce him to withdraw. Steadfast at his machine-gun, he continued to deliver fire until he was mortally wounded by an enemy grenade.

Charlton, a member of Company C, distinguished himself in action against the enemy on June 2, 1931, near Chipo-Ri, Korea. His platoon was attacking heavily defended hostile positions on commanding ground when the leader was wounded and evacuated. Carlton assumed command, rallied the men, and spearheaded the assault against the hill. Personally eliminating two hostile positions and killing six of the enemy with his rifle-fire and grenades, he continued up the slope until the unit suffered heavy casualties and was stalled. Regrouping the men, he led them forward, only to be again forced back by a shower of grenades. Despite a severe chest wound, Charlton refused medical attention and led a third daring charge that would advance to the crest of the ridge. He then charged a remaining enemy position on a nearby slope alone and, though hit by a grenade, raked the position with fire that eliminated it and routed the defenders. He died of wounds he received during his daring exploits.

### The Korean War Evolution

The early defeats American forces experienced in Korea prompted President Truman to replace his close friend, Secretary of Defense Louis A. Johnson. To succeed Johnson, President Truman selected retired General of the Army George C. Marshall, who had been Truman's Secretary of State during 1947-1949.

One of Marshall's first acts as Secretary of Defense was the creation of a new entity: Office of Assistant Secretary of Defense for Manpower and Reserves (OASD MPR). Marshall appointed Mrs. Anna M. Rosenberg, a forty-eight-year old New York City labor and public relations consultant, as head of this Office. In 1944, she had persuaded President Franklin D. Roosevelt to have Congress enact the education provisions of the World War II G.I. Bill of Rights. Dr. James C. Evans' Office of Special Assistant became a part of the OASD (MPR). This brought together two individuals knowledgeable in the rigors of discrimination—a Hungarian Jewish immi-

Black members of the 2nd Infantry Division, Korea, 1950.

grant woman and a black male college professor. Known affectionately in the Pentagon as "Aunt Anna," Mrs. Rosenberg's OASD (MPR) was responsible for industrial and military manpower, including Selective Service System policies. Secretary Rosenberg viewed military desegregation as an impetus for civilian society reform observing that, "In the long run, I don't think a man can live and fight next to one of another race and share experiences where life is at stake, and not have a strong feeling of understanding when he comes home."

The effective implementation of Executive Order No. 9981 turned on how well their hard-won opportunities were used by black military personnel. The one individual who was truly the mentor of the black military professional, especially black officers, was Dr. James C. Evans. During much of his tenure in the Pentagon, Dr. Evans' Executive Officer was Army Colonel John T. Martin, who later was Director of the Selective Service System for the District of Columbia. Commenting in 1993, Colonel Martin reflected that "James C. Evans and his associates accomplished much behind the scenes—and with no fingerprints—to advance the careers of all [black] personnel in the military." One bit of mentoring at which Dr. Evans excelled was "informal" career

counselling. A wise young black officer would heed an Evans "suggestion" to explore a certain military career field, complete a particular service school course, or obtain an advanced degree in a particular discipline. If a young officer hesitated, Dr. Evans might again "suggest" that a particular course of action would benefit the officer "in due course." The counsel came from a man able to accurately forecast future officer education and experience requirements. Many black generals and admirals owe their stars to the wise counsel of James C. Evans.

By the end of the Korean War, racial segregation had been totally removed from the United States armed services. In the years preceding the Vietnam War, blacks increasingly entered the services and opted for full careers. Between 1953 and 1961, there was a slow but steady increase in the number of black career officers in each service.

## ◆ THE VIETNAM WAR (1964-1973)

During the brief period of cease-fire between the end of the Korean War and the heightening of conflict in

Vietnam, the Kennedy Administration—prompted by Congressman Adam Clayton Powell, Jr., and others—sought to end any remaining discrimination in the Armed Forces. Through Secretary of Defense Robert McNamara, Kennedy stressed to military leaders the need for fostering friendship and equal opportunity for black servicemen, both on and off base.

Extensive American involvement in Vietnam began during the summer of 1964 following an attack on the

By the end of the Korean War, racial segregation had been totally removed from the United States armed services.

Between 1953 and 1961 there was a slow, but steady, increase in the number of black career officers. Pictured Major Jerome Cooper, 9th Marines.

*USS Maddox* by North Vietnamese naval vessels in the Gulf of Tonkin. Within four months, the United States had 23,000 soldiers fighting in Vietnam. Shortly thereafter, the Army, Navy, and Marine Corps of the United States were all engaged in the action in ever increasing numbers. While the American fighting force in Vietnam was composed of all American racial and ethnic groups, blacks were disporportionately represented and most likely to be placed in high-risk combat units. Although blacks consituted about 10.5 percent of the Army, they accounted for nearly 13 percent of those killed and wounded. By 1965, the conflict in Vietnam had escalated into a full-scale war to support both the South Vietnamese people and U.S. interests in Southeast Asia, a war that was deadlier than the Korean War and longer than any other in American history.

The uncertain objectives of the Vietnam War, the high casualties, and the disporportionate number of black U.S. soldiers in Vietnam caused tremendous controversy in the African American community. In 1965, Malcolm X claimed that the U.S. government was "causing American soldiers to be murdered every day, for no reason at all." Martin Luther King Jr., criticized African American involvement in Vietnam, remarking that "we are taking young black men who have been crippled by our society and sending them 8,000 miles away to guarantee liberties in Southeast Asia which they have not found in southwest Georgia or East Harlem."

With the assassinations of Dr. King and Senator Robert Kennedy in 1968, some black soldiers became increasingly demoralized and disenchanted. Their anger intensified as racial prejudice remained common in Vietnam, on military bases stateside, and onboard the aircraft carriers *Kitty Hawk, Constellation,* and *Franklin D. Roosevelt.* One of the most famous black protesters of the Vietnam War was heavyweight champion

Blacks increasingly entered the services and opted for full careers. Pictured Brigadier General Davis and Captain Murray, Vietnam.

Muhammad Ali. A Black Muslim, Ali declared himself a conscientious objector in 1968 on religious grounds. He was convicted of violating the Selective Service Act, stripped of his heavyweight boxing championship, and threatened with an extensive jail term. In 1970, the Supreme Court cleared Ali of wrongdoing.

Still, most young African American men were willing to answer the draft board's call when it came. Private First Class Milton Olive of Chicago was typical of African Americans who risked, and sometimes lost, their lives during the war. Olive was killed by an exploding grenade on which he had fallen to save the lives of his comrades; the government acknowledged his heroism by awarding a posthumous Congressional Medal of Honor.

By mid-1969, nine other African Americans had joined Olive as recipients of the Congressional Medal of Honor: Captain Riley L. Pitts; First Lieutenant Ruppert L. Sargent; Sergeants Rodney M. Davis, Matthew Leonard, and Donald R. Long; Specialists Five Lawrence Joel, Clarence E. Sasser, and Dwight H. Johnson; and Private First Class James Anderson, Jr.

According to the *New York Times* reporter Thomas Johnson, officers in the Military Assistance Command said that the 173rd Airborne Brigade, a crack outfit with a heavy black representation, was "the best performing unit in Vietnam." In such elite combat units, one out of every four combat troops was a black man.

In 1973, the United States withdrew all troops from Vietnam, ending on of the most painful chapters in American history.

## ◆ MILITARY PARTICIPATION IN THE 1970S AND 1980S

In 1972, a year before the final withdrawal of U.S. troops from Vietnam, the Defense Department issued "The Search for Military Justice." This report recognized that discrimination still existed in the military. In particular, it found that African Americans and Hispanics were involved in more disciplinary incidents and were often punished more severely.

General Colin Powell at the Vietnam Veterans Memorial, Washington, DC.

In the 1970s, blacks represented about 13 percent of discharged servicemen, but received 33 percent of the dishonorable discharges, 21 percent of bad conduct discharges, 16 percent of undesirable discharges, and 20 percent of general discharges. Less than honorable discharges can negatively affect a person for life, threatening one's civilian career, earning ability, and level of veteran's benefits.

Fortunately, high-ranking government and military officials are moving to eliminate racial prejudices and barriers. Today, in many ways, military life is less discriminatory than civilian life. Also, in the 1980s, increasing numbers of women joined the military and work side by side with men in a wide variety of areas. This helps to facilitate the breakdown of gender, as well as racial, obstacles to success in the military.

By the end of the 1980s, blacks represented 28 percent of the total enlisted Army force, while black women numbered nearly 45 percent of enlisted women. However, recruiting blacks as officers was difficult in the 1980s due, in part, to competition with industry, law schools, and other professions that can offer talented black men and women higher salaries than the military.

# ◆ THE PERSIAN GULF WAR (1991)

African Americans were deeply divided over American involvement in the Gulf War, with almost 50 percent of those polled at the time opposed to it. Several black leaders, including Representative Charles Rangel of New York, were concerned in particular about the high number of blacks fighting to liberate Kuwait from Iraq. Military leader Colin Powell himself initially favored economic sanctions (embargoes) over military actions,

Petty Officer First Class John T. Winstead holds the folded American flag.

until war became the stated policy of President George Bush. From then on, Powell earned credit for drafting and putting into action a brilliant campaign—which began with the largest single air attack in history—that minimized the loss of American lives.

About 104,000 of the 400,000 troops serving in the Persian Gulf were black. According to the Department of Defense, blacks accounted for 30 percent of the Army, 21 percent of the Navy, 17 percent of the Marines, and 14 percent of the Air Force personnel stationed in the Gulf (in 1991 blacks comprised only 12.4 percent of the U.S. population). For Powell, the high participation of blacks, as shown by the Gulf War numbers, is a positive, rather than a negative: "To those who question the proportion of blacks in the armed services, my answer is simple. The military of the United States is the greatest equal opportunity employer around." Since the end of the Persian Gulf War in 1991, African American military men and women have been well represented in peacekeeping missions in Somalia, Haiti, and Bosnia-Herzegovina.

## ◆ OUTSTANDING MILITARY FIGURES

### Ensign Jesse L. Brown (1926-1950)
*Naval Aviator*

Jesse Leroy Brown was the first African American to become a naval aviator and the first black naval officer to be killed in action during the Korean War.

Brown was born October 13, 1926 in Hattiesburg, Mississippi. He graduated from Eureka High School in 1944 and studied engineering at Ohio State University from 1944 to 1947. In 1946 Brown joined the Naval Reserve and in 1947 he became an aviation cadet.

Brown's flight training was at Pensacola, Florida and in 1948 he became the first African American to earn the Navy Wings. In 1949 Brown was assigned to the *USS Leyte* and won the Air Medal and the Korean Service Medal for his 20 air combat missions. On December 4, 1950 he was shot down while flying air support for United States Marines at the Battle of the Chosin Reservoir. He was posthumously awarded the Purple Heart and the Distinguished Flying Cross for exceptional courage, airmanship and devotion to duty. Brown was the first African-American naval officer to lose his life in combat.

In 1973 the *USS Jesse L. Brown*, a destroyer escort was named in his honor and launched at the Avondale Shipyard at Westwege, Louisiana.

### Sharian Grace Cadoria (1940- )
*Military Officer*

Born on January 26, 1940, in Marksville, Louisiana, Cadoria became the first black woman in the regular U.S. Army and the second African American female in history to rise to the rank of brigadier general. As a child, she and her two siblings helped pick cotton in the rural fields. After high school, Cadoria attended the state's Southern University, where, in the early 1960s, she was recruited for a four-week Women's Army Corp (WAC) training program conducted at Fort McClellan in Alabama. Thus began a 29-year-long, distinguished military career of "firsts," even after the WAC was dissolved in 1978 at which point she joined the male corp. Before fully devoting herself to the military, Cadoria earned her B.S. in Business Education from Southern and later obtained an M.A. in social work from the University of Oklahoma in 1974.

Among her marks of distinction, Cadoria was the first woman to command a male battalion; the first African American director of manpower and personnel for the Joint Chiefs of Staff—a position that required her to fill openings in all branches of the armed services, including the Army, Air Force, Navy, Marines, and affiliated reserve corps; the first black woman to attend the U.S. Army Command and General Staff College in addition to having attended the U.S. Army War College and having taken the Adjunct General School's advance course; and the first woman to achieve the rank of general through the military police rather than through the nursing corps.

Cadoria retired from the military in 1990, having spent the majority of her life breaking down the barriers presented by gender and racial discrimination. For outstanding contributions, Cadoria was awarded an Air Medal, an Army Commendation Medal, a Bronze Star, a Defense Superior Service Medal, a Distinguished Service Medal, and a Meritorious Service Medal during her career.

### Sergeant William H. Carney (1840-1908)
*First African American Medal of Honor Recipient*

William Carney was born a slave in Norfolk, Virginia, in 1840. Around 1856, Carney's father moved the family to New Bedford, Massachusetts. In 1863 Carney enlisted in the 54th Massachusetts Colored Infantry. On July 18, 1863, Carney and the 54th Massachusetts led an assault on Fort Wagner, South Carolina, during which Carney was severely wounded. On May 23, 1900, Carney was issued a Medal of Honor. He died in 1908.

### Lieutenant General Benjamin O. Davis, Jr. (1912- )
*First African American General, United States Air Force*

Born in Washington, DC, in 1912, Davis was educated in Alabama (his father taught military science at Tuskegee), and later, in Cleveland, where he graduated as president of his class. Davis went on to attend Western Reserve

University and the University of Chicago before accepting an appointment to the United States Military Academy in 1932. In 1936 Davis graduated 35th in his class of 276.

After serving in the infantry for five years, he transferred to the Army Air Corps in 1942 and was among the first six black air cadets to graduate from the Advanced Army Flying School.

As Commander of the 99th Fighter Squadron (and later commander of the all-black 332nd Fighter Group), Davis flew 60 missions in 224 combat hours during World War II, winning several medals, including the Silver Star.

In 1957 Davis was made chief of staff, of the 12th Air Force, United States Air Forces in Europe (USAFE). In 1961 he was made director of Manpower Organization, and in 1965 he became chief of staff for the United Nations Command and United States Forces in Korea. Davis was assigned as deputy commander in chief, US Strike Command in 1968. He retired from active duty in 1970.

### Brigadier General Benjamin O. Davis, Sr. (1877-1970)
*First African American General, United States Army*

Born in Washington, D.C., on July 1, 1877, Benjamin O. Davis, Sr. graduated from Howard University and joined the army in 1898 during the Spanish-American War. At the end of that war, he reenlisted in the 9th Cavalry and was made second lieutenant in 1901. Black promotions were rare in those years, but Davis rose through the officer's ranks until he was made a full colonel in 1930. During that time, in addition to his military commands, he was a professor of military science and tactics at Wilberforce and Tuskegee universities, military attache to Liberia, and instructor of the 372nd Infantry of the Ohio National Guard. After his promotion to brigadier general and his service in World War II, he became an assistant to the inspector general in Washington, D.C. until his retirement in 1948.

Among General Davis' many awards and decorations are the Distinguished Service Medal, the Bronze Star Medal, the Grade of Commander of the Order of the Star of Africa, from the Liberian government, and the French Croix de Guerre with palm. General Davis died on November 26, 1970.

### Lieutenant Henry Ossian Flipper (1856?-1940)
*First African American Graduate of the United States Military Academy*

Henry Ossian Flipper was born a slave in Thomasville, Georgia, on March 21, 1856; his father, a craftsman, bought his family's freedom. Flipper attended Atlanta University and in 1873 was appointed to the United States Military Academy.

Lieutenant General Benjamin O. Davis, Jr.

He graduated from the academy in 1877 and was commissioned as second lieutenant and assigned to the all-black 10th Cavalry. However, in 1881, Flipper became the victim of a controversial court-martial proceeding which cut short his career.

Flipper went on, as a civilian, to become a notable figure on the American frontier—as a mining engineer and consultant and later, as a translator of Spanish land grants. Flipper tried on many occasions to vindicate himself, befriending such prominent Washington officials as Senator A. B. Fall of New Mexico. When Fall became Secretary of the Interior, Flipper became his assistant until the infamous Teapot Dome affair severed their relationship.

Flipper returned to Atlanta at the close of his mining career, living with his brother, an AME bishop, until his death in 1940. His quest to remove the stain of "conduct unbecoming an officer and a gentleman" remained unfulfilled to his dying day.

### Vice Admiral Samuel L. Gravely, Jr. (1922- )
*First African American Admiral, United States Navy*

Samuel L. Gravely Jr. was born in Richmond, Virginia on June 4, 1922. He enrolled at Virginia Union Universi-

Brigadier General Benjamin O. Davis, Sr.

Lieutenant Henry O. Flipper

ty, but quit school to enlist in the U.S. Navy. He received naval training at the Great Lakes facility at Great Lakes, Illinois, the midshipmen school at Columbia University in New York, and Officer Training Camp at the University of California, Los Angeles. During World War II, Gravely served aboard a submarine chaser. After the war ended, he returned to school and received a B.A. in history from Virginia Union University in 1948.

Gravely was called back to active duty in 1949 and decided to make a career of the navy. During the Korean War, he served aboard the cruiser USS Toledo. He was steadily promoted through the ranks and, in 1962, he accepted command of the destroyer escort USS Falgout. Stationed at Pearl Harbor, Hawaii as part of the Pacific Fleet, he became the first African American to assume command of a navy combat ship. In 1971, while commanding the guided missile frigate USS Jouett, Gravely was promoted to admiral, the first African American to achieve that rank. In 1976, he was promoted to vice admiral and placed in command of the United States Navy's 3rd Fleet, a position he held until 1978. Gravely, now retired, has also served as director of the Defense Communications Agency from 1978 until 1980, and the executive director of education and training for the

Armed Forces Communications and Electronics Association.

While in the Navy, Gravely received many medals, including the Legion of Merit with Gold Star, Bronze Star, Meritorious Service Medal, Joint Service Commendation Medal, Navy Commendation Medal, World War II Victory Medal, Naval Reserve Medal for 10 years of service in the U.S. Naval Reserve, American Campaign Medal, Korean Presidential Unit Citation, National Defense Medal with one bronze star, China Service Medal, Korean Service Medal with two bronze stars, United Nations Service Medal, Armed Forces Expeditionary Medal, Vietnam Service Medal with six bronze stars, and the Antarctic Service Medal.

Gravely has also received numerous civilian awards, including the Founding Fathers Military Commands Award presented by the Masons (1975), Military Headliner of the Year Award given by the San Diego Press Club (1975) and Savannah State College's Award of Excellence (1974). In 1972, Gravely received the Distinguished Virginian Award presented by the Governor of Virginia. The Virginia Press Association named him Virginian of the Year in 1979. In 1991, Gravely was named Aide-de-Camp to the Governor of Virginia.

## General Daniel James, Jr. (1920-1978)

*First African American Four Star General, United States Air Force*

Appointed Commander of NORAD on August 29, 1975, Daniel "Chappie" James was the first African American four-star general in United States military history. Before coming to this post, he had been a flying ace in the Korean War, had served as deputy secretary of defense, and was vice commander of military airlift command.

Born on February 11, 1920 in Pensacola, Florida, he attended Tuskegee Institute, where he took part in the Army Air Corps program and was commissioned a second lieutenant in 1943. During the Korean War, James flew 101 combat missions in F-51 and F-80 aircraft. After the war, he performed various staff assignments until 1957, when he graduated from the Air Command and Staff College at Maxwell Air Force Base, Alabama. In 1966, he became deputy commander for operations of the 8th Tactical Fighter Wing stationed in Thailand, before promotion to commander of the 7272nd Flying Training Wing at Wheelus Air Force Base in Libya.

James became a brigadier general in 1970, a lieutenant general in 1973. He has received numerous civilian awards. His military awards include Legion of Merit with one oak leaf cluster, Distinguished Flying Cross, Air Medal with ten clusters, Distinguished Unit Citation, Presidential Unit Citation, and Air Force Outstanding Unit Award. In 1975 James was appointed commander in chief, NORAD/ADCOM, and was promoted to four-star general.

On February 25, 1978, James died of a heart attack at the age of fifty-eight in Colorado Springs.

## General Hazel W. Johnson (1927- )

*First African American Female General, United States Army*

Johnson was born in 1927 in West Chester, Pennsylvania and received nurses training at Harlem Hospital in New York. She enlisted in the United States Army in 1955 and in 1960 Johnson joined the Army's Nursing Corps as a first lieutenant. Johnson then went on to earn a bachelors degree in nursing from Villanova University, a masters degree in nursing education from Columbia University, and a doctorate in education administration from Catholic University in Washington, DC.

In 1979 Johnson was promoted to brigadier general, the first African-American woman to hold that rank and was placed in command of the Army Nurse Corps. In 1983 she retired from the service and began working for the American Nursing Association as director of their government affairs division. In 1986 she joined the faculty of George Mason University in Virginia as a professor of nursing.

Johnson is a recipient of the Army's Distinguished Service Medal, Legion of Merit, Meritorious Service Medal, and the Army Commendation Medal with oak leaf cluster.

## Sergeant Henry Johnson (1897-1929)

*369th Infantry Regiment, 93rd Division, United States Army*

Henry Johnson was born in 1897 in Winston-Salem, North Carolina. A member of the 15th National Guard of New York, which became the 369th Infantry, Henry Johnson was probably the most famous black soldier to have fought in World War I.

The 369th itself was the first group of black combat troops to arrive in Europe. After a summer of training, the group saw action at Champagne and fought its way to the Rhine River in Germany, receiving the Croix de Guerre from the French government. Johnson and another soldier (Needham Roberts) were the first Americans to receive this French medal for individual heroism in combat; Johnson was cited by the French as a "magnificent example of courage and energy." He was later promoted to sergeant. Johnson died on July 2, 1929.

## Dorie Miller (1919-1943)

*Mess Attendant Third Class, United States Navy*

A messman aboard the *USS Arizona*, Dorie Miller had his first taste of combat at Pearl Harbor on December 7, 1941, when he manned a machine gun and brought down four Japanese planes.

Born on a farm near Waco, Texas on October 12, 1919, Miller was the son of a sharecropper and grew up to become star fullback on the Moore High School football team in his native city. At 19, he enlisted in the United States Navy, and was nearing the end of his first hitch at the time of the Pearl Harbor attack.

For his heroism, Miller was awarded the Navy Cross, which was conferred by Admiral Chester W. Nimitz, the Commander in Chief of the Pacific Fleet.

He remained a messman during the hostilities, serving aboard the aircraft carrier *USS Liscome* Bay and being promoted to Mess Attendant Third Class. He was killed in action in the South Pacific in December of 1943.

General Daniel "Chappie" James, the first African American four star general.

Miller was commended for "distinguished devotion to duty, extreme courage, and disregard of his personal safety during attack."

### General Frank E. Petersen (1932- )
*First African American General in the United States Marine Corps*

Frank E. Petersen, Jr. was born March 2, 1932 in Topeka, Kansas. He attended Washington University, in St. Louis, and George Washington University, in Washington, DC, eventually earning a BS in 1967 and a MS in 1973. In 1951, Petersen entered the Naval Reserve as an aviation cadet.

In 1952, Petersen was commissioned as a second lieutenant in the United States Marine Corps. He was a designated naval aviator and received flight training at the United States Air Station at Pensacola, Florida. He also received flight training at Corpus Christie, Texas and the Marine Corps Air Station at Santa Ana, California.

Daniel James, Jr. seated in the cockpit of his jet fighter plane.

General Hazel Johnson

Petersen flew thirty-one air combat missions during the Korean War. In 1953 and 1954, he was assigned to the 1st Marine Aircraft Wing as its liaison officer. From 1954 to 1960, he was assigned to the Marine Corps' Santa Ana, California facility and, in 1968, he commanded the Marine Aircraft Group in Vietnam. In 1979, Petersen was promoted to the rank of brigadier general. From 1985 to 1988, he served as senior ranking pilot of the U.S. Navy & U.S. Marine Corps. He was also the senior pilot of the U.S. armed forces from 1986 to 1988. In 1989, Petersen retired from the service and became a vice president at DuPont.

As an African American Marine Corps officer, Petersen accomplished many firsts. He was the first African American to receive a commission as aviator, the first African American to attend the National War College, the first African American to command a tactical air squadron, and the first African American general in the U.S. Marine Corps.

Petersen is a recipient of over twenty individual medals for combat valor, including the Distinguished Flying Cross, the Air Medal with silver star, the Korean Service Medal, the Korean Presidential Citation, the National Defense Service Medal with bronze star, and the United Nations Service Medal.

Petersen is a member of the Tuskegee Airman and Business Executives for National Security. He is also on the board of directors for the National Bone Marrow Foundation and the Higher Education Assistance Foundation.

### General Colin L. Powell (1937- )
*First African American Chairman of the Joint Chiefs of Staff*

Colin L. Powell was born in New York City on April 5, 1937 and graduated from Morris High School in 1954. In 1958 he received a B.S. degree in geology from City College of New York; while in college Powell was very active in the ROTC program and attained the rank of cadet colonel.

Powell began his military career by accepting a second lieutenant's commission in the United States Army. In 1962, he served as a military advisor in South Vietnam and eventually became battalion executive officer and division operations officer in Vietnam in 1968. Returning to the United States, Powell earned an MBA degree from George Washington University in 1971. From 1972 to 1973, he served as assistant to the deputy director of the Office of Management and Budget. In 1973, he became a batallion commander in South Korea. Powell graduated from the National War College in 1976 and became commander of the Second Brigade of the 101st Airborne Division at Fort Campbell, Kentucky. In 1979, he became executive assistant to the Secretary of Energy and senior military assistant to the deputy Secretary

Admiral Nimitz awards Dorie Miller with the Navy Cross.

General Frank E. Petersen

of Defense. Powell served as assistant commander of the Fourth Infantry Division, at Fort Carson, Colorado from 1981 to 1983, when he became deputy commander of Fort Leavenworth, Kansas. From 1983 to 1986, he became military assistant to the Secretary of Defense. Powell went to Germany in 1986 to become commanding general of the Fifth Corps. He became assistant to the President for national security affairs in 1987, leaving this post in 1989 to become chairman of the Joint Chiefs of Staff, the highest military command in the United States. From this position, Powell received international recognition as one of the chief architects of the successful 1991 Gulf War against Iraq. Powell retired from the Joint Chiefs of Staff in 1993.

Powell wrote his memoir *My American Journey* and embarked on a nationwide tour in 1995 to promote the book. During the tour, there was widespread speculation that he would become a candidate for President in 1996. However, on November 9, 1995, Powell held a press conference and announced that he would not enter the race as a presidential candidate.

Powell remains active as a lecturer and guest speaker. In 1996, he was named to the board of trustees at Howard University.

During his tenure in the military, Powell was a recipient of several service medals, including the Purple Heart and the Bronze Star (1963), Legion of Merit Award (1969 and 1971), Distinguished Service Medal, Soldiers Medal, and the Secretary's Award (1988). He has received civilian honors as well. In 1993, former President Ronald Reagan presented Powell with the Ronald Reagan Freedom Award. That same year, he received an honorary doctoral degree from Yeshiva University.

### General Roscoe Robinson, Jr. (1928-1993)
*First African American Four Star General, United States Army*

Roscoe Robinson, Jr. was the first African American four-star Army general. He was born on October 11, 1928, in St. Louis, Missouri and graduated from the United States Military Academy with a bachelor's degree in military engineering. He also earned a master's degree in international affairs from the University of Pittsburgh and received further training at the National War College, the Army Command and General Staff College, and the Army's Infantry School.

After graduating from West Point, Robinson was commissioned a second lieutenant in the United States

General Colin Powell with Brigade Commander Kristin Baker.

Army. He served as a personnel management officer from 1965 to 1967, and in 1968 he was promoted to commanding officer of the 7th Cavalry. He became commanding officer of the 82nd Airborne Division's 2nd Brigade at Fort Bragg, North Carolina in 1972. Robinson was promoted to the rank of general in 1973 and was placed in command of forces in Okinawa. He served in this capacity until 1976, when he became commanding general of the 82nd Airborne Division. In 1978, he was placed in command of the 7th Army. He served in this post until 1980, when he commanded the U.S. Army in Japan. From 1982 to 1985 Robinson served as the United States representative to NATO. He also held the position of executive chief of staff, United States Pacific Command. Robinson retired from active service in 1985.

Robinson received numerous military awards, including the Silver Star with oak leaf cluster, Legion of Merit with oak leaf cluster, Bronze Star, 10 Air Medals, an Army Commendation Medal, Combat Infantryman Badge, Distinguished Flying Cross, Master Parachutist

Badge, Defense Distinguished Service Medal, and Army Distinguished Medal with oak leaf cluster.

On July 22, 1993, Robinson died of leukemia.

### Roderick K. von Lipsey (1959- )
*Fighter Pilot, United States Marine Corps.*

Roderick K. von Lipsey was born on January 13, 1959, in Philadelphia, Pennsylvania. He attended the U.S. Naval Academy in Annapolis, Maryland, graduating in 1980. In 1989, he completed a master of arts degree from Catholic University. He has also received further training at the Amphibious Warfare School in Quantico, Virginia.

In 1980, von Lipsey was commissioned as a second lieutenant in the U.S. Marine Corps and learned to fly various types of fighter aircraft. He was stationed at Fort Beaufort, South Carolina, in 1983, promoted to the rank of captain in 1984 and became the officer in charge of aircraft maintenance for the F-4 Phantom. Von Lipsey was then tapped for duty with NATO exercises in Europe and the Mediterranean in 1986. He was sent to the prestigious Navy Fighter Weapons School at Naval Station Miramar in California and completed the grueling six-week program. In 1989, von Lipsey was stationed with the Marine Fighter Attack Squadron at Kaneohe Bay, Hawaii.

On August 2, 1990, Iraq invaded Kuwait. Von Lipsey was sent to Saudi Arabia as part of Operation Desert Shield designed to prevent further Iraqi aggression. While in the Middle East, von Lipsey joined Marine Fighter Attack Squadron 235. On January 20, 1991, the start of Operation Desert Storm against Iraqi forces in Kuwait, von Lipsey led an attack of 35 aircraft from the Third Marine Aircraft Wing. All of the planes under von Lipsey's command returned safely. The attack was one of more than 40 sorties flown by von Lipsey during the Gulf War. For his meritorious service in the Gulf War, he was awarded with the Distinguished Flying Cross.

Following his return from the Middle East, von Lipsey was chosen as one of two aides-de-camp to Joint Chiefs of Staff Chairman Colin Powell. He remained in this assignment until 1993, when he was awarded a White House Fellowship. Eventually, he gained a position as a special assistant to White House Chief of Staff Thomas McLarty III in 1994. Von Lipsey was awarded a second fellowship in 1994 with the Council on Foreign Relations. When this fellowship ended during 1995, he was assigned to Marine Corps Air Squadron El Toro, based in Santa Ana, California.

*Appendix I*

# *Appendix*

## ◆ AFRICAN AMERICAN RECIPIENTS OF SELECTED AWARDS

### ACADEMY AWARD OF MERIT (OSCAR)— ACADEMY OF MOTION PICTURE ARTS AND SCIENCES

#### Best Performance by an Actor in a Leading Role

**1963**  Sidney Poitier, in *Lilies of the Field*

#### Best Performance by an Actor in a Supporting Role

**1982**  Louis Gossett, Jr., in *An Officer and a Gentleman*

**1989**  Denzel Washington, in *Glory*

#### Best Performance by an Actress in a Supporting Role

**1939**  Hattie McDaniel, in *Gone with the Wind*

**1990**  Whoopi Goldberg, in *Ghost*

#### Best Original Score

**1984**  Prince, for *Purple Rain*

**1986**  Herbie Hancock, for *'Round Midnight*

### AMERICAN ACADEMY AND INSTITUTE OF ARTS AND LETTERS AWARD

#### Art

**1946**  Richmond Barthe

**1966**  Romare Bearden

**1971**  Norman Lewis

#### Literature

**1946**  Gwendolyn Brooks; Langston Hughes

**1956**  James Baldwin

**1961**  John A. Williams

**1970**  James A. McPherson

**1971**  Charles Gordone

**1972**  Michael S. Harper

**1974**  Henry Van Dyke

**1978**  Lerone Bennett, Jr.; Toni Morrison

**1985**  John Williams

**1987**  Ernest J. Gaines

**1992**  August Wilson

#### Music

**1974**  Olly Wilson

**1981**  George Walker

**1988**  Hale Smith

**1991**  Tania J. Leon

### EMMY AWARD—ACADEMY OF TELEVISION ARTS AND SCIENCES

#### Outstanding Supporting Actor in a Comedy, Variety, or Music Series

**1985**  Robert Guillaume, in "Benson" (ABC)

**1979**  Robert Guillaume, in "Soap" (ABC)

#### Outstanding Lead Actor in a Drama Series

**1966**  Bill Cosby as Alexander Scott, in "I Spy" (NBC)

**1967**  Bill Cosby as Alexander Scott, in "I Spy" (NBC)

1968  Bill Cosby as Alexander Scott, in "I Spy" (NBC)

1991  James Earl Jones, in "Gabriel's Fire" (ABC)

## Outstanding Supporting Actor in a Miniseries or a Special

1991  James Earl Jones, in "Heatwave" (TNT)

## Outstanding Lead Actress in a Comedy Series

1981  Isabel Sanford, in "The Jeffersons" (CBS)

## Outstanding Supporting Actress in a Drama Series

1984  Alfre Woodard, in "Doris in Wonderland" episode of "Hill Street Blues" (NBC)

1991  Madge Sinclair, in "Gabriel's Fire" (ABC)

## Outstanding Supporting Actress in a Miniseries or a Special

1991  Ruby Dee, in "Decoration Day" (NBC)

## Outstanding Lead Actress in a Comedy or Drama Special

1974  Cicely Tyson, in "The Autobiography of Miss Jane Pittman" (CBS)

## Outstanding Lead Actress in a Miniseries or a Special

1991  Lynn Whitfield, in "The Josephine Baker Story" (HBO)

## Outstanding Achievement in Music Composition for a Series

1977  Quincy Jones and Gerald Fried, for "Roots" (ABC)

## Outstanding Directing in a Drama Series

1986  Georg Stanford Brown, for "Parting Shots," episode of "Cagney & Lacey" (ABC)

1990  Thomas Carter, for "Equal Justice" episode of "Promises to Keep" (ABC)

1991  Thomas Carter, for "Equal Justice" episode of "In Confidence" (ABC)

1992  Eric Laneuville, for "I'll Fly Away" episode of "All God's Children" (NBC)

## Outstanding Achievement in Music Composition

1971  Ray Charles, for "The First Nine Months Are the Hardest" (NBC)

1972  Ray Charles, for "The Funny Side of Marriage" (NBC)

# GRAMMY AWARD—NATIONAL ACADEMY OF RECORDING ARTS AND SCIENCES

## Record of the Year

1967  *Up, Up and Away*, by 5th Dimension

1969  *Aquarius/Let the Sun Shine In*, by 5th Dimension

1972  *The First Time Ever I Saw Your Face*, by Roberta Flack

1973  *Killing Me Softly with His Song*, by Roberta Flack

1976  *This Masquerade*, by George Benson

1983  *Beat It*, by Michael Jackson

1984  *What's Love Got To Do with It*, by Tina Turner

1985  *We Are the World*, by USA For Africa; produced by Quincy Jones

1988  *Don't Worry, Be Happy*, by Bobby McFerrin

1991  *Unforgettable*, by Natalie Cole with Nat "King" Cole

## Album of the Year

1973  *Innervisions*, by Stevie Wonder; produced by Stevie Wonder

1974  *Fulfillingness' First Finale*, by Stevie Wonder; produced by Stevie Wonder

1976  *Songs in the Key of Life*, by Stevie Wonder; produced by Stevie Wonder

1983  *Thriller*, by Michael Jackson; produced by Quincy Jones

1984  *Can't Slow Down*, by Lionel Richie; produced by Lionel Richie and James Anthony Carmichael

1990  *Back on the Block*, by Quincy Jones; produced by Quincy Jones

1991  *Unforgettable*, by Natalie Cole

# HEISMAN MEMORIAL TROPHY— DOWNTOWN ATHLETIC CLUB OF NEW YORK CITY, INC.

1961  Ernie Davis, Syracuse University, TB

1965  Michael Garrett, University of Southern California, TB

**1968** O. J. Simpson, University of Southern California, TB

**1971** Pat Sullilvan, Auburn University, QB

**1972** Johnny Rodgers, University of Nebraska, FL

**1974** Archie Griffin, University of Ohio State, HB

**1975** Archie Griffin, University of Ohio State, HB

**1976** Anthony Dorsett, University of Pittsburgh, HB

**1977** Earl Campbell, University of Texas, FB

**1978** Billy Sims, University of Oklahoma, HB

**1979** Charles White, University of Southern California, TB

**1980** George Rogers, University of South Carolina, HB

**1981** Marcus Allen, University of Southern California, TB

**1982** Herschel Walker, University of Georgia, HB

**1983** Mike Rozier, University of Nebraska, TB

**1985** Bo Jackson, Auburn University, TB

**1987** Tim Brown, University of Notre Dame, FL

**1988** Barry Sanders, Oklahoma State University, HB

**1989** Andre Ware, University of Houston, QB

**1991** Desmond Howard, University of Michigan, WR

## CLARENCE L. HOLTE LITERARY PRIZE (BIANNUAL)—CO-SPONSORED BY THE PHELPS-STOKES FUND AND THE SCHOMBURG CENTER FOR RESEARCH IN BLACK CULTURE OF THE NEW YORK PUBLIC LIBRARY

**1979** Dr. Chancellor Williams, for *The Destruction of Black Civililzation: Great Issues of a Race from 4500 B.C. to 2000 A.D.*

**1981** Ivan Van Sertima, for *They Came Before Columbus*

**1983** Vincent Harding, for *There Is a River: The Black Struggle for Freedom in America*

**1985** No award

**1986** John Hope Franklin, for *George Washington Williams: A Biography*

**1988** Arnold Rampersad, for *The Life of Langston Hughes, Volume 1 (1902-1941): I, Too, Sing America*

**1990** No award

**1992** No award

## KENNEDY CENTER HONORS—JOHN F. KENNEDY CENTER FOR THE PERFORMING ARTS

**1978** Marian Anderson

**1979** Ella Fitzgerald

**1980** Leontyne Price

**1981** William "Count" Basie

**1983** Katherine Dunham

**1984** Lena Horne

**1986** Ray Charles

**1987** Sammy Davis, Jr.

**1988** Alvin Ailey

**1989** Harry Belafonte

**1990** Dizzy Gillespie

**1991** Fayard and Harold Nicholas

**1992** Lionel Hampton

## MARTIN LUTHER KING, JR. NONVIOLENT PEACE PRIZE—MARTIN LUTHER KING, JR. CENTER FOR NONVIOLENT SOCIAL CHANGE, INC.

**1973** Andrew Young

**1974** Cesar Chavez

**1975** John Lewis

**1976** Randolph Blackwell

**1977** Benjamin E. Mays

**1978** Kenneth D. Kaunda; Stanley Levison

**1979** Jimmy Carter

**1980** Rosa Parks

**1981** The Hon. Ivan Allen, Jr.

**1982** Harry Belafonte

**1983** Sir Richard Attenborough; Martin Luther King, Sr.

**1984** No award

**1985** No award

**1986** Bishop Desmond Tutu

**1987** Corazon Aquino

**1988** No award

**1989** No award

**1990** Mikhail Gorbachev

**1991** No award

**1992** No award

1993   Jesse Jackson

# MEDAL OF HONOR

## Civil War

### Army

William H. Barnes, Private, Company C, 38th United States Colored Troops.

Powhatan Beaty, First Sergeant, Company G, 5th United States Colored Troops.

James H. Bronson, First Sergeant, Company D, 5th United States Colored Troops.

William H. Carney, Sergeant, Company C, 54th Massachusetts Infantry, United States Colored Troops.

Decatur Dorsey, Sergeant, Company B, 39th United States Colored Troops.

Christian A. Fleetwood, Sergeant Major, 4th United States Colored Troops.

James Gardiner, Private, Company 1, 36th United States Colored Troops.

James H. Harris, Sergeant, Company B, 38th United States Colored Troops.

Thomas R. Hawkins, Sergeant Major, 6th United States Colored Troops.

Alfred B. Hilton, Sergeant, Company H, 4th United States Colored Troops.

Milton M. Holland, Sergeant, 5th United States Colored Troops.

Alexander Kelly, First Sergeant, Company F, 6th United States Colored Troops.

Robert Pinn, First Sergeant, Company I, 5th United States Colored Troops.

<n.LEdward Radcliff, First Sergeant, Company C, 38th United States Colored Troops.

Charles Veal, Private, Company D, 4th United States Colored Troops.

### Navy

Aaron Anderson, Landsman, USS Wyandank.

Robert Blake, Powder Boy, USS Marblehead.

William H. Brown, Landsman, USS Brooklyn.

Wilson Brown, USS Hartford.

John Lawson, Landsman, USS Hartford.

James Mifflin, Engineer's Cook, USS Brooklyn.

Joachim Pease, Seaman, USS Kearsarge.

## Interim Period

### Navy

Daniel Atkins, Ship's Cook, First Class, USS Cushing.

John Davis, Seaman, USS Trenton.

Alphonse Girandy, Seaman, USS Tetrel.

John Johnson, Seaman, USS Kansas.

William Johnson, Cooper, USS Adams.

Joseph B. Noil, Seaman, USS Powhatan.

John Smith, Seaman, USS Shenandoah.

Robert Sweeney, Seaman, USS Kearsage, USS Jamestown.

## Western Campaigns

### Army

Thomas Boyne, Sergeant, Troop C, 9th United States Cavalry.

Benjamin Brown, Sergeant, Company C, 24th United States Infantry.

John Denny, Sergeant, Troop C, 9th United States Cavalry.

Pompey Factor, Seminole Negro Indian Scouts.

Clinton Greaves, Corporal, Troop C, 9th United States Cavalry.

Henry Johnson, Sergeant, Troop D, 9th United States Cavalry.

George Jordan, Sergeant, Troop K, 9th United States Cavalry.

William McBreyar, Sergeant, Troop K, 10th United States Cavalry.

Isaiah Mays, Corporal, Company B, 24th United States Infantry.

Issac Payne, Private (Trumpeteer) Seminole Negro Indian Scouts.

Thomas Shaw, Sergeant, Troop K, 9th United States Cavalry.

Emanuel Stance, Sergeant, Troop F, 9th United States Cavalry.

Augustus Walley, Private, Troop 1, 9th United States Cavalry.

John Ward, Sergeant, Seminole Negro Indian Scouts.

Moses Williams, First Sergeant, Troop 1, 9th United States Cavalry.

William O. Wilson, Corporal, Troop 1, 9th United States Cavalry.

Brent Woods, Sergeant, Troop B, 9th United States Cavalry.

## Spanish-American War

**Army**

Edward L. Baker, Jr., Sergeant Major, 10th United States Cavalry.

Dennis Bell, Private, Troop H, 10th United States Cavalry.

Fitz Lee, Private, Troop M, 10th United States Cavalry.

William H. Thompkins, Private, Troop G, 10th United States Cavalry.

George H. Wanton, Sergeant, Troop M, 10th United States Cavalry.

**Navy**

Robert Penn, Fireman, First Class, *USS Iowa*.

## World War I

**Army**

Freddie Stowers, Corporal, Company C, 371st Infantry Regiment, 93rd Infantry Division.

## Korean Conflict

**Army**

Cornelius H. Charlton, Sergeant, 24th Infantry Regiment, 25th Division.

William Thompson, Private, 24th Infantry Regiment, 25th Division.

## Vietnam Conflict

**Army**

Webster Anderson, Sergeant, Battery A, 2nd Battalion, 320th Artillery, 101st Airborne Division.

Eugene Ashley, Jr., Sergeant, Company C, 5th Special Forces Group (Airborne), 1st Special Forces.

William M. Bryant, Sergeant First Class, Company A, 5th Special Forces Group, 1st Special Forces.

Lawrence Joel, Specialist Sixth Class, Headquarters and Headquarters Company, 1st Battalion, 173d Airborne Brigade.

Dwight H. Johnson, Specialist Fifth Class, Company B, 1st Battalion, 69th Armor, 4th Infantry Division.

Garfield M. Langhorn, Private First Class, Troop C, 7th Squadron, 17th Cavalry, 1st Aviation Brigade.

Matthew Leonard, Platoon Sergeant, Company B, 1st Battalion, 16th Infantry, 1st Infantry Division.

Milton L. Olive III, Private First Class, Company B, 2nd Battalion 503d Infantry, 173d Airborne Brigade.

Charles C. Rogers, Lieutenant Colonel, 1st Battalion, 5th Infantry, 1st Infantry Division.

Donald R. Long, Sergeant, Troop C, 1st Squadron, 4th Cavalry, 1st Infantry Division.

Riley L. Pitts, Captain, Company C, 2nd Battalion, 27th Infantry, 25th Infantry Division.

Rupert L. Sargent, First Lieutenant, Company B, 4th Battalion, 9th Infantry, 25th Infantry Division.

Clarence E. Sasser, Specialist 5th Class, Headquarters Company, 3rd Battalion, 60th Infantry, 90th Infantry Division.

Clifford C. Sims, Staff Sergeant, Company D, 2nd Battalion, 501st Infantry, 101st Airborne Division.

John E. Warren, Jr., First Lieutenant, Company C, 2nd Battalion, 22d Infantry, 25th Infantry Division.

**Marines**

James A. Anderson, Jr. Private First Class, 2nd Platoon, Company F, 2nd Battalion, 3rd Marine Division.

Oscar P. Austin, Private First Class, Company E, 7th Marines, 1st Marine Division.

Rodney M. Davis, Sergeant, Company B, 1st Battalion, 5th Marines, 1st Marine Division.

Robert H. Jenkins, Jr., Private First Class, 3rd Reconnaissance Battalion, 3rd Marine Division.

Ralph H. Johnson, Private First Class, Company A, 1st Recon Battalion, 1st Marine Division.

## MISS AMERICA—MISS AMERICA ORGANIZATION

**1984** Vanessa Williams (New York); Suzette Charles (New Jersey)

**1990** Debbye Turner (Missouri)

## MISS BLACK AMERICA—J. MORRIS ANDERSON PRODUCTION COMPANY

**1968** Sandy Willliams (Pennsylvania)

**1969** G. O. Smith (New York)

**1970** Stephanie Clark (District of Columbia)

**1971** Joyce Warner (Florida)

**1972** Linda Barney (New Jersey)

**1973** Arnice Russell (New York)

**1974** Von Gretchen Sheppard (California)

**1975** Helen Ford (Mississippi)

**1976** Twanna Kilgore (District of Columbia)

**1977** Claire Ford (Tennessee)

1978 Lydia Jackson (New Jersey)

1979 Veretta Shankle (Mississippi)

1980 Sharon Wright (Illinois)

1981 Pamela Jenks (Massachusetts)

1982 Phyllis Tucker (Florida)

1983 Sonia Robinson (Wisconsin)

1984 Lydia Garrett (South Carolina)

1985 Amina Fakir (Michigan)

1986 Rachel Oliver (Massachusetts)

1987 Leila McBride (Colorado)

1989 Paula Swynn (District of Columbia)

1990 Rosie Jones (Connecticut)

1991 Sharmelle Sullivan (Indiana)

1992 Marilyn DeShields

1993 Pilar Ginger Fort

1994 Karen Wallace

1995 Asheera Ahmad

## MISS USA—MADISON SQUARE GARDEN TELEVISION PRODUCTIONS

1990 Carole Gist (Michigan)

1992 Shannon Marketic

1993 Kenya Moore (Michigan)

1994 Frances Louise "Lu" Parker

1995 Chelsi Smith (Texas)

1996 Ali Landry

## NATIONAL BASEBALL HALL OF FAME

1969 Roy Campanella

1962 Jackie Robinson

1971 Leroy R. "Satchel" Paige

1972 Josh Gibson; Walter "Buck" Leonard

1973 Roberto W. Clemente; Monford Irvin

1974 James T. "Cool Papa" Bell

1975 William "Judy" Johnson

1976 Oscar M. Charleston

1977 Ernest Banks; Martin Dihigo; John H. Lloyd

1979 Willie Mays

1981 Rube Foster; Robert T. Gibson

1982 Hank Aaron; Frank Robinson

1983 Jaun A. Marichal

1985 Lou Brock

1986 Willie L. "Stretch" McCovey

1987 Ray Dandridge; Billy Williams

1988 Willie Stargell

1990 Joe Morgan

1991 Rod Carew; Ferguson Jenkins

1993 Reggie Jackson

## NATIONAL BOOK AWARD—NATIONAL BOOK FOUNDATION

1953 Ralph Ellison, for *Invisible Man*, Fiction

1969 Winthrop D. Jordan, for *White over Black: American Attitudes toward the Negro, 1550-1812*, History and Biography

1983 Gloria Naylor, for *The Women of Brewster Place*, First Novel; Joyce Carol Thomas, for *Marked By Fire*, Children's Literature; Alice Walker, for *The Color Purple*, Fiction

1990 Charles Johnson, for *Middle Passage*, Fiction

1991 Melissa Fay Green, for *Praying for Sheetrock*, Nonfiction

1992 Edward P. Jones, for *Lost in the City*, Fiction

## NATIONAL MEDAL OF ARTS—NATIONAL ENDOWMENT FOR THE ARTS

1985 Ralph Ellison (writer); Leontyne Price (singer)

1986 Marian Anderson (singer)

1987 Romare Bearden (artist); Ella Fitzgerald (singer)

1988 Gordon Parks (photographer and film director)

1989 Katherine Dunham (choreographer); Dizzy Gillespie (musician)

1990 Riley "B. B." King (musician)

1991 James Earl Jones (actor); Billy Taylor (musician)

1994 Harry Belafonte (singer)

1995 Gwendolyn Brooks (poet); Ossie Davis (actor); Ruby Dee (actress)

## NATIONAL SOCIETY OF ARTS AND LETTERS GOLD MEDAL OF MERIT AWARD

1982 Andre Watts (music)

## NATIONAL TRACK AND FIELD HALL OF FAME—THE ATHLETICS CONGRESS OF THE USA

**1974** Ralph Boston; Lee Calhoun; Harrison Dillard; Rafer Johnson; Jesse Owens; Wilma Rudolph; Malvin Whitfield

**1975** Ralph Metcalfe

**1976** Robert Hayes; Hayes Jones

**1977** Robert Beamon; Andrew W. Stanfield

**1978** Tommie Smith; John Woodruff

**1979** Jim Hines; William DeHart Hubbard

**1980** Wyomia Tyus

**1981** Willye White

**1982** Willie Davenport; Eddie Tolan

**1983** Lee Evans

**1984** Madeline Manning Mims

**1986** Henry Barney Ewell

**1988** Gregory Bell

**1989** Milt Campbell; Edward Temple

**1990** Charles Dumas

**1994** Cornelius Johnson; Edwin Moses

## NEW YORK DRAMA CRITICS' CIRCLE AWARD

### Best American Play

**1959** *A Raisin in the Sun*, by Lorraine Hansberry

**1975** *The Taking of Miss Janie*, by Ed Bullins

**1982** *A Soldier's Play*, by Charles Fuller

**1996** *Seven Guitars*, by August Wilson

### Best New Play

**1985** *Ma Rainey's Black Bottom*, by August Wilson

**1987** *Fences*, by August Wilson

**1988** *Joe Turner's Come and Gone*, by August Wilson

**1990** *The Piano Lesson*, by August Wilson

## NOBEL PEACE PRIZE—NOBEL FOUNDATION

**1950** Ralph J. Bunche

**1964** Martin Luther King, Jr.

## ANTOINETTE PERRY (TONY) AWARD—LEAGUE OF AMERICAN THEATRES AND PRODUCERS

### Actor (Dramatic)

**1969** James Earl Jones, for *The Great White Hope*

**1975** John Kani, for *Sizwe Banzi*; Winston Ntshona, for *The Island*

**1987** James Earl Jones, for *Fences*

### Supporting or Featured Actor (Dramatic)

**1982** Zakes Mokae, for *Master Harold … and the Boys*

**1992** Larry Fishburne, for *Two Trains Running*

### Actor (Musical)

**1970** Cleavon Litte, for *Purlie*

**1973** Ben Vereen, for *Pippin*

**1982** Ben Harvey, for *Dreamgirls*

**1992** Gregory Hines, for *Jelly's Last Jam*

### Supporting or Featured Actor (Musical)

**1954** Harry Belafonte, for *John Murray Anderson's Almanac*

**1975** Ted Rose, for *The Wiz*

**1981** Hinton Battle, for *Sophisticated Ladies*

**1982** Cleavant Derricks, for *Dreamgirls*

**1983** Charles "Honi" Coles, for *My One and Only*

**1984** Hinton Battle, for *The Tap Dance Kid*

**1991** Hinton Battle, for *Miss Saigon*

### Supporting or Featured Actress (Dramatic)

**1977** Trazana Beverley, for *For Colored Girls Who Have Considered Suicide/When the Rainbow Is Enuf*

**1987** Mary Alice, for *Fences*

**1988** L. Scott Caldwell, for *Joe Turner's Come and Gone*

### Actress (Musical)

**1962** Diahann Carroll, for *No Strings*

**1968** Leslie Uggams, for *Hallelujah, Baby*

**1974** Virginia Capers, for *Raisin*

**1982** Jennifer Holliday, for *Dreamgirls*

**1989** Ruth Brown, for *Black and Blue*

### Supporting or Featured Actress (Musical)

**1950** Juanita Hall, for *South Pacific*

**1968** Lillian Hayman, for *Halleluja, Baby*

**1970** Melba Moore, for *Purlie*

**1975** Dee Dee Bridgewater, for *The Wiz*

**1977** Delores Hall, for *Your Arms's Too Short To Box with God*

**1978** Nell Carter, for *Ain't Misbehavin*

**1992** Tonya Pinkins, for *Jelly's Last Jam*

### Play

**1974** *The River Niger*, by Joseph A. Walker

**1987** *Fences*, by August Wilson

## PRESIDENTIAL MEDAL OF FREEDOM— UNITED STATES EXECUTIVE OFFICE OF THE PRESIDENT

**1963** Marian Anderson; Ralph J. Bunche

**1964** John L. Lewis; Leontyne Price; A. Philip Randolph

**1969** Edward Kennedy "Duke" Ellington; Ralph Ellison; Roy Wilkins; Whitney M. Young, Jr.

**1976** Jesse Owens

**1977** Dr. Martin Luther King, Jr. (posthumously)

**1981** James H. Eubie Blake; Andrew Young

**1984** Jack Roosevelt Robinson (posthumously)

**1985** William "Count" Basie (posthumously)

**1988** Pearl Bailey

**1991** General Colin L. Powell

**1992** Ella Fitzgerald

**1993** Colin L. Powell

**1994** Dorothy Height; Barbara Jordan

**1995** William T. Coleman, Jr.; John Hope Franklin; A. Leon Higginbotham, Jr.

## PRO FOOTBALL HALL OF FAME

**1967** Emlen Tunnell

**1968** Marion Motley

**1969** Fletcher "Joe" Perry

**1971** Jim Brown

**1972** Ollie Matson

**1973** Jim Parker

**1974** Richard "Night Train" Lane

**1975** Roosevelt Brown; Leonard "Lenny" Moore

**1976** Leonard "Len" Ford

**1977** Gale Sayers; Bill Willis

**1980** Herb Adderley; David "Deacon" Jones

**1981** Willie Davis

**1983** Bobby Bell; Bobby Mitchell; Paul Warfield

**1984** Willie Brown; Charley Taylor

**1985** O. J. Simpson

**1986** Ken Houston; Willie Lanier

**1987** Joe Greene; John Henry Johnson; Gene Upshaw

**1988** Alan Page

**1989** Mel Blount; Art Shell; Willie Wood

**1990** Junious "Buck" Buchanan; Franco Harris

**1991** Earl Campbell

**1992** Lem Barney; John Mackey

**1993** Larry Little; Walter Payton

**1994** Tony Dorsett, Leroy Kelly

**1995** Lee Roy Selmon

**1996** Charlie Joiner, Mel Renfro

## PULITZER PRIZE—COLUMBIA UNIVERSITY GRADUATE SCHOOL OF JOURNALISM

### Journalism: Commentary

**1996** E. R. Shipp

### Letters: Drama

**1970** *No Place To Be Somebody*, by Charles Gordone

**1982** *A Soldier's Play*, by Charles Fuller

**1987** *Fences*, by August Wilson

**1990** *The Piano Lesson*, by August Wilson

### Letters: Fiction

**1978** *Elbow Room*, by James Alan McPherson

**1983** *The Color Purple*, by Alice Walker

**1988** *Beloved*, by Toni Morrison

### Letters: Poetry

**1950** *Annie Allen*, by Gwendolyn Brooks

**1987** *Thomas and Beulah,* by Rita Dove

### Letters: Special Awards and Citations

**1977** Alexander Palmer Haley, for *Roots*

### Music: Special Awards and Citations

**1976** Scott Joplin

**1996** George Walker

## SPINGARN MEDAL—NATIONAL ASSOCIATION FOR THE ADVANCEMENT OF COLORED PEOPLE

**1915** Prof. Ernest E. Just—head of the department of physiology at Howard University Medical School.

**1916** Major Charles Young—United States Army.

**1917** Harry T. Burleigh—composer, pianist, singer.

**1918** William Stanley Braithwaite—poet, literary critic, editor.

**1919** Archibald H. Grimke—former U.S. Consul in Santo Domingo, president of the American Negro Academy, author, president of the District of Columbia branch of the NAACP.

**1920** William Edward Burghardt DuBois—author, editor, organizer of the first Pan-African Congress.

**1921** Charles S. Gilpin—actor.

**1922** Mary B. Talbert—former president of the National Association of Colored Women.

**1923** George Washington Carver—head of research and director of the experiment station at Tuskegee Institute.

**1924** Roland Hayes—singer.

**1925** James Weldon Johnson—former United States Consul in Venezuela and Nicaragua, author, editor, poet; secretary of the NAACP.

**1926** Carter G. Woodson—editor, historian; founder of the Association for the Study of Negro Life and History.

**1927** Anthony Overton—businessman; president of the Victory Life Insurance Company (the first black organization permitted to do business under the rigid requirements of the State of New York).

**1928** Charles W. Chestnutt—author.

**1929** Mordecai Wyatt Johnson—the first black president of Howard University.

**1930** Henry A. Hunt—principal of Fort Valley High and Industrial School, Fort Valley, Georgia.

**1931** Richard Berry Harrison—actor.

**1932** Robert Russa Moton—principal of Tuskegee Institute.

**1933** Max Yergan—secretary of the YMCA in South Africa.

**1934** William Taylor Burwell Williams—dean of Tuskegee Institute.

**1935** Mary McLeod Bethune—founder and president of Bethune Cookman College.

**1936** John Hope—president of Atlanta University.

**1937** Walter White—executive secretary of the NAACP.

**1939** Marian Anderson—singer.

**1940** Louis T. Wright—surgeon.

**1941** Richard Wright—author.

**1942** A. Philip Randolph—labor leader, international president of the Brotherhood of Sleeping Car Porters.

**1943** William H. Hastie—jurist, educator.

**1944** Charles Drew—scientist.

**1945** Paul Robeson—singer, actor.

**1946** Thurgood Marshall—special counsel of the NAACP

**1947** Dr. Percy Julian—research chemist.

**1948** Channing H. Tobias—,minister, educator.

**1949** Ralph J. Bunche—international civil servant, acting United Nations mediator in Palestine.

**1950** Charles Hamilton Houston—chairman of the NAACP Legal Committee.

**1951** Mabel Keaton Staupers—leader of the National Association of Colored Graduate Nurses.

**1952** Harry T. Moore—state leader of the Florida NAACP.

**1953** Paul R. Williams—architect.

**1954** Theodore K. Lawless—physician, educator, philanthropist.

**1955** Carl Murphy—editor, publisher, civic leader.

**1956** Jack Roosevelt Robinson—athlete.

**1957** Martin Luther King, Jr.—minister, civil rights leader.

**1958** Daisy Bates and the Little Rock Nine—for their pioneer role in upholding the basic ideals of American democracy in the face of continuing harassment and constant threats of bodily injury.

**1959** Edward Kennedy (Duke) Ellington—composer, musician, orchestra leader.

**1960** Langston Hughes—poet, author, playwright.

**1961** Kenneth B. Clark—professor of psychology at the City College of the City University of New York, founder and director of the Northside Center for Child Development, prime mobilizer of the resources of modern psychology in the attack upon racial segregation.

**1962** Robert C. Weaver—administrator of the Housing and Home Finance Agency.

**1963** Medgar Wiley Evers—NAACP field secretary for Mississippi, World War II veteran.

**1964** Roy Wilkins executive director of the NAACP.

**1965** Leontyne Price—singer.

**1966** John H. Johnson—founder and president of the Johnson Publishing Company.

**1967** Edward W. Brooke III—the first African-American to win popular election to the United States Senate.

**1968** Sammy Davis, Jr.—performer, civil rights activist.

**1969** Clarence M. Mitchell, Jr.—director of the Washington Bureau of the NAACP, civil rights activist.

**1970** Jacob Lawrence—artist, teacher, humanitarian.

**1971** Leon H. Sullivan—minister.

**1972** Gordon Alexander Buchanan Parks—writer, photographer, filmmaker.

**1973** Wilson C. Riles—educator.

**1974** Damon Keith—jurist.

**1975** Hank Aaron—athlete.

**1976** Alvin Ailey—dancer, choreographer, artistic director.

**1977** Alexander Palmer Haley—author, biographer, lecturer.

**1978** Andrew Young—United States Ambassador to the United Nations, diplomat, cabinet member, civil rights activist, minister.

**1979** Rosa Parks—community activist.

**1980** Rayford W. Logan—educator, historian, author.

**1981** Coleman A. Young—mayor of the City of Detroit, public servant, labor leader, civil rights activist.

**1982** Benjamin E. Mays—educator, theologian, humanitarian).

**1983** Lena Horn—performer, humanitarian.

**1984** Tom Bradley—government executive, public servant, humanitarian.

**1985** Dr. William H. Cosby—comedian, actor, educator, humanitarian.

**1986** Benjamin Lawson Hooks—executive director of The NAACP.

**1987** Percy Ellis Sutton—public servant, businessman, community leader.

**1988** Frederick Douglass Patterson—doctor of veterinary medicine, educator, humanitarian, founder of the United Negro College Fund.

**1989** Jesse Jackson—minister, political leader, civil rights activist.

**1990** L. Douglas Wilder—governor of Virginia.

**1991** General Colin L. Powell—chairman of the Joint Chiefs of Staff.

**1992** Barbara C. Jordan—educator, former congresswoman.

**1993** Dorothy I. Height—president of the National Council of Negro Woman

**1994** Maya Angelou—poet, author, performing artist

**1995** John Hope Franklin—historian

## UNITED STATES POET LAUREATE

**1993** Rita Dove

## WIMBLEDON—ALL ENGLAND LAWN TENNIS AND CROQUET CLUB

### Men's Singles

**1975** Arthur Ashe

### Ladies' Singles

**1957** Althea Gibson

**1958** Althea Gibson

**1990** Zina Garrison, runner-up

### Ladies' Doubles

**1957** Althea Gibson, with Darlene Hard

**1958** Althea Gibson, with Maria Bueno

# Appendix II

# *Appendix II*

◆ **1996 Olympic Games Medalists**

\* indicates African American athletes

## Archery

### MEN

**Individual**

GOLD—Justin Huish (Simi Valley, CA)
SILVER—Magnus Petersson (Sweden)
BRONZE—Oh Kyo-moon (South Korea)

**Team**

GOLD—United States: Justin Huish (Simi Valley, CA); Richard Johnson (Woodstock, CT); Rod White (Hermitage, PA)
SILVER—South Korea: Oh Kyo-moon; Kim Bo-ram; Jang Yong-ho
BRONZE—Italy: Matteo Bisiani; Michele Frangilli; Andrea Parenti

### WOMEN

**Individual**

GOLD—Kim Kyung-wook (South Korea)
SILVER—He Ying (China)
BRONZE—Olena Sadovnycha (Ukraine)

**Team**

GOLD—South Korea: Kim Jo-sun; Yoon Hye-young; Kim Kyung-wook
SILVER—Germany: Barbara Mensing; Cornelia Pfohl; Sandra Wagner
BRONZE—Poland: Iwona Dzieciol; Katarzyna Klata; Joanna Nowicka

## Track and Field

### MEN

**100 Meter**

GOLD—Donovan Bailey (Canada)
SILVER—Frank Fredericks (Namibia)
BRONZE—Ato Boldon (Trinidad)

**200 Meter**

GOLD—\*Michael Johnson (Rockwell, TX)
SILVER—Frank Fredericks (Namibia)
BRONZE—Ato Boldon (Trinidad)

**400 Meter**

GOLD—\*Michael Johnson (Rockwell, TX)
SILVER—Roger Black (Britain)
BRONZE—Davis Kamoga (Uganda)

**800 Meter**

GOLD—Vebjoern Rodal (Norway)
SILVER—Hezekiel Sepeng (South Africa)
BRONZE—Fred Onyancha (Kenya)

**1,500 Meter**

GOLD—Noureddine Morceli (Algeria)
SILVER—Fermin Cacho (Spain)
BRONZE—Stephen Kipkorir (Kenya)

**5,000 Meter**

GOLD—Venuste Niyongabo (Burundi)
SILVER—Paul Bitok (Kenya)
BRONZE—Khalid Boulami (Morocco)

## 10,000 Meter

GOLD—Haile Gebrselassie (Ethiopia)
SILVER—Paul Tergat (Kenya)
BRONZE—Salah Hissou (Morocco)

## 110 Hurdles

GOLD—*Allen Johnson (Chapel Hill, NC)
SILVER—Mark Crear (Valencia, CA)
BRONZE—Florian Schwarthoff (Germany)

## 400 Hurdles

GOLD—*Derrick Adkins (Atlanta, GA)
SILVER—Samuel Matete (Zambia)
BRONZE—*Calvin Davis (Eutaw, AL)

## 3,000 Steeplechase

GOLD—Joseph Keter (Kenya)
SILVER—Moses Kiptanui (Kenya)
BRONZE—Alessandro Lamruschini (Italy)

## 20km Walk

GOLD—Jefferson Perez (Ecuador)
SILVER—Ilya Markov (Russia)
BRONZE—Bernardo Sugura (Mexico)

## 50km Walk

GOLD—Robert Korzeniowski (Poland)
SILVER—Mikhail Schennikov (Russia)
BRONZE—Valentin Massana (Spain)

## Relay

GOLD—Canada: Donovan Bailey; Robert Esmie; Glenroy Gilbert; Bruny Surin; Carlton Chambers
SILVER—United States: *Tim Harden (Grandview, MT); *Jon Drummond (Culver City, CA); *Michael Marsh (Houston, TX); *Dennis Mitchell (Gainesville, FL); *Tim Montgomery (Gaffney, SC)
BRONZE—Brazil: Edson Ribeiro; Arnaldo Silva; Andre Silva; Robson da Silva

## 1,600 Relay

GOLD—United States: *LaMont Smith (Houston, TX); *Alvin Harrison (Salinas, CA); *Derek Mills (Marietta, GA); *Anthuan Maybank (Los Angeles, CA); *Jason Rouser (Norman, OK)

SILVER—Britain: Iwan Thomas; Jamie Baulch; Mark Richardson; Roger Black; Du'aine Ladejo
BRONZE—Jamaica: Michael McDonald; Roxbert Martin; Greg Haughton; Davian Clarke; Dennis Blake

## Decathlon

GOLD—Dan O'Brien (Moscow, ID)
SILVER—Frank Busemann (Germany)
BRONZE—Tomas Dvorak (Czech Republic)

## High Jump

GOLD—*Charles Austin (San Marcos, TX)
SILVER—Artur Partyka (Poland)
BRONZE—Steve Smith (Britain)

## Long Jump

GOLD—*Carl Lewis (Houston, TX)
SILVER—James Beckford (Jamaica)
BRONZE—Joe Greene (Westerville, OH)

## Triple Jump

GOLD—*Kenny Harrison (Bridgeton, MO)
SILVER—Jonathan Edwards (Britain)
BRONZE—Yoelbi Quesada (Cuba)

## Discus

GOLD—Lars Riedel (Germany)
SILVER—Vladimir Dubrovshchik (Belarus)
BRONZE—Vasiliy Kaptyukh (Belarus)

## Hammer

GOLD—Balazs Kiss (Hungary)
SILVER—Lance Deal (Eugene, OR)
BRONZE—Alexandr Krykun (Ukraine)

## Javelin

GOLD—Jan Zelezny (Czech Republic)
SILVER—Steve Backley (Britain)
BRONZE—Seppo Raty (Finland)

## Pole Vault

GOLD—Jean Galfione (France)
SILVER—Igor Trandenkov (Russia)
BRONZE—Andrei Tivontchik (Germany)

### Shot Put

GOLD—Randy Barnes (South Charleston, WV)
SILVER—John Godina (Los Angeles, CA)
BRONZE—Oleksandr Bagach (Ukraine)

### Marathon

GOLD—Josia Thugwane (South Africa)
SILVER—Lee Bong-ju (South Korea)
BRONZE—Eric Wainaina (Kenya)

## WOMEN

### 100 Meter

GOLD—*Gail Devers (Bridgeton, MO)
SILVER—Merlene Ottey (Jamaica)
BRONZE—*Gwen Torrence (Lithonia, GA)

### 200 Meter

GOLD—Marie-Jose Perec (France)
SILVER—Merlene Ottey (Jamaica)
BRONZE—Mary Onyali (Nigeria)

### 400 Meter

GOLD—Marie-Jose Perec (France)
SILVER—Cathy Freeman (Australia)
BRONZE—Falilat Ogunkoya (Nigeria)

### 800 Meter

GOLD—Svetlana Masterkova (Russia)
SILVER—Ana Quirot (Cuba)
BRONZE—Maria Mutola (Mozambique)

### 1,500 Meter

GOLD—Svetlana Masterkova (Russia)
SILVER—Gabriela Szabo (Romania)
BRONZE—Theresia Kiesl (Austria)

### 5,000 Meter

GOLD—Wang Junxia (China)
SILVER—Pauline Konga (Kenya)
BRONZE—Roberta Bruney (Italy)

### 10,000 Meter

GOLD—Fernanda Ribeiro (Portugal)
SILVER—Wang Junxia (China)
BRONZE—Gete Wami (Ethiopia)

### 100 Hurdles

GOLD—Ludmila Enquist (Sweden)
SILVER—Brigita Bukovec (Slovenia)
BRONZE—Patricia Girard-Leno (France)

### 400 Hurdles

GOLD—Deon Hemmings (Jamaica)
SILVER—*Kim Batten (McRae, GA)
BRONZE—*Tonja Buford Bailey (Dayton, OH)

### 10km Walk

GOLD—Yelena Ninikolayeva (Russia)
SILVER—Elisabetta Perrone (Italy)
BRONZE—Wang Yan (China)

### 400 Relay

GOLD—United States: *Gail Devers (Bridgeton, MO); *Chryste Gaines (San Leandro, CA); *Gwen Torrence (Lithonia, GA); *Inger Miller (Altadena, CA); *Carlette Guidry (Austin, TX)
SILVER—Bahamas: Chandra Sturrup; Eldece Clarke; Sevatheda Fynes; Pauline Davis; Debbie Ferguson
BRONZE—Jamaica: Michelle Freeman; Juliet Cuthbert; Nikole Mitchell; Merlene Ottey; Gillian Russell; Andrea Lloyd

### 1,600 Relay

GOLD—United States: *Rochelle Stevens (Memphis, TN); *Maicel Malone (Gainesville, FL); *Kim Graham (Austin, TX); *Jearl Miles (Gainesville, FL); *Linetta Wilson (Hawthorne, CA)
SILVER—Nigeria: Bisi Afolabi; Fatima Yusuf; Charity Opara; Falilat Ogunkoya
BRONZE—Germany: Uta Rohlaender; Linda Kisabaka; Anja Ruecker; Grit Breuer

### Heptathlon

GOLD—Ghada Shouaa (Syria)
SILVER—Natasha Sazanovich (Belarus)
BRONZE—Denise Lewis (Britain)

### High Jump

GOLD—Stefka Kostadinova (Bulgaria)

SILVER—Niki Bakoyianni (Greece)
BRONZE—Inga Babakova (Ukraine)

### Long Jump

GOLD—Chioma Ajunwa (Nigeria)
SILVER—Fiona May (Italy)
BRONZE—*Jackie Joyner-Kersee (Canoga Park, CA)

### Triple Jump

GOLD—Inessa Kravets (Ukraine)
SILVER—Inna Lasovskaya (Russia)
BRONZE—Sarka Kasparkova (Czech Republic)

### Discus

GOLD—Ilke Wyludda (Germany)
SILVER—Natalya Sadova (Russia)
BRONZE—Elya Zvereva (Belarus)

### Javelin

GOLD—Heli Rantanen (Finland)
SILVER—Louise McPaul (Australia)
BRONZE—Trine Hattestad (Norway)

### Shot Put

GOLD—Astrid Kumbernuss (Germany)
SILVER—Sui Xinmei (China)
BRONZE—Irina Khudorozhkina (Russia)

### Marathon

GOLD—Fatuma Roba (Ethiopia)
SILVER—Valentina Yegorova (Russia)
BRONZE—Yuko Arimori (Japan)

## Badminton
### MEN

### Singles

GOLD—Poul-Erik Hoyer-Larsen (Denmark)
SILVER—Dong Jiong (China)
BRONZE—Rashid Sidak (Malaysia)

### Doubles

GOLD—Rexy Mainaky and Ricky Subagja (Indonesia)
SILVER—Cheah Soon Kit and Yap Kim Hock (Malaysia)
BRONZE—S Antonius and Denny Kantono (Indonesia)

### WOMEN

### Singles

GOLD—Bang Soo-hyun (South Korea)
SILVER—Mia Audina (Indonesia)
BRONZE—Susi Susanti (Indonesia)

### Doubles

GOLD—Ge Fei and Gu Jun (China)
SILVER—Gil Young-ah and Jang Hye-ock (South Korea)
BRONZE—Qin Yiyuan and Tang Yongshu (China)

### Mixed Doubles

GOLD—Gil Young-ah and Kim Dong-moon (South Korea)
SILVER—Ra Kyung-min and Park Joo-bong (South Korea)
BRONZE—Liu Jianjun and Sun Man (China)

## Baseball

GOLD—Cuba: Omar Ajete, Miguel Caldes, Jose Ariel Contreras, Yobal Duenas, Jose Esrada, Jorge Fumero, Ernesto Guevara, Alberto Hernandez, Rey Isaac, Orestes Kindelan, Daniel Lazo, Pedro Luis Lazo, Omar Linares, Angel Lopez, Omar Luis, Juan Manrique, Eliecer Montes de Oca, Antonio Pacheco, Juan Padilla, Eduardo Paret, Osmany Romero, Antonio Scull, Luis Ulacia, Lazaro Vargas

SILVER—Japan: Naoto Adachi, Kosuke Fukudome, Tadahito Iguchi, Makoto Imaoka, Koichi Isobe, Takeo Kawamura, Jutaro Kimura, Takashi Kurosu, Takao Kuwamoto, Nobuhiko Matsunaka, Koichi Misawa, Masahiko Mori, Masao Morinaka, Daishin Nakamura, Kokoro Niida, Tomoaki Nishio, Masahiro Nojima, Hideaki Okubo, Hitoshi Ono, Yasuyuki Saigo, Tomoaki Sato, Masanori Sugiura, Takayuki Takabayashi, Yoshitomo Tani

BRONZE—United States: Chad Allen, Kris Benson, R.A. Dickey, Troy Glaus, Chad Green, Seth Greisinger, Kip Harkrider, A.J. Hingh, *Jacque Jones, Billy Koch, Mark Kotsay, Matt Lecroy, Travis Lee, Braden Looper, Brian Loyd, Warren Morris, Augie Ojeda, Jim Parque, Jeff Weaver, Jason Williams

## Basketball
### MEN

GOLD—United States: *Charles Barkley, *Anfernee Hardaway, *Grant Hill, *Karl Malone, *Reggie Miller, *Hakeem Olajuwon, *Shaquille O'Neal, *Gary Payton, *Scottie Pippen, *Mitch Richmond, *David Robinson, John Stockton

SILVER—Yugoslavia: Miroslav Beric, Dejan Bodiroga,

Nikola Bulatovic, Predrag Danilovic, Vlade Divac, Vladimir Djokic, Aleksandar Djordjevic, Predrag Drobnjak, Nikola Loncar, Sasa Obradovic, Zarko Paspalj, Zeljko Rebraca, Zoran Savic, Dejan Tomasevic, Zeljko Topalovic, Milenko Topic

BRONZE—Lithuania: Gintaras Einikis, Andrius Jurkunas, Arturas Karnisovas, Rimas Kurtinaitis, Darius Lukminas, Sarunas Marciulionis, Tomas Pacesas, Arvydas Sabonis, Saulius Stombergas, Rytis Vaisvila, Eurelijus Zukauskas, Mindaugas Zukauskas

## WOMEN

GOLD—United States: Jennifer Azzi, *Ruthie Bolton, *Teresa Edwards, *Venus Lacey, *Lisa Leslie, Rebecca Lobo, *Katrina McClain, *Nikki McCray, *Carla McGhee, *Dawn Staley, Katy Steding, *Sheryl Swoopes

SILVER—Brazil: Maria Angelica, Janeth Arcain, Roseli Gustavo, Silvia Luz, Hortencia Marcari Oliva, Alessandra Oliveira, Claudia Maria Pastor, Adriana Santos, Cintia Santos, Maria Paula Silva, Leila Sobral, Mart de Sooza Sobral

BRONZE—Australia: Carla Boyd, Michelle Brogan, Sandy Brondello, Michelle Chandler, Allison Cook, Trisha Fallon, Joanne Hill, Robyn Maher, Fiona Robinson, Shelley Sandie, Rachael Sporn, Georgina Stevens, Michele Timms, Jennifer Whittle

## Boxing

### Light Flyweight (106 pounds)

GOLD—Daniel Petrov (Bulgaria)

SILVER—Mansueto Velasco (Philippines)

BRONZE—Oleg Kiryukhin (Ukraine); Rafael Lozano (Spain)

### Flyweight (112 pounds)

GOLD—Maikro Romero (Cuba)

SILVER—Bolat Djumadilov (Kazakstan)

BRONZE—Albert Pakeev (Russia); Zoltan Lunka (Germany)

### Bantamweight (119 pounds)

GOLD—Istvan Kovacs (Hungary)

SILVER—Arnaldo Mesa (Cuba)

BRONZE—Raimkul Malakhbekov (Russia); and Vichairachanon Khadpo (Thailand)

### Featherweight (125 pounds)

GOLD—Somluck Kamsing (Thailand)

SILVER—Serafim Todorov (Bulgaria)

BRONZE—Pablo Chacon (Argentina); *Floyd Mayweather (Grand Rapids, MI)

### Lightweight (132 pounds)

GOLD—Hocine Soltani (Algeria)

SILVER—Tontcho Tontchev (Bulgaria)

BRONZE—Terrance Cauthen (Philadelpha, PA); Leonard Doroftei (Romania)

### Light Welterweight (139 pounds)

GOLD—Hector Vinent (Cuba)

SILVER—Oktay Urkal (Germany)

BRONZE—Bolat Niyazymbetov (Kazakstan); Fethi Missaoui (Tunisia)

### Welterweight (147 pounds)

GOLD—Oleg Saitov (Russia)

SILVER—Juan Hernandez (Cuba)

BRONZE—Marian Simion (Romania); Daniel Santos (Puerto Rico)

### Light Middleweight (156 pounds)

GOLD—David Reid (Philadelphia, PA)

SILVER—Alfredo Duvergel (Cuba)

BRONZE—Karim Tulaganov (Uzbekistan); Ermakhan Ibraimov (Kazakstan)

### Middleweight (165 pounds)

GOLD—Ariel Hernandez (Cuba)

SILVER—Malik Beyleroglu (Turkey)

BRONZE—*Rhoshii Wells (Riverdale, GA); Mohamed Bahari (Algeria)

### Light Heavyweight (178 pounds)

GOLD—Vassili Jirov (Kazakstan)

SILVER—Lee Seung-bao (South Korea)

BRONZE—Antonio Tarver (Orlando, FL); Thomas Ulrich (Germany)

### Heavyweight (201 pounds)

GOLD—Felix Savon (Cuba)

SILVER—David Defiagbon (Canada)

BRONZE—Nate Jones (Chicago, IL); Luan Krasniqi (Germany)

### Super Heavyweight (201-plus pounds)

GOLD—Vladimir Klitchko (Ukraine)
SILVER—Paea Wolfgramm (Tonga)
BRONZE—Alexei Lezin (Russia); Duncan Dokiwari (Nigeria)

# Canoe-Kayak

## MEN

### Canoe Single 500

GOLD—Martin Doktor (Czech Republic)
SILVER—Slavomir Knazovicky (Slovakia)
BRONZE—Imre Pulai (Hungary)

### Canoe Single 1000

GOLD—Martin Doktor (Czech Republic)
SILVER—Ivan Klementyev (Latvia)
BRONZE—Gyorgy Zala (Hungary)

### Canoe Double 500

GOLD—Gyorgy Kolonics and Csaba Horvath (Hungary)
SILVER—Nikolai Juravschi and Victor Reneischi (Moldova)
BRONZE—Gheorghe Andriev and Grigore Obreja (Romania)

### Canoe Double 1000

GOLD—Andreas Dittmer and Gunar Kirchbach (Germany)
SILVER—Marcel Glavan and Antonel Borsan (Romania)
BRONZE—Gyorgy Kolonics and Csaba Horvath (Hungary)

### Kayak Single 500

GOLD—Antonio Rossi (Italy)
SILVER—Knut Holmann (Norway)
BRONZE—Piotr Markiewicz (Poland)

### Kayak Single 1000

GOLD—Knut Holmann (Norway)
SILVER—Beniamino Bonomi (Italy)
BRONZE—Clint Robinson (Australia)

### Kayak Double 500

GOLD—Kay Bluhm and Torsten Gutsche (Germany)
SILVER—Beniamino Bonomi and Daniele Scarpa (Italy)
BRONZE—Andrew Trim and Danny Collins (Australia)

### Kayak Double 1000

GOLD—Antonio Rossi and Daniele Scarpa (Italy)
SILVER—Kay Bluhm and Torsten Gutsche (Germany)
BRONZE—Andrian Dushev and Milk Kazanov (Bulgaria)

### Kayak Fours 1000

GOLD—Detlef Hofmann, Olaf Winter, Thomas Reineck, and Mark Zabel (Germany)
SILVER—Attila Adrovicz, Ferenc Csipes, Gabor Horvath, and Andras Rajna (Hungary)
BRONZE—Sergey Verlin, Oleg Gorobiy, Anatoliy Tishchenko, and Georgiy Tsybulnikov (Russia)

## Women

### Kayak Single 500

GOLD—Rita Koban (Hungary)
SILVER—Caroline Brunet (Canada)
BRONZE—Josefa Idem (Italy)

### Kayak Double 500

GOLD—Agneta Andersson and Susanne Gunnarsson (Sweden)
SILVER—Birgit Fischer and Ramona Portwich (Germany)
BRONZE—Anna Wood and Katrin Borchert (Australia)

### Kayak Fours 500

GOLD—Ramona Portwich, Manuela Mucke, Birgit Fischer, and Anett Schuck (Germany)
SILVER—Daniela Baumer, Sabine Eichenberger, Ingrid Haralamow, and Gabi Mueller (Switzerland)
BRONZE—Agneta Andersson, Ingela Ericsson, Anna Olsson, and Susanne Rosenqvist (Sweden)

## MEN

### Canoe Singles

GOLD—Michal Martikan (Slovakia)
SILVER—Lukas Pollert (Czech Republic)
BRONZE—Patrice Estanguet (France)

### Canoe Doubles

GOLD—Frank Adisson and Wilfrid Forgues (France)
SILVER—Miroslav Simek and Jiri Rohan (Czech Republic)
BRONZE—Andre Ehrenberg and Michael Senft (Germany)

### Kayak Singles

GOLD—Oliver Fix (Germany)

SILVER—Andraz Vehovar (Slovenia)
BRONZE—Thomas Becker (Germany)

## WOMEN
### Kayak Singles

GOLD—Stepanka Hilgertova (Czech Republic)
SILVER—Dana Chladek (Kensington, MD)
BRONZE—Myriam Fox–Jerusalmi (France)

## Cycling
### MEN

#### Sprint

GOLD—Jens Fiedler (Germany)
SILVER—Marty Nothstein (Trexlertown, PA)
BRONZE—Curt Harnett (Canada)

#### Points Race

GOLD—Silvio Martinello (Italy)
SILVER—Brian Walton (Canada)
BRONZE—Stuart O'Grady (Australia)

#### Individual Pursuit

GOLD—Andrea Collinelli (Italy)
SILVER—Philippe Ermenault (France)
BRONZE—Bradley McGee (Australia)

#### Road Race

GOLD—Pascal Richard (Switzerland)
SILVER—Rolf Sorensen (Denmark)
BRONZE—Maximilian Sciandri (Britain)

#### Individual Time Trial

GOLD—Miguel Indurain (Spain)
SILVER—Abraham Olano (Spain)
BRONZE—Chris Boardman (Britain)

#### Mountain Bike

GOLD—Bart Jan Brentjens (Netherlands)
SILVER—Thomas Frischknecht (Switzerland)
BRONZE—Miguel Martinez (France)

#### 1km Time Trial

GOLD—Florian Rousseau (France)
SILVER—Erin Hartwell (Colorado Springs, CO)
BRONZE—Takanobu Jumonji (Japan)

#### Team Pursuit

GOLD—Christophe Capelle, Philippe Ermenault, Jean-Michel Monin, Francis Moreau, and Herve Thuet (France)
SILVER—Nikolay Kuznetsov, Aleksey Markov, Anton Chantyr, Eduard Gritsun, Yevgeniy Anashkin, Aleksandr Kirichenko, and Pavel Khamidulin (Russia)
BRONZE—Bradley McGee, Stuart O'Grady, Timothy O'Shannessey, and Dean Woods (Australia)

### WOMEN

#### Sprint

GOLD—Felicia Ballanger (France)
SILVER—Michelle Ferris (Australia)
BRONZE—Ingrid Haringa (Netherlands)

#### Points Race

GOLD—Nathalie Lancien (France)
SILVER—Ingrid Haringa (Netherlands)
BRONZE—Lucy Tyler Sharman (Australia)

#### Individual Pursuit

GOLD—Antonella Bellutti (Italy)
SILVER—Marion Clignet (France)
BRONZE—Judith Arndt (Germany)

#### Road Race

GOLD—Jeannie Longo–Ciprelli (France)
SILVER—Imelda Chiappa (Italy)
BRONZE—Clara Hughes (Canada)

#### Individual Time Trial

GOLD—Zulfiya Zabirova (Russia)
SILVER—Jeannie Longo-Ciprelli (France)
BRONZE—Clara Hughes (Canada)

#### Mountain Bike

GOLD—Paola Pezzo (Italy)
SILVER—Alison Sydor (Canada)
BRONZE—Susan DeMattei (Gunnison, CO)

## Diving
### MEN

#### Platform

GOLD—Dmitry Sautin (Russia)
SILVER—Jan Hempel (Germany)
BRONZE—Xiao Hailiang (China)

### Springboard

GOLD—Xiong Ni (China)
SILVER—Yu Zhuocheng (China)
BRONZE—Mark Lenzi (Bloomington, IN)

### WOMEN

### Platform

GOLD—Fu Mingxia (China)
SILVER—Annika Walter (Germany)
BRONZE—Mary Ellen Clark (Newtown Square, PA)

### Springboard

GOLD—Fu Mingxia (China)
SILVER—Irina Lashko (Russia)
BRONZE—Annie Pelletier (Canada)

## Equestrian

### Individual Dressage

GOLD—Isabell Werth on *Gigolo* (Germany)
SILVER—Anky Van Grunsven on *Bonfire* (Netherlands)
BRONZE—Sven Rothenberger on *Weyden* (Netherlands)

### Individual Jumping

GOLD—Ulrich Kirchhoff on *Jus de Pommes* (Germany)
SILVER—Willi Melliger on *Calvaro* (Switzerland)
BRONZE—Alexandra Ledermann on *Rochet M* (France)

### Individual Three-Day Event

GOLD—Blyth Tait on *Ready Teddy* (New Zealand)
SILVER—Sally Clark on *Squirrel Hill* (New Zealand)
BRONZE—Kerry Millikin on *Out and About* (Westport,MA)

### Team Dressage

GOLD—Germany: Isabell Werth on *Gigolo*; Monica Theodorescu on *Grunox*; Klaus Balkenhol on *Goldstern*; Martin Schuadt on *Durgo*
SILVER—Netherlands: Anky Van Grunsven on *Bonfire*; Sven Rothenberger on *Weyden*; Tineke Bartels-De Vries on *Olympic Barbria*; Gonnelien Rothenberger on *Dondolo*
BRONZE—United States: Robert Dover on *Metallic* (Wellington, FL); Steffen Peters on *Udon* (Escondido, CA); Michelle Gibson on *Peron* (Roswell, GA); Guenter Seidel on *Graf George* (Encinitas, CA)

### Team Jumping

GOLD—Germany: Ulrich Kirchhoff on *Jus De Pommes*;

Lars Nieberg on *For Pleasure*; Franke Sloothaak on *Joly*; Ludger Beerbaum on *Ratina*
SILVER—United States: Anne Kursinski on *Eros* (Flemington, NJ); Michael Matz on *Rhum* (Collegeville, PA); Peter Leone on *Legato* (Greenwich, CT); Leslie Burr-Howard on *Extreme* (Westport, CT)
BRONZE—Brazil: Rodrigo Pessoa on *Tomboy*; Andre Johannpeter on *Calei*; Luiz Azevedo Felipe on *Cassiana*; Alvaro Miranda Neto on *Aspen*

### Team Three-Day Event

GOLD—Australia: Wendy Schaeffer; Phillip Dutton; Andrew Hoy, Darien Powers
SILVER—United States: David O'Connor (The Plains, VA); Bruce Davidson, (Unionville, PA); Karen O'Connor (The Plains, VA); Jill Henneberg, (Voorhees, NJ)
BRONZE—New Zealand: Blyth Tait; Vaughn Jefferis; Andrew Nicholson; Vicky Latta

## Fencing

### MEN

### Individual Epee

GOLD—Aleksandr Beketov (Russia)
SILVER—Ivan Trevejo Perez (Cuba)
BRONZE—Geza Imre (Hungary)

### Individual Foil

GOLD—Alessandro Puccini (Italy)
SILVER—Lionel Plumenail (France)
BRONZE—Franck Boidin (France)

### Individual Sabre

GOLD—Stanislav Pozdnyakov (Russia)
SILVER—Sergey Sharikov (Russia)
BRONZE—Damien Touya (France)

### Team Epee

GOLD—Italy: Sandro Cuomo; Angelo Mazzoni; Maurizio Randazzo
SILVER—Russia: Aleksandr Beketov; Pavel Kolobkov; Valeriy Zakharevich
BRONZE—France: Jean-Michel Henry; Robert Leroux; Eric Srecki

### Team Foil

GOLD—Russia: Dmitriy Shevchenko; Ilgar Mamedov; Vladislav Pavlovich

SILVER—Poland: Piotr Kielpikowski; Adam Krzesinski; Ryszard Sobczak

BRONZE—Cuba: Elvis Gregory; Rolando Tucker Leon Samuel; Oscar Garcia Perez Manuel

### Team Sabre

GOLD—Russia: Stanislav Pozdnyakov; Grigoriy Kiriyenko; Sergey Sharikov

SILVER—Hungary: Csaba Koves; Jozsef Navarrete; Bence Szabo

BRONZE—Italy: Raffaello Caserta; Luigi Tarantino; Tonhi Terenzi

### WOMEN

### Individual Epee

GOLD—Laura Flessel (France)

SILVER—Valerie Barlois (France)

BRONZE—Gyoengyi Szalay Horvathne (Hungary)

### Individual Foil

GOLD—Laura Badea (Romania)

SILVER—Valentina Vezzali (Italy)

BRONZE—Giovanna Trillini (Italy)

### Team Epee

GOLD—France: (Laura Flessel; Sophie Moresee-Pichot; Valerie Barlois

SILVER—Italy: Laura Chiesa; Elisa Uga; Margherita Zalaffi

BRONZE—Russia: Mariya Mazina; Yuliya Garayeva; Karina Aznavuryan

### Team Foil

GOLD—Italy: Francesca Bortolozzi Borella; Giovanna Trillini; Valentina Vezzali

SILVER—Romania: Laura Badea; Reka Szabo; Roxana Scarlat

BRONZE—Germany: Anja Fichtel Mauritz; Sabine Bau; Monika Weber-Koszto

## Field Hockey

### MEN

GOLD—Netherlands: Floris Jan Bovelander, Danny Bree, Jacques Brinkman, Maurits Crucq, Teun de Nooijer, Marc Delissen, Jeroen Delmee, Ronald Jansen, Erik Jazet, Leo Klein Gebbink, Bram Lomans, Taco van den Honert, Rogier van der Wal, Tycho van Meer, Wouter van Pelt, Remco van Wijk, Stephan Veen, Guus Vogels

SILVER—Spain: Jaime Amat, Pablo Amat, Javier Arnau, Jordi Arnau, Oscar Barrena, Ignacio Cobos, Juan Dinares, Juan Escarre, Xavier Escude, Juantxo Garcia-Maruino, Antonio Gonzalez, Ramon Jufresa, Joaquin Malgosa, Victor Pujol, Ramon Sala, Pablo Usoz

BRONZE—Australia: Lee Bodimeade, Stuart Carruthers, Baeden Choppy, Stephen Davies, Damon Diletti, Lachlan Dreher, Darren Duff, Jason Duff, James Elmer, Lachlan Elmer, Brendan Garard, Paul Gaudoin, Mark Hager, Garry Jennison, Paul Lewis, Grant Smith, Matthew Smith, Daniel Sproule, Jay Stacy, Kenneth Wark, Michael York

### WOMEN

GOLD—Australia: Katie Allen, Michelle Andrews, Alyson Annan, Louise Dobson, Renita Farrell, Juliet Haslam, Rechelle Hawkes, Clover Maitland, Karen Marsden, Claire Mitchell-Taverner, Jenny Morris, Nikki Mott, Alison Peek, Jackie Pereira, Nova Peris-Kneebone, Katrina Powell, Lisa Powell, Danni Roche, Justine Sowry, Kate Starre, Liane Tooth

SILVER—South Korea: Eun-Jung Chang, Eun-Jung Cho, Eun-Kyung Choi, Mi-Soon Choi, Young-Sun Jeon, Deok-San Jin, Myung-Ok Kim, Soo-Hyun Kown, Chang-Sook Kwon, Eun-Kyung Lee, Eun-Young Lee, Ji-Young Lee, Jeong-Sook Lim, Seung-Shin Oh, Hyun-Jung Woo, Jae-Sook You

BRONZE—Netherlands: Ageeth Boomgaardt, Stelle de Heij, Wietske de Ruiter, Wilhelmina Donners, Willemijn Duyster, Wendy Fortuin, Eleonoor Holsboer, Nicole Koolen, Ellen Kuipers, Jeannette Lewin, Suzanne Plesman, Florentine Steenberghe, Josepha Teeuwen, Carole Thate, Jacqueline Toxopeus, Fleur van de Kieft, Dillianne van den Boogaard

## Gymnastics

### MEN

### All-Around

GOLD—Li Xiaoshuang (China)

SILVER—Alexei Nemov (Russia)

BRONZE—Vitaly Scherbo (Belarus)

### Floor Exercise

GOLD—Ioannis Melissanidis (Greece)

SILVER—Li Xiaoshuang (China)

BRONZE—Alexei Nemov (Russia)

### Horizontal Bar

GOLD—Andreas Wecker (Germany)

SILVER—Krasimir Dounev (Bulgaria)

BRONZE—Vitaly Scherbo (Belarus); Alexei Nemov (Russia); and Fan Bin (China)

### Parallel Bars

GOLD—Rustam Sharipov (Ukraine)
SILVER—*Jair Lynch (Washington, D.C.)
BRONZE—Vitaly Scherbo (Belarus)

### Pommel Horse

GOLD—Li Donghua (Switzerland)
SILVER—Marius Urzica (Romania)
BRONZE—Alexei Nemov (Russia)

### Rings

GOLD—Yuri Chechi (Italy)
SILVER—Dan Burinca (Romania); and Szilveszter Csollany (Hungary)
BRONZE—None awarded

### Vault

GOLD—Alexei Nemov (Russia)
SILVER—Yeo Hong-chul (South Korea)
BRONZE—Vitaly Scherbo (Belarus)

### Team

GOLD—Russia: Eugeni Podgorni; Nikolay Krukov; Dmitriy Trush; Sergei Charkov; Alexei Voropaev; Alexei Nemov
SILVER—China: Zhang Jinjing; Fan Bin; Shen Jian; Fan Hongbin; Li Xiaoshuang; Huang Huadong
BRONZE—Ukraine: Vladimir Shamenko; Rustam Sharipov; Alexandre Svetlichnyi; Igchinski; Yuri Yermakov; Grigory Misutin

## WOMEN

### All-Around

GOLD—Lilia Podkopayeva (Ukraine)
SILVER—Gina Gogean (Romania)
BRONZE—Simona Amanar (Romania); and Lavinia Milosovici (Romania)

### Balance Beam

GOLD—Shannon Miller (Edmond, OK)
SILVER—Lilia Podkopayeva (Ukraine)
BRONZE—Gina Gogean (Romania)

### Floor Exercise

GOLD—Lilia Podkopayeva (Ukraine)
SILVER—Simona Amanar (Romania)
BRONZE—*Dominique Dawes (Silver Spring, MD)

### Uneven Bars

GOLD—Svetlana Chorkina (Russia)
SILVER—Amy Chow (San Jose, CA); and Bi Wenjiing (China)
BRONZE-None awarded

### Vault

GOLD—Simona Amanar (Romania)
SILVER—Mo Huilan (China)
BRONZE—Gina Gogean (Romania)

### Team

GOLD—United States: Jaycie Phelps (Greenfield, IN); Amy Chow (San Jose, CA); Shannon Miller, (Edmond, OK); *Dominique Dawes (Silver Spring, MD); Dominique Moceanu (Hollywood, CA); Kerri Strug (Tucson, AZ)
SILVER—Russia: Oksana Liapina; Elena Grosheva; Svetlana Chorkina; Elena Dolgopolova; Dina Kochetkova; Rozalia Galiyeva
BRONZE—Romania: Ionela Loaies; Mirela Tugurlan; Gina Gogean; Alexandra Marinescu; Lavinia Milosovici; Simona Amanar

## Judo
### MEN

### Extra Lightweight

GOLD—Tadahiro Nomura (Japan)
SILVER—Girolamo Giovinazzo (Italy)
BRONZE—Richard Trautmann (Germany); and Dorjpalam Narmandakh (Mongolia)

### Half-Lightweight

GOLD—Udo Quellmalz (Germany)
SILVER—Yukimasa Nakamura (Japan)
BRONZE—Israel Hernandez (Cuba); and Henrique Guimares (Brazil)

### Lightweight

GOLD—Kenzo Nakamura (Japan)
SILVER—Kwak Dae-sung (South Korea)

BRONZE—Jimmy Pedro (Danvers, MA); and Christophe Gagliano (France)

### Half-Middleweight

GOLD—Djamel Bouras (France)
SILVER—Toshihiko Koga (Japan)
BRONZE—Soso Liparteliani (Georgia); and Cho In-chul (South Korea)

### Middleweight

GOLD—Jeon Ki-young (South Korea)
SILVER—Armen Bagdasarov (Uzbekistan)
BRONZE—Marko Spittka (Germany); and Mark Huizinga (Netherlands)

### Half-Heavyweight

GOLD—Pawel Nastula (Poland)
SILVER—Kim Min-soo (South Korea)
BRONZE—Stephane Traineau (France); and Miguel Fernandes (Brazil)

### Heavyweight

GOLD—David Douillet (France)
SILVER—Ernesto Perez (Spain)
BRONZE—Harry van Barneveld (Belgium); and Frank Moeller (Germany)

## WOMEN
### Extra Lightweight

GOLD—Kye Sun (North Korea)
SILVER—Ryoko Tamura (Japan)
BRONZE—Yolanda Soler (Spain); and Amarilis Savon (Cuba)

### Half-Lightweight

GOLD—Marie-Claire Restoux (France)
SILVER—Hyun Sook-hee (South Korea)
BRONZE—Noriko Sagawara (Japan); and Legna Verdecia (Cuba)

### Lightweight

GOLD—Driulis Gonzalez (Cuba)
SILVER—Jung Sun-yong (South Korea)
BRONZE—Isabel Fernandez (Spain); and Marisbel Lomba (Belgium)

### Half-Middleweight

GOLD—Yuko Emoto (Japan)
SILVER—Gella Van de Caveye (Belgium)
BRONZE—Jung Sung-sook (South Korea); and Jenny Gal (Netherlands)

### Middleweight

GOLD—Cho Min-sun (South Korea)
SILVER—Aneta Szczepanska (Poland)
BRONZE—Wang Xianbo (China); and Claudia Zwiers (Netherlands)

### Half-Heavyweight

GOLD—Ulla Werbrouck (Belgium)
SILVER—Yoko Tanabe (Japan)
BRONZE—Ylenia Scapin (Italy); and Diadenis Luna (Cuba)

### Heavyweight

GOLD—Sun Fuming (China)
SILVER—Estela Rodriguez (Cuba)
BRONZE—Johanna Hagn (Germany); and Christine Cicot (France)

## Modern Pentathlon

GOLD—Aleksandr Parygin (Kazakstan)
SILVER—Eduard Zenovka (Russia)
BRONZE—Janos Martinek (Hungary)

## Rhythmic Gymnastics
### Indvidual

GOLD—Yekaterina Serebryanskaya (Ukraine)
SILVER—Ianina Batyrchina (Russia)
BRONZE—Yelena Vitrichenko (Ukraine)

### Team

GOLD—Spain: Marta Baldo; Nuria Cabanillas; Estela Gimenez; Lorena Gurendez; Tania Lamarca; Estibaliz Martinez
SILVER—Bulgaria: Ivelina Taleva; Valentina Kevlian; Ina Deltcheva; Maja Tabakova; Maria Koleva; Vjara Vatachka
BRONZE—Russia: Evguenia Botchkareva; Irina Dziouba; Angelina Iouchkova; Olga Chtyrenko; Elena Krivochei; Ioulia Ivanova

# Rowing

## MEN

### Single Sculls

GOLD—Xeno Mueller (Switzerland)
SILVER—Derek Porter (Canada)
BRONZE—Thomas Lange (Germany)

### Double Sculls

GOLD—Davide Tizzano and Agostino Abbagnale (Italy)
SILVER—Kjetil Undset and Steffen Stoerseth (Norway)
BRONZE—Frederic Kowal and Samuel Barathay (France)

### Lightweight Double Sculls

GOLD—Michael Gier and Markus Gier (Switzerland)
SILVER—Maarten van der Linden and Pepjin Aardewijn (Netherlands)
BRONZE—Anthony Edwards and Bruce Hick (Australia)

### Quadruple Sculls

GOLD—Germany: Andre Steiner; Andreas Hajek; Stephan Volkert; Andre Willms
SILVER—United States: Tim Young (Moorestown, NJ); Brian Jamieson (Livingston, NJ); Eric Mueller (Cedarburg, WI); Jason Gailes (Webster, MA)
BRONZE—Australia: Janusz Hooker; Duncan Free; Ronald Snook; Boden Hanson

### Coxless Pair

GOLD—Steven Redgrave and Matthew Pinsent (Britain)
SILVER—David Weightman and Robert Scott (Australia)
BRONZE—Michel Andrieux and Jean-Christophe Rolland (France)

### Coxless Four

GOLD—Australia: Drew Ginn; James Tomkins; Nicholas Green; Michael McKay
SILVER—France: Gilles Bosquet; Daniel Fauche; Bertrand Vecten; Olivier Moncelet
BRONZE—Britain: Rupert Obholzer; Jonny Searle; Gregory Searle; Timothy Foster

### Lightweight Coxless Four

GOLD—Denmark: Niels Henriksen; Thomas Poulsen; Eskild Ebbesen; Victor Feddersen
SILVER—Canada: Jeffrey Lay; Dave Boyes; Gavin Hassett; Brian Peaker
BRONZE—United States: David Collins (Thousand Oaks, CA); Jeff Pfaendtner (Detroit, MI); Marcus Schneider (Everett, WA); William Carlucci (Rye Brook,NY)

### Eights

GOLD—Netherlands: Henk-Jan Zwolle; Diederik Simon; Michiel Bartman; Koos Maasdyk; Niels van der Zwan; Niels van Steenis; Ronald Florijn; Nico Rienks; Jeroen Duyster
SILVER—Germany: Frank Richter; Mark Kleinschmidt; Wolfram Huhn; Marc Weber; Detlef Kirchhoff; Thorsten Streppelhoff; Ulrich Viefers; Roland Baar; Peter Thiede
BRONZE—Russia: Anton Chermashentsev; Andrey Glukhov; Dmitriy Rozinkevich; Vladimir Volodenkov; Nikolay Aksyonov; Roman Monchenko; Pavel Melnikov; Sergey Matveyev; Aleksandr Lukyanov

## WOMEN

### Single Sculls

GOLD—Yekaterina Khodotovich (Belarus)
SILVER—Silken Laumann (Canada)
BRONZE—Trine Hansen (Denmark)

### Double Sculls

GOLD—Marnie McBean and Kathleen Heddle (Canada)
SILVER—Cao Mianying and Zhang Xiuyun (China)
BRONZE—Irene Eljs and Eeke van Nes (Netherlands)

### Lightweight Double Sculls

GOLD—Constantina Burcica and Camelia Macoviciuc (Romania)
SILVER—Teresa Z. Bell (Washington Crossing, NJ) Lindsay Burns (Big Timber, MT)
BRONZE—Rebecca Joyce and Virginia Lee (Australia)

### Quadruple Sculls

GOLD—Germany: Jana Sorgers; Katrin Rutschow; Kathrin Boron; Kerstin Koeppen
SILVER—Ukraine: Olena Ronzhina; Inna Frolova; Svitlana Maziy; Diana Miftakhutdinova
BRONZE—Canada: Laryssa Biesenthal; Marnie McBean; Diane O'Grady; Kathleen Heddle

### Coxless Pair

GOLD—Megan Still and Kate Slatter (Australia)
SILVER—Missy Schwen (Bloomington, IN) and Karen Kraft (San Mateo, CA)

BRONZE—Christine Gosse and Helene Cortin (France)

### Eights

GOLD—Romania: Anca Tanase; Vera Cochelea; Liliana Gafencu; Doina Spircu; Ioana Olteanu; Elisabeta Lipa; Marioara Popescu; Doina Ignat; Elena Georgescu

SILVER—Canada: Heather Mcdermid; Tosha Tsang; Maria Maunder; Alison Korn; Emma Robinson; Anna van der Kamp; Jessica Monroe; Theresa Luke; Lesley Thompson

BRONZE—Belarus: Natalya Lavrinenko; Aleksandra Pankina; Natalya Volchek; Tamara Davydenko; Valentina Skrabatun; Yelena Mikulich; Natalya Stasyuk; Marina Znak; Yaroslava Pavlovich

## Shooting
### MEN
#### Air Pistol

GOLD—Roberto Di Donna (Italy)
SILVER—Wang Yifu (China)
BRONZE—Tanu Kiriakov (Bulgaria)

#### Free Pistol

GOLD—Boris Kokorev (Russia)
SILVER—Igor Basinski (Belarus)
BRONZE—Roberto Di Donna (Italy)

#### Rapid Fire Pistol

GOLD—Ralf Schumann (Germany)
SILVER—Emil Milev (Bulgaria)
BRONZE—Vladimir Vokhmyanin (Kazakstan)

#### Running Target

GOLD—Yang Ling (China)
SILVER—Xiao Jun (China)
BRONZE—Miroslav Janus (Czech Republic)

#### Air Rifle

GOLD—Artem Khadzhibekov (Russia)
SILVER—Wolfram Waibel Jr. (Austria)
BRONZE—Jean-Pierre Amat (France)

#### Small-Bore Rifle Prone

GOLD—Christian Klees (Germany)
SILVER—Sergey Beliaev (Kazakstan)
BRONZE—Jozef Gonci (Slovakia)

#### Small-Bore Rifle 3-Position

GOLD—Jean-Pierre Amat (France)
SILVER—Sergey Beliaev (Kazakstan)
BRONZE—Wolfram Waibel Jr. (Austria)

#### Trap

GOLD—Michael Diamond (Australia)
SILVER—Josh Lakatos (Pasadena, CA)
BRONZE—Lance Bade (Ridgefield, WA)

#### Double Trap

GOLD—Russell Mark (Australia)
SILVER—Albano Pera (Italy)
BRONZE—Zhang Bing (China)

#### Skeet

GOLD—Ennio Falco (Italy)
SILVER—Miroslaw Rzepkowski (Poland)
BRONZE—Andrea Benelli (Italy)

### WOMEN
#### Air Pistol

GOLD—Olga Klochneva (Russia)
SILVER—Marina Logvinenko (Russia)
BRONZE—Mariya Grozdeva (Bulgaria)

#### Air Rifle

GOLD—Renata Mauer (Poland)
SILVER—Petra Horneber (Germany)
BRONZE—Aleksandra Ivosev (Yugoslavia)

#### Sport Pistol

GOLD—Li Duihong (China)
SILVER—Diana Yorgova (Bulgaria)
BRONZE—Marina Logvinenko (Russia)

#### Small-Bore Rifle Three Position

GOLD—Aleksandra Ivosev (Yugoslavia)
SILVER—Irina Gerasimenok (Russia)
BRONZE—Renata Mauer (Poland)

#### Double Trap

GOLD—Kim Rhode (El Monte, CA)
SILVER—Susanne Kiermayer (Germany)
BRONZE—Deserie Huddleston (Australia)

## Soccer

### MEN

GOLD—Nigeria: Daniel Amokachi, Emmanuel Amunike, Jonathan Apoborie, Tijani Babangida, Celestine Babayaro, Emmanuel Babayaro, Abiodun Baruwa, Joseph Dosu, Teslim Fatusi, Victor Ikpeba, Nwankwo Kanu, Garba Lawal, Ndubuisi Ndah, Abiodon Obafemi, Mobi Obaraku, Kingsley Obiekwu, Augustine Okocha, Sunday Oliseh, Wilson Oruma, Patrick Pascal, Okechukwu Uche, Taribo West

SILVER—Argentina: Matias Almeyda, Roberto Ayala, Guillermo Barros Schelotto, Christian Bassedas, Carlos Bossio, Pablo Cavallero, Jose Antonio Chamot, Hernan Crespo, Marcelo Delgado, Marcelo Gallardo, Javier Lavallen, Claudio Lopez, Gustavo Lopez, Hugo Morales, Ariel Ortego, Pablo Paz, Hector Pineda, Roberto Sensini, Diego Simeone, Juan Pablo Sorin, Juan Veron, Javier Zanetti

BRONZE—Brazil: Aldair, Amaral, Andre Luiz, Bebeto, Danrlei, Dida, Flavio Conceicao, Juninho, Luizao, Marcelinho Paulista, Narciso, Rivaldo, Roberto Carlos, Ronaldinho, Ronaldo, Savio, Ze Elias, Ze Maria

### WOMEN

GOLD—United States: Michelle Akers, Brandi Chastain, Amanda Cromwell, Joy Fawcett, Julie Foudy, Carin Gabarra, Mia Hamm, Mary Harvey, Kristine Lilly, Shannon MacMillan, Tiffeny Milbrett, Tracy Noonan, Carla Overback, Cindy Parlow, Tiffany Roberts, *Briànà Scurry, *Thori Staples, Jennifer Streiffer, Tisha Venturini, Saskia Webber, *Staci Wilson

SILVER—China: Yufeng Chen, Yunjie Fan, Hong Gao, Yating Li, Ailing Liu, Ying Liu, Lijie Niu, Guihong Shi, Qingxia Shui, Qingmei Sun, Wen Sun, Liping Wang, Haiying Wei, Lirong Wen, Huilin Xie, Hongqi Yu, Yan Zhang, Lihong Zhao, Yan Zhao, Honglian Zhong

BRONZE—Norway: Ann Kristin Aarones, Agnete Carlsen, Gro Espeseth, Tone Gunn Frustol, Tone Haugen, Linda Medalen, Merete Myklebust, Bente Nordby, Anne Nymark Andersen, Nina Nymark Anderson, Marianne Pettersen, Hege Riise, Brit Sandaune, Reidun Seth, Ingrid Sternhoff, Heidi Stoere, Tina Svensson, Trine Tangeraas, Kjersti Thun

## Softball

GOLD—United States: Laura Berg; *Gillian Boxx; Sheila Cornell; Lisa Fernandez; Michele Granger; Lori Harrigan; Dionna Harris; Kim Maher; Leah O'Brien; Dot Richardson; Julie Smith; Michele Smith; Shelly Stokes; Dani Tyler; Christa Williams

SILVER—China: Chunfang Zhang; Fang Yan; Xuging Liu; Ying Wang; Hua Tao; Hong Chen; Jian Xu; Zhongxin An; Qiang Wei; LiLei; Yaju Liu; Lihong Wang; Li Ou

BRONZE—Australia: Kim Cooper; Jocalyn Lester; Joanne Brown; Kerry Dienelt; Sally Modermin; Natalie Ward; Tanya Harding; Hayles Petrie; Petra Ededone; Leslie McDermid; Jen McRae; Shelly Richardson; Eve Roche; Laura Wilkins; Penny Crudgington

## Swimming

### MEN

50 Freestyle

GOLD—Alexander Popov (Russia)
SILVER—Gary Hall Jr. (Phoenix, AZ)
BRONZE—Fernando Scherer (Brazil)

100 Freestyle

GOLD—Alexander Popov (Russia)
SILVER—Gary Hall Jr. (Phoenix,AZ)
BRONZE—Gustavo Borges (Brazil)

200 Freestyle

GOLD—Danyon Loader (New Zealand)
SILVER—Gustavo Borges (Brazil)
BRONZE—Daniel Kowalski (Australia)

400 Freestyle

GOLD—Danyon Loader (New Zealand)
SILVER—Paul Palmer (Britain)
BRONZE—Daniel Kowalski (Australia)

1500 Freestyle

GOLD—Kieren Perkins (Australia)
SILVER—Daniel Kowalski (Australia)
BRONZE—Graeme Smith (Britain)

100 Backstroke

GOLD—Jeff Rouse (Fredericksburg, VA)
SILVER—Rodolfo Falcon (Cuba)
BRONZE—Neisser Bent (Cuba)

200 Backstroke

GOLD—Brad Bridgewater (Dallas, TX)
SILVER—Tripp Schwenk (Sarasota, FL)
BRONZE—Emanuele Merisi (Italy)

100 Breaststroke

GOLD—Fred Deburghgraeve (Belgium)

SILVER—Jeremy Linn (Harrisburg, PA)
BRONZE—Mark Warnecke (Germany)

### 200 Breaststroke

GOLD—Norbert Rozsa (Hungary)
SILVER—Karoly Guttler (Hungary)
BRONZE—Andrey Korneyev (Russia)

### 100 Butterfly

GOLD—Denis Pankratov (Russia)
SILVER—Scott Miller (Australia)
BRONZE—Vladislav Kulikov (Russia)

### 200 Butterfly

GOLD—Denis Pankratov (Russia)
SILVER—Tom Malchow (St. Paul, MN)
BRONZE—Scott Goodman (Australia)

### 200 Individual Medley

GOLD—Attila Czene (Hungary)
SILVER—Jani Sievinen (Finland)
BRONZE—Curtis Myden (Canada)

### 400 Individual Medley

GOLD—Tom Dolan (Arlington, VA)
SILVER—Eric Namesnik (Butler, PA)
BRONZE—Curtis Myden (Canada)

### 400 Medley Relay

GOLD—United States: Tripp Schwenk (Sarasota, FL); Kurt Grote (San Diego, CA); John Hargis (Clinton, AR); Josh Davis (San Antonio, TX); Gary Hall Jr. (Paradise Valley, AZ); Mark Henderson (Fort Washington, MD); Jeremy Linn (Harrisburg, PA); Jeff Rouse (Fredericksburg, VA)
SILVER—Russia: Vladimir Selkov; Stanislav Lopukhov; Denis Pankratov; Aleksandr Popov; Roman Ivanovskiy; Vladislav Kulikov; Roman Yegorov
BRONZE—Australia: Steven Dewick; Philip Rogers; Scott Miller; Michael Klim; Toby Haenen

### 400 Freestyle Relay

GOLD—United States: Jon Olsen (Jonseboro, AR); Josh Davis (San Antonio, TX); Bradley Schumacher (Bowie, MD); Gary Hall Jr. (Phoenix, AZ); Scott Tucker (Birmingham, AL); David Fox, Raleigh, NC)
SILVER—Russia: Roman Yegorov; Aleksandr Popov; Vladimir Predkin; Denis Pimankov; Vladimir Pyshnenko; Konstantin Ushkov

BRONZE—Germany: Christian Troger; Bengt Zikarsky; Bjorn Zikarsky; Mark Pinger; Alexander Luderitz

### 800 Freestyle Relay

GOLD—United States: Josh Davis (San Antonio, TX); Joe Hudepohl (Cincinnati, OH); Ryan Berube (Tequesta, FL); Bradley Schumacher (Bowie, MD); Jon Olsen (Jonesboro, AR)
SILVER—Sweden: Chriter Wallin; Anders Holmertz; Lars Frolander; Andre Lyrbring; Christer Walle
BRONZE—Germany: Aimo Heilmann; Christian Keller; Christian Troger; Steffen Zesner; Konstantin Dubrovin; Oliver Lampe

## WOMEN

### 50 Freestyle

GOLD—Amy Van Dyken (Englewood, CO)
SILVER—Le Jingyi (China)
BRONZE—Sandra Volker (Germany)

### 100 Freestyle

GOLD—Le Jingyi (China)
SILVER—Sandra Volker (Germany)
BRONZE—Angel Martino (Americus, GA)

### 200 Freestyle

GOLD—Claudia Poll (Costa Rica)
SILVER—Franziska van Almsick (Germany)
BRONZE—Dagmar Hase (Germany)

### 400 Freestyle

GOLD—Michelle Smith (Ireland)
SILVER—Dagmar Hase (Germany)
BRONZE—Kirsten Vlieghuis (Netherlands)

### 800 Freestyle

GOLD—Brooke Bennett (Plant City, FL)
SILVER—Dagmar Hase (Germany)
BRONZE—Kirsten Vlieghuis (Netherlands)

### 100 Backstroke

GOLD—Beth Botsford (Baltimore, MD)
SILVER—Whitney Hedgepeth (Rocky Mount, NC)
BRONZE—Marianne Kriel (South Africa)

### 200 Backstroke

GOLD—Krisztina Egerszegi (Hungary)

SILVER—Whitney Hedgepeth (Rocky Mount, NC)
BRONZE—Cathleen Rund (Germany)

### 100 Breaststroke

GOLD—Penny Heyns (South Africa)
SILVER—Amanda Beard (Irvine, CA)
BRONZE—Samantha Riley (Australia)

### 200 Breaststroke

GOLD—Penny Heyns (South Africa)
SILVER—Amanda Beard (Irvine, CA)
BRONZE—Agnes Kovacs (Hungary)

### 100 Butterfly

GOLD—Amy van Dyken (Englewood, CO)
SILVER—Liu Limin (China)
BRONZE—Angel Martino (Americus, GA)

### 200 Butterfly

GOLD—Susan O'Neill (Australia)
SILVER—Petria Thomas (Australia)
BRONZE—Michelle Smith (Ireland)

### 200 Individual Medley

GOLD—Michelle Smith (Ireland)
SILVER—Marianne Limpert (Canada)
BRONZE—Lin Li (China)

### 400 Individual Medley

GOLD—Michelle Smith (Ireland)
SILVER—Allison Wagner (Gainesville, FL)
BRONZE—Krisztina Egerszegi (Hungary)

### 400 Freestyle Relay

GOLD—United States: Jenny Thompson (Dover, NH); Catherine Fox (Shawnee Mission, KS); Angel Martino (Americus, GA); Amy Van Dyken (Englewood, CO); Lisa Jacob (Mission Viejo, CA); Melanie Valerio (Campbell, OH)
SILVER—China: Le Jingyi; Chao Na; Nian Yun; Shan Ying
BRONZE—Germany: Sandra Volker; Simone Osygus; Antje Buschschulte; Franziska van Almsick; Meike Freitag

### 400 Medley Relay

GOLD—United States: Beth Botsford (Baltimore, MD); Amanda Beard (Irvine, CA); Angel Martino (Americus, GA); Amy Van Dyken (Englewood, CO); Whitney Hedgepeth (Rocky Mount, NC); Kristine Quance (Northridge, CA); Jenny Thompson (Dover, NH); Catherine Fox (Shawnee Mission, KS)
SILVER—Australia: Nicole Stevenson; Samantha Riley; Susan O'Neill; Helen Denman; Angela Kennedy; Sarah Ryan
BRONZE—China: Chen Yan; Han Xue; Cai Huijue; Shan Ying

### 800 Freestyle Relay

GOLD—United States: Trina Jackson (Jacksonville, FL); Sheila Taormina (Livonia, MI); Cristina Teuscher (New Rochelle, NY); Jenny Thompson (Dover, NH); Lisa Jacob (Mission Viejo, CA); Ashley Whitney (Nashville, TN); Annette Salmeen (Ann Arbor, MI)
SILVER—Germany: Franziska van Almsick, Kerstin Kielgass, Anke Scholz, Dagmar Hase, Simone Osygus, Meike Freitag
BRONZE—Australia: Julia Greville, Nicole Stevenson, Emma Johnson, Susan O'Neill, Lise Mackie

## Synchronized Swimming

GOLD—United States: Tammy Cleland (Walnut Creek, CA); Becky Dyroen-Lancer (Campbell, CA); Heather Pease (Lafayette, C); Jill Savery (Concord, CA); Nathalie Schneyder (Walnut Creek, CA); Jill Sudduth (Morgan Hill, CA); Emily Lesueur (Mesa, AZ); Margot Thien (Berkeley, CA); Heather Simmons-Carrasco (Santa Clara, CA); Suzannah Bianco (Saratoga, CA)
SILVER—Canada: Karen Clark; Christine Larsen; Janice Bremner; Sylvie Frechette; Valerie Hould-Marchand; Karen Fonteyne; Kasia Kulesza; Cari Read; Erin Woodley; Lisa Alexander
BRONZE—Japan: Akiko Kawase; Miya Tachibana; Kaori Takahashi; Miho Takeda; Rei Jimbo; Raika Fujii; Miho Kawabe; Riho Nakajima; Junko Tanaka; Mayuko Fujiki

## Table Tennis
### MEN
### Singles

GOLD—Liu Guoliang (China)
SILVER—Wang Tao (China)
BRONZE—Joerg Rosskopf (Germany)

### Doubles

GOLD—Kong Linghui and Liu Guoliang (China)
SILVER—Lu Lin and Wang Tao (China)

BRONZE—Lee Chul-seung and Yoo Nam-kyu (South Korea)

## WOMEN

### Singles

GOLD—Deng Yaping (China)
SILVER—Chen Jing (Taiwan)
BRONZE—Qiao Hong (China)

### Doubles

GOLD—Deng Yaping and Qiao Hong (China)
SILVER—Liu Wei and Qiao Yunping (China)
BRONZE—Park Hae-jung and Ryu Ji-hae (South Korea)

## Team Handball

### MEN

GOLD—Croatia: Patrik Cavar, Valner Frankovic, Slavko Goluza, Bruno Gudelj, Vladimir Jelcic, Bozidar Jovic, Nenad Kljavic, Venio Losert, Valter Matosevic, Zoran Mikulic, Alvaro Nacinovic, Goran Perkovac, Iztok Puc, Zlatko Saracevic, Irfan Smajlagic, Vladimir Sujster
SILVER—Sweden: Magnus Andersson, Robert Andersson, Anders Backegren, Per Carlen, Martin Frandesjo, Peter Gentzel, Erik Hajas, Robert Hedin, Andreas Larsson, Ola Lindgren, Stafan Lofgren, Nicklas Martinsson, Mats Olsson, Staffan Olsson, Johan Pettersson, Thomas Sivertsson, Jan Stankiewicz, Thomas Svensson, Pierre Thorsson, Magnus Wislander
BRONZE—Spain: Talant Dujshebaev, Salvador Esquer, Aitor Etxaburu, Jesus Fernandez, Jaume Fort, Mateo Garralda, Raul Gonzalez, Rafael Guijosa, Fernando Hernandez, Jose Hombrados, Demetrio Lozano, Jordi Nunez, Jesus Olalla, Juan Perez, Inaki Urdangarin, Alberto Urdiales

### WOMEN

GOLD—Denmark: Anja Jul Andersen, Camilla Andersen, Kristine Anderson, Heidi Astrup, Tina Bottzau, Marianne Florman, Conny Hamann, Anja Hansen, Anette Hoffman, Tonje Kjaergaard, Janne Kolling, Susanne Lauritsen, Gitte Madsen, Lene Rantala, Rikke Solberg, Gitte Sunesen, Dorthe Tanderup
SILVER—South Korea: Eun-Hee Cho, Sun-Hee Han, Jeong-Ho Hong, Soon-Young Huh, Cheong-Shim Kim, Eun-Mi Kim, Jeong-Mi Kim, Mi-Sim Kim, Rang Kim, Hye-Jeong Kwag, Sang-Eun Lee, O-Kyeong Lim, Hyang-Ja Moon, Seong-Ok Oh, Yong-Ran Oh, Jeong-Rim Park
BRONZE—Hungary: Eva Erdos, Andrea Farkas, Rita Hochrajter, Beata Hoffmann, Aniko Kantor, Erzsebet Kocsis, Beatrix Kokeny, Eszter Matefi, Auguszta Matyas, Aniko Meksz, Aniko Nagy, Helga Nemeth, Ildiko Padar, Beata Siti, Anna Szanto, Katalin Szilagyi, Beatrix Toth, Melinda Tothne Szabo, Annamaria Vas, Zsuzsanna Viglasi

## Tennis

### MEN

#### Singles

GOLD—Andre Agassi (Las Vegas, NV)
SILVER—Sergi Bruguera (Spain)
BRONZE—Leander Paes (India)

#### Doubles

GOLD—Todd Woodbridge and Mark Woodforde (Australia)
SILVER—Neil Broad and Tim Henman (Great Britain)
BRONZE—Marc-Kevin Goellner and David Prinosil (Germany)

### WOMEN

#### Singles

GOLD—Lindsay Davenport (Newport Beach, CA)
SILVER—Arantxa Sanchez Vicario (Spain)
BRONZE—Jana Novota (Czech Republic)

#### Doubles

GOLD—Gigi Fernandez (Aspen, CO) and Mary Joe Fernandez (Miami, FL)
SILVER—Jana Novotna and Helena Sukova (Czech Republic)
BRONZE—Arantxa Sanchez Vicario and Conchita Martinez (Spain)

## Volleyball

### MEN

GOLD—Netherlands: Peter Blange, Markus Broere, Frank Denkers, Guido Gortzen, Rob Grabert, Henk-Jan Held, Misha Latuhihin, Reinder Nummerdor, Jan Posthuma, Brecht Rodenburg, Richard Schuil, Johannes van der Horst, Robert van Es, Bas van de Goor, Mike van de Goor, Olaf van der Meulen, Ron Zwerver
SILVER—Italy: Lorenzo Bernardi, Vigor Bovolenta, Marco Bracci, Luca Cantagalli, Andrea Gardini, Andrea Giani, Pasquale Gravina, Marco Meoni, Samuele Papi, Andrea Sartoretti, Paolo Tofoli, Andrea Zorzi
BRONZE—Yugoslavia: Vladimir Batez, Slobodan Boskan, Dejan Brdovic, Dorde Duric, Andrija Geric, Nikola Grbic,

Vladimir Grbic, Rajko Jokanovic, Slobodan Kovac, Strahinja Kozic, Dula Mester, Zarko Petrovic, Vanja Prtenjaca, Edin Skoric, Zeljko Tanaskovic, Goran Vujevic, Igor Vusurovic

### WOMEN

GOLD—Cuba: Taismari Aguero, Regla Bell, Magalys Carvajal, Marleny Costa, Ana Ibis Fernandez, Mirka Francia, Idalmis Gato, Lilia Izquierdo, Mireya Luis, Raiza O'Farrill, Yumilka Ruiz, Regla Torres

SILVER—China: Yongmei Cui, Qi He, Yawan Lai, Yan Li, Xiaoning Liu, Wenli Pan, Yue Sun, Lina Wang, Yi Wang, Ziling Wang, Yongmei Wu, Yunying Zhu

BRONZE—Brazil: Ana Ida Alivares, Leila Barros, Ericleia Filo Bodziak, Hilma Calderia, Ana Paula Connelly, Marcia Fu Cunha, Virna Dias, Ana Moser, Ana Flavia Sanglard, Heila Fofao Souza, Sandra Suruagy, Fernanda Venturini

## Beach Volleyball

### MEN

GOLD—Karch Kiraly (San Clemente, CA) and Kent Steffes (Pacific Palisades, CA)

SILVER—Mike Dodd (Manhattan Beach, CA) and Mike Whitmarsh (San Diego, CA)

BRONZE—John Child and Mark Heese (Canada)

### WOMEN

GOLD—Jackie Silva and Sandra Pires (Brazil)

SILVER—Monica Rodrigues and Adriana Samuel (Brazil)

BRONZE—Natalie Cook and Kerri Pottharst Ann (Australia)

## Water Polo

GOLD—Spain: Jose Maria Abarca, Angel Andreo, Daniel Ballart, Manuel Estiarte, Pedro Garcia, Salvador Gomez, Ivan Moro, Miguel Oca, Jorge Paya, Sergi Pedrerol, Jesus Rollan, Jordi Sans, Carlos Sanz

SILVER—Croatia: Maro Balic, Perica Bukic, Damir Glavan, Igor Hinic, Vjekoslav Kobescak, Josko Krekovic, Ognjen Krzic, Dubravko Simenc, Sinisa Skolnekovic, Ratko Stritof, Tino Vegar, Renato Vrbicic, Zdeslav Vrdoljak

BRONZE—Italy: Alberto Angelini, Francesco Attolico, Fabio Bencivenga, Alessandro Bovo, Alessandro Calcaterra, Roberto Calcaterra, Marco Gerini, Alberto Ghibellini, Luca Giustolisi, Amedeo Pomilio, Francesco Postiglione, Carlo Silipo, Leonardo Sottani

## Weightlifting

### 54kg (119 pounds)

GOLD—Halil Mutlu (Turkey)

SILVER—Zhang Xiangsen (China)

BRONZE—Sevdalin Minchev (Bulgaria)

### 59kg (130 pounds)

GOLD—Tang Ningsheng (China)

SILVER—Leonidas Sabanis (Greece)

BRONZE—Nikolay Pechalov (Bulgaria)

### 64kg (141 pounds)

GOLD—Naim Suleymanoglu (Turkey)

SILVER—Valerios Leonidis (Greece)

BRONZE—Xiao Jiangang (China)

### 70kg (154 pounds)

GOLD—Zhan Xugang (China)

SILVER—Kim Myong-nam (North Korea)

BRONZE—Attila Feri (Hungary)

### 76kg (167.5 pounds)

GOLD—Pablo Lara (Cuba)

SILVER—Yoto Yotov (Bulgaria)

BRONZE—Jon Chol (North Korea)

### 83kg (183 pounds)

GOLD—Pyrros Dimas (Greece)

SILVER—Marc Huster (Germany)

BRONZE—Anderzej Cofalik (Poland)

### 91kg (200.5 pounds)

GOLD—Aleksey Petrov (Russia)

SILVER—Leonidas Kokas (Greece)

BRONZE—Oliver Caruso (Germany)

### 99kg (218 pounds)

GOLD—Akakide Kakhiashvilis (Greece)

SILVER—Anatoli Khrapaty (Kazakstan)

BRONZE—Denis Gotfrid (Ukraine)

### 108 kg (238 pounds)

GOLD—Timur Taimazov (Ukraine)

SILVER—Sergey Syrtsov (Russia)

BRONZE—Nicu Vlad (Romania)

### 108kg-plus (238-plus pounds)

GOLD—Andrey Chemerkin (Russia)

SILVER—Ronny Weller (Germany)
BRONZE—Stefan Botev (Australia)

## Wrestling

### 48kg (105.5 pounds) Freestyle

GOLD—Kim Il (North Korea)
SILVER—Armen Mkrttchian (Armenia)
BRONZE—Alexis Vila (Cuba)

### 52kg (114.5 pounds) Freestyle

GOLD—Valentin Jordanov (Bulgaria)
SILVER—Namik Abdullaev (Azerbaijan)
BRONZE—Maulen Mamirov (Kazakstan)

### 57kg (125.5 pounds) Freestyle

GOLD—Kendall Cross (Raleigh, NC)
SILVER—Giya Sissauori (Canada)
BRONZE—Ri Yong Sam (North Korea)

### 62kg (136.5 pounds) Freestyle

GOLD—Tom Brands (Iowa City, IA)
SILVER—Jang Jae-sung (South Korea)
BRONZE—Elbrus Tedeev (Ukraine)

### 68kg (149.5 pounds) Freestyle

GOLD—Vadim Bogiev (Russia)
SILVER—Townsend Saunders (Phoenix, AZ)
BRONZE—Zaza Zazirov (Ukraine)

### 74kg (163 pounds) Freestyle

GOLD—Bouvaisa Satiev (Russia)
SILVER—Park Jang-soon (South Korea)
BRONZE—Takuya Ota (Japan)

### 82kg (180.5 pounds) Freestyle

GOLD—Khadzhimurad Magomedov (Russia)
SILVER—Yang Hyun-Mo (South Korea)
BRONZE—Amir Reza Khadem (Iran)

### 90kg (198 pounds) Freestyle

GOLD—Rasul Khadem (Iran)
SILVER—Makharbek Khadartsev (Russia)
BRONZE—Eldari Kurtanidze (Georgia)

### 100kg (220 pounds) Freestyle

GOLD—Kurt Angle (Pittsburgh, PA)
SILVER—Abbas Jadidi (Iran)
BRONZE—Arawat Sabejew (Germany)

### 130kg (286 pounds) Freestyle

GOLD—Mahmut Demir (Turkey)
SILVER—Alexei Medvedev (Belarus)
BRONZE—Bruce Baumgartner (Cambridge Springs, PA)

### 48kg (105.5 pounds) Greco-Roman

GOLD—Sim Kwon-Ho (South Korea)
SILVER—Alexander Pavlov (Belarus)
BRONZE—Zafar Gulyov (Russia)

### 52kg (114.5 pounds) Greco-Roman

GOLD—Armen Nazaryan (Armenia)
SILVER—Brandon Paulson (Anoka, MN)
BRONZE—Andriy Kalashnikov (Ukraine)

### 57kg (125.5 pounds) Greco-Roman

GOLD—Yuri Melnichenko (Kazakhstan)
SILVER—Dennis Hall (Stevens Point, WI)
BRONZE—Sheng Zetian (China)

### 62kg (136.5 pounds) Greco-Roman

GOLD—Wlodzimierz Zawadzki (Poland)
SILVER—Juan Luis Maren (Cuba)
BRONZE—Mahmet Pirim (Turkey)

### 68kg (149.5 pounds) Greco-Roman

GOLD—Ryszard Wolny (Poland)
SILVER—Ghani Yolouz (France)
BRONZE—Alexander Tretyakov (Russia)

### 74kg (163 pounds) Greco-Roman

GOLD—Feliberto Ascuy (Cuba)
SILVER—Marko Asell (Finland)
BRONZE—Josef Tracz (Poland)

### 82kg (180.5 pounds) Greco-Roman

GOLD—Hamza Yerlikaya (Turkey)
SILVER—Thomas Zander (Germany)
BRONZE—Valery Tsilent (Belarus)

### 90kg (198 pounds) Greco-Roman

GOLD—Vyacheslav Oleynyk (Ukraine)
SILVER—Jacek Fafinski (Poland)
BRONZE—Maik Bullman (Germany)

### 100kg (220 pounds) Greco-Roman

GOLD—Andrzej Wronski (Poland)
SILVER—Sergei Lishtvan (Belarus)
BRONZE—Mikael Ljungberg (Sweden)

### 130kg (286 pounds) Greco-Roman

GOLD—Alexander Karelin (Russia)
SILVER—Matt Ghaffari (Colorado Springs, CO)
BRONZE—Sergei Moureiko (Moldova)

# Yachting
## MEN

### Finn

GOLD—Mateusz Kusznierewicz (Poland)
SILVER—Sebastien Godefroid (Belgium)
BRONZE—Roy Heiner (Netherlands)

### Mistral

GOLD—Nikolaos Kaklamanakis (Greece)
SILVER—Carlos Espinola (Argentina)
BRONZE—Gal Fridman (Israel)

### 470

GOLD—Yevhen Braslavets and Ihor Matviyenko (Ukraine)
SILVER—John Merricks and Ian Walker (Great Britain)
BRONZE—Vitor Rocha and Nuno Barreto (Portugal)

## WOMEN

### Europe

GOLD—Kristine Roug (Denmark)

SILVER—Margriet Matthijsse (Netherlands)
BRONZE—Courtenay Becker-Dey (The Dalles, OR)

### Mistral

GOLD—Lee Lai-shan (Hong Kong)
SILVER—Barbara Kendall (New Zealand)
BRONZE—Alessandra Sensini (Italy)

### 470

GOLD—Theresa Zabell and Begona Via Dufresne (Spain)
SILVER—Yumiko Shige and Alicia Kinoshita (Japan)
BRONZE—Rusiana Taran and Olena Pakholchik (Ukraine)

## OPEN

### Laser

GOLD—Robert Scheidt (Brazil)
SILVER—Ben Ainslie (Great Britain)
BRONZE—Peer Moberg (Norway)

### Soling

GOLD—Germany: Jochen Schuemann; Thomas Flach; and Bernd Jaekel
SILVER—Russia: Georgiy Shayduko; Dmitriy Shabanov; and Igor Skalin
BRONZE—United States: Jeff Madrigali (San Anselmo, CA); Jim Barton (Fairfax, CA); and Kent Massey (Santa Barbara, CA)

### Star

GOLD—Torben Grael and Marcello Ferreira (Brazil)
SILVER—Hans Wallen and Bobby Lohse (Sweden)
BRONZE—Colin Beashel and David Giles (Australia)

### Tornado

GOLD—Fernando Leon and Jose Luis Ballester (Spain)
SILVER—Mitch Booth and Andrew Landenberger (Australia)
BRONZE—Lars Grael and Kiko Pellicano (Brazil)

# Appendix III

# Appendix III

## ♦ Selecting A Historically Black College (by Deborah Jones)

So you're ready to apply to the school of your choice—or are you? Applying to a college or university can be a costly and time-consuming venture—but it does not have to be. If you do enough digging, you can eliminate illogical choices, and spend your time and money wisely.

The key is to honestly evaluate your interests, strengths, and needs. The best person to do this is yourself; nobody knows you better.

## ASK YOURSELF THE TOUGH QUESTIONS

The first thing you'll want to do is ask yourself the following questions to pinpoint exactly which schools are in the running:

- Do I want a 2-year or a 4-year degree?

A 2-year—or associate's—degree is often a stepping stone to a 4-year—or bachelor's—degree. It's a good place to start if the field you plan to enter requires only an associate's degree or if you plan to earn a four-year degree, but need a firmer academic foundation before you are accepted into a four-year school. While a four-year bachelor's degree may be a bit more competitive in the job market, it requires more academic stamina and will cost you more money. Consider this when deciding whether you will attend a 2-year or 4-year school.

Talk with people who work in the professions you are interested in. Find out what kinds of people they want to hire, and what the academic requirements are for that field. Once you determine whether you will pursue a 2-year or 4-year degree, you will have eliminated a considerable number of schools from your search.

- Do I want to attend a school that is in-state or out-of-state?

Although this seems simple, it is a critical piece of information. Attending school in-state is often much less expensive than going out-of-state because schools tend to charge higher tuition to nonresidents. You'll also want to factor in the travel expenses you will incur going between home and school for breaks. If money is tight, you might want to limit your list of potential schools to in-state institutions. On the other hand, if your budget isn't so limited, then you might as well consider out-of-state institutions as well.

- Do I want to attend a small (2,500 or less), medium (2,500–8,000), large (8,000–15,000), or very large (more than 15,000) school?

If you don't mind the prospect of being in a class with more than 150 other people and perhaps never getting a chance to really have a chat with the instructor; if choosing from a wider range of course offerings and getting lost in a larger crowd is appealing, perhaps the larger institution is for you. On the other hand, if you feel you would thrive in an environment that would afford you more one-on-one attention, then a smaller school may be right for you.

- If I am attending school within-state, will I live at home and commute to school, or live on campus, away from home.

Again, if you are trying to go to college on the tightest budget, you should seriously consider commuting to a local college, if there is one that meets your needs. You could save yourself costly room and board expenses.

However, if you plan to commute from home, you need some mode of transportation in order to do so. Find out if you can reach your school of choice by public transportation or if you will need a car. Be sure to factor in the various expenses of running a car, including insurance, maintenance, and parking fees on campus.

## THE TOUGHEST QUESTION: WHO AM I?

- What kind of degree am I interested in?

Once you have answered the broadest practical questions, listed above, and have targeted your search accordingly, ask yourself who you are. What do you hope to accomplish with your degree? Although you probably won't know exactly what you want to do with your life just yet, you should have a fair understanding of what you enjoy and what you do well, or at least what you want to do well. Focus your energy there and explore the careers related to your interests and talents.

Your high school counselor should be able to help you with this decision. Now is the time to take inventory of your extracurricular activities, and your special skills and talents. Ask for evidence of your strengths from sources such as standardized tests, academic records, and other data in your school's counseling office, such as the Holland Self-Directed Search or the World of Work section on the ACT.

- What special needs do I have?

If there are specific features that you require in a school, such as excellent handicapped services, a large fraternity/sorority network, a sprawling green campus, or an excellent pre-veterinary medicine program, eliminate the schools that do not qualify immediately. Ask yourself if there is a special need that you have, and decide if it is important enough to drive your decision.

Once you know which schools you are interested in, you need to know how to apply. Below are requirements and some tips for freshmen, transfer students, and international students on the application process.

# PAPERWORK: PULLING THE PIECES TOGETHER

## Freshman Students

What you need:

- graduation from an accredited high school or a passing grade on the General Education Diploma examination (GED)
- completed applications to the schools of your choice. You can get blank applications from your high school counselor or contact the prospective schools' admissions department.
- the nonrefundable application fees
- scores for either the Scholastic Aptitude Test (SAT) or the American College Testing Program (ACT)

## Tips for Freshman Applicants

- You can begin applying to schools as early as the latter part of your junior year in high school. Sometimes, applying early will allow you a better chance at being admitted.
- Your high school academic preparation should be balanced, and should emphasize the five major academic areas, including English, history, mathematics, science, and foreign language.

- SAT or ACT scores are used both for admission and for placement counseling. Let these tests work for you.
- Once you're admitted, you might also need to submit the following: housing forms, physical examination forms, and proof of immunization.

## Transfer Students

What You Need:

- potentially, all of the above items listed under "Freshman Students: What You Need"
- transcripts of all credit earned
- often, if student has attended another institution for less than one year, she or he must submit a high school transcript along with a college transcript

## Tip for Transfers

- Upon acceptance, a transfer evaluator will assess previous college credits to be transferred. If you are dissatisfied with the evaluation, you may often request a review

## International Students

What You Need:

- completed application
- proof that you have received 12 years of elementary and secondary education
- an English Proficiency Report, which should be completed by a person who can verify that you have the ability to speak English
- Teaching of English as a Foreign Language (TOEFL) scores (only if your native language is not English)
- nonrefundable application fee
- foreign student financial aid statements

# LEVEL OF SELECTIVITY: EXACTLY HOW CHOOSY ARE THEY?

One of the most important pieces of information in making your decision is a college's level of selectivity. Be realistic about your qualifications and know which schools you are qualified for. To help you with this, *Black American Colleges and Universities* ranks the degree of competitiveness in the admissions' policy for each school profiled. Each school is ranked according to the number of requirements needed for admission which may include: minimum SAT or ACT scores, GED score or GPA; class rank; college preparatory units; high school recommendations; personal essay and statement of intent; and completion of 18 or more units. Competitive schools request four to six of the above requirements; moderately competitive schools require three to four; slightly competitive schools require two to three; and non-competitive schools ask for only one or two of the above requirements. Look for a handy breakdown of each school's level of selectivity and other key pieces of information, such as coed vs. single sex school and two-year vs. four-year, in the **Schools-at-a-Glance** section in this book. The chart will help you quickly identify key facts about schools of interest to you, and help you to narrow your search.

At some schools, conditional admissions are sometimes available to students who do not meet regular admission requirements. In this case, students are placed on probation for the first year while completing developmental courses to make up for deficiencies. Other admission policies include early admissions, early decision, advanced placement, and deferred entrance

## A WORD ABOUT THE PERSONAL ESSAY

The best advice you can get when you are preparing to write an essay for college entry is this: know what the assignment is. Read the instructions on your applications and ask yourself the question "what are they asking me to do here?" Then, do it. And do it well. In some cases reviewing your instructions will leave more questions than answers for you. For example, you might be instructed to write a 1,000-word personal essay. If that is all the guidance you are given, then it is your job to fill in the details of your discussion. Review your acheivements, your academic and professional goals, and seize this opportunity to reveal to an admissions officer what is not evident on a college applica-tion, just what makes you unique, an asset to his or her school. You might start with what you discovered about yourself when you asked "the tough questions" in deciding what kind of a degree you were looking for.

Start by writing a quick draft of whatever first comes to mind, if only to have something to rewrite. Write several drafts, and try setting your complete draft aside for a day, then go back and refine it. Once you have all of your thoughts down, reread your essay to ensure that it flows from beginning, to middle, to end.

## Technology is Your Friend

No matter what people tell you to the contrary, neat-ness counts. Unless the application stipulates that you hand-write it, type your essay, preferably on a word processor or computer so you can spell check it. Then proofread it again for those errors that only the human eye can detect. (Most software packages don't know enough to choose between to, too, and two for you.)

Lastly, ask someone—a professional writer, editor, or English teacher— to proofread it and give you their com-ments. It's better to know at this point—while it's still in your hands—if you have made some ugly grammatical snafu. While it is acceptable to get this type of technical advice on your essay, remember that this is your essay, and must be your work.

And while we're on the subject of outside help, a word of advice when you ask an adult to complete a teacher rec-ommendation form or write a letter of recommendation: GIVE THEM AT LEAST TWO WEEKS' NOTICE. Even if the people you are asking to recommend you are not ter-ribly busy, they will certainly appreciate your respect for their schedule. If they agree to write a letter on your behalf, send them a note of thanks after about a week. This will also serve as a tactful reminder to them of their commitment to you. And, if you want better letters of recommendation, do your letter-writers a favor by supplying them with a brief list of your achievements, special projects or activities, or anything that might help them write a more specific letter for you.

Finally, apply to more than one school; give yourself options. And, if you possibly can, make an effort to visit your prospective schools. If you call in advance you can even sit in on some relevant classes. Really explore the campus, and see if it feels like you.

## ◆ Funding Your College Education

You've lived through four years of high school, you've taken your SATs, you're about to embark on that great adventure called "college." So, again, you do your homework: you graze through college catalogs and you finally find "the one"—the perfect school for you. But how do you make it happen? Pursuing an education is a major investment of time, energy—and money.

According to a recent *Fortune* article, tuitions increased 9% annually during the 1980s and are expected to grow at an annual rate of 7% throughout the 1990s. What does this mean in real numbers? Well, according to national averages, a student entering college in the fall of 1993 will pay $77,000 for four years of tuition, room, and board at a private college; $36,000 for four years at a public university. Traditionally, tuitions at black colleges and universities are about half the national average, yet they are not immune to the average tuition hikes. For example, at Stillman—a private four-year college—tuition, room, and board for 1990–91 was $5,404. For 1993–94, college costs rose to $7,214, an increase of 33%.

Don't panic! These figures aren't meant to discourage you, they are only offered to make you aware of the reality of college costs. Although the primary obligation for college expenses lies with the family, keep in mind that at most schools almost all students receive some sort of financial aid. In addition, a number of other options exist to make your financial road a little less rocky. The following chapter is designed to let you know of viable alternatives and to help you devise a feasible financial aid plan.

### WHAT IS FINANCIAL AID?

You may be eligible to receive three types of financial aid:

- grants or scholarships (outright gifts that do not have to be repaid)
- loans (money that must be repaid at low interest after graduation or after leaving school)
- work-study programs/internships (employment opportunities that help defray tuition costs)

### FINANCIAL NEED: AM I ELIGIBLE?

The majority of colleges receive financial aid from the federal and state government. The various grants, loans, and work opportunity funds are provided to assist those students demonstrating the greatest need. For financial aid, need is defined as the difference between the amount of money a family may be expected to contribute and the total cost of education. Financial need is expressed as an equation:

Cost of Education
 – Expected Family Contribution
 = Financial Need

While cost may vary from school to school, the expected family contribution generally does not, since it is derived through a national formula. *(See* the Estimated Family Contribution chart located at the end of this section.)

### COST OF EDUCATION

The cost of education includes expenses that are reasonably related to education:

- Tuition and fees
- Room
- Board
- Books
- Supplies
- Transportation
- Personal Expenses

Cost may also include other expenses such as childcare for dependents; disability expenses not covered by other agencies; or participation in a program of study abroad. If you believe that you will incur extra expenses in order to attend college, write a letter explaining your circumstances to your college's financial aid officer.

### HOW DO I APPLY?— IT ALL STARTS WITH THE CORRECT FORM!

First, contact your high school guidance counselor or the financial aid director of the college that you are interested in attending. He/she will make sure that you know exactly which forms to complete, and the dates by which these forms must be returned. Do not wait for an admissions decision to apply for financial aid. Start your search early.

To apply for federal aid, all students must complete the Free Application for Federal Student Aid (FAFSA). No fee is charged in accordance with filling out the FAFSA (see example on page 11).

To be considered for non-federal aid, you may be required to fill out the following, all of which require a fee for each college that you list on the application:

- Financial Aid Form of the College Scholarship Service (FAF) (see example on page 10)
- Family Financial Statement of the American College Testing Service (FFS)
- Application form of the Pennsylvania Higher Education Assistance Agency (PHEAA)

In addition to the above, you may be required to complete individual state scholarship or grant program applications. Some colleges may require a campus application as well.

Complete the forms as soon as possible after January 1. (You will be required to file financial aid forms for each year of college that you attend.) You may file your applications using estimated income figures in order to meet the application deadlines. The records that you will need from the previous year to complete your FAFSA are:

- W-2 forms; income tax forms for you, your parents, and your spouse, if married

- records of social security benefits, veteran benefits, and other nontaxable income

- bank statements

- business/farm records

- statements of trust funds, money market funds, stocks, bonds, certificates of deposit, and similar assets

Save all your records after you have completed the applications in case you have to prove that the information is correct. Keep a copy of the applications you are filing for your records. For additional information about federal student financial aid, call the Federal Student Aid Information Center at 800-4 FED AID.

## Dependency Status

Income and asset information is used to determine eligibility for financial aid. The information you will be asked to provide is contingent on whether you are dependent or independent. If you are considered dependent, you must report your parent's income and assets, as well as your own. If you're independent, only your income and asset information (and that of your spouse) is needed. The definition of an independent student has changed.

You will be considered independent if you meet one of the following:

- you turn 24 by December 31 of the school year for which you are applying for financial aid (e.g., applying for aid for 1994–95, you must be born before January 1, 1970)
- veteran of U.S. Armed Forces
- graduate/professional student
- married
- orphan or ward of court
- have dependents other than a spouse

If you think you have some unusual circumstances that should be taken into consideration regarding your dependency status, contact your financial aid officer. Be prepared to document your case.

## FEDERAL FINANCIAL AID PROGRAMS: WHAT IS AVAILABLE?

### Federal Pell Grant

Depending on financial circumstances, undergraduate students from families with annual incomes of up to about $40,000 may qualify for a Pell Grant. For 1993-94, Pell Grants range from $400 to $2,300. Eligibility is based on financial need as determined by a national formula that takes into account total income; net assets, such as savings/checking accounts and real estate investments (not including your home); family size; and number of family members in college. Grant payments may be made for the period of time required to complete the first bachelor's degree.

## FEDERAL CAMPUS-BASED PROGRAMS

The three programs listed below are called "campus-based" programs because they are administered by individual colleges. Availability of funding is different at each institution.

### Federal Supplemental Educational Opportunity Grant (FSEOG)

The FSEOG is available for undergraduates with exceptional financial need. Priority is given to Pell Grant (*See* Federal Pell Grant above) recipients. The college determines award amounts based on the funds available at that college. Awards range from $100 to $4,000 and do not have to be repaid.

### Federal Perkins Loan Program

Under the guidelines of the Perkins Loan Program, undergraduate students may borrow up to $3,000 per year for a total of no more than $15,000 for undergraduate programs; up to $4,000 per year for graduate study; and up to $30,000 total for all years of study. This loan is interest-free while the student is enrolled at least half-time. Eligibility is based on exceptional financial need and availability of funds at each college. Repayment of interest and principal begins six to nine months after the student is no longer enrolled at least half-time. The interest rate is fixed at 5%.

### Federal Work-Study Program (FWS)

The FWS program provides job opportunities for undergraduate and graduate students to earn minimum wage or more. Eligibility is based on student's financial need. Students usually work 10 to 20 hours per week.

## FEDERAL FAMILY EDUCATION LOAN PROGRAMS

Some banks, credit unions, or savings and loan associations offer low-interest education loans that are insured by the federal government. Forms may be obtained from your lender, your college, or your state guaranty agency. For a list of lenders in your state, contact your state guaranty agency.

### Federal Stafford Student Loan (Subsidized)

As of July 1, 1993, the subsidized Stafford Student Loan limit for a new undergraduate student is $2,625 for the first year, $3,500 for the second, and $5,500 per academic year for the third through fifth years. Graduate students can borrow up to $8,500 a year. The total loan amount for undergraduate studies is $23,000. The total debt for graduate or professional study is $65,000, including any Federal Stafford Loans received as an undergraduate. The college certifies enrollment and loan eligibility on the loan application. Loans are subject to a origination fee and an insurance fee. The interest rate is variable and will change each year on July 1, but is capped at 9%. Repayment of interest and principal begins six months after the student is no longer enrolled at least half-time. Eligibility is based on need by completing the FAFSA.

## Federal Stafford Student Loan (Unsubsidized)

The terms and conditions of the unsubsidized loan are the same as for the subsidized loan (above), except that: 1) interest on the loan is due while the student is in school or the interest can be deferred, and 2) loan limits cover the cost of education minus any aid received up to the limits of the subsidized Stafford Loan. Accrued interest may be paid against or added to the loan (capitalized) as agreed by the borrower and the lender.

## Federal Supplemental Loans for Students (SLS)

Independent undergraduate students as of July 1, 1993, may borrow $4,000 per academic year for the first two years and $5,000 per academic year for the third through fifth years. The total loan amount for undergraduate studies is $23,000; for graduate students it is $10,000 per year with the total debt for graduate or professional study not to exceed $65,500 including Federal SLS loans made at the undergraduate level. An insurance fee of up to 3% and an origination fee of 5% are deducted from the amount borrowed. The interest rate on SLS loans is variable and will change each year on July 1—but is capped at 11%. Repayment begins within 60 days of receipt of the loan. Full-time undergraduate students may defer the principal but are responsible for the payment of interest while in school.

## Federal Parent Loans for Undergraduate Students (PLUS)

Parents may borrow up to the cost of education, minus any other aid received, per academic year on behalf of each dependent student. Eligibility is not based on need. PLUS loans can be used to meet all or part of the calculated family contribution. For new borrowers, the interest rate is variable, with a 10% cap. The interest rate is recalculated on July 1 of each year. An insurance fee of up to 3% on the amount borrowed and an origination fee of 5% are deducted from the amount borrowed. Repayment begins within 60 days of receipt of the loan. A credit check is required for loans disbursed after July 1, 1993.

# OTHER FEDERAL PROGRAMS
## Military Service Scholarships

The Army, Air Force, and Navy offer Reserve Officer Training Corps (ROTC) Scholarships and Armed Forces Health Professions Scholarships. Contact the appropriate military service recruiting office for specific information and a directory of participating colleges.

## National Science Scholars Program (NSSP)

This program awards funds to graduating high school seniors (or those who will obtain the equivalent of a certificate of graduation), who have demonstrated excellence and achievement in the physical, life, or computer sciences; mathematics; or engineering. The award is $5,000 per year for undergraduate study, or the cost of education, whichever is less, and is awarded to two students from each congressional district. For 1993-94, funding is expected to be $3,300. To obtain an application and additional information, contact your high school guidance counselor or your college's financial aid officer.

## Office of Vocational and Educational Services for Individuals with Disabilities (VESID)

Disabled students pursuing higher education may be eligible for assistance through the State Office of Vocational and Educational Services for Individuals with Disabilities (VESID). Criteria and funding vary. Applications and eligibility requirements may be obtained at the local VESID office.

## Paul Douglas Teacher Scholarship Program

This scholarship awards up to $5,000 per year for up to four years of full-time undergraduate study. To be eligible, students must be in the top 10% of their high school class or have high GED scores, and be matriculated in a degree program leading to certification in teaching. Students must teach two years for each year of aid received. To obtain an application and additional information contact your high school guidance counselor or your college's financial aid officer.

## Robert C. Byrd Honors Scholarship Program

The Byrd Program was established to recognize students with outstanding academic achievement who show promise of continued excellence. Students may receive $1,500 a year for up to four years at a college. At least 10 scholarships are available per state. To obtain an application and additional information, contact your high school guidance counselor or your college's financial aid officer.

# SAMPLE FREE APPLICATION FOR FEDERAL STUDENT AID

# Free Application for Federal Student Aid
## 1993-94 School Year    CCCCC  1

U.S. Department of Education
Student Financial
Assistance Programs

**WARNING:** If you purposely give false or misleading information on this form, you may be fined $10,000, sent to prison, or both.

"You" and "your" on this form always mean the student who wants aid.

FORM APPROVED
OMB NO. 1840-0110
APP. EXP. 6/30/94

## Section A: Yourself

1. Your name
   Last          First          M.I.

2. Your permanent mailing address
   (Mail will be sent to this address. See page 2 for State/Country abbreviation.)
   Number and Street (Include Apt. No.)
   City          State     ZIP Code

3. Your title *(optional)*
   ☐ Mr.    ☐ Miss, Ms., or Mrs.

4. Your State of legal residence ☐☐ State

   4a. When did you become a legal resident of the State you listed in Question 4? *(See the instructions on page 2.)*
   Month    Day    Year

5. Your social security number

6. Your date of birth
   Month    Day    Year

7. Are you a U.S. citizen?
   ₁ ☐ Yes, I am a U.S. citizen
   ₂ ☐ No, but I am an eligible noncitizen. *(See the instructions on page 3.)*
   [A] 
   ₃ ☐ No, neither of the above. *(See the instructions on page 3.)*

8. Will you have your first Bachelor's degree before July 1, 1993?
   ☐ Yes    ☐ No

9. As of today, are you married? *(Check only one box.)*
   ₁ ☐ I am not married. (I am single, widowed, or divorced.)
   ₂ ☐ I am married.
   ₃ ☐ I am separated from my spouse.

   9a. • If married or widowed, date married or widowed.
       • If currently divorced or separated, date separated.
       Month    Year

## Section B: Student Status

|  | Yes | No |
|---|---|---|
| 10. a. Were you born **before** January 1, 1970? | ☐ | ☐ |
| b. Are you a veteran of the U.S. Armed Forces? | ☐ | ☐ |
| c. Are you a graduate or professional student? | ☐ | ☐ |
| d. Are you married? | ☐ | ☐ |
| e. Are you a ward of the court or are both your parents dead? | ☐ | ☐ |
| f. Do you have legal dependents (*other than a spouse*) that fit the definition in the instructions on page 3? | ☐ | ☐ |

● If you answered "**No**" to **every** part of question 10, go to Section C, and fill out the **GREEN** and the **WHITE** areas on the rest of the form.

● If you answered "**Yes**" to **any** part of question 10, go to Section C and fill out the **GRAY** and the **WHITE** areas on the rest of the form.

## Section C: Household Information

### PARENTS

11. What is your parents' current marital status?
    ₁ ☐ single    ₃ ☐ separated    ₅ ☐ widowed
    ₂ ☐ married    ₄ ☐ divorced

12. What is your parents' State of legal residence? ☐☐ State

    12a. When did your parent(s) become legal resident(s) of the State you listed in Question 12? *(See the instructions on page 4.)*
    Month    Day    Year

13. Number of family members in 1993-94 ☐☐☐
    (Always include yourself [the student] and your parents. Include your parents' other children and other people only if they meet the definition in the instructions on page 4.)

14. Number of college students in 1993-94 ☐
    (Of the number in 13, write in the number of family members who will be in college at least half-time. Include yourself – the applicant. See the instructions on page 4.)

### STUDENT (& SPOUSE)

15. Number of family members in 1993-94 ☐☐
    (Always include yourself and your spouse. Include your children and other people only if they meet the definition in the instructions on page 4.)

16. Number of college students in 1993-94 ☐
    (Of the number in 15, write in the number of family members who will be in college at least half-time. Include yourself. See the instructions on page 4.)

**ED FORM 255**

## SAMPLE FAF

# FAF* Financial Aid Form — 1993-94                    ☐ ☐

This form is not required to apply for Title IV federal student aid. However, information from the FAF is used by some colleges and private organizations to award their own financial aid funds. CSS charges students a fee to collect and report this information. By filling out this form, you are agreeing to pay the fee, which is calculated in question 44.

**Section A — Student's Identification Information** — Be sure to complete this section. Answer the questions the same way you answered them in Section A of the Free Application for Federal Student Aid (FAFSA).

1. Your name
   Last          First          M.I.

3. Title (optional)
   1 ☐ Mr.   2 ☐ Miss, Ms., or Mrs.

2. Your permanent mailing address
   (Mail will be sent to this address.)
   Number, street, and apartment number
   City          State          Zip Code

4. Your date of birth
   Month   Day   Year

5. Your social security number

**Section B — Student's Other Information**

6. If you are now in high school, give your high school 6-digit code number.

7. What year will you be in college in 1993-94? (Mark only one box.)

   1 ☐ 1st (never previously attended college)
   2 ☐ 1st (previously attended college)
   3 ☐ 2nd
   4 ☐ 3rd
   5 ☐ 4th

   6 ☐ 5th or more undergraduate
   7 ☐ first-year graduate/professional (beyond a bachelor's degree)
   8 ☐ second-year graduate/professional
   9 ☐ third-year graduate/professional
   0 ☐ fourth-year or more graduate/professional

8. a. If you have previously attended any college or other postsecondary school, write in the total number of colleges and schools you have attended. ☐

   b. List below the colleges (up to five) that you have attended. Begin with the college you attended most recently. Use the CSS code numbers from the list in the FAF instruction booklet. If more space is needed, use Section M.

| Name, city, and state of college | Period of attendance From (mo./yr.) | To (mo./yr.) | CSS Code Number |
|---|---|---|---|
|  |  |  |  |
|  |  |  |  |
|  |  |  |  |
|  |  |  |  |

9. During the 1993-94 school year, you want institutional financial aid
   from ____ Month Year   through ____ Month Year

10. Mark your preference for institutional work and/or loan assistance.

    1 ☐ Part-time job only
    2 ☐ Loan only
    3 ☐ Will accept both, but prefer loan
    4 ☐ Will accept both, but prefer job
    5 ☐ No preference

11. If it is necessary to borrow money to pay for educational expenses, do you want to be considered for a Stafford Loan? (optional)
    Yes ☐ 1   No ☐ 2

    (If you mark "Yes," your information may be sent to the loan agency within your state.)

12. a. Your employer/occupation _____

    b. Employer's address _____

    c. Will you continue to work for this employer during the 1993-94 school year? Yes ☐ 1   No ☐ 2

13. If you have dependents other than a spouse, how many will be in each of the following age groups during 1993-94?
    Ages 0-5 ☐   Ages 6-12 ☐   Ages 13+ ☐

14. 1992 child support paid by you   $ _____ .00

**Section C — Student's Expected Summer/School-Year Income**

| | Summer 1993 3 months | School Year 1993-94 9 months | | Summer 1993 3 months | School Year 1993-94 9 months |
|---|---|---|---|---|---|
| 15. Income earned from work by you | $ ____ .00 | $ ____ .00 | 17. Other taxable income | $ ____ .00 | $ ____ .00 |
| 16. Income earned from work by spouse | $ ____ .00 | $ ____ .00 | 18. Nontaxable income and benefits | $ ____ .00 | $ ____ .00 |

## State Student Incentive Grant (SSIG)

These federal funds are allocated to states to encourage scholarship/grant assistance to college students who demonstrate need. Further information may be obtained from your high school guidance counselor or your college financial aid officer.

## Veterans Educational Benefits

Eligible veterans and children or spouses of eligible deceased or service-connected disabled veterans may be able to receive aid for approved college study. Information and application forms are available at all Veterans Administration Offices.

# INSTITUTIONAL GRANTS AND SCHOLARSHIPS

## Thurgood Marshall Scholarship

The Thurgood Marshall Scholarship fund provides a four-year scholarship to one entering freshman at each of the 37 historically black public college and universities including the University of the District of Columbia and the University of the Virgin Islands. To qualify, students need a high school GPA of 3.0, and a SAT score of 1000 or a ACT score of 24 or more. Students must be recommended by their high school counselor as exceptional or exemplary in the creative or performing arts. Students should contact the Thurgood Marshall Coordinators at each of the 37 historically black public colleges and universities listed in Appendix IX of *BACU*.

## United Negro College Fund (UNCF)

The United Negro College Fund program awards 300 scholarships through its 41 member schools. To be eligible students must attend one of the 41 UNCF schools listed in Appendix IV of *BACU* and must demonstrate financial need. UNCF scholarships range from $500 to $7,500 per year.

# COVERING THE BASES

Don't limit your search for financial aid to the federal and state levels. Explore all your options. Many grants and scholarships are available through individual colleges and universities. Some are based on academic achievement; others could be based on creative talent or athletic ability. Contact the financial aid office at the colleges where you are applying to find out:

1. What institutional grants and scholarships are available?

2. What are the eligibility requirements?

3. What is the criteria for selection?

4. What are the range of awards?

5. How and when can I apply?

## Not-So-Obvious Sources

- Companies that you or your parents are associated with may provide some type of assistance for pursuing post-secondary education.

- Contact local clubs, fraternal organizations (such as Elks, Kiwanas, etc.), and civic leagues. Community-based associations often have scholarships available.

- The local library or bookstore has myriad sourcebooks that provide information on locating funds for college.

Many private sector resources often go untapped because prospective students are simply not aware of them. All sources cited in the bibliography following this chapter are readily available at your local library.

# FINAL NOTE

It is important to note that it is never too early to begin your search for financial aid. In fact, it is not uncommon to begin two years prior to entering your freshman year in college. The search for financial aid should be an aggressive one, and although it may be an arduous journey, it is one that definitely pays off in the long run.

## ESTIMATED FAMILY CONTRIBUTION CHART

The following estimated family contribution chart provides an idea of what colleges expect families to contribute at various income levels. This is an estimate based on averages. The chart is also based on the following assumptions:

- Two-parent family
- Assets estimated at $20,000
- One family member in college

### ESTIMATED FAMILY CONTRIBUTION FOR A DEPENDENT STUDENT FROM A TWO-PARENT FAMILY 1993-94

| Total 1992 Family Income | Number of Family Members | | | |
|---|---|---|---|---|
| | 3 | 4 | 5 | 6 |
| $15,000 | 0 | 0 | 0 | 0 |
| 20,000 | 483 | 0 | 0 | 0 |
| 25,000 | 1,203 | 651 | 172 | 0 |
| 30,000 | 2,045 | 1,419 | 905 | 315 |
| 40,000 | 4,065 | 3,173 | 2,525 | 1,803 |
| 50,000 | 7,015 | 5,863 | 4,799 | 3,501 |
| 60,000 | 9,858 | 8,628 | 7,292 | 6,049 |
| 70,000 | 12,000 | 11,747 | 10,545 | 9,358 |
| 80,000 | 15,615 | 14,458 | 13,116 | 12,039 |
| 100,000 | 21,630 | 20,193 | 19,070 | 18,145 |

# SCHOOLS-AT-A-GLANCE

| UNIVERSITY OR COLLEGE NAME | TOTAL ENROLLMENT | 4-YEAR, 2-YEAR OR PROFESSIONAL | COED OR SINGLE SEX |
|---|---|---|---|
| **ALABAMA** | | | |
| Alabama Agricultural & Mechanical University | 5,215 | four-year | coed |
| Alabama State University | 5,490 | four-year | coed |
| Bishop State Community College | 2,144 | two-year | coed |
| Concordia College | 383 | two-year | coed |
| J. F. Drake State Technical College | 979 | two-year | coed |
| Lawson State Community College | 1,738 | two-year | coed |
| Lomax-Hannon Junior College | 60 | two-year | coed |
| Miles College | 751 | four-year | coed |
| Oakwood College | 1,334 | four-year | coed |
| Selma University | 287 | four-year | coed |
| Stillman College | 822 | four-year | coed |
| Talladega College | 615 | four-year | coed |
| Trenholm State Technical College | 704 | two-year | coed |
| Tuskegee University | 3,598 | four-year | coed |
| **ARKANSAS** | | | |
| Arkansas Baptist College | 291 | four-year | coed |
| Philander Smith College | 640 | four-year | coed |
| Shorter College | 120 | two-year | coed |
| University of Arkansas at Pine Bluff | 3,709 | four-year | coed |
| **CALIFORNIA** | | | |
| Charles R. Drew University of Medicine & Science | 140 | four-year | coed |
| Compton Community College | 5,700 | two-year | coed |
| **DELAWARE** | | | |
| Delaware State University | 2,882 | four-year | coed |
| **FLORIDA** | | | |
| Bethune-Cookman College | 2,301 | four-year | coed |

| ESTIMATED TOTAL COST PER YEAR | INCOMING FRESHMAN AVERAGE GPA | STUDENT/ TEACHER RATIO | LEVEL OF SELECTIVITY |
|---|---|---|---|
| $4,675 | 2.41 | 19:1 | slightly competitive |
| $4,333 | 2.49 | 21:1 | noncompetitive |
| $1,730 | n/a | 15:1 | noncompetitive |
| $6,362 | n/a | 28:1 | noncompetitive |
| $1,825 | n/a | n/a | noncompetitive |
| $1,550 | n/a | 20:1 | noncompetitive |
| $3,974 | n/a | 18:1 | noncompetitive |
| $7,150 | n/a | 18:1 | noncompetitive |
| $10,940 | 2.81 | 12:1 | noncompetitive |
| $6,265 | n/a | 11:1 | noncompetitive |
| $8,064 | n/a | 15:1 | noncompetitive |
| $7,444 | n/a | 13:1 | slightly competitive |
| $2,029 | n/a | 16:1 | noncompetitive |
| $10,655 | 2.7 | 13:1 | slightly competitive |
| $4,715 | n/a | 14:1 | noncompetitive |
| $5,660 | n/a | 16:1 | noncompetitive |
| $4,081 | n/a | 5:1 | noncompetitive |
| $3,885 | n/a | 19:1 | slightly competitive |
| $15,739 | n/a | 20:1 | competitive |
| $645 | n/a | 24:1 | noncompetitive |
| $5,696 | 2.49 | 15:1 | moderately competitive |
| $9,145 | 2.45 | 16:1 | slightly competitive |

# SCHOOLS-AT-A-GLANCE

| UNIVERSITY OR COLLEGE NAME | TOTAL ENROLLMENT | 4-YEAR, 2-YEAR OR PROFESSIONAL | COED OR SINGLE SEX |
|---|---|---|---|
| **FLORIDA** | | | |
| Edward Waters College | 634 | four-year | coed |
| Florida Agricultural & Mechanical University | 9,200 | four-year | coed |
| Florida Memorial College | 2,172 | four-year | coed |
| **GEORGIA** | | | |
| Albany State College | 3,106 | four-year | coed |
| Clark Atlanta University | 3,507 | four-year | coed |
| Fort Valley State College | 2,368 | four-year | coed |
| Interdenominational Theological Center | 383 | three-year | coed |
| Morehouse College | 2,992 | three-year | all-male |
| Morehouse School of Medicine | 140 | four-year | coed |
| Morris Brown College | 2,030 | four-year | coed |
| Paine College | 790 | four-year | coed |
| Savannah State College | 2,656 | four-year | coed |
| Spelman College | 1,906 | four-year | all-female |
| **ILLINOIS** | | | |
| Chicago State University | 8,648 | four-year | coed |
| Kennedy-King College | 3,137 | two-year | coed |
| **KENTUCKY** | | | |
| Kentucky State University | 2,500 | four-year | coed |
| Simmons University Bible College | 103 | four-year | coed |
| **LOUISIANA** | | | |
| Dillard University | 1,700 | four-year | coed |
| Grambling State University | 6,485 | four-year | coed |
| Southern University and Agricultural & Mechanical University at Baton Rouge | 8,941 | four-year | coed |
| Southern University (New Orleans) | 3,734 | four-year | coed |

| ESTIMATED TOTAL COST PER YEAR | INCOMING FRESHMAN AVERAGE GPA | STUDENT/ TEACHER RATIO | LEVEL OF SELECTIVITY |
|---|---|---|---|
| $7,466 | n/a | 12:1 | noncompetitive |
| $4,874 | 2.5 | 24:1 | moderately competitive |
| $7,900 | 2.5 | 17:1 | slightly competitive |
| $4,020 | n/a | 16:1 | slightly competitive |
| $11,252 | n/a | 19:1 | slightly competitive |
| $4,657 | n/a | 14:1 | slightly competitive |
| $6,695 | n/a | 13:1 | moderately competitive |
| $12,910 | n/a | 17:1 | slightly competitive |
| $25,962 | n/a | 4:1 | competitive |
| $11,298 | 2.5 | 13:1 | slightly competitive |
| $8,707 | 2.66 | 12.8:1 | noncompetitive |
| $4,375 | n/a | 22:1 | slightly competitive |
| $12,571 | 3.0 | 16:1 | moderately competitive |
| $1,528 | 2.39 | 30:1 | slightly competitive |
| $1,653 | n/a | 19:1 | noncompetitive |
| $4,702 | n/a | 13:1 | slightly competitive |
| $1,345 | n/a | n/a | noncompetitive |
| $9,815 | 2.5 | 15:1 | slightly competitive |
| $5,037 | n/a | 21:1 | noncompetitive |
| $4,747 | n/a | 17:1 | noncompetitive |
| $2,090 | n/a | 19:1 | noncompetitive |

# SCHOOLS-AT-A-GLANCE

| UNIVERSITY OR COLLEGE NAME | TOTAL ENROLLMENT | 4-YEAR, 2-YEAR OR PROFESSIONAL | COED OR SINGLE SEX |
|---|---|---|---|
| **LOUISIANA** | | | |
| Southern University (Shreveport) | 1,067 | two-year | coed |
| Xavier University of Louisiana | 3,330 | four-year | coed |
| | | | |
| **MARYLAND** | | | |
| Bowie State University | 4,437 | four-year | coed |
| Coppin State College | 2,816 | four-year | coed |
| Morgan State University | 5,034 | four-year | coed |
| Sojourner-Douglass College | 441 | four-year | coed |
| University of Maryland, Eastern Shore | 2,100 | four-year | coed |
| | | | |
| **MASSACHUSETTS** | | | |
| Roxbury Community College | 1,800 | two-year | coed |
| | | | |
| **MICHIGAN** | | | |
| Highland Park Community College | 2,335 | two-year | coed |
| Lewis College of Business | 346 | two-year | coed |
| Wayne County Community College | 11,123 | two-year | coed |
| | | | |
| **MISSISSIPPI** | | | |
| Alcorn State University | 3,526 | four-year | coed |
| Coahoma Community College | 1,373 | two-year | coed |
| Hinds Community College | 934 | two-year | coed |
| Jackson State University | 6,203 | four-year | coed |
| Mary Holmes Community College | 745 | two-year | coed |
| Mississippi Valley State University | 1,691 | four-year | coed |
| Rust College | 1,129 | four-year | coed |
| Tougaloo College | 1,003 | four-year | coed |
| | | | |
| **MISSOURI** | | | |
| Harris-Stowe State College | 1,881 | four-year | coed |

| ESTIMATED TOTAL COST PER YEAR | INCOMING FRESHMAN AVERAGE GPA | STUDENT/ TEACHER RATIO | LEVEL OF SELECTIVITY |
|---|---|---|---|
| $1,455 | 2.0 | 17:1 | noncompetitive |
| $10,950 | 2.78 | 16:1 | moderately competitive |
| $4,595 | 2.49 | 20:1 | slightly competitive |
| $5,483 | n/a | 25:1 | moderately competitive |
| $8,280 | n/a | 18:1 | moderately competitive |
| $3,930 | n/a | 10:1 | noncompetitive |
| $6,731 | 2.4 | 19:1 | slightly competitive |
| $2,080 | n/a | 25:1 | noncompetitive |
| $1,620 | n/a | 21:1 | noncompetitive |
| $2,875 | n/a | 13:1 | noncompetitive |
| $1,639 | n/a | 25:1 | noncompetitive |
| $2,762 | 2.495 | 20:1 | slightly competitive |
| $2,962 | n/a | 22:1 | noncompetitive |
| $3,367 | n/a | 19:1 | noncompetitive |
| $5,621 | n/a | 16:1 | slightly competitive |
| $8,300 | 2.495 | 20:1 | noncompetitive |
| $4,814 | n/a | 18:1 | slightly competitive |
| $6,100 | 2.5 | 18:1 | slightly competitive |
| $6,810 | 2.50 | 19:1 | slightly competitive |
| $2,253 | n/a | 18:1 | slightly competitive |

# SCHOOLS-AT-A-GLANCE

| UNIVERSITY OR COLLEGE NAME | TOTAL ENROLLMENT | 4-YEAR, 2-YEAR OR PROFESSIONAL | COED OR SINGLE SEX |
|---|---|---|---|
| **MISSOURI** | | | |
| Lincoln University (MO) | 4,101 | four-year | coed |
| | | | |
| **NEW YORK** | | | |
| LaGuardia Community College | 9,000 | two-year | coed |
| Medgar Evers College | 4,400 | four-year | coed |
| New York City Technical College | 10,426 | two-year | coed |
| | | | |
| **NORTH CAROLINA** | | | |
| Barber-Scotia College | 708 | four-year | coed |
| Bennett College | 568 | four-year | all-female |
| Elizabeth City State University | 1,762 | four-year | coed |
| Fayetteville State University | 3,903 | four-year | coed |
| Johnson C. Smith University | 1,256 | four-year | coed |
| Livingstone College | 654 | four-year | coed |
| North Carolina Agricultural & Technical State University | 7,119 | four-year | coed |
| North Carolina Central University | 5,385 | four-year | coed |
| Saint Augustine's College | 1,900 | four-year | coed |
| Shaw University | 2,149 | four-year | coed |
| Winston-Salem State University | 2,655 | four-year | coed |
| | | | |
| **OHIO** | | | |
| Central State University | 3,913 | four-year | coed |
| Cuyahoga Community College | 6,200 | two-year | coed |
| Wilberforce University | 758 | four-year | coed |
| | | | |
| **OKLAHOMA** | | | |
| Langston University | 3,323 | four-year | coed |
| | | | |
| **PENNSYLVANIA** | | | |
| Cheyney University of Pennsylvania | 1,607 | four-year | coed |

| ESTIMATED TOTAL COST PER YEAR | INCOMING FRESHMAN AVERAGE GPA | STUDENT/ TEACHER RATIO | LEVEL OF SELECTIVITY |
|---|---|---|---|
| $4,885 | n/a | 18:1 | noncompetitive |
| $2,704 | n/a | 18:1 | noncompetitive |
| $1,960 | n/a | 19:1 | noncompetitive |
| $1,600 | n/a | 10:1 | slightly competitive |
| $7,212 | 2.5 | 12:1 | noncompetitive |
| $8,924 | n/a | 10:1 | slightly competitive |
| $4,172 | 2.68 | 15:1 | noncompetitive |
| $4,125 | 2.85 | 18:1 | slightly competitive |
| $8,922 | n/a | 15:1 | slightly competitive |
| $9,100 | n/a | 15:1 | slightly competitive |
| $4,560 | n/a | 14:1 | moderately competitive |
| $5,119 | n/a | 13.5:1 | slightly competitive |
| $8,200 | n/a | 16:1 | slightly competitive |
| $9,146 | n/a | 16:1 | slightly competitive |
| $4,641 | 2.56 | 15:1 | slightly competitive |
| $7,493 | n/a | 21:1 | noncompetitive |
| $1,782 | n/a | 14:1 | noncompetitive |
| $10,838 | 2.5 | 20:1 | slightly competitive |
| $3,850 | n/a | 24:1 | noncompetitive |
| $6,813 | n/a | 16:1 | slightly competitive |

# SCHOOLS-AT-A-GLANCE

| UNIVERSITY OR COLLEGE NAME | TOTAL ENROLLMENT | 4-YEAR, 2-YEAR OR PROFESSIONAL | COED OR SINGLE SEX |
|---|---|---|---|
| **PENNSYLVANIA** | | | |
| Lincoln University of Pennsylvania | 1,458 | four-year | coed |
| | | | |
| **SOUTH CAROLINA** | | | |
| Allen University | 223 | four-year | coed |
| Benedict College | 1,469 | four-year | coed |
| Claflin College | 900 | four-year | coed |
| Clinton Junior College | 200 | two-year | coed |
| Denmark Technical College | 725 | two-year | coed |
| Morris College | 792 | four-year | coed |
| South Carolina State University | 5,145 | four-year | coed |
| Voorhees College | 600 | four-year | coed |
| | | | |
| **TENNESSEE** | | | |
| Fisk University | 867 | four-year | coed |
| Knoxville College | 1,200 | four-year | coed |
| Lane College | 562 | four-year | coed |
| LeMoyne-Owen College | 1,297 | four-year | coed |
| Meharry Medical College | 867 | professional | coed |
| Tennessee State University | 7,500 | four-year | coed |
| | | | |
| **TEXAS** | | | |
| Huston-Tillotson College | 536 | four-year | coed |
| Jarvis Christian College | 592 | four-year | coed |
| Paul Quinn College | 517 | four-year | coed |
| Prairie View Agricultural & Mechanical University | 5,590 | four-year | coed |
| Southwestern Christian College | 244 | four-year | coed |
| Texas College | 400 | four-year | coed |
| Texas Southern University | 10,777 | four-year | coed |
| Wiley College | 406 | four-year | coed |

| ESTIMATED TOTAL COST PER YEAR | INCOMING FRESHMAN AVERAGE GPA | STUDENT/ TEACHER RATIO | LEVEL OF SELECTIVITY |
|---|---|---|---|
| $6,702 | 2.50 | 15:1 | moderately competitive |
| $8,902 | n/a | 12:1 | noncompetitive |
| $7,776 | n/a | 17:1 | slightly competitive |
| $7,260 | n/a | 14:1 | moderately competitive |
| $3,710 | n/a | 17:1 | noncompetitive |
| $3,914 | n/a | 16:1 | noncompetitive |
| $7,170 | n/a | 14:1 | noncompetitive |
| $5,411 | 2.50 | 19:1 | slightly competitive |
| $6,628 | n/a | 15:1 | moderately competitive |
| $9,415 | n/a | 14:1 | slightly competitive |
| $8,595 | n/a | n/a | noncompetitive |
| $7,460 | n/a | 14:1 | slightly competitive |
| $6,825 | n/a | 18:1 | noncompetitive |
| $15,906 | n/a | 6:1 | competitive |
| $4,633 | 2.50 | 25:1 | moderately competitive |
| $8,639 | 2.50 | 13:1 | slightly competitive |
| $7,395 | 2.85 | 14:1 | noncompetitive |
| $6,275 | n/a | 12:1 | noncompetitive |
| $2,626 | 2.50 | 20:1 | slightly competitive |
| $6,093 | n/a | 10:1 | noncompetitive |
| $7,225 | n/a | 16:1 | noncompetitive |
| $4,985 | 2.50 | 18:1 | slightly competitive |
| $6,494 | 2.49 | 15:1 | noncompetitive |

# SCHOOLS-AT-A-GLANCE

| UNIVERSITY OR COLLEGE NAME | TOTAL ENROLLMENT | 4-YEAR, 2-YEAR OR PROFESSIONAL | COED OR SINGLE SEX |
|---|---|---|---|
| **VIRGIN ISLANDS** | | | |
| University of the Virgin Islands | 2,176 | four-year | coed |
| **VIRGINIA** | | | |
| Hampton University | 5,161 | four-year | coed |
| Norfolk State University | 8,624 | four-year | coed |
| Saint Paul's College | 750 | four-year | coed |
| Virginia Seminary | 40 | four-year | coed |
| Virginia State University | 4,585 | four-year | coed |
| Virginia Union University | 1,511 | four-year | coed |
| **WASHINGTON, DISTRICT OF COLUMBIA** | | | |
| Howard University | 11,222 | four-year | coed |
| Howard University School of Law | 380 | three-year | coed |
| University of the District of Columbia | 11,153 | four-year | coed |
| **WEST VIRGINIA** | | | |
| Bluefield State College | 2,907 | four-year | coed |
| West Virginia State College | 4,986 | four-year | coed |

| ESTIMATED TOTAL COST PER YEAR | INCOMING FRESHMAN AVERAGE GPA | STUDENT/ TEACHER RATIO | LEVEL OF SELECTIVITY |
|---|---|---|---|
| $6,415 | n/a | 15:1 | slightly competitive |
| $10,626 | 2.3 | 18:1 | competitive |
| $6,655 | n/a | 22:1 | noncompetitive |
| $9,218 | n/a | 17:1 | slightly competitive |
| $5,145 | n/a | n/a | noncompetitive |
| $8,749 | n/a | 18:1 | noncompetitive |
| $10,152 | 2.3 | 16:1 | slightly competitive |
| $11,300 | n/a | 15:1 | competitive |
| $12,730 | n/a | 8:1 | competitive |
| $1,589 | n/a | 10:1 | noncompetitive |
| $2,351 | 2.5 | 25:1 | noncompetitive |
| $2,906 | 2.0 | 21:1 | slightly competitive |

# Bibliography

# Bibliography

## Compiled by Donald Franklin Joyce

Included in this selected bibliography are titles which were published between 1990 and 1992, reviewed favorably in the reviewing media, and judged to be significant contributions to the study of black history and culture in the United States and in Africa. The titles are arranged under two major divisions: "Africana" and "African Americana." Within these two divisions titles are arranged alphabetically by author under categories indicative of their subject matter.

## ◆ AFRICANA

### Agriculture

Barnett, Tony, and Abbas Abdelkarim. *Sudan: The Gezira Scheme and Agricultural Transition*. London: Frank Cass, 1991.

Freeman, Donald B. *A City of Farmers: Informal Urban Agriculture in the Open Spaces of Nairobi, Kenya*. Montreal: McGill-Queen's University Press, 1991.

Gyllstrom, Bjorn. *State Administrative Rural Change: Agricultural Cooperatives in Rural Kenya*. New York: Routledge, 1991.

Kidane, Mengisteab. *Ethiopia: Failure of Land Reform and Agricultural Crisis*. Westport, CT: Greenwood Press, 1990.

### Apartheid

Burman, Sandra, and Pamela Reynolds, eds. *Growing Up In a Divided Society*. With forewords by Archbishop Desmond Tutu and Robert Coles. Evanston, IL: Northwestern University Press, 1992.

Cohen, Robin, Yvonne G. Muthien, and Abebe Zegeye, eds. *Repression and Resistance: Inside Accounts of Apartheid*. London; New York: Hans Zell Publishers, 1990.

Davis, R. Hunt, ed. *Apartheid Unravels*. Gainesville, FL: University of Florida Presses, 1991.

Dumor, E.K. *Ghana, OAU and Southern Africa: An African Response to Apartheid*. Accra: Ghana University Press, 1991.

Ellis, Stephen. *Comrades Against Apartheid: The ANC and the South African Communist Party in Exile*. London: James Currey/Indiana University Press, 1992.

Ellman, Stephen. *In a Time of Trouble: Law and Liberty in South Africa's State of Emergency*. New York: Oxford University Press, 1992.

Giliomee, Herman, and Laurence Schlemmer. *From Apartheid to Nation-Building*. Capetown, S.A.: Oxford University Press, 1990.

Grundy, Kenneth. *South Africa: Domestic Crisis and Global Challenge*. Boulder, CO: Westview Press, 1991.

Heard, Anthony Hazlett. *The Cape of Storms: A Personal History of the Crisis in South Africa*. Fayetteville: University of Arkansas Press, 1990.

Holland, Heidi. *The Struggle: A History of the African National Congress*. New York: Braziller, 1990.

Hull, Richard W. *American Enterprise in South Africa: Historical Dimensions of Engagement and Disengagement*. New York: New York University Press, 1990.

Human Rights Watch. *The Killings of South Africa: The Role of the Security Forces and the Response of the State*. New York: Human Rights Watch, 1991.

Johns, Sheridan, and R. Hunt Davis, eds. *Mandela, Tambo and the African National Congress: The Struggle Against Apartheid, 1948-1990: A Documentary Survey*. New York: Oxford University Press, 1991.

Kalley, Jacqueline A. *South Africa Road to Change, 1987-1990*. Westport, CT: Greenwood Press, 1991.

Lemon, Anthony, ed. *Homes Apart: South Africa's Segregated Cities*. Bloomington: Indiana University Press, 1991.

Maasdorp, Gavin, and Alan Whiteside, eds. *Towards a Post-Apartheid Future: Political and Economic Relations in South Africa*. New York: St. Martin's Press, 1992.

Mallaby, Sebastian. *After Apartheid: The Future of South Africa*. New York: Times Books, 1992.

Moss, Rose. *Shouting at the Crocodile: Popo Molefe, Patrick Lekota, and the Freeing of South Africa*. Boston: Beacon Press, 1990. (Dist. by Farrar, Strauss, Giroux)

Price, Robert M. *The Apartheid State in Crisis: Political Transformation in South Africa, 1975-1990*. New York: Oxford University Press, 1991.

Segal, Ronald. *The Black Diaspora: Five Centuries of the Black Experience Outside Africa*. New York: Farrar, Straus and Giroux, 1995.

Shepherd, George W., ed. *Effective Sanctions on South Africa: The Cutting Edge of Economic Intervention*. Westport, CT: Greenwood Press, 1991.

Sparks, Allister. *The Mind of South Africa*. New York: Knopf, 1990.

Spink, Kathryn. *Black Sash: The Beginning of a Bridge in South Africa*. With a foreword by Archbishop Desmond Tutu.

London: Methuen, 1991.

## Art

Courtney-Clarke, Margaret. *African Canvas: The Art of West African Women*. New York: Rizzoli, 1990.

Okediji, Mayo, ed. *Principles of "Traditional" African Art*. Ile Ife: Bard Book, 1992 (Dist. by Avon).

Smithsonian Institution. Libraries. National Museum of African Art Branch. *Catalog of the Library of the National Museum of African Art Branch of the Smithsonian Library*. Boston: G.K. Hall, 1991.

Vogel, Susan. *Africa Explores: Twentieth Century African Art*. New York: The Center for African Art, 1991.

Williams College Museum of Art. *Assuming the Guise: African Masks Considered and Reconsidered*. Williamstown, MA: Williams College Museum of Art, 1991.

Williamson, Sue. *Resistance Art in South Africa*. New York: St. Martin's Press, 1990.

## Autobiography and Biography

Appiah, Joseph. *Joe Appiah: The Autobiography of an African Patriot*. New York: Praeger, 1990.

Bunche, Ralph Johnson. *An African American in South Africa: The Travel Notes of Ralph J. Bunche, 28 September 1937 - 1 January 1938*. Edited by Roger R. Edgar. Athens: Ohio University Press, 1992.

Gastrow, Shelagh, ed., *Who's Who in South African Politics*. 3rd ed., London: Hans Zell Publishers, 1990.

Glickman, Harvey, ed., *Political Leaders of Contemporary Africa South of the Sahara: A Biographical Dictionary*. Westport, CT: Greenwood Press, 1992.

Harris, Eddy L. *Native Stranger: A Black American's Journey into the Heart of Africa*. New York: Simon & Schuster, 1992.

Isert, Paul Erdmann. *Letters on West Africa: Paul Erdmann Isert's Journey to Guinea and the Caribbean Islands in Columbia (1788)*. Translated by Selena Axelrod Winsnes. New York: Oxford University Press, 1992.

Lockot, Hans Wilhelm. *The Mission: The Life, Reign and Character of Haile Selassie I*. New York: St. Martin's Press, 1990.

Mashinini, Emma. *Strikes Have Followed Me All My Life: A South African Autobiography*. New York: Routledge, 1991.

Meer, Fatima. *Higher Than Hope: The Authorized Biography of Nelson Mandela*. New York: Harper & Row, 1990.

Mendelsohn, Richard. *Sammy Marks: the Uncrowned King of the Transvaal*. Athens: Ohio University Press, 1991.

Modisan, Blake. *Blame Me on History*. New York: Simon & Schuster, 1990.

Nkrumah, Kwame. *Kwame Nkrumah: The Conakry Years: His Life and Letters*. Compiled by June Milne. New York: Zed Books, 1991. (Dist. by Humanities Press)

Rake, Alan. *Who's Who in Africa: Leaders for the 1990s*. Metuchen, NJ: Scarecrow, 1992.

Rodney, Walter. *Walter Rodney Speaks: The Making of an African Intellectual*. With introduction by Robert Hill. Foreword by Howard Dodson. Trenton, NJ: Africa World Press, 1990.

Vaillant, Janet G. *Black, French and African: A Life of Leopold Sedar Senghor*. Cambridge: Harvard University Press, 1990.

Vige, Randolph, ed. *A Gesture of Belong: Letters from Bessie Head, 1965-1979*. Portsmouth, NH: Heinemann, 1991.

Wiseman, John A. *Political Leaders in Black Africa: A Biographical Dictionary of the Major Politicians Since Independence.* Brookfield, VT: Gower Publishing Co., 1991.

## Economics

Blumenfield, Jesmond. *Economic Interdependence in Southern Africa: From Conflict to Cooperation.* New York: Printer/St. Martin's Press, 1991.

Chole, Eschetu, ed. *Food Crisis in Africa: Policy and Management Issues.* New Delhi: Vikas Publishing House, 1990. (Dist. by Advent House)

Claessen, Henri J.M., and Pieter van de Velde, eds. *Early State Economies.* New Brunswick, NJ: Transaction Publishers, 1991.

Cock, Jacklyn, ed. *Going Green: People, Politics and the Environment in South Africa.* New York: Oxford University Press, 1991.

Crockcroft, Laurence. *Africa's Way: A Journey from the Past.* UK: Tauris, 1990. (Dist. by St. Martin's Press)

Crush, Jonathan, Alan Jeeves, and Donald Yudelman *Africa's Labor Empire: A History of Black Migrancy to the Gold Mines.* Boulder, CO: Westview Press/D. Philip, 1991.

Edington, J.A.S. *Rubber in West Africa.* Anaheim, CA: Collings, 1991.

Henige, David, and T.C. McCaskie, eds. *West African Economic and Social History: Studies in Memory of Marion Johnson.* Madison: African Studies Program, University of Wisconsin, 1990.

Hodd, Michael. *The Economies of Africa: Geography, Population, History, Stability, Performance, Forecasts.* Boston: G. K. Hall, 1991.

Mahjoub, Azzam, ed. *Adjustment or Delinking? The African Experience.* London: Zed Press, 1990. (Dist. by Humanities Press)

Martin, Matthew. *The Crumbling Facade of African Debt Negotiations: No Winners.* New York: St. Martin's Press, 1991.

Mingst, Karen A. *Politics and the African Development Bank.* Lexington: University of Kentucky Press, 1990.

Nyango'oro, Julius, and Timothy Shaw, eds. *Beyond Structural Adjustment in Africa: The Political Economy of Sustainable and Democratic Development.* New York: Praeger, 1992.

Okolo, Julius Emeka, and Stephen Wright, eds. *West African Regional Cooperation and Development.* Boulder, CO: Westview Press, 1990.

Peckett, James, and Hans Singer, eds. *Towards Economic Recovery in Sub-Saharan Africa: Essays in Honor of Robert Gardner.* New York: Routledge, 1991.

Pradervand, Pierre. *Listening to Africa: Developing Africa from the Grassroots.* New York: Praeger, 1990.

Pryor, Frederic L. *The Political Economy of Poverty, Equity and Growth: Malawi and Madagascar.* New York: Oxford University for the World Bank, 1990.

Rau, Bill. *From Feast to Famine: Official Cures and Grassroots Remedies to Africa's Food Crisis.* New York: Zed Books, 1991 (Dist. by Humanities Press).

Riddell, Roger C. *Manufacturing Africa: Performance and Prospects of Seven Countries in Sub-Saharan Africa.* Portsmouth, NH: Heinemann, 1990.

Sarhof, Joseph A. *Hydropower Development in West Africa: A Study in Resource Development.* New York: P. Lang, 1990.

Siddle, David, and Ken Swindell. *Rural Change in Tropical Africa: From Colonies to Nation-States.* Cambridge, MA: Basil Blackwell, 1990.

Stewart, Frances, ed. *Alternative Development Strategies in Sub-Saharan Africa.* New York: St. Martin's Press, 1992.

## Education

King, Kenneth, ed., *Botswana: Education, Culture and Politics.* Edinburgh: University of Edinburgh Press, 1990.

Mungazi, Dickson A. *Colonial Education for Africana: George Starks in Zimbabwe.* Westport, CT: Praeger, 1991.

Njobe, M.W. *Education for Liberation.* Johannesburg: Skotaville, 1990.

Okeem, E.O., ed. *Education in Africa: Search for Realistic Alternatives.* London: Institute for African Alternatives, 1990.

Okunor, Shiame. *Politics, Misunderstandings, Misconceptions: The History of Colonial Universities.* New York: P. Lang, 1991.

## Folklore and Folk Culture

Berry, Jack, comp. and trans. *West African Folktales.* Edited with introduction by Richard Spears. Evanston, IL: Northwestern University Press, 1991.

Gunter, Liz, and Mafika Gwala, eds. and trans., *Mushal: Zula*

*Popular Praises.* East Lansing: Michigan State University Press, 1991.

McDermott, Gerald. *Zomo the Rabbit: A Trickster Tale from West Africa.* San Diego: Harcourt Brace Jovanovich, 1992.

Mohindra, Kamlesh. *Folk Tales of West Africa.* New Delhi: Sterling Pubs., 1991. (Dist. by APT Books)

Njoku, John E. Eberegbulaum. *The Igbos of Nigeria: Ancient Rites, Changes and Survival.* Lewiston, NY: Edwin Mellen Press, 1990.

Schipper, Mineke. *Source of All Evil: African Proverbs and Sayings on Women.* Chicago: Ivan R. Dee, 1991.

Smith, Alexander McCall. *Children of Wax: African Folk Tales.* New York: Interlink Books, 1991.

Ugorji, Okechukwu K. *The Adventures of Torti: Tales from West Africa.* Trenton, NJ: Africa World Press, 1991.

## General Reference

Asante, Molafi Keto *The Book of African Names.* Trenton, NJ: Africa World Press, 1991.

Blackhurst, Hector, comp. *Africa Bibliography 1989.* Manchester, UK: Manchester University Press,

1991. (Dist. by St. Martin's Press, Inc.)

Fredland, Richard. *A Guide to African International Organizations.* New York: Hans Sell Publishers, 1991.

Morrison, Donald George, Robert Cameron Mitchell, and John Naber Paden. *Black Africa: A Comparative Handbook.* 2nd ed., New York: Paragon House/Irvington, 1990.

Moss, Joyce, and George Wilson. *Peoples of the World: Africans South of the Sahara.* Detroit: Gale Research Inc., 1991.

Sarfoh, Joseph A. *Energy in the Development of West Africa: A Selected Annotated Bibliography.* New York: Greenwood Press, 1991.

Thurston, Anne. *Guide to Archives and Manuscripts Relating to Kenya and East Africa in the United Kingdom.* New York: Hans Zell Publishers, 1991.

Zell, Hans M. *The African Studies Companion: A Resources Guide and Directory.* Providence, NJ: Hans Zell Publishers, 1990.

## Government and Politics

Bowman, Larry W. *Mauritius: Democracy and Development in the Indian Ocean.* Boulder, CO: Westview Press, 1991.

Charlick, Robert B. *Niger: Personal Rule and Survival in the Sahel.* Boulder, CO: Westview Press, 1991.

Clingman, Stephen, ed. *Regions and Repertoires: Topics in South African Politics and Culture.* Johannesburg: Raven Press, 1991. (Dist. by Ohio University Press.)

Clough, Marshall S. *Fighting Two Sides: Kenyan Chiefs and Politicians, 1918-1940.* Niwot, CO: University Press of Colorado, 1990.

Cowell, Alan. *Killing the Wizards: Wars of Power and Freedom from Zaire to South Africa.* New York: Simon & Schuster, 1992.

Deng, Frances M., and I. William Zartman, eds. *Conflict Resolution in Africa.* Washington: Brookings Institution, 1991.

Forrest, Joshua B. *Guinea-Bissau: Power, Conflict and Renewal in a West African Nation.* Boulder, CO: Westview Press, 1992.

Gambari, I.A. *Political and Comparative Dimensions of Regional Integration: The Case of ECOWAS.* New York: The Humanities Press, 1991.

Hanlon, Joseph. *Mozambique: Who Calls the Shots.* Bloomington: Indiana University Press, 1991.

Hansen, Holger Bernt, ed. *Changing Uganda: The Dilemmas of Structural Adjustment and Revolutionary Change.* Athens: Ohio University Press, 1991.

Henze, Paul B. *The Horn of Africa: From War to Peace.* New York: St. Martin's Press, 1991.

Herbst, Jeffrey. *State Politics in Zimbabwe.* Berkeley: University of California, 1990.

Hughes, Arnold, ed. *The Gambia: Studies in Society and Politics.* Birmingham, UK: University of Birmingham, Centre for African Studies, 1991.

Ingham, Kenneth. *Politics in Modern Africa: The Uneven Tribal Dimension.* New York: Routledge, 1990.

Johnson, Willard R. *West African Governments and Volunteer Development Organizations: Priorities for Partnerships.* Lanham, MD: University Press of America, 1990.

Khalid, Mansour. *The Government They Deserve: The Role of the Elite in Sudan's Political Evolution.* New York: Kegan Paul International, 1990.

Kriger, Norma J. *Zimbabwe's Guerrilla War: Peasant Voices.* New York: Cambridge University Press, 1991.

Machobane, L.B.B.J. *Government and Change in Lesotho, 1800-1966: A Study of Political Institutions.* New York: Macmillan, 1990.

Moss, Glenn, and Ingrid Obery, eds. and comps. *South Africa Contemporary Analysis.* London: Hans Zell Publishers, 1990.

Nyang'oro, Julius E., and Timothy M. Shaw, eds. *Beyond Structural Adjustment in Africa: The Political*

*Economy of Sustainable and Democratic Development.* New York: Praeger, 1992.

O'Brien, Donal B. Cruise, John Dunn, and Richard Rathbone, eds. *Contemporary West African States.* New York: Cambridge University Press, 1990.

Ogunsanwo, Alaba. *The Transformation of Nigeria: Scenarios and Metaphors.* Lagos: University of Lagos Press, 1991.

Reyna, Stephen P. *Wars Without End: The Political Economy of a Precolonial African State.* Hanover, NH: University Press of New England, 1990.

Riley, Eileen. *Major Political Events in South Africa, 1948-1990.* New York: Facts on File, 1991.

Schlosser, Dirk Berg, and Rainer Siegler. *Political Stability and Development: A Comparative Analysis of Kenya, Tanzania and Uganda.* Boulder, CO: Lynne Rienner, 1990.

Sklar, Richard L., and C. S. Whitaker. *African Politics and Problems in Development.* Boulder, CO: Lynne Rienner, 1991.

Tareke, Gebru. *Ethiopia, Power and Protest: Peasant Revolts in the Twentieth Century.* New York: Cambridge University Press, 1991.

Vines, Alex. *Renamo: Terrorism in Mozambique.* Bloomington: Indiana University Press, 1991.

Wunsch, James S., and Dele Olowu, eds. *The Failure of the Centralized State: Institutions and Self-Governance in Africa.* Boulder, CO: Westview Press, 1990.

Wylie, Diana. *A Little God: The Twilight of Patriarchy in a Southern Africa Chiefdom.* Hanover, NH: University Press of New England, 1990.

## Health

Baron, Vida C. *African Power: Secrets of the Ancient Ibo Tribe.* San Diego, Barez Publishing Co., 1992.

Falala, Toyin, ed. *The Political Economy of Health in Africa.* Athens: Ohio University for International Studies/Ohio University Press, 1992.

King, Richard D. *African Origin of Biological Psychiatry.* Germantown, TN: Seymour-Smith, Inc., 1990.

Turner, Edith L.B., et al. *Experiencing Ritual: A New Interpretation of African Healing.* Philadelphia: University of Pennsylvania Press, 1992.

Williams, A. Olufemi. *AIDS: An African Perspective.* Boca Rotan, FL: CRC Press, 1992.

Wolff, James, et. al. *Beyond Clinic Walls, Case Studies in Community-Based Distribution.* West Hartford, CT: Kumarian Press, 1990.

## History

Ayittey, George B.N. *Indigenous African Institutions.* Ardsley-on-Hudson, NY: Transnational Publishers, 1991.

Banbera, Tayiru. *A State of Intrigue: The Epic of Bamana Segu According to Tayiru Banbera.* Edited by David Conrad; transcribed and translated with the assistance of Soumaila Diakit'e. Oxford, UK: Oxford University Press, 1990.

Cammack, Diana. *The Rand at War, 1899-1902: The Witwatersrand and the Anglo-Boer War.* Berkeley: University of California Press, 1990.

Collelo, Thomas. *Angola: A Country Study* 3rd ed., Washington, DC: Government Printing Office, 1991.

Collins, Robert O. *Western African History.* New York: W. Wiener, 1990.

Crais, Clifton C. *White Supremacy and Black Resistance in Pre-Industrial South Africa: The Making of the Colonial Order in the Eastern Cape, 1770-1865.* Cambridge, UK: Cambridge University Press, 1992.

Digre, Brian. *Imperialism's New Clothes: The Repartition of Tropical Africa, 1914-1919.* New York: P. Lang, 1990.

Diop, Cheikh Anta. *Civilization or Barbarism: An Authentic Anthropology.* Translated by Yaa-Lengi Meema Ngemi; edited by Harold J. Salemson and Marjolijn de Jager. Brooklyn: Lawrence Hill Books, 1991.

Echenberg, Myron J. *Colonial Conscripts: The Tirailleurs S'en'egalais in French West Africa, 1857-1960.* Portsmouth, NH: Heinemann, 1991.

Friedman, Kajsa Ekholm. *Catastrophe and Creation: The Transformation of an African Culture.* Philadelphia: Hardwood Academic Publishers, 1991.

Gann, L.H., and Pete Duignan. *Hope for Africa.* Stanford, CA: Stanford University Press, 1991.

Gordon, April, ed. *Understanding Contemporary Africa.* Boulder, CO: Lynne Reinner Publishers, 1992.

Hair, P.E.H. *Black Africa in Time Perspective: Four Talks on Wide Historical Themes.* Liverpool, UK: Liverpool University Press, 1990. (Dist. by University of Pennsylvania Press).

Hair, P.E.H. *English Seamen and Traders in Guinea, 1553-1565: The New Evidence of their Wills.* Lewiston, NY: E. Mellen Press, 1992.

Hansen, Emmanuel. *Ghana Under Rawlings: Early Years.* Lagos: Malthouse Press, 1991.

Hassen, Mohammed. *The Oromo of Ethiopia: A History.* New York: Cambridge University Press, 1990.

Hudson, Peter. *Two Rivers: In the Footsteps of Mungo Park.* London: Chapmans Publishers, 1991.

Human Rights Watch. *Evil Days: Thirty Years of War and Famine in Ethiopia.* New York: Human Rights Watch, 1990.

Ki-Zerbo, J., ed. UNESCO General History of Africa, Vol. 1: Methodology and African Prehistory. Berkeley: University of California Press, 1990.

Lamphear, John. *The Scattering Time: Turkans Responses to Colonial Time.* New York: Oxford University Press, 1992.

Law, Robin. *The Slave Coast of West Africa, 1550-1750: The Impact of the Atlantic Slave Trade on African Society.* New York: Oxford University Press, 1991.

Manning, Patrick. *Slavery and African Life: Occidental, Oriental and African Slave Trades.* New York: Cambridge University Press, 1990.

Metaferia, Getchew. *The Ethiopian Revolution of 1974 and the Exodus of Ethiopia's Trained Human Resources.* Lewiston, NY: Edwin Mellen Press, 1991.

Mokhtar, G., ed. *UNESCO General History of Africa, Vol. II: Ancient History of Africa.* Berkeley: University of California Press, 1990.

Mooncraft, Paul L. *African Nemesis: War and Revolution in Southern Africa (1945-2010).* Riverside, NJ: Pergamon Press, 1990.

Morton, Fred. *Children of Ham: Freed Slaves and Fugitive Slaves on the Kenya Coast, 1873-1907.* Boulder, CO: Westview, 1990.

Mostert, Noel. *Frontiers: The Epic of South Africa's Creation and the Tragedy of the Xhosa People.* New York: Knopf, 1992.

Munford, Clarence J. *The Black Ordeal of Slavery and Slave Trading in the French West Indies, 1625-1715.* Lewiston, NY: Edwin Mellen Press, 1991.

Nasson, Bill. *Abraham Esau's War: A Black South African War in the Cape, 1899-1902.* New York: Cambridge University Press, 1991.

Obasanjo, Olusegun, and Hans d'Orville, eds. *The Impact of Europe in 1992 on West Africa.* New York: C. Russak, 1990.

Ochieng, William, ed. *Themes in Kenyan History.* Nairobi: Heinmann Kenya, 1990.

Ogot, B.A., ed. *Africa from the Sixteenth to the Eighteenth Century.* Berkeley: University of California Press, 1992.

Remmer, Douglas, ed. *Africa Thirty Years Ago.* Portsmouth, NH: Heinemann, 1991.

Shillington, Kevin. *History of Africa.* New York: St. Martin's Press, 1990.

Solow, Barbara L., ed. *Slavery and the Rise of the Atlantic System.* Cambridge, UK; New York: Cambridge University Press, 1991.

Stauton, Irene, comp. and ed. *Mothers of the Revolution: The War Experiences of Thirty Zimbabwean Women.* Bloomington: Indiana University Press, 1991.

Stedman, Stephen John. *Peacemaking in the Civil War: International Mediation in Zimbabwe, 1974-1980.* Boulder, CO: Lynne Rienner, 1991.

Temperley, Howard. *White Dreams, Black Africa: The Anti-Slavery Expedition to the River Niger, 1841-42.* New Haven: Yale University Press, 1991.

Thompson, Leonard. *A History of South Africa.* New Haven: Yale University Press, 1990.

Wyse, Akintola J.G., and H.C. Bankhole-Bight. *Politics in Colonial Sierra Leone, 1919-1958.* New York: Cambridge University Press, 1991.

Yarak, Larry W. *Asante and the Dutch, 1744-1873.* New York: Oxford University Press, 1990.

Young, John. *They Fell Like Stones: Battles and Casualties of the Zulu War, 1879.* Novato, CA: Presidio Press, 1991.

## International Relations

Kent, John. *The Internationalization of Colonialism: Britain, France and Black Africa.* New York: Oxford University Press, 1992.

Russell, Sharon Stanton, Karen Jacobsen, and William Deane Stanley. *International Migration and Development in Sub-Sahara Africa.* Washington, DC: The World Bank, 1991.

Thompson, Joseph E. *American Policy and African Famine: The Nigeria-Biafra War, 1966-1970.* New York: Greenwood Press, 1970.

Winros, Gareth M. *The Foreign Policy of GDR in Africa.* Cambridge, UK: Cambridge University Press, 1991.

## Language and Literature

Abraham, Cecils ed. *The Tragic Life: Bessie Head and Literature in South Africa.* Trenton, NJ: Africa World Press, 1990.

Achebe, Chinua. *Hopes and Impediments: Selected Essays.* New York: Doubleday, 1990.

Bjornson, Richard. *The African Quest for Freedom and Identity: Cameroonian Writing and the National Experience.* Bloomington: Indiana University Press, 1991.

Dram'e, Kandioura. *The Novel as Transformation Myth: A Study of the Novels of Mongo Beti and Ngugi wa Thiongo.* Syracuse, NY: Syracuse University, 1990.

Dunton, Chris. *Make Man Talk True: Nigerian Drama in English Since 1970.* New York: Hans Zell Publishers, 1992.

Elimimian, Isaac Iraber. *Theme and Style in African Poetry.* Lewiston, NY: E. Mellen, 1991.

February, V.A. *Mind Your Colour: The Coloured Stereotype in South African Literature.* London and New York: Kegan Paul International, 1991. (Dist. by Routledge, Chapman & Hall, Inc.).

Gikandi, Simon. *Reading Chinua Achebe: Language and Ideology in Fiction.* Portsmouth, NH: Heinemann, 1991.

Gunner, Liz, ed., and trans. *Musho!: Zulu Popular Praises.* East Lansing: Michigan State University Press, 1991.

Hale, Thomas A. *Scribe, Griot and Novelist: Narrative Interpreters of the Songhay Empire Followed by the Epic of Askia Mohammed Recounted,* Gainesville, FL: University of Florida Press/Center for African Studies, 1990.

Harrow, Kenneth, ed., *Faces of Islam in African Literature.* Portsmouth, NH: Heinemann, 1991.

Harrow, Kenneth, Jonathan Ngate, and Clarissa Zimra, eds. *Crisscrossing Boundaries in African Literatures, 1986.* Washington, DC: Three Continents Press/African Literature

Association, 1991.

Ikonne, Chidi, Emelia Oko, and Peter Onwudinjo, eds. *African Literature and African Historical Experience.* New York: Heinemann, 1991.

Innes, Catherine Lynette. *Chinua Achebe.* New York: Cambridge University Press, 1990.

Innes, Catherine Lynette. *The Devil's Own Mirror: The Irishman and the African Modern Literature.* Washington, DC: Three Continents Press, 1990.

James, Adeola, ed., *In Their Own Voices: African Women Writers Talk.* Portsmouth, NH: Heinemann, 1990.

Jones, Eldred Durosimi, ed. *The Question of Language in African Literature Today: Borrowing and Carrying: A Review.* Trenton, NJ: Africa World Press, 1991.

Julien, Eileen. *African Novels and the Question of Orality.* Bloomington: Indiana University Press, 1992.

Lazarus, Neil. *Resistance in Postcolonial African Fiction.* New Haven, CT: Yale University Press, 1991.

Lindfors, Bernth. *Popular Literature in Africa.* Trenton, NJ: Africa World Press, 1991.

Liyong, Taban Lo. *Another Last Word.* New York: Heinemann, 1990.

Miller, Christopher L. *Theories of Africans: Franco-Phone Literature and Anthropology in Africa.* Chicago: University of Chicago Press, 1990.

Mortimer, Mildred. *Journey Through the French African Novel.* Portsmouth, NH: Heinemann, 1990.

Nethersole, Reingard, ed. *Emerging Literature.* New York: P. Lang, 1990.

Ngara, Emmanuel. *Ideology and Form in African Poetry: Implications for Communication.* Portsmouth, NH: Heinemann, 1990.

Obiechina, Emmanuel N. *Language and Theme: Essays on African Literature.* Washington, DC: Howard University Press, 1990.

Orisawayi, Dele, et. al., eds. *Literature and Black Aesthetics.* New York: Heinemann, 1990.

Owomoyela, Onjekan. *Visions and Revisions: Essays on African Literatures and Criticisms.* New York: P. Lang, 1991.

*Research in African Literatures: Critical Theory and African Literature.* Bloomington: Indiana University Press, 1990.

*Research in African Literature: Dictatorship and Oppression.* Bloomington: Indiana University Press, 1990.

Roscoe, Adrian A., and Hangson Msika. *The Quiet Chameleon: Modern Poetry from Central Africa.* New York: Hans Zell Publishers, 1992.

Scheub, Harold. *The African Storyteller: Stories from African Oral Traditions.* Dubuque, IA: Kendell/Hunt, 1991.

Schipper, Mineke. *Beyond the Boundaries: Text and Context in African Literature.* Chicago: Ivan R. Dee, 1990.

Sicherman, Carol. *Ngugi wa Thiong: A Source Book on Kenyan Literature and Resistance.* New York: Hans Zell Publishers, 1990.

Soyinka, Wole. *Myth, Literature, and the African World.* New York: Cambridge University Press, 1990.

Trump, Martin, ed. *Rendering Things Visible: Essays on South African Literary Culture.* Athens: Ohio University Press, 1991.

Wilentz, Gay Alden. *Binding Cultures: Black Women Writers in Africa and the Diaspora.* Bloomington: Indiana University Press, 1992.

Wylie, Hal, Dennis Brutus, and Juris Silenieks, eds. *African Literature, 1988: New Masks.* Washington, DC: Three Continents Press/The African Literature Association, 1990.

## Law, Law Enforcement, Civil and Human Rights

Ahire, Philip Terdo. *Imperial Policing: The Emergence and Role of the Police in Nigeria, 1860-1960*. Philadelphia: Open University Press, 1991.

Bazille, Susan, ed. *Putting Women on the Agenda*. Johannesburg, S.A.: Raven Press, 1991. (Dist. by Ohio University Press).

Braham, Peter, ed. *Racism and Antiracism: Inequalities in Opportunities and Policies*. Philadelphia: Sage/Open University Press, 1992.

Hansson, Desiree, and Dirk van Zyl Smit, eds. *Toward Justice? Crime and State Control in South Africa*. New York: Oxford University Press, 1990.

Mann, Kristin, ed. *Law in Colonial Africa*. Portsmouth, NH: Heinemann, 1991.

Shepherd, George W., and Mark O.G. Anikpo, eds. *Emerging Human Rights: The African Political Economy Concept*. Westport, CT: Greenwood Press, 1990.

## Media

Faringer, Gunilla L. *Press Freedom in Africa*. Westport, CT: Praeger, 1991.

Harden, Blaine. *Africa: Dispatches from a Fragile Continent*. London: Harper Collins, 1990.

Hawk, Beverly G., ed. *Africa's Media Image*. New York: Praeger, 1992.

Sturges, Paul, and Richard Neill. *The Quiet Struggle: Libraries and Information for Africa*. New York: Mansell, 1990.

## Music

Arom, Simha. *African Polyphony and Polyrhythm: Musical Structure and Methodology*. Translated by Martin Thom and Barbara Tucker. New York: Cambridge University Press, 1991.

Bender, Wolfgang. *Sweet Mother: Modern African Music*. Translated by Wolfgang Freis. Chicago: University of Chicago Press, 1991.

Collins, John. *West African Pop Roots*. Philadelphia: Temple University Press, 1992.

Gray, John. *African Music: A Bibliographic Guide to the Traditional Popular Art and Liturgical Music of Sub-Saharan Africa*. Westport, CT: Greenwood Press, 1991.

Lems-Dworkin, Carol. *African Music: A Pan-African Annotated Bibliography*. New York: Hans Zell Publishers, 1991.

Stewart, Gary. *Breakout: Profiles in African Rhythm*. Chicago: University of Chicago Press, 1992.

Waterman, Christopher Alan. *Juju: A Social History and Ethnography of an African Popular Music*. Chicago: University of Chicago Press, 1990.

## Pan-Africanism

Agyeman, Opoku. *Nkrumah's Ghana and Esat Africa: Pan-Africanism and African Interstate Relations*. Cranbury, NJ: Fairleigh Dickinson University Press, 1992.

Clarke, John H. *Africans at the Crossroads: Notes for an African World Revolution*. Trenton, NJ: Africa World Press, 1992.

Staniland, Martin. *American Intellectuals and African Nationalists, 1950-1970*. New Haven: Yale University Press, 1991.

## Performing Arts

Diawara, Manthia. *African Cinema: Politics and Culture*. Bloomington: Indiana University Press, 1992.

Erlman, Veit. *African Stars: Studies in Black South African Performance*. Chicago: University of Chicago Press, 1991.

Lee, Jacques K. *Sega: The Mauritius Folk Dance*. London: Nautilus Publishing Co., 1990.

Orkin, Martin. *Drama and the South African State*. Manchester, UK: Manchester University Press, 1991. (Dist. by St. Martin's Press)

## Religion and Philosophy

Dankwa, Nano O., III. *Christianity and African Traditional Beliefs*. Edited by John W. Branch. New York: Power of the World Publishing Co., 1990.

Felder, Cain Hope, ed. *Stony the Road We Trod: African American Biblical Interpretation*. Minneapolis: Fortress Press, 1991.

Gbadegesin, Segun. *African Philosophy: Traditional Yoruba Philosophy and Contemporary African Realities*. New York: Lang, 1991.

Gifford, Paul. *The New Crusaders: Christianity and the New Right in Southern Africa*. London: Pluto, 1991.

Gray, Richard. *Black Christians and White Missionaries*. New Haven: Yale University Press, 1991.

Oldfield, J.R. *Alexander Crummell (1819-1898) and the Creation of an African-American Church in Africa*. Lewiston, NY: Edwin Mellin Press, 1990.

Olupona, Jacob K. *African Traditional Religions in Contemporary Society.* New York: Paragon, 1991.

Oruka, H. O. *Trends in Contemporary African Philosophy.* Nairobi, Kenya: Shirikon Publishers, 1990.

Peek, Philip M., ed. *African Divination Systems: Ways of Knowing.* Bloomington: Indiana University Press, 1991.

Prozesky, Martin, ed. *Christianity Amidst Apartheid* New York: London, Macmillan, 1990.

Soyinka, Wole. *The Credo of Being and Nothingness.* Ibadan: Spectrum Books, 1990.

Vanderaa, Larry A. *A Survey of Christian Reformed World Missions and Churches in West Africa.* Grand Rapids, MI: Christian Reformed World Missions, 1991.

## Sociology and Psychology

Barnes, James Franklin. *Gabon: Beyond the Colonial Legacy.* Boulder, CO: Westview Press, 1992.

Bell, Leland V. *Mental and Social Disorder in Sub-Saharan Africa: The Case of Sierra Leone, 1787-1990.* Westport, CT: Greenwood Press, 1991.

Carr-Hill, Roy A. *Social Conditions in Sub-Saharan Africa.* London; New York: Macmillan, 1991.

Cleaver, Tessa, and Marion Wallace. *Namibia: Women in War.* Foreword by Glenys Kinnock. Atlantic Highlands, NJ: Zed Books, 1990.

Cobley, Alan Gregord. *Class and Consciousness: The Black Petty Bourgeoisie in South Africa, 1924-1950.* Westport, CT: Greenwood Press, 1990.

Coles, Catherine, and Beverly Mack, eds. *Hausa Women in the Twentieth Century.* Madison: University of Wisconsin Press, 1991.

Gordon, Robert J. *The Bushman Myth: The Making of a Nambian Underclass.* Boulder, CO: Westview Press, 1992.

Hill, Martin J.D., ed. *The Harambee Movement in Kenya: Self-Help Development and Education Among the Kamba of Chat District.* Atlantic Highlands, NJ: Athlone Press, 1991.

Kilbride, Philip Leroy. *Changing Family Life in East Africa: Women and Children at Risk,* Philadelphia: Pennsylvania State University Press, 1990.

Mohammad, Duri, ed., *Social Development in Africa: Strategies, Policies and Programmes After the Lagos Plan.* Providence, NJ: H. Zell Publishers, 1991.

Moran, Mary. *Civilized Women: Gender and Prestige in Southeastern Liberia.* Ithaca, NY: Cornell University Press, 1991.

Nsamenang, A. Bame. *Human Development in Cultural Conflict.* Foreword by Michael Lamb. Newbury Park, CA: Sage Publications, 1992.

Ominde, S. H., ed. *Kenya' s Population Growth and Development to the Year 2000.* Columbus: Ohio University Press, 1990.

Reynolds, Pamela. *Dance Cat: Child Labour in the Zambezi Valley.* London: Hans Zell Books, 1991.

Riseman, Paul. *First Find Your Child A Good Mother: The Construction of Self in Two African Communities.* New Brunswick, NJ: Rutgers University Press, 1992.

Robertson, Struan. *The Cold Choice: Pictures of a South African Reality.* Grand Rapids, MI: Wm. B. Erdmans Publishing Co., 1992.

## ◆ AFRICAN AMERICANA

### Art, Architecture, and Photography

Bearden, Romare. *Memory and Metaphor: The Art of Romare Bearden, 1940-1987.* New York: Studio Museum of Harlem/Oxford University Press, 1991.

Durham, Michael S. *Powerful Days: The Civil Rights Photography of Charles Moore.* Introduction by Andrew Young. New York: Stewart, Tabori & Chang, 1991.

Easter, Eric, D. Michael Cheers, and Dudley M. Brooks, eds. *Songs of My People: African Americans: A Self-Portrait.* Introduction by Gordon Parks. Essays by Sylvester Monroe. Boston: Little, Brown, 1992.

*Gumbo Ya Ya: Anthology of Contemporary African-American Women Artists,* New York: Mid-March Arts Press, 1995.

McElroy, Guy C. *Facing History: The Black Image in American Art, 1710-1940.* Edited by Christopher C. French. Washington, DC: Bedford Arts/Corcoran Gallery, 1990.

Powell, Richard J. *Homecoming: The Art and Life of William H. Johnson.* New York: National Museum of American Art/Rizzoli, 1991.

Rozelle, Robert V., et. al. eds. *Black Art: Ancestral Legacy: The African-American Impulse in African-American Art.* New York: Abrams, 1990.

Thomison, Dennis, comp. *The Black Artist in America: An Index to Reproductions.* Metuchen, NJ: Scarecrow Press, 1991.

Travis, Jack, ed. *African-American Architects in Current Practice.* New York: Princeton Architecture Press, 1991.

## Autobiography and Biography

Baker, Donald P. *Wilder: Hold Fast to Dreams: A Biography of L. Douglas Wilder.* Cabin John, MD: Seven Locks, 1990.

Baldwin, Lewis V. *There Is a Balm in Gilead: The Cultural Roots of Martin Luther King, Jr.* Minneapolis: Fortress Press, 1991.

Bigelow, Barbara Carlisle, ed. *Contemporary Black Biography.* Detroit: Gale Research Inc., 1992.

Bjarkman, Peter C. *Ernie Banks.* Introduction by Jim Murray. New York: Chelsea House, 1992.

Brown, Drew T., III. *You Gotta Believe!: Education + Hard Work - Drugs = The American Dream.* New York: Morrow, 1991.

Brown, James, and Bruce Tucker. *James Brown: The Godfather of Soul.* New York: Thunder's Mouth Press, 1990.

Buchmann-Moller, Frank. *You Just Fight for Your Life: The Story of Lester Young.* New York: Praeger, 1990.

Campbell, James. *Talking at the Gate: A Life of James Baldwin.* New York: Viking, 1991.

Carson, Clayborne. *Malcolm X; The FBI File.* Introduction by Spike Lee. Edited by David Gallen. New York: Carroll & Graf Publishers, Inc., 1991.

Carson, Clayborne, ed. *The Papers of Martin Luther King, Jr.* Berkeley: University of California Press, 1991.

Chilton, John. *The Song of the Hawk: The Life and Recordings of Coleman Hawkins.* New York: St. Martin's Press, 1990.

Davis, Benjamin O., Jr. *Benjamin O. Davis, Jr., American: An Autobiography.* Washington, DC: Smithsonian Institution, 1991.

Davis, Miles, and Quincy Troupe. *Miles, The Autobiography.* New York: Simon & Schuster, 1990.

Deane, Bill. *Bob Gibson.* Introduction by Jim Murray. New York: Chelsea House, 1992.

Dees, Morris. *A Season for Justice: The Life and Times of Civil Rights Lawyer Morris Dees.* New York: Scribner, 1991.

Faser, Jane. *Walter White.* New York: Chelsea House, 1991.

Goldman, Roger, and David Gallen. *Thurgood Marshall: Justice for All.* New York: Carroll & Graf, 1992.

Hamilton, Charles V. *Adam Clayton Powell, Jr.: The Political Biography of an American Dilemma.* New York: Atheneum, 1991.

Hawkins, Walter L. *African American Biographies: Profiles of 558 Current Men and Women.* Jefferson, NC: McFarland & Co., 1992.

Hayes, Bob. *Run, Bullet, Run.* New York: Harper Collins, 1990.

Kranz, Rachel C. *The Biographical Dictionary of Black Americans.* New York: Facts on File, 1992.

Kremer, Gary R. *James Milton Turner and the Promise of America: The Public Life of a Post-Civil War Black Leader.* Columbia: University of Missouri Press, 1991.

Levi, Darrell E. *Michael Manley: The Making of a Leader.* Athens: University of Georgia Press, 1990.

McFeely, William S. *Frederick Douglass.* New York: Norton, 1990.

Mosby, Dewey F., and Darrel Sewell. *Henry Ossawa Tanner.* New York: Rizzoli, 1991.

Naughton, Jim. *Taking to the Air: The Rise of Michael Jordan.* New York: Warner Books, 1992.

Pallister, Janis L. *Aime Cesaire.* New York: Twayne, 1991.

Perry, Bruce. *Malcolm: The Life of a Man Who Changed Black America.* Barrytown, NY: Station Hill, 1991.

Pfieffer, Paula F. *A. Philip Randolph, Pioneer of the Civil Rights Movement.* Baton Rouge: Louisiana State University Press, 1990.

Phelps, J. Alfred. *Chappie: America's First Black Four-Star General.* Novato, CA: Presidio Press, 1991.

Phelps, Shirelle, ed. *Who's Who Among Black Americans, 1993-94.* 7th ed., William C. Matney, Jr., Consulting Editor.

Detroit: Gale Research Inc., 1993.

Pickens, William. *Bursting Bonds: Enlarged edition (of) The Heir of Slaves: The Autobiography of a "New Negro".* Edited by William L. Andrews. Bloomington: Indiana University Press, 1991.

Rattenbury, Ken. *Duke Ellington, Jazz Composer.* New Haven: Yale University Press, 1991.

Rivlin, Benjamin, ed. *Ralph Bunche, The Man and His Times.* Foreword by Donald F. Henry. New York: Holmes & Meier, 1990.

Rose, Cynthia. *Living in America: The Soul Saga of James Brown.* London: Serpent Tale, 1990 (Dist. by Consortium Book Sales Distribution.)

Rout, Kathleen. *Eldridge Cleaver.* Boston: Twayne/G.K. Hall, 1991.

Schwartzman, Myron. *Romare Bearden: His Life and Art.* New York: Abrams, 1990.

Shapiro, Leonard. *Big Man on Campus: John Thompson and the Georgetown Hoyas.* New York: Holt, 1991.

Shapiro, Miles. *Bill Russell.* Introductory essay by Coretta Scott King. New York: Chelsea House, 1991.

Sifford, Charlie. *Just Let Me Play: The Story of Charlie Sifford: The First Black PGA Golfer.* Latham, NY: British American Publishers, 1992.

Smith, Eric Ledell. *Bert Williams: A Biography of the Pioneer Black Comedian.* Jefferson, NC: McFarland, 1992.

Stewart, James Brewer. *William Lloyd Garrison and the Challenge of Emancipation.* Arlington Heights, IL: Harlan Davidson, 1992.

Strode, Woody, and Sam Young. *Goal Dust: An Autobiography.* Lantham, MD: Madison Books, 1990.

Tucker, Ken. *Ellington: The Early Years.* Champaign: University of Illinois Press, 1991.

Urban, Wayne J. *Black Scholar: Horace Mann Bond, 1904-1972.* Athens: University of Georgia Press, 1992.

Vache, Warren W. *Crazy Fingers: Claude Hopkins' Life in Jazz.* Washington, DC: Smithsonian Institution Press, 1992.

Watts, Jill. *God, Harlem U.S.A.: The Father Divine Story.* Berkeley: University of California Press, 1992.

Weland, Gerald. *Of Vision and Valor: General O. O. Howard, A Biography.* Canton, OH: Daring Publishing Group, 1991.

Wells, Dicky. *The Night People: The Jazz Life of Dicky Wells.* As told to Stanley Dance. rev. ed., Washington, DC: Smithsonian Institution Press, 1991.

Wills, Maury, and Mike Celizic. *On the Run: The Never Dull and Often Shocking Life of Maury Wills.* New York: Carroll & Graf, 1991.

## Black Nationalism and Pan-Africanism in the United States

Crosby, Edward W., and Linus A. Hoskins, eds. *Africa for the Africans: Selected Speeches of Marcus Mosiah Garvey; Malcolm X; and Nelson Kolihlahla Mandela.* Kent, OH: The Institute for African American Affairs, Department of Pan-African Studies, Kent State University, 1991.

Crummell, Alexander. *Destiny and Race: Selected Writings, 1840-1898.* Edited with introduction by Wilson J. Moses. Amherst: University of Massachusetts Press, 1992.

Drake, St. Clair. *Black Folks Here and There: An Essay in History and Anthropology.* 2 vols. Los Angeles: University of California, Los Angeles, Center for Afro-American Studies, 1991.

Harris, Robert, et. al. *Carlos Cooks: And Black Nationalism from Garvey to Malcolm.* Dover, MA: Majority Press, 1992.

Jacques, Geoffrey. *The African-American Movement Today.* New York: Watts, 1992.

Lemelle, Sid. *Pan-Africanism for Beginners.* New York: Writers and Readers Publishing, Inc., 1992.

Lewis, Rupert, ed. *Garvey: His Work and Impact.* Trenton, NJ: Africa World Press, 1991.

Martin, Tony, comp. and ed. *African Fundamentalism: A Literary and Cultural Anthropology of Garvey's Harlem Renaissance.* Dover, MA: Majority Press, 1991.

Moses, Wilson J. *Alexander Crummell: A Study of Civilization and Discontent.* Amherst: University of Massachusetts Press, 1992.

## Civil Rights, Law, and Civil Protests

*Administrative History of the Civil Rights Division of the Department of Justice During the Johnson Administration.* 2 vol., New York: Garland Publishing Co., 1991.

Aguirre, Adalberto, Jr., and David V. Baker. *Race, Racism and the Death Penalty in the United States.* Barrien Springs, MI: Vande Vere Publishers, 1992.

Belknap, Michal. *Racial Violence and Law Enforcement in the South.* New York: Garland Publishing Co., 1991.

Belknap, Michal. *Securing the Enactment of Civil Rights Legislation, 1965-1968.* New York: Garland Publishing Co., 1991.

Belknap, Michal. *Urban Race Riots.* New York: Garland Publishing Co., 1991.

Belknap, Michal. *Voting Rights.* New York: Garland Publishing Co., 1991.

Belz, Herman. *Equality Transformed: A Quarter-Century of Affirmative Action.* New Brunswick, NJ: Transaction, 1991.

Blumberg, Rhoda L. *Civil Rights, the Freedom Struggle.* rev. ed., Boston: Twayne G.K. Hall, 1991.

Bolick, Clint. *Unfinished Business: A Civil Rights Strategy for America's Third Century.* San Francisco: Research Institute of Public Policy, 1990.

Cagin, Seth, and Philip Dray. *We Are Not Afraid: The Story of Goodman, Schwerner and Chaney and the Civil Rights Campaign for Mississippi.* New York: Bantam Books, 1991.

Capeci, Dominic, and Martha Wilkerson. *Layered Violence: the Detroit Rioters of 1943.* Jackson: University Press of Mississippi, 1991.

Carson, Clayborne, et. al. eds. *"The Eyes on the Prize" Civil Rights Reader: Documents, Speeches, and Firsthand Accounts from the Black Freedom Struggle, 1954-1990.* New York: Viking, 1991.

Cashman, Sean Dennis. *African-Americans and the Quest for Civil Rights, 1900-1990.* New York: New York University Press, 1991.

Cashmore, Ellis, and Eugene McLaughlin, eds. *Out of Order?: Policing Black People.* New York: Routledge, 1991.

Cone, James H. *Martin and Malcolm and America: A Dream or a Nightmare.* New York: Orbis Books, 1991.

Cook, Anthony. *Law, Race and Social Theory.* Boston: New England School of Law, 1991.

Detefsen, Robert R. *Civil Rights Under Reagan.* San Francisco: ICS Press, 1991.

*Encyclopedia of African American Civil Rights: From Emancipation to the Present.* Westport, CT: Greenwood Press, 1992.

Epstein, Richard Allen. *Forbidden Grounds: The Case Against Employment Discrimination Laws.* Cambridge: Harvard University Press, 1992.

Ezorsky, Gertrude. *Racism and Justice: The Case for Affirmative Action.* Ithaca, NY: Cornell University Press, 1991.

Fendrich, James Max. *Ideal Citizens: The Legacy of the Civil Rights Movement.* Albany: State University of New York Press, 1993.

Finkelman, Paul, ed. *African Americans and the Law.* New York: Garland Publishing Co., 1991 (*Race, Law and American History, 1700-1900. The African American Experience.*)

Finkelman, Paul, ed. *African-Americans and the Legal Profession in Historical Perspective.* New York: Garland Publishing Co., 1991 (*Race, Law, and American History, 1700-1990. The African American Experience.* vol. 10).

Finkelman, Paul, ed. *African-Americans and the Right to Vote.* Edited by Paul Finkelman. New York: Garland Publishing Co., 1992. (*Race, Law, and American History, 1700-1900. The African-American Experience.* vol. 6).

Finkelman, Paul, ed. *Lynching, Racial Violence, and Law.* New York: Garland Publishing Co., 1992. (*Race, Law, and American History, 1700-1990. The African-American Experience,* vol. 9.)

Finkelman, Paul, ed. *Race and Criminal Justice.* New York: Garland Publishing Co., 1992. (*Race, Law, and American History, 1700-1900. The American Experience,* vol. 8.)

Finkelman, Paul, ed. *Race and Law Before Emancipation.* New York: Garland Publishing Co., 1992. (*Race, Law and American History, 1700-1990. The African American Experience,* vol. 2.)

Finkelman, Paul, ed. *The Era of Integration and Civil Rights, 1930-1990.* New York: Garland Publishing Co., 1992. (*Race, Law, and American History, 1700-1990. The African American Experience* vol. 5).

Fiscus, Ronald Jerry. *The Constitutional Logic of Affirmative Action.* Edited by Stephen Wasby. Durham, NC: Duke University Press, 1992.

Fisher, Sethard. *From Margin to Mainstream: The Social Progress of Black Americans.* 2nd ed., Savage, MD: Rowman & Littlefield, 1992.

Goings, Kenneth W. *The NAACP Comes of Age: The Defeat of Judge Parker.* Bloomington: Indiana University Press, 1990.

Goldwin, Robert A. *Why Blacks, Women and Jews Are Not Mentioned in the Constitution, and Other Unorthodox Views.* Washington, DC: American Enterprise Institute, 1990.

Graetz, Robert S. *Montgomery, A White Preachers Memoir.* Minneapolis: Fortress Press, 1991.

Grafman, Bernard, ed. *Controversies in Minority Voting: The Voting Rights Act in Perspective.* Washington, DC: Brookings Institute, 1992.

Graham, Hugh Davis. *The Civil Rights Era: Race, Gender and National Policy, 1960-1972.* New York: Oxford University Press, 1990.

Hampton, Henry, and Steve Fayer, comps. *Voices of Freedom: An Oral History of the Civil Rights Movement from the 1950s Through the 1980s.* New York: Bantam Books, 1990.

Harding, Vincent. *Hope and History: Why We Must Share the Story of the Movement.* Maryknoll, NY: Orbis Books, 1990.

Harris, Jacqueline. *A History of the NAACP.* New York: Watts, 1992.

Jackson, James E. *The Bold Bad '60s: Pushing the Point for Equality Down South and Out Yonder.* New York: International Publishers, 1992.

James, Hunter. *They Didn't Put That on the Huntley-Brinkley Report!: A Vagabound Reporter Encounters the New South.* Athens: University of Georgia, 1993.

*Justice Department Briefs in Crucial Civil Rights Cases.* 2 vols., New York: Garland, 1991.

Kapur, Sudarshan. *Raising Up a Prophet: The African-American Encounter with Gandhi.* Boston: Beacon, 1992.

King, Richard. *Civil Rights and the Idea of Freedom.* New York: Oxford University Press, 1992.

Kull, Andrew. *The Color-Blind Constitution.* Cambridge: Harvard University Press, 1992.

Levy, Peter B., ed. *Dictionary History of the Modern Civil Rights Movement.* New York: Greenwood Press, 1992.

Levy, Peter B., ed. *Let Freedom Ring: A Documentary History of the Modern Civil Rights Movement.* New York: Praeger, 1992.

Lyon, Danny. *Memories of the Civil Rights Movement.* Text and photographs by Danny Lyon; foreword by Julian Bond. Chapel Hill: University of North Carolina Press, 1992.

Meier, August, et. al. eds. *Black Protest in the Sixties.* New York: M. Wiener, 1991.

Meier, August. *A White Scholar and the Black Community, 1945-1965: Essays and Reflections.* Afterword by John H. Bracey, Jr. Amherst: University of Massachusetts Press, 1992.

Mills, Nicolaus. *Like a Holy Crusade: Mississippi, 1964—The Turning of the Civil Rights Movement in America.* Chicago: I.R. Dee, 1992.

Nieli, Russell, ed. *Racial Preference and Racial Justice: The New Affirmative Action Controversy.* Washington, DC: Ethics and Public Policy Center, 1991 (Dist. by National Book Network.)

Nieman, Donald G. *Promises to Keep: African Americans and the Constitutional Order, 1776 to the Present.* New York: Oxford University Press, 1991.

O'Reilly, Kenneth. *Racial Matters: The FBI's Secret File on Black America, 1960-1972.* New York: Free Press, 1991.

Powledge, Fred. *Free At Last?: The Civil Rights Movement and the People Who Made It.* Boston: Little, Brown, 1990.

Reed, Merl E. *Seedtime for the Modern Civil Rights Movement: The President's Committee on Fair Employment Practice, 1941-1946.* Baton Rouge: Louisiana State University Press, 1991.

Robinson, Amelia Boynton. *Bridge Across Jordan.* rev. ed., Washington, DC: Schiller Institute, 1991.

Robinson, Armistead L., and Patricia Sullivan, eds. *New Directions in Civil Rights Studies.* Charlottesville: University Press of Virginia, 1991.

Sigelman, Lee, and Susan Welch. *Black Americans' Views of Racial Inequality: The Dream Deferred.* New York: Cambridge University Press, 1991.

Sikora, Frank. *Until Justice Rolls Down: The Birmingham Church Bombing Case* Tuscaloosa: University of Alabama Press, 1991.

Stern, Mark. *Calculating Visions: Kennedy, Johnson and Civil Rights.* New Brunswick, NJ: Rutger University Press, 1992.

Swift, Jeanne, ed. *Dream and Reality: The Modern Black Struggle for Freedom and Equality.* New York: Greenwood Press, 1991.

Thomas, Clarence. *Clarence Thomas: Confronting the Future: Selections from the Senate Confirmation Hearing and Prior Speeches.* Washington, DC: Regnery Gateway, 1992.

Urofsky, Melvin I. *A Conflict of Rights: The Supreme Court and Affirmative Action.* New York: Scribners, 1991.

Watson, Denton L. *Lion in the Lobby: Clarence Mitchell, Jr.'s Struggle for the Passage of Civil Rights Laws.* New York: Morrow, 1990.

Wright, Roberta Hughes. *The Birth of the Montgomery Bus Boycott.* Southfield, MI: Charro Book Co., 1991.

## Economics, Entrepreneurship, and Labor

Broadnax, Derek. *The Black Entrepreneurs Guide to Million Dollar Business Opportunities.* Austin, TX: Black Entrepreneurs Press, 1990.

Broadnax, Derek. *The Black Entrepreneurs Guide to Money Sources: How to Get Your Share.* Austin, TX: Black Entrepreneurs Press, 1990.

Butler, John Sibley. *Entrepreneurship and Self-Help Among Black Americans: A Reconsideration of Race and Economics.* Albany: State University of New York Press, 1991.

Dewart, Janet, ed. *The State of Black America, 1991.* New York: National Urban League, 1991.

Duncan, Mike. *Reach Your Goals In Spite of the Old Boy Network: A Guide for African American Employees.* Edgewood, MD:

M.E. Duncan and Co., 1990.

Grant, Nancy L. *TVA and Black Americans: Planning for the Status Quo.* Philadelphia: Temple University Press, 1990.

Green, Shelley, and Paul Pryde. *Black Entrepreneurship in America.* Brunswick, NJ: Transactions Publishers, 1990.

Greenberg, Jonathan D. *Staking a Claim: Jake Simmons and the Making of an African-American Oil Dynasty.* New York: Atheneum, 1991.

Reed, Wornie, ed. *Social, Political and Economic Issues in Black America.* Amherst: University of Massachusetts, William Monroe Trotter Institute, 1990.

Rosen, George H. *Black Money.* Chelsea, MI: Scaraborough House, 1990.

## Education

Allen, Walter R., Edgar Epps, and Nesha Z. Haniff, eds. *College in Black and White: African American Students in Predominately White and Historically Black Public Universities.* Albany: State University of New York Press, 1991.

Altbach, Philip G., and Kofi Lomotey, eds. *The Racial Crisis in American Higher Education.* Albany: State University of New York Press, 1991.

Bowman, J. Wilson. *America's Black Colleges.* South

Pasadena, CA: Sandcastle Publishing Co., 1992.

Fife, Brian L. *Desegregation in American Schools: Comparative Intervention Strategies.* New York: Praeger, 1992.

Finkelman, Paul, ed. *The Struggle for Equal Education.* New York: Garland Publishing Co., 1992. (*Race, Law, and American History, 1700-1990. African-American Experience,* vol. 7.)

Formisano, Ronald P. *Boston Against Busing: Race, Class, and Ethnicity in the 1960s and 1970s.* Chapel Hill: University of North Carolina Press, 1991.

Harmon, Marylen E. *The Infusion of African and African American Studies into the Curriculum.* Roanoke, VA: Absolute Writings Ltd., 1991.

Irvine, Jacqueline Jordan. *Black Students and School Failure: Policies, Practices, and Prescriptions.* Westport, CT: Greenwood Press, 1990.

Lomotey, Kofi, ed. *Going to School: The African-American Experience.* Albany: State University of New York Press, 1990.

Lusane, Clarence. *The Struggle for Equal Education.* New York: F. Watts, 1992.

Margo, Robert A. *Race and Schooling in the South, 1880-1950.* Chicago: University of Chicago Press, 1991.

National Afro-American Museum and Cultural Center. *From Victory to Freedom: The African American Experience: Curriculum Guide, Secondary School Course of Study.* Wilberforce, OH: National Afro-American Museum and Cultural Center, 1991.

Neufeldt, Harvey G., and Leo McGee, eds. *Education of the African American Adult: An Historical Overview.* Westport, CT: Greenwood, 1990.

Pratt, Robert A. *The Color of Their Skin: Education and Race in Richmond, Virginia, 1954-89.* Charlottesville: University of Virginia Press, 1992.

Sachar, Emily. *Shut Up and Let the Lady Teach: A Teacher's Year in a Public School.* New York: Poseidon Press, 1991.

Thompkins, Susie Powers. *Cotton-Patch Schoolhouse.*

Tuscaloosa: University of Alabama Press, 1992.

Willie, Charles V., Anatoine M. Garibaldi, and Wornie L. Reed, eds. *The Education of African Americans.* Westport, CT: Auburn House/Greenwood Publishing Group, 1991.

## Folklore and Folk Culture

Abrahams, Roger D. *Singing the Master: The Emergence of African American Culture in the Plantation South.* New York: Pantheon Books, 1992.

Hall, Gwendolyn Midlo. *Africans in Colonial Louisiana: The Development of Afro-Creole Culture.* Baton Rouge: Louisiana State University Press, 1992.

Hazzard-Gordon, Katrina. *Jookin': The Rise of Social Dance Formation in African-American Culture.* Philadelphia: Temple University Press, 1990.

Hill, James L., ed. *Studies in African and African American Culture.* New York: P. Lang, 1990.

Holloway, Joseph E., ed. *Africanisms in American Culture.* Bloomington: Indiana University Press, 1990.

Njeri, Itabari. *Every Good-Bye Ain't Gone: Family Portraits and Personal Escapades.* New York: Times Books, 1990.

Roberts, John W. *From Trickster to Badman: The Black Folk Hero in Slavery and Freedom.* Philadelphia: University of Pennsylvania Press, 1990.

Spalding, Henry D., comp. and ed. *Encyclopedia of Black Folklore and Humor.* Introduction by J. Mason Brewer. Middle Village, NY: Jonathan David Publishers, 1990.

Sundquist, Eric J. *The Hammers of Creation: Folk Culture in Modern African-American Culture.* Athens: University of Georgia Press, 1992.

Twining, Mary A., and Keith E. Baird, eds. *Sea Island Roots: African Presence in Carolina and Georgia.* Trenton, NJ: Africa World Press, 1991.

## General Reference

Asante, Molefi K. *The Historical and Cultural Atlas of African Americans*. New York: Macmillan, 1991.

*The Black Resource Guide, 1990-1991 Edition*. Washington, DC: Black Resource Guide, Inc., 1991.

Bogle, Donald, ed. *Black Arts Annual, 1988/89*. New York: Garland, 1990.

Donovan, Richard X. *Black Scientists of America*. Portland, OR: National Book Co., 1990.

Fitzpatrick, Sandra, and Maria Godwin. *The Guide to Black Washington: Places and Events of Historical and Cultural Significance in the Nation's Capital*. New York: Hippocrene, 1990.

Furtaw, Julia C., ed. *Black American Information Directory*. 2nd ed., Detroit: Gale Research Inc., 1992.

Hancock, Sybil. *Famous Firsts of Black Americans*. Gretna, LA: Pelican Publishing Co., 1991.

Horton, Carrell Peterson, and Jessie Carney Smith, comps. and eds. *Statistical Record of Black America*. 2nd ed., Detroit: Gale Research Inc., 1991.

Smithsonian Institution. *African and African American Resources at the Smithsonian*. Washington, DC: Smithsonian Institution, 1991.

Southern, Eileen, and Josephine Wright, comps. *African American Traditions in Song, Sermon, Tale, and Dance, 1600s-1920: An Annotated Bibliography of Literature, Collections, and Artworks*. Westport, CT: Greenwood Press, 1990.

Thum, Marcella. *Hippocrene U.S.A. Guide to Black America: A Directory of Historic and Cultural Sites Relating to Black America*. New York: Hippocrene Books, 1992.

## Health

Bailey, A. Peter. *The Harlem Hospital Story: 100 Years of Struggle Against Illness*. Richmond, VA: Native Sun Publishers, 1991.

Bailey, Eric J. *Urban African American Health Care*. Lantham, MD: University Press of America, 1991.

*The Black Women's Health Book: Speaking for Ourselves*. Seattle: Seal Press, 1990.

Dixon, Barbara M., with Josleen Wilson, *Good Health for African-American Kids,*, Crown Trade Paperbacks, 1995.

Duh, Samuel V. *Blacks and AIDS: Genetic or Environmental Causes*. Newbury Park, CA: Sage Publications, 1991.

*Health of Black Americans from Post Reconstruction to Integration, 1871-1960: An Annotated Bibliography of Contemporary Sources*. Westport, CT: Greenwood Press, 1990.

McBride, David. *From TB to AIDS: Epidemics Among Urban Blacks Since 1900*. Albany: State University of New York Press, 1991.

*National Black Health Leadership Directory, 1990-91*. Washington, DC: NRW Associates, 1991.

Villarosa, Linda, ed. *Body & Soul: The Black Woman's Guide to Physical Health and Mental Well-Being*. HarperCollins, 1994.

## History

*The African American Experience: A History*. Sharon Harley, Stephen Middleton, and Charlotte Stokes, Consultants. Englewood Cliffs, NJ: Prentice-Hall, 1992.

America, Richard, ed. *The Wealth of Races: The Present Value of Benefits from Past Injustices*. Westport, CT: Greenwood Press, 1991.

Anderson, Eric, and Alfred Moss, Jr., eds. *The Facts of Reconstruction: Essays in Honor of John Hope Franklin*. Baton Rouge: Louisiana State University Press, 1991.

Andrews, George Reid. *Blacks and Whites in Sao Paulo Brazil, 1888-1988*. Madison: University of Wisconsin Press, 1992.

Aptheker, Herbert. *Anti-Racism in U.S. History: The First Hundred Years*. New York: Greenwood Press, 1992.

Aptheker, Herbert. *To Be Free: Pioneering Studies in Afro-American History*. Introduction by John Hope Franklin. New York: Citadel Press, 1991.

Bailey, Richard. *Neither Carpetbaggers Nor Scalawags: Black Officeholders During the Reconstruction in Alabama*. Montgomery, AL: R. Bailey Publishers, 1991.

Beeth, Howard, and Cary E. Wintz, eds. *Black Dixie: Afro-Texan History and Culture in Houston*. College Station, TX: Texas A&M University Press, 1992.

Berlin, Irs, and Philip D. Morgan, eds. *The Slaves' Economy: Independent Production by Slaves in the Americas*. London: F. Cass, 1991.

Berlin, Irs, et. al., eds. *Slaves No More: Three Essays on Emancipation and the Civil War*. New York: Cambridge University Press, 1992.

*The Black Abolitionist Papers, Vol. 3: The United States, 1830-1846*. Chapel Hill: University of North Carolina Press, 1991.

Boney, F.N., Richard L. Hume, and Rafia Zafar. *God Made Man, Man Made the Slave.* Macon, GA: Mercer University Press, 1990.

Bryan, Patrick. *The Jamaican People, 1880-1902: Race and Social Control.* New York: Macmillan, 1991.

Bush, Barbara. *Slave Women in Caribbean Society, 1650-1838.* Bloomington: University of Indiana Press, 1990.

Campbell, Randolph B. *An Empire for Slavery: The Peculiar Institution in Texas, 1821-1865.* Baton Rouge: Louisiana State University Press, 1991.

Cantor, George. *Historic Landmarks of Black America.* Detroit: Gale Research Inc., 1991.

Cohen, William. *At Freedom Edge: Black Mobility at the Southern Quest for Racial Control, 1861-1915.* Baton Rouge: Louisiana State University Press, 1991.

Cornelius, Janet Duitsman. *"When I Can Read My Title Clear": Literacy, Slavery, and Religion in the Antebellum South.* Columbia: University of South Carolina Press, 1991.

Counter, S. Allen. *North Pole Legacy: Black, White and Eskimo.* Amherst: University of Massachusetts Press, 1991.

Crouch, Berry A. *The Freedmen's Bureau and Black Texans.* Austin: University of Texas Press, 1992.

Davis, Lenwood G. *A Travel Guide to Black Historical Sites and Landmarks in North Carolina.* Winston-Salem, NC: Bandit Books, 1991.

*Deromantizing Black History: Critical Essays and Reappraisals.* Knoxville: University of Tennessee Press, 1991.

Dillon, Merton L. *Slavery Attacked: Southern Slaves and Their Allies, 1619-1865.* Baton Rouge: Louisiana State University Press, 1990.

Downey, Dennis B., and Raymond M. Hyser. *No Crooked Death: Coatsville, Pennsylvania, and the Lynching of Zachariah Walker.* Champaign: University of Illinois Press, 1991.

Drago, Edmund L., ed. *Broke by the War: Letters of a Slave Trader.* Columbia: University of South Carolina Press, 1991.

Dykstra, Robert. *Bright Radical Star: Black Freedom and White Supremacy on the Hawkeye Frontier.* Cambridge: Harvard University Press, 1993.

Fede, Andrew. *People Without Rights: An Interpretation of the Fundamentals of the Law of Slavery in the U.S. South.* New York: Garland Publishing Co., 1992.

Ferguson, Leland G. *Uncommon Ground: Archaeology and Early African America, 1650-1800.* Washington, DC: Smithsonian Institution Press, 1992.

Finkelman, Paul, ed. *The Age of Jim Crow: Segregation from the End of Reconstruction to the Great Depression.* New York: Garland Publishing Co., 1992. (*Race, Law, and American History, 1760-1990. The African American Experience*, vol. 4.)

Finkelman, Paul, ed. *Emancipation and Reconstruction.* New York: Garland Publishing Co., 1992. (*Race, Law and American History, 1700-1990. The African American Experience.* vol. 3.)

Franklin, Vincent P. *Black Self-Determinism: A Cultural History of African-American Resistance.* 2nd ed., Brooklyn, NY: Lawrence Hill Books, 1992.

Frey, Sylvia. *Water from the Rock: Black Resistance in a Revolutionary Age.* Princeton, NJ: Princeton University Press, 1992.

Gatewood, Willard B. *Aristocrats of Color: The Black Elite, 1880-1920.* Bloomington: Indiana University Press, 1990.

Genovese, Eugene D. *The Slaveholders' Dilemma: Freedom and Progress in Southern Conservative Thought, 1820-1860.* Columbia: University of South Carolina Press, 1992.

Greenberg, Cheryl Lynn. *"Or Does It Explode?": Black Harlem in the Great Depression.* New York: Oxford University Press, 1991.

Hamilton, Kenneth Marvin. *Black Towns and Profit, Promotion and Development in the Trans-Appalachian West, 1877-1915.* Champaign: University of Illinois Press, 1991.

Harley, Sharon. *The African American Experience: A History.* Englewood Cliffs, NJ: Globe, 1992.

Harris, Richard S. *Politics & Prejudice: A History of Chester, Pennsylvania Negroes.* Apache Junction, AZ: Relmo Pubs., 1991.

Harrison, Alfredteen, ed. *Black Exodus: The Great Migration from the American South.* Oxford: University Press of Mississippi, 1991.

Henry, Paget, and Paul Buhle, eds. *C.L.R. James' Caribbean.* Durham, NC: Duke University Press, 1992.

Hornsby, Jr., Alton. *Chronology of African-American History: Significant Events and People from 1619 to the Present.* Detroit: Gale Research Inc., 1991.

Horton, James Oliver. *Free People of Color: Inside the African American Community.* Washington, DC: Smithsonian Institution, 1993.

Inikoroi, Joseph E., and Stanley L. Engerman, eds. *The Atlantic Slave Trade: Effects on Economic Societies, and Peoples in Africa, the Americas and Europe.* Durham, NC: Duke University Press, 1992.

Jackson, Terrance. *Putting It All Together: World Conquest, Global Genocide and African Liberation.* Bronx, NY: AKASA, 1991.

Jones, Howard. *The Red Diary: A Chronological History of Black Americans in Houston and Some Neighboring Harris County Communities-122 Years Later.* Austin, TX: Nortex Press, 1992.

Jones, Norrece T. *Born a Child of Freedom, Yet A Slave: Mechanisms of Control and Strategies of Resistance in Antebellum South Carolina.* Middletown, CT: Wesleyan University Press, 1990.

Jordan, Winthrop. *Tumult and Silence at Second Creek: An Inquiry into a Civil War Slave Conspiracy.* Baton Rouge: Louisiana State University Press, 1993.

Katz, William Loren. *Breaking the Chains: African American Slave Resistance.* New York: Atheneum, 1990.

Lane, Roger. *William Dorsey's Philadelphia and Ours: On the Origins and Future Prospects of Urban Black America.* New York: Oxford University Press, 1991.

Lesko, Kathleen M., ed. *Black Georgetown Remembered: A History of Its Black Community from the Founding of "The Town of George" in 1751 to the Present Day.* Washington, DC: Georgetown University Press, 1991.

Malone, Ann Patton. *Sweet Chariot: Slave Family and Household Structure in Nineteenth Century Louisiana.* Chapel Hill: University of North Carolina Press, 1992.

McLaurin, Melton A. *Celia, a Slave.* Athens: University of Georgia Press, 1991.

McMillen, Sally Gregory. *Southern Women: Black and White in the Old South.* Arlington Heights, IL: Harlan Davidson, 1992.

Meillassaux, Claude. *The Anthropology of Slavery: The Womb of Iron and Gold.* Translated by Alide Dasnois. Chicago: University of Chicago Press, 1991.

Meyer, Mary K. *Free Blacks in Hartford, Somerset, and Talbort Counties, Maryland.* Mt. Airy, MD: Pipe Creek Publications, 1991.

Middleton, Stephen. *The Black Laws in the Old Northwest: A Documentary History.* New York: Greenwood Press, 1992.

Munford, Clarence J. *The Black Ordeal of Slavery and Slave Trading in the French West Indies, 1625-1715.* Lewiston, ME: Edwin Mellen, 1991.

Nash, Gary B. *Freedom by Degrees: Emancipation in Pennsylvania and Its Aftermath.* New York: Oxford University Press, 1991.

Nash, Gary B. *Race and Revolution.* Madison, WI: Madison House, 1990.

Oakes, James. *Slavery and Freedom: An Interpretation of the Old South.* New York: Knopf, 1990.

Pearson, Edward. *Slave Work and Culture in Town and Country.* Williamsburg, VA: Institute of Early American History and Culture, 1991.

Perdue, Charles L., ed. *Weevils in the Wheat: Interviews with Virginia Ex-Slaves.* Charlottesville: University Press of Virginia, 1992.

Reidy, Joseph. *From Slavery to Agrarian Capitalism in the Cotton Plantation South: Central Georgia, 1800-1880.* Chapel Hill: University of North Carolina Press, 1992.

Richardson, Bonham C. *The Caribbean in the Wide World, 1492-1922.* New York: Cambridge University Press, 1992.

Richter, William L. *Overreached on All Sides: The Freedmen's Bureau Administrators in Texas, 1865-1868.* College Station: Texas A&M University Press, 1991.

Schwartz, Stuart B. *Slaves, Peasants, and Rebels: Reconsidering Brazilian Slavery.* Champaign: University of Illinois Press, 1992.

Schweninger, Loren. *Black Property Owners in the South, 1790-1915.* Champaign: University of Illinois Press, 1990.

Slaughter, Thomas P. *Bloody Dawn: The Christiana Riot and Racial Violence in Antebellum North.* New York: Oxford University Press, 1991.

Solow, Barbara L., ed. *Slavery and the Rise of the Atlantic System.* New York: Cambridge University Press/W.E.B. DuBois Institute for Afro-American Research, 1991.

Stanisland, Martin. *American Intellectuals and African Nationalists; 1955-1970.* New Haven, CT: Yale University Press, 1991.

Stevenson, Lisbeth Gant. *African-American History: Heroes in Hardship.* Cambridge, MA: Cambridgeport Press, 1992.

Stone, Albert E. *The Return of Nat Turner: History, Literature, and Cultural Politics in Sixties America.* Athens: University of Georgia, 1992.

Stone, Frank Andrews. *African American Connecticut: African Origins, New England Roots.* Storrs, CT: Isaac N. Thut World Education Center, 1991.

Terry, Ted. *American Black History: Reference Manual.* Tulsa, OK: Myles Publishing Co., 1991.

Thomas, Richard W. *Life for Us: Building Black Community in Detroit, 1915-1945.* Bloomington: Indiana University Press, 1992.

Thornton, John. *Africa and Africans in the Making of the Atlantic World, 1400-1680.* New York: Cambridge University Press, 1992.

White, Shane. *Somewhat More Independent: The End of Slavery in New York City 1770-1870.* Athens: University of Georgia Press, 1991.

Williams, Jacob C. *Lillie: Black Life in Martins Ferry, Ohio During the 1920s and 1930s.* Ann Arbor, MI: Braun-Brumfield, 1991.

Williams, Lee E. *Post-War Riots in America, 1919 and 1946: How the Pressures of War Exacerbated American Urban Tensions to the Breaking Points.* Lewiston, NY: E. Mellen, 1991.

## Language, Literature, and Drama

Babb, Valerie Melissa. *Ernest Gaines.* Boston: Twayne/G.K. Hall, 1991.

Bailey, Guy, Natalie Maynor, and Patricia Cukor-Avila, eds. *The Emergence of Black English: Text and Commentary.* Philadelphia: J. Benjamins Publishing Co., 1991.

Baker, Houston A., and Patricia Redmond, eds. *Afro-American Literary Study in the 1990s.* Chicago: University of Chicago Press, 1990.

Baraka, Imamu Amiri. *The Leroi Jones/Amiri Baraka Reader.* Edited William J. Harris. New York: Thunder's Mouth Press, 1991.

Barksdale, Richard K. *Praisesong of Survival: Lectures and Essays, 1957-1989.* Introduction by R. Baxter Miller. Urbana: University of Illinois, 1992.

Bassett, John E. *Harlem in Review: Critical Reactions to Black American Writers, 1917-1939.* Selinsgrove, PA: Susquehanna University Press, 1992.

Benitoz-Rojo, Antonio. *The Repeating Island: The Caribbean and the Postmodern Perspective.* Durham, NC: Duke University Press, 1992.

Blackshire-Belay, Carol Aisha, ed. *Language and Literature in the African American Imagination.* Westport, CT: Greenwood Press, 1992.

Bloom, Harold, ed. *Bigger Thomas.* New York: Chelsea House, 1990.

Brown, Stewart, ed. *The Art of Derek Walcott.* UK: Seren Books, 1992. (Dist. by Dufour Editions, Inc.)

Busby, Mark. *Ralph Ellison.* Boston: Twayne/G.K. Hall, 1991.

Butler, Robert. *Native Son: The Emergence of a New Black Hero.* Boston: Twayne/G.K. Hall, 1991.

Cartey, Wilfred. *Whispers form the Caribbean: I Going Away,*

*I Going Home.* Los Angeles: University of California, Los Angeles, Center for Afro-American Studies, 1991.

DeJongh, James. *Vicious Modernism: Black Harlem and the Literary Imagination.* New York: Cambridge University Press, 1990.

Dieke, Ikenna. *The Primordial Image: African, Afro-American, and Caribbean Mythopoetic Text.* New York: P. Lang, 1991.

Draper, James P., ed. *Black Literature Criticism: Excerpts from Criticism of the Most Significant Works of Black Authors over the Past 200 Years.* 3 vols., Detroit: Gale Research Inc., 1992.

Edwards, Walter F., and Donald Winford, eds. *Verb Phrase Patterns in Black English and Creole.* Detroit: Wayne State University Press, 1991.

Fabre, Michel. *Richard Wright: Books and Writers.* Oxford: University Press of Mississippi, 1990.

Gates, Henry Louis, Jr. *Loose Canons: Notes on the Culture Wars.* New York: Oxford University Press, 1992.

Hamalian, Leo, and James V. Hatch, eds. *The Roots of African American Drama: An Anthology of Early Plays, 1858-1938.* Detroit: Wayne State University Press, 1991.

Hord, Fred L. *Reconstructing Memory: Black Literary Criticism.* Chicago: Third World Press, 1991.

Johnson, Dianne. *Telling Tales: The Pedagogy and Power of African American Literature for Youth.* New York: Greenwood Press, 1990.

Jones, Gayl. *Liberating Voices: Oral Tradition in African American Literature.* Cambridge, MA: Harvard University Press, 1991.

Joseph, Margaret Paul. *Caliban in Exile: The Outsider in Caribbean Fiction.* New York: Greenwood Press, 1992.

Kinnamon, Kenneth, ed. *New Essays on Native Son.* New York: Cambridge University Press, 1990.

Metzger, Linda, Hal May, Deborah A. Straub, and Susan M. Trotsky, eds. *Black Writers.* Detroit: Gale Research Inc., 1989.

Mikolyzk, Thomas A. comp. *Langston Hughes: A Bio-Bibliography.* Westport, CT: Greenwood Press, 1990.

Miller, R. Baxter. *The Art and Imagination of Langston Hughes.* Lexington: University of Kentucky Press, 1990.

Morrison, Toni. *Playing in the Dark: Whiteness and the Literary Imagination.* Cambridge, MA: Harvard University Press, 1992.

Newby, James Edwards. *Black Authors: A Selected Annotated Bibliography.* New York: Garland, 1990.

Ntire, Daphne Williams, ed., and comp. *Roots and Blossoms; African American Plays for Today*. Troy, MI: Bedford Publishers, 1991.

Peterson, Bernard L. *Early Black American Playwrights and Dramatic Writers: A Biographical Dictionary and Catalog of Plays, Films and Broadcasting Scripts*. Westport, CT: Greenwood Press, 1990.

Rajiv, Sudhi. *Forms of Black Consciousness*. New York: Advent Books, 1992.

Rollock, Barbara. *Black Authors and Illustrators of Children's Books: A Biographical Dictionary*. 2nd ed., New York: Garland, 1992.

Smith, Valerie. *Self-Discovery and Authority in Afro-American Narrative*. Cambridge, MA; Harvard University Press, 1991.

Stepto, Robert B. *From Behind the Veil: A Study of Afro-American Narrative*. 2nd ed., Urbana: University of Illinois Press, 1991.

Thurman, Wallace. *Infants of the Spring*. With foreword by Amritjit Singh. Boston: Northeastern University Press, 1992.

Toomer, Jean. *Essentials*. Edited by Rudolph P. Bird.

Athens: University of Georgia Press, 1991.

Washington, Mary Helen, ed. *Memory of Kin: Stories About Family by Black Writers*. New York: Doubleday, 1991.

Wilson, August. *Two Trains Running*. New York: Dutton, 1992.

## Media, Publishing, and Book Collecting

Chester, Thomas Morris. *Thomas Morris Chester, Black Civil War Correspondent: His Dispatches from the Virginia Front*. With Biographical Essay and Notes by R.J.M. Blackett. New York: DeCapo Press, 1991.

Dates, Jannette L., and William Barlow. *Split Image: African Americans in the Mass Media*. Washington, DC: Howard University Press, 1990.

Hill, George. *Black Women in Television: An Illustrated History and Bibliography*. New York: Garland Publishing Co., 1990.

Joyce, Donald Franklin. *Black Book Publishers in the United States: A Historical Dictionary of the Press, 1817-1990*. Westport, CT: Greenwood Press, 1991.

Schuyler, George S. *Black Empire: George S. Schuyler Writing As Samuel I. Brooks*. Edited by Robert A. Hill and R. Kent Rasmussen. Boston: Northeastern University, 1991.

Silk, Catherine, and John Silk. *Racism and Anti-Racism in*

*American Popular Culture: Portrayals of African-Americans in Fiction and Film*. Manchester, UK: Manchester University Press, 1990. (Dist. by St. Martin's Press)

Sinnette, Elinor Des Verney, W. Paul Coates, and Thomas C. Battle, eds. *Black Bibliophiles and Collectors: Preservers of Black History*. Washington, DC: Howard University Press, 1990.

## Military Participation

**Collum, Danny Duncan, ed.** *African Americans in the Spanish Civil War: "This Ain't Ethiopia, but It'll Do"*. New York: G.K.Hall, 1992.

Cox, Clinton. *Undying Glory: The Story of the Massachusetts 54th Regiment*. New York: Scholastic, Inc., 1991.

Donaldson, Gary. *The History of African-Americans in the Military: Double V*. Malabar, FL: Krieger Publishing Co., 1991.

Gooding, James Henry. *On the Alter of Freedom: A Black Soldier's Civil War Letters from the Front*. Edited by Virginia Matzke Adams. Amherst: University of Massachusetts Press, 1991.

Johnson, Charles. *African American Soldiers in the National Guard: Recruitment and Deployment During Peacetime and War*. New York: Greenwood Press, 1992.

Redkey, Edwin S., ed. *A Grand Army of Black Men: Letters from African-American Soldiers in the Union Army*. New York: Cambridge University Press, 1992.

## Music

Allen, Ray. *Singing in the Spirit: African-American Sacred Quartets in New York City*. Philadelphia: University of Pennsylvania Press, 1991.

Boggs, Vernon W. *Salsiology: Afro-Cuban Music and the Evolution of Salsa in New York City*. Westport, CT: Greenwood Press, 1992.

Booth, Stanley. *Rhythm Oil: A Journey Through the Music of the American South*. New York: Pantheon, 1991.

Cantor, Louis. *Wheelin' on Beale*. Foreword by B.B. King. New York: Pharos, 1992.

Costello, Mark, and David Foster Wallace. *Signifying Rappers: Rap and Race in the Urban Present*. New York: Ecco Press, 1990.

Donovan, Richard X. *Black Musicians of America*. Portland, OR: National Book Co., 1991.

Finn, Julio. *The Bluesman: The Musical Heritage of Black Men and Women in the Americas.* New York: Interlink Books, 1991.

Floyd, Samuel A., ed. *Black Music in the Harlem Renaissance: A Collection of Essays.* Westport, CT: Greenwood Press, 1990.

Friedwall, Will. *Jazz Singing: America's Great Voices from Bessie Smith to Bebop and Beyond.* New York: Scribner's, 1990.

Harris, Michael W. *The Rise of Gospel Blues: The Music of Thomas Andrew Dorsey in the Urban Church.* New York: Oxford University Press, 1992.

Horne, Aaron, comp. *Keyboard Music of Black Composers: A Bibliography.* Westport, CT: Greenwood Press, 1992.

Horne, Aaron, comp. *String Music of Black Composers: A Bibliography.* Westport, CT: Greenwood Press, 1991.

Horne, Aaron. comp. *Woodwind Music of Black Composers* Westport, CT: Greenwood Press, 1990.

Jackson, John A. *Big Beat Heat: Alan Freed and the Early Years of Rock & Roll.* New York: Schirmer/Macmillan, 1991.

Merrill, Hugh. *The Blues Route.* New York: Morrow, 1990.

Morgan, Thomas L. *From Cakewalk to Concert Hall: An Illustrated History of African American Popular Music from 1895 to 1930.* Washington, DC: Elliott & Clark Publishers, 1992.

Morton, David C. and Charles K. Wolfe. *DeFord Bailey: A Black Star in Early Country Music.* Knoxville: University of Tennessee Press, 1991.

Peretti, Burton W. *The Creation of Jazz: Music, Race and Culture in Urban America.* Urbana: University of Illinois Press, 1992.

Perry, Frank. *Afro-American Vocal Music: A Select Guide to Fifteen Composers.* Berrien Springs, MD: Vande Verde Publishers, 1991.

Porter, Lewis, ed. *A Lester Young Reader.* Washington, DC: Smithsonian Institution Press, 1991.

Price, Sammy. *What Do They Want: A Jazz Autobiography.* Edited by Caroline Richmond. Chronological discography compiled by Bob Weir. Urbana: University of Illinois Press, 1990.

Roach, Hildred. *Black American Music Past and Present: Pan-African Composers.* 2nd ed., Malabar, FL: Kruger, 1992.

Rosenthal, David H. *Hard Bop: Jazz and Black Music, 1955-1965.* New York: Oxford University Press, 1992.

Scott, Frank. *The Down Home Guide to the Blues.* Pennington, NJ: A Capella Books, 1990.

Spencer, Jon Michael, ed. *The Emergency Black and the Emergence of Rap.* Durham: Duke University Press, 1991.

Spencer, Jon Michael, ed. *Sacred Music of the Secular City: From Blues to Rap.* Durham: Duke University Press, 1992.

Story, Rosalyn. *And So I Sing: African American Divas of Opera and Concert.* New York: Warner Books, 1990.

Tate, Greg. *Flyboy in the Buttermilk: Essays on Contemporary America.* New York: Simon and Schuster, 1992.

Turner, Patricia. *Dictionary of Afro-American Performers: 78 RPM and Cylinder Recordings of Opera, Choral Music and Song, ca. 1900-1949.* New York: Garland, 1990.

Walker-Hill, Helen. *Piano-Music by Black Women Composers: A*

*Catalogue of Solo and Ensemble Works.* New York: Greenwood Press, 1992.

Wright, Josephine, and Samuel A. Floyd, Jr., eds. *New Perspectives on Music: Essays in Honor of Eileen Southern.* Warren, MI: Harmonie Park Press, 1992.

## Performing Arts

Adamczke, Alice J. *Black Dance: An Annotated Bibliography.* New York: Garland Publishing Co., 1990.

Ely, Melvin Patrick. *The Adventures of Amos 'n' Andy: A Social History of an American Phenomenon.* New York: Free Press, 1991.

Gray, John, comp. *Black Theatre and Performance: A PanAfrican Bibliography.* Westport, CT: Greenwood Press, 1990.

Gray, John, comp. *Blacks in Film and Television: A Pan-African Bibliography of Films, Filmmakers, and Performers.* Westport, CT: Greenwood Press, 1990.

Hansberry, Lorraine. *A Raisin in the Sun: The Unfilmed Original Screenplay.* Edited by Robert Nemiroff. Foreword by Jewell Gres. Afterword by Spike Lee. New York: Dutton, 1992.

Hughes, Langston, and Zora Neale Hurston. *Mule Bone: A Comedy of Negro Life.* Edited by George H. Bass and Henry L. Gates. New York: Harper Collins, 1991.

Jhally, Sut, and Justin Lewis. *Enlightened Racism: The Cosby Show, Audiences, and the Myth of the American Dream.* Boulder, CO: Westview Press, 1992.

Jones, G. William. *Black Cinema Treasurey: Lost and Found.* Denton, TX: University of North Texas Press, 1991.

Klotman, Phyllis Rauch, ed. *Screenplays of the African American Experience.* Bloomington: Indiana University Press, 1991.

Mapp, Edward. *Directory of Blacks in the Performing Arts.* 2nd ed., Metuchen, NJ: Scarecrow Press, 1990.

## Politics

Barker, Lucius J., ed. *Ethnic Politics and Civil Liberties.* New Brunswick, NJ: Transaction Books, 1992.

Clavel, Pierre, and Wim Wiewel, eds. *Harold Washington and the Neighborhoods: Progressive City Government in Chicago, 1983-1987.* New Brunswick, NJ: Rutgers University Press, 1991.

Gomes, Ralph C., and Linda Faye Williams eds. *From Exclusion to Inclusion: The Long Struggle for African American Political Power.* Westport, CT: Greenwood Press, 1992.

Henry, Charles P. *Culture and African American Politics.* Bloomington: Indiana University Press, 1990.

Henry, Charles P. *Jesse Jackson: The Search for Common Ground.* Oakland, CA: Black Scholar Press, 1990.

Jennings, James. *The Politics of Black Empowerment: The Transformation of Black Activism in Urban America.* Detroit: Wayne State University Press, 1992.

Joint Center for Political and Economic Studies. *Black Elected Officials: A National Roster.* Washington, DC: Joint Center for Political and Economic Studies Press, 19–.

Kimball, Penn. *Keep Hope Alive: Super Tuesday and Jesse Jackson's 1988 Campaign for the Presidency.* Washington, DC: Joint Center for Political and Economic Studies, 1992.

Lawson, Steven. *Running for Freedom: Civil Rights and Black Politics in America Since 1941.* Philadelphia: Temple University Press, 1990.

Marable, Manning. *The Crisis of Color and Democracy: Essays on Race, Class and Power.* Monroe, ME: Common Courage Press, 1992.

McCartney, John T. *Black Power Ideologies: An Essay in African American Political Thought.* Philadelphia: Temple University Press, 1992.

Natanson, Nicholas. *The Black Image in the New Deal: The Politics of FSA.* Knoxville: University of Tennessee Press, 1992.

Orfield, Gar, and Carole Ashkinaze. *The Closing Door: Conservative Policy and Black Opportunity.* Chicago: University of Chicago Press, 1991.

Parker, Frank R. *Black Votes Count: Political Empowerment in Mississippi After 1965.* Chapel Hill: University of North Carolina Press, 1990.

Rees, Matthew. *From the Deck to the Sea: Blacks and the Republican Party.* Wakefield, NH: Longwood Press, 1991.

Rivlin, Gar. *Fire on the Prairie: Chicago's Harold Washington and the Politics of Race.* New York: Holt, 1992.

Van DeBurg, William L. *New Day in Babylon: The Black Power Movement and American Culture.* Chicago: University of Chicago Press, 1992.

## Race Relations

Brady, Paul L. *A Certain Blindness: A Black Family's Quest for the Promise of America.* Atlanta: ALP Publishers, 1990.

Brooks, Roy L. *Rethinking the American Race Problem.* Berkeley: University of California, 1991.

Collier, Peter, ed. *Second Thoughts About Race in America.* Lanham, MD: Madison Books, 1991.

Crouch, Stanley. *Notes of a Hanging Judge: Essays and Reviews.* New York: Oxford University Press, 1990.

Davis, F. James. *Who Is Black: One Nation's Definition.* University Park: Pennsylvania State University Press, 1991.

DeSantis, John. *For the Color of His Skin: The Murder of Yusuf Hawkins and the Trial of the Bensonhurst.* Introduction by Alan M. Dershowitz. New York: Pharos Books, 1991.

Essed, Philomena. *Understanding Racism: An Interdisciplinary Theory.* Newbury Park, CA: Sage, 1991.

Hacker, Andrew. *Two Nations: Black and White, Separate, Hostile, Unequal.* New York: Scribner's, 1992.

Horowitz, Irving Louis. *Daydreams and Nightmares: Reflections on a Harlem Childhood.* Jackson: University Press of Mississippi, 1990.

Hynes, Charles J., and Bob Drury. *Incident at Howard Beach: The Case for Murder.* New York: Putnam, 1990.

Leiman, Melvin M. *Racism in the U.S.A.: History and Political Economy.* Concord, MA: Paul & Co., 1992.

Lewis, Earl. *In Their own Interests: Race, Class, and Power in Twentieth-Century Nolf, Virginia.* Berkeley: University of California Press, 1991.

McFadden, Robert, et. al. *Outrage: The Story Behind the Tawana Brawley Hoax.* New York: Bantam, 1990.

Pemberton, Gayle. *The Hottest Water in Chicago: One Family, Race, Time and American Culture.* Winchester, MA: Faber & Faber, 1992.

Perlmutter, Philip. *Divided We Fall: A History of Ethnic, Religious, and Racial Prejudice in America.* Ames: Iowa State University Press, 1992.

Rasberry, William. *Looking Backward at Us.* Jackson: University Press of Mississippi, 1991.

Salzman, Jack, ed. *Bridges and Boundaries: African Americans and American Jews.* New York: Braziller, 1992.

Steele, Shelby. *The Contest of Our Character: A New Vision of Race in America.* New York: St. Martin's Press, 1990.

Stepan, Nancy Leys. *The Hour of Eugenics: Race, Gender, and Nation.* Ithaca, NY: Cornell University Press, 1991.

Terkel, Studs. *Race: How Blacks and Whites Think and Feel About the American Obsession.* New York: New Press/Norton, 1992.

Welch, Susan, and Lee Sigelman. *Black America's Views of Racial Equality: The Dream Deferred.*, New York: Cambridge University Press, 1991.

Zegeye, Abebe, ed. *Exploitation and Exclusion: Race and Class in Contemporary U.S. Society.* London: Hans Zell Publishers, 1991.

Zweigenhaft, Richard L., and G. William Domhoff. *Blacks in the White Establishment: A Study of Race and Class in America.* New Haven, CT: Yale University Press, 1991.

**Religion and Philosophy**

Baer, Hans, and Merrill Singer. *African-American Religion in the Twentieth Century: Varieties of Protest and Accommodation.* Knoxville: University of Tennessee, 1992.

Davis, Lenwood G. *Daddy Grace: An Annotated Bibliography.* New York: Greenwood Press, 1992.

Dvorak, Katherine L. *An African-American Exodus: the Segregation of Southern Churches.* With preface by Jerald C. Brauer. Brooklyn, NY: Carlson Publishing Co., 1991.

Harris, Leonard, ed. *The Philosophy of Alain Locke.* Philadelphia: Temple University Press, 1990.

Haynes, Lemuel. *Black Preacher to White America: the Collected Writings of Lemuel Haynes, 1774-1833.* Edited by Richard Newman. New York: Carlson Publishing Co., 1990.

Hopkins, Dwight N., and George C.L. Cummings, eds. *Cut Loose Your Stammering Tongue: Black Theology in the Slave Narratives.* Maryknoll, NY: Orbis Books, 1991.

Howard, Victor B. *Conscience and Slavery: the Evangelistic Calvinistic Domestic Missions, 1837-1861.* Kent, OH: Kent State University Press, 1990.

Irvin, Dona L. *The Unsung Heart of Black America: A Middle-Class Church at Midcentury.* Columbia: University of Missouri Press, 1992.

Jacobs, Claude F., and Andrew J. Kaslow. *The Spiritual Churches of New Orleans: Origins, Beliefs and Rituals of an African-American Religion.* Knoxville: University of Tennessee Press, 1991.

Johnson, John L. *Black Biblical Heritage.* Nashville: Winston-Derek Publishers, 1990.

Lincoln, C. Eric, and Lawrence H. Mamiya. *The Black Church in the American Experience.* Durham: Duke University Press, 1990.

Martin, Sandy D. *Black Baptists and African Missions: the Origins of a Movement, 1880-1915.* Macon: Mercer University Press, 1990.

Ochs, Stephen J. *Desegregating the Alter: The Josephites and the Struggle for Black Priests, 1871-1960.* Baton Rouge: Louisiana State University Press, 1990.

Payne, Wardell J., ed. *Directory of African American Religious Bodies: A Compendium by the Howard University School of Divinity.* Prepared under the auspices of the Research Center on Black Religious Bodies, Howard University School of Divinity. Washington, DC: Howard University Press, 1991.

Seymour, Robert E. *Whites Only: A Pastor's Retrospective on Signs of a New South.* Valley Forge, PA: Judson Press, 1991.

Spencer, Jon Michael. *Black Hymnody: A Hymnological History of the African-American Church.* Knoxville: University of Tennessee Press, 1992.

Spencer, Jon Michael. *Protest and Praise: Sacred Music of Black Religion.* Minneapolis: Augsburg Fortress Publishers, 1990.

Walker, Theodore, Jr. *Empower the People: Social Ethics for the African-American Church.* Maryknoll, NY: Orbis Books, 1991.

Walker, Wyatt Tee. *Spirits That Dwell in Deep Woods III: The Prayer and Praise Hymns of the Black Religious Experience.* New York: Martin Luther King Press, 1991.

Wood, Forrest G. *The Arrogance of Faith: Christianity and Race in America from the Colonial Era to the Twentieth Century.* New York: Knopf, 1990.

## Sociology and Psychology

Andersen, Margaret L. *Race, Class and Gender: An Anthology.* Belmont, CA: Wadsworth Publishing Co., 1992.

Anderson, Elijah. *Streetwise: Race, Class and Social Change in an Urban Community.* Chicago: University of Chicago Press, 1990.

Baer, Hans, and Yvonne Jones, eds. *African Americans in the South: Issues of Race, Class and Gender.* Athens: University of Georgia Press, 1992.

Benjamin, Lois. *The Black Elite: Facing the Color Line in the Twentieth Century.* Chicago: Nelson-Hall, 1991.

Billingsley, Andrew. *Climbing Jacob's Ladder: The Future of*
*the African-American Family* New York: Simon and Schuster, 1991.

Blackwell, James Edward. *The Black Community: Diversity and Unity.* 3rd ed., New York: Harper Collins, 1991.

Bowser, Benjamin, ed. *Black Male Adolescents: Parenting and Education in Community Context.* Latham, MD: University Press of America, 1991.

Consortium for Research on Black Adolescence Staff and Patricia Bell-Scott. *Black Adolescence: Current Issues and Annotated Bibliography.* Boston: G.K. Hall, 1990.

Edelman, Marian Wright. *The Measure of Our Success: A Letter to My Children and Yours.* Boston: Beacon Press, 1992.

Hay, Fred J. *African-American Community Studies from North America. A Classified, Annotated Bibliography.* New York: Garland, 1991.

Hopson, Darlene, and Derek Hopson. *Different and Wonderful: Raising Black Children in a Race Conscious Society.* New York: Simon and Schuster, 1992.

Jones, Howard, and Wanda Jones. *Heritage and Hope: The Legacy and Future of the Black Family in America.* Wheaton, IL: Victor Books, 1992.

Kunjufu, Jawanza. *Countering the Conspiracy to Destroy Black Boys.* Chicago: African American Images, 1990.

Leigh, Wilhemina A., ed. *The Housing Status of Black Americans.* New Brunswick, NJ: Transaction Books, 1992.

Lemann, Nicholas. *The Promised Land: The Great Black Migration and How It Changed America.* New York: Knopf, 1991.

Platat, Anthony M. *E. Franklin Frazier Reconsidered.* New Brunswick, NJ: Rutgers University Press, 1991.

Trotter, Joe William, ed. *The Great Migration in Historical Perspective: New Dimensions of Race, Class and Gender.* Bloomington: Indiana University Press, 1991.

## Sports

Cooper, Michael L. *Playing America's Game: The Story of Negro League Baseball.* New York: Lodestar Books, 1993.

Page, James A. *Black Olympian Medalists.* Englewood, CO: Libraries Unlimited, 1991.

## Women

Alexander, Adele Logan. *Free Women of Color in Rural Georgia, 1789-1879.* Fayetteville: University of Arkansas Press, 1991.

Baker, Houston A. *Working of the Spirit: The Poetics of Afro-American Women's Writings.* Chicago: University of Chicago Press, 1991.

The Black Women Oral History Project. *Guide to the Transcripts.* Edited by Ruth E. Hill. Westport, CT: Meckler, 1991.

Braxton, Joanne M. *Black Women Writing Autobiography: A Tradition Within a Tradition.* Philadelphia: Temple University Press, 1990.

Braxton, Joanne M., and Andree Nicola McLaughlin, eds. *Wild Women in the Whirlwind: Afro-American Culture and the Contemporary Literary Renaissance.* New Brunswick, NJ: Rutgers University Press, 1990.

Brown, Karen McCarthy. *Mama Lola: A Voodoo Priestess in Brooklyn.* Berkeley, University of California Press, 1991.

Brown-Guillory, Elizabeth, ed., and comp. *Wines in the Wilderness: Plays by African American Women from the Harlem Renaissance to the Present.* Westport, CT: Greenwood Press, 1990.

Bundles, A'Lelia Perry. *Madam C. J. Walker.* New York: Chelsea House, 1991.

Busby, Margaret, ed. *Daughters of Africa: An International Anthology of Words and Writings by Women of African Descent; From the Ancient World to Present.* New York: Pantheon, 1992.

Butler-Evans, Elliott. *Race, Gender, and Desire: Narrative Strategies in the Fiction of Toni Cade Bambara, Toni Morrison, and Alice Walker.* Philadelphia: Temple University Press, 1990.

Caraway, Nancie. *Segregated Sisterhood: Racism and the Politics of American Feminism.* Knoxville: University of Tennessee Press, 1991.

Celsi, Teresa N. *Rosa Parks and the Montgomery Bus Boycott.* Brookfield, CT: Millbrook Press, 1991.

Crawford, Vicki L. Crawford, Jacqueline Anne Reese, and Barbara Woods, eds. *Women in the Civil Rights Movement: Trailblazers and Torchbears, 1941-1965.* Brooklyn, NY: Carlson Publishing Co., 1990. (*Black Women in United States History*, vol. 16.)

Davis, Michael D. *Black American Women in Olympic Track and Field: A Complete Illustrated Reference.* Jefferson, NC: McFarland, 1992.

Gates, Henry Louis, Jr. *Reading Black, Reading Feminist.* New York: Meridan, 1991.

Glassman, Steve, and Kathryn Lee Seidel, eds. *Zora in Florida.* Gainesville: University Presses of Florida, 1991.

Guy-Sheftall, Beverly. *Daughters of Sorrow: Attitudes Toward Black Women.* New York: Carlson Publishing Co., 1990. (*Black Women in United States History*, vol. II.)

Guy, Sheftall, Beverly. *Words of Fire: An Anthology of African American Feminist Thought.* New Press, 1995.

Harris, Trudier. *Fiction and Folklore: The Novels of Toni Morrison.* Knoxville: University of Tennessee Press, 1991.

Hine, Darlene Clark, ed. *Black Women in American History, From Colonial Times Through the Nineteenth Century.* Brooklyn, NY: Carlson Publishing Co., 1990.

Hooks, Bell. *Black Looks: Race and Representation.* Boston: South End Press, 1992.

Ihle, Elizabeth L., ed. *Black Women in Higher Education: An Anthology of Essays, Studies and Documents.* New York: Garland Publishing Co., 1992.

Jackson, Carlton. *Hattie: The Life of Hattie McDaniel.* Lantham, MD: Madison Books, 1990.

Jones, Adrienne Lash. *Jane Edna Hunter: A Case Study of Black Leadership.* Brooklyn, NY: Carlson Publishing Co., 1990.

(*Black Women in United States History*, vol. 12)

Jones, Beverly Washington. *Quest for Equality: The Life and Writing of Mary Eliza Church Terrell, 1863-1954.* Brooklyn, NY: Carlson Publishing Co., 1990. (*Black Women in United States History*, vol. 13.)

Kent, George E. *A Life of Gwendolyn Brooks.* Lexington: University of Kentucky Press, 1990.

King, Joyce Elaine, and Carolyn Ann Mitchell. *Black Mothers to Sons: Juxtaposing African American Lit-erature and the Social Practice.* New York: Peter Lang, 1990.

Kubitschek, Missy Dehn. *Claiming the Heritage: African-American Women Novelists and History.* Oxford: University Press of Mississippi, 1991.

Mabalia, Dorethea Drummond, *Toni Morrison's Developing Class*

*Consciousness.* Cranbury, NJ: Susquehanna University

Press/Associated University Presses, 1991.

Morton, Patricia. *Disfigured Images: The Historical Assault on Afro-American Women.* Westport, CT: Greenwood Press, 1991.

Nathiri, N.Y., ed. *Zora! Zora Neale Hurston: A Woman and Her Community.* Orlando, FL: Sentinel Books, 1991.

Neverdon-Morton, Cynthia. *Afro-American Women of the South and the Advancement of the Race, 1895-1925.* Knoxville: University of Tennessee Press, 1990.

Otfinoski, Steven. *Marian Wright Edelman—Defender of Children's Rights.* New York: Rosen Publishing Group, 1991.

Reckley, Ralph. *Twentieth Century Black Women in Print: Essays.* Acton, MA: Copley Publishers, 1991.

Roses, Lorraine Elena, and Ruth Elizabeth Randolph. *Harlem Renaissance and Beyond: Literary Biographies of 100 Black Women Writers, 1900-1945.* Boston: G.K. Hall, 1990.

Salem, Dorothy. *To Better Our World: Black Women in Organized Reform.* Brooklyn, NY: Carlson Publishing Co., 1990. (*Black Women in United States History*, vol. 14.)

Samuels, Wilfred D., and Clenora Hudson-Weems. *Toni Morrison.* Boston: G.K. Hall, 1990.

Scott, Kesho Yvonne. *The Habit of Surviving: Black Women's Strategies for Life.* New Brunswick, NJ: Rutgers University Press, 1991.

Smith, Jesse Carney, ed. *Notable Black American Women.* Detroit: Gale Research Inc., 1991.

Smith, Rita Webb, and Tony Chapelle. *The Woman Who Took Back Her Streets: One Woman Fights the Drug*

*Wars and Rebuilds Her Community.* Far Hill, NJ: New Horizon, 1991.

Thompson, Mildred I. *Ida B. Wells-Barnett: An Exploratory Study of An American Black Woman, 1893-1930.* Brooklyn, NY: Carlson Publishing Co., 1990. (*Black Women in United States History*, vol. 15)

Walker, Melissa. *Down From the Mountaintop: Black Women's Novels in the Wake of the Civil Rights Movement, 1966-1989.* New Haven, CT: Yale University Press, 1991.

Walker, Robbie Jean, ed. *The Rhetoric of Struggle: Public Addresses by African American Women.* New York: Garland Publishing Co., 1992.

Werner, Craig. *Black American Women Novelists: An Annotated Bibliography.* Englewood Cliffs, NJ: Salem Press, 1990.

Williams, Constance Willard. *Black Teenage Mothers: Pregnancy and Child Rearing from Their Perspective.* Lexington, MA: Lexington Books, 1991.

Woody, Bette. *Black Women in the Workplace: Impacts of Structural Change in the Economy.* Westport, CT: Greenwood Press, 1992.

Yee, Shirley J. *Black Women Abolitionists: A Study in Activism, 1828-1860.* Knoxville: University of Tennessee Press, 1992.

# Picture and Text Credits

# Photo and Text Credits

## Photographs

**Courtesy of ABC Records/Ron Rogers,** used with permission: p. 931 (King, B. B., performing). **Courtesy of ABC-TV:** p. 739 (Goode, Mal, photograph). **A. Phillip Randolph Institute,** used with permission: p. 375 (African Americans in front of Voter Registration Headquarters, photograph). **AP/Wide World Photos,** reproduced by permission: pp. 29 (Randolph, Asa Philip, photograph); 33 (Segregation sign "White Waiting Room", photograph); 36 (Parks, Rosa, being fingerprinted, photograph); 39 (Student sit-in , Atlanta, GA, photograph); 49 (1967 Detroit Riots, aerial view, photograph); 51 (King, Martin Luther, Jr., King's funeral, photograph); 57 (J. Bruce Llewellyn); 58 (Chisholm, Shirley, photograph); 61 (Bakke Decision March, photograph); 67 (Hooks, Benjamin L., photograph); 67 (Wilson, Margaret Bush, speaking, photograph); 70 (Black leaders urging sanctions against South Africa, photograph); 75 (Wilder, Lawrence Douglas, photograph); 78 (Powell, Colin, visiting troops during Gulf War, photograph); 82 (Brown, Jesse L., Clinton, Bill, photograph); 95 (*U.S.S. Harmon,* photograph); 96 (Campanella, Roy, photograph); 102 (Alexander, Clifford, photograph); 102 (Harris, Patricia Roberts, photograph); 103 (Dinkins, David, photograph); 103 (Wilder, Lawrence, photograph); 104 (Mosely-Braun, Carol, at Democratic Convention, photograph); 125 (Frederick Douglass); 136 (Ku Klux Klan, cross burning, photograph); 141 (Segregation sign, man placing segregation sign, photograph; 152 (Federal troops escorting four black students, photo-

graph); 160 (Johnson, Lyndon B., photograph); 175 (Tuskegee Institute, view of chapel, photograph); 176 (Central High School, Little Rock, AR, photograph); 183 (Ebenezer Baptist Church, photograph); 188 (Attucks, Crispus, photograph); 193 (Lincoln University, photograph); 196 (Abysinnian Baptist Church, photograph); 197 (Apollo Theater, photograph); 207 (Harper's Ferry National Park, photograph); 302 (Douglass, Frederick, photograph); 316 (Civil Rights Protest in Birmingham, AL, photograph); 317 (Rustin, Bayard, photograph); 318 (Rights Protest in Birmingham, AL, photograph); 321 (King, Martin Luther, Jr., riding on bus, photograph); 322 (Bates, Daisy, photograph); 322 (Carmichael, Stokley, photograph); 325 (Evers, Medgar, photograph); 326 (Hamer, Fannie Lou, photograph); 328 (Coretta Scott King); 330 (King, Martin Luther, Jr., with group of people, photograph); 334 (Sharpton, Al, photograph); 349 (Farrakhan, Louis, photograph); 361 (King, Martin Luther, Jr., facing microphone, photograph); 362 (Chavis, Benjamin Franklin, Jr., photograph); 363 (Carmichael, Stokley, photograph); 364 (Seale, Bobby, photograph); 365 (Robinson, Randall, with Nelson Mandela, photograph); 366 (Chavis, Benjamin Franklin, Jr., photograph); 367 (Farmer, James, photograph); 369 (Hooks, Benjamin L., photograph); 370 (Innis, Roy, photograph); 371 (Jacob, John E., photograph); 372 (Jordan, Vernon E., Jr., photograph); 373 (Lowery, Joseph E., photograph); 376 (Robinson, Randall, photograph); 421 (Thomas, Clarence, photograph); 437 (Busing Protests/Segregation Ends, photograph); 438 (Lunch counter sit-in, photograph); 439 (Lewis, Woodrow T., with Albert L. Dunn, photograph); 425 (Segregation sign at Rail-

"Newspaper Boy"); 1023 (William H. Johnson's "Going to Chruch"); 1033 (Augusta Savage's "Gamin"). **National Park Service, Department of the Interior:** p. 180 (Douglass, Frederick, two story house, photograph). **National Portrait Gallery/Smithsonian,** used with permission: pp. 293 (Pennsylvania Abolition Society, photograph); 312 (Allen, Richard, photograph). **National Urban League:** p. 378 (Young, Whitney M., Jr., photograph). **NBC-TV,** used with permission: p. 1108 (Lewis, Carl, photograph). **Carl Nesfield,** courtesy of: p. 1096 (Clay, Cassius, photograph). *New York Amsterdam News,* used with permission: pp. 164 (Black Panthers demonstrating outside of courthouse, photograph); 332 (King, Martin Luther, Jr.); 362 (McKissick, Floyd B., photograph). *New York Daily News,* used with permission: p. 674 (Black Rabbi, photograph). **New York Historical Society:** p. 725 (Vassa, Gustavus, photograph). **New York Public Library Picture Collection,** reproduced by permission: pp. 312 (Allen, Richard, photograph); 662 (Allen, Richard, photograph); 941 (Smith, Bessie, photograph). **Andy Roy:** p. 565 (Freedom National Bank). **Courtesy of Ron Scherl:** p. 812 (Jones, James Earl, cast of "Fences," photograph). **Schomburg Center for Black Culture,** reproduced by permission: pp. 204 (Haley's boyhood home); 616 (New York African Free School No. 2, photograph); 696 (Fauset, Jessie, photograph); 837 (Horne, Lena, photograph); 863 (Jones, Matilda Sisieretta). **Stanley B. Burns, M.D. and the Burns Archive,** used with permission: pp. 524 (Rural black family in Savannah, GA, photograph); 664 (A.M.E. Church Reunion, photograph); 923 (Hampton, Lionel, photograph). **Susan Stetler:** pp. 545 (White collar worker); 551 (Woman using computer). **Tony Brown Productions, Inc.:** p. 744 (Brown, Tony, photograph). **Turner Broadcasting System Management:** p. 751. **United Nations:** pp. 212 (Pan-African Movement leaders); 220 (Angolans celebrating independence); 224 (Woman husking corn, photograph); 225 (Central Africa family, photograph); 226 (Rural farmers in Chad, photograph); 230 (Children in Equitorial Guinea, photograph); 231 (Selassie, Haile, photograph); 232 (Ethiopia, market, photograph); 233 (Cattleherders in rural Gambia, photograph); 234 (Jawara, Prime Minister, photograph); 236 (Masai tribesman, Kajiado, Kenya, photograph); 242 (Morocccan dancers, photograph); 245 (Minaret in Agadez, Niger, photograph); 249 (South African youths, photograph); 250 (South African children, photograph); 252 (South African village of Cross Roads, photograph); 253 (Swazi woman, South Africa, photograph); 256 (Togolese woman, photograph); 266 (Santo Domingo, Dominican Republic, photograph); 267 (Stevedores carrying bananas, photograph); 270 (Workers on banana plantation, photograph); 271 (Jamaican children, Hope Gardens, photograph); 273 (Nicaragua, open air market, photograph); 507 (Sampson, Edith, photograph). **UPI/Bettmann,** used with permission: pp. 29 (Scottsboro Boys, photograph); 32 (Marian Anderson); 206 (Washington, Booker T., boyhood home, photograph); 436 (Lunch counter sit-in, photograph); 711 (Haley, Alex, photograph); 845 (McDonald, Hattie); 1072 (Jemison, Mae C., photograph). **Courtesy of the U.S. Air Force:** p. 1155 (Davis, Benjamin O., Jr., photograph). **Courtesy of the U.S. Army:** p. 1143 (Davis, Benjamin O., Sr., photograph); 1144 (Davis, Benjamin O., Sr. pins medal on his son, photograph); 1146 (Soldiers from the 92nd Division, 1944, photograph); 1150 (Korean Conflict, photograph); 1156 (Davis, Benjamin O., Sr., portrait). **Courtesy of the U.S. Marine Corps:** p. 1151 (Cooper, Capt. Jerome, photograph); 1152 (Military officers). **Courtesy of the U.S. National Aeronautics and Space Administration:** pp. 550 (Caw, Lawrence, photograph). **Courtesy of the U.S. Navy:** p. 1153 (Winstead, John T., photograph); 1160 (Miller, Dorie, photograph). **Courtesy of the U.S. Senate Historical Office:** pp. 480 (Bruce, Blanche K., photograph); 506 (Revels, Hiram Rhodes, photograph). **U.S. Signal Corps-National Archives:** p. 23 (Freed slaves waiting for work opportunities, photograph); 1137 (Ninth U.S. Calvalry, 1889, photograph). **Walker Collection of A'Lelia Perry Bundles:** p. 567 (Madame C. J. Walker). **Courtesy of the U.S. War Department General Staff National Archives:** pp. 27 (Black soldiers leaving for war, photograph); 1140 (Black sailors, photograph). **The Washington Post Writers Group,** used with permission: p. 759 (Raspberry, William, photograph). **Alix B. Williamson:** p. 895 (Watts, Andre, photograph). **William Morris Agency:** p. 917 (Davis, Miles). **Edwin L. Wilson, Sr.:** p. 601 (Children playing basketball).

Text

# Index

# *Index*

Index

# J

# M

# N

Robinson, Bill "Bojangles"  808, 810, 850, 1039
Robinson, David  1089
Robinson, Eddie  1086, 1113
Robinson, Frank  99, 1085, 1103, 1113
Robinson, H. Alexander  589
Robinson, Jackie Roosevelt  1084
Robinson, Johnny  1060
Robinson, John Roosevelt "Jackie"  198
Robinson, Joseph C.  415
Robinson, Lavaughn  814
Robinson, Max  375, 743, 758
Robinson, Randall  83, 362, 375, 469
Robinson, Roscoe, Jr.  1160
Robinson, Sallie  415
Robinson, Sandra  589
Robinson, Smokey  191, 971, 972, 987, 990
Robinson, Sugar Ray  1086, 1087, 1115
*Robinson v. Memphis & Charleston Railroad*  414, 415
Robinson, William, Jr.  987
Rochon, Lela  719, 975
rock and roll  512, 914, 953, 955, 956, 962-964, 970, 982, 984, 987, 988
Rockefeller, Nelson  37, 368, 578
Rockin' Dopsie  901
Rock, John  90, 419
*Rock Kill Black View*  780
rock music  886, 906, 973
Rodgers, Jonathan  743
Rodgers, Moses  176
Rodgers, Norman  985
Rogers, Joel Augustus  343
Rogers, Rod  814
Rollins, Sonny  906, 912, 930, 940
Rollins, Theodore Walter  940
Romare, Eleo  814
Roosevelt, Franklin D.  147, 181, 315, 333, 419, 446, 690, 1142, 1147, 1149, 1151
Roosevelt, Theodore  25, 199, 873, 1121, 1137
Roosters, The  982
*Roots*  60, 79, 203, 288, 315, 322, 343, 383, 389, 485, 567, 599, 636, 671, 699, 700, 710-712, 819, 826, 832, 834, 841, 848, 850, 853, 854, 859, 899, 906, 943, 952, 955, 961, 978, 997, 998, 1003, 1023, 1083, 1138
Rose, Edward  193
Ross, Diana  857, 929, 933, 958, 961, 962, 972, 987, 988, 990, 991
Ross, Ted  813
Rotardier, Kelvin  814
Roundtree, Richard  850
Roussell, Norward  74
Rowe, William L.  97
Rowley, Laetitia  419
Roxbury Community College  645
Royal African Company  282

Royal Knights Savings and Loan Association  566
Royal Niger Company  244
Royal Sons, The  953
Roy, Charlotte E.  91
Rudder, John Earl  94
Rudolph, Wilma  1092, 1116, 1117
Ruffin, David  979
Ruffin, George  456
*Rufus Rastus*  806
Run-DMC  960, 973, 988
*Runnin' Wild*  808, 810, 929
*Runyon v. McCrary*  431
RuPaul  589
Rush, Bobby L.  472
Rush, Christopher  662
Rushing, Jimmy  910, 941
Rush, Otis  901, 940
Russell, Bill  98, 1089, 1117
Russwurm, John B.  117, 738, 759
Rust College  645
Rustin, Bayard  54, 330, 376, 589
Ruthless Records  968, 981
Rwanda  223, 245, 246

# S

Saar, Betye  1005, 1032
*Sacramento Observer*  770
Saddler, Joseph  960
*Sad-Faced Boy*  702
St. Andrew's African Methodist Episcopal Church  176
Saint Augustine's College  645, 1049
Saint Christopher  259, 274
Saint Croix  277
Saint-Gaudens, Augustus  188
St. George's Episcopal Church  198
Saint Helena  246
St. Jacques, Raymond  811
Saint John  277
St. John, Keith  589
Saint Kitts and Nevis  274
*St. Louis Argus*  776
"St. Louis Blues"  855
*St. Louis Crusader*  776
*St. Louis Sentinel Newspaper*  777
*St. Louis Woman*  808, 819
Saint Lucia  274
Saint Luke Bank and Trust Company  580
*Saint Luke Herald*  580
Saint Luke Penny Savings Bank  207
St. Luke's Protestant Episcopal Church  347
Saint Paul's College  645
*St. Paul Recorder*  776